ScottForesman Spanish Program

PASO A PASO

Teacher's Edition

2

Myriam Met
Coordinator of Foreign Languages
Montgomery County Public Schools
Rockville, MD

Richard S. Sayers
Niwot High School
Longmont, CO

Carol Eubanks Wargin
Glen Crest Junior High School
Glen Ellyn, IL

ScottForesman

Editorial Offices: Glenview, Illinois

Regional Offices: San Jose, California • Atlanta, Georgia
Glenview, Illinois • Oakland, New Jersey • Dallas, Texas

Visit ScottForesman's Home Page at http://www.sf.aw.com

ADDITIONAL WRITERS AND CONTRIBUTORS

The following individuals contributed their expertise and creativity in developing the many notes and features in this Teacher's Edition.

Lynn Andersen
Chattahoochee High School
Alpharetta, GA

Mary Louise Carey
Natick (MA) High School

JoAnn DiGiandomenico
Natick (MA) High School

Susan Dobinsky
Niles North High School
Skokie, IL

Gail Glover
Cheyenne Mountain
   Junior High School
Colorado Springs, CO

Marjorie Hall Haley, Ph. D.
George Mason University
Fairfax, VA

Thomasina Pagán Hannum
Albuquerque, NM

Mary Maggi
Bristow, OK

Lucía Nuñez
Stanford University
Stanford, CA

Bernadette M. Reynolds
Parker, CO

Luz Nuncio Schick
Naperville, IL

ISBN: 0-673-21673-X

Copyright © 1996

Scott, Foresman and Company, Glenview, Illinois

1.800.554.4411
http://www.sf.aw.com

45678910-RW-03020100999897

TABLE OF CONTENTS

PHILOSOPHY OF THE PROGRAM

Welcome to *PASO A PASO!*

This program is based on the belief that the purpose of learning Spanish is to communicate with the people who speak it and to understand their cultures. *PASO A PASO* is designed to help your students achieve that goal by getting them to communicate right from the start.

PASO A PASO reflects the most current thinking in the foreign language field. It reflects state-of-the-art research on how students learn languages and what teachers and materials need to do to help them become proficient language users, whether they are using their new language for oral or written communication.

Let's take a look at some basic premises about language and language learning, the components of *PASO A PASO,* and how each of these components contributes to developing language proficiency.

What is communication?

Communication is an authentic exchange of information for a real purpose between two or more people. By this we mean that people tell each other (through speech or writing) something the other person doesn't already know.

Communicating meaning has several aspects. Students need to learn to listen to and read Spanish in order to interpret intended meanings, to express meaning by conveying their own messages for a purpose and to a real audience, and to negotiate meaning through the natural give-and-take involved in understanding and in making oneself understood (Savignon, 1991). Research tells us that classroom activities must provide students practice in interpreting, expressing, and negotiating meaning through extensive and frequent peer interactions, preferably in pairs or small groups.

Communication is driven not only by meaning, but also by purpose. In real life, people communicate to get things done. They may communicate to transact business, to get to know someone

else, or to find out something they really need to know. In authentic communication, people give and get new ideas or information. The information that one partner has and the other doesn't is often called an *information gap* or an *opinion gap.* How unlike the classrooms of old, where we typically asked students questions to which we (and everyone else) already knew the answer, questions such as, "Tom, what's your name?" and "Sally, are you a boy or a girl?" These questions are not heard in real life because they lack a communicative purpose: there is no information or opinion gap.

PASO A PASO is organized around the principle that just as meaning and purpose drive all language use, so too should they drive all language learning. Students are engaged in understanding messages, in sending their own messages, and thus in communicating on every page of every chapter. Because *PASO A PASO* structures almost all activities for pair or group interaction, students find themselves active participants in every lesson, every day. They communicate real ideas and real meanings for real purposes. Every component of *PASO A PASO* is designed with the goal of communication in mind.

Interpreting meaning

In the last decade we have learned more than ever before about how language is acquired. We know that students learn best when they have ample opportunities to internalize meanings before they have to produce them. That is, we know that comprehension precedes production. Many teachers will be familiar with the term "comprehensible input," first used by Stephen Krashen, who suggests that learners acquire language by understanding what they hear. Students need many opportunities to match what they hear with visual cues (pictures, video, or teacher pantomime) or experiences (physical actions) so that they can associate meanings with forms. This is as true for comprehending language structure and syntax as it is for vocabulary development.

In keeping with research on the importance of matching language with meaning, *PASO A PASO* gives students many opportunities to comprehend new language before producing it. The video allows students to hear native speakers using the language in a new and exciting soap-opera format. Students learn by matching what they hear with what they see. Numerous activities for providing comprehensible input are suggested in this Teacher's Edition, activities that involve visuals (transparencies and pictures) and that physically engage students as they acquire new language. Whenever possible, in the pupil's text, vocabulary is visualized, providing examples of language in context.

What kind of practice promotes communication skills?

The first and most critical step in the language development process is getting meaning—learning to understand by matching what is heard with what is seen or experienced. But by itself, understanding is not enough. Students also need to use their new knowledge.

Research tells us that students need extensive practice in using their new language to create and convey their own messages. While there may be a legitimate role for simply drilling new structures or vocabulary, the most valuable practice comes from using them to send messages that have meaning for the learner and serve a legitimate communicative purpose. When teachers (or texts) structure activities so there is only one right answer, clearly students are sending messages that convey someone else's thoughts, not their own, and are serving someone else's communicative purpose. In these kinds of activities students are *practicing* language, but they are not really *using* language to communicate.

In contrast, when the answers are determined by the students themselves—and are therefore unpredictable, with no single correct response—students are involved in authentic communica-

tion. In these information- or opinion-gap activities, answers will vary. Research suggests that these types of activities are extremely important. After all, if the purpose of learning Spanish is to communicate, then students will need practice in doing just that! In contrast, if practice consists only (or mainly) of producing right answers determined by others, students will have difficulty spontaneously creating their own messages when needed. Thus language activities and tasks should not proceed from rote or de-contextualized to meaningful practice. All practice should be meaningful, with a predominance of activities that are truly communicative, activities in which students' answers will vary.

Research also tells us that pair and group language practice is far more effective than student-teacher practice alone. Cooperative learning and pair and group work both provide increased time for communicative language practice and promote the give-and-take necessary for negotiating meaning.

Working with a partner to make and share meaning lies at the heart of *PASO A PASO*. Everything students learn in each chapter is tied together in a meaningful way. The parts of language are taught and practiced (with a partner) within the context of the whole, with vocabulary and related grammar closely intertwined. Students use language in context to convey meaning and for a real purpose. All activities involve meaning, and most allow students to choose the meanings they want to convey. These are the kinds of information- and opinion-gap events that are characteristic of real-life communication. Even in structured activities designed to provide specific practice of forms and to elicit certain responses, teachers will find that students may still respond in ways that are personal and true for them. The activities are, however, focused, and you will often find "answers will vary, but look for correct use of ..." in the answer keys.

To promote the development of communicative ability, *PASO A PASO* integrates vocabulary and grammar. They are then re-integrated continually, with gradually increasing complexity. In addition to the personalized and open-ended responses found in the vocabulary and grammar sections of the chapter, the *Todo junto* feature specifically focuses on weaving together newly learned material with material from previous chapters. It promotes the use of all the language students have learned to that point, in oral tasks and through reading and writing.

Teaching for understanding:
The whole is greater than the parts

In many academic disciplines today, instructional practices are based on constructivist theory, which suggests that learners are more likely to be successful when instruction focuses on making meaning, on students' pursuing their natural inclination to try to make sense of what they are experiencing, and on ensuring that the parts are carefully integrated. In foreign languages, we traditionally taught the parts (grammar rules, vocabulary, pronunciation) hoping that eventually students would have the opportunity and ability to integrate them into the "whole" of communicating their own ideas. Today, integration of the parts of language takes place right from the start. It has been suggested that the relationship between learning the parts vs. integration with the whole is like learning to play a musical instrument. The focus is always on making music, and from the outset, learners need to have many experiences producing it. But they can't learn to play an instrument without knowing something about how to produce sounds (e.g., use the violin bow or play scales) or without practice.

Just as students learn the specific skills they need to produce a piece of music in learning to play an instrument, in language-learning we proceed today by identifying the learner's communicative needs (that is, the "music" they want to be able to produce) and then identifying the vocabulary, structures, and cultural skills needed to accomplish their purpose. Vocabulary and grammar are thus taught in the context of the situations in which students will be communicating or the topics they will be communicating about. Everything ties together naturally.

All effective learning is rooted in a meaningful context. We know from research that information is most likely to be retained when it is connected to other information in a meaningful way. Thus, language learning is more successful and retention more likely when we present new language organized into topics or by situations. This also means that some things we have taught in the past may not get taught at the same point or in the same way. For example, students may need to learn the stem-changing verbs *jugar, perder,* and *querer* to describe leisure or sports activities. However, since *dormir, morir,* and *pedir* do not naturally fit with the theme of sports or leisure, they may not be introduced until another theme or situation arises that will logically involve the use of one or more of them.

PASO A PASO is organized into thematic chapters. All material—vocabulary, grammar, culture—is rooted in a context and used meaningfully. All the elements of a chapter tie together. Students learn the vocabulary related to the theme, the grammar they need to communicate about the theme, and the information that helps anchor language in its cultural context. The themes have been chosen to reflect what students want or need to talk about. And the end-of-chapter vocabulary list is organized to reflect how the new words are used to create and convey meaning.

Critical thinking:
Understanding and making meaning

We know from research that language learners are active makers of meaning. They learn by creating their own understandings, not by memorizing ours. This means that students are more likely to remember vocabulary when they have acquired it by figuring out its meaning in a logical context (video situation, visual, teacher pantomime). Grammar is most likely to be understood and rules applied when students have been guided to discover underlying patterns or have formulated the rules for themselves. In contrast, retention and applicability are greatly reduced when students simply memorize lists or rules without real understanding.

In order for students to construct their own understandings and generate rules of language usage, they need to be guided through interaction with teacher and text. Strategic questioning (in the text or by the teacher) plays an important role in this process, a process that is not at all the same as groping blindly to make a random discovery. Rather, through well-chosen examples and appropriate, inductive questioning, students can be led to make significant discoveries on their own, leading to a deep understanding that is much more likely to stay with them and be reflected in their own language use.

Understanding grammar

Understanding and critical thinking are reflected throughout *PASO A PASO*. This text is unique in its approach to the development of grammar skills, emphasizing as it does the critical roles that comprehensible input and student construction of knowledge play in language learning. New structures are foreshadowed through lexical presentation in the vocabulary section, and by the use of the *yo / tú* verb forms in vocabulary practice prior to the grammar presentation. Vocabulary activities familiarize students with new grammar before it is formally presented, allowing them to construct their own understanding.

To further facilitate grammar learning, students observe patterns of use in the comprehensible input that introduces the grammar section. This is done through a visualized context and strategic inductive questions. Through interaction with the teacher and the text, observation and analysis lead students to understand grammar, not merely to memorize formulas to be applied in rote fashion.

Understanding culture

Guided discovery is also an effective means of helping students construct an understanding of culture. Not only do we want our students to know about the cultures of the people who speak Spanish, we also want them to understand the cultural framework that determines what people say or do. In other words, we want students to understand the *why* of culture that determines the *what*. Whenever and wherever students may encounter speakers of Spanish, they will likely confront cultural practices and behaviors that are new to them. Cultural understanding begins with developing sensitivity to the possibility that people vary in how they think, live, and behave. Students must learn to observe other cultures without judging and to use what they see to help them discover the meanings that underlie cultural practices or behaviors. Specific information provides knowledge that aids in understanding the system of attitudes, values, and beliefs that frames cultural practices or behaviors. Students also need to understand other cultures in relation to their own, so that they may gain a deeper understanding of why they think, live, and behave as they do.

Background knowledge can serve as an important tool for the construction of meaning. It may be contextual (What normally happens in a restaurant?), topical (What are some typical leisure activities?), linguistic (What words do I already know that look like this new word?), or cultural (I know that interpersonal relationships are very important in Hispanic cultures, so that may be why people put so much value on greeting one another). This can serve to help students interpret new cultural information or contrast that information with values and practices common to their own culture. Students should be encouraged to understand the close relationship between language and culture. The social / cultural meanings of words (What does "friendship" mean in Hispanic cultures?) should be taught along with their dictionary meanings.

PASO A PASO develops important cultural understandings through a unique guided-discovery approach.

PASO A PASO provides students with a progression of activities that leads them from thoughtful observation to knowledge and understanding of Hispanic cultures and then to reflection on their own culture. A photo essay with strategic inductive questions leads them to reflect on what they are observing. An informative reading then provides cultural information or insights that expand upon the visual information and allows students to validate or reject the ideas they formulated at the beginning. They are then asked thought-provoking questions to lead to reflection upon their own culture and their own cultural perspectives.

Strategies for success

Effective learners not only construct their own understanding of new concepts, they also know how to help themselves be successful learners. One way they do this is by using specific problem-solving strategies. When confronted with unknown words in a reading passage, successful learners don't run for a dictionary or just give up. They know how to get around that obstacle.

PASO A PASO teaches students to use strategies to be effective listeners, readers, and writers. Each reading selection takes students through a multi-step process (Phillips, 1984). Before reading, they are encouraged to use their background knowledge to help them predict or anticipate information they are likely to encounter in the text. A first reading helps them focus on general ideas (gist) without getting mired in details or difficult expressions. Reading closely for specific information, with specific strategies for dealing with difficult aspects of a text, is a strategy frequently emphasized in the reading sections. Students are then encouraged to use what they have learned in the reading by applying it in a new way. Thus, from the start, students are empowered to deal with authentic print materials.

Effective writing is promoted through a process approach in *PASO A PASO*. In the pre-writing stage, students think about the topic, generate needed language, and organize their ideas. They then write a first draft. Reviewing this draft with a peer yields insights into needed revisions or clarification and results in a revision that may be published or placed in a portfolio. This approach is consistent with the ways in which many students are learning to write in their English classes. It also provides them with a strategy or model for independent writing.

Authenticity in language learning

Language teaching today places great value on authenticity. The content that students are expected to learn and how they practice it (objectives and tasks) should be authentic to the learner's interests and to real-life uses. Tasks should require an authentic exchange of meaning (an information or opinion gap) and should have an authentic purpose. Students should be taught authentic, not "textbook," language. Most important, information and, to the extent possible, materials should be culturally authentic.

PASO A PASO opens authentic avenues to communication and culture. Students continually engage in authentic communicative tasks. Pair and group activities in which students fill information or opinion gaps constitute the great majority of exercises. These activities allow students to express their own views on topics and questions of interest to them. The language presented is culturally accurate. Videos, photos, realia, and readings provide authentic contacts with the cultures of Spanish speakers.

PASO A PASO and the student

PASO A PASO is a learner-friendly series. It is friendly to the interests of students and provides extensive opportunities for them to talk about themselves, to explore with peers, and to be engaged, thoughtful learners. Each chapter opens with clearly stated communicative objectives that help focus on what students are expected to learn. Knowing what's expected of them makes students more comfortable.

Because we know that it is impossible for students to learn all the vocabulary related to a given theme at one time, and because we know that it is unusual for students to "master" the grammar the first time they are exposed to it, *PASO A PASO* reviews each Book 1 theme in Book 2. However, the review is not simply repetition, re-entry, or recycling. Rather, our approach is recursive: Each review allows students to expand to new levels of achievement, so that their language becomes more refined, more elaborate, and more complex. Students will find comfort in knowing that there is more than one chance to learn the material and that they don't need to know everything perfectly all at once. *PASO A PASO* is a program in which students are continually getting better at communicating in Spanish and are regularly made aware of their progress at specific points in every chapter.

The pupil's edition and tests convey a powerful message. Both emphasize knowledge in action. Students are asked to use what they know to communicate real messages to a real audience for a real purpose. Practice activities make it clear to students that they are expected to learn to communicate in the language. End-of-chapter tests reinforce the message, assessing students' ability to use what they have learned for receptive and productive purposes and allowing them to demonstrate their understanding of related aspects of Hispanic cultures.

We know more today than ever about how foreign languages are learned. Using that knowledge to help students become proficient communicators, and to acquire an understanding and appreciation of other cultures, can be facilitated by appropriate instructional materials. *PASO A PASO* is based on solid research on second-language acquisition, on accepted theories about the teaching of culture, and on sound pedagogical

practices that are common to all disciplines. We are sure that you and your students will find this an exciting, engaging, and enormously successful approach to learning Spanish.

Bibliography

Adair-Hauck, Bonnie, Richard Donato and Philomena Cumo. 1994. "Using a Whole Language Approach to Teach Grammar," in Eileen Glisan and Judith Shrum, Eds. *Contextualized Language Instruction,* Boston: Heinle and Heinle Publishers. pp. 90–111.

Brooks, Jacqueline and Martin G. Brooks. 1993. *In Search of Understanding: The Case for Constructivist Classrooms.* Alexandria, VA: Association for Supervision and Curriculum Development.

Doughty, Catherine and Teresa Pica. 1986. "Information Gap Tasks: Do They Facilitate Second Language Acquisition?" *TESOL Quarterly.* 20:3, 305–325.

Ellis, Rod. 1993. "The Structural Syllabus and Second Language Acquisition." *TESOL Quarterly.* 27:1, 91–112.

Kagan, Spencer. 1992. *Cooperative Learning.* San Juan Capistrano, CA: Resource for Teachers Inc.

Krashen, Stephen. 1982. *Principles and Practice in Second Language Acquisition.* Oxford: Pergamon Press.

Nunan, D. 1991. "Communicative Tasks and the Language Curriculum." *TESOL Quarterly.* 25:2, 279–295.

Phillips, June K. "Practical Implication of Recent Research in Reading," *Foreign Language Annals* 17:4 (September 1984), pp. 285–299.

Resnick, Lauren B. 1989. *Knowing, Learning, and Instruction: Essays in Honor of Robert Glaser.* Hillsdale, New Jersey: Lawrence Erlbaum Associates, Publishers.

Savignon, S. J. Communicative Language Teaching: State of the Art. *TESOL Quarterly,* 1991, 25:2, 261–277.

Swain, Merrill. 1985. "Communicative Competence: Some Roles of Comprehensible Input and Comprehensible Output in Its Development." In Susan Gass and Madden, C. (Eds.) *Input in Second Language Acquisition.* Rowley, Mass.: Newbury House.

COMPONENTS OF THE PROGRAM

PASO A PASO is a complete, three-level series with a full range of ancillary components that allow you to tailor the materials to the needs of your students and to your teaching style.

Pupil's Edition

Presentation material begins with maps of Spanish-speaking countries and *Pasodoble,* a unique magazine-format contextual review of basic Book 1 material (regular verbs, *ir, querer, gustar,* and the like). This is followed by fourteen thematic chapters and an appendix offering verb charts, Spanish-English / English-Spanish vocabularies, and a grammar index.

Teacher's Edition

This Teacher's Edition contains the student text in slightly reduced form, with answers, teaching suggestions, and cross references to ancillary materials. Each chapter presents an extensive array of Teacher Notes that includes:

- a scope and sequence chart with communicative, cultural, and grammar objectives

- an overview of components available for use in the chapter

- on-page cultural information for photos and realia

- on-page Learning Spanish Through Action notes (a modified version of Total Physical Response)

- on-page notes for Spanish-speaking students, students needing extra help, enrichment, cooperative learning, multicultural perspectives, cross-curricular activities, using the video, critical thinking, class starter reviews, reteach / review, and re-enter / recycle.

Ancillaries
Multisensory / Technology

Overhead Transparencies: A package of 90 full-color overhead visuals that reproduce the vocabulary-teaching illustrations without labels or captions. Also included are maps, a pronoun chart, the realia from the *Gramática en contexto,* and additional teaching transparencies. Suggestions for use are provided in a separate booklet.

Audio Cassettes / CDs: A set of ten 60-minute audio tapes on cassette or CD containing listening activities for each chapter and separate tapes for assessment, pronunciation and vocabulary, and songs. The primary focus is on developing listening comprehension, with secondary emphasis on supporting the intermediate stages of speaking, including practice with pronunciation of new words and some focused speaking opportunities.

Vocabulary Art Blackline Masters for Hands-On Learning: All teaching vocabulary art reproduced on blackline masters, ideal for making manipulatives or flashcards.

Classroom Crossword: A wall-size crossword puzzle to be completed over the course of the school year.

La Catrina: A storyline video series taped on location in Mexico. Available on both tape and disc, *La Catrina* incorporates the chapter themes, vocabulary, and grammar into an engaging tale of romance, intrigue, and adventure. A Teacher's Guide is included with complete transcriptions, cultural information, teaching suggestions, and reduced reproductions of the Video Activities pages *(see next page)* with overprinted answers.

La Catrina: **Interactive CD-ROM:** Real-world activities based on *La Catrina* offer creative, interactive practice opportunities for listening, speaking, reading, and writing, while extending students' knowledge of Hispanic cultures.

Print

 Practice Workbook: (with separate Teacher's Answer Key): Worksheets for basic, one-step writing practice for all vocabulary and grammar sections of the student text. Exercises include the support of learning strategies. Each chapter also has an Organizer that allows students to record and keep track of new vocabulary and structures.

 Writing, Audio & Video Activities: Writing Activities provide chapter-by-chapter practice that is at the same level as (or slightly higher level than) that in the student text. Audio Activities offer exercises necessary to focus attention on listening comprehension as students work with the audio tapes. Video Activities focus attention as students view the video. Follow-up activities verify and extend their understanding of what they have seen.

Teacher's Edition: Writing, Audio & Video Activities: Student material with overprinted answers and a complete tapescript of the audio tapes and CDs.

 Communicative Activities Blackline Masters (Pair and Small-Group Activities with Situation Cards): Oral activities for pair and group practice.

 Un paso más: Actividades para ampliar tu español: A worktext for Spanish-speaking students designed to supplement the textbook activities.

Assessment

 Assessment Program: Blackline master quizzes *(Pruebas)* for each vocabulary section and each grammar topic in the student text; fourteen chapter quizzes *(Pruebas cumulativas);* fourteen chapter proficiency tests *(Exámenes de habilidades);* a chapter test for *Pasodoble (Prueba Pasodoble);* and *Bancos de ideas,* several sets of cumulative proficiency sections for use in creating mid-term and special end-of-year tests to highlight teachers' own objectives or areas of concern. Suggestions for administering and scoring proficiency tests are included.

 Test Generator: A multiple-choice test generator. Teachers can add their own questions to the question bank.

Teacher's Resource File: This convenient, desk-top organizer contains the Teacher's Edition of the Writing, Audio & Video Activities, the Assessment Program, and the Communicative Activities Blackline Masters.

CHAPTER ORGANIZATION

Organization of the Text

PASO A PASO 2 contains a review section *(Pasodoble)* and 14 thematically organized chapters in which students learn to communicate about their own lives and how to interact with Hispanic cultures. The 14 themes are:

CAPÍTULO 1 **School**

CAPÍTULO 2 **Daily routine**

CAPÍTULO 3 **Clothing**

CAPÍTULO 4 **Leisure activities**

CAPÍTULO 5 **Childhood**

CAPÍTULO 6 **Special occasions**

CAPÍTULO 7 **Luxuries and necessities**

CAPÍTULO 8 **Shopping**

CAPÍTULO 9 **Health**

CAPÍTULO 10 **Movies and TV**

CAPÍTULO 11 **The future**

CAPÍTULO 12 **Travel**

CAPÍTULO 13 **Food**

CAPÍTULO 14 **Nature**

Using *Pasodoble*

The magazine-format review, *Pasodoble,* is designed to help students recall certain major vocabulary sets and structure taught in Chapters 1–12 of *PASO A PASO 1.* Previously taught concepts are uniquely integrated to provide meaningful communication combined with purposeful review.

Chapter organization

The 14 chapters follow a consistent organization that increases student confidence while allowing for easy classroom management. Chapters are organized according to the latest research on how students learn a second language and follow a clear pedagogical model:

1 Introduce/Preview **4** Apply
2 Present **5** Summarize/Assess
3 Practice

Each chapter follows this model:

Chapter Sections	Pedagogical Support
Objectives	Introduce
¡Piénsalo bien!	Preview
Vocabulario para conversar	
• *Visualized vocabulary*	Present
• También necesitas . . .	Present
• Empecemos a conversar	Practice
• Empecemos a escribir (y a leer)	Apply
• ¡Comuniquemos!	Practice
• ¿Qué sabes ahora?	Practice / Assess
Perspectiva cultural	Preview / Present
•La cultura desde tu perspectiva	Apply
Gramática en contexto	Preview / Present / Practice
•Ahora lo sabes	Practice / Assess
Todo junto	
•Actividades	Apply
•¡Vamos a leer!	Apply
•¡Vamos a escribir!	Apply
¿Lo sabes bien?	Apply / Assess
Resumen del capítulo	Summarize

USING A CHAPTER

Chapter Opener *(Introduce)*

The chapter theme is introduced through a photograph and related communicative and cultural objectives.

Teaching ideas for the Chapter Opener

Wrap-around notes give many suggestions. Here are a few basic ideas for these two pages:

1 Prior to discussing the objectives, have students look at the photos and skim the chapter. Ask them to suggest objectives based upon what they have seen. Write these on the chalkboard and see if they compare with those listed.

2 Show additional pictures, posters, or slides that preview the chapter theme.

Objectives:
Relate to real-life, purposeful communication and relevant cultural information. These will be referred to throughout the chapter so that students can monitor their own progress. Chapter assessment is based on the objectives.

CAPÍTULO 5

¿Qué te gustaba hacer de pequeño?

OBJECTIVES

At the end of this chapter, you will be able to:

- tell what you were like as a child
- tell what you used to like to do
- talk about what you learned to do
- understand how experiences in José Martí's early life affected his later life

Festival de cometas en Guatemala   159

¡Piénsalo bien! *(Preview)*

This section continues to preview the chapter theme. Students use their own experiences and background information to interact with the photographs.

Teaching ideas for *¡Piénsalo bien!*

1 Ask students to study the photographs and to suggest as many words, phrases, or short sentences as they can about them. Focus on previously taught vocabulary.

2 Use the inductive questions to elicit the similarities and differences. Focus on the similarities.

3 At the end of the chapter, return to these photos. See how extensively students can describe the pictures. Choose a photo and have students bring it to life by acting out the situation.

Questions:
Students use critical thinking to answer inductive questions.

¡Piénsalo bien!

Mira las fotos. Los niños que vemos están haciendo sus actividades favoritas. ¿Qué te gustaba hacer cuando eras niño(a)?

"Aquí está mi nueva tarjeta de Juan González."

Cuando eras niño(a), ¿coleccionabas algo? ¿Tenías una colección grande? ¿Todavía la tienes?

Un niño de Caracas les muestra su colección de tarjetas de béisbol a unos amigos.

"¡Dos y dos son cuatro; cuatro y dos son seis; seis y dos son ocho y ocho dieciséis!"

¿Qué te gustaba jugar de niño(a)? Si saltabas a la cuerda, ¿cantabas canciones como ésta?

Niños hondureños saltando a la cuerda

160 Capítulo 5

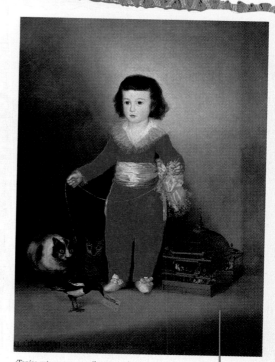

¿Tenías gatos, perros o pájaros cuando eras niño(a)?

Don Manuel Osorio Manrique de Zúñiga (1788); Francisco de Goya

161

Captions:
Easy-to-guess cognates and recycled vocabulary help build students' confidence. New vocabulary and structures are previewed.

Painting:
Photos of a wide variety of art and handicrafts reinforce the chapter theme and broaden knowledge of Hispanic cultures.

Vocabulario para conversar (*Present, Practice & Apply*)

New vocabulary is presented in a visualized context in two short, manageable sections.

Teaching ideas

1 Use the Overhead Transparencies, the Vocabulary Audio Tape, and /or the Vocabulary Art Blackline Masters to introduce the new vocabulary.

2 Combine auditory, visual, and kinesthetic activities. Present the vocabulary using comprehensible input. Here are several suggestions:

A. Getting meaning from comprehensible input

The purpose of these activities is to allow students to match new language with its meaning.

- Using the Overhead Transparency, point to pictures as you simply and clearly name and talk about them in Spanish. Students should be able to understand new vocabulary from your body language and gestures. For example: *Aquí hay unos animales de peluche. Hay un oso de peluche, un gato de peluche y una tortuga de peluche.*

- You might also pantomime new vocabulary.

- As you progress through *PASO A PASO,* your descriptions will expand to include previously learned language.

Visualized vocabulary:
Research indicates that we learn best in logical sets or categories and through immediately associating words with objects.

¡No olvides!:
This recycling feature reminds students at appropriate moments of previously taught concepts and vocabulary.

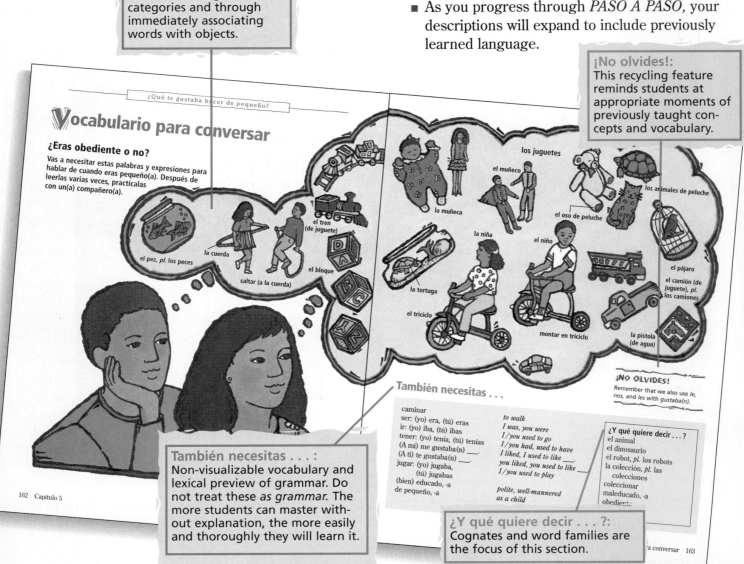

¿Qué te gustaba hacer de pequeño?

Vocabulario para conversar

¿Eras obediente o no?

Vas a necesitar estas palabras y expresiones para hablar de cuando eras pequeño(a). Después de leerlas varias veces, practícalas con un(a) compañero(a).

el pez, *pl.* los peces
la cuerda
saltar (a la cuerda)
el tren (de juguete)
el bloque
la tortuga
el triciclo
los juguetes
el muñeco
la muñeca
la niña
el niño
el oso de peluche
los animales de peluche
el pájaro
el camión (de juguete), *pl.* los camiones
montar en triciclo
la pistola (de agua)

¡NO OLVIDES!
Remember that we also use *le, nos,* and *les* with *gustaba(n).*

162 Capítulo 5

También necesitas . . .

caminar — to walk
ser: (yo) era, (tú) eras — I was, you were
ir: (yo) iba, (tú) ibas — I/you used to go
tener: (yo) tenía, (tú) tenías — I/you had, used to have
(A mí) me gustaba(n) ___. — I liked, I used to like ___
(A ti) te gustaba(n) ___. — you liked, you used to like ___
jugar: (yo) jugaba, (tú) jugabas — I/you used to play
(bien) educado, -a
de pequeño, -a — polite, well-mannered / as a child

¿Y qué quiere decir . . . ?
el animal
el dinosaurio
el robot, *pl.* los robots
la colección, *pl.* las colecciones
coleccionar
maleducado, -a
obediente

También necesitas . . . :
Non-visualizable vocabulary and lexical preview of grammar. Do not treat these *as grammar.* The more students can master without explanation, the more easily and thoroughly they will learn it.

¿Y qué quiere decir . . . ?:
Cognates and word families are the focus of this section.

...a conversar 163

B. Demonstrating comprehension through physical response

The purpose of these activities is to allow students to demonstrate their comprehension non-verbally.

■ After presenting two or three pictures of new vocabulary, review by asking yes / no questions: *¿Es un pájaro? ¿Es una cuerda? ¿Tenías un triciclo?* Students may respond as a group with thumbs up / down *(sí / no)*. Individuals may also be asked to respond in this way.

■ As students become more proficient, vocabulary from previous chapters can be used in these questions: *¿Dónde viven las tortugas? ¿Y los peces?*

■ Continue alternating the steps in the first two paragraphs until all new vocabulary has been presented.

■ Distribute Vocabulary Art BLMs. As you name each new item, point to it on the transparency. Have students point to the corresponding picture. Tell students: *Señalen el tren. Señalen la muñeca.* This time, do not point to the picture on the transparency until students have pointed to it on their worksheet. Confirm student responses on the transparency.

■ Have students point to pictures on the Overhead Transparency as you describe the picture: *Al niño le encanta montar en triciclo* (student points to picture of tricycle).

■ Have students open their books and point to pictures you name or describe: *Señalen su juguete favorito. ¿Qué animal de peluche es mejor para una niña de tres años?*

■ Have students pantomime vocabulary.

■ Have students respond to commands: *Dale el bloque a Matilde. Muestra el tren a la clase.*

■ Provide each student with a worksheet from the Vocabulary Art BLMs. Direct them to cut out each picture. Have students move the pictures as you direct: *Pongan el bloque a la derecha de los peces. Pongan el tren entre el bloque y los peces. Pongan los juguetes en tres columnas: Juguetes para niños, niñas o los dos.* Or students may use them to make your sentence true by arranging pictures to match your oral description: *El tren y el camión están en la mesa.*

Each chapter provides suggestions for Learning Spanish Through Action (TPR).

C. Limited verbal response

Once students have had an opportunity to internalize meaning and to demonstrate comprehension of new language physically, they may respond verbally.

■ Ask yes / no or true / false questions: *¿Saltabas a la cuerda? Un pez sabe saltar a la cuerda.*

■ Ask questions that require comprehension of new vocabulary but do not require using it in the answer. Responses will use language from previous chapters: *¿De qué color era tu triciclo?*

■ Ask questions in which the correct answer is embedded: *¿Es un pez o un pájaro? ¿Preferías jugar con muñecas o con animales de peluche?*

■ Have students repeat after you for pronunciation practice.

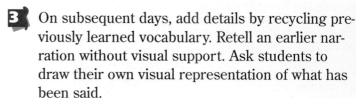 On subsequent days, add details by recycling previously learned vocabulary. Retell an earlier narration without visual support. Ask students to draw their own visual representation of what has been said.

Empecemos a conversar (Practice)

Students practice the new vocabulary in paired activities that provide models for real-life language.

Teaching ideas for *Empecemos a conversar*

1 Place students in pairs. (There are many ways of doing this.) You may want to pair students of different abilities. Assign "study buddies" for each week or chapter. They are not only pair-practice partners, but they also keep track of each other's papers and assignments. (Be sure they exchange phone numbers.) You might award extra credit for partners who work well together and show improvement.

2 Always model the pair practice. Quickly review the vocabulary so that students can be more successful.

3 Set a time limit. Finish an activity when approximately three fourths of the class have finished. Walk around the class, listening for areas of difficulty such as pronunciation or grammar. Focus on these at a later time.

4 Ask pairs of students to do selected items for the whole class.

5 Have students work in pairs to answer the questions, then with another group to compare responses. Ask individuals to write this section as homework. Use the more open-ended questions as one-on-one questions with students or as topics for class discussion.

6 See the list of ancillaries for additional resources to help students work with the new vocabulary.

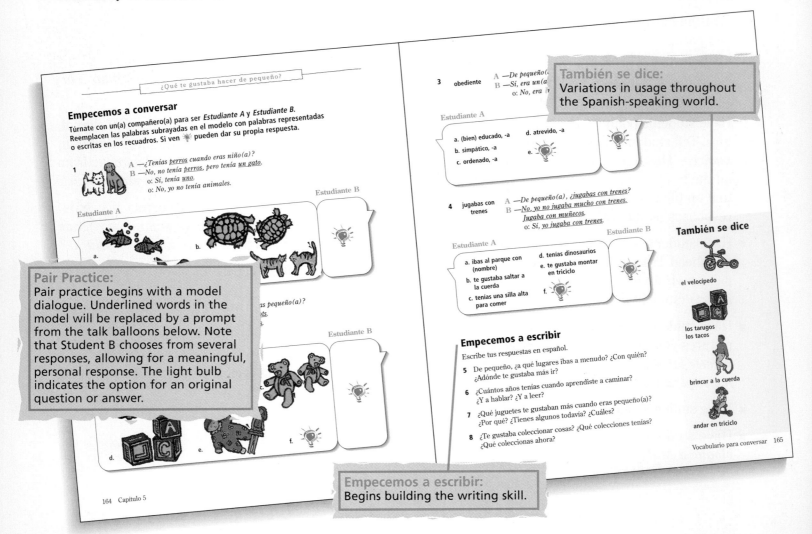

Pair Practice:
Pair practice begins with a model dialogue. Underlined words in the model will be replaced by a prompt from the talk balloons below. Note that Student B chooses from several responses, allowing for a meaningful, personal response. The light bulb indicates the option for an original question or answer.

También se dice:
Variations in usage throughout the Spanish-speaking world.

Empecemos a escribir:
Begins building the writing skill.

¡Comuniquemos! (Practice)

This section offers additional practice with the new vocabulary. The varied activities guide students to personalized communication.

Teaching ideas

Follow the guidelines for paired practice. At this point, students are familiar with the new vocabulary and the activities should go quickly, but choose from among them. Do not attempt to do them all.

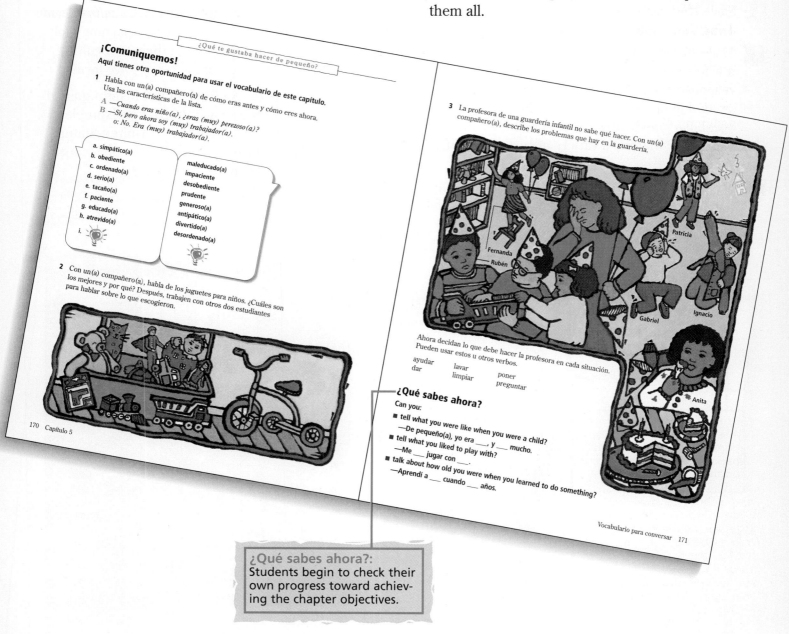

¿Qué te gustaba hacer de pequeño?

¡Comuniquemos!

Aquí tienes otra oportunidad para usar el vocabulario de este capítulo.

1 Habla con un(a) compañero(a) de cómo eras antes y cómo eres ahora. Usa las características de la lista.

A —Cuando eras niño(a), ¿eras (muy) perezoso(a)?
B —Sí, pero ahora soy (muy) trabajador(a)?
o: No. Era (muy) trabajador(a).

a. simpático(a)
b. obediente
c. ordenado(a)
d. serio(a)
e. tacaño(a)
f. paciente
g. educado(a)
h. atrevido(a)
i.

maleducado(a)
impaciente
desobediente
prudente
generoso(a)
antipático(a)
divertido(a)
desordenado(a)

2 Con un(a) compañero(a), habla de los juguetes para niños. ¿Cuáles son los mejores y por qué? Después, trabajen con otros dos estudiantes para hablar sobre lo que escogieron.

170   Capítulo 5

3 La profesora de una guardería infantil no sabe qué hacer. Con un(a) compañero(a), describe los problemas que hay en la guardería.

Patricia
Fernanda
Rubén
Gabriel
Ignacio
Anita

Ahora decidan lo que debe hacer la profesora en cada situación. Pueden usar estos u otros verbos.

ayudar   lavar
dar   limpiar   poner
                       preguntar

¿Qué sabes ahora?

Can you:

■ tell what you were like when you were a child?
   —De pequeño(a), yo era ___, y ___ mucho.
■ tell what you liked to play with?
   —Me ___ jugar con ___.
■ talk about how old you were when you learned to do something?
   —Aprendí a ___ cuando ___ años.

Vocabulario para conversar   171

¿Qué sabes ahora?:
Students begin to check their own progress toward achieving the chapter objectives.

Perspectiva cultural (*Preview, Present & Apply*)

This section offers a unique perspective into understanding the richness of Hispanic cultures. Using a combination of a photographic and narrative essay, it asks students to think about culture in such a way as to develop real cross-cultural understanding and sensitivity.

Teaching ideas for the *Perspectiva cultural*

1 Have students answer the inductive questions as a whole-class or small-group activity. Write their responses on the board. This will activate background information, prompt and recycle related vocabulary, and show that, even in their own class, they will find a variety of customs and traditions.

2 Use the photographs to encourage students to make observations about cultural perspective. Describe the photo(s) in Spanish, adding more information.

3 Add personal information or anecdotes. If any students have personal knowledge about the cultural topic, let them share their experiences. Ask Spanish speakers to share family traditions.

4 In small groups or as a whole class, have students answer the questions in *La cultura desde tu perspectiva*. This is your best opportunity for helping students understand their own culture and the beliefs and attitudes they have formed.

5 Ask students to use the cultural insight gained to reflect on their own culture. For example, whom would students cite as a United States figure similar to José Martí if a Spanish-speaking student should ask?

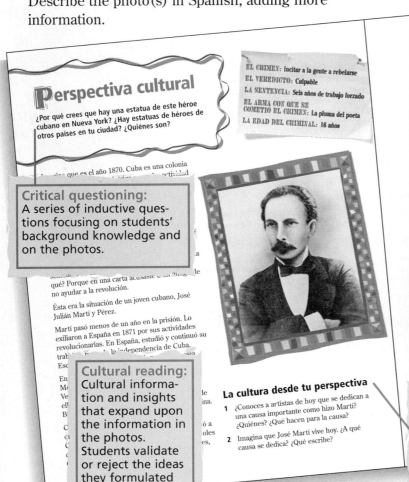

Critical questioning:
A series of inductive questions focusing on students' background knowledge and on the photos.

Cultural reading:
Cultural information and insights that expand upon the information in the photos. Students validate or reject the ideas they formulated earlier.

La cultura desde tu perspectiva:
Students reflect upon and interact with new cultural information from the perspective of their own culture.

Gramática en contexto (*Preview, Present & Practice*)

A realia-based reading provides comprehensible input for the new grammar. This gives students meaningful understanding of the structures by letting them intuit the rules. This inductive approach allows students to internalize and gain a deeper understanding of the grammar. Students were shown these structures in the vocabulary presentation and have practiced using them. They should not be uncomfortable with the structures themselves.

Realia-based reading:
The reading combines cognates and previously learned vocabulary with the chapter's key grammar concepts.

Teaching ideas for *Gramática en contexto*

1 Show the Overhead Transparency. Activate students' own experience by asking questions such as: How many students have studied about colonial life in America? How was life different then? Have they ever visited a site of colonial life that has been preserved or reconstructed?

2 Have students read the captions and study the pictures. Have them answer the questions individually or in pairs. Let them verify their answers with another pair or as a whole-class activity.

3 As students generate explanations, write them on the chalkboard along with examples from the reading.

¿Qué te gustaba hacer de pequeño?

Gramática en contexto

¿Cómo era la época colonial?

Mucha gente vivía en fincas. La gente hacía su propia ropa y comía lo que la finca producía.

Los niños iban a la escuela a pie. Generalmente caminaban largas distancias para llegar allí.

Los niños usaban juguetes hechos a mano y jugaban con otros niños de la familia. Todos se divertían.

A menudo el padre o la madre le leía algo a la familia por la noche. Muchas veces alguien tocaba un instrumento y los otros cantaban o bailaban.

A When reading about what colonial families used to do, what endings do you find on the verbs *caminar, usar, jugar, tocar,* and *cantar*?

B Find the sentence that tells how children used to go to school. What is the verb? What is its infinitive form?

C The writer uses the words *vivía, hacía, comía,* and *se divertían*. What verbs do you think they come from?

174   Capítulo 5

Inductive questions:
Students scan for information that leads them to produce their own explanation for the structures used.

El imperfecto de los verbos que terminan en *-ar*

You have already learned to talk about the past using the preterite tense for actions that began and ended at a definite time.

> Ana **cantó** en la fiesta anoche.
> *Ana **sang** at the party last night.*

The imperfect tense is another way to talk about the past. We use it to describe past actions without any indication of their beginning or end.

> Ana **cantaba**.
> *Ana **was singing**.*

Esta niña venezolana se divierte mucho durante el recreo.

• We use the imperfect to talk about actions that happened repeatedly in the past. In English we often say "used to" or "would" to express this idea.

> Generalmente **caminaban** mucho.
> *Generally **they would walk** a lot.*

> **Jugaban** con otros niños de la familia.
> *They **used to play** with other children in the family.*

• Expressions such as *generalmente, a menudo, muchas veces, todos los días, siempre,* and *nunca* can cue us to use the imperfect.

Here are all the forms of *-ar* verbs in the imperfect. Notice the accent mark on the *nosotros* form.

caminar

(yo)	caminaba	(nosotros) (nosotras)	caminábamos
(tú)	caminabas	(vosotros) (vosotras)	caminabais
Ud. (él) (ella)	caminaba	Uds. (ellos) (ellas)	caminaban

• Since the *yo* and the *Ud. / él / ella* forms are the same, we often use the subject pronouns to avoid confusion.

Easy-to-understand grammar explanations:
Rules developed by the student are reinforced in easily understood explanations. Grammar terminology is kept to a minimum.

Gramática en contexto   175

In a truly thematic approach, grammar is tied to the communicative objectives. What is not relevant is not presented. Here, for example, students work with understanding and using the imperfect in the context of what they were like as children and what they used to do. Students focus on content relevant to the theme. Students will, in later chapters, continue to work with the imperfect as related to other themes. This thematic approach builds in regular review and recycling as students are reminded of structures and vocabulary sets through the *¡No olvides!* feature. There are three to four grammar topics per chapter, each followed by a variety of activities.

¿Qué te gustaba hacer de p

3 Túrnate con un(a) compañero(a) para hablar de lo que t
personas cuando Uds. eran pequeños(as).

tus abuelos   **A** —¿Qué tenían tus abuelos
              B —Tenían un proyector d

a. tus tíos   d. tus hermanos
b. tus primos   e. tu vecino(a)
c. tú   f. ☀

4 Pregúntale a dos compañeros(as) qué
en la escuela primaria.

obedecer siempre   **A** —¿Uds. obedecían
a sus padres   **B** —Sí, obedecíamo
                   o: No, desobed

a. comer en la cafetería todos lo
b. hacer fila antes de las clases
c. ver videos en las clases
d. leer libros en la biblioteca a
e. tener tarea
f. soler visitar museos
g. escribir cartas a estudian
   de otras escuelas
h. mentir mucho o siempr
   decir la verdad
i. ☀

178   Capítulo 5

El imperfecto de los
terminan en -er e -ir

Here are all the forms of -er a
have the same pattern of endi

comer / vivir

(yo)	comía vivía
(tú)	comías vivías
Ud. (él) (ella)	comía vivía

• The verb *ver* is irreg
  are added to the ste

(yo)	veía
(tú)	veías
Ud. (él) (ella)	veía

• *Haber* is a sp
  know the pre
  form is *habí*

  En la esc
  En mi c

Unas niñas españolas saltan a la cuerda
delante de su casa en Andalucía.

Ahora lo sabes

Can you:

■ talk about your life as a child?

—De pequeño(a) ___ en
un apartamento muy pequeño.
Me ___ jugar con trenes.

■ tell what people used to do regularly?

—Los vecinos ___ de lunes a viernes.
Y los fines de semana ___ de pesca.

■ compare what people used to do with
what they do now?

—Cuando ___ pequeño(a), yo ___ los
platos. Ahora ___ la comida.

Gramática en contexto   181

Este mes

CRECER *feliz*

• TU PELO, TU SONRISA...
¿Qué heredará
tu hijo de ti?

• JUGUETES
INTELIGENTES
Informática
para bebés

92 PAPILLAS
PARA ELEGIR
LA MEJOR

• SUS DIBUJOS
HABLAN
Aprende a
descifrarlos

• ALERGIAS
Cómo afectan
al embarazo

REGALO
Una cuchara
para comidas muy divertidas

Ahora lo sabes *(Assess):*
Students continue assessing their
progress toward achieving the
chapter objectives.

⒯odo junto (Apply)

Todo junto is composed of three integrative sections: *Actividades, ¡Vamos a leer!*, and *¡Vamos a escribir!*

Teaching ideas for *Actividades*

1 To complement what students have learned up to this point, use the video segments for *La Catrina*. (See pp. T35–T36 for details.) See the Teacher's Guide that accompanies the video program for teaching suggestions.

2 You may want to use different activities for different ability groupings. Better students might work together on Ex. 3 while others do either Ex. 1 or 2. Assess students on their effort, completion of the task, creativity, and ability to communicate rather than on accuracy.

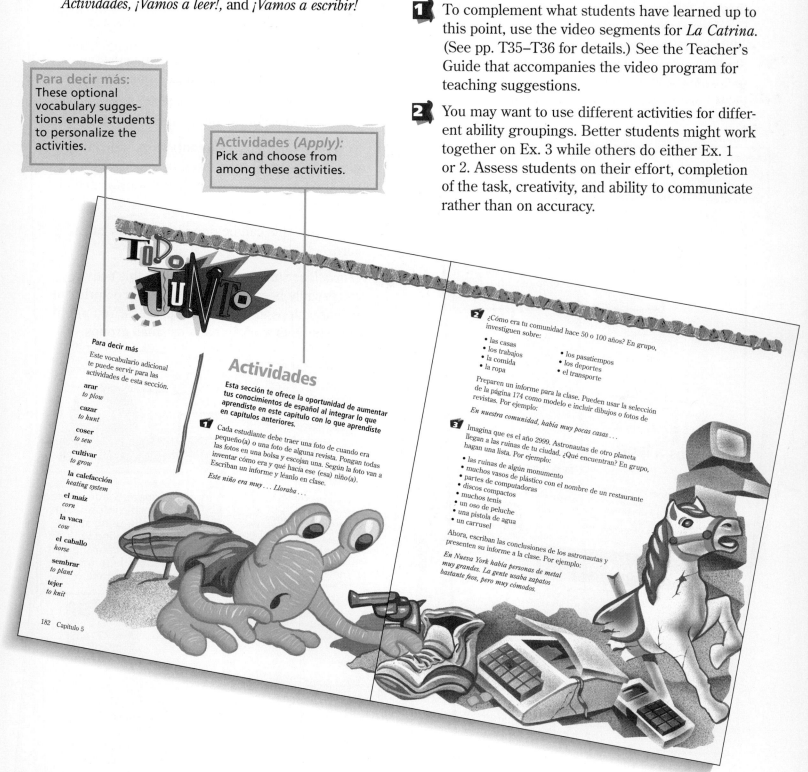

Para decir más

Este vocabulario adicional te puede servir para las actividades de esta sección.

arar
to plow

cazar
to hunt

coser
to sew

cultivar
to grow

la calefacción
heating system

el maíz
corn

la vaca
cow

el caballo
horse

sembrar
to plant

tejer
to knit

Actividades

Esta sección te ofrece la oportunidad de aumentar tus conocimientos de español al integrar lo que aprendiste en este capítulo con lo que aprendiste en capítulos anteriores.

1 Cada estudiante debe traer una foto de cuando era pequeño(a) o una foto de alguna revista. Pongan todas las fotos en una bolsa y escojan una. Según la foto van a inventar cómo era y qué hacía ese (esa) niño(a). Escriban un informe y léanlo en clase.

Este niño era muy ... Lloraba ...

2 ¿Cómo era tu comunidad hace 50 o 100 años? En grupo, investiguen sobre:

- las casas
- los trabajos
- la comida
- la ropa
- los pasatiempos
- los deportes
- el transporte

Preparen un informe para la clase. Pueden usar la selección de la página 174 como modelo e incluir dibujos o fotos de revistas. Por ejemplo:

En nuestra comunidad, había muy pocas casas ...

3 Imagina que es el año 2999. Astronautas de otro planeta llegan a las ruinas de tu ciudad. ¿Qué encuentran? En grupo, hagan una lista. Por ejemplo:

- las ruinas de algún monumento
- muchos vasos de plástico con el nombre de un restaurante
- partes de computadoras
- discos compactos
- muchos tenis
- un oso de peluche
- una pistola de agua
- un carrusel

Ahora, escriban las conclusiones de los astronautas y presenten su informe a la clase. Por ejemplo:

En Nueva York había personas de metal muy grandes. La gente usaba zapatos bastante feos, pero muy cómodos.

182 Capítulo 5

¡ **V**amos a leer! *(Apply)*

Students learn how to become efficient readers through a four-step process. Real comprehension is achieved through strategies, questions, and activities in the *Infórmate* and *Aplicación*. Students encounter unknown vocabulary, but gain confidence by realizing they don't need to know every word to read successfully.

Teaching ideas

1 *Antes de leer:* Use the globe on p. 185 or the maps on the Overhead Transparencies to point out where Nicaragua is located. Ask students if anyone has heard of Roberto Clemente. Does anyone have one of his baseball cards? Encourage answers to the questions to activate prior knowledge. Write responses on the chalkboard.

2 *Mira la lectura:* Have students work individually or in groups and report back to the class. Compare their answers to what they brainstormed in *Antes de leer.*

3 *Infórmate:* This can be done individually or in pairs.

4 *Aplicación:* Students will complete this activity successfully because of the careful structuring of the early steps in the reading process. You might have students work in pairs or small groups.

> **• Step 1**
> *Antes de leer:* Activates students' background knowledge to help them predict or anticipate.

> **• Step 2**
> *Mira la lectura:* Pre-reading section focusing on a specific reading strategy.

> **• Step 3**
> *Infórmate:* Students read for specific information or details, using strategies for dealing with difficult aspects of the text. Questions help focus on key information.

> **• Step 4**
> *Aplicación:* Students use what they have learned by applying it in a different way.

Todo junto

¡ **V**amos a leer!

Antes de leer
STRATEGY ▶ Using prior knowledge

Have you ever known a really amazing athlete? What was he or she like? What information would you expect to find in the life story of an outstanding athlete? How is a biography usually organized?

Mira la lectura

Read the story through quickly. Did you find the information you expected?

Esta estatua de Roberto Clemente queda enfrente del estadio en Pittsburgh.

El campeón

—¡Roberto! ¡Roberto, ven! ¡Ya es hora de comer!

El pequeño Roberto no prestaba atención. Era un muchacho obediente, pero en ese momento, sólo pensaba en lo que hacía—jugar béisbol.

Roberto Clemente nació en 1934 en la pequeña comunidad de Carolina, Puerto Rico. Jugaba béisbol todos los días, pero también tenía que ir a la escuela y trabajar. Trabajaba porque quería comprarse una bicicleta. Después de trabajar tres años, tuvo bastante dinero para comprarse una. En la escuela secundaria, Roberto era un muchacho tímido, pero en el campo de béisbol su timidez desaparecía.

En 1953 representantes de los Brooklyn Dodgers fueron a

Puerto Rico para observar y contratar a nuevos jugadores.
—¡Tenía que contratarlo! Era el mejor atleta innato que había visto,— dijo el scout de los Dodgers cuando vio al joven Roberto jugar. Los Dodgers lo mandaron a su equipo de Montreal, Canadá. De allí pasó a los Piratas de Pittsburgh en 1955. Cinco años más tarde los Piratas ganaron el campeonato de la Liga Nacional y la Serie Mundial. Clemente fue nombrado el Jugador Más Valioso de la liga en 1966. El 24 de julio de 1970 se celebró la Noche de Robert... en el estadio Three... Pittsburgh para ho... pelotero más fam... querido del equip...

En diciembre de ... un terrible terrem...

Nicaragua. En seguida Clemente organizó un vuelo de ayuda. Llevaba alimentos, ropa y medicina para las víctimas del desastre. El avión era viejo y pequeño y pesaba mucho, pero Clemente insistió ...

Infórmate
STRATEGY ▶ Recognizing time expressions

Time expressions will help you understand writing that is organized chronologically, as a biography usually is. Some of the time expressions in this biography are:

- ... en 1934 ...
- Cinco años más tarde ...
- En diciembre de 1972 ...

Other expressions can help you to keep track of time by referring to activities associated with a certain stage of life. For example:

- ... tenía que ir a la escuela ...
- En la escuela secundaria, ...

1. Now reread the biography. When you come ... an expression that helps you fix the time, st... and quickly calculate how old Roberto was ...

2. Why is Roberto Clemente one of baseball's ... most honored players? Why is he considered ... a great humanitarian?

Managua, Nicaragua

La ciu...

18

Aplicación

Write three to five sentences with time expressions about a famous athlete or other famous person. Then read one sentence to a partner and ask him or her to guess who it is about. If your partner can't guess, read the next sentence, ...nd so on. For example, these statements are about Nancy López.

1. Ganó el Torneo de Golf Femenino de Nuevo México cuando tenía 12 años.
2. En 1978 ganó nueve torneos de golf, entre ellos el de la Asociación de Mujeres Golfistas Profesionales (LPGA en inglés).
3. Siete años después, ganó cinco torneos, entre ellos el LPGA una vez más.

¡Vamos a leer! 185

T24   184 Capítulo 5

¡ Vamos a escribir! *(Apply)*

As with reading, students develop effective writing through a process approach consistent with the way they are learning to write in their English classes. It also provides a strategy or model for writing independently. Each writing task provides a creative, personalized opportunity to expand the chapter theme.

> **• Step 1**
> Pre-writing questions have students think about the topic, generate needed language, and organize their ideas. They then write the first draft.

> **• Steps 2 & 3**
> Through peer review students gain insights into needed revisions or clarifications for preparing the final draft.

Teaching ideas

1 This may be done in class or as homework. Students can work individually, in pairs, or in small groups to brainstorm the topic and needed vocabulary. Be sure to review the model interviews that accompany the photographs. They can jot down answers to the questions and share them with other students. They then use the questions and responses as a starting point for writing their first draft. Have students skip lines on the first draft so that there is room for comments during the peer review.

2 Have students share their first draft with one or more partners. Peer reviewers should check for thoroughness and comprehensibility, as well as for errors in spelling, grammar, and punctuation. (Each reviewer should say at least one good thing about the writing sample.)

3 Students may might want to include final drafts in their writing portfolios.

Todo junto

¡ Vamos a escribir!

Todos tenemos una persona especial en la vida. Puede ser un(a) pariente(a), un(a) amigo(a) o un(a) profesor(a). Vamos a escribir una biografía breve de una persona especial.

1 Primero entrevista a la persona o a alguien que la conoce. Contesta estas preguntas:

* ¿Cuándo y dónde nació?
* ¿Dónde vivía la familia cuando nació?
* ¿Cómo era de pequeño(a)?
* ¿Qué hacía de pequeño(a)? ¿De joven?
* ¿Cómo es ahora?
* ¿Qué hace ahora?

2 Organiza tus ideas en orden cronológico. Escribe el primer borrador. Sigue los pasos del proceso de escribir.

Ahora escribe una anécdota de la vida de la persona que escogiste. Debe ser una anécdota que revele algo de su carácter. Por ejemplo, ¿hizo alguna vez algo muy difícil? ¿Algo increíble?

3 Para distribuir las biografías y anécdotas, pueden:

* enviarlas a las personas de quienes escribieron
* enviarlas al periódico o a la revista literaria escolar
* incluirlas en un libro titulado *Personas especiales*
* ponerlas en sus portafolios

186 Capítulo 5

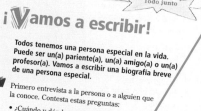
Un gaucho de San Antonio de Areco, Argentina

Entrevista con un gaucho

ESTUDIANTE	¿Qué es un gaucho?
GAUCHO	Somos vaqueros.
ESTUDIANTE	¿La ropa que usa es típica?
GAUCHO	Sí. El poncho, el sombrero negro, los pantalones flojos, el cinturón de plata y las botas son muy típicos.

Entrevista con mi abuela

NIETA	¿Dónde vivía tu familia cuando naciste?
ABUELA	Aquí en esta misma vecindad. Sólo a unas cuadras de donde vivo hoy.
NIETA	¿Qué hacías cuando eras niña?
ABUELA	Recuerdo que iba a recoger flores y frutas con mis hermanos. A mi mamá—tu bisabuela—le encantaba tener flores frescas en la casa.

Una niña en los brazos de su abuelita en Argentina

Un ecuatoriano en camino a su trabajo

Entrevista con un profesor de español

ESTUDIANTE	¿Puede Ud. decirme cuándo y dónde nació?
SR. ALLENDE	Nací en Ecuador. Ayer cumplí 30 años. ¡Tú puedes calcular el año!
ESTUDIANTE	¿Qué hacía de pequeño?
SR. ALLENDE	A mí y a mis amigos nos encantaba montar en bicicleta. También pasábamos muchas horas pescando.

¿o sabes bien? *(Apply, Assess & Summarize)*

In this section students practice tasks similar to those they will encounter on the *Examen de habilidades*. They focus on the chapter objectives and show what they can do with the language.

Teaching ideas

1 Point out how this pre-test and the vocabulary on the following page prepare for the *Examen de habilidades*.

2 Do this as a whole-class activity or have pairs complete the sections at home and then compare their responses with those of a partner. Or, with a partner, they can work through each section in class and then compare their answers with those of another pair.

3 Students who do well should feel confident about performing well on the test. Those having difficulty will know where they need to focus attention as they study for the test.

Resumen del capítulo *(Summarize)*

This section organizes the chapter vocabulary to reflect how it can be used to meet the communicative objectives. The objectives were stated in the chapter overview, and students have been given regular opportunities to assess their progress in the *¿Qué sabes ahora?*, *Ahora lo sabes,* and *¿Lo sabes bien?*

¿Lo sabes bien?

Esta sección te ayudará a prepararte para el examen de habilidades.

Listening
Can you understand when people talk about what they were like as children? Listen as your teacher reads a sample similar to what you will hear on the test. How were Tina and her sister different? Why were they different?

Reading
Read the following fragment of an autobiography. Then complete the sentences with the right time expressions. (One choice will not be used.)

Cuando yo era niño, mi mamá me hacía animales de peluche. Mi papá me hacía juguetes de madera. ___ me hizo una casa de madera en un árbol. Yo no entendía por qué mis padres no me compraban juguetes de plástico, como los de mis compañeros. ___ por fin entendí. Estudiamos el medio ambiente y la importancia de reciclar los materiales. Mis padres estaban reciclando las cosas. ___ yo también hago juguetes de madera para mi hija.

Writing
Clara is going to spend a year in Guatemala as an exchange student. A Guatemala City newspaper has asked for a brief description of her as a child. This is what a long-time friend wrote. Write a similar description of *your* best friend.

> Recuerdo que Clara era una niña muy simpática y trabajadora. Cuando no conocía a la gente, era un poco tímida, pero después era sociable. Éramos vecinos. Íbamos a la misma escuela. Los fines de semana jugábamos en el parque. Yo sé que Clara va a tener muchos amigos en Guatemala.

Culture
If you had been a friend of José Martí, would you have helped him fight for Cuban independence? Why?

Speaking
With a partner, talk about your childhood. Ask one another some questions to find out what you were like as young children. Here is a sample dialogue.

A —*Cuando tenías cinco años, ¿cómo eras?*
B —*Obediente pero a veces un poco travieso. ¿Y tú?*
A —*Casi siempre me portaba bien, pero también era traviesa. ¿Con qué te gustaba jugar?*
B —*Me gustaban los bloques, los trenes eléctricos y las pistola de agua. ¿Qué preferías tú?*
A —*A mí me encantaba montar en triciclo y saltar a la cuer*

a. cuando estaba en la escuela secundaria
b. el año pasado
c. ahora
d. cuando cumplí ocho años

188   Capítulo 5

Teaching ideas

1 Have pairs review the vocabulary. They might make up a sentence or dialogue in each category. For example, *Tenía un pez cuando era niño* or:
—*¿Tenías un pájaro cuando eras niño?*
—*No, pero tenía una tortuga.*

2 If students have created flashcards, have them organize these according to the communicative categories.

3 Have students quiz each other using the list in the book or their flashcards. Ask them to indicate any words their partner had trouble with by writing them on a sheet of paper or placing a check on the flashcard. This will focus their test preparation on problem areas.

Assessment options

1 The *Prueba cumulativa* is a prochievement instrument that focuses on students' knowledge of the chapter vocabulary and grammar in a communicative context.

2 The *Examen de habilidades* is a proficiency-oriented instrument that focuses on what students can do with the language in a real-world context.

3 The Test Generator provides a test bank of multiple-choice questions to which you can add your own questions.

Resumen del capítulo 5

el vocabulario de este capítulo para:
ell what you were like as a child
ell what you used to like to do
talk about what you learned to do

talk about animals
animal, *pl.* los animales
pájaro
pez, *pl.* los peces
tortuga

talk about people
pequeño, -a
niño, la niña
vecino, la vecina
bediente
esobediente
bien) educado, -a
naleducado, -a
onsentido, -a
ímido, -a
ravieso, -a

o name toys
el juguete
la muñeca
el muñeco
el robot, *pl.* los robots
el animal de peluche, *pl.* los animales de peluche
el oso de peluche
el dinosaurio
el camión, *pl.* los camiones
el tren (de juguete)
el bloque
la pistola (de agua)

to discuss things you used to do
ser: (yo) era, (tú) eras
caminar
montar en triciclo
el triciclo
saltar (a la cuerda)
la cuerda
ir: (yo) iba, (tú) ibas
recordar *(o → ue)*
coleccionar
la colección, *pl.* las colecciones
la verdad
mentir *(e → ie)*
obedecer *(c → zc)*
desobedecer *(c → zc)*
portarse (bien / mal)
molestar
pelearse (con)
llorar

to talk about places children go
la guardería infantil
el kindergarten
la escuela primaria

to talk about playground equipment
el patio de recreo
el cajón de arena, *pl.* los cajones de arena
el carrusel
el columpio
el sube y baja
el tobogán, *pl.* los toboganes

Resumen 189

USING THE TEACHER'S EDITION

This Teacher's Edition provides all the support needed to work with the wide range of students in today's Spanish classes.

Each teacher chapter begins with a spread that provides organizational and cultural information for instructional planning.

Additional information and insight into the chapter's cultural theme

List of the chapter communication, culture, and grammar objectives

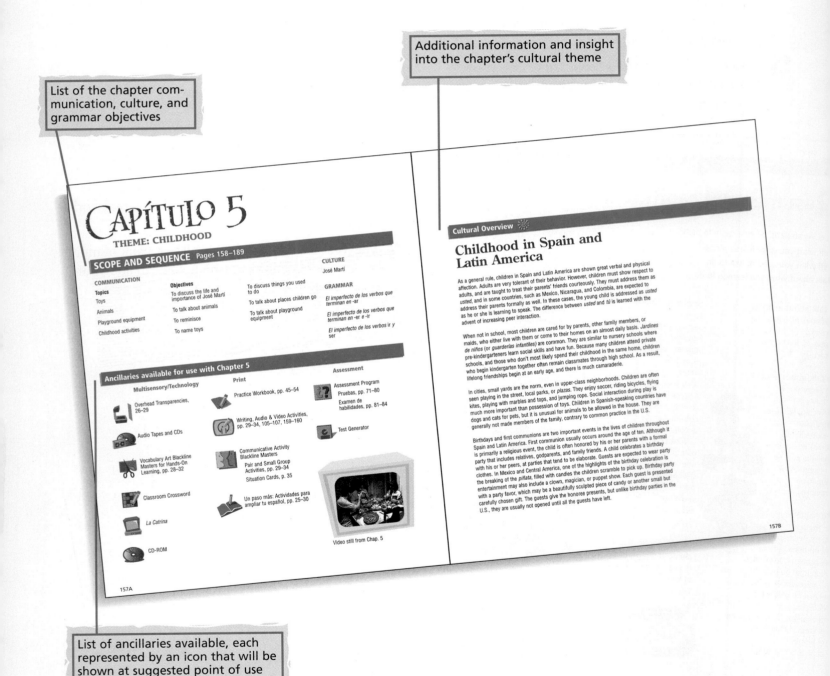

CAPÍTULO 5
THEME: CHILDHOOD

SCOPE AND SEQUENCE Pages 158–189

COMMUNICATION

Topics	Objectives		CULTURE
Toys	To discuss the life and importance of José Martí	To discuss things you used to do	José Martí
Animals	To talk about animals	To talk about places children go	**GRAMMAR**
Playground equipment	To reminisce	To talk about playground equipment	El imperfecto de los verbos que terminan en -ar
Childhood activities	To name toys		El imperfecto de los verbos que terminan en -er e -ir
			El imperfecto de los verbos ir y ser

Ancillaries available for use with Chapter 5

Multisensory/Technology

- Overhead Transparencies, 26–29
- Audio Tapes and CDs
- Vocabulary Art Blackline Masters for Hands-On Learning, pp. 28–32
- Classroom Crossword
- La Catrina
- CD-ROM

Print

- Practice Workbook, pp. 45–54
- Writing, Audio & Video Activities, pp. 29–34, 105–107, 159–160
- Communicative Activity Blackline Masters
  Pair and Small Group Activities, pp. 29–34
  Situation Cards, p. 35
- Un paso más: Actividades para ampliar tu español, pp. 25–30

Assessment

- Assessment Program
  Pruebas, pp. 71–80
  Examen de habilidades, pp. 81–84
- Test Generator

Video still from Chap. 5

157A

Cultural Overview

Childhood in Spain and Latin America

As a general rule, children in Spain and Latin America are shown great verbal and physical affection. Adults are very tolerant of their behavior. However, children must show respect to adults, and are taught to treat their parents' friends courteously. They must address them as usted, and in some countries, such as Mexico, Nicaragua, and Colombia, are expected to address their parents formally as well. In these cases, the young child is addressed as usted as he or she is learning to speak. The difference between usted and tú is learned with the advent of increasing peer interaction.

When not in school, most children are cared for by parents, other family members, or maids, who either live with them or come to their homes on an almost daily basis. Jardines de niños (or guarderías infantiles) are common. They are similar to nursery schools where pre-kindergarteners learn social skills and have fun. Because many children attend private schools, and those who don't most likely spend their childhood in the same home, children who begin kindergarten together often remain classmates through high school. As a result, lifelong friendships begin at an early age, and there is much camaraderie.

In cities, small yards are the norm, even in upper-class neighborhoods. Children are often seen playing in the street, local parks, or plazas. They enjoy soccer, riding bicycles, flying kites, playing with marbles and tops, and jumping rope. Social interaction during play is much more important than possession of toys. Children in Spanish-speaking countries have dogs and cats for pets, but it is unusual for animals to be allowed in the house. They are generally not made members of the family, contrary to common practice in the U.S.

Birthdays and first communions are two important events in the lives of children throughout Spain and Latin America. First communion usually occurs around the age of ten. Although it is primarily a religious event, the child is often honored by his or her parents with a formal party that includes relatives, godparents, and family friends. A child celebrates a birthday with his or her peers, at parties that tend to be elaborate. Guests are expected to wear party clothes. In Mexico and Central America, one of the highlights of the birthday celebration is the breaking of the piñata, filled with candies the children scramble to pick up. Birthday party entertainment may also include a clown, magician, or puppet show. Each guest is presented with a party favor, which may be a beautifully sculpted piece of candy or another small but carefully chosen gift. The guests give the honoree presents, but unlike birthday parties in the U.S., they are usually not opened until all the guests have left.

157B

List of ancillaries available, each represented by an icon that will be shown at suggested point of use

This Teacher's Edition is organized to provide for maximum ease of use. The student page is slightly reduced. Teacher notes appear regularly in the same place on the page.

Sidenotes are organized around the five-step pedagogical model used throughout *PASO A PASO:*

- **Introduce / Preview**
- **Present**
- **Practice**
- **Apply**
- **Summarize / Assess**

Notes provide answers, teaching suggestions, ancillary cross-references, recycling references, and other useful information.

Previously taught vocabulary sets that are re-entered in the chapter

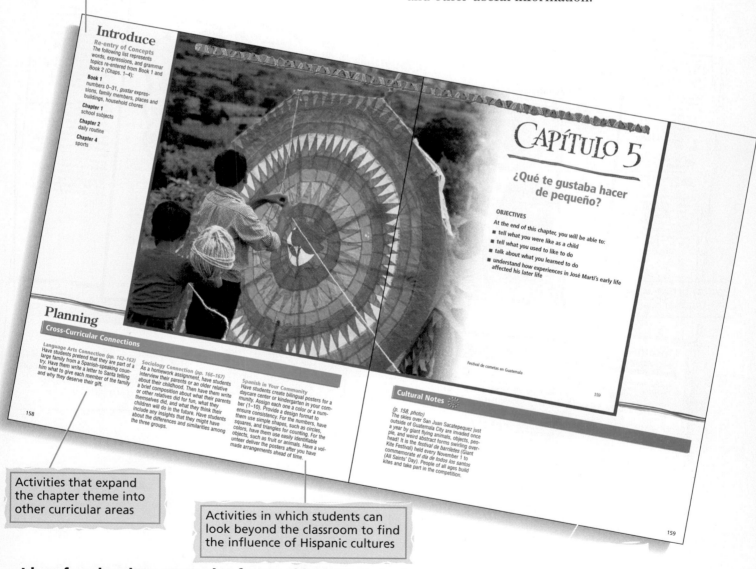

Activities that expand the chapter theme into other curricular areas

Activities in which students can look beyond the classroom to find the influence of Hispanic cultures

Ideas for planning, strategies for reaching all students, and expansions on cultural themes

References to help with planning and instruction

Chapter theme

Communicative objectives

Ideas for recycling previously taught material

Icons for ancillary references

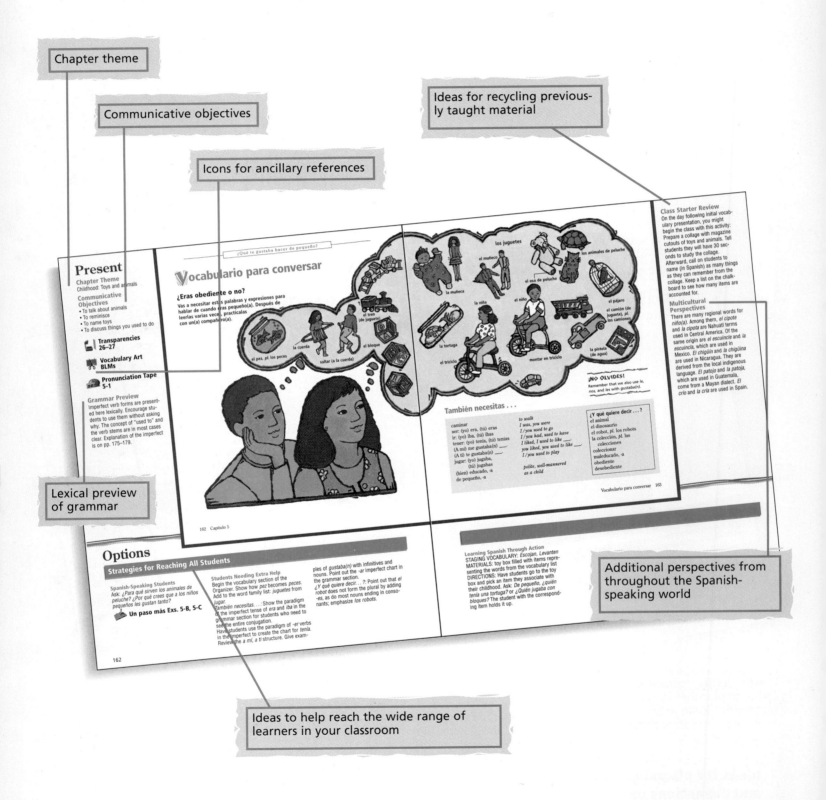

Lexical preview of grammar

Additional perspectives from throughout the Spanish-speaking world

Ideas to help reach the wide range of learners in your classroom

MANAGEMENT AND PACING

Management and pacing have frustrated many foreign language teachers in the past. Several factors affect pacing in a typical classroom:

1 Reduced or interrupted instructional time. The amount of class time for teachers across the country varies from 38 to 60 minutes. Of that, time is lost due to the inevitable interruptions (assemblies, fire drills, announcements, etc.). In addition, flexible scheduling may change the amount of instructional time from day to day.

2 Wider range of students in the classroom. Many students are coming to the Spanish classroom with weak English skills and poor study skills. The pace of instruction must change to include more repetition and greater variety in teaching strategies.

3 Time for building proficiency. Our goals for language teaching today recognize the need for more time. Memorizing a conjugation is one thing. Gaining the ability to use it with some ease is another thing altogether. Pair and small-group practice—the most effective and long-lasting tool for learning a language—requires time. Though less material may be covered, what is learned is more likely to be retained.

4 Amount of content in textbooks. Many teachers are concerned that too much is presented in textbooks, especially in the first and second years. The combination of varying instructional time, the wide range of students, and more emphasis on communicative activities and proficiency contribute to a slower pace of instruction than in the past.

PASO A PASO 2 has been carefully developed to provide the instructional materials for one school year. The authors had as a goal the development of a realistically paced and easy-to-manage program that would relieve teacher and student frustration. There is flexibility and choice among the textbook activities and ancillaries. To help work with the wide variety of learners in your classroom, *PASO A PASO 2* offers unprecedented support on every page. We developed the Scope and Sequence to give students the tools needed to communicate about their interests. Thematic chapter organization allows for real integration of vocabulary, grammar, and culture, while avoiding unneeded grammatical content.

We present vocabulary in logical sets and, when possible, with visuals. Research shows that both of these approaches lead to more efficient and more permanent learning. Above all, lexical and contextual introduction of grammar allows students to learn structures in a truly natural way. *Fui* is not "the first-person singular preterite of the verb *ir*," but, quite simply, "I went"—a concept that presents no difficulty. (This is particularly true for students who neither know nor care that "I went" is a past-tense form of the verb "to go.")

We would urge you to allow this process to unfold. Avoid explanations in the vocabulary section. Allow students to use the words naturally. By the time they reach the explanations they will feel confident in their ability to use the language.

Bridging from *PASO A PASO 1*
Pacing for the review section, *Pasodoble*

Students begin the new school year with a renewed excitement about learning. In order to encourage this energy, we are offering students a motivating, engaging review of selected content from *PASO A PASO 1. Pasodoble* provides a unique, integrative review of some of the major vocabulary sets and structures presented in the first year. See pp. 1A–1B for a list of the vocabulary and grammar integrated in the *Pasodoble*.

Do not spend more than two weeks on this section. You will find these concepts re-entered throughout *PASO A PASO 2,* thereby offering still more opportunities for review.

Pacing for *PASO A PASO 2*
Pacing for Chapters 1–14

We suggest that approximately 11–13 instructional days be spent on each chapter, including assessment. This time will vary based upon the amount of instructional time and the range of students in the class.

As you begin teaching with *PASO A PASO 2,* you will sense a rhythm, a flow within each chapter that helps students move smoothly and successfully. The thematic integration and spiraling within a chapter, the extensive use of context and comprehensible input for vocabulary and grammar, the inductive questioning that leads to real understanding, and the recycling of previously taught material are part of the carefully thought-out chapter design. You should be able to move quickly through the chapters in the suggested time period.

Bridging to PASO A PASO 3

As students move into *PASO A PASO 3,* it is expected that they will have completed the content in Chapters 1–12 of Book 2. The grammar and vocabulary in Chapters 13–14 will be retaught as if new in *PASO A PASO 3.*

Review and reteaching

As students move into *PASO A PASO 3,* they will continually be exposed to material they will have learned in this book.

PASO A PASO 3 begins with a lively, communicative magazine-like section entitled *Pasodoble* that reactivates the major vocabulary sets and structures of the early chapters of *PASO A PASO 2.*

The charts on the following pages show the reteaching and expansion of specific grammar points from book to book.

Block Scheduling

In recent years, some school districts have adopted block scheduling. While there are many variations in this type of scheduling, the most common change from the traditional 45- or 50-minute class period is to one of longer duration, typically from 70 to 90 minutes. In some schools, these classes meet daily and complete the year-long program in 4.5 to 6 months. In others, they meet every other day for the entire school year.

Some teachers have expressed concerns about the extended period of time that students are in a given session. How can one avoid their becoming bored? The answer lies in the variety of engaging activities offered during a given class period. Using *PASO A PASO,* teachers have at hand a wealth of varied activities that allow students to learn using paired and large- and small-group activities (open-ended and personalized), unusually engaging audiotape material, video-viewing activities, Total Physical Response, and inductive approaches both to culture and to grammar—all in addition to the unique ideas and approaches that each teacher brings to the classroom.

Another question raised by block scheduling is that of retention rate. In one approach, students have to remember a day's lesson from, say, Monday to Wednesday; in the other, they may have a six-month time lag between levels of language study. Research demonstrates that when material has been thoroughly acquired, the retention rate is significantly higher. Returning students are more quickly able to return to the level of language where they left off the year before. *PASO A PASO's* in-depth thematic emphasis enables students to make this transition as smoothly as possible.

PASO A PASO is designed to offer the best possible instructional opportunities for either approach to scheduling.

rammar

Grammar	PASO A PASO 1	PASO A PASO 2
ser	1, **5***	*Pasodoble,* **4, 5, 7**
adjectives	**1,** 3, **4, 5, 6, 7, 8, 9**	*Pasodoble,* **1, 3**
negatives	**1,** 2, **14**	**8**
regular *-ar* verbs	**2**	*Pasodoble*
tener	2, 4, **5**	*Pasodoble,* **1**
ir	**3**	*Pasodoble,* **5**
estar	**3**	*Pasodoble,* **8**
stem-changing verbs: *o→ue*	3, **7, 9**	**2**
stem-changing verbs: *e→ie*	3, 4, **7, 8**	**2**
regular *-er* verbs	**4**	*Pasodoble*
possessive adjectives	**5, 8**	*Pasodoble,* **7**
demonstrative adjectives	**6**	**1,** 3
direct object pronouns	**6,** 10, **11,** 12, 13	**1,** 9
preterite	6, 7, 9, **10, 11, 12,** 13	**3, 4, 6, 9, 10**
salir	**7**	**1**
personal *a*	**7**	*Pasodoble*
regular *-ir* verbs	**8**	*Pasodoble*
hacer	**8**	*Pasodoble*
poner	**8**	**9**
indirect object pronouns	**9, 11, 12**	2, 3, 5, 9
dar	11, **14**	**6**
comparatives / superlatives	**11**	*Pasodoble,* **1,** 3
stem-changing verbs: *e→i*	**12**	**2, 6**
traer	**12**	**1,** 9
saber	**13**	**4,** 8
decir	**13**	*Pasodoble,* **7**
tú affirmative commands	**13**	**12, 13**
conocer	**14**	**1,** 5
present progressive	**14**	**8,** 9

*Lightface numbers represent lexical introduction or quick review;
boldface numbers represent presentation of the grammar point.

Grammar

Grammar	PASO A PASO 2	PASO A PASO 3
ir	*Pasodoble*	*Pasodoble*
hacer	*Pasodoble*	*Pasodoble*
tener	*Pasodoble,* **1***	*Pasodoble*
comparatives / superlatives	*Pasodoble,* **1, 3**	*Pasodoble*
demonstratives	1, **3**	*Pasodoble*
ser	*Pasodoble,* **4, 5, 7**	*Pasodoble*
possession	*Pasodoble,* **7**	*Pasodoble*
estar	*Pasodoble,* **8**	*Pasodoble*
direct object pronouns	**1,** 9	*Pasodoble,* **1, 6**
indirect object pronouns	2, 3, 5, 9	*Pasodoble,* **1, 6**
reflexive verbs	**2, 4,** 6	*Pasodoble*
stem-changing verbs: $e \rightarrow i$	**2, 6**	*Pasodoble,* 8
preterite	**3, 4, 6, 9, 10**	*Pasodoble,* **3, 4,** 11, 12
imperfect	**5, 6, 10**	*Pasodoble,* **2**
negatives	**8**	*Pasodoble*
present progressive	**8,** 9	**5**
imperfect progressive	**9**	**3**
future	**11**	**6**
tú commands	**12, 13,** 14	*Pasodoble,* **1, 9**
subjunctive	**13, 14**	**7, 8, 9, 10, 11, 12**

*Lightface numbers represent lexical introduction or quick review; boldface numbers represent presentation of the grammar point.

ROLE OF THE VIDEO: *La Catrina*

La Catrina is the storyline video program that accompanies *PASO A PASO 2*. Why a storyline video? For many students, the second year of language learning is especially difficult and they lose motivation. We have thus developed an energizing, motivating, teen-centered *telenovela* that will help students feel a sense of accomplishment as they work their way through the 14 episodes (and the 14 chapters). It is performed by professional actors, most of them well known to Mexican television viewers.

Students can benefit in many ways from viewing *La Catrina*. They expand their ability to understand native speakers of Spanish as they move beyond the textbook. They experience the integration and recycling of previously learned vocabulary and grammar. They grow in confidence as they encounter and understand new content embedded in a meaningful context. They gain in cultural understanding as they observe contemporary Mexican culture, with special emphasis on the day-to-day lives of young adults. Students improve in proficiency as they work with the video's content and the activities that accompany *La Catrina*. In addition, students' motivation to learn Spanish grows as they become involved in the engaging plot and characters that bring *La Catrina* to life.

The plot of *La Catrina*

Jamie González, a bilingual high-school student from Los Angeles, spends the summer in Querétaro, Mexico. A scholarship from the Comité de Intercambio Cultural has made this trip possible. Accompanying her on the trip is a classmate, Philip Armstrong. While there, Jamie hopes to learn about her great-grandmother, La Catrina, who lived in Querétaro during the time of the Mexican Revolution. To help in this search, Jamie brings the family's only connection to this mysterious relative: an old, faded photograph. Awaiting Jamie is a summer of mystery, adventure, and romance . . . and the discoveries involving La Catrina, which will change her life forever.

The organization of *La Catrina*

Each of the 14 episodes is organized around three segments. In the first chapter, segment 1 is an introduction to the story. In subsequent chapters, it is entitled *¿Recuerdas?*, and is a brief summary of the plot up to that point to help students prepare for the upcoming episode. The second segment, approximately eight minutes long, contains the episode itself. The third segment, *Para entender mejor,* is a one-minute review focusing on a key plot concept. It includes additional narration and on-screen text to support students' understanding. The Teacher's Guide accompanying the video contains plot synopses as well as a complete video transcript.

Using *La Catrina* with *PASO A PASO 2*

La Catrina incorporates the themes and vocabulary of *PASO A PASO 2*. But the video moves the students well beyond the book as they experience Spanish in real-world contexts. Each of the 14 episodes corresponds to the similarly numbered chapter in the text. The chapter theme and some of its vocabulary are integrated into the plot. For example, the theme in Chapter 2 of *PASO A PASO 2* is school. In episode 2 of *La Catrina,* Jamie is getting to know María Linares, with whose family she will live while in Mexico. The two girls talk about their school experiences and how schools differ in the United States and Mexico.

You might find it most successful to show *La Catrina* as students begin working with the chapter section entitled *Todo junto*, where chapter vocabulary and grammar are integrated with previously learned content. This philosophy is reflected in *La Catrina,* where students continually build upon language they already know.

As you work with *La Catrina,* we suggest you use the material in the video section of the student Writing, Audio & Video Activities workbook, which contains both pre- and post-viewing activities. Before viewing, have students recall the previous episode by brainstorming what happened.

Then show segment 1 to verify their recall. Let students see segment 2 several times. You might want to break the episode up by scenes and show them over several days, first showing portions with the sound off. Encourage students to brainstorm what the episode might be about. What are the locales? Who are the characters? What are they doing? Use segment 3 after students have viewed the episode in its entirety. After they view this video explanation of a key concept, they might want to see the entire episode again, as they will have still more insight into the plot. After completing the entire episode, you might focus on the scenes that integrate the chapter theme. See the Video Teacher's Guide for additional teaching ideas.

There is an additional workbook of activities based on *La Catrina*. It contains different and more extensive activities than those in the Writing, Audio & Video Activities workbook.

While it is certainly possible to teach *PASO A PASO 2* without using the video, you will find it a powerful tool in promoting the development of the listening skills students need to function outside the sheltered environment of the classroom, and in bringing the culture of Mexico into the classroom in a vivid and motivating way.

STRATEGIES FOR REACHING ALL STUDENTS

PASO A PASO 2 provides teachers the support and strategies needed to reach all students in the Spanish classroom. We offer an unprecedented commitment to providing materials that help meet the realities of today's classroom. This article focuses on strategies from *PASO A PASO 2* that will help you and all of your students enjoy a successful year learning Spanish . . . step by step!

1 Material that builds upon students' experiences

Language students learn best by using what they know, by building new knowledge on old, and by experiencing and doing. As you use the text, you will see that *PASO A PASO 2* provides for an authentic, meaningful experience for the learner. The fourteen chapter themes were developed by asking, "What do students want to talk about?" The vocabulary taught is high-frequency language that students want to learn. The grammar supports communication and is practiced communicatively. The cultural content provides a means toward understanding and a global perspective that will be meaningful to all students. The activities ask students to interact, to become active participants in the learning process, and to express real ideas and real meanings for real purposes.

2 A multisensory approach to learning

Each student enters the Spanish classroom with different learning styles and abilities. Some work best with an aural / oral approach; others need a strong visual approach. Many need to touch and be physically involved in learning. An approach that addresses the needs and strengths of each student lays the groundwork for reaching all.

PASO A PASO 2 provides a strong multisensory approach to language learning. Students have varied opportunities for success by working with activities that recognize different learning styles and employ more than one modality. Each chapter provides suggestions for incorporating TPR, which we call Learning Spanish Through Action. The *Todo junto* offers activities that involve different learning skills and interests (creating a collage, preparing a skit, drawing a house).

The cornerstone of success in ScottForesman's foreign language programs has always been our strong visual approach. We have expanded this in *PASO A PASO 2*. Each chapter opens with culturally authentic photographs (*¡Piénsalo bien!*) that call upon students' background knowledge in discussing the chapter theme. Vocabulary presentation is facilitated by contextual visualization that is then recycled in the practice activities to reinforce learning. This approach is supported by the Overhead Transparencies and the Vocabulary Art Blackline Masters. We have enhanced the visual approach through a photo essay in the *Perspectiva cultural*. A new, realia-based approach offers students an opportunity to study grammar in a real-life context. And reading and writing practice are made more accessible through the strong use of visual cues.

The multisensory approach is further expanded through use of the chapter-by-chapter audio tapes, video, and the interactive multimedia CD-ROM. The video program brings the culture to students through a story that represents language in a truly authentic context. The *La Catrina:* Interactive CD-ROM provides opportunities for students to work at their own pace while engaging all learning styles.

3 Learning strategies

PASO A PASO 2 reinforces the strategies and skill-building techniques that students are using in their other classes. Some of these may be new to you but are easily implemented in the Spanish classroom. Strategies include building on background knowledge and experience, making lists or webs to organize their learning, inductive questioning, and consistent application of reading strategies and process writing.

Higher-order and inductive thinking

It sometimes seems that every day researchers are discovering new facts about the workings of the brain. We now know that information is stored in many areas of the brain and connected by a rich network of neurons. The goal of instruction should be to maximize the use of this network by helping students make connections and to learn information from a variety of perspectives and in a variety of ways. Activities aimed toward this goal are inherently interesting and motivating.

Students learn more successfully when they create their own understanding. Throughout *PASO A PASO 2* you will find activities that ask students to do just this. Inductive questions, for example, are the starting point of the following chapter features: *¡Piénsalo bien!, Perspectiva cultural, Gramática en contexto,* and *¡Vamos a leer!* Activities that engage students in higher-level thinking skills are the initial focus in each of these sections, as well as in the *Actividades* and *¡Vamos a escribir!* We sequence these activities so that all students can be successful.

Another important learning strategy, informed guessing, is embedded in the vocabulary section entitled *¿Y qué quiere decir . . . ?* and is focused on in the inductive questions about photographs, as well as in the process reading and writing sections of each chapter.

Multiple learning opportunities

We know that students will improve at different rates and will be stronger in some areas than in others. In addition, developing proficiency takes time for everyone, no matter how gifted. Therefore, instruction must provide multiple opportunities for learning and improvement.

PASO A PASO 2 offers these opportunities. New vocabulary is presented, practiced, and recycled throughout a chapter and in subsequent chapters. Students are first exposed to grammar lexi-

cally, use it as they practice, and have some degree of understanding and control of it before it is presented and practiced as grammar. It is presented in easy-to-deal-with increments. The imperfect, for example, is first explained in Chapter 5, with additional information being presented in Chapters 6 and 10. Similarly, reflexive constructions are explained in Chapter 2, with reminders or additional information in Chapters 4, 6, and 8. In addition, recursive themes from one level to the next allow for regular review, expansion, and elaboration.

Throughout the text you will find reminder notes to students entitled *¡No olvides!* These focus on previously learned concepts that students will need to do a particular exercise or to understand better an extension of a given structure. These reminders are not crutches, but rather important tools for mastery.

Additional opportunities for students who need them

A regular on-page feature of this Teacher's Edition entitled "Strategies for Reaching All Students" provides you support for working with:

- Spanish-speaking students
- those having difficulty learning
- the gifted

For working with Spanish speakers, there are suggestions throughout the text, as well as a specially written supplemental worktext, *Un paso más: Actividades para ampliar tu español.* Notes under the heading "Students Needing Extra Help" suggest adaptations of the textbook activities or grammar explanations for those with real learning difficulties. Enrichment suggestions allow students who are capable of doing so to move beyond the textbook. You will also find notes for cooperative learning, an excellent strategy for reaching all students.

7 Varied assessment options

Students will do better in assessment situations if they have a clear understanding of the objectives, of how they will be assessed, and if they are assessed in such a way as to focus on their strengths.

PASO A PASO 2 offers a variety of options. Besides the *Pruebas* and *Exámenes de habilidades* in the Assessment Program, the *Actividades* in the integrative *Todo junto* offer you different types of opportunities for assessment, asking students to draw upon auditory, visual, and kinesthetic strengths. The Communicative Activities Blackline Masters include Situation Cards that are ideal for use in assessing speaking proficiency. (For additional ideas, see the article on assessment, pp. T40–T45, and the Introduction to the Assessment Program itself.)

Through the clearly stated objectives at the beginning of each chapter and the mini-assessments within the chapter *(¿Qué sabes ahora?* and *Ahora lo sabes),* students are able to monitor their own progress. In addition, the end-of-chapter pretest *(¿Lo sabes bien?)* gives them a clear picture of how they will be assessed on the *Examen de habilidades.*

PASO A PASO 2 is committed to helping every teacher reach every student in the Spanish class. By providing materials that are strategy-based and that have built-in teacher support, we believe that we are enabling both you and your students to experience real enjoyment and unparalleled success.

ASSESSMENT

Assessment in a communicative classroom can take many forms: informal daily assessments, short quizzes that check knowledge of vocabulary or grammar, longer end-of-chapter assessments that verify what students know and can do in Spanish, and student portfolios. To be most effective, assessment should be based on the following criteria: (1) clear objectives that allow for meaningful and purposeful communication; (2) student understanding of what is expected of them when assessed; (3) assessment that reflects what students have done in the chapter; and (4) varied assessment options that utilize the strengths of each student. *PASO A PASO 2* provides you a wide variety of assessment options.

At the beginning of each chapter, students see the objectives expressed as what they will be able to do by the end of the chapter. They have multiple opportunities to verify their progress toward achieving these objectives in the *¿Qué sabes ahora?, Ahora lo sabes,* and *¿Lo sabes bien?* sections. The end-of-chapter vocabulary list organizes vocabulary based upon the chapter objectives. Thus, students are told at the start what is expected of them, given opportunities to check their progress, and given a pre-test that models the *Examen de habilidades.*

Informal daily assessment

Class performance and homework are key elements in assessment. Throughout, the pupil's book offers a wide variety of daily assessment opportunities. Regular informal assessment builds self confidence, particularly for students who do not perform well in more formal or traditional testing situations. Encouraging creativity in activities and homework assignments often evokes rewarding results for the individual, the class, and the teacher.

At all stages of *PASO A PASO 2,* students participate in meaningful, purposeful activities that are ideal for informal assessment. The abundant ancillaries that accompany *PASO A PASO 2* also provide for flexibility and variety.

Expanding the textbook: Ideas for creative homework

The following are creative ideas for expanding on the various chapter sections.

Vocabulario para conversar

Students can:

- make collages of the vocabulary words and present them to the class
- make flashcards showing pictograms of the vocabulary
- create crossword puzzles, word searches, and scrambled word lists, including answer keys, with new vocabulary; share these with a partner
- find and describe additional photographs related to the vocabulary theme; present descriptions to the class
- photograph or videotape people and objects representative of the chapter vocabulary; write captions for the photographs or narrate the video
- write expanded captions for the photographs in the textbook and explain them to a partner
- use a computer to create word games using chapter vocabulary

Empecemos a conversar

Students can:

- practice conversations on the phone and then present them to a small group or to the class
- produce videotapes with props and then present them to the class
- write new dialogues using pictures or talk bubbles and then present the dialogues in class

Empecemos a escribir
Empecemos a escribir y a leer

Students can:

- make up original questions and then interview a partner; the results of the interviews can be written up as interviews or as summaries of what they learned from one another

- create new questions or dialogues, including illustrations such as talk balloons or magazine cutouts; practice and then perform the dialogues in class

- interview a student or someone in the community who speaks Spanish; write out the interview and then report what was learned to the rest of the class

¿Qué sabes ahora? / Ahora lo sabes

Students can:

- illustrate the sentences or dialogues, including talk balloons that show what the characters are saying

- create collages representing the answers to the questions

- record the answers on an audio cassette

- create dialogues, practicing them with a partner on the telephone and then presenting them to a small group or to the class

Perspectiva cultural

Students can:

- make original posters that illustrate the main idea

- create travel brochures with illustrations and captions

- interview someone who is knowledgeable about the topic; make videos or audio cassettes of the interview; write illustrated summaries

- make posters showing similarities and differences between cultures

- find photographs that illustrate the cultural theme and write a caption or description

Gramática en contexto

Students can:

- write modified versions of the realia-based readings

- make charts illustrating one or more of the grammar rules presented, color-coding the essential points

- create mnemonic devices that will help them remember the grammar points

- compose simple lyrics or poems illustrating a grammar rule

¿Lo sabes bien?

Students can:

- create short listening passages with questions; have partners listen and then answer the questions, correcting one another whenever appropriate

- write advertisements, post cards, or conversations with questions; have partners read and then answer the questions

- make collages of the cultural topic, explaining them to the class or to partners

- create new dialogues using the one in the Speaking section as a model

There are several ways to evaluate student performance on informal assessment, including the above ideas for creative homework. You might want to evaluate some assignments or, at other times, let students evaluate each other's work or their own. There are several criteria you can use for informal assessment, including: completion of task, quantity of information, appropriateness, comprehensibility, originality, promptness, variety, quality above and beyond base expectations, individual improvement, accuracy, and fluency.

Formal assessment

Quizzes

PASO A PASO 2 provides blackline master quizzes, *Pruebas,* for each chapter vocabulary and grammar section. Feel free to use some or all of the quizzes based on the needs of your students.

End-of-chapter assessment

At the end of each chapter, you have several assessment options.

1 *Prueba cumulativa:* A contextualized, comprehensive chapter quiz that assesses student knowledge of vocabulary and grammar.

2 *Examen de habilidades:* A thematic, contextualized assessment of listening and reading comprehension, writing and speaking proficiency, and cultural knowledge. The vocabulary and grammar are fully integrated as opposed to being tested in isolation.

3 Test Generator (multiple-choice questions): A test generator provides a bank of questions per chapter. You can add your own questions to the test bank.

Final examinations

The Assessment Program offers you *Bancos de ideas,* several banks of test items that you can copy, cut, and paste to develop an end-of-semester/quarter or final exam.

See the introduction to the Assessment Program for a complete explanation of the formal assessment options.

Student portfolios

In addition to the informal and formal assessment, and the creative homework already described, another way to check student performance is through the use of student portfolios.

Portfolios in the second-language classroom

The portfolio should contain samples of a student's work collected over a period of time. This enables both you and the student to observe the progress being made. The portfolio should provide students the opportunity to examine and reflect upon what they have produced so that they become more involved in improving their work. The portfolio can be useful to determine grade / level placement.

Contents of the portfolio

- written work, such as short paragraphs, compositions, or journals
- audio and / or video cassettes of student performance
- quizzes and tests
- evidence of reading comprehension
- evidence of listening comprehension
- individual student projects
- pair or group projects
- art work
- cultural projects
- picture dictionaries
- story boards
- evidence that the language skills were practiced outside of the classroom
- evidence of contact with Hispanic cultures in the community
- original creative writing, such as poems, short stories, narratives, or explanations
- student-produced newspapers
- evidence of student reflection on his or her own writing or speaking

Introducing the portfolio

If the portfolio is to be used in the assessment of progress and proficiency in the language, then students must know that it is more than just a collection of materials. They need to know that it will be integrated with daily, weekly, or monthly activities. The following is one example of how to introduce the portfolio to your students:

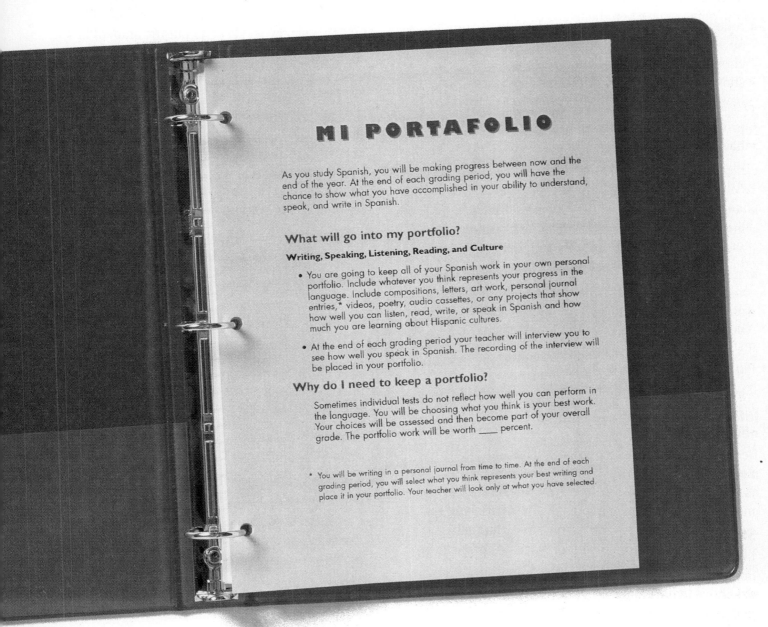

MI PORTAFOLIO

As you study Spanish, you will be making progress between now and the end of the year. At the end of each grading period, you will have the chance to show what you have accomplished in your ability to understand, speak, and write in Spanish.

What will go into my portfolio?
Writing, Speaking, Listening, Reading, and Culture

- You are going to keep all of your Spanish work in your own personal portfolio. Include whatever you think represents your progress in the language. Include compositions, letters, art work, personal journal entries,* videos, poetry, audio cassettes, or any projects that show how well you can listen, read, write, or speak in Spanish and how much you are learning about Hispanic cultures.

- At the end of each grading period your teacher will interview you to see how well you speak in Spanish. The recording of the interview will be placed in your portfolio.

Why do I need to keep a portfolio?

Sometimes individual tests do not reflect how well you can perform in the language. You will be choosing what you think is your best work. Your choices will be assessed and then become part of your overall grade. The portfolio work will be worth _____ percent.

* You will be writing in a personal journal from time to time. At the end of each grading period, you will select what you think represents your best writing and place it in your portfolio. Your teacher will look only at what you have selected.

Assessing the portfolio

The portfolio could be used as the sole means of assessing student progress, as an integral part of the overall grade, or only as a showcase of what students have accomplished. The following are some ways in which students could construct and edit the contents of their portfolio for eventual assessment by the teacher.

The students could:

- rewrite compositions after peer or teacher correction

- redo an oral performance, such as an interview, summary, or dramatization

- reflect on their writing and speaking by writing an analysis of their work or by filling out a checklist; this list could include columns to show what areas need improvement, those that have improved, and those showing real mastery

- provide written or spoken evidence that they have mastered the objectives of each chapter; this evidence could be assessed along with what they demonstrate on the tests

- select samples of work that illustrate their improvement, with the improvement being assigned a grade, but not the samples

- include notes taken in class as they learn vocabulary that is not a part of the text, or notes on cultural information; these can become a part of the assessment package

- include as evidence of improvement or mastery whatever they produce after working with a given chapter section

Informal assessment for students needing extra help

Because language production is a skill and involves considerable risk on the part of students as they try to perform well, it is important to encourage their participation and use a variety of assessment options whenever possible. Students should be acknowledged with positive remarks and by receiving credit for:

- doing activities outside of the classroom

- participating voluntarily in class activities

- trying to use Spanish rather than English

- completing assignments

- showing improvement

Acknowledgment of these efforts will help maintain students' enthusiasm.

Formal assessment

Students with learning problems have a particularly difficult time taking quizzes and tests. Apprehension, insecurity, lack of preparedness and / or mastery all serve to put the student in a less-than-desirable position prior to test time. Help students perform optimally by following these suggestions:

- provide a pre-quiz or pre-test practice opportunity that is identical in format to the actual quiz or test (be sure directions are also the same; this is adhered to in the *¿Lo sabes bien?* test preparation in the student text and the *Examen de habilidades* in the Assessment Program)

- provide students with test-preparation guides that focus on what will be tested; tell them what they need to know and exactly how you will grade them

- allow extra time for quizzes and tests

- explain all directions on tests and give examples (in English if necessary)

- underline important words in directions and test items

- allow some students to take the test orally or to dictate answers to you

- if possible, tape record questions so that students can read and hear them simultaneously

- weight the scoring of the test to reflect individual strengths; do not require all students to do the entire test (allow them to do every other item or even skip certain sections)

- when appropriate, be lenient with spelling

- avoid unannounced quizzes and tests

- require a certain level of performance and retest if necessary

- be willing to accept projects or demonstrations as an alternative to a final test; give quizzes a cumulative grade

- use a grading system that rewards effort and participation

- allow students to write verb, pronoun, and other charts on their test papers so they don't have to rethink paradigms for each question

- before copying the quizzes and tests for your students, add models and cut and paste pictures and icons; in question-and-answer sections, add pronouns

Specific suggestions for the
Examen de habilidades

1 Listening Comprehension
Play the tape more than once, or read the manuscript so that students hear a familiar voice. Remember that many students do not have auditory strengths.

2 Reading Comprehension
Read the questions first, or have students read one question and then look for the answer. The length of the reading may discourage some students.

3 Writing Proficiency
Determine specific learning objectives. If you are looking for students' ability to manipulate the language, allow them to use their Organizers. Alternatively, the writing section of the test could be a separate grade, scored in accordance with the fact that they can use their books and Organizers. You may want to prepare a form in which you have given the first few words of each sentence. Students then fill in the remainder.

4 Culture
Although students have taken notes, they may not remember to review them. Go over the notes in class or have students review their notes in pairs.

5 Speaking Proficiency
Choose the easiest of the topics. Offer extra credit if you elect to give both topics or the more difficult one. This section may be especially stressful for some students. Allow students to write some of their thoughts down and speak from notes. Allow students to use their Organizers.

INDEX OF CULTURAL REFERENCES

ScottForesman Spanish Program

PASO A PASO

2

Myriam Met
Coordinator of Foreign Languages
Montgomery County Public Schools
Rockville, MD

Richard S. Sayers
Niwot High School
Longmont, CO

Carol Eubanks Wargin
Glen Crest Junior High School
Glen Ellyn, IL

ScottForesman

Editorial Offices: Glenview, Illinois

Regional Offices: San Jose, California • Atlanta, Georgia
Glenview, Illinois • Oakland, New Jersey • Dallas, Texas

Visit ScottForesman's Home Page at http://www.scottforesman.com

En el Parc Güell, Barcelona

ISBN: 0-673-21670-5
Copyright © 1996
Scott, Foresman and Company, Glenview, Illinois
All Rights Reserved. Printed in the United States of America.

This publication is protected by Copyright and permission should be obtained from the publisher prior to any prohibited reproduction, storage in a retrieval system, or transmission in any form or by any means, electronic, mechanical, photocopying, recording, or otherwise.

For information regarding permission, write to:
Scott, Foresman and Company, 1900 East Lake Avenue, Glenview, Illinois 60025.

1.800.554.4411
http://www.scottforesman.com

45678910DQ0403020100999897

Acknowledgments

Chapter 4, p. 144: Biographies of Gloria Estefan and Jon Secada. Reprinted by permission of Foreign Imported Productions & Publishing, Inc.

Chapter 8, pp. 286–287: *¿De qué país es esta bandera?*, map and flags. Adapted from MATERIALES QUINTO CENTENARIO, NOVIEMBRE-DICIEMBRE 1992, page 22. Text, p. 287, adapted from "Tarjetas de Información" from MATERIALES QUINTO CENTENARIO, NOVIEMBRE-DICIEMBRE 1992. Copyright © 1992 Consejería de Educación - Embajada de España. Reprinted by permission.

Chapter 9, p. 320: "Chana y su rana" from CHANA Y SU RANA by Cecilia Ávalos. Text copyright © 1992 Scholastic Inc. Reprinted by permission of Scholastic Inc.

Chapter 13, p. 450: From "El aceite de oliva" from DA QUE HABLAR, Número 14, Octubre-Noviembre 1993, page 13. Reprinted by permission of Consejería de Educación - Embajada de España.

Acknowledgments for illustrations and photographs appear on pages 526–527. That acknowledgments section should be considered an extension of the copyright page.

The modernist style of Spanish architect Antonio Gaudí (1852–1926) is reflected in these benches found in Parc Güell, an unfinished hillside park that Gaudí designed for his most important patron, Eusebio Güell. Gaudí favored using the richest, most colorful textures possible, and he often created mosaics made of broken tile scraps. Gaudí's work inspired a twentieth-century revival in the use of tile in architecture.

Contributing Writers

Eduardo Aparicio
Miami, FL

Margaret Juanita Azevedo
Stanford University
Palo Alto, CA

Louis Carrillo
New York City, NY

Thomasina Pagán Hannum
Albuquerque, NM

Mary de López
University of Texas
El Paso, TX

Reader Consultants

The authors and editors would like to express our heartfelt thanks to the following team of reader consultants. Each of them read the manuscript, chapter by chapter, offering suggestions and providing encouragement. Their contribution has been invaluable.

Rosario Martínez-Cantú
Northside Health Careers High School
San Antonio, TX

Greg Duncan
InterPrep
Marietta, GA

Walter Kleinmann
Sewanhaka Central High School District
New Hyde Park, NY

Bernadette M. Reynolds
Parker, CO

Rudolf L. Schonfeld, Ph.D.
Brooklawn Middle School
Parsippany, NJ

Connie Johnson Vargas
Apple Valley High School
Apple Valley, CA

Marcia Payne Wooten
Starmount High School
Boonville, NC

Tabla de materias

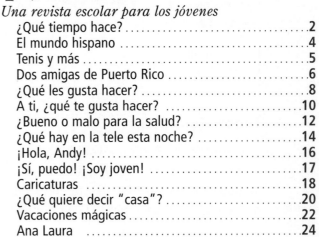

PASODOBLE
Una revista escolar para los jóvenes

IV

Capítulo 1

¿Cómo es tu escuela?

Capítulo 2

¿Qué haces todos los días?

CAPÍTULO 3

¿Qué ropa está de moda?

CAPÍTULO 4

¿Cómo te diviertes?

CAPÍTULO 5

¿Qué te gustaba hacer de pequeño?

CAPÍTULO 6

¡Celebremos!

CAPÍTULO 7

¿Es un lujo o una necesidad?

CAPÍTULO 8

¿Dónde sueles hacer tus compras?

CAPÍTULO 9

¿Tuviste un accidente?

CAPÍTULO 10

¿De qué se trataba la película?

CAPÍTULO 11

¿Cómo será el futuro?

CAPÍTULO 12

¡El pasaporte, por favor!

CAPÍTULO 13

¿Qué sugieres que pida?

CAPÍTULO 14

¡Me encanta la naturaleza!

Tijuana • Mexicali

BAJA
CALIFORNIA
NORTE

Nogales •

Ciudad
Juárez

Río Bravo

Río Grande

ESTADOS UNIDOS

GOLFO DE MÉXICO

Hermosillo •

SONORA

CHIHUAHUA

Chihuahua •

Río Conchos

SIERRA MADRE OCCIDENTAL

COAHUILA

Nuevo Laredo •

MÉXICO

NUEVO
LEÓN

Monterrey •

SIERRA MADRE ORIENTAL

DURANGO

TAMAULIPAS

—Trópico de Cáncer—

Durango •

SINALOA

ZACATECAS

Baja California

Golfo de California

Baja
California Sur

Mazatlán •

AGUASCALIENTES

SAN LUIS
POTOSÍ

NAYARIT

San Luis Potosí •

Tampico •

Río Pánuco

La Habana ⊛

Aguascalientes •

León •

GUANAJUATO

Iztaccíhuatl
(5286 m)

Golfo de
Campeche

Mérida •

YUCATÁN

Isla de la
Juventud

Río Grande
de Santiago

Guadalajara •

Querétaro •

Popocatépetl
(5452 m)

Península de
Yucatán

—20°—

QUERÉTARO

HIDALGO

QUINTANA
ROO

JALISCO

México D. F. ⊛

TLAXCALA

Campeche •

CAMPECHE

COLIMA

Cuernavaca •

MÉXICO

Taxco •

Puebla •

Veracruz •

Citlaltépetl
(5700 m)

TABASCO

MICHOACÁN

Río Balsas

PUEBLA

MORELOS

VERACRUZ

Río Usumacinta

Belmopan •

BELICE

SIERRA MADRE
DEL SUR

GUERRERO

Oaxaca •

OAXACA

CHIAPAS

Acapulco •

OCÉANO
PACÍFICO

Golfo de
Tehuantepec

GUATEMALA

HONDURAS

Tegucigalpa ⊛

Guatemala ⊛

San Salvador ⊛

EL SALVADOR

NICARAGUA

Lago de
Managua

Lago de
Nicaragua

Managua ⊛

San José ⊛

COSTA
RICA

**México, América Central
y el Caribe**

Símbolo	Descripción
——	Límites internacionales
—	Límites estatales
⊛	Capitales nacionales
•	Otras ciudades
▲	Picos montañosos

N
O — E
S

0   300   600 kilómetros
0   300   600 millas

© SF

XII

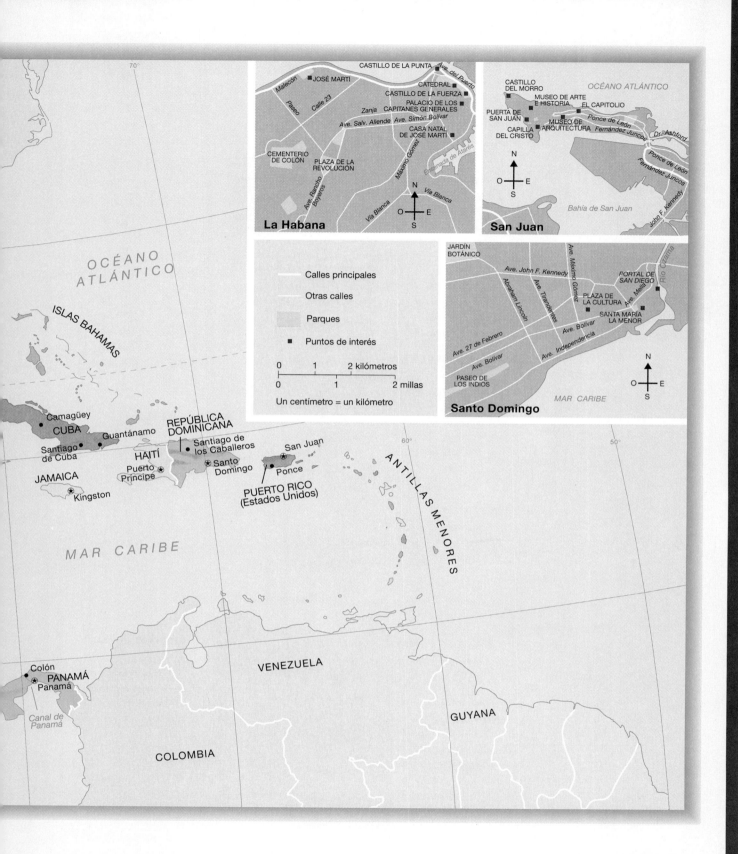

La Habana

CASTILLO DE LA PUNTA
Malecón
JOSÉ MARTÍ
Paseo
Calle 23
Zanja
Ave. Salv. Allende   Áve. Simón Bolívar
CEMENTERIO DE COLÓN
PLAZA DE LA REVOLUCIÓN
Ave. Rancho Boyeros
Vía Blanca
Vía Blanca
Máximo Gómez
Ensenada de Atarés
CATEDRAL
CASTILLO DE LA FUERZA
PALACIO DE LOS CAPITANES GENERALES
CASA NATAL DE JOSÉ MARTÍ
Ave. del Puerto

San Juan

OCÉANO ATLÁNTICO
CASTILLO DEL MORRO
MUSEO DE ARTE E HISTORIA
EL CAPITOLIO
PUERTA DE SAN JUAN
MUSEO DE ARQUITECTURA
CAPILLA DEL CRISTO
Ponce de León
Fernández Juncos
Ponce de León
Fernández Juncos
Dr. Ashford
John F. Kennedy
Bahía de San Juan

Calles principales
Otras calles
Parques
■ Puntos de interés

0   1   2 kilómetros
0   1   2 millas

Un centímetro = un kilómetro

Santo Domingo

JARDÍN BOTÁNICO
Ave. John F. Kennedy
Abraham Lincoln
Ave. Tiradentes
Ave. Máximo Gómez
PORTAL DE SAN DIEGO
PLAZA DE LA CULTURA
Ave. Mella
Río Ozama
SANTA MARÍA LA MENOR
Ave. Bolívar
Ave. 27 de Febrero
Ave. Bolívar
Ave. Independencia
PASEO DE LOS INDIOS
MAR CARIBE

OCÉANO ATLÁNTICO

ISLAS BAHAMAS

Camagüey
CUBA
Guantánamo
Santiago de Cuba
JAMAICA
Kingston

REPÚBLICA DOMINICANA
Santiago de los Caballeros
HAITÍ
Puerto Príncipe
Santo Domingo
Ponce
San Juan
PUERTO RICO (Estados Unidos)

ANTILLAS MENORES

MAR CARIBE

Colón
PANAMÁ
Panamá
Canal de Panamá

VENEZUELA

GUYANA

COLOMBIA

Mapas   XIII

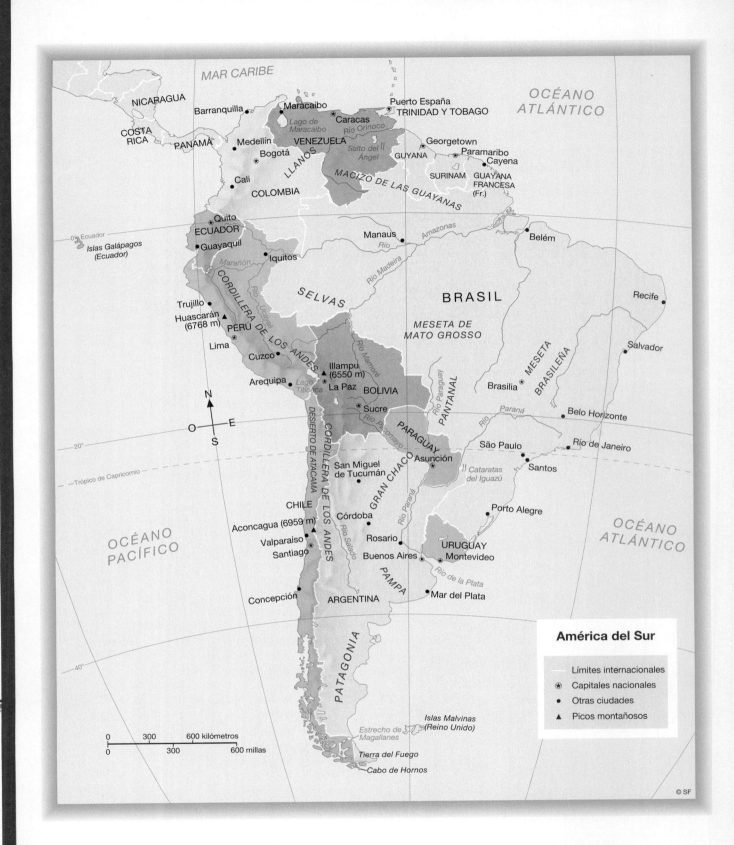

América del Sur

— Límites internacionales
✸ Capitales nacionales
● Otras ciudades
▲ Picos montañosos

MAR CARIBE

OCÉANO ATLÁNTICO

NICARAGUA

COSTA RICA

PANAMÁ

Barranquilla
Maracaibo
Lago de Maracaibo
Caracas
Puerto España
TRINIDAD Y TOBAGO
VENEZUELA
Río Orinoco
Salto del Ángel
Medellín
Bogotá
LLANOS
Georgetown
Paramaribo
Cayena
GUYANA
SURINAM
GUAYANA FRANCESA (Fr.)
Cali
COLOMBIA
MACIZO DE LAS GUAYANAS

0° Ecuador
Islas Galápagos (Ecuador)
Quito
ECUADOR
Guayaquil
Manaus
Río Amazonas
Belém
Marañón
Iquitos

CORDILLERA DE LOS ANDES
Río Ucayali
SELVAS
BRASIL
Recife

Trujillo
Huascarán (6768 m)
PERÚ
MESETA DE MATO GROSSO
Río Madeira
Salvador

Lima
Cuzco
Río Mamoré
MESETA BRASILEÑA
Illampu (6550 m)
La Paz
BOLIVIA
Brasilia
Arequipa
Lago Titicaca
Sucre
Río Pilcomayo
Río Paraguay
PANTANAL
Belo Horizonte

DESIERTO DE ATACAMA
CORDILLERA DE LOS ANDES
PARAGUAY
Río Paraná
20°
São Paulo
Río de Janeiro
Trópico de Capricornio
San Miguel de Tucumán
Asunción
GRAN CHACO
Cataratas del Iguazú
Santos

CHILE
Aconcagua (6959 m)
Córdoba
Río Salado
Río Paraná
Porto Alegre
OCÉANO ATLÁNTICO

Valparaíso
Santiago
Rosario
URUGUAY
Montevideo

N
O   E
S

Concepción
Buenos Aires
Mar del Plata
ARGENTINA
PAMPA
Río de la Plata

OCÉANO PACÍFICO

PATAGONIA

40°

0   300   600 kilómetros
0   300   600 millas

Islas Malvinas (Reino Unido)
Estrecho de Magallanes
Tierra del Fuego
Cabo de Hornos

© SF

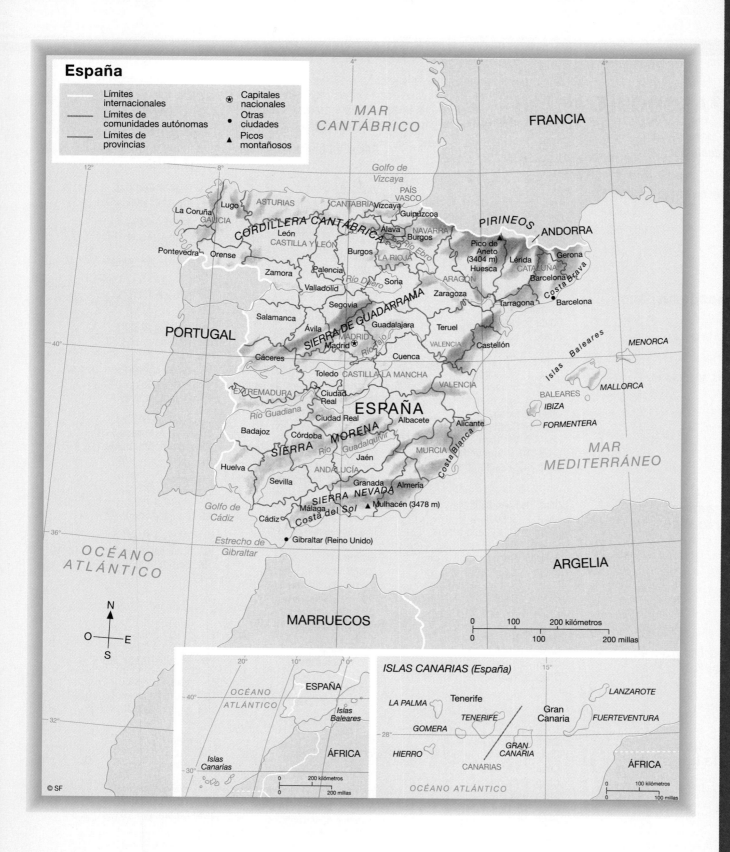

España

Límites internacionales
Límites de comunidades autónomas
Límites de provincias

⊛ Capitales nacionales
● Otras ciudades
▲ Picos montañosos

FRANCIA

MAR CANTÁBRICO

Golfo de Vizcaya

La Coruña
Lugo
ASTURIAS
CANTABRIA
Vizcaya
PAÍS VASCO
Guipúzcoa
PIRINEOS
ANDORRA

GALICIA
CORDILLERA CANTÁBRICA
León
CASTILLA Y LEÓN
Álava
NAVARRA
Pico de Aneto (3404 m)
Lérida
Gerona

Pontevedra
Orense
Burgos
LA RIOJA
Río Ebro
Huesca
CATALUÑA
Barcelona

Zamora
Palencia
Soria
ARAGÓN
Barcelona
Costa Brava

Valladolid
Río Duero
Zaragoza
Tarragona

Segovia
SIERRA DE GUADARRAMA
Guadalajara
Teruel

PORTUGAL
Ávila
MADRID
Madrid ⊛
VALENCIA
Castellón

Salamanca
Río Tajo
Cuenca
Islas Baleares
MENORCA

Cáceres
Toledo
CASTILLA-LA MANCHA
VALENCIA
BALEARES
MALLORCA

EXTREMADURA
Ciudad Real
ESPAÑA
IBIZA

Río Guadiana
Ciudad Real
Albacete
Alicante
FORMENTERA

Badajoz
Córdoba
SIERRA MORENA
RÍO Guadalquivir
MURCIA
Costa Blanca
MAR MEDITERRÁNEO

Huelva
Jaén
ANDALUCÍA

Sevilla
Granada
Almería
SIERRA NEVADA

Golfo de Cádiz
Málaga
Costa del Sol
▲ Mulhacén (3478 m)

Cádiz
Gibraltar (Reino Unido)

Estrecho de Gibraltar

OCÉANO ATLÁNTICO

ARGELIA

N
O—E
S

MARRUECOS

0   100   200 kilómetros
0   100   200 millas

OCÉANO ATLÁNTICO
ESPAÑA
Islas Baleares
ÁFRICA
Islas Canarias

0   200 kilómetros
0   200 millas

ISLAS CANARIAS (España)

LA PALMA
Tenerife
LANZAROTE

TENERIFE
Gran Canaria
FUERTEVENTURA

GOMERA
GRAN CANARIA

HIERRO
CANARIAS
ÁFRICA

OCÉANO ATLÁNTICO

0   100 kilómetros
0   100 millas

© SF

Mapas   XV

XV

**PASODOBLE**

This motivating magazine-style section recycles some of the major themes and concepts from *PASO A PASO 1*. The following chart shows the integrative review of vocabulary and grammar. You will also find references to the ancillary materials for *Pasodoble*. Some of the Communicative Activities from *PASO A PASO 1* are listed to provide additional review.

Pasodoble Sections	Thematic Review from *PASO A PASO 1*	Recycled Concepts	Ancillary Support Materials
¿Qué tiempo hace?	*El primer paso:* Spanish-speaking world Chap. 3: Sports and leisure Chap. 7: Vacation Chap. 10: Community	**Vocabulary:** countries and capitals, numbers, calendar expressions, seasons, weather, directions **Grammar:** *estar*	*PASO A PASO 2:* Practice Wkbk. PD-1 *PASO A PASO 1:* Transparencies 14, 17, 27, 38–40 Comm. Act. BLM 7-1
El mundo hispano	*El primer paso:* Spanish-speaking world Chap. 5: Family Chap. 7: Vacation Chap. 10: Community	**Vocabulary:** countries and capitals, physical characteristics, nature, directions, *estar*	*PASO A PASO 2:* Practice Wkbk. PD-2 *PASO A PASO 1:* Transparencies 78–81
Tenis y más	Chap. 1: Friendship Chap. 2: School Chap. 3: Sports and leisure Chap. 5: Family Chap. 6: Clothing Chap. 7: Vacation Chap. 10: Community Chap. 12: Restaurants	**Vocabulary:** personal questions, personality traits, school subjects, leisure activities, colors **Grammar:** *gustar, -ar* verbs, *jugar*, age, *ser*, adjective agreement, personal *a*, preterite tense	*PASO A PASO 2:* Practice Wkbk. PD-3 Writing Activity A *PASO A PASO 1:* Transparencies 8–10 Comm. Act. BLMs 1-1, 1-2, 1-3
Dos amigas de Puerto Rico	Chap. 1: Friendship Chap. 2: School Chap. 3: Sports and leisure Chap. 4: Food Chap. 5: Family Chap. 7: Vacation Chap. 8: Home Chap. 9: Health	**Vocabulary:** school subjects, leisure activities, household chores **Grammar:** *gustar, ir a* + inf., *poder, querer, -er* verbs, *encantar*, age, *ser, quisiera, pensar, tener que, hacer, vivir*, indirect object pronouns	*PASO A PASO 2:* Practice Wkbk. PD-4 *PASO A PASO 1:* Transparencies 16, 18, 42, 45 Comm. Act. BLMs 3-1, 3-3
¿Qué les gusta hacer?	Chap. 1: Friendship Chap. 3: Sports and leisure Chap. 8: Home	**Vocabulary:** leisure activities **Grammar:** *gustar, estar*, possessive adjectives	*PASO A PASO 2:* Practice Wkbk. PD-5 *PASO A PASO 1:* Transparencies 18, 19, 42 Comm. Act. BLM 2-3
A ti, ¿qué te gusta hacer?	Chap. 1: Friendship Chap. 3: Sports and leisure Chap. 7: Vacation Chap. 8: Home Chap. 9: Health Chap. 10: Community Chap. 12: Restaurants	**Vocabulary:** leisure activities, household chores **Grammar:** *ni . . . ni, poder, pensar*, negative constructions, preterite tense	*PASO A PASO 2:* Practice Wkbk. PD-6 Writing Activity B *PASO A PASO 1:* Transparencies 18, 19, 42 Comm. Act. BLMs 3-2, 8-1
¿Bueno o malo para la salud?	Chap. 2: School Chap. 3: Sports and leisure Chap. 4: Food Chap. 6: Clothing Chap. 8: Home Chap. 9: Health Chap. 11: Movies and TV	**Vocabulary:** leisure activities, food, health **Grammar:** *-ar* verbs, *comer, deber, -er* verbs, demonstrative adjectives, *hacer, tener que*, comparatives, superlatives	*PASO A PASO 2:* Practice Wkbk. PD-7 Writing Activity C *PASO A PASO 1:* Transparencies 21–24 Comm. Act. BLM 4-1

Pasodoble Sections	Thematic Review from *PASO A PASO 1*	Recycled Concepts	Ancillary Support Materials
¿Qué hay en la tele esta noche?	*El primer paso:* Spanish-speaking world Chap. 1: Friendship Chap. 2: School Chap. 3: Sports and leisure Chap. 4: Food Chap. 5: Family Chap. 7: Vacation Chap. 13: Environment	**Vocabulary:** calendar expressions **Grammar:** *hay, se dice, leer,* time-telling, *poder, creer, llamarse, pensar, hay que* + inf.	*PASO A PASO 2:* Practice Wkbk. PD-8 Writing Activity D *PASO A PASO 1:* Transparencies 13, 16, 56–60 Comm. Act. BLM 11-1
¡Hola, Andy!	Chap. 5: Family Chap. 10: Community Chap. 11: Movies and TV Chap. 12: Restaurants	**Vocabulary:** family members **Grammar:** preterite tense, comparatives	*PASO A PASO 1:* Transparencies 29–30 Comm. Act. BLMs 10-2, 10-3
¡Sí, puedo! ¡Soy joven!	Chap. 1: Friendship Chap. 3: Sports and leisure Chap. 5: Family Chap. 9: Health	**Vocabulary:** personality traits, physical characteristics **Grammar:** *ir a* + inf., *querer, poder,* negative expressions	*PASO A PASO 1:* Transparencies 8, 10, 28–29 Comm. Act. BLM 7-2
Caricaturas	Chap. 3: Sports and leisure Chap. 4: Food Chap. 9: Health Chap. 11: Movies and TV	**Grammar:** *estar, deber,* negative expressions, indefinite pronouns	*PASO A PASO 2:* Writing Activity E
¿Qué quiere decir "casa"?	Chap. 5: Family Chap. 6: Clothing Chap. 8: Home Chap. 13: Environment	**Vocabulary:** rooms in a house, furniture **Grammar:** *tener,* direct object pronouns, *decir*	*PASO A PASO 2:* Practice Wkbk. PD-9 *PASO A PASO 1:* Transparencies 41–43 Comm. Act. BLM 8-3
Vacaciones mágicas	Chap. 3: Sports and leisure Chap. 4: Food Chap. 5: Family Chap. 7: Vacation Chap. 10: Community Chap. 11: Movies and TV Chap. 12: Restaurants Chap. 13: Environment	**Vocabulary:** leisure activities, travel, environmental terms **Grammar:** *gustar* expressions, *poder, preferir, tener, pensar,* preterite tense, superlatives	*PASO A PASO 2:* Practice Wkbk. PD-10 Writing Activity F *PASO A PASO 1:* Transparencies 36–37, 40 Comm. Act. BLM 7-3
Ana Laura	Chap. 1: Friendship Chap. 4: Food Chap. 5: Family Chap. 6: Clothing Chap. 7: Vacation	**Vocabulary:** personality traits, physical characteristics **Grammar:** *-er* and *-ir* verbs, adjective agreement, *quisiera*	*PASO A PASO 2:* Writing Activity G Audio Activities P.1, P.2, P.3, P.4 *PASO A PASO 1:* Transparencies 8–10, 28–29

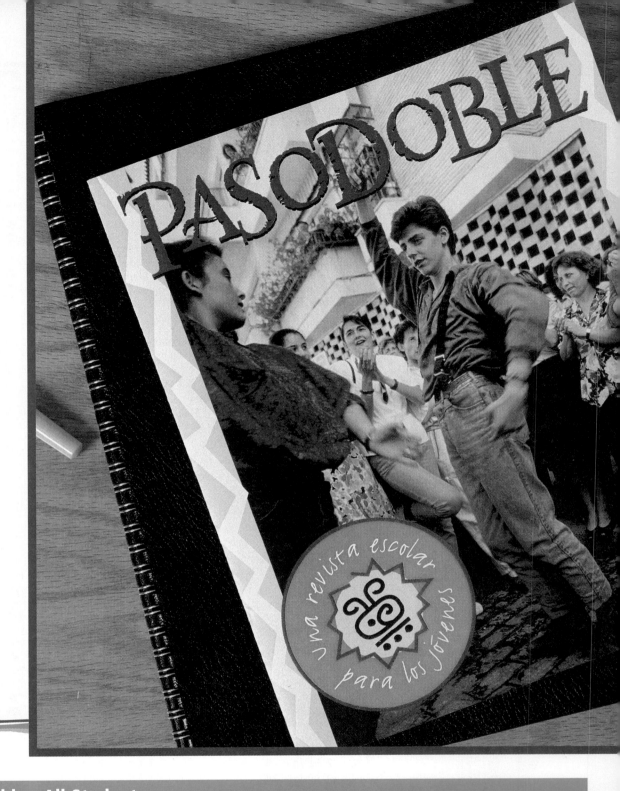

Options

Strategies for Reaching All Students

Students Needing Extra Help
Point out the magazine format to those who
do not recognize it. Emphasize that just as
magazines reprint popular articles, the
authors have re-entered important concepts
studied the previous year.

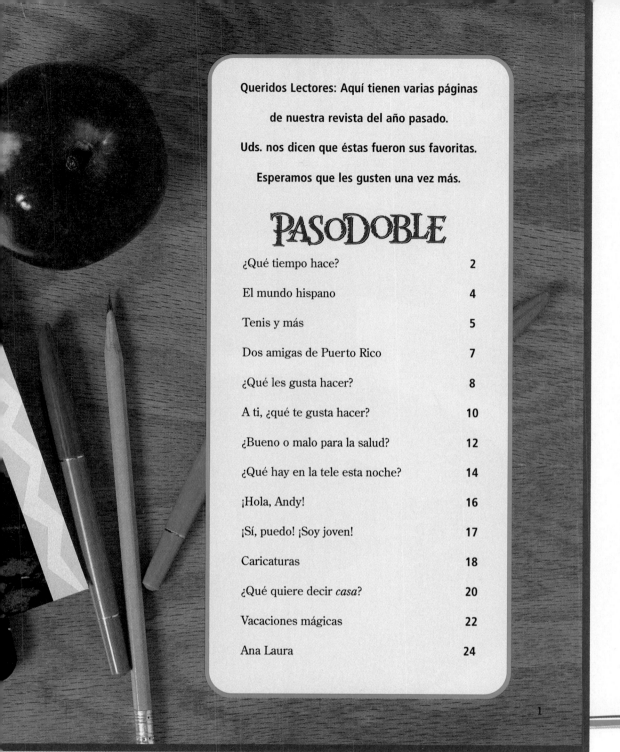

Queridos Lectores: Aquí tienen varias páginas

de nuestra revista del año pasado.

Uds. nos dicen que éstas fueron sus favoritas.

Esperamos que les gusten una vez más.

PASODOBLE

1

Cultural Notes

(p. xvi, photo)
El pasodoble, a familiar ballroom dance, actually refers to the dramatic march music played at bullfights and other public events in Spain. Each measure of its music consists of eight beats in 2/4 time, creating an even rhythm. Although the term literally means "two-step," the dance is a march step accentuated by movements reminiscent of the *torero.* The popular meaning came into use as professional dancers of the 1920s and '30s used the music to improvise encores after classical dance performances.

Review

Recycled Concepts
Countries and capitals, calendar expressions *(El primer paso)*; numbers *(El primer paso* and Chaps. 2, 5, 6, and 10); *estar* and seasons (Chap. 3); weather (Chap. 7); directions (Chaps. 8 and 10)

Ancillaries available for use with *Pasodoble*

 Practice Wkbk. PD-1

Ancillaries suggested from *PASO A PASO 1*

 Transparencies 14, 17, 27, 38–40

 Comm. Act. BLM 7-1

de la edición de enero

¿Qué tiempo hace?

Maricao, Puerto Rico

La Parva, Chile

Una playa chilena

Pronto vas a planear tus vacaciones del verano. A menudo nuestros lectores nos preguntan qué tiempo hace en los meses de julio y agosto en varios países de habla española y en ciudades donde hay mucha gente de origen hispano. Este mapa puede ayudarte a planear tus vacaciones.

2   Pasodoble

Options

Strategies for Reaching All Students

Spanish-Speaking Students
¿Has vivido en otro país o estado? ¿Cuál era el promedio de temperatura en ese lugar en julio?

Students Needing Extra Help
Remind students that they already know this material. Emphasize that they don't need to understand every word to comprehend the material.
Ex. 1: Have a map available for students having difficulty identifying the states and countries. You may also want to make this a homework assignment after students have tried it in class.

Ex. 3: Make sure students realize that *meses* is the plural of *mes.*
Ex. 4: Brainstorm words that describe your community in the chosen season. Give students a definite number of sentences to create.

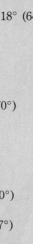

*e*n el mes de julio, la temperatura promedio de estas ciudades es diferente. ¿Puedes decir por qué? ¿Por qué hay dos temperaturas para cada ciudad? (El símbolo ° se dice "grado.")

Bariloche: 3° (38°)

Buenos Aires: 11° (51°)

Caracas: 22° (72°)

Ciudad de México: 18° (64°)

Houston: 34° (93°)

La Paz: 9° (48°)

Los Ángeles: 21° (70°)

Madrid: 24° (75°)

Miami: 32° (89°)

Montevideo: 10° (50°)

Nueva York: 25° (77°)

Quito: 14° (67°)

San Juan: 27° (80°)

Aguadilla, Puerto Rico

1. ¿Puedes decir en qué país o estado está cada una de las ciudades mencionadas?

2. ¿Cuántos países de habla española pueden nombrar tú y un(a) compañero(a)? ¿Cuántos pueden indicar en el mapa?

3. ¿Qué tiempo hace en tu ciudad en el verano? ¿Y en el invierno? ¿Nieva mucho? ¿Hay meses en que llueve mucho? ¿Cuáles?

4. Si pensamos ir de vacaciones a tu ciudad, ¿en qué estación debemos ir: en la primavera, en el verano, en el otoño o en el invierno? Trabaja con un(a) compañero(a) para escribir una tarjeta postal en que describes la estación más bonita del lugar donde vives.

3

Cultural Notes

(p. 2, center photo)
Maricao, located in the Cordillera Central of Puerto Rico, is known for its coffee plantations. Every February the *plaza* is transformed into a coffee plantation of the past, in the colorful three-day celebration of the coffee harvest. Townspeople dress in indigenous costumes, and folkloric *trovadores* entertain the crowds with their musical improvisations.

(p. 2, photos)
Chile is a land of extreme climatic variation, due in great part to its 5,000-mile length. During the summer months of January and February, many Chileans spend time at beach resorts. From June to September, skiing is a popular activity.

(p. 3, photo)
These fishing boats are on Crashboat Beach, one of Aguadilla's most beautiful beaches, with sparkling white sand, calm waters, and sunny weather. Its beauty is clouded, however, by the mystery of the Bermuda Triangle, which supposedly touches the area around the beach. Divers frequently discover sunken boats about a mile offshore.

Review

Recycled Concepts
Countries and capitals, *(El primer paso)*; physical characteristics (Chap. 5); nature (Chap. 7); directions (Chaps. 8 and 10)

Ancillaries available for use with *Pasodoble*

 Practice Wkbk. PD-2

Ancillaries suggested from *PASO A PASO 1*

 Transparencies 78–81

Activate Prior Knowledge
To prepare students for this reading, have a wall map available or use the overhead. Ask students to identify various Spanish-speaking countries and capitals. For example: *¿Dónde está Paraguay? ¿Es Lima la capital de Paraguay? ¿Qué países hispanos son islas?*

Answers
1. d; 2. c; 3. c; 4. a; 5. b; 6. b; 7. a; 8. b; 9. a; 10. c

Writing Extensions
As homework or an in-class writing assignment, have students create five additional multiple-choice questions for this survey. Have pairs exchange surveys and try to answer them.

---

de la edición de febrero

El mundo hispano

1 ¿Cuál de estos países no está en América Central?

   a. Costa Rica
   b. El Salvador
   c. Honduras
   d. México

2 Tres capitales tienen el nombre de un santo: San José, San Juan y Santiago. Son las capitales de:

   a. Honduras, El Salvador y Uruguay
   b. Colombia, Bolivia y Ecuador
   c. Costa Rica, Puerto Rico y Chile
   d. Nicaragua, Paraguay y Perú

3 Montevideo es:

   a. la montaña más alta de América del Sur
   b. un videojuego muy popular
   c. la capital y la ciudad más grande de un país
   d. el país más pequeño de las Américas

4 Hay más de veinte países donde el español es la lengua oficial. En área, ¿cuál es el más grande?

   a. Argentina
   b. Brasil
   c. España
   d. México

5 Managua es:

   a. el nombre de la selva en Ecuador
   b. una ciudad y capital centroamericana
   c. una isla en el Caribe
   d. una pirámide azteca en México

6 La República Dominicana queda en una isla. ¿Qué otro país está en esa isla?

   a. Cuba
   b. Haití
   c. Panamá
   d. Puerto Rico

7 ¿Cuál de estos países no está al lado de Perú?

   a. Argentina
   b. Bolivia
   c. Chile
   d. Colombia

8 La capital de Colombia es:

   a. Asunción
   b. Bogotá
   c. La Paz
   d. Lima

9 ¿Cuál de estos países es una isla?

   a. Cuba
   b. Guatemala
   c. Paraguay
   d. Uruguay

10 El país de habla española que está más cerca de los Estados Unidos es:

   a. Colombia
   b. Cuba
   c. México
   d. Puerto Rico

4   Pasodoble

Options

Strategies for Reaching All Students

Spanish-Speaking Students
El mundo hispano: Escribe tres a cinco preguntas más acerca de los países hispanohablantes. Hazles las preguntas a tus compañeros. ¿Eran tus preguntas demasiado fáciles o difíciles? ¿Las contestaron bien?

Tenis y más: Have students write and discuss with other Spanish-speaking students, if possible: *Usa esta información para escribir sobre tu compañero(a). No des el nombre. Léeles la descripción a otros compañeros para ver si pueden adivinar de quién escribes.*

Students Needing Extra Help
El mundo hispano: Have maps and other research materials available. Have pairs of students answer the questions.
Tenis y más: Read the information about Conchita Martínez aloud as students follow along in their texts.

TENIS y más

de la edición de marzo

Conchita Martínez juega tenis profesional desde los dieciséis años. En 1994 ganó el torneo internacional de Wimbledon.

Nació en: *España, el 18 de abril de 1972*

Vive en: *Barcelona*

Colores favoritos: *el negro y el blanco*

Actor favorito: *Patrick Swayze*

Pasatiempo favorito: *ir al cine*

Le gusta: *jugar golf y fútbol, montar a caballo, escuchar toda clase de música, estar con sus amigos y su familia y trabajar como voluntaria*

No le gusta: *la guerra*

Admira a: *la gente que ayuda a otros*

Característica principal: *es perfeccionista*

Le interesa: *la psicología y la literatura*

Mejor momento en la cancha de tenis: *cuando venció a Gabriela Sabatini 7-5, 6-1 en Roma en mayo de 1994.*

Entrevista a un(a) compañero(a). Puedes usar estas preguntas u otras:

1 ¿Cuándo es tu cumpleaños?

2 ¿Cuál es tu dirección?

3 ¿Cuál es tu color favorito?

4 ¿Quiénes son tu actor y actriz favoritos?

5 ¿Cuáles son tus pasatiempos favoritos?

6 ¿Qué no te gusta hacer?

7 ¿A quién o a quiénes admiras?

8 ¿Cómo eres? ¿paciente o impaciente? ¿atrevido(a) o prudente? ¿ordenado(a) o desordenado(a)? ¿perezoso(a) o trabajador(a)? ¿gracioso(a) o serio(a)? ¿Eres artístico(a)? ¿deportista? ¿callado(a)? ¿amable?

5

Review

Recycled Concepts
Question words (*El primer paso* and Chaps. 1–2); personality traits (Chap. 1); leisure activities (Chaps. 1 and 3); *gustar* (Chaps. 1 and 5); school subjects and *-ar* verbs (Chap. 2); *jugar* (Chap. 3); age and *ser* (Chap. 5); colors and adj. agreement (Chap. 6); personal *a* (Chap. 7); preterite tense (Chaps. 10 and 12)

Ancillaries available for use with *Pasodoble*

 Practice Wkbk. PD-3

Ancillaries suggested from *PASO A PASO 1*

 Transparencies 8–10

 Comm. Act. BLMs 1-1, 1-2, 1-3

Activate Prior Knowledge
Brainstorm what information would likely be in an interview. Have students determine which information is most important, and when in the interview it should be requested.

Answers
1–8 Answers will vary.

Writing Extensions

 Writing Activity A

Enrichment
El mundo hispano: As a homework assignment, ask students to research Hispanic countries and then make up three more multiple-choice questions regarding them. Have them write one of their questions on the chalkboard for the entire class to try to answer.

Tenis y más: Encourage students to make up additional questions regarding likes or dislikes in music, books, sports, etc. Students may also want to ask questions about their subject's place of birth, family, or career plans.

Cultural Notes

(p. 5, photo)
Spain's Conchita Martínez is one of the world's most successful women tennis players. Together with her countrywoman, Arantxa Sánchez-Vicario, she consistently ranks in the top five players in terms of earnings. In 1994, Martínez became the first Spanish woman to win at Wimbledon.

Review

Recycled Concepts

Leisure activities (Chaps. 1 and 3); school subjects (Chap. 2); *ir a +* inf. (Chap. 3); *poder* and *querer* (Chaps. 3 and 7); *-er* verbs (Chap. 4); *gustar, encantar, ser,* and age (Chap. 5); *quisiera* (Chap. 7); *pensar* (Chaps. 7 and 11); *tener que, hacer, vivir,* and household chores (Chap. 8); indirect object pronouns (Chap. 9)

Ancillaries available for use with *Pasodoble*

 Practice Wkbk. PD-4

Ancillaries suggested from *PASO A PASO 1*

 Transparencies 16, 18, 42, 45

 Comm. Act. BLMs 3-1, 3-3

Querido Pasodoble.

¡Hola! Somos seis amigos de la clase de español de segundo año de El Toro High School, en El Toro, California. Nos encanta Pasodoble. Todos los artículos de su revista son interesantes y originales.

Queremos leer más sobre los jóvenes de diferentes países de América Latina: qué ropa llevan, qué música les gusta, qué hacen para divertirse y si tienen algunos intereses especiales, como la ecología.

Saludos a todos los lectores de Pasodoble. ¡Y muchas gracias por una revista fantástica!

Options

Strategies for Reaching All Students

Spanish-Speaking Students

Have students work in pairs, if possible, to respond either orally or in writing: *Imaginen que contestan estas preguntas. ¿Qué dirían Uds.? Para las últimas preguntas, sustituyan Puerto Rico con los Estados Unidos u otro país donde hayan vivido.*

Students Needing Extra Help

Remind students that they don't need to know every word to understand the material. If necessary, explain *lo que.* Divide students into groups of three to conduct interviews similar to this one. When the class has completed *Pasodoble,* have students write a letter similar to this one, commenting on the magazine.

Enrichment

As an in-class written assignment, students can answer the questions in this section as if they were being interviewed. For the last question, they can say what they like best about living where they do.

DOS AMIGAS
de Puerto Rico

Gretel Cathiard es una joven de quince años. Su amiga Magda Ramos tiene dieciséis años. Las dos viven en San Juan, la capital de Puerto Rico. A Gretel le encantan las ciencias, y a Magda el inglés y las ciencias sociales. Lo que más les gusta es ir a la playa, tomar el sol, nadar y jugar vóleibol. **Pasodoble** habla con las dos amigas.

PD: ¿Qué les gusta hacer los fines de semana?

Gretel: Nos gusta estar con nuestros amigos. Vamos al cine o a la playa donde jugamos vóleibol, nadamos y paseamos en bote.

Magda: Y cuando no podemos estar juntos, hablamos por teléfono.

PD: ¿Adónde van Uds. con sus familias?

Magda: A veces vamos a pasear al parque. Y por supuesto vamos juntos a la iglesia los domingos. También vamos al centro comercial, pero sólo cuando necesito ir de compras. Cuando no tengo que comprar cosas, voy allí con amigos.

PD: ¿Qué piensan hacer después de terminar la escuela secundaria?

Gretel: Todavía no sé, pero me interesa mucho la medicina.

Magda: Quiero ser psicóloga. Quisiera ayudar a otros, y creo que tengo el potencial para hacerlo.

PD: ¿Qué no les gusta hacer?

Gretel: No me gustan nada los quehaceres de la casa: pasar la aspiradora, sacudir los muebles, lavar platos . . . ¡Bah!

Magda: A mí no me gusta hacer mi tarea de matemáticas. Afortunadamente, Gretel me ayuda a hacerla.

PD: ¿Qué diferencias ven Uds. entre los jóvenes de los Estados Unidos y los de Puerto Rico?

Gretel: Creo que los puertorriqueños somos menos nerviosos.

Magda: En los Estados Unidos un muchacho y una muchacha pueden ser novios a los doce años. Aquí no es común tener novio antes de los catorce.

PD: ¿Qué es lo que más les gusta de la vida en Puerto Rico?

Gretel: ¡El tiempo y el campo! Es un lugar muy bonito, ¿no?

Magda: A mí lo que más me gusta es la gente de mi país. Los puertorriqueños son generosos y simpáticos. De veras comprenden lo que es importante en la vida.

7

Answers

Answers to inductive questions will vary.

Writing Extensions

As an in-class written assignment, have students interview a classmate. Each interview should contain five questions about what the person likes to do, and why. Have students write out the questions beforehand, leaving space between them for answers.

 **Writing Activity B**

Review

Recycled Concepts
Leisure activities (Chaps. 1 and 3); *gustar* (Chaps. 1 and 5); *estar* (Chap. 3); possessive adjectives (Chap. 8)

Ancillaries available for use with *Pasodoble*

 Practice Wkbk. PD-5

Ancillaries suggested from *PASO A PASO 1*

 Transparencies 18, 19, 42

 Comm. Act. BLM 2-3

de la edición de mayo

¿QUÉ LES GUSTA HACER?

unos jóvenes de Caracas, Venezuela, nos envían una lista de sus actividades favoritas. ¿Cuáles son?

1. Escuchar música
2. Ir al cine
3. Ver la televisión
4. Practicar deportes
5. Ir de compras
6. Hablar por teléfono
7. Leer
8. Dormir

Y tú, ¿estás de acuerdo con ellos? ¿Cuáles de sus actividades favoritas te gustan también a ti? ¿Hay actividades en la lista que a ti no te gustan?

8   Pasodoble

Options

Strategies for Reaching All Students

Spanish-Speaking Students
Responde a las preguntas por escrito.

Students Needing Extra Help
Review *estar de acuerdo.*

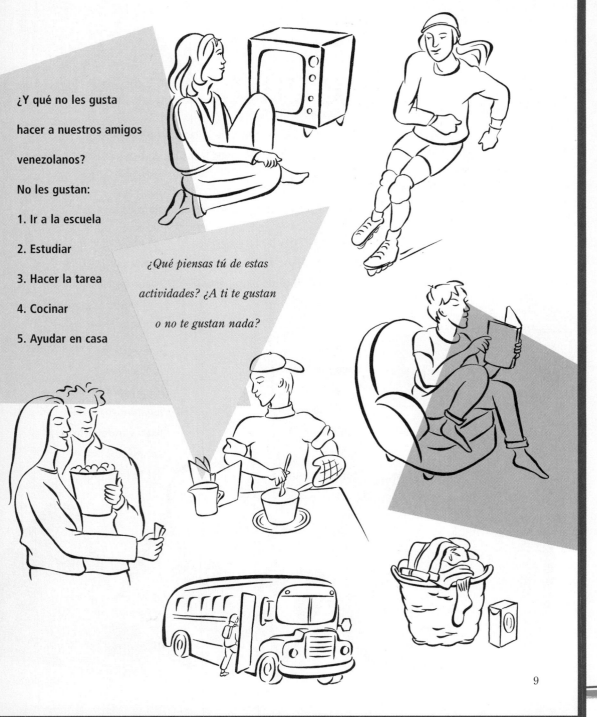

¿Y qué no les gusta hacer a nuestros amigos venezolanos?

No les gustan:

1. Ir a la escuela

2. Estudiar

3. Hacer la tarea

4. Cocinar

5. Ayudar en casa

¿Qué piensas tú de estas actividades? ¿A ti te gustan o no te gustan nada?

9

Review

Recycled Concepts
Ni . . . ni (Chap. 1); leisure activities (Chaps. 1 and 3); *poder* (Chaps. 3 and 7); household chores (Chap. 8); negative constructions (Chap. 9); preterite tense (Chaps. 10 and 12); *pensar* (Chap. 11)

Ancillaries available for use with *Pasodoble*

 Practice Wkbk. PD-6

Ancillaries suggested from *PASO A PASO 1*

 Transparencies 18, 19, 42

 Comm. Act. BLMs 3-2, 8-1

de la edición de junio

A ti, ¿qué te gusta hacer?

El mes pasado un grupo de jóvenes venezolanos nos enviaron una lista de sus actividades favoritas. Este mes tú puedes hacer una lista similar.

Aquí tienes varias actividades. ¿Qué piensas de ellas?

ayudar en casa (sacar la basura, lavar platos, hacer la cama, sacudir los muebles, pasar la aspiradora, etc.)	estudiar/hacer la tarea
	hablar por teléfono
	hacer ejercicio
	ir al centro comercial
cocinar	ir al cine
comer	ir al parque de diversiones
comprar cosas (ropa, libros, etc.)	ir al museo
	ir de pesca
cortar el césped	jugar videojuegos
dibujar	practicar deportes
dormir	sacar fotos
escuchar música	ver la televisión

Options

Strategies for Reaching All Students

Spanish-Speaking Students
Responde a las preguntas por escrito. Después de decidir cuáles de las actividades son quehaceres, di con cuáles deben ayudar todos y por qué.

Students Needing Extra Help
Review the present tense.
Ex. 2: Make sure students understand how the parentheses are used. Review *ni . . . ni*.

1. ¿Cuáles de estas actividades te gustan más? ¿Cuáles no te gustan nada? ¿Cuáles son pasatiempos y cuáles son quehaceres? Haz dos listas: *Me gusta mucho* y *No me gusta nada.* Escribe por lo menos cinco actividades en cada lista.

2. Con un(a) compañero(a), hablen de las actividades que sí les gustan y de las que no les gustan. ¿Cuáles no les gustan ni a él (ella) ni a ti?

3. Haz una encuesta (*poll*) para decidir cuáles son las actividades favoritas y las menos favoritas de la clase.

11

Activate Prior Knowledge
Brainstorm additional activities that can be included in the list on p. 10 *(bailar, pasear en bote, dibujar, lavar ropa, nadar, poner la mesa, jugar béisbol).*

Answers
1 Answers will vary but may include:
pasatiempos: comer, comprar cosas, dibujar, dormir, escuchar música, hablar por teléfono, ir al centro comercial, ir al cine, ir al museo, ir al parque de diversiones, ir de pesca, jugar videojuegos, practicar deportes, sacar fotos, ver la televisión
quehaceres: ayudar en casa, cocinar, cortar el césped, estudiar, hacer la tarea, hacer ejercicio

2–3 Answers will vary.

Writing Extensions

Writing Activity B

Review

Recycled Concepts

Leisure activities (Chaps. 1 and 3);
-ar verbs (Chap. 2); *comer, deber,
-er* verbs, and food (Chap. 4); demonstrative adjectives (Chap. 6);
hacer, and *tener que* (Chap. 8);
health (Chap. 9); comparatives
and superlatives (Chap. 11)

**Ancillaries available for
use with *Pasodoble***

 Practice Wkbk. PD-7

**Ancillaries suggested
from *PASO A PASO 1***

 **Transparencies
21–24**

 Comm. Act. BLM 4-1

de la edición de julio

¿*Bueno* o *malo* para la salud?

¿Qué debes comer y qué debes hacer para tener buena salud? Y, lo que es más importante, ¿comes esa comida y haces esas actividades?

¿Haces ejercicio cada día? ¿Nadas o patinas? ¿Juegas básquetbol, vóleibol, fútbol o béisbol? ¿Esquías en el invierno?

¿Cuántas frutas (manzanas, naranjas, plátanos, uvas, etc.) comes al día?

¿Cuántas clases de verduras comes (guisantes, judías verdes, lechuga, tomates, zanahorias)? ¿Te gustan las ensaladas?

¿Comes pan, arroz o papas más o menos tres veces al día?

Cuando tienes sed, ¿tomas agua, leche o jugo de naranja o de manzana? ¿O bebes siempre un refresco, café o té?

Compara lo que comes en el desayuno con lo que come un(a) compañero(a).

1. Haz una encuesta para decidir quién come el mejor desayuno. ¿Por qué creen Uds. que ese desayuno es el mejor?

2. Mira el menú. En tu opinión, ¿cuál de estas pizzas es mejor para la salud?

3. Para comprar la pizza más saludable, ¿qué tienes que hacer?

12   Pasodoble

Options

Strategies for Reaching All Students

Spanish-Speaking Students
Have students respond orally or in writing:
*De las meriendas que comes todos los días,
¿cuál crees que es la más nutritiva y cuál es
la menos nutritiva? ¿Por qué?*

Students Needing Extra Help
After answering the questions, have students discuss how healthy or unhealthy their habits are as a class. Also discuss the health aspects of skipping breakfast.
Ex. 1: Review the vocabulary necessary to talk about breakfast. If available, use the vocabulary section of the Book 1, Chap. 4 Organizer. Categorize the words according to food groups. Have a food pyramid available.

Ex. 3: Remind students to read the fine print on the menu. Refer them to the questions discussing exercise earlier in the selection for clues.

Activate Prior Knowledge

To prepare students for this reading, brainstorm healthy foods from each food group. Have a food pyramid available so that students can categorize foods correctly.

Answers

Answers to inductive questions will vary, but look for correct use of the present tense.

1–2 Answers will vary.

3 (printed upside down on the bottom of p. 13) To buy the healthiest pizza, walk to the pizza parlor. You need the fresh air!

Writing Extensions

As an in-class written assignment, have pairs of students create a list of their ten favorite foods, indicate to which food groups they belong, and how frequently students eat them in a week. Pairs should share this information with the class, to see which pair has the healthiest eating habits.

Writing Activity C

Enrichment

Conduct a class discussion on the Telepizza ad, asking students to comment on similarities and differences between this ad and pizza ads they see in the local newspaper. Encourage students to comment on the different kinds of pizza listed, saying which they would order. You may want to have pairs of students act out a call to the pizza place in front of the class, with one student ordering and the other taking the order, writing it down, and reading it back for verification.

Review

Recycled Concepts

Hay, se dice, and calendar expressions *(El primer paso); leer* (Chap. 1); time-telling (Chap. 2); *poder* (Chaps. 3 and 7); *creer* (Chap. 4); *llamarse* (Chap. 5); *pensar* (Chap. 11); *hay que* + inf. (Chap. 13)

Ancillaries available for use with *Pasodoble*

 Practice Wkbk. PD-8

Ancillaries suggested from *PASO A PASO 1*

 Transparencies 13, 16, 56–60

 Comm. Act. BLM 11-1

¿Qué hay en la tele esta noche?

Aquí tienes dos páginas del *Teleprograma* de Barcelona del mes de mayo pasado. ¿Cuántos de estos programas reconoces?

¿Eres buen lector?
Vamos a ver . . .

1. No hay que leer nada para saber cuántos programas deportivos hay esta noche. ¿Cuántos hay?

2. ¿Y cuántos programas hay en que las personas pueden ganar dinero?

3. ¿Por qué crees que hay símbolos sólo para esas dos clases de programas?

4. ¿Qué piensan los editores de la película *Agárralo como puedas 2 1/2?*

14   Pasodoble

VIERNES 14 MAYO

18.00
- **18.00** 2-TVE BALONCESTO NBA
- **18.00** ANTENA-3 COSAS DE CASA
- **18.20** CANAL+ AVANCE. REDACCIÓN
- **18.25** CANAL+ PREVIO TOROS
- **18.30** ANTENA-3 LA MERIENDA
  Espacio infantil en el que se ofrecen varios concursos y la serie CHICHO TERREMOTO.

19.00
- **19.00** TELE-5 HABLANDO SE ENTIENDE LA BASCA

Jesús Vázquez entabla cada tarde una interesante conversación con sus jóvenes invitados.

- **19.00** CANAL+ TOROS. FERIA DE SAN ISIDRO (Codificado)
- **19.25** TVE-1 NOTICIAS
- **19.30** TVE-1 MacGYVER: "COSECHA AMARGA"
  El coche de MacGyver se para en la localidad de Kasabian, donde un grupo de trabajadores del campo se enfrentan a los propietarios de las tierras que trabajan.
  INTÉRPRETES: RICHARD DEAN ANDERSON, DANA ELCAR, ABE VIGODA, DICK BUTKUS.
- **19.30** 2-TVE JARA Y SEDAL

- **19.30** ANTENA-3 NUEVOS POLICÍAS
  El oficial Penhall y Hoffs investi la muerte de un atleta olímpico consumo de anabolizantes.
- **19.30** TELE-5 LA RULETA DE LA FORTUNA

20.00
- **20.00** 2-TVE EL INFORME DEL DÍA
- **20.00** TELE-5 PRIMER AMOR (Cap. 7
  Armando da su aprobación adopción de la niña de Ros Rossana visita al médico y és dice que está embarazada.
- **20.30** TVE-1 VUELTA CICLISTA A ESPAÑA (Resumen)
- **20.30** 2-TVE DÍAS DE CINE
- **20.30** ANTENA-3 NOTICIAS
- **20.30** 2-TVE (Canarias) A TODA VELA
- **20.45** TELE-5 TELECUPÓN

21.00
- **21.00** TVE-1 TELEDIARIO-2
- **21.00** 2-TVE LOS PRIMEROS
- **21.00** 2-TVE (Canarias) CAMPUS
- **21.05** TELE-5 SU MEDIA NARANJA
- **21.15** ANTENA-3 BUSCAVIDAS
- **21.25** TVE-1 EL TIEMPO
- **21.25** CANAL+ INFORMACIÓN METEOROLÓGICA
- **21.30** TVE-1 UN, DOS, TRES...: "EL LEJANO OESTE"
  En esta ocasión se cuenta con l sencia de Cher, La Frontera, Din pa los pollos y Abuelo Jones.
- **21.30** 2-TVE TAL CUAL

86   ☺☺☺☺ EXCELENTE   ☺☺☺ MUY BUENA   ☺☺ BUENA   ☺ REG

Options

Strategies for Reaching All Students

Spanish-Speaking Students
¿Has visto algunos de estos mismos programas? ¿Cuáles recomiendas? ¿Por qué?

Students Needing Extra Help
Emphasize that this listing is for people watching TV in Barcelona. Point out context clues for students having difficulty with *baloncesto.* If necessary, help students find the icons representing sports and game shows, as well as the film rating guide at the bottom left-hand page.

TV Guide (realia)

14 MAYO VIERNES

CANAL +	REDACCIÓN. NOTICIAS
2 - TVE	(Canarias) CANARIOS EN SU RINCÓN
ANTENA-3	CINE ...OS JACKSON (Cap. 2 y último)
CANAL +	INFORMACIÓN ...EPORTIVA

TELE-5 SENSACIÓN DE VIVIR: ...PERFECTAMENTE PERFECTO'
...erie estadounidense. Mientras ...elly sigue obsesionada con su ...xceso de peso, sus amigos están ...reparando para ella una gran fies-...a de cumpleaños.
Reportaje en páginas 8 a 11)

CANAL + AGÁRRALO ...OMO PUEDAS 2 1/2 ◆◆
...STRENO (Codificado)
...roducción estadounidense de ...990. Título original: "Nacked gun ...2: the smell of fear". Duración: ...2 minutos. Color. Comedia. ...NTÉRPRETES: LESLIE NIELSEN, ...RISCILLA PRESLEY, GEORGE ...ENNEDY. Director: D. ZUCKER.

TELE-5 MELROSE PLACE (Cap.30)
...erie estadounidense. Billy y Alli-...on quieren que su relación se ...antenga en secreto.

Los chi-cos de Melrose Place tie-nen mul-titud de proble-mas sen-timenta-les.

23.00

23.00 2-TVE PAVAROTTI Y SUS AMIGOS
Gran gala concierto, celebrada en Modena (Italia), en la que intervie-nen intérpretes de los más diver-sos estilos musicales: Pavarotti, Sting, Zucchero, Lucio Dalla, Nevi-lle Brothers, Aaron Neville, Suzan-ne Vega, Mike Oldfield, Brian May, Bob Geldof y Patricia Kaas.

23.20 CANAL + SOLO EN CASA
CINE (Codificado) (Repetición)

23.30 ANTENA-3 CON USTEDES ...
PEDRO RUIZ

23.50 TELE-5 CONTACTO, CON TACTO

24.00

24.00 TVE-1 PARA ELISA (Capítulo 14)
Vicente consigue que Laura acce-da a encontrarse con él fuera de Madrid. Por otro lado, Óscar y Na-talia siguen con su romance sin que Claudio sepa nada. Se va a celebrar en Madrid el premio "la señorita España" y Jana está se-gura de que será nominada.
INTÉRPRETES: ASSUMPTA SER-NA, XABIER ELORRIAGA, FER-NANDO VALVERDE.

24.00 2-TVE DOCTOR EN ALASKA (3)
Serie estadounidense que comenzó a emitirse el pasado 30 de Abril sin previo aviso. Shelly se queda emba-razada y Holling se ve obligado a casarse con ella. En el pueblo todos preparan la ceremonia y en el último momento Holly no se presenta. Pe-se a todo, Shelley vuelve a aceptar la propuesta de matrimonio.
INTÉRPRETES: ROB MORROW, BARRY CORBIN, JOHN CORBETT, JANINE TURNER.

00.35 TELE-5 ENTRE HOY Y MAÑANA

00.45 ANTENA-3 NOTICIAS

87

Questions

5. ¿Cómo se llama el programa "Wheel of Fortune" en España?

6. ¿Cómo se llama "Doctor en Alaska" en los Estados Unidos?

7. ¿Cómo se dice "básquetbol" en España?

8. Jesús Vázquez entrevista a jóvenes invitados a su programa. ¿Cómo se llama su programa? ¿A qué hora pueden verlo los barceloneses?

9. ¿A qué hora hay que ver la televisión para saber qué tiempo va a hacer mañana? ¿En qué canales puedes ver esos programas?

10. Imagina que la fecha de hoy es el 14 de mayo. Con un(a) compañero(a), hablen de los programas que quieren ver. Después, hablen con otro grupo y decidan qué van a ver esta noche.

15

Cultural Notes ☼

(pp. 14–15, realia)
Many popular U.S. television programs shown in Barcelona retain their original names: "MacGyver" and "Melrose Place," for example. Others are given new titles: *Sensación de vivir* is "Beverly Hills 90210." *Su media naranja* means, colloquially, "your better half."

La ruleta de la fortuna, the Spanish equiva-lent of "Wheel of Fortune," is as popular as the show is in the U.S. The variety game show *Un, dos, tres* is thematic: *El lejano oeste* is the theme listed for this day, so contestants are required to wear western wear. For more information about this game show, see p. 329.

Review

Recycled Concepts
Family members (Chap. 5); preterite tense (Chaps. 10 and 12); comparatives (Chap. 11)

Ancillaries suggested from *PASO A PASO 1*

 Transparencies 29–30

 Comm. Act. BLMs 10-2, 10-3

Activate Prior Knowledge
Brainstorm vocabulary that would be used in a performer's biography *(estudió, trabajó, vivió, película, jugó, televisión, cantó).*

Writing Extensions
Have students write a short biography about their favorite performer, using the format shown here and the vocabulary they came up with in the **Activate Prior Knowledge** section.

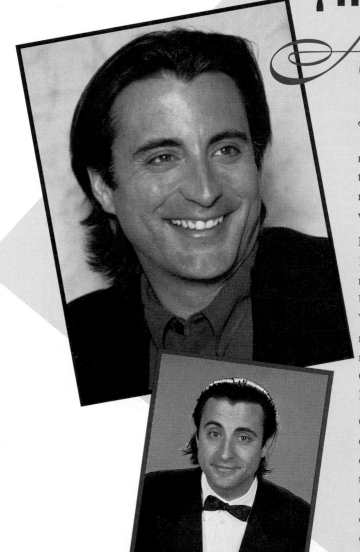

¡HOLA, Andy!

¿Quién es Andy García? Es un actor del cine norteamericano, famoso por su talento y por su amabilidad natural. Pero, ¿quién es en la vida real?

Nació en La Habana, Cuba, el 12 de abril de 1956. Cinco años más tarde, llegó a los Estados Unidos con sus padres. Vivieron en Miami, donde reside la comunidad cubana más grande de este país. Cuando decidió ser actor, fue a Los Ángeles.

Cuando no trabaja, Andy se dedica a su familia—su esposa, que también es cubana, y sus tres hijas. Para Andy, la familia es lo más importante. En su casa se habla español y él quiere educar a sus hijas en la tradición en que le enseñaron sus padres a él—con mucha dedicación y disciplina.

16   Pasodoble

Options

Strategies for Reaching All Students

Spanish-Speaking Students
¡Hola, Andy!: ¿Conoces a otro(a) artista hispano(a)? ¿Quién es?
¡Sí, puedo! ¡Soy joven!: ¿Tienes la misma confianza que este(a) poeta? ¿Qué quieres ser y hacer tú?

Students Needing Extra Help
¡Hola, Andy!: Review preterite-tense verb forms. Discuss any other well-known Spanish-speaking people students may know (Jimmy Smits, Paul Rodríguez, Rosie Pérez, José Canseco).
¡Sí, puedo! ¡Soy joven!: Review *nada* and *nadie.* Students do not yet know the future tense, but context should make it clear here. Emphasize the theme rather than poetic language and style.

Enrichment
¡Sí, puedo! ¡Soy joven!: For a homework assignment, ask students to write a paragraph or poem in which they tell what they want to do to improve the world.

¡Sí, puedo!
¡Soy joven!

de la edición de octubre

Puedo ser lo que quiero ser.
¡Soy joven!
Soy trabajador.
No hay nadie mejor.
¡Sí, puedo!

Quiero hacer lo que puedo hacer.
¡Soy joven!
Soy atrevido.
Nada me da miedo.
¡Sí, puedo!

Mi cabeza guarda fotos,
fotos del futuro,
fotos en que yo curo
los dolores, las enfermedades.
Quiero construir ciudades,
ciudades con casas felices
donde puedo vivir y construir un país
que será el más grande de todos.

¿Qué voy a ser?
¿Qué voy a hacer?
No sé.
Pero sí, yo sé quién será
el héroe de mi vida.
Seré yo—
yo que puedo,
yo el joven.

Review

Recycled Concepts
Ir a + inf. Chap. 3; *querer* and *poder* (Chaps. 3 and 7); negative expressions (Chaps. 5 and 9)

Ancillaries suggested from *PASO A PASO 1*

 Transparencies 8, 10, 28–29

 Comm. Act. BLM 7-2

Activate Prior Knowledge
To prepare students for this reading, have each write a short description of his or her future goals, and what qualities they possess that will help them achieve those goals. Ask for volunteers to share their descriptions with the class.

Cultural Notes

(p. 16, photos)
Andy García's popularity skyrocketed in 1990 with the release of *Godfather Part III, A Show of Force,* and *Internal Affairs.* He co-wrote the latter. The plot of *A Show of Force* revolves around the true story of the fatal political shooting of two young pro-independence Puerto Ricans, one of whom was the son of novelist Pedro Juan Soto. García is one of the first Hispanics, along with Edward James Olmos and Paul Rodríguez, to enter the U.S. film production business.

Review

Recycled Concepts
Estar (Chap. 3); *deber* (Chap. 4); negative expressions (Chaps. 5 and 9); *alguien* (Chap. 14)

CARICATURAS

Aquí tienes algunas de las caricaturas que más nos gustaron el año pasado.

—Ahora que he terminado el retrato debo encontrar a alguien que se le parezca.

¡Mira qué contento está de ver el mar!

—Ahora, las últimas noticias.

18   Pasodoble

Options

Strategies for Reaching All Students

Spanish-Speaking Students
¿Cuál de las caricaturas crees que es más cómica? ¿Por qué?

Students Needing Extra Help
Review the concept of cartoons making points rather than just being humorous. Before discussing the cartoon of the painter, emphasize that the subject of a portrait is always a person.

HOVIV

—¡Me aburro! ¡No hay nada interesante en la tele!

19

Activate Prior Knowledge
Have some local political or satirical cartoons available to share with students. Discuss how to read these types of cartoons to understand the point the artist was making. Point out that the artwork is often used to complement the text, not only to illustrate it. Students do not know the verb forms in the cartoon showing the painter. Help them as they work to figure out its meaning.

Writing Extensions
Students might enjoy drawing their own cartoons and generating captions for them.

 Writing Activity E

Review

Recycled Concepts
Tener (Chap. 5); rooms in a house and furniture (Chap. 8); *decir* (Chap. 13)

Ancillaries available for use with *Pasodoble*

 Practice Wkbk. PD-9

Ancillaries suggested from *PASO A PASO 1*

 Transparencies 41–43

 Comm. Act. BLM 8-3

de la edición de noviembre

¿Qué quiere decir "casa"?

Maracaibo, Venezuela

Una casa no es *a house.* La imagen que tiene una persona española cuando dice "mi casa" normalmente no incluye ni césped grande ni garaje ni sótano con lavadero y sala de estar. Pero sí puede incluir un patio bonito (muchas veces en el centro de la casa) con flores y sillas. El patio es un "cuarto" muy importante en una casa española o latinoamericana.

¿Qué ves tú cuando dices *house*?

San Cristóbal de las Casas, México

Córdoba, España

20 Pasodoble

Options

Strategies for Reaching All Students

Spanish-Speaking Students
Ask students to write a paragraph answering the following questions: *El primer párrafo dice que el patio es un "cuarto" importante. ¿Por qué será? ¿Cómo se usa el patio de una casa en España o en América Latina? ¿Qué se usa en los Estados Unidos para las mismas actividades?*

Students Needing Extra Help
Use the vocabulary section of the Book 1, Chap. 8 Organizer, if available. Have students use extra-large paper so they can spread out their work. Have magazines available for them to cut out pictures of furniture or rooms of a house. Give students guidelines as to what you expect the description to include.

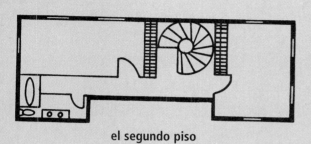

el segundo piso

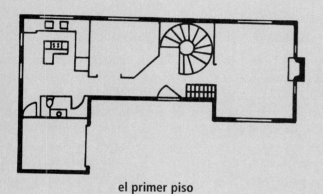

el primer piso

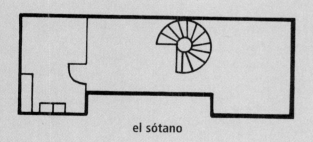

el sótano

Mira las fotos de las casas y patios. Mira también el plano de una casa típica de los Estados Unidos. Trabaja con dos o tres compañeros(as) para diseñar la casa ideal. Pueden combinar aspectos de los dos tipos de casas.

Uno de ustedes debe dibujar la casa. Después, descríbanla. ¿Dónde están las puertas y ventanas? Una persona puede describir los muebles de la sala o de la sala de estar (sofás, sillones, sillas, mesas, lámparas). Otra persona debe describir los dormitorios (camas, cómodas, guardarropas, etc.). ¿Hay escritorio? ¿Equipos de sonido? ¿Videocaseteras? ¿Dónde hay espejos o carteles o fotos?

Con otro grupo hablen de los dos diseños.

Cuando una persona hispanohablante dice, "Mi casa es su casa," ¿qué quiere decir? ¿Hay una expresión de hospitalidad similar en inglés?

21

Activate Prior Knowledge
Brainstorm with students the components of a typical house, including number and types of rooms and their locations. List on the chalkboard the types of rooms and the furniture usually found in them.

Answers
Answers will vary, but students may mention that *mi casa es su casa* is roughly the equivalent of "make yourself at home."

Review

Recycled Concepts
Leisure activities (Chaps. 1 and 3);
gustar expressions (Chap. 3);
poder (Chaps. 3 and 7); *preferir*
(Chaps. 4 and 8); *tener* (Chap. 5);
travel (Chap. 7); *pensar* (Chaps. 7
and 11); preterite tense (Chaps. 10
and 12); superlatives (Chap. 11);
environmental terms (Chap. 13)

**Ancillaries available for
use with *Pasodoble***

 **Practice Wkbk.
PD-10**

**Ancillaries suggested
from *PASO A PASO 1***

 **Transparencies
36–37, 40**

 Comm. Act. BLM 7-3

de la edición de diciembre

Vacaciones mágicas ¿Adónde piensas ir de vacaciones? ¿Qué tipos de lugares y qué actividades prefieres? En América Latina hay una gran variedad de lugares interesantes y divertidos.

Para el deportista

¿Te gustaría esquiar en verano? Puedes ir a Chile o a Argentina, donde es invierno cuando es verano en los Estados Unidos. El mes de agosto es cuando hay mejor nieve para esquiar. El lugar más popular para esquiar está en Bariloche, un centro turístico en el sur de Argentina. Es similar a Suiza por su arquitectura y su belleza natural. Sólo necesitas llevar la ropa apropiada. Los esquís, las botas . . . puedes alquilar allí todo lo que necesitas.

Para el ecólogo

Si prefieres el clima tropical y la ecología, puedes pasar unas vacaciones ideales en Costa Rica. Muchos turistas van para tomar el sol en sus playas del Caribe y del Pacífico, para pasear en bote por sus ríos o para explorar la selva. Si te interesa la ecología, puedes ir a la provincia de Guanacaste para ver la gran variedad de animales y plantas en los parques nacionales.

Y para los más aventureros, hay programas donde pueden trabajar como voluntarios ayudando a proteger el medio ambiente.

Para el antropólogo

Imagina una ciudad muy moderna, donde también hay arquitectura colonial y ruinas de ciudades de hace quinientos años. Si te interesan las civilizaciones precolombinas, el lugar ideal para ti es la Ciudad de México. Tienes que visitar el Museo Nacional de Antropología para ver los antiguos artefactos de esas civilizaciones indígenas. Cerca de la plaza del Zócalo, puedes ver las ruinas del Templo Mayor de Tenochtitlán, la ciudad más importante de los aztecas, que descubrieron unos trabajadores en 1978. ¿Hay más ruinas debajo de esta ciudad moderna? ¡Claro que sí! Pero qué son y cuándo las vamos a descubrir es todavía un misterio.

22 Pasodoble

Options

Strategies for Reaching All Students

Spanish-Speaking Students
Describe otro lugar que atraería a los turistas. Menciona los lugares de interés y la mejor estación para visitar.

Students Needing Extra Help
Refer to pp. 2–3 where Bariloche is mentioned. Have visuals available to help students understand the concepts of anthropology, pre-Columbian civilizations, etc.

1. ¿Cuál de estos lugares te gustaría visitar? ¿Por qué?

2. ¿Cuál no te gustaría visitar? ¿Por qué?

3. Con un(a) compañero(a), hablen del país de América Latina que más les gustaría visitar y digan por qué.

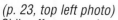

Activate Prior Knowledge

Have students write captions describing the photos on p. 23.

Answers

1–3 Answers will vary, but look for a wide variety of appropriate vocabulary.

Writing Extensions

As a homework assignment, have students write a paragraph similar to the ones in the reading about a vacation spot in or near their community. They should include information about what activities are available there, the best time to go, and what type of person would most enjoy going there on vacation.

Writing Activity F

Cultural Notes

(p. 23, top left photo)
Chile offers many impressive ski resorts. Valle Nevado, near Santiago, is the largest in South America, with almost 50 ski lifts and 22,000 acres of Andean ski slopes. Some runs are 10 miles long and 17,908 feet high. Other popular ski resorts are Chillán, Farellones, Lagunillas, and Portillo.

(p. 23, top right photo)
Mexico City's *metro* system is quiet, smooth, and efficient. During the construction of the Pino Suárez station in the city's center, engineers unearthed an Aztec pyramid, which has been left in the station. Modern Mexico is juxtaposed with the ancient past as commuters stream past the little pyramid.

(p. 23, bottom photo)
Leatherback turtles, the largest existing sea turtles, have a flexible shell made of small bones embedded in soft, leathery skin. Weighing over 1,600 pounds and reaching lengths of over 7 feet, they maintain a constant body temperature in or out of the water. Leatherbacks go ashore to lay their eggs, and tourists often visit Costa Rican beaches to watch the hatchlings work their way into the water.

23

Review

Recycled Concepts

Personality traits (Chap. 1); *-er* and *-ir* verbs (Chap. 4); physical characteristics (Chap. 5); adjective agreement (Chap. 6); *quisiera* (Chap. 7)

Ancillaries suggested from *PASO A PASO 1*

Transparencies 8–10, 28–29

Éste es un bio-poema. El poeta (la poetisa) describe su personalidad y sus emociones. Aquí tienes la estructura de un bio-poema. Síguela y ¡tú también puedes ser poeta!

Escribe tu nombre: ___ .

Escribe 4 adjetivos que te describen: ___ .

Escribe el nombre de uno de tus padres: ___ .

Escribe: A quien le encantan: ___ , ___ y ___ .

Escribe: Quien se siente: ___ , y ___ .

Escribe: Quien necesita: ___ , ___ y ___ .

Escribe: Quien ofrece *(offers):* ___ y ___ .

Escribe: Quien teme a *(fears):* ___ , ___ y ___

Escribe: Quien quisiera tener: ___ , ___ y ___ .

Escribe: Quien quisiera ver: ___ y ___ .

Escribe: Quien vive en: ___ (tu ciudad), ___ (tu dirección).

Escribe tu apellido: ___ .

24   Pasodoble

Ana Laura

Alta, impaciente, cariñosa y callada.

Hija de Adriana.

A quien le encantan:
los elefantes, la lluvia y los ojos de Daniel.

Quien se siente:
emocionada por la generosidad, y triste por los
que tienen hambre.

Quien necesita:
la música, el océano y a su amiga Raquel.

Quien ofrece:
puerta abierta a los amigos
y hamburguesas sabrosas.

Quien teme a:
la ignorancia, la tacañería
y la contaminación de la Tierra.

Quien quisiera tener:
la visión del poeta, la vida de un rockero
y un perro labrador de color chocolate.

Quien quisiera ver:
cómo se hace una película
y a Paula lavar los platos.

Quien vive en:
Gilboa, calle Blossom.
Cáceres León.

Options

Strategies for Reaching All Students

Students Needing Extra Help
Brainstorm other vocabulary in each category for students to use in the poem.

Activate Prior Knowledge

To prepare students for this activity, brainstorm vocabulary describing personality traits and physical characteristics.

Answers

Answers will vary, but look for a wide variety of appropriate vocabulary.

Writing Extensions

 Writing Activity G

 Audio Activities P. 1, P. 2, P. 3, P. 4

Cultural Notes ☀

(p. 25, photo)
This Guatemalan woman looks out over Lake Atitlán, known for its beaches, mountains, and volcanoes. Volcán San Pedro, in the background, rises 9,920 feet above sea level. The other two volcanoes overlooking the lake are Tolimán (10,340 feet) and Atitlán (11,560 feet). Temperatures around this tropical shoreline range narrowly from 50° to 70° F.

CAPÍTULO 1
THEME: SCHOOL

SCOPE AND SEQUENCE Pages 26–57

COMMUNICATION

Topics

School subjects

School equipment

School activities

Homework

Objectives

To compare schooling in Spanish-speaking countries and in the U.S.

To name school subjects

To name people who work at a school

To name places in a school

To describe school equipment

To talk about activities associated with school

To talk about homework

To make comparisons

CULTURE

Schooling

GRAMMAR

El verbo salir

La forma comparativa: tan ... como

Repaso: La forma superlativa

Repaso: El complemento directo

Ancillaries available for use with Chapter 1

Multisensory/Technology

 Overhead Transparencies, 6–10

 Audio Tapes and CDs

 Vocabulary Art Blackline Masters for Hands-On Learning, pp. 8–12

 Classroom Crossword

 La Catrina

 CD-ROM

Print

 Practice Workbook, pp. 1–11

 Writing, Audio & Video Activities, pp. 5–10, 93–95, 151–152

 Communicative Activity Blackline Masters

Pair and Small Group Activities, pp. 1–6

Situation Cards, p. 7

 Un paso más: Actividades para ampliar tu español, pp. 1–6

Assessment

 Assessment Program

Pruebas, pp. 9–20

Examen de habilidades, pp. 21–24

 Test Generator

Video still from Chap. 1

25A

High School in Latin America

Although there are similarities between the high-school experience in the U.S. and in Spanish-speaking countries, there are also some striking differences.

In the U.S., high-school students take between five and seven subjects per year, but in Latin America, students usually take between ten and twelve. These classes do not meet each day, however. A geography class may meet only three days a week; a music class, twice a week. As a result, student schedules vary from day to day. Furthermore, although physical education is taught, team athletics do not form part of the curriculum. On the other hand, the study of English is mandatory in many schools.

Schools in Latin America rarely have the amenities that students take for granted in the U.S. For example, most schools are not equipped with lockers. As a result, many students use *mochilas* (backpacks) or *bolsos* (book bags) to carry their books and personal items. As a rule, Latin American students have much more homework than American students, thus providing another reason for owning a good, sturdy backpack or book bag.

The grading scale varies from country to country, but letter grades are rarely used. For example, in Mexico grades range from 0–10; in Ecuador, the scale is 1–20; and in Chile, it is 1–7. Although in this chapter we use the terms *nota* (grade, as in evaluation of work) and *año* (grade, as in year in school), the word *grado,* to mean both, is current in some Spanish-speaking regions of the U.S.

Private schools are common in Latin America. Many are Roman Catholic and run by specific orders of nuns and priests. Parochial schools in Latin America are usually not coeducational. But there are many coed private schools that are not church-affiliated. Many of these are associated with ethnic or cultural traditions and require the study of the appropriate foreign language. In this category are many American, German, British, Italian, and French schools.

The most obvious difference between our school system and that of Spanish-speaking countries is the use of uniforms. In some cases the uniform is the same throughout the country, but usually a school—especially a private school—can be identified by the uniform. For girls, this may consist of a jumper, a blouse, and tie, or a pleated skirt, a blouse, and a vest or blazer. Boys must wear slacks, a shirt with a tie, and sometimes a sweater or blazer as well. Some schools have variations of the girls' uniforms for special occasions, such as honor roll assemblies or celebrations honoring the patron saint of their institution.

Introduce

The following list represents words, expressions, and grammar topics re-entered from Book 1: numbers 0–31, physical characteristics, school subjects, school supplies, *gustar* expressions, time-telling, food, family, pets, clothing, personal hygiene items, places and buildings, health-care items

Planning

Cross-Curricular Connections

Art Connection *(pp. 31–32)*
Have students design textbook covers. Let them choose one of the subjects listed in the *Vocabulario para conversar.* Encourage them to be as creative as possible. Display the completed covers or have students use them to cover their books.

Journalism Connection *(pp. 40–41)*
Have pairs of students write an article about an imagined conversation between a Mexican student and an American student who is visiting Mexico. With each student assuming one of the roles, have them compare experiences and tell about the advantages and disadvantages of attending their particular schools.

Career Connection *(pp. 50–51)*
Have individuals pretend that they are interviewing for the position of high-school principal. The screening committee has asked them to provide the following: a) a description of the types of teachers they will hire; b) five main rules for students and staff; and c) a list of extracurricular activities to be offered.

CAPÍTULO 1

¿Cómo es tu escuela?

OBJECTIVES

At the end of this chapter, you will be able to:

- talk about your classes and homework
- describe your school and your school day
- compare the subjects you like the most and the least
- talk about similarities and differences between your schooling and that of a student in Mexico City

Una escuela en Izcuchaca, Perú

27

Preview

¡Piénsalo bien!

Mira las fotos. Los estudiantes que vemos están hablando de su escuela, de sus clases y de sus tareas.

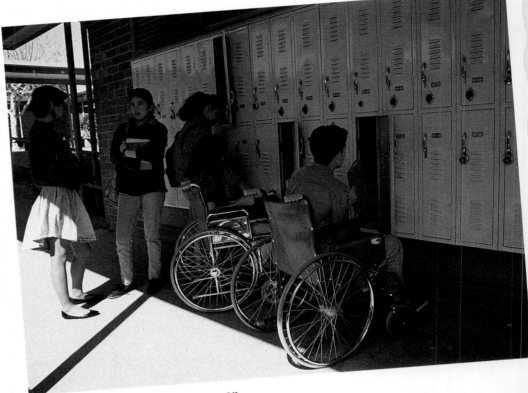

"¿Cuál es el número de tu armario?"

¿Tienes un armario en tu escuela? ¿Qué contiene? ¿Cómo te gustaría decorarlo?

28   Capítulo 1

Options

Strategies for Reaching All Students

Spanish-Speaking Students
Ask: *¿Has estudiado en otra secundaria? ¿Cómo era igual y cómo era diferente? ¿Te gustaría seguir estudiando después de graduarte de la escuela secundaria? ¿Por qué?*

 Un paso más Ex. 1-A

Students Needing Extra Help
(p. 29, top left photo): Students may not have the vocabulary to answer questions about biology, chemistry, or physics. Let them move ahead to find the necessary words.
(p. 29, top right photo): Tell students briefly about *Don Quijote* or have them research the subject. Bring in some Spanish literature.
(p. 29, bottom photo): Review Book 1, Chap. 2, for school-related words.

Cultural Notes

(p. 28, photo)
In U.S. high schools, students may often chat with friends between classes at their lockers. Students in Latin America don't usually have lockers; they carry their class materials with them. Most students remain in their classroom and the teachers travel from class to class. Study groups are commonly formed within a classroom, and individuals may meet outside of school for cooperative study sessions and test preparation.

"Tenemos que estudiar tres capítulos para el examen de biología."

¿Tomas alguna clase de ciencias este año? ¿Cuál? ¿Te gustan las ciencias?

En un laboratorio de biología en Madrid

Don Quixote (1955), Pablo Picasso

"Esta semana vamos a empezar a leer Don Quijote."

¿Qué sabes de la literatura española o latinoamericana?

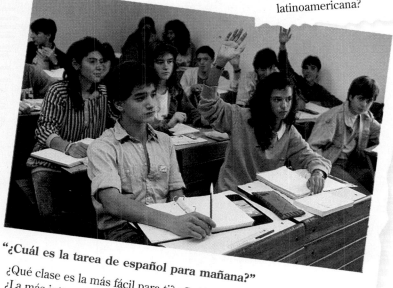

"¿Cuál es la tarea de español para mañana?"

¿Qué clase es la más fácil para ti? ¿Cuál es la más difícil? ¿La más interesante? ¿La más aburrida? ¿Por qué?

Estudiantes en una clase en Buenos Aires

29

(p. 29, top left photo)
These students are carrying out a lab assignment under their teacher's supervision. In Spain, two major paths of secondary education are available. The *Bachillerato Unificado y Polivalente* (BUP) provides students with general liberal arts and technical training. The *Curso de Orientación Universitaria* (COU) consists of one-third general studies, one-third scientific studies, and one-third professional subjects.

(p. 29, top right photo)
Don Quijote de la Mancha has long been a favorite folk hero in Spanish literature. He and his squire, Sancho Panza, are rendered in this lithograph by Pablo Picasso, who examined literary themes during the 1950s. *El ingenioso hidalgo, Don Quijote de la Mancha* was originally published in two parts, the first in 1605 and the second in 1615. Cervantes's story is often considered to be the first true novel in Western literature.

(p. 29, bottom photo)
Class time in Argentina's high schools is usually teacher centered. Students are expected to respond to lecture material through highly structured oral questioning, written assignments, and tests. Final exams are often cumulative and students are expected to demonstrate mastery of an entire year's worth of information. They must pass the final exam to advance to the next level of study.

Present

Chapter Theme
School: Subjects and equipment

Communicative Objectives
- To name school subjects
- To describe school equipment
- To make comparisons

 Transparencies 6-7

 Vocabulary Art BLMs

 Pronunciation Tape 1-1

Grammar Preview
El / la más and *el / la menos* + adj. are reviewed here lexically. A review of superlatives appears on pp. 44–45.

Teaching Suggestions
Preparing students to speak: Use one or two options from each of the categories of Comprehensible Input, Physical Response, or Limited Verbal Response. For a complete explanation of these categories and some sample activities, see pp. T16–T17.

Vocabulario para conversar

¿Cuándo tienes geografía?

Vas a necesitar estas palabras y expresiones para hablar sobre tus clases. Después de leerlas varias veces, practícalas con un(a) compañero(a).

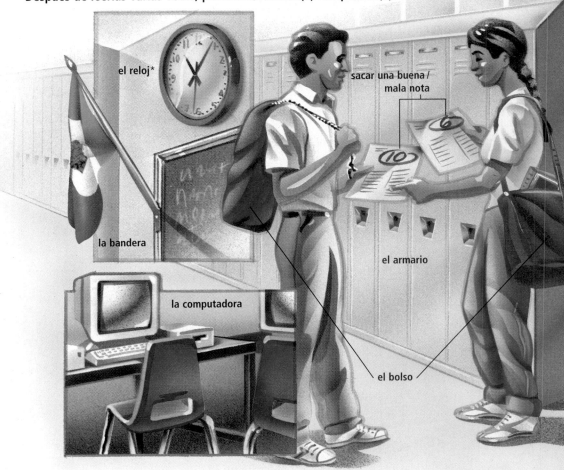

el reloj*

sacar una buena / mala nota

la bandera

el armario

la computadora

el bolso

* We also use the word *el reloj* or *el reloj pulsera* for "wristwatch."

30   Capítulo 1

Options

Strategies for Reaching All Students

Spanish-Speaking Students
 Un paso más Exs. 1-B, 1-C

Students Needing Extra Help
Have students begin to fill in their Organizers. Review reading directions in the target language. Remind students that names of languages are not capitalized. Give some examples of *sacar: ¿Por qué sacas buena nota en la clase de español?* Get a sample report card to encourage discussion. Give some examples using *álgebra* so that students can manipulate the adjective: *El álgebra es aburrida.*

If necessary, refer to Book 1, Chap. 11, to review superlatives. Give some examples with *el problema* so that students can use the proper form of the adjective.

el laboratorio

la literatura

la geografía

el álgebra (f.)*

el alemán

la geometría

el francés

la biología

la química

la historia

la página

También necesitas . . .

el idioma[†]	language
la materia	school subject
el informe	report
próximo, -a	next
alguno (algún), -a	some
repasar	to review
por suerte	luckily
tan + adj. + como	as + adj. + as

¿Y qué quiere decir . . . ?

escribir	el examen
el capítulo	la lección
la composición	el problema[†]
el ejercicio	la prueba

* Note that *álgebra* is a feminine noun. However, we use the article *el* with feminine nouns beginning with stressed *a* or *ha.*
† Note that *el idioma* and *el problema* are masculine nouns although they end in *a.*

Vocabulario para conversar   31

Class Starter Review
On the day following the initial vocabulary presentation, you might begin the class with this activity:
Have students ask three class-mates for their favorite and least favorite classes. Record responses to see which received the most votes.

Multicultural Perspectives
In ancient Mexico, education was important to the Aztecs. Students attended a temple-school called a *telpochcalli,* where they received instruction on temple services and also learned to prepare for war. The children of the nobles attend-ed *calmecac.* Students of other classes were allowed to attend these schools if they exhibited certain special abilities. The *cuica-calli* were special schools for music and dance for those stu-dents who showed talents in these areas. Ask students to share any information they may have about the educational systems of other past or present cultures.

Learning Spanish Through Action
STAGING VOCABULARY: *Levanten, Pongan*
MATERIALS: students' books
DIRECTIONS: Direct students to put all the books they have with them on their desks. Ask them to hold up a book for the class you mention. You might choose to review locations by giving directions to put books in certain places.

Practice & Apply

Reteach / Review: Vocabulary

Ex. 1: To extend this dialogue, *Estudiante A* can respond to *Estudiante B*'s news with expressions of disappointment, disbelief, or relief (*¡Vaya! ¡Qué bueno! ¡Qué lástima!*).

Ex. 2: To extend this dialogue *Estudiante A* can react to *Estudiante B*'s reply and then name the subject that is most interesting in his or her opinion. Encourage students to begin their extended responses with an expression of surprise or interest (*¡No me digas! ¿De veras?*).

Answers: Empecemos a conversar

1 ESTUDIANTE A

a. ¿Cuál es la tarea de historia?

b. ...de química?

c. ...de biología?

d. ...de literatura?

e. ...de geografía?

f. ...de álgebra?

g. ...de español?

h. Questions will vary, but look for *de* + school subject.

ESTUDIANTE B

a.–h. Answers will vary, but look for *tenemos que* + inf.

Empecemos a conversar

Túrnate con un(a) compañero(a) para ser *Estudiante A* y *Estudiante B*. Reemplacen las palabras subrayadas en el modelo con las palabras representadas o escritas en los recuadros. Si ven 💡 pueden dar su propia respuesta.

1

A —¿Cuál es la tarea de <u>geometría</u>?
B —Tenemos que <u>hacer los problemas 20 y 21 de la página 10</u>.
   o: *Por suerte no tenemos tarea.*

Estudiante A   **Estudiante B**

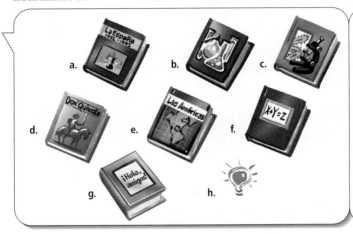

Estudiante B recuadro:

hacer los problemas 20 y 21 de la página 10

escribir una composición

hacer un informe

repasar la lección

leer un capítulo

estudiar dos páginas

hacer algunos ejercicios

2   interesante

A —*Para ti, ¿qué materia es la más <u>interesante</u>?*
B —*Para mí, <u>la química</u>.*

Estudiante A   **Estudiante B**

a. fácil   e. importante

b. difícil

c. aburrida   f.

d. divertida

32   Capítulo 1

Options

Strategies for Reaching All Students

Students Needing Extra Help

Ex. 3: Brainstorm the location of these objects before beginning the exercise.

Exs. 4–5: Brainstorm possible responses to *¿Por qué?*

Ex. 5: Remind students that they can use the preterite (*Saqué buena nota porque estudié mucho*) or the present (*Saco buena nota porque estudio mucho*).

Ex. 6: Brainstorm why learning another language is important. Review *para* + inf. Give some examples.

Ex. 7: Review adjectives describing color, size, and material (Book 1, Chap. 9).

Enrichment

Ex. 2: Once students have finished this exercise, have the class vote on which subject they consider most interesting, important, etc., by raising their hands as you call out subjects. Keep a tally on the chalkboard. Discuss the results, asking individuals whether they agree or disagree with what the majority of the class said. Ask them to justify their opinions.

3

A —¿Hay _bandera_ en la sala de historia?

B —Claro que sí. En (casi) todas las salas hay _una bandera_.

o: _No, en esa sala no hay bandera._

¡NO OLVIDES!

Este, esta; estos, estos = this; these
Ese, esa; esos, esas = that; those

Estudiante A   **Estudiante B**

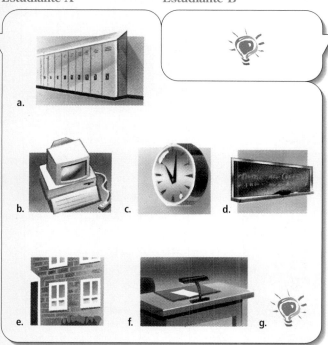

Empecemos a escribir

Escribe tus respuestas en español.

4 ¿Qué materia te gusta más? ¿Y cuál te gusta menos? ¿Por qué?

5 ¿En qué materias sacas buena nota? ¿Y en cuáles sacas mala nota? ¿Por qué?

6 ¿Hay clases de alemán y francés en tu escuela? ¿Crees que es importante aprender otro idioma? ¿Por qué?

7 ¿Usas una mochila o un bolso para llevar tus cosas? ¿Cómo es? ¿Cuántos compartimientos tiene? Generalmente, ¿qué llevas allí?

También se dice

Con frecuencia, en los países donde se habla español, se usan palabras diferentes para decir lo mismo. En esta sección puedes ver algunas de esas palabras.

el computador
el ordenador

el guardarropa
el guardalibros
el casillero
el ropero

la bolsa
la cartera

For _la materia_, we can also say _la asignatura_.

For _el informe_, we can also say _la presentación_ or _el reporte_.

Vocabulario para conversar   33

Present

Chapter Theme
School: Locations

Communicative Objectives
- To name places in a school
- To talk about activities associated with school
- To name people who work at a school

 Transparencies 8–9

 Vocabulary Art BLMs

 Pronunciation Tape 1-2

Grammar Preview
Conozco / conoces are presented here lexically. The paradigm of present-tense *conocer* is presented on p. 48.

Vocabulario para conversar

¿Conoces a todos los profesores?

Aquí tienes el resto del vocabulario que necesitas en este capítulo para hablar sobre tus clases.

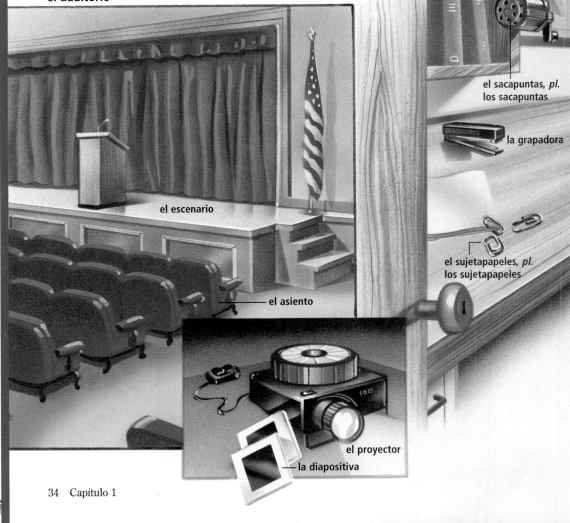

el auditorio

el mapa

el sacapuntas, *pl.* los sacapuntas

la grapadora

el escenario

el sujetapapeles, *pl.* los sujetapapeles

el asiento

el proyector

la diapositiva

34   Capítulo 1

Options

Strategies for Reaching All Students

Spanish-Speaking Students
 Un paso más Ex. 1-D

Students Needing Extra Help
También necesitas . . . : Show how *escolar* is used as an adjective: *el año escolar, el periódico escolar.*
Because *entregar* follows *escolar,* emphasize that this is a verb. Give an example of how it is used.
Show the entire *conocer* paradigm to those who need to see the whole conjugation.

Learning Spanish Through Action
STAGING VOCABULARY: *Apunten, Señalen, Toquen*
MATERIALS: transparency of vocabulary and / or drawings of items listed that are not in the room
DIRECTIONS: Direct students to point to or touch items in the room. As each item is shown, make a true or false statement about it. *(El sacapuntas está a la derecha del escritorio.)* The class signals with thumbs up for true or thumbs down for false.

34

la oficina

hacer fila

el bufet de ensaladas

la pared

la cafetería

Teaching Suggestions
Preparing students to speak: Use one or two options from each of the categories of Comprehensible Input, Physical Response, or Limited Verbal Response. For a complete explanation of these categories and some sample activities, see pp. T16–T17.

Point out the similarity between *el mapa* and previous vocabulary in this chapter *(el idioma, el problema)*.

Class Starter Review
On the day following initial vocabulary presentation, you might begin the class with this activity: Have pairs of students take turns naming objects in the classroom.

También necesitas . . .

escolar	*school* (adj.)	se prohibe	*it's prohibited*
entregar	here: *to hand in*	la respuesta	*answer*
hacer una pregunta	*to ask a question*	el consejero,	*counselor*
contestar	*to answer*	la consejera	
explicar	*to explain*	el director,	*principal*
conocer *(c → zc)*:	*to know, to be*	la directora	
	acquainted with:		
(yo) conozco	*I know*		
(tú) conoces	*you know*		
se permite	*it's allowed*		

¿Y qué quiere decir . . . ?

usar	preguntar
la pregunta	el edificio

Vocabulario para conversar   35

Practice & Apply

Reteach / Review: Vocabulary

Ex. 8: Students can extend this dialogue and review their vocabulary for directions by having *Estudiante A* ask *Estudiante B* where the room in question is located.

Answers: Empecemos a conversar

8 ESTUDIANTE A

a. ¿Qué hay en la cafetería?
b. . . . en la oficina?
c. . . . en la sala de clase?
d. . . . en la biblioteca?
e. . . . en la escuela?
f. Questions will vary.

ESTUDIANTE B

a.–f. Answers will vary.

9 ESTUDIANTE A

a. Necesito un proyector. ¿Dónde hay uno?
b. . . . un mapa. . . . uno?
c. . . . una bandera. . . . una?
d. . . . un diccionario. . . . uno?
e. . . . una grapadora. . . . una?
f. . . . unos sujetapapeles. . . . unos?
g. Questions will vary, but look for correct use of the indefinite article.

ESTUDIANTE B

a.–g. Answers will vary.

Empecemos a conversar

8
A —*¿Qué hay en el auditorio?*
B —*Muchos asientos y un escenario grande.*

Estudiante A

Estudiante B

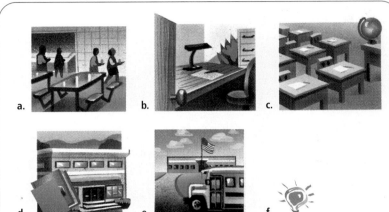

9
A —*Necesito un sacapuntas. ¿Dónde hay uno?*
B —*Hay uno en la sala de arte.*
o: *No sé. Lo siento.*

Estudiante A

Estudiante B

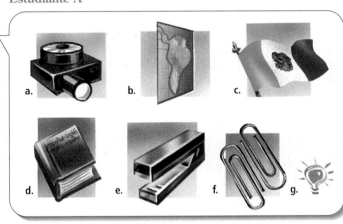

en la sala de ___
en la oficina de ___
en el escritorio de ___

36   Capítulo 1

Options

Strategies for Reaching All Students

Spanish-Speaking Students

Ex. 8: After this exercise, ask: *¿En qué clase dan más tarea? ¿En qué clase tienes poca tarea? ¿Por qué es importante hacer la tarea? ¿Siempre la haces?*
Ex. 15: After this exercise, have Spanish-speaking students respond in writing: *Describe tu escuela. ¿Es nueva o vieja? ¿Es de un piso o de varios? ¿Tiene gimnasio, auditorio o teatro u otros salones especiales?*

 Un paso más Ex. 1-E

Students Needing Extra Help

Ex. 8: Brainstorm what things could be found in these rooms.
Ex. 9: Brainstorm in what area of the building you could find these. If you find them all in the room you are in, review location words so that students can say *Hay uno cerca del libro,* etc.
Ex. 10: Brainstorm possible answers. These responses require a lot of vocabulary and some sophisticated structures. There could be many responses for students to formu-

10 entregar la tarea tarde   A —¿*Se permite entregar la tarea tarde?*
B —*No. Debemos entregar la tarea a tiempo.*
    o: *Sí, se permite.*

Estudiante A   **Estudiante B**

a. usar las computadoras después de las clases

d. escuchar música en clase

b. llevar pantalones cortos

e. contestar en inglés en la clase de español

c. hacer preguntas en un examen

f.

Empecemos a escribir y a leer

Escribe tus respuestas en español.

11 ¿Qué se prohibe en la escuela? ¿Y en la clase de español?

12 En tu escuela, ¿tienes que hacer fila en la cafetería? ¿Para qué más debes hacer fila?

13 ¿A qué hora empieza el día escolar? ¿A qué hora termina? ¿Cuántas horas estás en la escuela?

14 ¿Dónde queda la oficina del director (de la directora)? ¿Y la oficina de los consejeros? ¿Cómo se llama el director (la directora)? ¿Conoces a los consejeros? ¿Cómo son?

15 ¿Qué clase es? Lee las frases y escribe la respuesta.

a. Hay diccionarios en dos idiomas sobre el escritorio del profesor y un mapa de América Central en la pared. Las preguntas del profesor y las respuestas de los estudiantes son en otro idioma.

b. Hay una regla en el escritorio de la profesora. La profesora explica un problema. Algunos estudiantes usan sus calculadoras. Estudian círculos y triángulos.

c. Hay mapas de todos los países en las paredes. El profesor tiene diapositivas de océanos y montañas. Los estudiantes van a la biblioteca a menudo. Deben hacer muchos informes.

También se dice

el tajador
el sacaminas

formar fila
hacer cola

el salón de actos

la butaca

el comedor

el foro

10 ESTUDIANTE A
a. ¿Se permite usar las computadoras después de las clases?
b. …llevar pantalones cortos?
c. …hacer preguntas en un examen?
d. …escuchar música en clase?
e. …contestar en inglés en la clase de español?
f. Questions will vary, but should include *Se permite* + inf.
ESTUDIANTE B
a.–f. Answers will vary; look for *Debemos* + inf.

Answers: Empecemos a escribir y a leer

11 Answers will vary; look for the expression *Se prohibe* + inf.

12 Answers will vary, but look for use of *tengo*.

13 Answers will vary, but look for correct use of time expressions.

14 Answers will vary.

15 a. español; b. geometría; c. geografía

 Practice Wkbk. 1-3, 1-4

 Audio Activity 1.2

 Writing Activities 1-A, 1-B, 1-C

Pruebas 1-3, 1-4

late, depending on your school's environment and individual teacher rules.
Ex. 11: Start with responses from Ex. 10 and brainstorm others: eating in class, etc.
Ex. 12: If students can't think of any situations in which they stand in line, remind them of middle and elementary school, sporting events, movies, etc.
Ex. 14: Review location words.

Enrichment
Ex. 10: As a homework assignment, have students go to their public library and report on the rules of a specific department (children's, young adult, adult, audiovisual). Students can list the rules under either of two columns: *Se prohibe* and *Se permite.* If they wish, students can also write what they think of these rules and suggest changes. As a class, discuss what students wrote, comparing the rules of the various departments of the library.

Practice

Answers:
¡Comuniquemos!

1 Answers will vary. Look for correct use of *el señor / la señora / la señorita* and a variety of appropriate adjectives.

2 Answers will vary. Look for correct use of time expressions and *nos gustaría*.

3 Answers will vary. Look for a variety of appropriate adjectives and nouns and logical verbs for the rooms being discussed. For example: *el auditorio (ver / escuchar / hablar), la biblioteca (buscar / leer / estudiar / hacer tarea), la cafetería (cocinar / comer / hablar con), la oficina de los consejeros (hablar / aprender)*

¡Comuniquemos!

Aquí tienes otra oportunidad para usar el vocabulario de este capítulo.

1 Haz una lista de las tres materias que te gustan más. Compárala con la lista de un(a) compañero(a). Hablen de:

- por qué les gustan más esas tres clases
- quiénes son los profesores y cómo son
- cuánta tarea tienen que hacer

2 Compara tu horario con el de un(a) compañero(a). Hablen de:

- a qué hora empieza y a qué hora termina el día escolar
- qué clases toman juntos *(together)* y cuáles no
- qué les gustaría cambiar *(change)* en sus horarios para tener un horario ideal

Pueden escribir su horario ideal y compararlo con los horarios de otros compañeros.

3 Con un(a) compañero(a) discutan sobre algunas salas de la escuela, por ejemplo: el auditorio, la biblioteca, la cafetería, la oficina de los consejeros. Hablen de:

- cómo es la sala
- qué hay en esa sala
- qué hacen las personas allí

Dos muchachas mexicanas se preparan para un examen de inglés.

Horario de un estudiante en Madrid

38   Capítulo 1

Options

Strategies for Reaching All Students

Spanish-Speaking Students
Ex. 1: Have Spanish-speaking students survey the class and report the results orally or in writing. *Haz una encuesta. Ve de grupo en grupo para aprender cuáles son las clases más populares y qué características tienen en común los profesores de estas clases. Después de hablar con cada grupo, presenta tus resultados a la clase entera oralmente o en forma escrita.*

Students Needing Extra Help
Rather than have students do all exercises, divide them into groups, assign an activity to them, and have them report back to the class. Ex. 1 is the easiest; Ex. 2 is the most challenging.
Use the vocabulary sections from Book 1 Organizers.
¿Qué sabes ahora?: Have students write out this section so they can check off what they have mastered.

Enrichment
Ex. 2: To extend this dialogue, *Estudiante A* can ask *Estudiante B* which school he or she prefers and why.

ENGLISH SUMMER S.A. SCHOOLS

UN VERANO "EXCLUSIVO" PARA SUS HIJOS

COLEGIOS RESIDENCIALES DE INGLES EN VERANO
(ESPAÑA)

- Empresa familiar, dirigida por Mrs. Margaret Wright.
- 14 años de Experiencia.
- 6.000 familias de toda España nos avalan.
- INGLES, deporte, diversión, formación humana y convivencia.
- Centros de propiedad en la provincia de Tarragona.
- Antiguo Hotel-Balneario "La Capella" (a 200 m. Monasterio de Poblet).
- Casa Señorial de Vallclara.
- Estancias de 4 o 3 semanas.
- Edades: De 6 a 13 y de 14 a 18 años.

PARA MAS INFORMACION: Solicite nuestro folleto

Oficinas centrales:
ENGLISH SUMMER, S.A.
Rambla vella 2. Edif. Hotel Imperial Tárraco - 43003 TARRAGONA.

Tfno. 977/ 23.45.08. Fax: 977/ 23.45.19

ACADEMIAS DE LENGUA INGLESA - CURSOS DE IDIOMAS EN EL EXTRANJERO - COLEGIOS DE INGLES EN VERANO

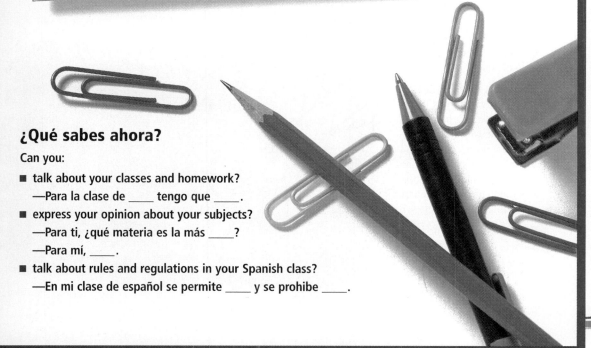

¿Qué sabes ahora?

Can you:

- talk about your classes and homework?
  —Para la clase de ____ tengo que ____.
- express your opinion about your subjects?
  —Para ti, ¿qué materia es la más ____?
  —Para mí, ____.
- talk about rules and regulations in your Spanish class?
  —En mi clase de español se permite ____ y se prohibe ____.

Answers: ¿Qué sabes ahora?
- Answers will vary, but the first should be a school subject and the second an infinitive.
- Answers will vary, but the first should be an adjective and the second a definite article + school subject.
- Answers will vary, but both should be infinitives.

 Audio Activity 1.3

Cultural Notes

(p. 39, realia)
This advertisement from a Spanish publication asks parents to consider enrolling their children in a summer English-language program. Students live on campus, experiencing immersion in the foreign language. The ability to speak English has acquired added value in Europe in recent years, as countries continue to integrate their economies in the European Economic Community.

Present & Apply

Cultural Objective
- To compare schooling in Spanish-speaking countries and the U.S.

Critical Thinking: Identifying Stereotypes

After students have read the *Perspectiva cultural,* review the term "stereotype." Make sure they understand that not all high schools in Mexico are like the one attended by Gilda and her friends. In rural Mexico, schools are less formal and have fewer amenities. Have students offer suggestions as to how a rural school in Mexico and in the U.S. might be different from one in a large city.

Multicultural Perspectives

One of the major reforms of the Mexican Revolution of 1910 was to change the educational system so that all children could receive a free public education. Today, the educational system is divided into levels: elementary, secondary, and higher education. At the elementary level, children first attend a kindergarten, or *jardín de niños.* They then go on to *la primaria,* which takes six years, and then to *la enseñanza media básica (secundaria),* which takes three years. After finishing this basic

Perspectiva cultural

¿A qué hora llegas a la escuela? Imagina un día escolar en que los estudiantes llegan a las dos de la tarde. ¿Cómo es su día? ¿A qué hora regresan a la casa?

Gilda va a la escuela por la tarde. Sus clases empiezan a las dos de la tarde y terminan a las ocho de la noche. Hay tantos estudiantes en la Ciudad de México que la mayoría de las escuelas tienen que ofrecer dos sesiones. La sesión de la mañana, el turno matutino, es para estudiantes menores de once años. La sesión de la tarde, el turno vespertino, es para estudiantes mayores de once años.

"Me encanta ir a la escuela por la tarde," dice Gilda. "Puedo levantarme tarde."

Gilda toma doce clases y pasa 30 horas por semana en la escuela. Sus clases incluyen español, historia, geografía de México, educación cívica, biología, química, física, inglés, arte y educación física. Las clases de computadoras y de matemáticas son sus clases favoritas. Gilda estudia las mismas materias durante todo el año.

La escuela de Gilda tiene reglas muy estrictas. Por ejemplo, las muchachas pueden llevar pantalones sólo cuando hace frío. Y nunca pueden llevar maquillaje ni tacones altos. Los muchachos no pueden llevar ni gorras ni aretes.

Gilda siempre sale de la escuela con Sonia y Enrique, que son hermanos y viven cerca de su casa. Inmediatamente después de salir de la escuela, Gilda y Sonia se maquillan y Enrique se pone su gorra de béisbol.

La cultura desde tu perspectiva

1 Para ti, ¿quiénes tienen un horario más difícil, los estudiantes mexicanos o tú y tus compañeros? ¿Por qué?

2 ¿Te gustaría tomar clases por la tarde y por la noche? ¿Por qué? ¿Cuáles crees que son las ventajas *(advantages)* y las desventajas de un sistema de dos sesiones al día?

Jóvenes colombianos escuchando cintas en un laboratorio de idiomas en Cali

40 Capítulo 1

Options

Strategies for Reaching All Students

Spanish-Speaking Students
Have Spanish-speaking students respond in writing: *¿Tienes las mismas clases que Gilda? ¿Cuáles tienen en común? ¿Cómo sería tu día si tuvieras clases en turno vespertino?*

 Un paso más Ex. 1-F

Students Needing Extra Help
Have students take notes to use as they study for the chapter test.
Discuss cultural differences with regard to strictness and discipline.
Exs. 1–3: Review comparatives (Book 1, Chap. 11).
The last question may pose a challenge for some students. Guide them through it.

Jóvenes ecuatorianas en camino a la escuela

Un grupo de muchachas van a la escuela en la Ciudad de México.

cycle, students can elect to continue to receive their *bachillerato* or *preparatoria*. This will prepare students for such careers as nursing, social work, or vocational jobs. Students who have finished their *preparatoria* can select from among universities, teachers' colleges, or technical educational institutions. Encourage students to share any knowledge they may have of the educational systems of other countries.

Answers

Answers to inductive questions will vary, but may include some time between 7:30 and 9:00 A.M. / Students in the *turno vespertino* return home some time late in the evening.

Answers: La cultura desde tu perspectiva

1–2 Answers will vary.

Cultural Notes

(p. 40, photo)
Almost all Colombian high-school students study a foreign language. The most commonly studied are English, French, and German. Many young people attend private high schools, approximately 40 percent of which are bilingual. In addition, various institutes in Colombia offer private instruction in a second language.

(p. 41, photos)
Students in Latin America often wear uniforms, such as those worn by the girls in these photos. Both public and private school students wear uniforms, which tend to be conservative in appearance. Girls usually wear skirts and boys wear dark slacks and a tie. School uniforms are often viewed as a way to contribute a sense of community and equality within a student body.

Preview

Answers

A There are four forms of *salir: salgo, sales, salimos, salir. Salgo* is the *yo* form. Verbs with a similar *yo* form include *hacer (hago), traer (traigo),* and *tener (tengo).*

B The word that comes before *bonita* is *tan.* The word that comes after is *como.* / The new employee is not as pretty as Marianela.

Gramática en contexto

42 Capítulo 1

Options

Strategies for Reaching All Students

Students Needing Extra Help
Have students begin to fill in the grammar section of the Organizer.

¿Qué va a hacer Pablo? ¿Va a salir con Marianela o con la empleada nueva? ¡Vea el próximo capítulo de *Marianela* mañana, a la misma hora y en el mismo canal!

A As you know, *salir* means "to leave, to go out." How many forms of *salir* can you find in the scenes of this *telenovela?* Which is the *yo* form? What other verbs do you know that have a similar *yo* form?

B One way to make comparisons is by using *más / menos* + adjective + *que*. We can also make other kinds of comparisons. Find the sentence in Frame 4 in which Pablo compares Marianela to the new employee. What word comes before *bonita?* And after? What do you think Pablo is saying?

El verbo *salir*

Salir follows the pattern of regular *-ir* verbs except in the *yo* form, *salgo*. Here are all its present-tense forms:

(yo)	sal**go**	(nosotros) (nosotras)	sal**imos**
(tú)	sal**es**	(vosotros) (vosotras)	sal**ís**
Ud. (él) (ella)	sal**e**	Uds. (ellos) (ellas)	sal**en**

Gramática en contexto   43

Present & Practice

Class Starter Review

On the day following the presentation of comparatives, you might begin the class with this activity: Post pairs of pictures with obvious similarities on the chalkboard (two famous actresses, two ugly dogs, two tall basketball stars, etc.). Have students develop comparative statements. *(Sally Field es tan famosa como Whoopi Goldberg.)*

Answers

1 ESTUDIANTE A

a. ¿A qué hora sale de la casa tu padre (madre)?
b. ...salen tus abuelos?
c. ...sale tu hermano(a) mayor (menor)?
d. ...sales tú?
e. ...salen tú y tu hermano(a)?

ESTUDIANTE B

Answers will vary, but look for correct use of time expressions.
a. Sale ...
b. Salen ...
c. Sale ...
d. Salgo ...
e. Salimos ...

2 ESTUDIANTE A

Questions may vary, but may include: *¿A qué hora sales de tu (la) casa por la mañana en un día escolar? ¿Cuánto tiempo necesitas para llegar a la escuela?*

1 Habla de un sábado típico con un(a) compañero(a). Imagina que todas estas personas viven contigo. ¿A qué hora sale de la casa cada *(each)* persona y qué hace cuando sale?

tu hermano
A —¿A qué hora sale de la casa tu hermano?
B —Sale a las nueve de la mañana para practicar deportes.

a. tu padre / tu madre
b. tus abuelos
c. tu hermano(a) mayor / menor
d. tú
e. tú y tu hermano(a)

2 Ahora pregunta a tres personas a qué hora salen de su casa por la mañana en un día escolar. ¿Cuánto tiempo necesitan para llegar a la escuela?

La forma comparativa: *tan ... como*

To compare things that are the same, we use *tan* + adjective + *como*. In English we use "as ... as."

Elena es **tan** alta **como** su madre, pero no es **tan** deportista **como** ella.

3 Con un(a) compañero(a), comparen a los estudiantes de su clase. Usen los dibujos.

A —*(Patricia) es tan trabajadora como (Daniel), ¿no?*
B —*Sí, tienes razón.*
  o: *No, no tienes razón. (Patricia) es más / menos trabajadora que (Daniel).*

a.   b.   c.

¡NO OLVIDES!
• To make unequal comparisons, we use *más / menos* + adj. + *que*. *El álgebra es **más** fácil **que** la química.*
• We do not use *más / menos* with the words *mayor / menor* and *mejor / peor*. *Juan es **menor que** su hermano Luis.*

44   Capítulo 1

Options

Strategies for Reaching All Students

Students Needing Extra Help
Ex. 1: Use the vocabulary sections of the Book 1 Organizers to help determine which activities the people can do when they leave. Remind students that the exercise specifies activities done on Saturday.
Review how verb forms change when going from a question to an answer.
Ex. 2: Model. Remind students to use the *tú* form.
La forma comparativa: Students may find this concept and structure difficult.

Elaborate on *tan ... como*. Give some examples in English.
¡No olvides!: If available, review the grammar section of the Organizer from Book 1, Chap. 11.
Give a model using *menos*.
Review meanings of *mayor / menor* and *mejor / peor*. Give examples.
Emphasize by example that the noun can be dropped.
Give a sample using the English "good, better, best."

La forma superlativa: Write this formula on the chalkboard or overhead for each kind of noun: masculine singular, feminine singular, etc. Write it out in one straight line. Have students come to the chalkboard and fill in the formula with the information you have given them. Then add *de* to the formula. Emphasize this because students want to use *en*. Review *del*.
Ex. 4: Help students see that this exercise is not a linear match for answers: They can combine any noun from the first column

44

d.

e.

f.

g.

h.

i.

Repaso: La forma superlativa

Remember that to say something is the "most" or the "least," we use:

el / la / los / las + noun + *más / menos* + adjective

la prueba **más** difícil
el informe **menos** interesante

• To say something is the "most" or the "least" in a group or category, we use *de* after the adjective. For example:

Esta prueba es **la más** difícil **de** todas.
Estos informes son **los menos** interesantes **del** día.

4 Túrnate con un(a) compañero(a) para combinar palabras de las tres listas y expresar tu opinión. Por ejemplo:

Central Park es el parque más grande de la ciudad de Nueva York.

a. el profesor / la profesora	alto, -a	los Estados Unidos
b. el edificio	bonito, -a	la escuela
c. la persona	viejo, -a	(nombre de un país)
d. la escuela	grande	(nombre de una comunidad)
e. el almacén	simpático, -a	(nombre de una ciudad)
f. el actor / la actriz	guapo, -a	
g. 💡	pequeño, -a	
	💡	

Gramática en contexto   45

¡NO OLVIDES!

We also use the irregular forms *mejor* and *peor, mayor* and *menor* in the superlative.
Pepe es **el mejor** estudiante **de** la clase.
Pepe es **el menor de** la familia.

ESTUDIANTE B
Answers will vary, but look for *salgo* and a correct time expression.

3 ESTUDIANTE A
Look for the construction *tan* + adj. + *como* and adjective agreement.
a. ...es tan paciente como...
b. ...es tan atrevido(a) como...
c. ...es tan artístico(a) como...
d. ...es tan deportista como...
e. ...es tan serio(a) como...
f. ...es tan generoso(a) como...
g. ...es tan ordenado(a) como...
h. ...es tan desordenado(a) como...
i. ...es tan prudente como...

ESTUDIANTE B
Answers will vary, but may include the construction *más / menos* + adj. + *que*. Look for adjective agreement.

4 Answers will vary, but should follow the model and the construction *el / la / los / las* + noun + *más / menos* + adj. + *de*. Look for adjective agreement.

 Practice Wkbk 1-5, 1-6, 1-7

Writing Activities 1-E, 1-F

 Pruebas 1-5, 1-6, 1-7

with any logical adjective or noun from the second and third columns.

45

Present & Practice

Reteach / Review: Vocabulary

Ex. 5: To extend this dialogue, have *Estudiante A* ask *Estudiante B* for directions to the store.

Answers

5 ESTUDIANTE A
Adjectives may vary.
a. ¡Qué (bonitos) son tus jeans! / ¿Dónde los compraste?
b. ¡Qué (bonito) es tu suéter! / ¿Dónde lo compraste?
c. ¡Qué (bonitos) son tus calcetines! / ¿Dónde los compraste?
d. ¡Qué (bonita) es tu camiseta! / ¿Dónde la compraste?
e. ¡Qué (bonitos) son tu camisa y tus pantalones! / ¿Dónde los compraste?
f. ¡Qué (bonitas) son tus botas! / ¿Dónde las compraste?
g. ¡Qué (bonito) es tu bolso! / ¿Dónde lo compraste?
h. ¡Qué (bonita) es tu chaqueta! / ¿Dónde la compraste?
i. Questions will vary, but should follow the model. Look for correct adjective agreement and verb form with proper placement of correct direct object pronoun.

Repaso: El complemento directo: los pronombres *lo, la, los, las*

Remember that a direct object tells who or what receives the action of the verb. Here are the direct object pronouns in Spanish:

lo	*him, it, you* (formal)	**los**	*them, you* (m. pl.)
la	*her, it, you* (formal)	**las**	*them, you* (f. pl.)

• Direct object pronouns agree in number and gender with the nouns they replace. They usually come right before the verb.

—¿Tomaste **la prueba** la semana pasada?
—Sí, **la** tomé el viernes.

• When a pronoun replaces both a masculine and a feminine noun, we use *los.*

—¿Tomaste **la prueba** y **el examen**?
—Sí, **los** tomé.

5   Admira algo que tiene uno(a) de tus compañeros(as). Luego pregúntale dónde lo compró. Usa los dibujos.

A —*¡Qué (bonitos) son tus zapatos!*
B —*Gracias.*
A —*¿Dónde los compraste?*
B —*Los compré en el almacén Rogers.*

a.   b.   c.   d.

e.   f.   g.   h.   i.

46   Capítulo 1

Options

Strategies for Reaching All Students

Students Needing Extra Help
Ex. 5: Avoid replacing *bonitos* with another adjective. Simply remind students of the four forms of direct object pronouns so that they won't be concerned about which adjective to use. The emphasis should be on direct object pronouns.

Review *tener, traer,* and *conocer.* If students have them available, they can use the Organizers from Book 1, Chaps. 5, 8, 9, 12, and 14.
El complemento directo: Refer to Book 1, Chap. 6, for a review.

Repaso: Los verbos *tener* y *traer*
El verbo *conocer*

Review the present-tense forms of *tener*.

(yo)	**tengo**	(nosotros) (nosotras)	**tenemos**
(tú)	**tienes**	(vosotros) (vosotras)	**tenéis**
Ud. (él) (ella)	**tiene**	Uds. (ellos) (ellas)	**tienen**

- Remember that we use *tener* in many different expressions:

  —¿Cuántos años **tienes**?
  —Dieciséis.

  —**Tengo** hambre / sed.
  —Pues **tienes que** comer / beber algo.

Review the present-tense forms of *traer*.

(yo)	**traigo**	(nosotros) (nosotras)	**traemos**
(tú)	**traes**	(vosotros) (vosotras)	**traéis**
Ud. (él) (ella)	**trae**	Uds. (ellos) (ellas)	**traen**

  —¿Qué **traes** en la mochila?
  —**Traigo** libros, lápices, bolígrafos y un sacapuntas.

En un restaurante mexicano,
Novato, California

ESTUDIANTE B
a. Los compré en . . .
b. Lo compré en . . .
c. Los compré en . . .
d. La compré en . . .
e. Los compré en . . .
f. Las compré en . . .
g. Lo compré en . . .
h. La compré en . . .
i. Answers will vary, but look for correct verb form with proper placement of correct direct object pronoun.

 Practice Wkbk. 1-8

 Writing Activity 1-G

 Prueba 1-8

Present & Practice

Answers

6 ESTUDIANTE A
a. Tengo que comprar un libro. ¿Adónde puedo ir?
b. ...comestibles...
c. ...zapatos...
d. ...pasta dentífrica...
e. ...un sello...
f. ...una falda...
g. Statements will vary.

ESTUDIANTE B
a. Yo conozco una librería por aquí.
b. ...un supermercado...
c. ...una zapatería...
d. ...una farmacia...
e. ...un correo...
f. ...una tienda (de ropa) / un almacén...
g. Answers will vary.

7 ESTUDIANTE A
a. ¿Quién trae el queso?
b. ...los refrescos?
c. ...la ensalada?
d. ...las frutas?
e. ...el pollo?
f. ...la leche?
g. ...la limonada?
h. ...el pan?
i. ...las naranjas?

Here are the present-tense forms of *conocer* ("to know, to be acquainted with").

(yo)	**conozco**	(nosotros) (nosotras)	**conocemos**
(tú)	**conoces**	(vosotros) (vosotras)	**conocéis**
Ud. (él) (ella)	**conoce**	Uds. (ellos) (ellas)	**conocen**

- Remember that we use *a* before the direct object if it refers to a person or an animal (especially a pet).

  Conozco a María Teresa. *but:* **Conozco** Madrid.

6 Pregúntale a un(a) compañero(a) si conoce algún lugar que quede cerca. Usa los dibujos.

A —*Tengo que comprar un regalo. ¿Adónde puedo ir?*
B —*Yo conozco una tienda (de regalos) por aquí.*

a.   b.   c.

d.   e.   f.   g.

48   Capítulo 1

Options

Strategies for Reaching All Students

Students Needing Extra Help
Ex. 7: Remind students that there may be two changes: one to the direct object and one to the verb.
Use the subject pronoun icon overhead transparency.
Ahora lo sabes: Have students write out this section so they can check off what they have mastered.

7 La clase planea un picnic. Túrnate con tu compañero(a) para decir qué va a traer cada persona.

A —¿Quién trae el jamón?
B —Pedro y Sara lo traen.

(dos nombres)

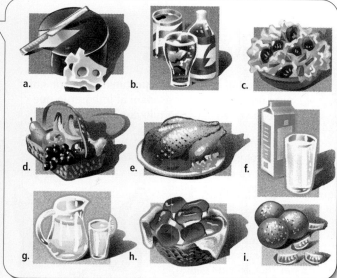

a. b. c.

d. e. f.

g. h. i.

(nombre)
(dos nombres)

Ahora lo sabes

Can you:

- talk about the time you leave a place?
  —Nosotros _____ de la escuela a las tres de la tarde.
- make equal comparisons of people or things?
  —Margarita está _____ cansada _____ Pablo.
- talk about the most or the least in a certain category?
  —Este libro es _____ interesante _____ la biblioteca.

Practice Wkbk. 1-9, 1-10

Audio Activities 1.4, 1.5

Writing Activity 1-H

Prueba 1-9

Comm. Act. BLM 1-2

Pronunciation Tape 1-3

Introducción

Play

Video Activity A

Using the Video

In this initial presentation of *La Catrina*, we meet Jamie González, a high school student from Los Angeles. Jamie has a grant to spend the summer in Querétaro, Mexico. She wants to find out about her paternal great-grandmother, "La Catrina," who disappeared during the Mexican Revolution.

In Spanish class at Jamie's school, the teacher wishes Jamie and fellow classmate Philip Armstrong (also a grant recipient) a good trip. After the plane flight to Mexico City, Jamie and Philip (Felipe) travel by train to Querétaro, where they meet their host families. The Navarro family is surprised to learn that the boy they were expecting, "Jaime," is a girl named "Jamie."

Meanwhile, at the local library, Demetrio Alcocer receives a phone call from Santana, who has been

Para decir más

Aquí tienes vocabulario adicional que te puede servir para hacer las actividades de esta sección.

bravo, -a
brave, fierce

el pájaro
bird

la tortuga
turtle

el pez
fish

el conejo
rabbit

el hámster
hamster

el pato
duck

Actividades

Esta sección te ofrece la oportunidad de aumentar tus conocimientos de español al integrar lo que aprendiste en este capítulo con lo que ya sabes.

1 ¡Tu mascota—perro, gato, etc.—va a participar en un concurso *(contest)!* Trae una foto de tu mascota para exhibir en clase. Luego, la clase va a votar y a preparar medallas. Por ejemplo:

el /la más feo(a)
el /la más grande
el /la más pequeño(a)
el /la más perezoso(a)
el /la más inteligente
el /la más . . .

La gata más bonita de la clase

50   Capítulo 1

Options

Strategies for Reaching All Students

Spanish-Speaking Students
Ex. 1: Give this assignment to Spanish-speaking students: *Prepara un artículo de periódico que describe este concurso. Debes incluir dónde y cuándo tuvo lugar, los premios que se dieron y las mascotas que los recibieron.*

 Un paso más Exs. 1-G, 1-H

Students Needing Extra Help
Actividades: Assign one of these to a group of students if time is limited.
Ex. 1: Put the formula on the chalkboard so students can fill it in.
Ex. 2: Use the Organizer to brainstorm other vocabulary possibilities.
Ex. 3: Brainstorm other categories: use the Organizer from Book 1, Chap. 1, if available.

Cooperative Learning
Tan + adj. + *como* can also be used to construct similes such as "She is as quiet as a mouse." Explain what a simile is and how to construct one, then divide the class into groups of three or four. Have them use *tan* + adj. + *como* to create five or six similes. For example: *"La geometría es tan divertida como leer una guía telefónica"* or *"La química es tan interesante como arreglar mi cuarto."* Collect the similes and read the most humorous ones to the class.

2 Túrnate con un(a) compañero(a) para describir tu escuela primaria. Pueden hablar de:

- su tamaño *(size)*
- las salas que tiene
- los profesores y profesoras
- el lugar donde está

3 La clase va a preparar un "Guinness Book of Class Records." El libro debe tener un nombre en español. Puedes usar estas categorías. Piensa también en otras.

¿Quién es el (la) estudiante más / menos atrevido(a)?

¿Quién tiene el pelo más largo / más corto?

¿Quién escribe más rápido en la computadora?

¿Quién dibuja mejor?

¿Quién saca las mejores notas?

Cada estudiante debe traer una foto. Todos deben comparar las fotos y decidir qué información van a escribir debajo de cada una. Pueden exhibir el libro en la sala de clases o en la biblioteca escolar.

En Santiago, Chile, unos jóvenes deportistas celebran una victoria.

Actividades   51

spying on Jamie and Felipe on the train.

In subsequent episodes, each chapter's video is divided into three segments: a) a summary of the previous episode, b) the main story, and c) a review of a difficult concept from the second segment. These video notes will focus on giving a synopsis of the main story for each chapter.

La Catrina: Capítulo 1

Play

Video Activity B

Para entender mejor

Play

Video Activity C

Answers: Actividades
1–2 Answers will vary.

3 Answers will vary, and may include the construction *(nombre) es el / la estudiante más / menos + adj. + de la clase.*

Comm. Act. BLMs 1-3, 1-4, 1-5

Apply

Process Reading

Make sure students understand the four headings in this section and the tasks they represent:

• *Antes de leer:* prereading activity for activating prior knowledge; emphasis on one or more strategies for overcoming the tendency to read slowly, word by word, and instead to focus on receiving the message being communicated in the text

• *Mira la lectura:* scanning / skimming for general ideas or information, looking for cognates, proper nouns, headings, numbered or bulleted items, familiar words, etc.

• *Infórmate:* reading for more detailed information

• *Aplicación:* post-reading activity

Answers
Antes de leer
Answers will vary.

Mira la lectura
Answers will vary, but students may say that the play will be a comedy.

¡Vamos a leer!

Antes de leer

STRATEGY ➤ Using prior knowledge

This is a play about an unusual mosquito. How do you feel about insects? How do you react when you see one?

Mira la lectura

STRATEGY ➤ Using the title and illustrations as context clues

Read the title and look at the illustrations. What do you think the play will be like?

Infórmate

STRATEGY ➤ Using context clues

Now read the play. When you come to something you don't know, use the words you do know and your knowledge of the situation to help you figure it out. For example, toward the end of the play, the word *grita* occurs twice in stage directions. Both times it comes before something Eduardo says. And what Eduardo says begins and ends with exclamation marks, which tells you that he is speaking louder than normal. Read the stage directions to see what word makes sense. Is your answer confirmed when Alfonso asks, "*¿Por qué gritas?*" That is a natural question if you can't understand why someone is excited.

El EXTRAÑO caso del mosquito

EDUARDO ROBLES BOZA (TÍO PATOTA)

Acto I

(Eduardo está en su dormitorio escuchando música. Lleva un libro en la mano mientras da vueltas por el cuarto. Abre, repasa y cierra el libro continuamente. Está nervioso. Es de noche.)

EDUARDO: Mañana tengo examen y no sé nada.

(Eduardo da vueltas otra vez; trata de leer y memorizar. Ve un mosquito. Pone el libro en la cama, recoge un periódico y va a la pared a matar el mosquito. Pero el mosquito empieza a hablar.)

MOSQUITO: ¡No me mates, por favor!

EDUARDO: ¿Tú hablas?

52   Capítulo 1

Options

Strategies for Reaching All Students

Spanish-Speaking Students
Add: *Después de leer "El extraño caso del mosquito," piensa en los refranes que siguen: "Nunca dejes para mañana lo que puedas hacer hoy" y "Lo mal ganado se lo lleva el diablo." ¿Cuál es un buen refrán para Eduardo? ¿Por qué?*

Students Needing Extra Help
Infórmate: Explain the concept of stage directions.
As an example of using prior knowledge, show students where *grita* is. See if they pick up on the exclamation points *before* you read the *Infórmate* to them. Discuss what they mean. Emphasize that they have taken something they already know (that exclamation points are used to show excitement, a raised voice, etc.) and transferred it to *this* situation. Show them how you have to guess sometimes and try again.
Aplicación 2: When students make suggestions, help them with the vocabulary they need and add it to the story.

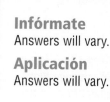

MOSQUITO: Sí, y en dos idiomas. Soy bilingüe.

EDUARDO: ¡Caramba! No lo puedo creer . . . Pues, tengo que matarte. *(Levanta el periódico.)*

MOSQUITO: ¡No! ¡No! Puedo ayudarte.

EDUARDO: ¿Ayudarme? ¿Tú? ¿A qué?

MOSQUITO: A estudiar. Tengo memoria y sé leer también.

(Eduardo coloca el mosquito, con cuidado, en la palma de su mano. Lo lleva y lo pone sobre el libro abierto que está en la cama.)

EDUARDO: Bueno, lee lo que hay en esa página.

MOSQUITO: Aquí dice que Cristóbal Colón fue un navegante español que . . .

EDUARDO: ¡Está bien, está bien! Eres un mosquito muy preparado.

MOSQUITO: ¿No me vas a matar?

EDUARDO: No sé. ¿Cómo vas a ayudarme?

MOSQUITO: Muy fácil. Yo estudio esta noche. Tú duermes y mañana me escondo en tu oreja, . . . y te explico todo. *(Eduardo no contesta.)* Bueno, ¿cuándo empiezo?

EDUARDO: *(Recoge el libro, lo pone sobre el escritorio y lo abre en una página.)* Puedes empezar ahora. Tienes que estudiar desde esta página y hasta terminar el libro . . . y yo me voy a dormir. ¡Hasta mañana, compañero!

Acto II

(Es de día. Eduardo duerme. La luz del escritorio todavía está encendida. Entra un muchacho.)

ALFONSO: ¡Eduardo! ¡Hoy tenemos examen! ¿Estudiaste?

EDUARDO: ¿Cómo dices? ¡Sí, sí, claro que estudié!

(Eduardo se levanta, recoge su ropa y entra en el baño. Alfonso da vueltas por el cuarto.)

ALFONSO: Veo que estudiaste mucho porque la luz todavía está encendida y el libro abierto.

EDUARDO: *(Grita desde el baño.)* ¡Sí, hoy sé todo!

(Alfonso recoge el libro y lo cierra. Eduardo sale del baño y ve lo que está haciendo Alfonso. Se pone las manos en la cara y le grita.)

EDUARDO: ¡Qué horror! ¿Qué haces, Alfonso?

ALFONSO: ¿Por qué gritas? Sólo cerré tu libro.

EDUARDO: *(Corre rápido adonde está Alfonso y toma el libro, busca nerviosamente en las páginas y ve que el mosquito está aplastado.)* Creo que no voy a poder tomar el examen . . . ¡Ya olvidé todo!

Aplicación

Make a list of three to five new words you figured out from the context. Discuss them with a classmate to see if he or she agrees. Then look them up in a dictionary to see if you were right.

If you were Eduardo at the end of the play, what would you do? In a small group, decide on some suggestions for him.

Apply

Process Writing

Inform students in advance that their work will be kept in a portfolio of their writing. Explain that their portfolio will help them keep a record of their progress throughout the year.

Portfolios represent a systematic process involving both learner and teacher. They document progress toward specific standards by applying clearly stated criteria in selecting, monitoring, and evaluating significant products and performance. (For a more detailed explanation of portfolio writing and assessment, see pp. T42–T45.)

In preparation for the writing assignment, you may wish to briefly review adjective agreement. For step 5, remind students about correct accent placement, question marks, and exclamation points. For spelling checks, tell students that they may always refer back to the vocabulary sections or the *Resumen del capítulo* at the end of the chapter.

Before beginning this exercise, you may want to review the five steps of process writing with your students.

NOTE: *¡Vamos a escribir!* offers two related activities. The first is more basic; the second is an

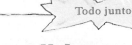

¡Vamos a escribir!

Con un(a) compañero(a), prepara un folleto *(pamphlet)* en español sobre tu escuela. El folleto va a servirles a los estudiantes que sólo hablan español.

 Primero, contesta estas preguntas con un(a) compañero(a).

* El horario
  ¿A qué hora empieza el día escolar? ¿A qué hora termina? ¿Cuánto dura cada clase?

* Las salas
  ¿Hay cafetería, auditorio, gimnasio, piscina? ¿Cómo son? ¿Dónde quedan?

* Las materias
  ¿Qué materias toman los estudiantes de tu año?

* Las actividades
  ¿Qué deportes pueden practicar? ¿En qué otras actividades pueden participar?

* El personal
  ¿Cómo se llaman el (la) director(a) y los consejeros? ¿Dónde están sus oficinas? ¿Cuáles son sus números de teléfono? ¿Cómo se llama el (la) enfermero(a)? ¿Dónde está la enfermería?

* Las reglas
  ¿Qué se prohíbe hacer? ¿Hay ropa que se prohíbe llevar? ¿Qué debes hacer si te sientes mal y no puedes ir a la escuela? ¿Y si te sientes mal en la escuela?

Usa tus respuestas para preparar el folleto. Si quieres, puedes hacer un dibujo de la mascota u otra insignia de tu escuela.

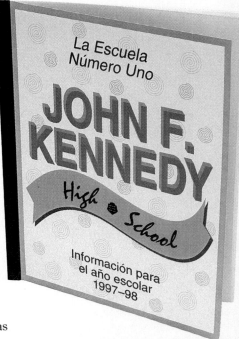

La Escuela Número Uno

JOHN F. KENNEDY High School

Información para el año escolar 1997–98

¡NO OLVIDES!

Hay cinco pasos.
1. Primero, piensa en el tema *(topic)* y escribe tus ideas.
2. Luego, escribe el primer borrador *(draft)*.
3. Comparte *(share)* tu borrador con un(a) compañero(a) y pídele recomendaciones o ideas. Escribe el segundo borrador.
4. Revisa tu trabajo para corregir los errores de ortografía y puntuación.
5. Ahora, distribuye tu trabajo entre las personas a quienes pueda interesar, y guarda otra copia en tu portafolio.

Options

Strategies for Reaching All Students

Students Needing Extra Help
Because students are used to having the directions given in English, turn to a *Vamos a escribir* section from the end of Book 1. Show students how similar and consistent the formats are.
Have students keep a list in their notebooks of words such as *el tema, el borrador*, etc., that will keep reappearing in this section throughout the book.

If students have them available, they can use the vocabulary sections of the Organizers from Book 1, Chap. 2, and this chapter.
Review sports vocabulary (Book 1, Chap. 3). Have students use *guitarra, música, periódico,* etc.
El personal: Have a student handbook available.
Las reglas: Use the Organizer from this chapter.

Step 2: If you do this activity, supply some vocabulary. Do this as a large group and brainstorm.
This is a sophisticated format. Students can supply the vocabulary while you provide the structure of the sentences and the grammar.

2 Ahora, tú y tu compañero(a) deben preparar una carta para enviarles con el folleto a las familias que hablan español. En la carta pueden incluir:

- una bienvenida a la escuela
- quién escribió el folleto
- para quién es el folleto
- una invitación a visitar la escuela

La carta debe empezar con la fecha y un saludo formal. Al final, escriban una despedida (Cordialmente o Atentamente).

_____ de septiembre de 199 _____

Estimada familia _____
¡Bienvenidos a la escuela _____ !
xxxxxxxxxxxxxxxxxxxxxxx
xxxxxxxxxxxxxxxxxxxxxx
xxxxxxxxxxxxxxxxxxxx
xxxxxxxxxxxxxxxxxxxx

Atentamente,

_____
(firma)

Estudiantes en Ambato, Ecuador, se preparan para los Juegos Nacionales.

3 Ahora pueden:

- darles folletos a los estudiantes nuevos de la escuela que hablan español
- enviarles folletos a los estudiantes de la escuela media *(middle)* que hablan español
- exhibir los folletos en la sala de clases
- incluirlos en su portafolio

inglés en **QUICK LEARNING**
¡hablas o hablas!
como aprendiste a hablar el español, sin tareas en casa, sin reglas gramaticales, ¡ así de fácil !, ¡ así de natural !
346-87-18
GARANTIZAMOS RESULTADOS O TE DEVOLVEMOS TU DINERO
INICIAMOS CURSOS LUNES 17 DE ENERO
CENTROS DE INFORMACION: • • • Mty: 346-87-18 y 346-87-19
D. F.: 538-71-80 • Gdl: 625-75-55 • Tij: 84-24-23

¡Vamos a escribir!   55

extension and should be reserved for more able students. The second is also appropriate for any native speakers of Spanish who may be in your class. (If your school doesn't have any Spanish-speaking students, ask students to share their pamphlet with someone they know who speaks Spanish.)

Using Realia
Using context clues, ask students if they can figure out what the phrase *¡hablas o hablas!* means ("You will speak, no matter what!" or "We guarantee you will speak English!").

Cultural Notes

(p. 55, photo)
Each year a different Ecuadoran province sponsors these games in which young people and adults from around the country participate.

(p. 55, realia)
A traditional approach to learning a foreign language is to study grammar rules and to memorize vocabulary out of context. This advertisement in a Mexican publication promises that students will learn English in the same natural way they learned their native language. The ad offers four information centers in Mexico: Monterrey (Mty), Distrito Federal (D.F. / Ciudad de México), Guadalajara (Gdl), and Tijuana (Tij).

Assess & Summarize

You may want to assign parts of this section as written homework or as an in-class writing activity prior to administering the *Examen de habilidades*.

Answers

Listening: *Tomo muchas materias este año. Y todos los días tengo que entregar tareas. En geometría tenemos que hacer problemas y todos los viernes hay prueba. Tomo química también, pero no es tan interesante. Para mí, la historia es la materia más interesante y más fácil de todas.* / History is the easiest subject. / The student expects a weekly test in geometry.

Reading: The picture of the dejected soccer player does not agree with the student's note, which says the soccer team is in first place.

Writing: Letters will vary.

¿Lo sabes bien?

Esta sección te ayudará a prepararte para el examen de habilidades, donde tendrás que hacer tareas semejantes. Recuerda, sin embargo, que en el examen no habrá *(there won't be)* modelos.

Listening

Can you understand when people talk about their classes and assignments? Listen as your teacher reads a sample similar to what you will hear on the test. According to this student, which subject is the easiest? In which subject does the student expect a weekly test?

Reading

Can you understand a written description in which a student compares one school with others? Which picture does not agree with this student's note to a friend?

Me gusta mucho mi escuela. No es tan grande como otras, pero es muy moderna. Tenemos computadoras en todas las salas de clase. Tomamos las mismas materias que en otras escuelas. Pero también podemos estudiar varios idiomas y ciencias avanzadas. ¡Y el equipo de fútbol está en el primer lugar de la liga!

56   Capítulo 1

Writing

Can you write a letter in which you describe your school to someone else? Here is a sample.

Culture

Can you explain how the school day of a Mexican student might differ from yours?

Speaking

Can you talk about your school and your classes? With a partner, create a dialogue between an old student and a new one. What are some questions a new student might ask about your school? Here is a sample dialogue:

Querida Toña,

Hay muchas cosas que me gustan de esta escuela nueva. Primero, no está tan lejos de mi casa y salgo casi media hora más tarde por la mañana. Hay armarios también, y no tengo que llevar todo en mi bolso. ¡Y se permite salir a comer al mediodía! Ya conozco a muchos de los profesores. Creo que son mejores que los del año pasado, pero ninguno de ellos es tan divertido como el Sr. Gómez.

Tu amiga,

María

A —¿*Cómo es la clase de matemáticas?*
B —*No es mi clase favorita, pero la profesora explica bien y se permite hacerle preguntas.*
A —*Y los exámenes, ¿son muy difíciles?*
B —*No mucho. Por suerte, a la profesora le encanta repasar.*
A —¿*Y hay mucha tarea?*
B —*Ah, eso sí. Todos los días tenemos que hacer tres páginas de ejercicios.*

Options

Strategies for Reaching All Students

Students Needing Extra Help
Have students write out this section so they can check off what they have mastered. Present this as a sample test or a pretest. Be sure that students understand that this is not the actual test. Some students will study *only* what they see here.
Listening: Read slowly, pausing after each sentence so that students can absorb the material. Remember that many of your students are visual, and that listening, without visual input, is difficult.

Remind students that they are only listening for two pieces of information. See if they can suggest some of the words they might hear.
Reading: Have the students look at the three pictures first so they can get an idea of what they are looking for. Again, emphasize that they don't have to know each word in order to understand.
Writing: Have students use the Organizer and write a sample letter as practice.

Culture: Have students review any notes they may have taken during their first reading of the *Perspectiva cultural*.
Speaking: Use the Organizer to create some dialogues.
Review the *¡Comuniquemos!* section, where students created a similar dialogue.

Resumen del capítulo 1

Usa el vocabulario de este capítulo para:

- talk about your classes and homework
- describe your school and your school day
- compare the subjects you like the most and the least

to name school subjects
el alemán *German*
el álgebra (f.)
la biología
el francés
la geografía
la geometría
la historia
el idioma *language*
la literatura
la materia *subject*
la química *chem*

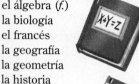

to name people who work at a school
el consejero, la consejera
el director, la directora

to name places in a school
el auditorio
el bufet de ensaladas
la cafetería
el escenario *stage*
el laboratorio
la oficina

to describe school equipment
el armario
el asiento
la bandera
el bolso
la computadora

la diapositiva *slide*
la grapadora *stapler*
el mapa
la pared *wall*
el proyector
el reloj *clock*
el sacapuntas,
    pl. los sacapuntas
el sujetapapeles,
    pl. los sujetapapeles
el edificio

to talk about activities associated with school
conocer *(c → zc):* *know*
    (yo) conozco
    (tú) conoces
contestar
escribir
explicar
hacer fila *line up*
hacer una pregunta *ask?*
preguntar
repasar *review*
sacar una buena / mala nota
la pregunta
la respuesta *answer*
se permite
se prohibe
usar
escolar

to talk about homework
entregar *hand in*
el capítulo *chapter*
la composición
el ejercicio
el examen
el informe *report*
la lección
la página
el problema
la prueba *quiz*

to make comparisons
tan + *adj.* + como

other useful words and expressions
alguno (algún), -a
por suerte
próximo, -a *next*

Culture: Answers will vary, but students may say that in a Mexican school, the school day is divided into a morning session and an afternoon session, that students take more classes, have more homework, etc.

Speaking: Dialogues will vary.

¿? **Prueba cumulativa**

¿? **Examen de habilidades**

c **Test Generator**

CAPÍTULO 2
THEME: DAILY ROUTINE

SCOPE AND SEQUENCE   Pages 58–89

COMMUNICATION

Topics

Personal hygiene items

Before-school activities

After-school activities

Musical instruments

Objectives

To compare students' extracurricular activities in Guatemala and in the U.S.

To describe daily routine

To indicate time

To discuss extracurricular activities

To discuss music

CULTURE

Extracurricular activities in Guatemala

GRAMMAR

Los verbos reflexivos

Repaso: Verbos con los cambios o → ue, e → ie, *y* e → i

Antes de / después de + *inf.*

Ancillaries available for use with Chapter 2

Multisensory/Technology

 Overhead Transparencies, 11–15

 Audio Tapes and CDs

 Vocabulary Art Blackline Masters for Hands-On Learning, pp. 13–17

 Classroom Crossword

 La Catrina

 CD-ROM

Print

 Practice Workbook, pp. 12–22

 Writing, Audio & Video Activities, pp. 11–16, 96–98, 153–154

 Communicative Activity Blackline Masters

Pair and Small Group Activities, pp. 8–13

Situation Cards, p. 14

 Un paso más: Actividades para ampliar tu español, pp. 7–12

Assessment

 Assessment Program

Pruebas, pp. 25–34

Examen de habilidades, pp. 35–38

 Test Generator

Video still from Chap. 2

¿Qué haces todos los días?

Although daily routines and activities of young people in Spanish-speaking countries vary from place to place and from one socioeconomic group to another, many of these activities are shared among them.

As in the U.S., school plays an important role. Much of young people's social life stems from the relationships they establish there. Many students, particularly those in private schools, have been classmates since grade school. Because of this, the few extracurricular activities that are offered take on added significance. Among these activities are school performances, field trips, and dances.

Unlike young people in the U.S., teens in most Spanish-speaking countries rarely hold outside jobs. Families sometimes employ maids and gardeners—even middle-class families. Teenagers are expected to dedicate time at home to their studies. As in the U.S., they are sometimes provided special tutors to ensure that they do well.

In large Spanish-speaking cities, many young people study English, French, German, or other languages at language academies. This instruction is in addition to the foreign language education offered in the schools. There are also educational opportunities away from school. Many students study dance, voice, guitar, art, or gymnastics.

Young Hispanics enjoy socializing in groups—giving or attending parties is one important aspect of this. They can often be seen at *cafés,* public parks, town *plazas,* as well as at the local shopping mall. Weekend activities might include camping, going to the beach, or going on a skiing trip (depending on the country or season).

Eating habits and schedules for teens in Spanish-speaking countries differ considerably from those of young people in the U.S. Most eat a light breakfast of bread and jam with juice and coffee. Lunch, however, includes several courses: soup, a meat dish with vegetables and / or salad, dessert, fruit, and coffee. Lunch may take place as late as 1:30 or 2:00 in the afternoon. It is a time considered important for the family to come together and relax. For most families, the evening meal is light because of the heavy and late lunch, but some families have a complete dinner around 9:00 P.M. or later.

Introduce

Re-entry of Concepts
The following list represents words, expressions, and grammar topics re-entered from Book 1 and Book 2 (Chap. 1):

Book 1
numbers 0–31, calendar terms, *gustar* expressions, time-telling, seasons, leisure-time activities, places in a community, vacation activities, chores, recycling activities

Chapter 1
school subjects

Planning

Cross-Curricular Connections

Career / Home Economics Connection (pp. 66–67)
Have pairs or small groups of students role play being instructors for a parenting class. Using dolls or stuffed animals, they will instruct the class or another group on how to care for a new baby and also how to treat older siblings. They may want to make posters as a follow-up. Brainstorm with students additional necessary vocabulary before beginning.

Art / Business Connection (pp. 74–75)
Have students create an ad poster for a new personal hygiene item. Have them use reflexive verbs and vocabulary from the first *Vocabulario para conversar* to create ads such as these: *Debe bañarse con jabón Fiesta. ¡Es el mejor!* or *Yo me lavo el pelo con el champú Color Bonito. ¡Me encanta!* Display the posters around the classroom.

Spanish in Your Community
Have students find out what type of Spanish music is available in their community. If possible, have them listen to a Spanish-language radio station for at least 15 minutes and take notes on what they hear. What do they recognize (advertisements, newscasts, DJ "talk")? What could they understand (store names, addresses)? Have students visit a local store that sells CDs and cassettes to find out the names of popular Hispanic bands or singers.

CAPÍTULO 2

¿Qué haces todos los días?

OBJECTIVES

At the end of this chapter, you will be able to:

- describe your day before and after school
- talk about which extracurricular activities you prefer
- compare your extracurricular activities with those of another student
- compare students' extracurricular activities in Guatemala and the United States

Haciendo una alfombra de serrín *(sawdust)* en Antigua, Guatemala

59

(p. 58, photo)
On Maundy Thursday (Holy Thursday) in Guatemala, teens from different churches work into the night making decorative carpets out of sawdust for the next day's procession—rather like rolling out the red carpet. They lay wood cutouts on the pavement and fill in the holes with colored sawdust, until they have completed the carpet. The next day, Good Friday, the churches form a procession and walk over the decorative sawdust carpets.

Preview

¡Piénsalo bien!

Mira las fotos. Los estudiantes que vemos aquí están hablando de lo que hacen antes y después de las clases. ¿Qué haces tú?

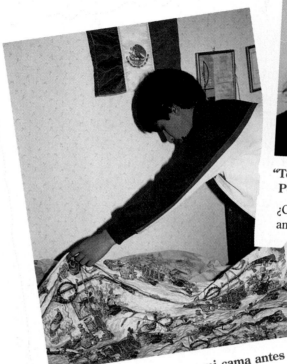

"Tengo hambre y necesito desayunar. Pero primero debo cepillarme el pelo."

¿Cuánto tiempo necesitas para prepararte antes de ir a la escuela?

"Siempre tengo que hacer mi cama antes de salir para la escuela."

¿Hay quehaceres de la casa que tú tienes que hacer por la mañana? ¿Cuáles?

60   Capítulo 2

Options

Strategies for Reaching All Students

Spanish-Speaking Students
Ask: *¿Por qué crees que a los estudiantes les falta tiempo para hacer lo que tienen que hacer? Además de ir a clases, ¿qué otras cosas tienes que hacer todos los días? ¿Qué haces después de las clases?*

 Un paso más Ex. 2-A

Tres músicos (<u>Three Musicians</u>)
(1921), Pablo Picasso

"¡Nos encanta tocar en la banda!"

A estos jóvenes en San Sebastián, España, les gusta mucho esta actividad extracurricular.
¿Hay banda en tu escuela? ¿Tocas tú algún instrumento musical?

61

Cultural Notes

(p. 61, photo)
"The Three Musicians" is an example of Picasso's cubist style. Musicians and instruments are rendered here as geometric forms on one plane. The genre of cubism assigns geometric shapes to natural forms. In this painting, for example, the center musician's legs and torso are represented by triangles. The guitar is a composite of geometric shapes, yet remains recognizable as a guitar.

Present

Chapter Theme
Before-school activities

Communicative Objectives
• To describe daily routine
• To indicate time

 Transparencies 11–12

 Vocabulary Art BLMs

 Pronunciation Tape 2-1

Grammar Preview
Reflexive verbs; verbs with the stem change o → ue, e → ie, and e → i; and antes de / después de + inf. are presented lexically. Their explanation appears in the grammar section. Avoid explaining or treating these as grammar at this point. Allow students to use them naturally, and the grammar will be much more readily comprehended later.

Vocabulario para conversar

¿Te despiertas temprano?

Vas a necesitar estas palabras y expresiones para hablar sobre lo que haces antes y después de la escuela. Después de leerlas varias veces, practícalas con un(a) compañero(a).

despertarse (e → ie)

levantarse

la cara

lavarse la cara

cepillarse los dientes

ducharse

lavarse el pelo

62   Capítulo 2

Options

Strategies for Reaching All Students

Spanish-Speaking Students

 Un paso más Exs. 2-B, 2-C

Students Needing Extra Help
Begin to fill in the vocabulary section of the Organizer.
Reflexive verbs may be difficult for some students. Point out that these are -ar and -ir verbs with -se attached at the end.
Remind them that e → ie and e → i are boot verbs. Review this concept. Show them the sample in También necesitas . . . .
También necesitas . . . : Provide some expressions using hay que, antes de, después de, and soler with regular verbs

and reflexives. Remind students that they have seen me and te used before with gusta(n), encanta(n), etc.
This vocabulary may seem complicated to some. Postpone explanations until later in the chapter. Keep in mind, however, that some students may need to understand concepts before they can manipulate the words.
Give examples of de buen / mal humor.

secarse el pelo | cepillarse el pelo | peinarse

vestirse *(e → i)* | bañarse | acostarse *(o → ue)*

Teaching Suggestions
Preparing students to speak: Use one or two options from each of the categories of Comprehensible Input, Physical Response, or Limited Verbal Response. For a complete explanation of these categories and some sample activities, see pp. T16–T17.

Class Starter Review
On the day following initial vocabulary presentation, you might begin the class with this activity: Prepare a transparency with five or six morning activities in the infinitive form. Have students put them in logical order.

También necesitas . . .

hay que + *inf.*	*It's necessary to ___.*	antes de + *inf.*	*before* + verb + *-ing*
(yo) me despierto	*I wake up*	después de + *inf.*	*after* + verb + *-ing*
(tú) te despiertas	*you wake up*	de buen / mal humor	*in a good / bad mood*
(yo) me levanto	*I get up*	mismo, -a	*same*
(tú) te levantas	*you get up*	soler *(o → ue)* + *inf.*	*to be in the habit of*
uno	*here: one, a person*		
sin	*without*		
según	*according to*		
por lo menos	*at least*		

> **¿Y qué quiere decir . . . ?**
>
> depender   es necesario
> desayunar   fácilmente

Vocabulario para conversar 63

Enrichment
Present this vocabulary in conjunction with a game of charades. You can play the game with the entire class, having individuals or groups of students perform a given action in front of the class as you call out a word or expression and then having a vote for who did the clearest pantomime, the funniest, etc.

Learning Spanish Through Action
STAGING VOCABULARY: *Hagan pantomimas*
MATERIALS: copies of the Vocabulary Art BLMs or actual items to represent vocabulary: toothbrush, shampoo, comb, brush, alarm clock, etc.
DIRECTIONS: Direct students to use the props, if available, to act out the activities that you mention: *Hay que lavarse el pelo. Hay que cepillarse los dientes,* etc.

Practice & Apply

Reteach / Review: Vocabulary

Ex. 1: As an extension exercise, have students redo this exercise with *Estudiante A* and *Estudiante B* talking about whether various people or pets have breakfast early or late, or whether they have breakfast at all. Encourage students to extend their dialogues as best they can by asking each other what they eat and why they eat breakfast when they do *(porque me despierto temprano, porque tengo que ir a la escuela temprano)*, and any other appropriate questions.

Answers: Empecemos a conversar

1 ESTUDIANTE A

a. ¿A qué hora te levantas los días de semana?

b. . . . en el verano?

c. . . . en las vacaciones?

d. . . . el sábado?

e. . . . el domingo?

ESTUDIANTE B

a.–e. Answers will vary, but look for *me levanto* and a correct time expression.

Empecemos a conversar

Túrnate con un(a) compañero(a) para ser *Estudiante A* y *Estudiante B.* Reemplacen las palabras subrayadas en el modelo con palabras representadas o escritas en los recuadros. Si ven  pueden dar su propia respuesta.

1 los fines de semana

A —*¿A qué hora te levantas los fines de semana?*
B — *Depende. Algunas veces me levanto a las 8:00, otras a las 9:00.*

Estudiante A   **Estudiante B**

a. los días de semana

b. en el verano

c. en las vacaciones

d. el sábado

e. el domingo

2 temprano

A —*¿Te despiertas temprano?*
B —*Sí, me despierto temprano.*
  o: *No, no me despierto temprano.*
  o: *No, me despierto tarde.*

Estudiante A   **Estudiante B**

a. de buen humor

b. fácilmente

c. sin despertador

d. siempre a la misma hora

e.

Options

Strategies for Reaching All Students

Spanish-Speaking Students

Ex. 7: After this exercise, ask Spanish-speaking students: *¿Cuándo preparas la ropa que vas a llevar a la escuela? ¿Cuándo te bañas? ¿Cuándo preparas tus libros y cuadernos? ¿Quién te prepara el desayuno?*

 **Un paso más Exs. 2-D, 2-E**

Students Needing Extra Help

Ex. 1: Give *Estudiante B* time to develop appropriate responses. Review time-telling. Remind students that not only will the verb form change in the answer, but also the reflexive pronoun. Give them extra practice, both oral and written.

Ex. 2: Do this exercise three times. Do each example answering *sí* to everything, then with the first negative response, and finally answer all examples with the last response. In this way, students can focus on the *me /*

te changes and the verb endings.

Ex. 3: Show students that they only have to change the verb and number.

Exs. 4 and 6: Students may need some help with the vocabulary in order to answer the *¿por qué?* portions of these exercises.

Ex. 5: Allow students time to do a quick survey to answer these questions.

Ex. 7: Many students probably don't eat breakfast or may eat at a free breakfast program provided by the school. Emphasize the importance of breakfast.

3

A —¿*Cuánto tiempo necesita uno para* _vestirse_?
B —*Pues, por lo menos* _veinte_ *minutos.*

Estudiante A   **Estudiante B**

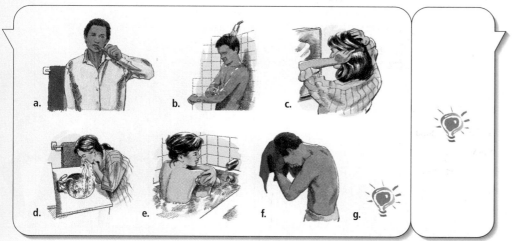

a.   b.   c.

d.   e.   f.   g.

Empecemos a escribir

Escribe tus respuestas en español.

4 ¿Te despiertas de buen humor? ¿Es fácil o difícil despertarse temprano? ¿Crees que es importante levantarse temprano? ¿Y acostarse temprano? ¿Por qué?

5 ¿Cuántas personas de tu clase suelen bañarse por la mañana? ¿Y antes de acostarse?

6 ¿Es necesario cepillarse los dientes por lo menos tres veces al día? Según los dentistas, ¿cuándo hay que cepillarse los dientes? ¿Y hay que lavarse las manos antes de comer? ¿Por qué?

7 ¿Desayunas siempre a la misma hora? ¿Sueles desayunar antes de salir de casa? ¿Con quién? Si no, ¿cuándo y dónde desayunas?

También se dice

lavarse los dientes

tomar un baño /una ducha
darse un baño /una ducha

Vocabulario para conversar   65

2 ESTUDIANTE A
a. ¿Te despiertas de buen humor?
b. . . . fácilmente?
c. . . . sin despertador?
d. . . . siempre a la misma hora?
e. Questions will vary; look for the construction ¿*Te despiertas . . .* ?
ESTUDIANTE B
a.–e. Answers will vary, but look for *Me despierto . . . .*

3 ESTUDIANTE A
a. ¿Cúanto tiempo necesita uno para cepillarse los dientes?
b. . . . ducharse?
c. . . . peinarse?
d. . . . lavarse la cara?
e . . . bañarse?
f. . . . secarse el pelo?
g. Questions will vary.
ESTUDIANTE B
a.–g. Answers will vary, but should be logical.

Answers: Empecemos a escribir
4–7 Answers will vary.

Practice Wkbk. 2-1, 2-2

Audio Activity 2.1

Pruebas 2-1, 2-2

Comm. Act. BLM 2-1

Enrichment
Ex. 4: As a follow-up assignment, have students write a note for a baby-sitter, giving instructions on the bedtime routine for a five-year-old. Tell students to name their child and to be creative and thorough as they tell the sitter what grooming activities must be done and in what order, and when the child must go to bed.

Present

Chapter Theme
After-school activities

Communicative Objectives
• To discuss extracurricular activities
• To discuss music

 Transparencies 13–14

 Vocabulary Art BLMs

 Pronunciation Tape 2-2

Teaching Suggestions
Preparing students to speak: Use one or two options from each of the categories of Comprehensible Input, Physical Response, or Limited Verbal Response. For a complete explanation of these categories and some sample activities, see pp. T16–T17.

Vocabulario para conversar

¿Qué haces después de las clases?

Aquí tienes el resto del vocabulario que necesitas en este capítulo para hablar sobre lo que haces antes y después de las clases.

Las actividades extracurriculares

el coro

el anuario

las artes marciales *(pl.)*

el periódico (de la escuela)

la revista (literaria)

Viajes

Options

Strategies for Reaching All Students

Students Needing Extra Help
También necesitas . . . : Remind students that *ganar* also means "to win."

Learning Spanish Through Action
STAGING VOCABULARY: *Señalen*
MATERIALS: large calendar with various activities from the vocabulary list and *También necesitas . . .* pictured under various dates
DIRECTIONS: Make several true / false statements about routines and activities,

using days of the week: *El jueves toco en la banda. El coro practica sólo los lunes. Los viernes los estudiantes trabajan en el anuario.* Students will signal thumbs up for true statements and thumbs down for false ones.

La banda
Los instrumentos musicales

la flauta

la trompeta

el clarinete

el violín,
pl. los violines

el contrabajo

el saxofón, *pl.* los saxofones

el tambor

el piano

la canción, *pl.* las canciones

Ojos negros

cantar

También necesitas . . .

ganar	here: *to earn* (money)	
cuidar niños	*to baby-sit*	
repartir	here: *to deliver*	
el equipo	*team*	
el miembro	*member*	

¿Y qué quiere decir . . . ?

el club, *pl.* los clubes	literario, -a
el consejo estudiantil	participar (en)
la orquesta	ser miembro de
el tutor, la tutora	trabajar como voluntario(a)

Vocabulario para conversar   67

Class Starter Review
On the day following initial vocabulary presentation, you might begin the class with this activity: Ask students to list five extracurricular activities offered at your school. Keep a list of their responses on the chalkboard for reporting purposes.

Cooperative Learning
Divide students into groups of four. Ask them to rank the extracurricular activities on p. 66 from most to least popular. Have them add other activities if they know them in Spanish. Call on each group to report results, and tally them on the chalkboard.

Practice & Apply

Re-enter / Recycle
Ex. 9: school subjects from Chap. 1

Answers: Empecemos a conversar

8 ESTUDIANTE A
a. ¿Qué haces de pasatiempo?
b ...como voluntario(a)?
c. ...después de las clases?

ESTUDIANTE B
a.–c. Answers will vary, but may include any of the following: *Practico artes marciales. Toco los tambores. Participo en el anuario. Trabajo en el hospital. Canto en el coro.*

9 ESTUDIANTE A
a. ¿Qué clases son las más populares de la escuela?
b. ...deportes son los más populares ...?
c ...profesores son los más populares ...?
d. ...pasatiempos son los más populares ...?
e. ...clubes son los más populares ...?
f. Questions will vary, but should include the construction *de la escuela.*

ESTUDIANTE B
a.–f. Answers will vary.

Empecemos a conversar

8 después de las clases

A —¿Qué haces <u>después de las clases</u>?
B —<u>Practico artes marciales todos los miércoles</u>.

Estudiante A

a. de pasatiempo
b. como voluntario(a)
c. después de las clases

Estudiante B

practicar

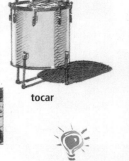
tocar

participar en

trabajar en

cantar en

9 actividades extracurriculares

A —¿Qué <u>actividades extracurriculares</u> son <u>las más populares de la escuela</u>?
B —Creo que <u>son la revista literaria y la banda</u>.

Estudiante A

a. clases
b. deportes
c. profesores
d. pasatiempos
e. clubes
f.

Estudiante B

EL CLUB DE ESPAÑOL

Options

Strategies for Reaching All Students

Spanish-Speaking Students
Ex. 15: After this exercise, have students respond to the following in writing: *¿Cuáles son los beneficios de participar en actividades extracurriculares? ¿En actividades para voluntarios? ¿Participan todos Uds. en estas actividades? ¿Por qué?*

Students Needing Extra Help
Ex. 8: Remind students that *haces* is rarely answered with *hago*. Tell them to look for a logical answer, not just to go straight across.
Ex. 9: Ask students what will happen to *las* when you do a sentence with a masculine subject.

Ex. 10: Brainstorm possible work places for response *b*.
Ex. 11: Brainstorm possible responses to *¿por qué?*
Ex. 13: Emphasize the cultural concept of singing. Stress that it is acceptable to sing.
Ex. 14: Students will need help with the structures needed to express these ideas.

10 cuidar niños

A —*¿Cuidas niños para ganar dinero?*
B —*No. Trabajo en un supermercado.*
      o: *No. No hago nada para ganar dinero.*

Estudiante A   **Estudiante B**

a. ayudar en casa

b. trabajar en ____

c. repartir periódicos

d. trabajar de tutor(a)

e. tocar un instrumento

f. cortar céspedes

Empecemos a escribir y a leer

Escribe tus respuestas en español.

11 ¿Qué actividades extracurriculares te gustan más? ¿En cuál(es) no participas? ¿Por qué? ¿Haces algo para ganar dinero? ¿Qué?

12 En tu comunidad, ¿dónde puede uno trabajar como voluntario?

13 ¿Hay banda u orquesta en tu escuela? ¿Tocas algún instrumento musical o te gustaría tocar alguno? ¿Cuál? ¿Te gusta cantar? ¿Qué canciones sabes cantar o tocar?

14 ¿Qué día de la semana estás más ocupado(a)? ¿Por qué? ¿Estás de buen o de mal humor cuando estás ocupado(a)? ¿Por qué?

15 Lee las frases siguientes con un(a) compañero(a). ¿Con cuáles están de acuerdo? ¿Con cuáles no?

- A los estudiantes de hoy no les gusta trabajar.
- Las actividades extracurriculares ayudan a formar líderes *(leaders)*.
- El consejo estudiantil es la actividad más importante de la escuela.
- Los estudiantes de hoy deben jugar menos y estudiar más.
- Una persona ocupada es una persona contenta.
- Los deportes son buenos para la salud.

Si no están de acuerdo con estas frases, cámbienlas *(change them)* y escriban otras.

También se dice

la memoria

Vocabulario para conversar   69

10 **ESTUDIANTE A**
a. ¿Ayudas en casa para ganar dinero?
b. ¿Trabajas en ___ ...
c. ¿Repartes periódicos ...
d. ¿Trabajas de tutor(a) ...
e. ¿Tocas un instrumento ...
f. ¿Cortas el césped ...
ESTUDIANTE B
a.–f. Answers will vary

Answers: Empecemos a escribir y a leer
11–15 Answers will vary.

 Practice Wkbk. 2-3, 2-4

 Audio Activity 2.2

 Writing Activities 2-A, 2-B, 2-C

 Pruebas 2-3, 2-4

 Comm. Act. BLM 2-2

Enrichment
Ex. 9: Have students redo this exercise with *Estudiante A* asking *Estudiante B* which activities or classes are least popular.
Ex. 10: You may want to keep a class tally of how many students do various things to earn money.
Exs. 12–14: Additional questions: *¿En qué actividades extracurriculares te gustaría participar? ¿Por qué? ¿Hay estas actividades extracurriculares en tu escuela? ¿Por qué sí o no?*

Practice

Answers:
¡Comuniquemos!

1 Answers will vary, but look for *puede* + inf. and logical time expressions.

2 Answers will vary.

¡Comuniquemos!

Aquí tienes otra oportunidad para usar el vocabulario de este capítulo.

1 El día escolar empieza a las 8 de la mañana y Luz suele llegar tarde todos los días. Con un(a) compañero(a), digan qué puede hacer Luz para llegar a tiempo a la escuela. Usen las palabras y expresiones de las dos columnas para formar frases.

acostarse	por la noche
despertarse	a las (6:45)
levantarse	en (5) minutos
ducharse	antes de ...
lavarse el pelo	temprano
secarse el pelo	en seguida
cepillarse los dientes	después de ...
peinarse	a la misma hora
vestirse	puntualmente
desayunar	
salir de su casa	
llegar a la escuela	

Luz puede despertarse a las seis y cuarenta
y cinco y levantarse en seguida.
Puede ducharse por la noche ...
Puede ...

2 Con un(a) compañero(a), hablen de sus tareas escolares y de sus actividades extracurriculares.

A —¿Cuándo haces tus tareas?
B —Creo que es mejor ...
A —¿Por qué?
B —Porque ...
A —Y después de las clases, ¿qué haces?

Options

Strategies for Reaching All Students

Spanish-Speaking Students
Ex. 3: As an alternative to this exercise, give this assignment: *Haz una descripción corta de cada actividad ilustrada aquí. Luego, di qué características debe tener una persona para participar en cada una.*

 Un paso más Ex. 2-F

Students Needing Extra Help
Ex. 1: Finish the model, giving students more of a framework. Assign a minimum number of sentences to be produced.
Ex. 2: If students respond that they don't do homework, have them respond when they *should* do homework. Complete this model. Help students organize their thoughts and develop correct responses to *¿por qué?*
Ex. 3: If available, use the vocabulary section from the Book 1, Chap. 1 Organizer.

Because some students may not participate in these activities, they may not see the connections between some of these traits and the corresponding activity. Explain the connections.
¿Qué sabes ahora?: Have students write out this section so they can check off what they have mastered.

3 Recomiéndales a las siguientes personas alguna actividad extracurricular según sus características. Puedes usar las ideas del dibujo u otras.

> **A** —*Soy serio y me gusta escribir. ¿Qué actividad crees que me gustaría?*
> serio(a) / escribir
> **B** —*La revista literaria.*

a. ordenado(a) / dibujar

b. deportista / hacer ejercicio

c. atrevido(a) / sacar fotos

d. paciente / tocar la flauta

e. trabajador(a) / leer

f.

¿Qué sabes ahora?

Can you:

■ describe typical morning routines?
—Antes de ir a la escuela, es necesario ___, ___ y ___.

■ talk about which extracurricular activities you prefer?
—A mí me gusta(n) ___ y ___.

■ tell what you do after school?
—Después de las clases, hago la tarea, ___ y ___.

---

3 **ESTUDIANTE A**

a. Soy ordenado(a) y me gusta dibujar. ¿Qué actividad crees tú que me gustaría?

b. . . . deportista . . . hacer ejercicio . . .

c. . . . atrevido(a) . . . sacar fotos . . .

d. . . . paciente . . . tocar la flauta . . .

e. . . . trabajador(a) . . . leer . . .

f. Answers will vary.

ESTUDIANTE B

Answers will vary, but may include:

a. El anuario.

b. El equipo de fútbol.

c. El periódico (de la escuela).

d. La banda. / La orquesta.

e. El periódico (de la escuela).

f. Answers will vary, but look for logical answers.

Answers: ¿Qué sabes ahora?

• Answers will vary, but should include a variety of reflexive verbs.

• Answers will vary, but should include chapter vocabulary.

• Answers will vary, but look for logical verbs in the first person singular.

 Audio Activity 2.3

Cultural Notes

Enrichment
Ex. 3: Have students choose three friends and write two sentences about each, describing his or her personality and the activities he or she enjoys most.

(p. 70, realia)
This advertisement for a teeth-whitening system offers the potential user a dazzling smile. The ad's headlines, *Si tus dientes no están blancos es porque no quieres,* uses the *tú* form of address to imply intimacy with the reader, while promising a "natural" method of whitening teeth.

Present & Apply

Cultural Objective
• To compare students' extra-curricular activities in Guatemala and in the U.S.

Multicultural Perspectives

What young people do after school in Guatemala depends on whether they live in a small *aldea* in the highlands or if they live in Guatemala City. In rural towns, young boys may help their fathers in the *milpa,* planting, tending, and harvesting corn for their families' use. Rural girls might work at home weaving *huipiles* (dresses), *servilletas* (cloths used to wrap tortillas and bread), and other items that their families will then sell. On religious holidays and other special days, everyone in town helps prepare for a *fiesta.* Men's associations called *cofradías* organize and conduct many of the ceremonies during a *fiesta.* Have students familiar with other cultures share information about how holidays are celebrated.

Answers

Answers to inductive questions will vary, but students may say a student council provides students a voice in decision-making and gives students a sense of power and self-esteem.

Perspectiva cultural

¿Hay muchos estudiantes que quieren estar en el consejo estudiantil de tu escuela? ¿Por qué? ¿Cómo puede un consejo estudiantil mejorar una escuela?

"Vamos a mejorar la escuela," dice Maya. "Por ejemplo," dice Javier, "el próximo año queremos tener un club de inglés." Éstas son las palabras de dos candidatos al consejo estudiantil del Colegio Interamericano, una escuela privada en la Ciudad de Guatemala. Es una escuela bilingüe donde todos los estudiantes toman unas clases en inglés y otras en español. Por eso, la idea de un club de inglés es muy popular.

Hay dos grupos rivales que esperan ganar el consejo estudiantil. El grupo de Maya y Javier es el más organizado. Su equipo tiene cuatro estudiantes: Maya es candidata a presidenta, Javier a vicepresidente, Luis Enrique a secretario y Margarita a tesorera.

En el Colegio Interamericano hay muchas actividades extracurriculares. La mayoría de los estudiantes participan en algún deporte. Muchos trabajan en el periódico escolar o en la nueva revista literaria. También hay un club de teatro. A veces los grupos hacen fiestas o venden dulces, pasteles o frutas para ganar dinero para algún proyecto.

"El próximo año voy a estar muy ocupada," dice Maya, "y no voy a poder participar en el club de teatro. Para mí el club es muy importante, pero ser presidenta del consejo estudiantil es todavía más importante."

72 Capítulo 2

En una biblioteca escolar, tres jóvenes mexicanos hablan de lo que debe hacer el consejo estudiantil.

La cultura desde tu perspectiva

1 ¿Qué actividades extracurriculares tiene tu escuela? ¿Hay actividades en el colegio de Maya que no hay en tu escuela? ¿Y viceversa? ¿Cuáles?

2 ¿Hay un programa bilingüe en tu escuela? ¿Quiénes participan en ese programa? ¿Cómo es el programa bilingüe en el Colegio Interamericano? ¿Qué piensas de él?

Options

Strategies for Reaching All Students

Spanish-Speaking Students
After reading the *Pespectiva cultural,* have Spanish-speaking students make campaign posters based on the following questions: *Si fueras candidato(a) a presidente(a) del consejo estudiantil de tu escuela, ¿qué prometerías? ¿Por qué?* Display the posters around the classroom and encourage the other students to read them.

 Un paso más Ex. 2-G

Students Needing Extra Help
Explain what a student council tries to accomplish and how. Students will need some additional vocabulary.
Ex. 1: Some students may not participate in extracurricular activities. In order to get a response, ask if they work after school, or baby-sit a younger brother or sister. If not, elicit negative responses. Help them with the vocabulary.

Ex. 2: Some students may not be aware of the bilingual program. This would be a good opportunity to have bilingual students or the director come in and talk about the program. If your school doesn't have a bilingual (or ESL) program, brainstorm with students what they would need to do to start one.

Después de las clases, un joven gana dinero trabajando en una librería en Mérida, México.

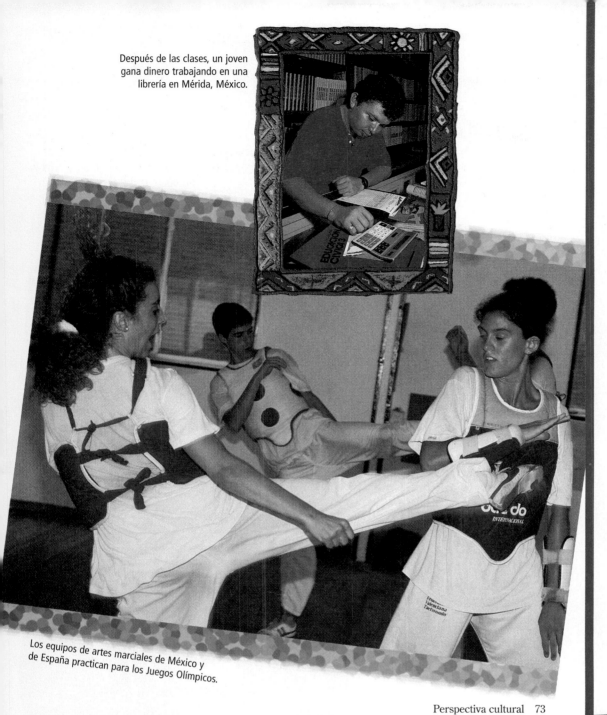

Los equipos de artes marciales de México y de España practican para los Juegos Olímpicos.

Cultural Notes

(p. 72, photo)
These students are meeting to discuss student council matters. Education is free of cost and compulsory for students between the ages of 6 and 14 in Mexico. While the quality of public education in rural Mexico has improved in recent years, urban areas continue to offer greater educational opportunities, especially for study above the *primaria* level. About 80 percent of university students study in Mexico City.

(p. 73, top photo)
It is more common than it once was for high-school students in Latin America to work part-time after school. Among other school expenses, Mexican students must purchase all of their own textbooks which are not provided by the schools. Specialized *librerías* in Latin America sell primarily school texts and supplies.

Preview

🖨 **Transparency 15**

Answers

A Other forms of *despertarse: se despiertan, nos despertamos; cepillarse: se cepillan, nos cepillamos; bañarse: se bañan, nos bañamos.* The words that precede the forms of these verbs are pronouns, *se* and *nos.* The *nosotros* form of *levantarse: nos levantamos;* the *Uds. / ellos / ellas* form: *se levantan.*

B *Despertarse* is an *e → ie* stem-changing verb. *Dormir* is an *o → ue* verb. The stem doesn't change in the *nosotros* form.

Gramática en contexto

Entrevista con un astronauta

REPORTERO Hoy está con nosotros un astronauta, el señor Montero. Señor Montero, ¿es muy difícil trabajar en el espacio?

ASTRONAUTA No tanto. Uno se acostumbra rápido.

REPORTERO ¿Duermen en camas?
ASTRONAUTA Bueno, dormimos en sacos de dormir atados a la pared.

REPORTERO ¿Cómo se despiertan?
ASTRONAUTA Nos despertamos con música.

REPORTERO ¿Y cómo se cepillan los dientes?
ASTRONAUTA Nos cepillamos los dientes con pasta dentífrica, como todo el mundo.

REPORTERO ¿Y cómo se bañan?
ASTRONAUTA Nos bañamos con una esponja y un poco de agua.

REPORTERO ¿Dónde se lavan las manos?
ASTRONAUTA En una fuente de agua que está debajo de una cúpula de plástico.

REPORTERO Bueno. Gracias por su visita, Sr. Montero. Y gracias a ustedes por ver este programa. Hasta la próxima semana.

A Can you find in the interview two other forms of each of these verbs: *despertarse, cepillarse,* and *bañarse?* What words precede those forms? What would be the *nosotros* form of *levantarse?* And the *Uds. / ellos / ellas* form?

B You know that *querer* is an *e → ie* stem-changing verb and *poder* is an *o → ue* stem-changing verb. Which verb in the interview is an *e → ie* verb? Which one is an *o → ue* verb? In which form do you <u>not</u> see the stem change?

74   Capítulo 2

Options

Strategies for Reaching All Students

Students Needing Extra Help
Begin to fill in the grammar section of the Organizer.
A: When students find the forms, put them on the chalkboard. Have them note what is unusual.
B: Have students write out the paradigms for *querer* and *poder* (Book 1, Chap. 7). If they have difficulty, refer them to letter A. Have them start with those three verbs to look for a stem change.

Los verbos reflexivos: 1) Write *levantarse,* drawing a line through the *-se.* 2) Now write out the subject pronoun chart underneath the infinitive. 3) Draw a blank space after each subject pronoun. 4) After each blank space, place the correct conjugated form of *levantar,* pointing out that it is a regular *-ar* verb. 5) Fill in the reflexive pronouns in the blanks next to the corresponding subject pronoun. Point out that students have seen a similar construction in Book 1, Chaps. 7

and 11 (Chap. 12 with infinitives), and in Book 2, Chap. 1.
Provide more examples of placing the reflexive in both positions. Emphasize the use of the definite article. This may be confusing for students because the translation from English suggests using *mi, tu,* etc., instead of *el, la,* etc. Show them that the possession is in the reflexive pronoun because you are doing the action to yourself.

74

Saturno

Present

Class Starter Review
On the day following presentation of reflexive verbs, you might begin class with this activity:
Have students list three morning activities *(levantarse, ducharse, cepillarse los dientes)*. They then ask three classmates at what time they do each activity (nine questions total). Record the responses.

Los verbos reflexivos

Reflexive verbs are generally used to tell that a person does something to or for him- or herself. A reflexive verb has two parts: a reflexive pronoun *(me, te, se, nos, os)* and a verb form. Here are all the present-tense forms of *levantarse:*

(yo)	**me** levanto	(nosotros) (nosotras)	**nos** levantamos
(tú)	**te** levantas	(vosotros) (vosotras)	**os** levantáis
Ud. (él) (ella)	**se** levanta	Uds. (ellos) (ellas)	**se** levantan

- Except for *se*, the reflexive pronouns are the same as the indirect object pronouns. They usually come before the verb, but they may also be attached to an infinitive.

  Me voy a lavar el pelo.
  Voy a lavar**me** el pelo.

- When using reflexive verbs to talk about parts of the body, we usually use the definite article.

  Nos lavamos **el** pelo.   *We're washing our hair.*
  ¿Te cepillas **los** dientes?   *Are you brushing your teeth?*

¡NO OLVIDES!
Do you remember the expression *debes quedarte en la cama?* It uses the reflexive verb *quedarse,* "to remain, to stay."

¡NO OLVIDES!
You know the indirect object pronouns.

me	*(to / for) me*
te	*(to / for) you*
le	*(to / for) him, her, it, you (formal)*
nos	*(to / for) us*
os	*(to / for) you (pl.)*
les	*(to / for) them, you (pl.)*

Gramática en contexto   75

Cooperative Learning
Divide the class into groups of three or four. Have them make charts with the following headings: *bañarse (ducharse), vestirse, peinarse, cepillarse los dientes, secarse el pelo.* Under each heading, have the groups list the amount of time it takes to perform each activity. Have groups tabulate their results and report to the class.

Practice

Answers

1 Answers will vary, but look for a logical progression of actions and the correct reflexive construction. Answers may include: *Primero me levanto. Segundo me cepillo los dientes. Luego me ducho. Después me seco el pelo. Luego me peino.*

Using Realia

Ask: *¿Qué quiere decir "se limpian solas"?*

1 Dile a tu compañero(a) qué haces por la mañana.
Puedes usar *a las (6:00), primero, segundo, después, luego.*

Me despierto a las 6:00.

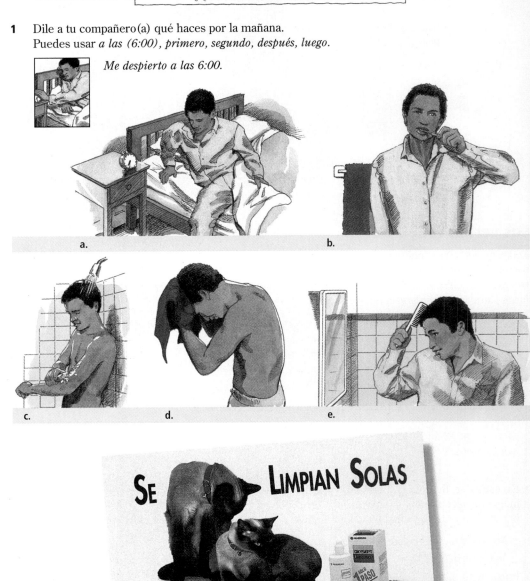

a.

b.

c.

d.

e.

Se LIMPIAN SOLAS

CON **OXYSEPT COMFORT** TUS **LENTES** DE **CONTACTO**
TAMBIÉN SE LIMPIAN SOLAS
Y EN... **1** SOLO **PASO**
ALLERGAN S.A.

DUERMA DE NOCHE. DESCANSE DE DIA.

76   Capítulo 2

Options

Strategies for Reaching All Students

Students Needing Extra Help
Ex. 2: Have students match the verbs to the pictures and then go back and conjugate the verbs according to the people (or animals) shown. As a reference for students, project the transparency of the reflexive vocabulary pictures.

Ex. 3: Remind students of compound subjects and that the verb form as well as the reflexive pronoun will change in the answer. Model a few of these sentences. If students seem uncertain, do this as a whole-class exercise on the chalkboard or with pairs of students formulating answers.

2 ¿Qué ocurre en estos dibujos? Usa los verbos de la lista para decirle a tu compañero(a) lo que pasa en cada uno.

Rosario y Mónica se secan el pelo.

acostarse	lavarse	quedarse
cepillarse	peinarse	secarse
despertarse		

Rosario y Mónica

a. ellos   b. Carlos y Ricardo   c. Pilar

d. yo   e. nosotros   f. tú

3 Túrnate con un(a) compañero(a) para hacer preguntas y respuestas.

a qué hora
levantarse / tú y
tus hermanos

A —¿A qué hora se levantan tú y tus hermanos?
B —Nos levantamos temprano.
  o: No tengo hermanos, pero yo me levanto temprano.

a. con qué lavarse las manos / María

b. con qué lavarse el pelo / Manuel y Óscar

c. cuántas veces al día cepillarse los dientes / Uds.

d. cuándo ducharse / tú

e. en cuánto tiempo secarse el pelo / Silvia

a las 7:00

con champú

con jabón

media hora

temprano

tres veces al día

Gramática en contexto   77

2 Answers
a. Ellos se lavan.
b. Carlos y Ricardo se peinan.
c. Pilar se lava el pelo.
d. Yo me despierto.
e. Nosotros nos cepillamos el pelo.
f. Tú te quedas en la cama.

3 ESTUDIANTE A
a. ¿Con qué se lava María las manos?
b. ¿Con qué se lavan Manuel y Óscar el pelo?
c. ¿Cúantas veces al día se cepillan Uds. los dientes?
d. ¿Cúando te duchas?
e. ¿En cúanto tiempo se seca Silvia el pelo?

ESTUDIANTE B
a. Se lava las manos con jabón.
b. Se lavan el pelo con champú.
c. Nos cepillamos los dientes tres veces al día.
d. Me ducho temprano (a las 7:00).
e. Se seca el pelo en media hora.

 Practice Wkbk. 2-5, 2-6

 Writing Activity 2-D

 Prueba 2-5

Cultural Notes

(p. 76, realia)
Note that this advertisement employs both informal and formal forms of address. The *S.A.* following the manufacturer's name stands for *sociedad anónima:* a publicly held corporation with stock holders. The abbreviation is the equivalent of "Inc." in the U.S.

Present & Practice

Class Starter Review

On the day following the presentation of stem-changing verbs, you might begin the class with this activity:

Have students make two columns: 1) *durante las vacaciones* and 2) *durante el año escolar.* Using *acostarse, despertarse,* and *vestirse,* have them write sentences describing at what time they do these activities during vacation and during the school year.

Answers

4 ESTUDIANTE A

a. ¿A qué hora crees que se despierta un actor (una actriz)?
b. ...se despierta una persona muy trabajadora?
c. ...se despierta una persona perezosa?
d. ...se despierta un(a) profesor(a)?
e. ...se despierta un(a) médico(a)?
f. ...nos despertamos mi familia y yo los fines de semana?

ESTUDIANTE B

a.–f. Answers will vary, but look for logical times and proper use of the reflexive construction. In *f.,* the answer will be in the *Uds.* form *(Creo que Uds. se despiertan ...).*

Repaso: Verbos con los cambios *o → ue,* *e → ie* y *e → i*

You know three kinds of stem-changing verbs:

o → ue   *(poder)*   e → ie   *(pensar)*   e → i   *(pedir)*

Here are all the present-tense forms of *acostarse (o → ue), despertarse (e → ie),* and *vestirse (e → i).*

(yo)	me ac**ue**sto	(nosotros) (nosotras)	nos acostamos
(tú)	te ac**ue**stas	(vosotros) (vosotras)	os acostáis
Ud. (él) (ella)	se ac**ue**sta	Uds. (ellos) (ellas)	se ac**ue**stan

(yo)	me desp**ie**rto	(nosotros) (nosotras)	nos despertamos
(tú)	te desp**ie**rtas	(vosotros) (vosotras)	os despertáis
Ud. (él) (ella)	se desp**ie**rta	Uds. (ellos) (ellas)	se desp**ie**rtan

(yo)	me v**i**sto	(nosotros) (nosotras)	nos vestimos
(tú)	te v**i**stes	(vosotros) (vosotras)	os vestís
Ud. (él) (ella)	se v**i**ste	Uds. (ellos) (ellas)	se v**i**sten

78   Capítulo 2

Options

Strategies for Reaching All Students

Students Needing Extra Help

Verbos con los cambios ... : Have students review the *poder* paradigm from Book 1, Chap. 7. Then have them write out the *acostar* paradigm based on their review of *poder.* Follow this with a review of *pensar* (Book 1, Chap. 7). Then write out *despertar.* Finally, review *pedir* (Book 1, Chap. 12), writing out *vestir.* Let them discover similar patterns. Show them the pattern of "boot" verbs.

Exs. 4–5: Show students what stays the same and what changes.

Brainstorm the times for each kind of personality or job.

Remind students to be careful with *f.* because of the verb change to *nosotros / Uds.* Have students answer, using the second choice, so they can practice attaching the pronoun to the infinitive.

Ex. 6: Brainstorm what activities would need particular clothing. Then conjugate the verb. Add pictures of clothing if it helps students to focus.

78

Después de jugar jai alai, hay que descansar.

4 ¿A qué hora crees que se despiertan estas personas? Trabaja con un(a) compañero(a).

un(a)
camarero(a)

A —*¿A qué hora crees que se despierta un(a) camarero(a)?*
B —*Creo que se despierta a las cinco de la mañana.*
   o: *Depende. Puede despertarse a las seis o las siete de la mañana.*

a. un actor, una actriz
b. una persona muy trabajadora
c. una persona perezosa

d. un(a) profesor(a)
e. un(a) médico(a)
f. mi familia y yo los fines de semana

5 Ahora, trabaja con un(a) compañero(a) para decir a qué hora se acuestan las personas del Ejercicio 4.

un(a)
camarero(a)

A —*¿A qué hora crees que se acuesta un(a) camarero(a)?*
B —*Creo que se acuesta a las diez y media de la noche.*
   o: *Depende. Puede acostarse a medianoche.*

6 Túrnate con un(a) compañero(a). Digan para qué se visten estas personas. Usen expresiones de las dos columnas.

a. yo   para practicar ___
b. mis compañeros y yo   para cantar en ___
c. (nombre)   para ir a ___
d. los miembros del (de la) ___   para jugar ___
e. tu profesor(a) de español   para 💡

Gramática en contexto   79

5 ESTUDIANTE A
a. ¿A qué hora crees que se acuesta un actor (una actriz)?
b. ... se acuesta una persona muy trabajadora?
c. ... se acuesta una persona perezosa?
d. ... se acuesta un(a) profesor(a)?
e. ... se acuesta un(a) médico(a)?
f. ... nos acostamos mi familia y yo los fines de semana?
ESTUDIANTE B
a.–f. Answers will vary, but look for the proper use of the reflexive or *puede* + reflexive *inf.*

6 Answers will vary, but should begin in the following manner:
a. Yo me visto para ...
b. Mis compañeros y yo nos vestimos para ...
c. (Nombre) se viste para ...
d. Los miembros del coro se visten para ...
e. Mi profesor(a) de español se viste para ...

 Practice Wkbk. 2-7, 2-8

 Writing Activity 2-E

 Prueba 2-6

Cultural Notes ☼

(p. 79, photo)
The game of jai alai was first played by the Spanish Basques who named this sport *pelota vasca.* Around 1900 the game was introduced to Cuba and from there has become popular in Spain, France, Italy, Mexico, the Philippines, and Indonesia, and in parts of the U.S. There is an international jai alai federation that holds championship games every four years.

Present & Practice

Class Starter Review

On the day following presentation of *antes de / después de,* you might begin the class with this activity:

Have students form groups of three and then take turns playing three roles: *Estudiante A* gives a reflexive verb, *Estudiante B* says what he or she does before the verb mentioned *(Antes de lavarme el pelo, yo me levanto),* and *Estudiante C* says what he or she does afterward.

Answers

7 ESTUDIANTE A
a. ¿Qué haces antes de pasar la aspiradora?
b. . . . nadar en la piscina?
c. . . . ir al centro comercial?
d. . . . salir para la escuela?
e. . . . acostarte?
f. Questions will vary, but look for the construction *antes de* + inf.

ESTUDIANTE B
Answers will vary, but may include the following:
a. Sacudo los muebles.
b. Me ducho (me baño).
c. Saco dinero.
d. Me visto. / Me cepillo los dientes.
e. Me cepillo los dientes.
f. Answers will vary, but may include a reflexive verb in the first person singular.

Antes de /después de + infinitivo

When *antes de* or *después de* is followed by a verb, the verb is in the infinitive form.

Me gusta leer **antes de acostarme.**
Después de preparar la mochila, salgo de la casa.

7 Pregúntale a un(a) compañero(a) qué hace antes de hacer estas actividades.

ir al dentista
A —¿*Qué haces antes de ir al dentista?*
B —*Me cepillo los dientes.*

Estudiante A

a. pasar la aspiradora
b. nadar en la piscina
c. ir al centro comercial
d. salir para la escuela
e. acostarse
f.

Estudiante B

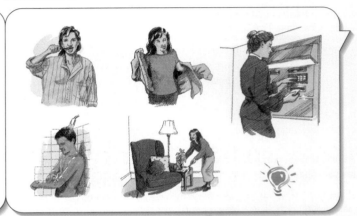

A esta joven española le encanta cuidar niños.

80   Capítulo 2

Options

Strategies for Reaching All Students

Students Needing Extra Help
Ex. 7: Remind students that *hace* is usually answered with another verb.
Use the vocabulary sections from the Book 1 Organizers, if available.
Ex. 8: Give additional models, showing students the combination of regular and reflexive verbs in a dialogue.
Ex. 9: Remind students that the verb form won't change if the answer involves com-

pound subjects. However, if only one student answers a question, the verb form will change. Everyone should keep a list in order to answer the questions in Ex. 10.
Ex. 10: Remind students to answer in the *nosotros* form.
Ahora lo sabes: Have students write out this list so they can record what they have mastered.

8 Ahora pregúntale a tu compañero(a) qué hace después de hacer estas actividades.

levantarse   A —¿Qué haces después de levantarte?
                B —Hago la cama.

Estudiante A

a. ducharse   d. lavarse el pelo

b. practicar artes marciales   e. desayunar

c. poner la mesa

f.

Estudiante B

hacer la cama   ducharse

comer algo   vestirse

secarse el pelo

9 Trabajen en grupo. Un miembro del grupo va a hacer estas preguntas. Escriban el nombre de los estudiantes que contestan cada pregunta.

a. ¿Quiénes se levantan antes de las 6:30?
b. ¿Quiénes se acuestan después de las 10:30 los días de semana?
c. ¿Quiénes hacen la tarea antes de la cena?
d. ¿Y quiénes la hacen después de la cena?
e. ¿Quiénes se visten antes de desayunar el sábado?
f. ¿Quiénes se cepillan los dientes después del desayuno?

10 Luego, compara las respuestas del Ejercicio 9 y dile a un(a) compañero(a) el nombre de un(a) estudiante que dio la misma respuesta que tú.

Pablo y yo nos levantamos antes de las 6:30.

Ahora lo sabes

Can you:

■ talk about your daily routine?

—Todas las mañanas ___ levanto temprano, me ___ y me ___ para ir a la escuela.

■ talk about people's habits?

—Mi hermanito nunca ___ los dientes ni ___ la cara.

■ talk about a sequence of events?

—Es necesario cepillarse los dientes ___ de comer.

Gramática en contexto   81

Cultural Notes ☀

(p. 80, photo)
This Spanish girl is helping care for her younger brother. While child care has traditionally been considered to be a woman's responsibility, gender roles in Spanish society are gradually changing. Today many men also perform such domestic tasks as child care, cleaning, and cooking.

Apply

Answers: Actividades

1 Answers will vary, but look for correct use of reflexive verbs.

2–3 Answers will vary.

 ¿Recuerdas?

Play

 Video Activity A

Using the Video

Episode 2 begins as Jamie arrives at the Navarro family's house in Querétaro. The Navarros had previously agreed to Jamie's sharing a bedroom with their son Carlos because they thought she was a boy named *Jaime*. On discovering the truth, the Navarros send Jamie to stay with the family of Carlos' former girlfriend, María Linares. Meanwhile, in the Querétaro Central library, the mysterious figure who appeared on the train in Episode 1, Santana, is meeting privately with the library's director, Demetrio. Santana has been spying on Jamie, secretly following her everywhere. Demetrio tells Santana to continue keeping an eye on Jamie.

Para decir más

Aquí tienes vocabulario adicional que te puede servir para hacer las actividades de esta sección.

actuar
to act, to perform

aburrirse
to be bored, to get bored

divertirse *(e → ie)*
to have fun, to have a good time

casarse
to get married

divorciarse
to get divorced

prepararse
to get ready

tardar
to take time

trasnochar
to stay up late

la rutina
routine

82   Capítulo 2

Actividades

Esta sección te ofrece la oportunidad de aumentar tus conocimientos de español al integrar lo que aprendiste en este capítulo con lo que aprendiste en capítulos anteriores.

 Escribe las respuestas a estas preguntas:

- ¿A qué hora te levantas para ir a la escuela?
- ¿A qué hora sales de casa?
- ¿A qué hora regresas a casa después de la escuela?
- ¿A qué hora te acuestas por la noche?

Luego, en grupo, compara tus respuestas con las de los otros estudiantes para hacer una tabla con la siguiente información:

- ¿Quién se levanta más temprano? ¿Y más tarde?
- ¿Quién sale de la casa más temprano? ¿Y más tarde?
- ¿Quién regresa a la casa más temprano? ¿Y más tarde?
- ¿Quién se acuesta más temprano? ¿Y más tarde?

Compartan *(share)* los resultados con los otros grupos. Después, pueden hacer una tabla con los resultados de toda la clase.

La sección de tambores de una banda en Cartagena, Colombia

Options

Strategies for Reaching All Students

Spanish-Speaking Students
Ex. 3: After this activity, have Spanish-speaking students answer in writing: *¿Qué personas famosas te interesan más? ¿Por qué? ¿Por qué crees que nos interesan tanto las vidas de personas famosas?*

 Un paso más Ex. 2-H

Students Needing Extra Help
If pressed for time, divide the class into groups. Assign an activity to each group.
Ex. 1: Have a chart ready for students to record their own responses. Then have one student ask others for their responses while another student records. Now the second group of questions can be answered with the help of all students while they look at the chart.

Ex. 2: This could be a whole-class activity. Use the vocabulary section of the Organizer. Offer a model for the list of activities.
Ex. 3: If available, use the vocabulary sections of the Book 1 Organizers for help with words relating to families, activities, pastimes, etc.
Brainstorm how to form the questions the interviewer will ask.

2 En grupo, hagan una lista de las actividades extracurriculares que ofrece la escuela.

- Hablen de las actividades más populares.
- Digan por qué son tan populares.
- Digan qué es necesario hacer para participar en estas actividades.
- Díganles a otros estudiantes por qué deben participar.

3 En grupos pequeños, inventen una entrevista con una persona famosa. Pregúntenle sobre:

- cuándo se levanta y se acuesta
- sus actividades por la mañana
- su familia
- sus pasatiempos
- sus planes para el futuro

Escojan (choose) a dos personas del grupo para practicar la entrevista. Grábenla (record it) si es posible. Luego, preséntenla a la clase.

El básquetbol es muy popular en los países hispanos.

En Cali, Colombia, dos muchachos practican el tiro al arco.

In the final scene, don Silvestre Aguilar, a powerful local politician, makes a secret visit to María's house, where Jamie is now staying.

 La Catrina: Capítulo 2

Play

 Video Activity B

 Para entender mejor

Play

 Video Activity C

 Writing Activities 2-G, 2-H

 Comm. Act. BLMs 2-4, 2-5

Cultural Notes ☀

(p. 83, top photo)
Basketball is beginning to rival soccer as a sport without national boundaries. The only sport whose origins are wholly within the U.S., basketball was invented in 1891 by James A. Naismith in Springfield, Massachusetts. In recent years, it has gained greatly in popularity throughout the world.

(p. 83, left center photo)
Cartagena, the fifth-largest city in Colombia, is located on the Caribbean coast. Founded in 1533, the city includes shipbuilding and transportation among its principal industries. The members of this band reflect Cartagena's multiethnic population.

Apply

Process Reading

For a description of process reading, see p. 52.

Multicultural Perspectives

Fútbol is not the same game played by the San Francisco 49ers or Green Bay Packers. It is, however, one of the most popular games in Latin America and the most popular worldwide. Soccer, as it is called in the U.S., is only beginning to become popular here. The World Cup *(la Copa Mundial),* soccer's international championship tournament, was held for the first time in the U.S. in the summer of 1994. This event takes place only every four years, and millions follow their favorite team from even the most remote areas. The Hispanic American countries of Argentina, Bolivia, Colombia, and Mexico all had qualifying teams for the 1994 World Cup. (Brazil defeated Italy for the championship.) Since the tournament began in 1930, two Spanish-speaking countries have won the World Cup: Uruguay (1930, 1950) and Argentina (1978, 1986). Ask students who are familiar with other cultures to share their knowledge of popular sports in those cultures.

¡Vamos a leer!

Antes de leer

STRATEGY ➤ Using prior knowledge

Which sports are the most popular at your school? Are you on a sports team? How long do you practice each day?

Mira la lectura

STRATEGY ➤ Identifying the main idea

Skim this article to see if you can identify the main idea. Which of these would make the best title for the selection?

• Mi deporte favorito
• Me encanta nadar
• Menos práctica, por favor
• ¡Abajo los deportes!

¿De Acuerdo?

¿Cómo son los deportes en las escuelas secundarias de los Estados Unidos? Creo que tomamos los deportes demasiado en serio.

Soy nadadora. Me paso todo el día en mis clases y en la piscina, y el resto durmiendo. Tengo que levantarme a las seis de la mañana y acostarme a las nueve de la noche o antes. Mi equipo practica dos horas antes de entrar a clase y dos horas y media después de salir de la escuela. Las prácticas son muy duras. En una tarde,

nadamos más de 9.000 yardas y tenemos sólo seis minutos para descansar. ¡Pero no estamos entrenando para las olimpiadas!

No comprendo por qué los deportes son tan importantes. Es posible que las escuelas quieran tener una buena reputación, pero el resultado es la tensión innecesaria y a veces los accidentes. Creo que se debe fijar un máximo de tiempo para el entrenamiento de los atletas. Si hay deportistas

que quieren practicar más, pueden hacerlo en clubes fuera de la escuela.

84   Capítulo 2

Options

Strategies for Reaching All Students

Spanish-Speaking Students

Aplicación: After this activity, have Spanish-speaking students answer in writing: *¿Crees que es mejor tener equipos para varios deportes en la escuela o sólo en clubes fuera de la escuela? ¿Por qué?*

Students Needing Extra Help

Antes de leer: Remind students to follow the four-step procedure (predict, skim, reread, summarize) recommended in Chap. 1. A cooperative learning method appropriate for this reading selection is to form teams of three students. Each team member is responsible for reading and answering the questions in one of the three *¡Vamos a leer!* sections. After each student has completed his or her individual section, the team meets together, and the three members report on

the content of their sections to the rest of the team. However, each member is responsible for reading all parts.

Mira la lectura: Be sure students understand the meaning of the four possible title selections. Bring students back to the four titles. They may lose track of the assignment as they skim through.

Infórmate: Be sure students understand the four attitudes.

Aplicación: Ask for volunteers to approach the athletes, or use the athletes in your own

Infórmate

STRATEGY> Identifying the writer's attitude

A reading selection can not only tell us what the writer *thinks* about a subject, but also what he or she *feels* about it. However, the writer's attitude is often not stated directly. We have to figure it out from clues that might include choice of words, choice of details, and what is left out.

Read the article carefully. Which of these statements best expresses the writer's attitude toward sports?

1. Le gustan los deportes, pero no todos.
2. No le gustan los deportes escolares.
3. Le gustan los deportes. Sobre todo le gusta nadar.
4. Le gustan los deportes, pero quiere darles menos énfasis.

Aplicación

Take a poll of ten members of your school's athletic teams. Ask them if the amount of practice required is too much, too little, or just enough. Then report the results to the class.

For example:

Hay (número) personas que están de acuerdo con la autora.

Hay (número) personas que creen que no practican demasiado.

Hay (número) personas que creen que practican muy poco tiempo.

¡Vamos a leer!   85

class to answer this. Also, this might spark a great discusion with members of non-athletic clubs who put in as much practice time, but are not recognized for doing so.

Apply

Process Writing
For more information regarding developing a writing portfolio, see p. 54.

¡Vamos a escribir!

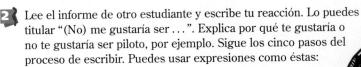

1 ¿Quieres ser jugador(a) de béisbol? ¿Conoces a algunos médicos? Piensa en el horario de una persona con una profesión interesante (policía, actor, actriz, etc.). Si puedes, entrevista a la persona. Contesta estas preguntas.

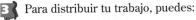

- ¿Cuándo se levanta?
- ¿Trabaja por la noche?
- ¿A qué hora sale para el trabajo?
- ¿Qué hace en el trabajo?
- ¿A qué hora regresa a casa?
- ¿Cómo se siente al final del día?

Luego escribe un informe con el título "Un día en la vida de..." Sigue los cinco pasos del proceso de escribir. (Si es necesario, mira la página 54.)

2 Lee el informe de otro estudiante y escribe tu reacción. Lo puedes titular "(No) me gustaría ser...". Explica por qué te gustaría o no te gustaría ser piloto, por ejemplo. Sigue los cinco pasos del proceso de escribir. Puedes usar expresiones como éstas:

- porque soy (muy)...
- fácil / difícil
- prefiero...

3 Para distribuir tu trabajo, puedes:

- incluirlo en un libro titulado *Un día en la vida de...*
- enviarlo a la revista literaria de la escuela
- incluirlo en un boletín para los padres
- exhibirlo en la sala de clases
- incluirlo en tu portafolio

Un soldador ecuatoriano construyendo un edificio

Options

Strategies for Reaching All Students

Students Needing Extra Help
Step 1: Give students time to think about how to respond to these questions. Model using the student's own life. Interview school personnel in your building: custodians, nurse, administrator, etc. Send students in pairs.

Assign this in advance and give enough time. Remind students that the essay will be written using the reflexive *se*.
Step 2: If students wrote an essay as suggested in Step 1, the class could respond to it here. They may need more vocabulary to write the essay.

Cultural Notes

(p. 86, photo)
This man in Quito, Ecuador, is practicing *soldadura* (welding). The frequent use of sheet metal in the construction of Latin American housing calls for the skills of trained welders at construction sites. Door and window frames in homes are often constructed of steel, and the internal support structure typically is constructed in part with iron rods.

Un policía mexicano contestando preguntas

Un astronauta explorando el espacio

Un camarógrafo filmando una película en Barcelona

Una ingeniera mexicana

¡Vamos a escribir!   87

(p. 87, top left photo)
Mexico has both national and local police forces. In Mexico City, local police often work out of small *cabinas* situated at traffic intersections. The *cabinas* are staffed 24 hours a day.

(p. 87, bottom left photo)
These filmmakers are shooting on location in Barcelona, which is one of the filmmaking centers of Spain. Barcelona vies with Madrid as the cultural capital. Barcelona is a bilingual city, with most residents speaking both Castillian and Catalan.

(p. 87, bottom right photo)
This young Mexican woman is using her engineering skills on a project. In Mexico, as in many other countries, women are participating in formerly male-dominated occupations in ever-increasing numbers. The enrollment of women in technical university courses is on the upswing. More women work outside the home, and more than ever, families have both parents working.

Assess & Summarize

You may want to assign parts of this section as homework or as an in-class writing activity prior to administering the *Examen de habilidades.*

Answers

Listening: *Yo siempre me levanto temprano. Me levanto a las cinco porque tengo que repartir el periódico antes de las seis. Casi todos los días cuido niños después de la escuela. No puedo practicar deportes ni tocar en la banda como tú. Pero estoy de buen humor. Sé que en dos o tres meses voy a poder comprarme una computadora nueva.* The student is talking about after-school activities. The student is unable to participate in sports or play in the band because he or she is earning money for a new computer through a paper route and a baby-sitting job.

Reading: The writer of the second passage probably enjoys his or her morning routine; he or she seems less rushed.

Writing: Letters will vary.

¿Lo sabes bien?

Esta sección te ayudará a prepararte para el examen de habilidades, donde tendrás que hacer tareas semejantes. Recuerda, sin embargo, que en el examen no habrá *(there won't be)* modelos.

Listening
Can you understand when people talk about the things they do before and after school? Listen as your teacher reads a sample similar to what you will hear on the test. Is this student talking about extracurricular activities or outside-of-school activities? What is this student not able to do and why?

Reading
Can you understand a writer's attitude? Which of the two writers probably enjoys his or her morning routine?

1. Todos los días el despertador me despierta a la misma hora. Tengo que levantarme inmediatamente. Me ducho, me cepillo los dientes y me visto rápido porque mi hermana tiene que usar el baño después.

2. Todos los días el despertador me despierta a la misma hora. Me baño, me cepillo los dientes y me visto. Luego preparo el desayuno. Desayuno y repaso mis lecciones antes de salir para la escuela.

Writing
Can you write a letter to a friend describing what you do during the week? Here is a sample.

> Querido Alonso,
>
> Mi semana es bastante típica. Antes de regresar a casa practico con la banda los lunes, miércoles y viernes. Los martes y jueves trabajo como tutor voluntario. Enseño flauta y clarinete en una escuela que está cerca. Me gusta despertarme tan tarde como posible porque siempre me acuesto tarde.
>
> Tu amigo,
>
> Sebastián

Culture
Can you describe what teenagers in Guatemala might do as extracurricular activities? Which of these are similar to what you and your friends do?

Speaking
Can you talk with someone about your day before or after school? Create a dialogue with your partner. Here is a sample:

A —¿A qué hora te despiertas de lunes a viernes?
B —Me despierto a las seis y media. Por suerte, los fines de semana puedo levantarme más tarde.
A —¿Qué haces por la mañana?
B —Antes de ir a la escuela me ducho y me visto. Después de desayunar salgo para la escuela.
A —¿Participas en alguna actividad extracurricular?
B —Sí, en la banda y también escribo para la revista literaria. ¿Y tú?

Options

Strategies for Reaching All Students

Students Needing Extra Help
Have students write out this section so they can keep track of what they have mastered. Remind them that this is just a sample of what the test will be like.
Listening: Ask students for which information they should be listening. What words do they think will be used?
Emphasize that they don't have to understand everything in order to be successful in this exercise.
Allow students to jot down words as they hear them. Many with poor auditory processing might hear the word but have difficulty recalling it. Read the sample more than once.
Another method is to let students write down the words they think might be contained in the paragraph and then check them off as they hear them.
Reading: If this is too subtle for some students to pick up, add words to the second paragraph that mean the opposite of *inmediatamente* and *rápido.*

Writing: Use the vocabulary section of the Organizer.
Culture: Have students review the *Perspectiva cultural.* Follow up with a discussion of important points.
Speaking: Review both sections of *Empecemos a conversar* in order to find expressions that would be useful here. Set a specific time for this assignment.

Resumen del capítulo 2

Usa el vocabulario de este capítulo para:

- describe your day before and after school
- talk about which extracurricular activities you prefer
- compare your extracurricular activities with those of another student

to indicate daily routine
acostarse *(o → ue)*
bañarse
la cara
cepillarse (los dientes / el pelo)
desayunar
el despertador
despertarse *(e → ie)*
ducharse
lavarse (la cara / el pelo)
levantarse
peinarse
secarse (el pelo)
soler *(o → ue) + inf.*
vestirse *(e → i)*

to indicate time
antes de + *inf.*
después de + *inf.*

to discuss extracurricular activities
la actividad extracurricular
el anuario
las artes marciales
el club, *pl.* los clubes
el consejo estudiantil
cuidar niños
el equipo
ganar
literario, -a
el miembro
participar (en)
el periódico (de la escuela)
repartir
la revista (literaria)
ser miembro de
trabajar como voluntario(a)
el tutor, la tutora

to discuss music
la banda
la canción, *pl.* las canciones
cantar
el coro
la orquesta
el instrumento musical
  el clarinete
  el contrabajo
  la flauta
  el piano
  el saxofón, *pl.* los saxofones
  el tambor
  la trompeta
  el violín, *pl.* los violines

other useful words and expressions
depender
de buen / mal humor
fácilmente
es necesario
hay que + *inf.*
mismo, -a
por lo menos
según
sin
uno

 Prueba cumulativa

 Examen de habilidades

 Test Generator

CAPÍTULO 3
THEME: CLOTHING

SCOPE AND SEQUENCE Pages 90–123

COMMUNICATION

Topics
Clothing

Currency

Objectives

To understand relative values of currencies

To indicate articles of clothing

To describe clothing in detail

To describe fabrics and patterns

To indicate sizes

To indicate clothing preferences and make comparisons

To discuss ways of paying for purchases

CULTURE

Currency in Spain and Latin America

GRAMMAR

Repaso: El pretérito de los verbos regulares

Adjetivos y pronombres demostrativos

Los comparativos: tanto(a) ... como

Ancillaries available for use with Chapter 3

Multisensory/Technology

 Overhead Transparencies, 16–20

 Audio Tapes and CDs

 Vocabulary Art Blackline Masters for Hands-On Learning, pp. 18–22

 Classroom Crossword

 La Catrina

 CD-ROM

Print

 Practice Workbook, pp. 23–33

 Writing, Audio & Video Activities, pp. 17–22, 99–101, 155–156

 Communicative Activity Blackline Masters
  Pair and Small Group Activities, pp. 15–20
  Situation Cards, p. 21

 Un paso más: Actividades para ampliar tu español, pp. 13–18

Assessment

 Assessment Program
  Pruebas, pp. 39–50
  Examen de habilidades, pp. 51–54

 Test Generator

Video still from Chap. 3

¿Qué ropa está de moda?

School uniforms show school affiliation and are very practical. Many Latin American and Spanish teens wear them. Away from school, however, these teens are often fashionable and enjoy wearing trendy clothing.

Many of the same clothes that are "in" in the U.S. are also popular in Spanish-speaking countries. For example, teens love T-shirts and sweatshirts. Those sporting the names of American universities or that have some writing in English are always in vogue. Athletic shoes are also considered fashionable for informal occasions, and blue jeans are as popular there as here. However, even though the casual look is acceptable, sloppiness is frowned upon. Generally, shorts, other than for children, are considered improper anywhere except the beach or a resort town.

Teens in Spanish-speaking countries often express their individuality through clothing styles. Leather boots and jackets are common in cold climates, and accessories might include scarves, thick leather belts and, for girls, more jewelry than a typical U.S. teen might wear. Colors are generally subdued. In tropical countries, embroidered, bright-colored cotton clothing is popular. Each Spanish-speaking country is different. You are likely to see more teens dressed in up-to-date fashions in countries with a heavy European influence and a large middle class, such as Argentina and Chile, than in countries whose populations are heavily Indian or part Indian such as Bolivia or Peru.

It would be amiss to speak of clothing in Latin America and fail to mention the beautiful native clothing worn by many indigenous people. For example, the colorful and intricate patterns worn by the Mayas of Guatemala are hand-woven on looms designed centuries ago. Throughout Latin America, Indian villages have their own unique style of dress, and on market days, when villagers from a specific region converge on the market town, one can identify their origins by the clothing they wear. Today, this is more true of the women than the men, but in areas where there is less contact with urban areas, the men, too, wear the clothing of their village. Traditional costumes may be worn on *días de fiesta*.

Introduce

Re-entry of Concepts

The following list represents words, expressions, and grammar topics re-entered from Book 1 and Book 2 (Chaps. 1–2):

Book 1
numbers 0–61, *gustar* expressions, school supplies, colors, clothing, vacation places, household chores, formal attire

Chapter 1
school activities
school supplies

Chapter 2
daily routine

Planning

Cross-Curricular Connections

Consumer Education Connection (pp. 98–99)
Ask students to put together a wardrobe for school with a budget of $150. Have them consider these factors: Can the item be worn with more than one thing? Is the fabric durable? Is the item multifunctional (for example, a scarf that doubles as a waist wrap)? Have students present their wardrobe choices to the class.

Career Connection (pp. 108–109)
In small groups, have students create a line of clothing on a large piece of construction paper. Have them include a designer name, a logo, and a category of clothing for the current season. Students can draw or use magazine pictures to illustrate their line, and they should write a brief description of each item or ensemble and give it a price in dollars and *pesos* (or another currency used in the Spanish-speaking world).

Math Connection (pp. 116–117)
Provide students with a chart comparing the cost of common items (for example, a ballpoint pen, a soft drink, etc.) in U.S. currency and currency from Spanish-speaking countries. Using a currency conversion chart from a newspaper, compare the actual cost of the items in U.S. currency and calculate the percentage difference.

¿Qué ropa está de moda?

School uniforms show school affiliation and are very practical. Many Latin American and Spanish teens wear them. Away from school, however, these teens are often fashionable and enjoy wearing trendy clothing.

Many of the same clothes that are "in" in the U.S. are also popular in Spanish-speaking countries. For example, teens love T-shirts and sweatshirts. Those sporting the names of American universities or that have some writing in English are always in vogue. Athletic shoes are also considered fashionable for informal occasions, and blue jeans are as popular there as here. However, even though the casual look is acceptable, sloppiness is frowned upon. Generally, shorts, other than for children, are considered improper anywhere except the beach or a resort town.

Teens in Spanish-speaking countries often express their individuality through clothing styles. Leather boots and jackets are common in cold climates, and accessories might include scarves, thick leather belts and, for girls, more jewelry than a typical U.S. teen might wear. Colors are generally subdued. In tropical countries, embroidered, bright-colored cotton clothing is popular. Each Spanish-speaking country is different. You are likely to see more teens dressed in up-to-date fashions in countries with a heavy European influence and a large middle class, such as Argentina and Chile, than in countries whose populations are heavily Indian or part Indian such as Bolivia or Peru.

It would be amiss to speak of clothing in Latin America and fail to mention the beautiful native clothing worn by many indigenous people. For example, the colorful and intricate patterns worn by the Mayas of Guatemala are hand-woven on looms designed centuries ago. Throughout Latin America, Indian villages have their own unique style of dress, and on market days, when villagers from a specific region converge on the market town, one can identify their origins by the clothing they wear. Today, this is more true of the women than the men, but in areas where there is less contact with urban areas, the men, too, wear the clothing of their village. Traditional costumes may be worn on *días de fiesta*.

Introduce

The following list represents words, expressions, and grammar topics re-entered from Book 1 and Book 2 (Chaps. 1–2):

Book 1
numbers 0–61, *gustar* expressions, school supplies, colors, clothing, vacation places, household chores, formal attire

Chapter 1
school activities
school supplies

Chapter 2
daily routine

Planning

Cross-Curricular Connections

Consumer Education Connection (pp. 98–99)
Ask students to put together a wardrobe for school with a budget of $150. Have them consider these factors: Can the item be worn with more than one thing? Is the fabric durable? Is the item multifunctional (for example, a scarf that doubles as a waist wrap)? Have students present their wardrobe choices to the class.

Career Connection (pp. 108–109)
In small groups, have students create a line of clothing on a large piece of construction paper. Have them include a designer name, a logo, and a category of clothing for the current season. Students can draw or use magazine pictures to illustrate their line, and they should write a brief description of each item or ensemble and give it a price in dollars and *pesos* (or another currency used in the Spanish-speaking world).

Math Connection (pp. 116–117)
Provide students with a chart comparing the cost of common items (for example, a ball-point pen, a soft drink, etc.) in U.S. currency and currency from Spanish-speaking countries. Using a currency conversion chart from a newspaper, compare the actual cost of the items in U.S. currency and calculate the percentage difference.

CAPÍTULO 3

¿Qué ropa está de moda?

OBJECTIVES

At the end of this chapter, you will be able to:

■ describe clothing in detail

■ indicate clothing preferences and make comparisons

■ say how you paid for purchases

■ talk about the currency in Spain and in various Latin American countries

Una tienda de ropa en Guatemala

91

Cultural Notes

Spanish in Your Community
Have students visit a large bank to obtain a credit card application in Spanish and see how much they understand. They might want to compare it to an application in English. Have them find out whether the credit cards used in the U.S. are accepted in Spanish-speaking countries and how the exchange rate is converted.

(p. 90, photo)
After arranging displays of merchandise in her store, this young woman writes out the prices and tags each item by hand. Some items are hung from a rotating wheel, which customers turn to examine the articles of clothing. Service in Latin American shops is often more personal than in the U.S. The clerk will exchange greetings with cus-

tomers and give advice and suggestions regarding purchases. In smaller shops particularly, it is often appropriate for buyer and seller to bargain *(regatear)* over the sale price.

Cultural Objective

• To discuss students' clothes-purchasing habits and preferences

Critical Thinking: Classifying Information

Ask students what factors they consider when making a clothing purchase. After writing each response on the chalkboard, poll students to find out the three most important factors.

¡Piénsalo bien!

Mira las fotos. Los estudiantes que vemos aquí están hablando de la ropa que usan.

"¿Quieres entrar en esta tienda o en ésa?"

¿Te gusta ir al centro comercial los fines de semana? ¿Qué tiendas de ropa prefieres?

De compras en el centro comercial Plaza Flamingo, Cancún, México

92   Capítulo 3

Options

Strategies for Reaching All Students

Spanish-Speaking Students

Ask: *¿Quién te compra ropa o te da dinero para comprarla? ¿Qué tipo de ropa te gusta llevar? ¿Por qué crees que a muchos jóvenes les gusta la ropa un poco exagerada? ¿Cuál es el estilo más popular ahora?*

 Un paso más Ex. 3-A

"Creo que prefiero esta camisa a rayas."

¿Gastas mucho dinero en ropa? ¿Pagas con tarjeta de crédito o siempre en efectivo?

Un joven chileno compra una camisa.

"¡Qué lástima! Uso la talla 30, pero no encuentro jeans en esa talla."

¿Qué haces cuando no encuentras tu talla? ¿Vas a otra tienda? ¿Le pides ayuda al (a la) vendedor(a)?

En El Corte Inglés, Barcelona

93

Cultural Notes

(p. 92, photo)
As international trade agreements, such as NAFTA, between the U.S., Mexico, and Canada are put into effect, more consumer products are exchanged between countries. Aproximately two thirds of Mexico's exports go to the U.S. and about 67 percent of Mexico's imports are from the U.S. Thus, shopping malls in different countries may carry many of the same products and have a similar appearance.

(p. 93, bottom photo)
El Corte Inglés is a well-known department store chain in Spain. Here a young man examines blue jeans in the Barcelona store. Jeans are the quintessential U.S. export product. Although they were first produced as heavy-duty work pants, jeans are popular casual attire throughout the world. In Spain, jeans are called *tejanos* or *vaqueros,* while in other places they may be referred to as simply *jeans.*

Present

Chapter Theme
Clothing

Communicative Objectives
- To indicate articles of clothing
- To describe fabrics and patterns

Transparencies 16–17

Vocabulary Art BLMs

Pronunciation Tape 3-1

Teaching Suggestions
Preparing students to speak: Use one or two options from each of the categories of Comprehensible Input, Physical Response, or Limited Verbal Response. For a complete explanation of these categories and some sample activities, see pp. T16–T17.

Multicultural Perspectives
Dyed fabrics from Guatemala, alpaca sweaters from Peru, woven fabrics from Nigeria—what do these items have in common? Chances are you'll see these items and others incorporated into the fashions of some of the most renowned designers. From the friendship bracelets made by Guatemalan Indians to the woven

Vocabulario para conversar

¿Qué va bien con este chaleco?

Vas a necesitar estas palabras y expresiones para hablar sobre la ropa que usas. Después de leerlas varias veces, practícalas con un(a) compañero(a).

el suéter de cuello alto

la gorra

la corbata

el pañuelo

la cartera

el traje

el cinturón, *pl.* los cinturones

el bolso

el chandal

el chaleco

el mocasín, *pl.* los mocasines

el botín, *pl.* los botines

el chaquetón, *pl.* los chaquetones

los zapatos de tacón alto

94   Capítulo 3

Options

Strategies for Reaching All Students

Spanish-Speaking Students
Ask: *¿Puedes añadir otras palabras a las que están aquí? ¿Cuál(es) de las variaciones usas o prefieres tú?*

 Un paso más Exs. 3-B, 3-C

Students Needing Extra Help
Make a clear distinction between words with similar spellings such as *chaquetón, chaleco,* and *chandal;* and *lona* and *lana.*
Remind students that *un gorro* is a ski cap and *una gorra* is a baseball cap.
También necesitas . . . : Give some examples of *¿De qué es . . . ?* and *Es de . . . .*
Write out the *probar* (verb) forms.
¿Y qué quiere decir . . . ?: Give examples and write out all the forms for *estar de moda.*

Learning Spanish Through Action
STAGING VOCABULARY: *Apunten, Levántense, Siéntense*
MATERIALS: none
DIRECTIONS: Direct students to stand if they are wearing the items you mention. Tell them to sit if the item is a certain color or is made of a certain material, such as cotton or wool. Tell them to point to a classmate who's wearing a certain item of clothing.

94

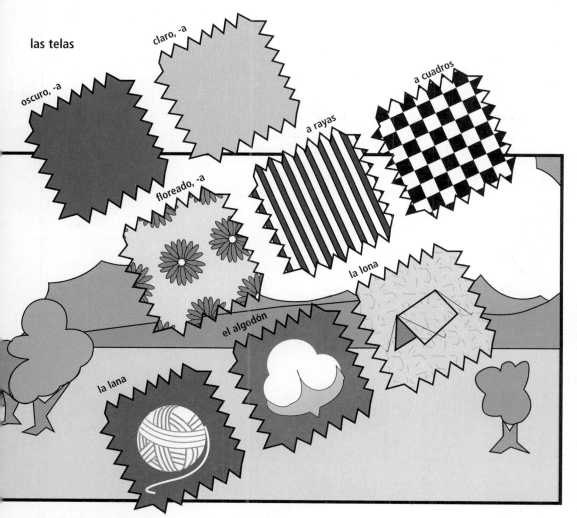

las telas

oscuro, -a

claro, -a

a cuadros

a rayas

floreado, -a

la lona

el algodón

la lana

También necesitas . . .

la moda	*fashion*	
liso, -a	*plain*	
sencillo, -a	*simple*	
probarse *(o → ue)*	*to try on*	
usar	here: *to wear*	
¿De qué es ___?	*What's (it) made of?*	
Es de ___.	*It's made of . . .*	

¿Y qué quiere decir . . . ?
estar de moda
el nilón
el plástico
elegante
sintético, -a

Vocabulario para conversar   95

hats worn by the Rastafari in Jamaica, these accessories are part of a "global" look popular with many young people. Ask students to think about what is fashionable today and to trace the origin of those fashions.

Class Starter Review

On the day following initial presentation, begin the class with either of these activities:

1) Have a volunteer write the three categories *Hombres, Mujeres,* and *Los dos* on the chalkboard. As you call out each clothing item, have the class respond with the correct category. The volunteer then writes each in the appropriate column.

2) Have students form pairs and have one face toward the class and the other away from the class. *Estudiante A,* who is facing the class, describes someone's clothing to *Estudiante B,* who draws the outfit and then turns around to guess whose clothing he or she has drawn.

Practice & Apply

Teaching Suggestions

Review clothing (Book 1, Chap. 6), before presenting new vocabulary.

Answers: Empecemos a conversar

1 **ESTUDIANTE A**

a. ¿Qué va bien con este pañuelo floreado?

b. ...este traje (de color) oscuro?

c. ...esta corbata a rayas?

d. ...esta cartera?

e. ...estos botines rosados?

f. Questions will vary.

ESTUDIANTE B

a.–f. Answers will vary, but should begin *Yo creo que* ....

2 **ESTUDIANTE A**

a. ¿De qué son estos mocasines?

b. ...es este chaquetón?

c. ...es esta cartera?

d. ...es esta gorra?

e. ...es este chandal?

f. Questions will vary.

ESTUDIANTE B

Answers will vary, but may include the following:

a. Son de plástico. Yo prefiero los de cuero.

b. Es de tela sintética. ...los de lana.

c. Es de plástico. ...los de cuero.

d. Es de lona. ...las de algodón.

e. Es de nilón. ...los de algodón.

f. Answers will vary.

Empecemos a conversar

Túrnate con un(a) compañero(a) para ser *Estudiante A* y *Estudiante B.* Reemplacen las palabras subrayadas en el modelo con palabras representadas o escritas en los recuadros. Si ven 💡 pueden dar su propia respuesta.

1 A —¿Qué va bien con <u>este chaleco a cuadros</u>?
B —Yo creo que <u>un suéter de cuello alto liso</u>, ¿no?

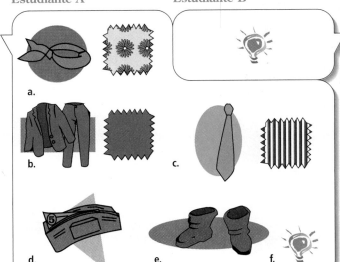

Estudiante A

Estudiante B

a.
b.
c.
d.
e.
f.

2  A —¿De qué <u>es este cinturón</u>?
B —<u>Es de plástico</u>. Yo prefiero <u>los de cuero</u>.

Estudiante A

Estudiante B

a.
b.
c.
d.
e.
f.

plástico   nilón
cuero   algodón
lona
lana
tela sintética

¡NO OLVIDES!

When comparing two similar things, we can avoid repeating the noun:

—*Prefieres la corbata roja o **la amarilla**?*

—***La roja.***

The definite article and adjective agree with the noun they refer to. Similarly with expressions that include *de*:

*No me gusta ni el bolso de Juana ni **el de María**.*

96   Capítulo 3

Options

Strategies for Reaching All Students

Spanish-Speaking Students

Ex. 6: After this exercise, ask: *Algunas personas creen que la ropa refleja la personalidad del que la lleva. ¿Crees que es verdad? ¿Por qué? ¿Qué ropa llevas tú que refleja o indica cómo eres?*

 Un paso más Ex. 3-D

Students Needing Extra Help

Empecemos a conversar: Begin to fill in the vocabulary section of the Organizer.
Give students time to describe the articles of clothing with the patterns.
¡No olvides!: Give additional examples of agreement, using masculine and feminine and singular and plural.
Ex. 2: Remind students that names of materials are always in the singular form: *los de cuero.*

Ex. 3: To practice the use of indefinite pronouns, have students repeat this exercise, using the third choice in the model: *No, pero me gustaría comprar uno.*
Ex. 5: Review colors from Book 1, Chap. 6.
Ex. 6: Be aware that this discussion may be uncomfortable for students of limited economic means. Provide additional vocabulary for students to answer *¿Por qué?*

3

A —¿Tienes _chaquetón_?

B —_Sí, tengo un chaquetón de lona._

    o: _No. No uso chaquetón._

    o: _No. Pero me gustaría comprar uno._

Estudiante A   Estudiante B

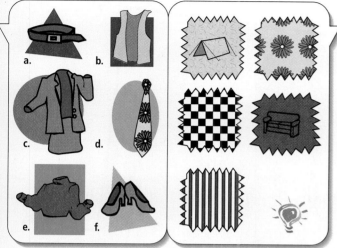

Empecemos a escribir

Escribe tus respuestas en español.

4 Generalmente, ¿qué ropa usas cuando vas a la escuela? ¿Usas la misma ropa los fines de semana?

5 ¿Qué colores de ropa sueles usar más? ¿Prefieres los colores claros o los oscuros? ¿Prefieres la ropa floreada, a cuadros o a rayas? ¿O prefieres ropa muy sencilla de sólo un color?

6 ¿Qué ropa está de moda ahora? ¿Crees que es necesario o importante estar de moda? ¿Por qué?

7 ¿Sueles probarte la ropa antes de comprarla? ¿Por qué?

¡NO OLVIDES!

You can also use _uno / una_ to avoid repeating a noun.

—_¿Tienes mochila?_

—_No, necesito **una.**_

También se dice

el cincho
la faja
el cinto

el monedero
la billetera
el portamonedas

el suéter de cuello de tortuga

el tailleur
el saco
el paltó

Vocabulario para conversar   97

---

3 **ESTUDIANTE A**

a. ¿Tienes cinturón?

b. . . . chaleco?

c. . . . traje?

d. . . . corbata?

e. . . . suéter de cuello alto?

f. . . . zapatos de tacón alto?

ESTUDIANTE B

Answers will vary, but may include the following:

a. Sí, tengo un cinturón de cuero; No. No uso cinturón; No. Pero me gustaría comprar uno.

b. . . . un chaleco a rayas . . . uno.

c. . . . un traje a cuadros . . . uno.

d. . . . una corbata floreada de algodón . . . una.

e. . . . un suéter de cuello alto de lana . . . uno.

f. unos zapatos de tacón alto de cuero . . . unos.

Answers: Empecemos a escribir

4–7 Answers will vary.

 Practice Wkbk. 3-1, 3-2

 Audio Activity 3.1

 Pruebas 3-1, 3-2

 Comm. Act. BLM 3-1

Present

Chapter Theme
Clothing sizes

Communicative Objectives
- To describe clothing in detail
- To indicate sizes
- To discuss ways of paying for purchases

 Transparencies 18–19

 Vocabulary Art BLMs

 Pronunciation Tape 3-2

Teaching Suggestions
Preparing students to speak: Use one or two options from each of the categories of Comprehensible Input, Physical Response, or Limited Verbal Response. For a complete explanation of these categories and some sample activities, see pp. T16–T17.

Vocabulario para conversar

¿Qué talla usas?

Aquí tienes el resto del vocabulario que necesitas en este capítulo para hablar sobre la ropa que usas.

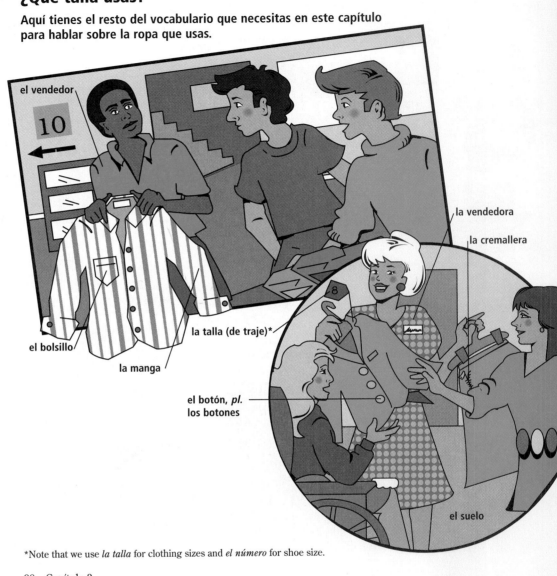

el vendedor

la vendedora

la cremallera

la talla (de traje)*

el bolsillo

la manga

el botón, pl. los botones

el suelo

*Note that we use *la talla* for clothing sizes and *el número* for shoe size.

98   Capítulo 3

Options

Strategies for Reaching All Students

Spanish-Speaking Students

 Un paso más Ex. 3-E

Students Needing Extra Help
Explain that *tamaño, pequeño, mediano,* and *grande* can refer to many things besides clothes. However, the word *talla* refers only to clothes and accessories.
También necesitas . . . : Give examples of half sizes (*Mi número de zapato es siete y medio*).
Show the connection between *guardarropa* (closet) and *guardar* (to put away).
Give examples in which *(me) da igual* would be an appropriate answer. Refer to Ex. 11.

Learning Spanish Through Action
STAGING VOCABULARY: *Cuelguen, Encuentren, Guarden, Pongan*
MATERIALS: items of clothing labeled either *sucio(a)* or *limpio(a)* scattered on the floor; hangers; boxes; laundry hamper (or a box with label: *ropa sucia*)
DIRECTIONS: Direct students to find the items you call out. If the item is clean, direct them to hang it up or put it away. If the item is dirty, direct them to put it in the laundry hamper.

el cajero

la cajera

la tarjeta de crédito

TARJETA

595812 2456 7891230

BANCO CENTRAL

el cheque

el cesto de la ropa sucia

el tamaño

M mediano

G

P pequeño

10 1/2 — el número

grande

el catálogo

Class Starter Review
On the day following initial presentation, you might begin the class with this activity:
Post pictures of shoes of varying sizes: well-known athletes sporting their basketball shoes, actresses in high heels, toddlers in their first walking shoes. Have students guess the size shoe the person is wearing: *Yo creo que Shaquille O'Neal usa número 14; creo que Cher usa número 7 y medio; el bebé usa número 1.*

También necesitas . . .

(el dinero) en efectivo	*cash*	la liquidación,	*sale*
flojo, -a	*loose (clothing)*	*pl.* las liquidaciones	
apretado, -a	*tight (clothing)*	la fiesta	*party*
(número) y medio	*(number) and a half*	(me) da igual	*it's all the same (to me)*
	(in sizes)	por todas partes	*all over, everywhere*
colgar *(o → ue)*	*to hang*	lo que	*what*
encontrar *(o → ue)*	*to find*		
escoger*	*to choose*		
guardar	*to put away, to keep*		
alguien	*someone*		

¿Y qué quiere decir . . . ?
estar en liquidación

* *Escoger* is a regular -*er* verb. However, the *g* changes to *j* in the *yo* form: *(yo) escojo.*

Vocabulario para conversar   99

Practice

Grammar Preview
Encontraste is used lexically in Ex. 9. A review of the preterite of *-ar* verbs is on p. 109.

Answers: Empecemos a conversar

8 ESTUDIANTE A
a. ¿Qué número de zapato (tenis) usas?
b. ...tamaño (talla) de chandal...
c. ...tamaño (talla) de cinturón...
d. ...tamaño (talla) de chaquetón...
e. ...tamaño (talla) de traje...
f. ...tamaño (talla) de vestido...
g. Questions will vary.

ESTUDIANTE B
a.–g. Answers will vary.

9 ESTUDIANTE A
a. ¿Encontraste el chaleco?
b. ...la cartera?
c. ...el pañuelo?
d. ...la corbata?
e. ...el suéter de cuello alto?
f. Questions will vary.

ESTUDIANTE B
Answers will vary, but look for logical fabrics or materials and adjectives that agree with them rather than with the article of clothing.
a. Sí. Esogí uno de lana blanca.
b. ...una de...
c. ...uno de...
d. ...una de...
e. ...uno de...
f. Answers will vary.

Empecemos a conversar

8
A —¿Qué talla de <u>pantalones</u> usas?
B —Uso <u>la talla treinta y cuatro.</u>

Estudiante A   Estudiante B

a.   b.

talla 30, 32, 34, ...
tamaño pequeño / mediano / grande
talla 4, 6, 8, ...
número 6, 6½, 7, ...

c.   d.   e.   f.   g.

9
A —¿Encontraste <u>los mocasines</u>?
B —Sí. Escogí <u>unos de cuero rojo.</u>

Estudiante A   Estudiante B

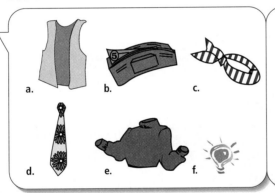

a.   b.   c.

d.   e.   f.

Zapatos hechos a mano en un mercado mexicano

100   Capítulo 3

Options

Strategies for Reaching All Students

Students Needing Extra Help
Ex. 8: Review when to use *talla* versus *número*, and *talla* versus *tamaño*.
Ex. 9: Give students time to come up with combinations of patterns and materials. Since the model uses the plural, model a question in the singular.
Ex. 10: Point out that item *e* is plural.

Enrichment
Ex. 8: Point out that this exercise uses American sizes. However, many Spanish-speaking countries use a different sizing system. In Spain, for example, a size 38 dress, blouse, or coat is equivalent to a U.S. size 6; a 40 is equal to size 8; 42 to size 10, and so on. For both men's and women's shoes, the sizes are 36, 37, 38, and so on. Use the chart on p. 101 so students can figure out what sizes they wear in Spanish-speaking countries.

10

A —¿Cómo me queda *este chandal*?
B —Te queda muy *apretado*.

¡NO OLVIDES!

Remember that the verb *quedar* is like *gustar*, and that we use it with the indirect object pronouns *me, te, nos,* and *le(s)*.

Estudiante A

Estudiante B

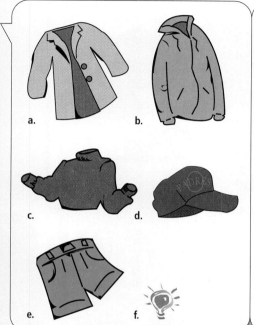

a. b.

c. d.

e. f.

10 ESTUDIANTE A

a. ¿Cómo me queda este chaquetón?
b. . . . queda esta chaqueta?
c. . . . queda este suéter de cuello alto?
d. . . . queda esta gorra?
e. . . . quedan estos pantalones cortos?
f. Questions will vary, but look for the correct use of *me queda(n)*.

ESTUDIANTE B

a. Te queda muy flojo.
b. . . . queda muy floja.
c. . . . queda apretado (pequeño).
d. . . . queda apretada (pequeña).
e. . . . quedan muy bien.
f. Answers will vary, but look for the correct use of *te queda(n)* and adjective agreement.

Cultural Notes ☀

(p. 101 photo)
Mexico has a tradition of skilled leather work both in folk arts and in manufacturing. Shoes are a major product from the states of Jalisco and Guanajuato. In Guadalajara, Jalisco, a major commercial center and Mexico's second-largest city, an entire district is devoted to shoe stores. Cow hide is not a commodity native to the Americas: cattle were first introduced to Mexico in 1519 by the Spanish explorer Cortez.

TALLAS	blusas y vestidos						
españolas	36	38	40	42	44	46	
norteamericanas	4	6	8	10	12	14	
	pantalones para hombre y mujer						
españolas	36	38	40	42	44	46	
norteamericanas	35	36	37	38	39	40	
	camisas para hombre						
españolas	36	37	38	40	41	42	43
norteamericanas	14	14½	15	15½	16	16	17
NÚMEROS	zapatos para hombre y mujer						
españoles	36	37	38	39	40	41	42
norteamericanos	5	6	7	8	9	9½	10

Practice & Apply

11 ESTUDIANTE A

a. ¿Te gusta usar ropa de algodón?

b. . . . pantalones con cremallera?

c. . . . suéteres sin bolsillos?

d. . . . zapatos de tacón alto?

e. . . . vestidos de tela sintética?

f. Questions will vary.

ESTUDIANTE B

a.–f. Answers will vary.

Answers: Empecemos a escribir y a leer

12–15 Answers will vary.

11 camisas de manga larga

A —¿Te gusta usar *camisas de manga larga*?

B —*Depende, pero prefiero las de manga corta en el verano.*

o: *Me da igual.*

o: *No, nunca uso camisas de manga larga.*

Estudiante A

a. ropa de algodón

b. pantalones con cremallera

c. suéteres sin bolsillos

d. zapatos de tacón alto

e. vestidos de tela sintética

f.

Estudiante B

Empecemos a escribir y a leer

Escribe tus respuestas en español.

12 En tu cuarto, ¿está la ropa en el suelo por todas partes? ¿Dónde pones la ropa sucia? ¿Dónde guardas la ropa limpia? ¿Qué ropa cuelgas en el guardarropa?

13 ¿Qué ropa te gusta usar cuando vas a fiestas? ¿Te ayuda alguien a escoger lo que vas a llevar?

14 ¿Sueles comprar cosas que están en liquidación? ¿Por qué? ¿Qué te gusta comprar en liquidación?

15 ¿Compras a veces por catálogo? ¿Qué compras? ¿Pagas con tarjeta de crédito? ¿O paga alguno de tus padres con cheque? Generalmente, ¿qué cosas pagas en efectivo?

102   Capítulo 3

Options

Strategies for Reaching All Students

Spanish-Speaking Students

Ex. 13: Ask: *¿Tienes ropa diferente para cada estación del año? ¿Cuál te gusta más usar: la de la primavera, del verano, etc.? ¿Por qué?*

 Un paso más Ex. 3-F

Students Needing Extra Help

Ex. 11: Discourage students from always answering with *Me da igual*. Encourage them to give reasons for the kind of clothing they prefer: *Prefiero la ropa de lana porque me gusta la ropa cómoda. Prefiero los suéteres con bolsillos para poner mi dinero*, etc.

Ex. 12: Make a distinction between *el suelo* and *yo suelo* if it presents a problem for students. Explain that they are homonyms,

like the word "rose" in the sentence "He rose to hand her a pink rose." If available, use the vocabulary section of the Book 1, Chap. 6 Organizer.

Ex. 15: Be sensitive to socioeconomic issues.

Ex. 16: Discuss the dialogue that usually occurs between a customer and a salesperson or cashier. Be sure everyone is starting with the correct sentence.

Una tienda de ropa en Puerto Rico

16 [CL = clienta;
V = vendedor(a); CA = cajero(a).]
Order of dialogue is as follows:
CL —Perdón, señor, busco un
suéter de cuello alto.
V —Tenemos unos en liquidación,
señorita . . . .
CL —Quiero dos, . . .
CA —Depende. ¿Tiene Ud. . . .
CL —No, no tengo.
CA —Entonces sólo puede
pagar . . .

**Practice Wkbk. 3-3,
3-4**

Audio Activity 3.2

**Writing Activities
3-A, 3-B, 3-C**

Pruebas 3-3, 3-4

También se dice

el cierre
el cierre relámpago
el síper

la bolsa

el canasto de la ropa sucia
el ropasuciero

16 Lee las frases de este diálogo y ponlas en un orden lógico. Después, decide quién dice cada frase. Puede ser el cajero (la cajera), el vendedor (la vendedora) o la clienta.

2 —Tenemos unos en liquidación, señorita. Son muy baratos. Mire, dos por $30.

6 —Entonces sólo puede pagar en efectivo o con tarjeta de crédito.

5 —No, no tengo.

4 —Depende. ¿Tiene Ud. alguna identificación con foto?

3 —Quiero dos, uno rojo mediano y otro azul pequeño. ¿Puedo pagar con cheque?

1 —Perdón, señor, busco un suéter de cuello alto.

Vocabulario para conversar 103

Cultural Notes ☀

(p. 102, realia)
This advertisement from El Corte Inglés, a trend-setting Spanish department store, promotes Italian clothing and personal accessories. Spain and Italy maintain strong commercial ties. Italy continues to be a leader in European fashion, and Italian styles frequently set the pace in Spain.

Practice

Answers:
¡Comuniquemos!

1 ESTUDIANTE A

a. ¿Qué ropa usas cuando vas a la playa?

b. ...a las montañas?

c. ...al teatro?

d. ...a una fiesta?

e. ...a la iglesia (al templo)?

f. Questions will vary, but should begin *¿Qué ropa usas cuando vas a...*.

ESTUDIANTE B

a.–f. Answers will vary, but should be logical.

2 Answers will vary, but should include a wide variety of chapter vocabulary.

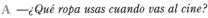

¡Comuniquemos!

Aquí tienes otra oportunidad para usar el vocabulario de este capítulo.

1 Dile a un(a) compañero(a) qué ropa usas cuando vas a estos lugares.

A —¿Qué ropa usas cuando vas al cine?
B —Generalmente uso algo sencillo: jeans, camiseta y una chaqueta.

 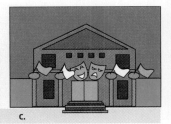

a. b. c.

d. e. f.

2 Con un(a) compañero(a) hablen de la última prenda de ropa *(article of clothing)* que compraron. Hablen de:

- qué es
- cómo es (el color, etc.)
- dónde la compraron
- cómo pagaron
- si la compraron en liquidación o no
- cuándo la usan

104   Capítulo 3

Options

Strategies for Reaching All Students

Spanish-Speaking Students
Ex. 3: Have students write out this exercise. *Lee las instrucciones. En vez de decirle a tu compañero(a) cómo organizar su guardarropa, escríbele tus recomendaciones.*

 Un paso más Ex. 3-G

Students Needing Extra Help
Ex. 1: If available, use the vocabulary sections from the Book 1, Chaps. 6, 7, and 14 Organizers.
Ex. 2: Students may need help constructing their narrative. Provide them with an opening sentence and give them time to prepare. Use the vocabulary section of the Organizer.
Ex. 3: Brainstorm other expressions of emotion. Use the vocabulary section of the

Organizer. Review commands for some words that students might want to use: *separar, lavar,* etc.
Review furniture from Book 1, Chap. 9.
¿Qué sabes ahora?: Have students write out this list so that they can record what they have mastered.

3 ¡Qué desastre! Dile a un(a) compañero(a) cómo organizar
su dormitorio. Puedes usar las siguientes expresiones u otras.

Guarda ___ en ___   Pon ___ en ___   Hay que colgar ___

cómoda

¿Qué sabes ahora?

Can you:

■ describe clothing in detail?

—La blusa es de manga ___ y de color verde ___.

■ indicate clothing preferences?

—Prefiero los suéteres de ___ y los zapatos ___.

■ say how you paid for your purchases?

—Compré estas dos camisetas en ___, pero pagué
por el chaquetón con ___.

Vocabulario para conversar   105

3 Answers will vary, but should
be logical.

**Answers: ¿Qué sabes
ahora?**
• corta (larga) / claro (oscuro)
• Answers will vary.
• efectivo / cheque (tarjeta de
crédito)

 Audio Activity 3.3

Enrichment
Ex. 1: Have students redo this exercise with
Estudiante B saying that he or she plans to
wear clothes that are obviously unsuitable
for the situation mentioned. *Estudiante A*
can then react in a shocked manner and
suggest more appropriate clothes.

Cooperative Learning
In groups of three or four, tell students they
have each been given $500. Have them cre-
ate a list of clothing that they would buy for
themselves or for a family member or a
friend. Tell them to include details such as
style, material, and cost. Have them explain
their choices. Groups should then tabulate
the results to find the most popular item.
Call on groups to report results.

Present & Apply

Cultural Objective
- To understand relative values of currencies

Teaching Suggestions
If possible, go to a major bank and exchange a few dollars' worth of U.S. money for currency from Spanish-speaking countries. Bring in coins from your trips to Spanish-speaking countries.

Answers
Answers to inductive questions will vary.

Perspectiva cultural

¿Cuánto cuestan las cosas en las fotos?
¿Piensas que son baratas o no?

Tabla de Monedas Oficiales

Argentina	peso	El Salvador	colón	Paraguay	guaraní
Bolivia	peso	España	peseta	Perú	sol
Chile	peso	Guatemala	quetzal	Puerto Rico	dólar
Colombia	peso	Honduras	lempira	República Dominicana	peso
Costa Rica	colón	México	peso	Uruguay	peso
Cuba	peso	Nicaragua	córdoba	Venezuela	bolívar
Ecuador	sucre	Panamá	balboa		

Options

Strategies for Reaching All Students

Spanish-Speaking Students
Ask: ¿Has visto el dinero de otro(s) país(es)? ¿Cuál es el más interesante? ¿Por qué?

 Un paso más Ex. 3-H

Students Needing Extra Help
Have students take notes to help them when reviewing for the chapter test.
Bring in a currency-conversion table from a newspaper. Explain the concept of the difference in the value of money from country to country. Explain the "weight" concept of currency. You might give the example of weighing a gold chain to determine its price.

Enrichment
Explain the origin of the currency from other Spanish-speaking countries: the *guaraní* was named for the indigenous people and language of Paraguay. *Lempira* was a fallen hero in Honduras' battle against the Spaniards. The *sol* was originally called *inti*, after the sun god of the people inhabiting what is now Peru.

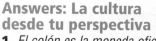

La respuesta a las preguntas de la izquierda depende del país en que se sacaron las fotos. Por ejemplo, un paraguas que cuesta 1.500 pesetas en España no es caro. Una peseta vale más o menos tres cuartos de un centavo americano. Por eso, el paraguas sólo cuesta diez dólares estadounidenses.

Si estás en un país extranjero, siempre tienes que saber el valor de la moneda para saber si lo que compras es una ganga. ¡Y no olvides que el valor puede cambiar de un día a otro!

La moneda oficial no es la misma en cada país. En España se usa *la peseta*. En México y en algunos otros países se usa *el peso*. ¿Sabías que esas dos palabras están relacionadas con el verbo *pesar,* que quiere decir *"to weigh"*? Hace muchos años una moneda de oro o de plata valía lo que pesaba. Piensa, por ejemplo, en la moneda inglesa—¡*pound!*

La moneda puede decirte mucho sobre un país. La moneda oficial panameña, por ejemplo, se llama *el balboa* y la de Nicaragua se llama *el córdoba.* ¿Por qué? Vasco Nuñez de Balboa era el conquistador que llevó a los primeros soldados españoles por Panamá hasta el Océano Pacífico. Francisco Hernández de Córdoba fundó las ciudades nicaragüenses de Léon y Granada.

En el dinero de muchos países puedes ver a personajes literarios, líderes políticos y animales y paisajes locales. Mirando con cuidado su dinero, puedes aprender mucho sobre un país.

A este joven chileno le interesan las liquidaciones.

La cultura desde tu perspectiva

1 Mira la tabla de monedas. ¿Cómo se llaman las monedas costarricense y salvadoreña? ¿Por qué se llaman así? ¿De qué país es el quetzal la moneda oficial? ¿Y el guaraní? Si no las conoces, busca esas palabras en un diccionario de inglés.

2 Imagina que el dinero de nuestro país va a cambiar y que tú puedes sugerir un nuevo nombre y un nuevo diseño. ¿Qué nombre va a tener la moneda oficial? ¿Qué símbolos vas a poner en el dinero para reflejar nuestros valores más importantes?

Estos zapatos en México se venden muy baratos ahora.

Perspectiva cultural   107

Cultural Notes

Preview

 Transparency 20

Reteach / Review: Direct Object Pronouns

A: Point out the direct object pronoun *los* in these phrases: *los busqué, los llevaste, los lavé.* Remind students that direct object pronouns usually come before the verb.

Answers:

A The forms are *lavé* and *lavo:* "I washed" (preterite), "I wash" (present). The endings change the meanings.

B Two *ellos / ellas* forms (panel 5): *entraron, salieron. Entraron* is an *-ar* verb *(entrar); salieron* is an *-ir* verb *(salir).*

C *Busqué* (panel 2) is a verb whose infinitive ends in *-car (buscar).* The preterite *yo* form differs from that of other *-ar* verbs because the consonant *(c)* changes (to *qu).* The preterite *yo* form of *tocar* is *toqué.*

Gramática en contexto

¡Los busqué por toda la casa!

108   Capítulo 3

A The boy uses two forms of *lavar* to talk about washing clothes. What are they? How do they differ in meaning? What is it about these two verb forms that changes the meaning?

B Find the two *ellos / ellas* forms of the preterite. Which one is an *-ar* verb and which is an *-ir* verb?

C Find a verb whose infinitive ends in *-car.* How is its *yo* form in the preterite different from that of other *-ar* verbs? What do you think the preterite *yo* form of *tocar* would be?

Options

Strategies for Reaching All Students

Students Needing Extra Help
Begin to fill in the grammar section of the Organizer. Review Book 1, Chaps. 10 and 12. Students will more likely remember the preterite of irregular verbs, which they saw in the latter part of their previous academic year; they will therefore need to review the preterite of regular verbs.

C: If students are having trouble identifying the *-car* verbs, have them give the present tense of *buscar* and *lavar.* Now have them compare these verb forms to the corresponding ones in the reading.

Repaso: El pretérito de los verbos regulares

You have learned to use the preterite tense to talk about things that happened in the past. Remember that, in general, verb endings tell who did an action and when it was done. Here are all the preterite forms of regular *-ar, -er,* and *-ir* verbs:

comprar

(yo)	compr**é**	(nosotros) (nosotras)	compr**amos**
(tú)	compr**aste**	(vosotros) (vosotras)	compr**asteis**
Ud. (él) (ella)	compr**ó**	Uds. (ellos) (ellas)	compr**aron**

comer

(yo)	com**í**	(nosotros) (nosotras)	com**imos**
(tú)	com**iste**	(vosotros) (vosotras)	com**isteis**
Ud. (él) (ella)	com**ió**	Uds. (ellos) (ellas)	com**ieron**

vivir

(yo)	viv**í**	(nosotros) (nosotras)	viv**imos**
(tú)	viv**iste**	(vosotros) (vosotras)	viv**isteis**
Ud. (él) (ella)	viv**ió**	Uds. (ellos) (ellas)	viv**ieron**

Colores siempre alegres con Micolor

Micolor
elimina la suciedad protege los colores

Gramática en contexto   109

Present

Using Realia
Remind students that they saw *alegre* in Chap. 4 as meaning "happy, festive." Have them brainstorm to figure out what *alegre* means in this advertisement ("bright, sunny").

Practice

Re-enter / Recycle

Ex. 1: school activities from
Chap. 1
Ex. 2: daily routine from Chap. 2

Answers

1 Answers will vary, but look for
the correct preterite forms.

2 ESTUDIANTE A

a. Pepe encontró los chandales,
¿verdad?

b. Julia lavó la ropa sucia . . .

c. Tú guardaste la ropa limpia . . .

d. Mi padre buscó su corbata . . .

e. Tú y tu hermano compraron los
mocasines . . .

f. Tía Carmen escogió el
pañuelo . . .

g. José colgó los chaquetones . . .

ESTUDIANTE B

a.–g. Answers may vary, but look
for the correct preterite forms and
direct object pronouns.

• Remember that -ar and -er verbs that have a stem change in the present
tense do *not* have a stem change in the preterite.

cerrar *(e → ie):*
C**ie**rro las ventanas de mi cuarto
todas las noches.
Pero ayer no c**e**rré las ventanas.

devolver *(o → ue):*
Siempre dev**ue**lvo los libros
los miércoles.
Ayer dev**o**lví tres libros.

• Remember that in the preterite, verbs
whose infinitive ends in -*gar* or -*car* have
a spelling change in the *yo* form. All of
their other preterite forms are regular.

pa**gar**	yo pa**gué**
lle**gar**	yo lle**gué**
ju**gar**	yo ju**gué**
sa**car**	yo sa**qué**
bus**car**	yo bus**qué**
to**car**	yo to**qué**

1 Formen grupos para describir lo que
hicieron Uds. y otras personas en
el pasado. Usen una expresión de
cada columna. Den *(Give)* más
información si pueden.

    Mario   *Mario tocó el violín anoche.*

a. mis amigos   tocar el violín   anoche
b. mi hermano(a)   ver la televisión   ayer
c. tú y tu tío   practicar deportes   hace una hora
d. yo   comer tacos   el año pasado
e. tú   entregar el informe   el mes pasado
f. nosotros   cerrar la puerta   la semana pasada
g. 💡   encontrar la cartera   el (día de la semana)
       💡   💡

En un mercado de San Blas, Panamá,
se vende ropa típica de los indios cuna
además de ropa hecha para los turistas.

Options

Strategies for Reaching All Students

Students Needing Extra Help
El pretérito de los verbos regulares: Give
additional examples of stem changes that
occurred in the present but won't in the
preterite. Write them on the chalkboard.
Point out that the *yo* form is irregular.
Ex. 1: Remind students to form logical
answers; this is not a linear match.
Review the preterite of the verbs in column
2 and words that indicate past in column 3.

Ex. 2: Review object pronouns. Model the
exercise, choosing the correct pronoun.
Then go through it again, changing the
verbs to the preterite.
Ex. 3: Explain that the parenthetical phrase
in the model is optional. Brainstorm words
that mean the opposite of the words given:
mañana (tarde); elegante (sencillo).

2 Trabaja con un(a) compañero(a) para corregir estos malentendidos (*misunderstandings*).

tú /pagar   A —*Pagaste la cuenta, ¿verdad?*
la cuenta   B —*No, yo no la pagué. Anita la pagó.*

a. Pepe /encontrar los chandales   mi padre
b. Julia /lavar la ropa sucia   Miguel y Roberto
c. tú /guardar la ropa limpia   mi madre
d. mi padre /buscar su corbata   Tomás
e. tú y tu hermano /comprar   la abuela
   los mocasines   Anita
f. tía Carmen /escoger el pañuelo   yo
g. José /colgar los chaquetones   nosotros

3 Túrnate con un(a) compañero(a) para hablar sobre algo que no suelen hacer pero que hicieron ayer.

salir de casa   *Generalmente salgo de casa a las 7:00. Pero ayer salí a las*
a las 7:00   *cinco de la mañana (para ir de pesca con mi padre).*

a. repartir periódicos por la mañana   f. usar vestidos de colores claros
b. llevar ropa elegante   g. ver la televisión durante el día
c. sacar una buena nota   h. pagar en efectivo
d. desayunar temprano   i.
e. llegar a casa a las 8:00

Gramática en contexto   111

---

3 Answers will vary, but may include the following:
a. Generalmente reparto periódicos por la mañana. Pero ayer repartí periódicos por la tarde.
b. ... llevo ropa elegante. ... llevé ropa sencilla.
c. ... saco una buena nota. ... saqué una mala nota.
d. ... desayuno temprano. ... desayuné tarde.
e. ... llego a casa a las 8:00. ... llegué a las 9:00.
f. ... uso vestidos de colores claros. ... usé uno (un vestido) de color oscuro.
g. ... veo la televisión durante el día. ... vi la televisión durante la noche.
h. ... pago en efectivo. ... pagué con un cheque.
i. Statements will vary.

 Practice Wkbk. 3-5, 3-6, 3-7

 Writing Activity 3-D

 Pruebas 3-5, 3-6

 Comm. Act. BLM 3-2

Cultural Notes ☀

(p. 110, photo)
Panama's Cuna Indians are known for their *molas,* colorful reverse-appliquéd fabrics. Panama's population is highly diverse. Nearly half of the country's inhabitants are of African descent, about a third are *mestizos* (of mixed Indian and black or white heritage), and about seven percent are indigenous peoples.

(p. 111, realia)
A sense of humor increases the consumer's interest in these personalized sew-on labels. The choice of "Francisco de Goya," "Don Juan Tenorio," etc., reflect the prominence of these figures in Spanish culture. The purchaser can call the manufacturer or fill out a mail-in order form to take advantage of this offer.

Present & Practice

Re-enter / Recycle

Ex. 4: school supplies from
Chap. 1

Adjetivos y pronombres demostrativos

Remember that we use demonstrative adjectives to point out people or things that are nearby. A demonstrative adjective always comes before the noun and agrees with it in gender and number.

este bolso	*this bag*	**estos** bolsos	*these bags*
esta cartera	*this wallet*	**estas** carteras	*these wallets*
ese bolso	*that bag*	**esos** bolsos	*those bags*
esa cartera	*that wallet*	**esas** carteras	*those wallets*

- To point out things that are farther away, we use these demonstrative adjectives.

| **aquel** chaleco | *that vest* | **aquellos** chalecos | *those vests* |
| **aquella** chaqueta | *that jacket* | **aquellas** chaquetas | *those jackets* |

- Demonstrative adjectives can also be used as pronouns to replace nouns. In that case they have a written accent.

  Este chaleco no me gusta; me gusta **ése.**
  No voy a comprar **ésta.** Prefiero **aquélla.**

112   Capítulo 3

Options

Strategies for Reaching All Students

Students Needing Extra Help

Adjetivos y pronombres demostrativos: For a quick review, refer to Book 1, Chap. 6. Emphasize gender agreement; students tend to use only the masculine form. Demonstrate *aquel* as "over there" (the farthest one from you). Provide additional examples. Sress the importance of the accents on the pronouns (i.e., when the noun is not used).

Ex. 4: Provide an assortment of school supplies that represent the masculine, feminine, singular, and plural forms.
Start with a simple model: *este libro.* Then present the pronouns: *éste, ése.* Repeat until all supplies have been mentioned.

Here are all of the demonstrative adjectives and pronouns.

	Close to you		Closer to the person you are talking to		Far from both of you	
Adjectives	este	estos	ese	esos	aquel	aquellos
	esta	estas	esa	esas	aquella	aquellas
Pronouns	éste	éstos	ése	ésos	aquél	aquéllos
	ésta	éstas	ésa	ésas	aquélla	aquéllas

4 Pon varios útiles escolares *(school supplies)* sobre la mesa. Describe los de tu mesa, los de la mesa de tu compañero(a) y los de una mesa que está un poco más lejos.

Este libro es negro y grande.
Ése es gris y pequeño.
Aquél es un diccionario.

Esta joven chilena trabaja de cajera en una tienda.

En Santiago de Chile, unos jóvenes admiran las chaquetas en el almacén Falabella.

Gramática en contexto   113

Class Starter Review
On the day after reviewing demonstrative adjectives and pronouns, you might begin the class with this activity:
Cut out pictures of various fashion models from magazines. Have students form groups of three, and hand out three pictures to each group. Each group takes turns describing the differences in clothing among the three photos. *(Esta mujer lleva . . . Ésa lleva . . . Aquélla lleva . . .)*

4 Answers will vary, but look for correct agreement of subject and verb, correct adjective agreement, and correct use of demonstrative adjectives and pronouns.

Practice Wkbk. 3-8, 3-9

Writing Activity 3-E

Pruebas 3-7, 3-8

Cultural Notes

(p. 113, top photo)
Store clerks in Latin America often play a different role than their U.S. counterparts. In the U.S., customers typically search through merchandise and select their own purchases. In Latin America, the clerk often locates and shows goods to the customer in a one-on-one interchange with more personalized service.

(p. 113, bottom photo)
Santiago is the cultural, political, and financial capital of Chile. Over 90 percent of the population lives in and around the capital in the central part of the country. The Chilean economy has rebounded in recent years, and many Chileans have acquired a greater amount of disposable income.

Present & Practice

Answers

5 Order of questions and answers will vary, but may include the following:

MAMÁ

¿De quién son estos pantalones azules oscuros?

... son estos jeans blancos?

... son estos jeans negros?

... es esta sudadera verde clara?

... es esta sudadera roja?

... es este suéter rosado?

... es este suéter verde oscuro?

VÍCTOR

Ésos son de Pedro.

Ésos son de Julia.

Ésos son de Pedro.

Ésa es de Julia.

Ésa es de Pedro.

Ése es de Julia.

Ése es de Pedro.

MAMÁ

¿De quién es aquella sudadera anaranjada clara?

... es aquel suéter rojo?

... son aquellos tenis blancos?

... son aquellos tenis negros?

VÍCTOR

¿Aquélla? Es de Julia.

¿Aquél? Es de Pedro.

¿Aquéllos? Son de Julia.

¿Aquéllos? Son de Pedro.

5 Víctor ayuda a su madre a guardar la ropa después de lavarla. La ropa de su hermano Pedro es de colores oscuros. La de su hermana Julia es de colores claros. Con un(a) compañero(a) digan de quién es la ropa de los dibujos.

Mamá —*¿De quién son estos pantalones marrones claros?*
Víctor —*Ésos son de Julia.*

Mamá —*¿De quién son aquellos pantalones verdes oscuros?*
Víctor —*¿Aquéllos? Son de Pedro.*

Los comparativos: *tanto(a) ... como*

You know that we use *tan* + adjective + *como* ("as ... as") to make equal comparisons of people or things. To make the same kind of comparison with nouns, we use *tanto(a)* + noun + *como*.

Rosa es **tan** elegante **como** su prima.	*Rosa is **as** elegant **as** her cousin.*
Tiene **tanto** dinero **como** su prima.	*She has **as much** money **as** her cousin.*
Compró **tantas** blusas **como** faldas.	*She bought **as many** blouses **as** skirts.*

Since *tanto* is an adjective, it agrees in number and gender with the noun.

114   Capítulo 3

Options

Strategies for Reaching All Students

Spanish-Speaking Students

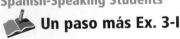 **Un paso más Ex. 3-I**

Students Needing Extra Help
Los comparativos: Provide a few more examples with *tan,* stressing its use with an adjective. Then give some masculine, feminine, singular, and plural examples of *tanto,* stressing its use with a noun.
To emphasize that *tanto* refers to objects, provide examples with objects in the room: *Marcos tiene tantos libros como Rosa.* If there is confusion with *tan,* review examples from Chap. 1.

Ex. 5: Point out that in the first sentence of the sample dialogue, the adjective is used; in the second, the pronoun is used.
Review the concept of distance (over there). Instruct students to pay close attention to the illustration.

6 Túrnate con un(a) compañero(a) para decir qué hicieron estas personas.

Julia sacó tanto dinero como Juan.
o: *Juan sacó tanto dinero como Julia.*

Julia / Juan / sacar

a. Susana / Rosita / escoger   b. Felipe / Anita / tocar   c. Rosario / Pablo / comprar

d. María / Roberto / repartir   e. Lucía / Tomás / escribir   f. Diego / Luis / comer

Ahora lo sabes

Can you:

- tell what happened in the past?

—Ayer compré un(a) ___ y lo (la) ___ con tarjeta de crédito.

- refer to people and things at various distances from you?

—Ese chaleco es bonito, pero ___ es más elegante.

- compare quantities that are the same?

—Julio tiene ___ gorras ___ su hermano.

Gramática en contexto   115

---

6 a. Susana (Rosita) escogió tantos cinturones como Rosita (Susana).
b. Felipe (Anita) tocó tanta música como Anita (Felipe).
c. Rosario (Pablo) compró tantas corbatas como Pablo (Rosario).
d. María (Roberto) repartió tantos periódicos como Roberto (María).
e. Lucía (Tomás) escribió tantas tarjetas postales como Tomás (Lucía).
f. Diego (Luis) comió tantos sandwiches como Luis (Diego).

Answers: Ahora lo sabes
- *Answers will vary.* / pagué
- éste (aquél)
- tantas / como

 Practice Wkbk. 3-10

 Audio Activities 3.4, 3.5

 Writing Activity 3-F

 Pruebas 3-9

 Comm. Act. BLM 3-3

Ex. 6: Go through the exercise, using only
tanto + noun + *como: tantos cinturones
como*. Then form the verb in the preterite:
escogió. Finally, put the two together:
escogió tantos cinturones como.
Ahora lo sabes: Have students write out this
section so they can record what they have
mastered.

Actividades

Esta sección te ofrece la oportunidad de aumentar tus conocimientos de español al integrar lo que aprendiste en este capítulo con lo que aprendiste en capítulos anteriores.

1 Es el cumpleaños del director (o de la directora). Le gusta mucho la ropa. Con un(a) compañero(a) decidan qué regalarle. Hablen de:

- lo que pueden comprarle
- tamaño, tela, color
- cuánto cuesta
- cómo van a pagar

Después, comparen el regalo que escogieron ustedes con el de otros grupos. Decidan cuál es el mejor regalo que le puede comprar toda la clase.

A esta joven argentina le gusta la ropa a cuadros.

116   Capítulo 3

2 Piensa en un día muy especial. Túrnate con un(a) compañero(a) para hablar de lo que hiciste ese día. Puedes hablar de:

- las actividades del día
- la hora, el lugar
- las personas que participaron
- lo que ocurrió

3 Hagan una "tienda de ropa" en la clase. Pueden traer ropa de su casa o fotos de revistas. Usen toda la sala. Pongan algunas cosas cerca de ustedes y otras más lejos. Inventen diálogos entre vendedores, cajeros y clientes. Usen estas u otras ideas en sus diálogos:

- saludar *(to greet)* y preguntar al cliente (a la clienta) qué busca
- hablar de la tela, de la talla (del número) y del color
- si puede probarse la ropa
- decir el precio y preguntar cómo quiere pagar
- dar las gracias y despedirse *(say good-by)*

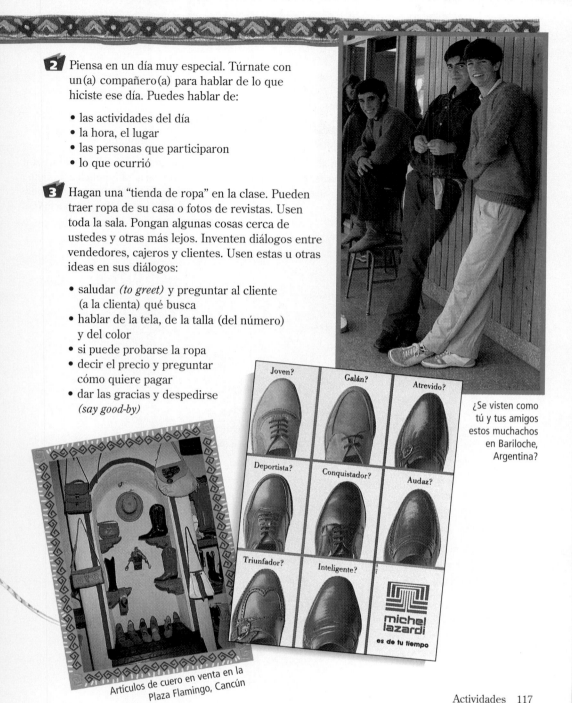

Joven? Galán? Atrevido?
Deportista? Conquistador? Audaz?
Triunfador? Inteligente?

michel lazardi
es de tu tiempo

Artículos de cuero en venta en la Plaza Flamingo, Cancún

¿Se visten como tú y tus amigos estos muchachos en Bariloche, Argentina?

Actividades 117

Later María, Carlos and Jamie shop for clothes. Afterward they go to a hotel restaurant, where they are spied on again by don Silvestre Aguilar. He tells his companions that Jamie poses a threat to his political campaign, since she is the heir to all of La Catrina's property, and Demetrio Alcocer, the librarian, has the will.

 La Catrina: Capítulo 3

Play

 Video Activity B

 Para entender mejor

Play

 Video Activity C

 Writing Activities 3-G, 3-H

 Comm. Act. BLMs 3-4, 3-5

Enrichment
Ex. 2: Before doing this exercise, brainstorm activities that someone may do on a special day: a party, a trip, a visit to the museum or to visit relatives, for example. Follow up this exercise by having students take notes on the narrative and write about their classmate's day.
Ex. 3: For extra credit, have groups of students prepare a videotape of their dialogue at home.

Cooperative Learning
Divide the class into groups of three or four. Photocopy pictures from magazines and distribute a different one to each group. On one sheet of paper, each group member should write one descriptive sentence about the picture and then pass the paper to the right. After each student has written three sentences, have the groups organize the sentences to create a story or logical description. Call on groups to share their stories with the class.

Cultural Notes

(p. 117, realia)
"Shoes make the man," implies this advertisement taken from a Spanish publication. The advertising agency most likely translated this ad directly from Italian to Spanish: note the absence of the inverted initial question marks.

Apply

Process Reading
For a description of process reading, see p. 52.

Answers
Antes de leer
Answers will vary. Students may say that advice columns deal with relationship problems, finances, health and beauty, or consumer issues.

Mira la lectura
Answers will vary.

¡Vamos a leer!

Antes de leer

STRATEGY➤ Using prior knowledge

What kinds of problems are discussed in advice columns? What advice might you give someone who was unhappy about his or her wardrobe?

Mira la lectura

STRATEGY➤ Skimming

Skim the column to get an overall idea of what it is about. Were some parts of it not clear? Make a list of three to five words that seemed to prevent you from understanding something important.

Querida Aurora...

Aurora:

Por favor, ¡dime qué debo hacer! Mis hermanitos y yo vivimos con mi papá. Él trabaja desde temprano por la mañana hasta tarde por la noche para mantenernos. El problema es que mi ropa está vieja, descolorida y me queda muy apretada. Pero no tengo dinero para comprar ropa nueva. Me da envidia cuando veo a mis amigas tan bien vestidas. Yo solamente tengo 17 años y ya me siento infeliz.

Alma Rosa Calderón

Alma Rosa:

Hay varias cosas que puedes hacer para no sentirte infeliz y para mejorar tu situación. Primero, ¡cambia de actitud! Claro que sí es normal querer ropa nueva, pero no olvides que hay otras cosas más importantes. Segundo, ¿por qué no encuentras una manera de ganar dinero? Puedes cuidar niños o trabajar en un restaurante o en una tienda. Además de comprar la ropa que necesitas, también vas a sentirte mejor porque podrás ayudar a tu padre. Sobre todo, ¡no descuides tus estudios! Recuerda que son más importantes que nada.

Aurora

118   Capítulo 3

Options

Strategies for Reaching All Students

Spanish-Speaking Students
Aplicación: Have students respond in writing: *Imagina que Alma Rosa te escribió a ti con su problema. ¿Qué le dirías? Escribe una carta dándole consejos.*

Students Needing Extra Help
Mira la lectura: If students come up with too many words that they don't know, show them which ones aren't important to getting the gist of the reading.
Infórmate: Provide examples of prefixes in English. This is a concept with which they are probably familiar. Have students work in pairs to figure out the meaning of the words listed.

Aplicación: Be alert to the mention of illegal means of earning money. It is easier to change Alma Rosa's letter first; then change Aurora's response. Brainstorm ways that Alma Rosa's letter can change: complaints against a disorganized sibling, an impatient parent, unmanageable school work, etc.

Infórmate

STRATEGY ➤ Understanding prefixes

Your list may have included the words *infeliz, descolorida,* and *descuides.* These words begin with a prefix that changes the meaning of the base word to its opposite. For example, you already know these pairs of opposites.

cómodo   incómodo
ordenado   desordenado
paciente   impaciente

Here are some other words with the negative prefixes *des-* and *in-/im-*.

necesario   innecesario
ocupado   desocupado
posible   imposible
prudente   imprudente

Use the meanings of these words to figure out the words with the prefixes in the reading.

feliz   *happy*
colorida   *colorful*
cuidar   *to take care of*

¿NECESITA AYUDA CON LOS NIÑOS?

Mi nombre es Alma Rosa Calderón. Tengo 17 años de edad y busco trabajo cuidando niños los fines de semana. Como soy la hermana mayor en mi familia, tengo mucha experiencia con los niños pequeños y con los quehaceres de la casa.

Soy honesta, responsable y muy buena estudiante. Por favor llame al teléfono (745) 555-2341

¡NO BUSQUE MÁS!

Aplicación

What do you think of Aurora's advice? How do teenagers earn money in your community? Change Aurora's letter to reflect the way things are where you live. Use the pairs of opposites in *Infórmate* and this section if you can.

Use the meanings of these words to figure out their opposites:

cansar   descansar *(to rest)*
contento *(happy)*   descontento
justo   injusto *(unfair)*
maduro *(mature)*   inmaduro

¡Vamos a leer!   119

Enrichment

Aplicación: Additional activities: 1) Imagine you are the brother or sister of the young woman who wrote the letter. Write to Aurora to explain your sister's problem from your perspective. 2) Write to Aurora to explain the problem from the point of view of a friend or parent. 3) Write to Aurora about a problem of your own.

Apply

Process Writing
For information regarding developing a writing portfolio, see p. 54.

¡Vamos a escribir!

Imagina que tu escuela necesita uniformes nuevos: uno para usar en clase, uno para un equipo deportivo y uno para la banda.

1 Primero, escoge un uniforme para diseñar. Piensa en estas cosas:

- las telas
- los colores
- el costo

Luego escribe una descripción del uniforme. Haz un dibujo para acompañar la descripción. No olvides ponerle el nombre o el símbolo de la escuela. Sigue los cinco pasos del proceso de escribir. (Si es necesario, mira la página 54.)

A estos jóvenes mexicanos les quedan bien los uniformes escolares.

Estudiantes de camino a la escuela en Quito, Ecuador

Estudiantes en Santiago, República Dominicana

120   Capítulo 3

Options

Strategies for Reaching All Students

Students Needing Extra Help
Ex. 1: Students need design only one uniform.
Ex. 2: Help students with the words *afectar* and *mejorar*. Remind them of the *tanto . . . como* formula and demonstrative adjectives.

Unos deportistas corren cerca de las montañas en Ecuador.

2 Ahora en grupo escriban un artículo para el periódico escolar sobre la importancia de los uniformes. Usen expresiones como éstas:

- bonito(a) / guapo(a)
- práctico(a)
- barato(a) / caro(a)
- afectar la disciplina
- mejorar el espíritu escolar

En Caracas, Venezuela, unas jóvenes juegan *kickball.*

3 Para distribuir su trabajo, pueden:

- exhibir las descripciones y los dibujos en la sala de clases
- exhibirlos en el vestíbulo o la biblioteca escolar
- enviar el artículo al periódico escolar
- enviarlo al director o a la directora de la escuela
- poner todo en el portafolio

¡Vamos a escribir! 121

Cultural Notes ☀

(p. 120–121, photos)
Uniforms contribute to a sense of equality and common purpose within a group. For this reason, athletic teams employ uniforms that identify their members. School uniforms contribute to this same goal. In Latin America, many schools enforce a dress code in which girls wear dark skirts or dresses, while boys wear ties and conservative style slacks.

(p. 121, photo)
Kickball is popular in many parts of Latin America. The game is similar to baseball, except that the "pitcher" bowls the ball to the "batter," who kicks it into play.

Assess & Summarize

Test Preparation
You may want to assign parts of this section as written homework or as an in-class writing activity prior to administering the *Examen de habilidades.*

Answers:
Listening: *¡Mamá! Luz María me invitó a pasar una semana en el campo con ella y su familia. Me gustaría llevar esta chaqueta de cuero, pero ya no está de moda. Creo que debo llevar aquel suéter de cuello alto y los pantalones de lana. ¿Están limpios? También necesito un chandal. Ese de tela sintética ya no me queda bien. ¡Mamá! ¡Tenemos que ir de compras!*
Answers may vary, but students should mention cold or cool weather.

Reading: The bottom right picture

Writing: Answers will vary.

Culture: Answers will vary, but students may say they'd need to know the exchange rate before buying something. / By looking carefully at a country's currency one can see literary figures, political leaders, and national flora and fauna: the *quetzal,* the currency of Guatemala, is also the name of that country's national bird.

¿Lo sabes bien?

Esta sección te ayudará a preparrate para el examen de habilidades, donde tendrás que hacer tareas semejantes. Recuerda, sin embargo, que en el examen no habrá modelos.

Listening
Can you understand when someone talks about clothes in detail? Listen as your teacher reads a sample similar to what you will hear on the test. Based on the clothing mentioned, what do you think the weather will be like in the country?

Reading
Can you understand written descriptions of clothes? Which picture matches one of the articles described?

Pagué veinte dólares por esta blusa a cuadros y me queda floja. Estos pantalones de algodón no tienen bolsillos, y no me gusta la chaqueta porque los botones son demasiado pequeños. Los zapatos que llegaron para papá son de color marrón, y no negro, y el cinturón para mi hijo no es de la talla que él usa.

Querida Mónica,

Debes traer ropa sencilla y cómoda. Por aquí está muy de moda usar jeans con un chaleco, también los suéteres de cuello alto y las camisas lisas de algodón. ¿Compraste aquel chaquetón que vimos en el almacén González? Por la noche hace frío. No tienes que traer traje de baño. Aquí hay tres de tamaño mediano. Me regalaron dos y compré uno. Pero papá dice que necesitas una tarjeta de crédito si quieres comprar algo muy caro. Hasta pronto.

Tu amiga,
Gloria

Writing
Can you write a letter to a friend about an upcoming visit? See the sample above.

Culture
If you were planning to visit several Latin American countries, what would you need to know before buying something? What can you tell about a country by looking carefully at its currency? Give an example from a Spanish-speaking country.

Speaking
Can you ask and answer questions about clothes? Create a dialogue with your partner between a salesperson and a customer. Here is a sample dialogue:

A —*¿De qué son estos cinturones?*
B —*Éstos son de cuero y aquéllos de lona.*
A —*Este cinturón me queda apretado. ¿Lo tiene en la talla mediana?*
B —*Sí. Aquí hay uno. ¿Necesita algo más?*
A —*Me gustarían unos pantalones flojos y oscuros.*
B —*Éstos a rayas están muy de moda.*

Options

Strategies for Reaching All Students

Students Needing Extra Help
Have students write out this section so they can check off what they have mastered.
Listening: Review weather expressions. Ask students what they would wear in different types of weather: *¿Qué llevas cuando hace frío?* Review the vocabulary section of the Organizer.
Reading: Have students first look at the pictures so that they know what to look for. Read slowly so students pick up subtleties.

Writing: Brainstorm other activities that require special clothing because of the weather. Limit the number of sentences.
Culture: Have students review the *Perspectiva cultural.*
Speaking: Use the vocabulary section of the Organizer. Review dialogues in the *Vocabulario para conversar* and *Todo junto* sections.

Resumen del capítulo 3

Usa el vocabulario de este capítulo para:
- describe clothing in detail
- indicate clothing preferences and make comparisons
- say how you paid for purchases

Speaking: Dialogues will vary.

 Prueba cumulativa

 Examen de habilidades

 Test Generator

to indicate articles of clothing
el bolso
el botín, *pl.* los botines
la cartera
el chaleco
el chandal
el chaquetón, *pl.* los chaquetones
el cinturón, *pl.* los cinturones
la corbata
la gorra
el mocasín, *pl.* los mocasines
el pañuelo
el suéter de cuello alto
el traje
los zapatos de tacón alto

to indicate parts of clothing
el bolsillo
el botón, *pl.* los botones
la cremallera
la manga

to discuss making purchases
el cajero, la cajera
el catálogo
el cheque
(el dinero) en efectivo
la liquidación, *pl.* las liquidaciones
estar en liquidación
la tarjeta de crédito
el vendedor, la vendedora
encontrar *(o → ue)*
escoger

to discuss clothing
apretado, -a
flojo, -a
elegante
sencillo, -a
la moda
estar de moda
probarse *(o → ue)*
usar

to discuss fabrics and patterns
¿De qué es ___?
Es de ___.
la tela
el algodón
la lana

la lona
el nilón
el plástico
sintético, -a
a cuadros
a rayas
floreado, -a
liso, -a
claro, -a
oscuro, -a

to indicate sizes
el número (de zapatos)
(número) y medio
la talla
el tamaño
    grande
    mediano, -a
    pequeño, -a

other useful words and expressions
alguien
el cesto de la ropa sucia
el suelo
la fiesta
colgar *(o → ue)*
guardar
lo que
(me) da igual
por todas partes

Resumen 123

123

CAPÍTULO 4

THEME: LEISURE-TIME ACTIVITIES

SCOPE AND SEQUENCE   Pages 124–157

COMMUNICATION

Topics
Sports and sports equipment

Music

Games

Objectives
To discuss the paintings of Frida Kahlo and Diego Rivera

To discuss sports

To discuss leisure activities

To describe people or things

To discuss activities in the past

CULTURE

The paintings of Frida Kahlo and Diego Rivera

GRAMMAR

El pretérito del verbo ser

El pretérito de los verbos hacer, poder *y* tener

Repaso: El verbo saber

El pretérito de verbos reflexivos

Ancillaries available for use with Chapter 4

Multisensory/Technology

 Overhead Transparencies, 21–25

 Audio Tapes and CDs

 Vocabulary Art Blackline Masters for Hands-On Learning, pp. 23–27

 Classroom Crossword

 La Catrina

 CD-ROM

Print

 Practice Workbook, pp. 34–44

 Writing, Audio & Video Activities, pp. 23–28, 102–104, 157–158

 Communicative Activity Blackline Masters

    Pair and Small Group Activities, pp. 22–27

    Situation Cards, p. 28

 Un paso más: Actividades para ampliar tu español, pp. 19–24

Assessment

 Assessment Program

    Pruebas, pp. 55–66

    Examen de habilidades, pp. 67–70

 Test Generator

Video still from Chap. 4

123A

Outdoor Fun

Most leisure-time activities in Spanish-speaking countries take place in the streets, parks, and cafés in the commercial areas of the cities—often in the downtown areas. Because towns and cities are designed with the pedestrian in mind, street life is full of things to see and do.

People of all ages commonly enjoy each other's company in local outdoor cafés, or in the many parks, often replete with monuments, fountains, and gazebos. Vendors selling ice cream, fresh fruit, cold beverages, and brightly colored balloons add to the liveliness of the parks and *plazas*. Occasionally entertainment may be provided by a group of musicians playing songs of the region, or by a clown juggling, or by a city-organized concert. Local artists and artisans display paintings, jewelry, and other handicrafts in outdoor areas. Some locales with temperate climates offer year-round art fairs.

One of Latin America's most renowned parks lies in the heart of Mexico City. It is called Chapultepec, which is the Aztec, or Nahuatl, word for "grasshopper hill." Chapultepec Park contains spacious areas for walking and playing, a small lake for boating, outdoor restaurants, and the city zoo. It is also the site of several museums, including the historical museum known as *El Castillo*—former home of the French-imposed emperor and empress Maximiliano and Carlota, who ruled Mexico between 1864 and 1867. Other museums include the *Museo Nacional de Antropología,* which houses the most complete collection of pre-Columbian art and artifacts in the world, and *El Museo de Arte Moderno,* which features twentieth-century paintings by Mexico's most accomplished artists. In all Spanish-speaking countries, the citizens are very proud of their rich cultural heritage, and museums are considered to be important and enjoyable places to relax and learn.

Undoubtedly, the most popular team sport throughout Spain and most of Latin America is soccer *(fútbol).* Youngsters of all ages can be seen playing it in parks, on sports fields, or neighborhood streets. As a spectator sport, soccer is also extremely important. People fill the stadiums for games, and many of the events are televised. In countries that have not adopted soccer as a national sport, such as the Dominican Republic and Nicaragua, baseball is the preferred game. Skiing is popular during the winter months in Argentina, Chile, and Spain. Each of these nations boasts several internationally known ski resorts. In addition, of course, beaches are popular in all Spanish-speaking countries except the two landlocked South American nations of Bolivia and Paraguay.

Introduce

Re-entry of Concepts
The following list represents words, expressions, and grammar topics re-entered from Book 1 and Book 2 (Chaps. 1–3):

Book 1
calendar expressions, *gustar* expressions, time-telling, family members, places and buildings, television shows

Chapter 1
school activities

Chapter 2
daily routine

Planning

Cross-Curricular Connections

Physical Education Connection
(pp. 128–129)
Have pairs of students choose a favorite sport or invent a new one. Have them make a poster and / or prepare an oral report in Spanish stating the rules, the equipment needed, and the reasons that this sport is so much fun.

Communications Connection
(pp. 146–147)
In small groups, have students prepare a TV sportscast. Each student should report on a different game from that day or evening. They should include key plays, errors, and other crucial information. If time permits, you might want to videotape some of the best reports to share with other classes.

Literature / History Connection
(pp. 154–155)
Have each student choose a famous person, past or present, and write a short biography using the past tense. Focus should be on the person's most significant moment or success and the factors that led to it.

CAPÍTULO 4

¿Cómo te diviertes?

OBJECTIVES

At the end of this chapter, you will be able to:

- talk about past and present activities
- extend, accept, or reject an invitation
- discuss and evaluate a leisure-time activity
- talk about the paintings of two Mexican artists and what their work tells us about them and their culture

Mural dedicado a Carlos Santana, San Francisco, California

125

Cultural Notes

Spanish in Your Community
Have students select three activities from the chapter vocabulary and name at least one Hispanic person famous for each. For example, they might name Seve Ballesteros, a Spaniard, for golf. Afterwards, have each student ask five people outside of the classroom to provide additional names for the categories. Have students share the results of their surveys with the class and discuss the contributions of Hispanics to sports and other activities.

(p. 124, photo)
This mural *Inspire to Aspire,* located in San Francisco's Mission District, was painted in 1987 by Mike Ríos. It depicts musician Carlos Santana, the son of a *mariachi* violinist who taught him to play violin and guitar. Ríos has symbolized Santana's musical roots through portraits of *mariachis* and salsa musicians. The two indigenous profiles behind Santana point to his racial and cultural *mestizaje.*

Santana is considered to be the father of fusion Latin rock and was one of the first Latino musicians to become popular with mainstream audiences in the U.S. He made his first major appearance at the Woodstock festival in 1969. Ríos was a member of the *Galería de la Raza* and an active muralist during the early 1970s at the start of the contemporary mural movement. Ríos and his peers are influenced by the work of Rivera and other Mexican muralists.

Preview

Cultural Objective
• To discuss leisure-time activities in Spanish-speaking countries

Critical Thinking: Synthesizing
Have students write one or two descriptive sentences about the photographs. Refer to Book 1, Chap. 3, to review leisure-time activities.

¡Piénsalo bien!

Mira las fotos. Las personas están hablando de varias diversiones. ¿Qué pasatiempos te gustan a ti?

"Ayer fuimos al parque para jugar ajedrez."

El ajedrez es un pasatiempo muy popular por todas partes. ¿Sabes jugar?

Jugando ajedrez en Caracas, Venezuela

"Dicen que el último disco compacto de Los Lobos tiene muchas canciones muy buenas."

¿Qué clase de música te gusta más? ¿Conoces algunos artistas que cantan en inglés y en español? ¿Te gusta su música?

Una tienda de discos compactos en Buenos Aires

126   Capítulo 4

Options

Strategies for Reaching All Students

Spanish-Speaking Students
Ask students to respond orally or in writing: *Describe tus actividades favoritas cuando estabas en la escuela primaria. ¿En qué participabas fuera de la escuela? ¿Te gustaban los deportes, los videos, los videojuegos y el baile? ¿En qué quisieras participar después de terminar tus estudios?*

 Un paso más Ex. 4-A

Sports were just as important to
the people of ancient Mesoamerica as they are today. Some
of these sports, however, were
more than simple *diversiones*. For
example, the ancient ball game of
ulama, a version of which is still
played today in rural Mexico, may
have had a religious significance.
Players had to hit the ball, which
may have represented the sun,
through a stone ring in order to
score. The sport was much more
physical than modern football or
rugby. In fact, players sometimes
died from injuries suffered during
what was aptly called *el juego de
vida y muerte.* Ask students to
analyze current sports and
describe what significance they
have to a given culture.

Answers: ¡Piénsalo bien!
Answers to inductive questions
will vary. Some names of artists
who sing in English and in
Spanish may include: Santana,
Plácido Domingo, The Barrio
Boyzz, Lisette Meléndez, and
Selena.

"No sé por qué a tantos jóvenes no les gusta el ballet.
¡Los bailarines son atletas fantásticos!"

¿Crees que es más difícil meter un gol en fútbol o bailar por una hora?

El Ballet Nacional de Cuba

127

Cultural Notes

(p. 127, photo)
El Ballet Nacional de Cuba, based in Havana,
was founded in 1960 by ballerina Alicia
Alonso (1921–). Although she was allowed
to study ballet, her parents did not intend
for her to dance professionally. However, at
the age of 15, she defied them by eloping
with a fellow classmate, Fernando Alonso, to
New York City, where they both wished to
pursue a career in ballet. She joined the
American Ballet Theater and was with the
theater from 1941–1960. In 1960, the couple returned to Cuba with the dream of creating their own company. They started by
forming a ballet school in each of the
island's six provinces and training a corps of
dancers. By 1966, Cuban dancers were winning recognition in competitions all over
Europe. El Ballet Nacional de Cuba, headed
by its star and founder, performed all over
the world, except in the U.S, where she was
not allowed to perform because of her political affiliation. Then, in 1975, in a gesture of
international goodwill, Alonso was allowed
to perform once again in the city that had
made her a star: she danced *Swan Lake*
with the American Ballet Theater at Lincoln
Center. At the end of her performance, she
received an 18-minute standing ovation.
Before returning to Havana, she said: *El
arte no tiene fronteras. Le pertenece al
mundo, y el mundo somos tú y yo.*

Present

Chapter Theme
Sports and sports equipment

Communicative Objectives
• To discuss sports
• To discuss activities in the past

 Transparencies 21–22

 Vocabulary Art BLMs

 Pronunciation Tape 4-1

Teaching Suggestions
Preparing students to speak: Use one or two options from each of the categories of Comprehensible Input, Physical Response, or Limited Verbal Response. For a complete explanation of these categories and some sample activities, see pp. T16–T17.

Vocabulario para conversar

¿Me prestas tu raqueta?

Vas a necesitar estas palabras y expresiones para hablar sobre las diversiones. Después de leerlas varias veces, practícalas con un(a) compañero(a).

el palo (de golf, de hockey)
el casco
el disco (de hockey)

los bolos   el golf   el hockey

el entrenador
las pesas

la bicicleta
el patín, pl. los patines

montar en bicicleta   patinar sobre hielo   levantar pesas

la entrenadora

correr   el campeón, pl. los campeones; la campeona

128   Capítulo 4

Options

Strategies for Reaching All Students

Spanish-Speaking Students
Ask: *¿Usas otras palabras para estos deportes o este equipo? ¿Cuáles son? Haz una lista.*

 Un paso más Exs. 4-B, 4-C

Students Needing Extra Help
Vocabulario para conversar: Have students begin filling in the vocabulary section of the Organizer.
Distinguish between *pelota* and *balón:* *pelota* is a small ball, such as a baseball or tennis ball; *balón* is a large, inflated ball such as a basketball or volleyball. Remind students to use *jugar* with sports words. Point out word families such as *patinar / patín,* etc.

También necesitas . . . : Distinguish between *prestar* (to lend) and *pedir prestado* (to borrow).

empatar perder *(e → ie)* ganar

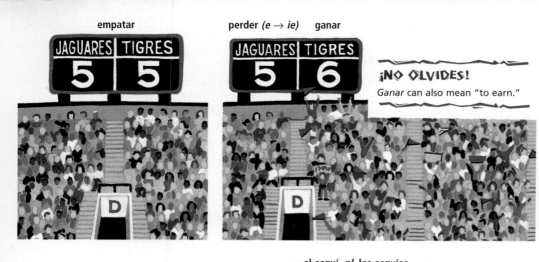

¡NO OLVIDES!
Ganar can also mean "to earn."

el esquí, *pl.* los esquíes

la jugadora (de golf)

la raqueta (de tenis)

el bate

el jugador (de béisbol)

el balón, *pl.* los balones

la pelota (de golf, de béisbol)

el guante (de béisbol)

También necesitas . . .

prestar	*to lend*	el partido	*match, game*
pedir prestado, -a (a)	*to borrow*	meter un gol	*to score a goal*
tener que:			
(yo) tuve que	*I had to*		
(tú) tuviste que	*you had to*		
la liga	*league*		

¿Y qué quiere decir . . . ?
el campeonato

Vocabulario para conversar   129

Explain to students that this chapter is about leisure-time activities. They should be prepared to state what they are in the habit of doing (using *soler*) on weekends.

Grammar Preview
(Yo) tuve que / (tú) tuviste que are presented here lexically. The complete paradigm of *tener* in the preterite is found on p. 146. Avoid grammar discussion at this point.

Class Starter Review
On the day following initial vocabulary presentation, you might begin the class with either of these activities:
1) In pairs, have students take turns naming a sport and listing the equipment necessary for it.
2) Prepare a transparency listing outcomes of sports matches, real or imaginary *(Los Leones 21, Los Tigres 20)*. In pairs, students take turns reading the scores and then saying who won *(ganó, ganaron)*, who lost *(perdió, perdieron)*, or if it was a tie *(empataron)*.

Learning Spanish Through Action
STAGING VOCABULARY: *Busquen, Levanten*
MATERIALS: envelopes containing pictures of vocabulary items
DIRECTIONS: Pass out envelopes to groups. Direct them to look for and then hold up pictures of sports equipment related to the sport that you mention.

Practice

Reteach / Review: Time-telling

Ex. 1: Pairs of students can extend this dialogue by having *Estudiante A* ask *Estudiante B* at what time he or she would like to do the activity named.

Answers: Empecemos a conversar

1 ESTUDIANTE A
a. Tengo un palo de golf nuevo. ¿Jugamos golf mañana?
b. Tengo esquíes nuevos. ¿Esquiamos mañana?
c. Tengo un (balón de) básquetbol nuevo. ¿Jugamos básquetbol mañana?
d. Tengo patines nuevos. ¿Patinamos sobre hielo mañana?
e. Tengo una raqueta de tenis nueva. ¿Jugamos tenis mañana?
f. Tengo un (balón de) fútbol nuevo. ¿Jugamos fútbol mañana?

ESTUDIANTE B
a.–f. Answers will vary, but encourage students to use a variety of answers.
You might want students to note the use of the present tense implying future. It is the same as the English "are we playing tomorrow?"

Empecemos a conversar

Túrnate con un(a) compañero(a) para ser *Estudiante A* y *Estudiante B*. Reemplacen las palabras subrayadas en el modelo con palabras representadas o escritas en los recuadros. Si ven pueden dar su propia respuesta.

1
A —*Tengo un palo de hockey nuevo.*
   ¿Jugamos hockey mañana?
B —*¡Por supuesto!*

Estudiante A   Estudiante B

Sí, me gustaría mucho.

No, yo nunca ___.

No, mañana no puedo. Tengo que ___.

No, mañana no. ¿Por qué no jugamos ___?

Pero yo no sé ___.

¡Por supuesto!

Levantando pesas,
Palos Verdes, California

130   Capítulo 4

Options

Strategies for Reaching All Students

Students Needing Extra Help
Ex. 1: Discuss what kinds of words will go in the blank for *Estudiante B*.
Ex. 2: Remind students that this is not a linear match for answers.

2

A —¿Me prestas tu _pelota de béisbol_?
B —Claro que sí. ¿Necesitas _el bate_ también?

Estudiante A   Estudiante B

a.   b.

c.   d.

e.   f.

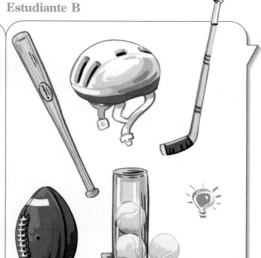

Patinando afuera de
un centro comercial,
Santiago, Chile

2 ESTUDIANTE A
a. ¿Me prestas tu bicicleta?
b. . . . guante de béisbol?
c. . . . raqueta de tenis?
d. . . . casco de fútbol americano?
e. . . . disco de hockey?
f. Questions will vary.
ESTUDIANTE B
a. Claro que sí. ¿Necesitas el
casco de bicicleta también?
b. . . . el bate (de béisbol)
también?
c. . . . las pelotas de tenis
también?
d. . . . el balón de fútbol americano
también?
e. . . . el palo de hockey también?
f. Answers will vary.

Cultural Notes

(p. 131, photo)
Santiago, Chile, has many shopping malls:
two of the largest are Parque Arauco and
Alto de los Condes. Malls have become a
popular place for socializing or to enjoy
such unconventional activities as roller
skating.

Practice & Apply

Answers:
Empecemos a conversar

3 ESTUDIANTE A

a. ¿Quién ganó el partido de fútbol?

b. ... hockey?

c. ... tenis?

d. ... básquetbol?

e. ... bolos?

f. Questions will vary.

ESTUDIANTE B

a.–f. Answers will vary, but encourage students to use a variety of answers. Be alert for appropriate use of preterite forms.

4 ESTUDIANTE A

a. ¿Fuiste a patinar sobre el hielo el sábado pasado?

b. ... a montar en bicicleta ...

c. ... a jugar bolos ...

d. ... a levantar pesas ...

e. ... a esquiar ...

f. Questions will vary, but should include *a* + inf.

ESTUDIANTE B

a.–f. Answers will vary, but encourage students to use a variety of excuses. Look for the construction *tuve que* + inf.

3

A —*¿Quién ganó el partido de béisbol?*
B —*Nosotros ganamos (cuatro a dos).*

Estudiante A

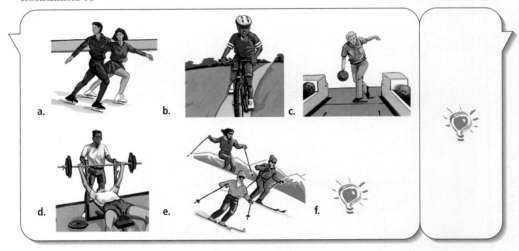

Estudiante B

(nombre) ___.

El otro equipo ___.

Nosotros perdimos.

Nadie ___. Empatamos.

Nosotros. Metimos ___ goles.

4

A —*¿Fuiste a correr el sábado pasado?*
B —*No, tuve que llevar a mi hermano menor al parque.*

Estudiante A

Estudiante B

132   Capítulo 4

Options

Strategies for Reaching All Students

Spanish-Speaking Students

Ex. 8: After this exercise, ask: *¿Juegan fútbol en tu escuela? ¿Participas tú? ¿Cómo es el equipo? ¿Cuándo practican? ¿Cuándo son los partidos? ¿Tienen que viajar mucho para los partidos?*

Students Needing Extra Help

Ex. 3: In the list of possible responses for *Estudiante B,* explain what will go in the blanks and how the *nombre* response fits in.

Ex. 4: Brainstorm possible responses for *Estudiante B.* Have students alternate *Estudiante A* and *Estudiante B* parts in order to practice both constructions.

Ex. 5: Explain the general nature of the first question and how the second question is really asking if there was a variance in routine during the past weekend. Students may see this as redundant. Remind them that the first question is answered in the present tense, while the second is answered in the preterite.

Ex. 7: You may need to get some information from the athletic director in order to answer these questions.

Empecemos a escribir

Escribe tus respuestas en español.

5 Generalmente, ¿qué tienes que hacer los fines de semana? ¿Y qué tuviste que hacer el fin de semana pasado?

6 Cuando no tienes algo, ¿sueles pedirlo prestado? ¿A quién? Generalmente, ¿qué cosas pides prestado?

7 ¿Qué equipos hay en tu escuela? ¿Cuántos jugadores hay en cada equipo? ¿Quiénes son los entrenadores?

8 ¿Quiénes son los campeones de la liga escolar de fútbol americano? ¿Y de béisbol? ¿Cuándo ganaron el campeonato?

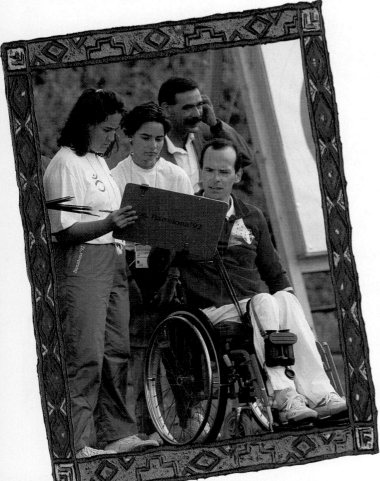

Un participante de los Juegos Paralímpicos en Barcelona

También se dice

el boliche
el bowling

hacer pesas
hacer halterofilia

la manopla

la bola

Vocabulario para conversar   133

Answers: Empecemos a escribir

5 Answers will vary, but look for *tengo que / tuve que* + inf.

6–8 Answers will vary, but encourage use of chapter vocabulary.

Practice Wkbk. 4-1, 4-2

Audio Activity 4.1

Pruebas 4-1, 4-2

Comm. Act. BLM 4-1

Enrichment
Ex. 4: Encourage *Estudiante B* to use a variety of excuses: *estudiar, ir a la biblioteca, ayudar en casa, cocinar, ir a una fiesta,* etc., or you may want to brainstorm excuses.

Cooperative Learning
Divide the class into groups of three. One student will be a world-class athlete in one of the sports mentioned in this chapter. Another student will be a clothing designer, and the third will be a graphic designer. As a group, they should develop a new line of clothing for the sport, to be promoted by the athlete. The ad should include such things as a logo, name, and description of the line. Have them present their ad on a poster to be displayed in the classroom.

Cultural Notes

(p. 133, photo)
The ninth *paralímpicos* (Paralympics), or Olympic Games for the Disabled, were held in Barcelona following the 1992 Olympics. Sixteen events, including fencing, cycling, judo and wheelchair basketball, were included in the '92 games. Volunteers from all parts of Spain contributed translation, technical, and information services to the event. Queen Sofía of Spain hosted the games as Honorary President.

Present

Chapter Theme
Games and music

Communicative Objectives
• To discuss leisure-time activities
• To discuss activities in the past

 Transparencies 23–24

 Vocabulary Art BLMs

 Pronunciation Tape 4-2

Teaching Suggestions

Preparing students to speak: Use one or two options from each of the categories of Comprehensible Input, Physical Response, or Limited Verbal Response. For a complete explanation of these categories and some sample activities, see pp. T16–T17.

Vocabulario para conversar

¿Cómo estuvo el concierto?

Aquí tienes el resto del vocabulario que necesitas en este capítulo para hablar sobre las diversiones.

la fiesta de disfraces

la obra de teatro

la exposición, *pl.* las exposiciones (de arte)

la música clásica

la música rock

el desfile

(hacer) un picnic

las damas

134   Capítulo 4

Options

Strategies for Reaching All Students

Students Needing Extra Help
Vocabulario para conversar: Review the forms of *hacer.*
También necesitas . . . : Write out the two reflexive paradigms. Give examples of *soportar, pasarlo bien / mal* and *bastante.* Write out the entire *saber* paradigm for students who need to see all six forms.
¿Y qué quiere decir . . . ?: Give some examples of *tener tiempo de* + inf.

Learning Spanish Through Action
STAGING VOCABULARY: *Señalen, Levántense*
MATERIALS: transparency of the vocabulary page
DIRECTIONS: Direct students to decide which is their favorite activity. Ask them to stand if the activity you mention is their favorite. Write the number of standing students on the transparency. Make comments

about the favorite activities of the class. If you have other classes of the same level, you might use different-colored markers for each class so that you can make comparisons between classes.

134

(hacer) un crucigrama

(hacer) un rompecabezas

el ajedrez

el disco compacto

el casete

el video musical

También necesitas . . .

saber: (yo) sé	*to know: I know,*	alegre	*happy, festive*
(tú) sabes	*you know*	último, -a	*last*
divertirse *(e → ie)*	*to have fun*	bastante	here: *quite*
aburrirse	*to be bored*		
soportar	*to tolerate, to stand*		
pasarlo bien / mal	*to have a good /*		
	bad time		
estuvo *(from:* estar*)*	*he / she / it was*		
fue *(from:* ser*)*	*he / she / it was*		

> **¿Y qué quiere decir . . . ?**
> tener tiempo de + *inf.*
> la diversión, *pl.* las diversiones
> el desastre
> el horror

Vocabulario para conversar   135

Grammar Preview
(Yo) sé / (tú) sabes are presented here lexically. The paradigm of present-tense *saber* is reviewed on p. 148.
Fue is presented here lexically. The paradigm of *ser* in the preterite is on p. 145. Alert students may realize that it is the same as the preterite form of *ir.*

Class Starter Review
On the day following initial vocabulary presentation, you might begin the class with this activity: Have students rank the activities from this and the previous vocabulary section in order of preference. Have a volunteer keep a class tally on the chalkboard.

Practice

Reteach / Review: Vocabulary
Ex. 9: You may want to review vocabulary from Book 1, Chap. 11 before doing this exercise.

Teaching Suggestions
Ex. 10: To review direct object pronouns, ask students questions such as these: *¿Viste la película Jurassic Park? (Sí la vi.) ¿Hiciste la tarea de matemáticas? (No, no la hice.) ¿Quién corta el césped en tu casa? (Mi hermano lo corta or Yo lo corto.)*

Answers: Empecemos a conversar

9 ESTUDIANTE A

a. ¿Cómo estuvo el último programa de entrevistas que viste?
b. ...la última película...
c. ...la última obra de teatro...
d. ...la última exposición de arte...
e. ...la última telenovela...
f. Questions will vary, but look for adjective agreement.

ESTUDIANTE B

a.–f. Answers will vary, but look for logical answers and adjective agreement.

Empecemos a conversar

9
A —¿Cómo estuvo *el último video musical* que viste?
B —*Bastante divertido.*

Estudiante A

a. b. c.

d. e. f.

Estudiante B

> genial
> **bastante divertido(a)**
> **(muy) aburrido(a)**
> **horrible**
> **Me encantó.**
> **No me gustó nada.**
> **(muy) bueno(a) / malo(a)**

10
A —*¿Te gustan los picnics?*
B —*Sí, son muy divertidos.*
  o: *No, son demasiado aburridos.*
  o: *No, no los soporto.*

Estudiante A

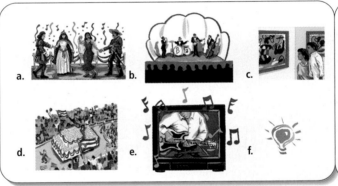

a. b. c.

d. e. f.

Estudiante B

> aburrido(a)
> alegre
> divertido(a)
> interesante
> largo(a)

136   Capítulo 4

Options

Strategies for Reaching All Students

Students Needing Extra Help
Ex. 9: Show how *último, divertido,* and *aburrido* will change with a feminine noun.
Ex. 11: Brainstorm what kinds of words will go in the blank for the second response.

Enrichment
Ex. 10: Have students justify their answers about what they like or don't like by explaining their own tastes or personalities.

11

A —¿Fuiste _a la exposición de arte de tus amigos_?
B —Sí. Y _lo pasé muy bien_.
  o: _No, no fui. Fui a ___._

de tus amigos

Estudiante A

a. del 4 de julio b. de la escuela c. de (nombre)

d. de (nombre) e. con tu familia f.

Estudiante B

me encantó

(no) me gustó

me aburrí

(no) me divertí

fue un desastre / horror

Estos carteles anuncian presentaciones de grupos de baile peruanos, dominicanos, mexicanos y colombianos.

Una orquesta sinfónica en el Teatro Real de Madrid

10 ESTUDIANTE A
a. ¿Te gustan las fiestas de disfraces?
b. ...los conciertos?
c. ...las exposiciones de arte?
d. ...los desfiles?
e. ...los videos musicales?
f. Questions will vary, but look for _te gustan_ + _los / las_ + plural noun.

ESTUDIANTE B
a.–f. Answers will vary, but look for adjective agreement.

11 ESTUDIANTE A
a. ¿Fuiste al desfile del 4 de julio?
b. ...a la obra de teatro de la escuela?
c. ...a la fiesta de disfraces de _(nombre)_?
d. ...al concierto de _(nombre)_?
e. ...al picnic con tu familia?
f. Questions will vary.

ESTUDIANTE B
a.–f. Answers will vary.

Cultural Notes

(p. 137, left photos)
Mexico City, with a population of approximately 8,236,700, is a cosmopolitan site to which performers come from all over the world, as these posters from the Salón Riviera demonstrate. The city has communities of immigrants from many other places in Latin America who support performers from their native countries.

(p. 137, right photo)
Madrid's Teatro Real is one of Spain's most important cultural institutions. Symphonic music and _zarzuelas_ (the unique Spanish operetta form) are often performed there.

Practice & Apply

Answers:
Empecemos a conversar

12 ESTUDIANTE A
a. ¿Prefieres las películas o las obras de teatro?
b. ...los discos compactos o los casetes?
c. ...los desfiles o los picnics?
d. ...los rompecabezas o los crucigramas?
e. ...la música rock o la música clásica?
f. Questions will vary, but should include logical pairs.

ESTUDIANTE B
a.–f. Answers will vary.

Answers: Empecemos a escribir y a leer
13–17 Answers will vary.

 Practice Wkbk. 4-3, 4-4

 Audio Activity 4.2

 Writing Activities 4-A, 4-B, 4-C

 Pruebas 4-3, 4-4

12

A —¿Prefieres _jugar damas_ o _ajedrez_?
B —Prefiero _jugar ajedrez_. Pero a veces _juego damas_.
  o: _No me gustan ni las damas ni el ajedrez._

Estudiante A   Estudiante B

a.   b.   c.   d.   e.   f.

Empecemos a escribir y a leer

Escribe tus respuestas en español.

13 ¿Qué diversiones prefieres tú? ¿Tienes tiempo para todas las diversiones que te gustan?

14 ¿Qué tipo de música sueles escuchar? ¿Vas a conciertos? ¿Con quién? La última vez que fuiste a un concierto, ¿cómo lo pasaste?

15 ¿Piensas que es difícil hacer crucigramas? ¿Por qué? ¿Sabes jugar ajedrez? ¿Quién te enseñó a jugar? ¿Con quién juegas? En tu opinión, ¿es fácil aprender?

138   Capítulo 4

Options

Strategies for Reaching All Students

Spanish-Speaking Students
Ex. 14: _¿Qué tipo de música es más popular en tu comunidad?_
Ex. 16: _Describe la última película que viste. Debes dar el nombre de la película y de los artistas, un resumen de la acción, y decir si te gustó o no y por qué._

 Un paso más Ex. 4-D

Students Needing Extra Help
Ex. 12: Have students go through the exercise once using the infinitives and then using the second response. Brainstorm which infinitives will go with movies, CDs, etc.
Ex. 14: Review possible kinds of music.
Ex. 15: Students will need help with the vocabulary to answer _¿Por qué?_ If no one plays chess, ask _¿Por qué?_

Ex. 17: Brainstorm other possibilities of things to do with little or no money. Bring in the section of the weekend newspaper relating to this theme.

16 ¿Sueles ver películas en el cine o en video? ¿Cuál prefieres? ¿Por qué?

17 Lee este párrafo sobre diversiones que cuestan muy poco o nada. Luego describe una diversión similar.

Quieres salir con tus amigos y no tienes dinero. ¿Qué haces? Pues, la diversión no tiene que costar mucho. En muchos museos la entrada es gratis por lo menos un día a la semana. Además, siempre hay exposiciones en bancos, bibliotecas y agencias del gobierno que son gratis. Y si hace buen tiempo, ¿por qué no vas a un parque o al zoológico? Sólo necesitas buscar en el periódico local para ver qué hay y pasar un día muy divertido.

También se dice

la cinta
el caset

el CD

la muestra (de arte)

Linda Ronstadt a menudo se viste de charra en sus conciertos.

Miles de Discos Compactos Diferentes
Usted puede escoger su música latina favorita y **nosotros se la enviamos** a cualquier lugar del país o del extranjero el mismo día que recibimos su orden.

MÚSICA LATINA DE TODOS LOS PAÍSES Y TODAS LAS ÉPOCAS

CASA DE DISCOS
7249 Point Loma Blvd. N.
San Diego, CA 92165
TEL: (800) 555-7979

Aceptamos las principales tarjetas de crédito.

Cultural Notes ☀

Practice

Reteach / Review: Accepting and declining invitations

Ex. 1: Have students name creative ways to accept and decline invitations. Write the expressions on the chalkboard as they are said. Some suggestions: *¡Sí! ¡Cómo no! / ¡Por supuesto! / ¡Me gustaría mucho! / ¡Genial!* or *No puedo. Tengo que. . . / ¿No podemos otro día? / ¡Qué lástima! Debo . . . / Me gustaría mucho, pero . . . / Lo siento mucho, pero . . .*

Answers:
¡Comuniquemos!

1 ESTUDIANTE A

a. ¿Quieres ir al concierto el domingo? . . . (a las siete)

b. . . . a la fiesta de disfraces el viernes? . . . (a las ocho)

c. . . . al parque de diversiones el sábado? . . . (al mediodía)

d. . . . al restaurante el miércoles? . . . (a las siete y media)

e. Questions will vary.

ESTUDIANTE B

a.–e. Answers will vary, but look for a variety of acceptances and refusals. If students use *¿A qué hora?* in their responses, look for correct use of time-telling by *Estudiante A*.

2 Answers will vary.

¡Comuniquemos!

Aquí tienes otra oportunidad para usar el vocabulario de este capítulo.

1 Túrnate con un(a) compañero(a) para aceptar o rechazar *(refuse)* las siguientes invitaciones.

A —¿Quieres ir a jugar fútbol el sábado?
B —¡Claro que sí! (¿A qué hora? ¿Dónde?)
  o: Lo siento. No juego fútbol.
  o: El sábado no puedo. ¿Podemos ir . . . ?

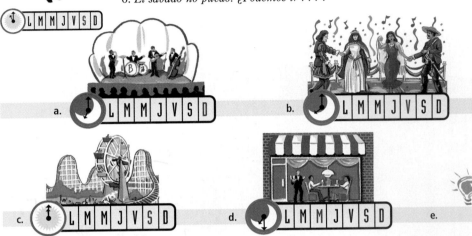

2 La nueva revista para jóvenes *¡Ya!* pregunta a sus lectores qué les gustaría leer. Con un(a) compañero(a), escojan dos de las secciones siguientes:

- televisión
- deportes
- cine y video
- moda
- música

¿Qué les gustaría ver en las secciones que escogieron?

—Me gustaría leer algo sobre ___ porque ___.
—A mí me gustaría saber más sobre ___. Creo que ___.

Después, hablen con otros grupos que escogieron las mismas secciones.

En la sección de deportes nos gustaría encontrar / leer / aprender / saber más sobre . . .

140 Capítulo 4

Options

Strategies for Reaching All Students

Spanish-Speaking Students

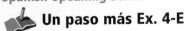 **Un paso más Ex. 4-E**

Students Needing Extra Help
Ex. 1: Use the vocabulary section of the Organizer. Brainstorm *dónde* responses. Review days of the week. Discourage students from responding with only *lo siento*.
Ex. 3: Model. Show students that *encontrar, leer, aprender,* and *saber* are interchangeable. Brainstorm the possibilities for the blanks. If available, use the vocabulary sections of Level 1, Chaps. 1 and 11, to help students express why they like to read these sections. Have each group do only two sections.
¿Qué sabes ahora?: Have students write this out so they can record what they have mastered.

3 Ayuda al recepcionista del hotel con las maletas de estos jugadores. Túrnate con un(a) compañero(a) para ser el recepcionista y el ayudante. Por ejemplo:

A —*¿De quién es esta maleta?*
B —*Es de un jugador de . . .*
A —*¿Cómo lo sabes?*
B —*Porque aquí hay un(a) . . .*
A —*¿Y aquel(la) . . . ?*

¿Qué sabes ahora?

Can you:

■ compare what you usually do with what you did?

 —**Generalmente ___ los sábados, pero el sábado pasado ___ .**

■ extend, accept, or reject an invitation?

 —**¿Quieres ir a ___ ?**

 —**___ .**

■ discuss and evaluate a leisure-time activity?

 —**¿Cómo ___ la fiesta de ___ ?**

 —**(No) Me ___ . Estuvo muy ___ .**

Vocabulario para conversar 141

3 ESTUDIANTE B
Es de un jugador de béisbol. / Porque aquí hay una pelota de béisbol, un bate y un guante de béisbol.
. . . de tenis. / . . . una raqueta, una pelota y zapatos de tenis.
. . . de golf. / . . . palos de golf.
. . . de hockey. / . . . patines, un palo y un disco de hockey.
. . . de básquetbol. / . . . un balón y una camiseta de básquetbol.
. . . de fútbol americano. / . . . un balón y un casco de fútbol americano.
. . . de fútbol. / . . . un balón y una camiseta de fútbol.

Answers: ¿Qué sabes ahora?

• Answers will vary, but look for the *yo* form of the present tense in the first blank and of the preterite in the second.
• Answers will vary, but should be logical.
• *estuvo* / Answers will vary. / *aburrí or divertí* / Answers will vary.

 Audio Activity 4.3

Enrichment
Ex. 2: After pairs of students have completed this activity, have them share their ideas with other groups or with the class: *En la sección de deportes a nosotros nos gustaría . . . Nos gustaría saber más sobre . . . .*

Present & Apply

Cultural Objective
• To discuss the paintings of Diego Rivera and Frida Kahlo, and what their work tells about them and their culture

Critical Thinking: Identifying Stereotypes
Diego Rivera is a world-renowned artist, most famous for his enormous murals depicting facets of Mexican life. Discuss the different ways of looking at Rivera's work. Stress that these are his viewpoints and that they don't necessarily reflect a national consciousness.

Multicultural Perspectives
Muralismo in Mexico dates back to ancient times when artists portrayed important events on the walls of temples and palaces. Twentieth-century muralists such as Diego Rivera and José Clemente Orozco, recording Mexico's past, present, and future, took this indigenous art form to truly remarkable levels. Rivera's murals depict clear messages of the poverty of the Indians, of the failure of land redistribution, and of corrupt politicians. Orozco's powerful fresco of Cortés and Malinche shows Mexico's roots. Have students find examples of

Perspectiva cultural

¿Qué quieren expresar los artistas en estas pinturas? ¿Cómo comunican las pinturas esas ideas? Míralas con cuidado. ¿Te dicen algo sobre las personas que las pintaron?

Roberto es un estudiante mexicano que está pasando un año en Detroit. Tiene un nuevo amigo, Mauricio, que espera visitar a Roberto en México en la primavera.

—Primero vamos a visitar el Palacio Nacional— dice Roberto—. Tienes que ver los murales de Diego Rivera. Te ayudarán a comprender la historia y la gente de México. Y después vas a ver varios de los autorretratos maravillosos de Frida Kahlo, su esposa.

—Los conozco a los dos—dice Mauricio—. Hay murales increíbles de Rivera aquí, en el museo de arte.

142 Capítulo 4

—Sí, es un pintor muy importante. ¡Y la obra de Kahlo es única! No hay nadie como ella.

Diego Rivera es conocido sobre todo por los grandes murales que pintó. Quería ayudar a la gente a apreciar la historia de su país.

Kahlo es igualmente conocida. Vivió una vida muy triste. De niña, tuvo polio y, de mujer joven, casi murió en un accidente de tranvía *(trolley)*. Después, siempre sufrió de un dolor extremo. En su obra vemos la tristeza y los dolores que tan bien conocía.

Mira con cuidado las obras de arte. Pueden decirte mucho.

Options

Strategies for Reaching All Students

Spanish-Speaking Students
Ask: *¿Conoces a otros pintores? Haz una investigación sobre un pintor hispano. Luego escribe uno o dos párrafos sobre su vida y su obra.*

 Un paso más Ex. 4-F

Students Needing Extra Help
Perspectiva cultural: Students may not have much information about artists. Ask the art teacher to help them gain an appreciation. Ex. 1: If your community doesn't have outdoor art, talk about places students have visited that do, and / or cities near you that do have this type of art. Contact the Visitors' Bureau or the Chamber of Commerce. They may be able to give you pictures.

Cultural Notes ☀

(pp. 142–143, photo)
The Alameda Central is the oldest public park in Mexico City and the setting for this Diego Rivera mural, in which he visually summarizes Mexican history from the pre-Colombian era until the early twentieth century. From left to right: *(man with top hat)* **Manuel Gutiérrez Nájera,** poet and precursor of modernist poetry; **Lucecita Díaz,** daughter of Porfirio Díaz, who was president of Mexico (1876–1880 and 1884–1911); **Carmen Romero Rubio de**

Detalle del *Sueño de una tarde dominical en la Alameda Central* (1947-1948), Diego Rivera

Las Dos Fridas (1939), Frida Kahlo

La cultura desde tu perspectiva

1 Mirando *La Alameda* de Diego Rivera, ¿qué puedes decir sobre la historia de México? ¿Hay murales en tu comunidad? ¿Son similares a o diferentes de los de Rivera?

2 ¿Qué atracciones culturales hay en tu ciudad o estado? ¿Qué comunican sobre la historia de la comunidad y sus habitantes?

Perspectiva cultural   143

Answers: La cultura desde tu perspectiva

1 Answers will vary, but students may make references to *La Catrina*—subject of the video they are watching—the skeleton with the feather boa around her neck. Through this character, Rivera pokes fun at the upper class of society. Students may mention the images of wealth and poverty, issues that still confront Mexico today.

2 Answers will vary.

Díaz, Porfirio Díaz's second wife; *(man tipping hat)* **José Martí,** poet who led the fight for Cuba's independence; **Diego Rivera** as a boy and, behind him, **Frida Kahlo,** his wife; *(skeleton)* **La Calavera Catrina,** character created by artist **José Guadalupe Posada** (represented at the far right of the mural) to poke fun at the aristocracy of the Díaz era. Rivera embellished the character with a feather boa, symbol of Quetzalcóatl ("plumed serpent" in Nahuatl), a pre-Colombian god.

(p. 143, bottom photo)
This double self portrait by Frida Kahlo was created during her divorce from Diego Rivera in 1940. (They were later remarried in 1941.) The Frida whom Diego no longer loves wears a white dress that is ripped. Her heart is broken and bleeding. The other Frida is still loved by Rivera. Her heart is connected to his small portrait. Kahlo represents her dual European and indigenous heritage through the dress and features of the two figures.

Preview

 Transparency 25

Multicultural Perspectives

In Latin America, tastes in music are diverse and vary from region to region. In the Caribbean, *salsa, soca, calypso,* and *merengue* are popular. The Mighty Sparrow, a well-known entertainer in the Caribbean, is best known for *calypso,* a type of music that dates back to the days of slavery. The slaves passed information from person to person through these simple rhythmic tunes. Juan Luis Guerra, a popular performer in the Dominican Republic, combines the rhythms of *merengue* and *salsa* with social commentary about the country's economic woes. Ask students if they are familiar with other kinds of music from Latin America.

Answers

A Elicit *nació, trabajó, ganó, sacó,* and *llegó.* The accented final *o* is a clue.

B *Fue a vivir: ir; Fue estudiante: ser; Fue después: ir; Fue representante: ser*

C *Tuvo un accidente:* He had an accident, *tener; Tuvo su primer gran hit:* She had her first great hit, *tener; Tuvo un accidente:* She had an accident, *tener; Hizo una donación:* She made a donation, *hacer*

Gramática en contexto

¿Quiénes son?

¿Sabes quiénes son estas personas famosas? (Sus nombres están al pie de la página.)

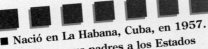

- Nació en La Habana, Cuba, en 1957.
- Llegó con sus padres a los Estados Unidos dos años después.
- Tuvo su primer gran hit, "Conga," en 1985.
- Fue después a Inglaterra, Holanda, Japón, México, Canadá y Bélgica, donde ganó discos de oro y plata en 1989.
- Tuvo un accidente de autobús muy grave en 1990.
- Hizo una donación de $2.000.000 para las víctimas del huracán Andrew en 1992.
- Fue representante de los Estados Unidos ante las Naciones Unidas también en 1992.

★ Nació en La Habana, Cuba, en 1962.

★ Fue a vivir con sus padres a Miami, Florida, en 1970.

★ Fue estudiante en la Universidad de Miami.

★ Trabajó en el restaurante de sus padres antes de ser famoso.

★ Ganó un "Grammy" en 1992 por su álbum, *Otro día más sin verte.*

★ Tuvo un accidente en el escenario cantando para la Copa Mundial en 1994.

★ Sacó su segundo álbum llamado *Si te vas* en 1994.

A Look at the verbs at the beginning of every sentence in the biographies. Which ones have regular preterite endings? What helps you recognize them?

B Look at the four sentences that begin with *fue.* In these sentences the verb *fue* has two different meanings. In each case, what is the infinitive form of the verb?

C Find the preterite verb forms *tuvo* and *hizo.* Can you figure out what they mean? What are their infinitive forms?

Respuestas: Gloria Estefan; Jon Secada

Options

Strategies for Reaching All Students

Students Needing Extra Help

Gramática en contexto: Begin the grammar section of the Organizer.
A: Find the verbs. If students have difficulty, review preterite endings.
B: Use context clues. If available, have students look at the Organizer from Level 1, Chap. 10. Write the four examples on the chalkboard. Point out that two examples have *fue + a.*

C: Point out specific clues.
El pretérito del verbo ser: Have students call out the present tense of *ser* and *ir* as you write the words on the chalkboard. Then write the preterite next to it. Write *hoy* and *ayer* next to the appropriate tenses.
Ex. 1: Again, emphasize that *fue + a* = went.

El pretérito del verbo *ser*

Here are all the preterite forms of *ser.* They are identical to the preterite forms of *ir.* The context makes the meaning clear.

(yo)	**fui**	(nosotros) (nosotras)	**fuimos**
(tú)	**fuiste**	(vosotros) (vosotras)	**fuisteis**
Ud. (él) (ella)	**fue**	Uds. (ellos) (ellas)	**fueron**

Compare the following sentences:

Jon Secada **fue** estudiante en la Universidad de Miami.
*Jon Secada **was** a student at the University of Miami.*

Gloria Estefan **fue** a Inglaterra y Holanda en 1989.
*Gloria Estefan **went** to England and Holland in 1989.*

1 Túrnate con un(a) compañero(a) para decir cuándo fue la última vez que fuiste a los siguientes lugares. Por ejemplo:

A —*¿Cuándo fue la última vez que fuiste a un restaurante?*
B —*La última vez fue hace dos días.*
  o: *Nunca voy a restaurantes.*

a.   b.   c.   d.

e.   f.   g.   h.

Gramática en contexto   145

Present

Answers

1 ESTUDIANTE A
a. ¿Cuándo fue la última vez que fuiste a un concierto?
b. ...a un desfile?
c. ...al cine?
d. ...a una exposición de arte?
e. ...a una fiesta de disfraces?
f. ...a una biblioteca?
g. ...a un picnic?
h. Questions will vary.

ESTUDIANTE B
a.–h. Answers will vary, but look for *fue* + time expression or the correct use of *hace* + time expression.

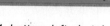

Cultural Notes

(p. 144, bottom left photo)
Gloria Estefan was born in Cuba and moved with her family to Miami after Fidel Castro came to power. In 1976 she began her career with the Miami Sound Machine, led by her then future husband Emilio Estefan, performing songs in English and Spanish.

Their song "Conga" was the first to place on pop, dance, black, and Latin music charts. She is shown here performing at the 1994 *Premio Lo Nuestro a la Música Latina,* an awards show honoring international performers of Latin music. It is produced in Miami by Univisión.

(p. 144, right photo)
Jon Secada received a Master of Arts degree in jazz vocal performance from the University of Miami. He sang backup vocals for Miami Sound Machine before making his first solo album in 1991. His first two hits, "Just Another Day" *(Otro día más)* and "Angel" *(Ángel),* reached the top 40 in both the Spanish- and English-language pop charts simultaneously.

Present & Practice

Re-enter / Recycle
Ex. 3: daily routine from Chap. 2
Ex. 4: school activities from Chap. 1

Answers
2 Questions and answers will vary, but look for correct preterite forms of *ir*.

 Practice Wkbk. 4-5, 4-6

 Writing Activity 4-D

 Prueba 4-5

3 ESTUDIANTE A

a. ¿Melba no tuvo tiempo de lavarse el pelo?
b. ¿(Tú) no tuviste tiempo de secarte el pelo?
c. ¿Sara y María no tuvieron tiempo de correr?
d. ¿Tomás no tuvo tiempo de hacer el crucigrama?
e. ¿Ud. no tuvo tiempo de cepillarse los dientes?
f. ¿Enrique y tú no tuvieron tiempo de desayunar?

ESTUDIANTE B

a. No, no pudo lavarse el pelo.
b. No, no pude secarme el pelo.
c. No, no pudieron correr.
d. No, no pudo hacer el cruci-grama.

---

2 Túrnate con un(a) compañero(a) para hablar de un viaje que hiciste con tu familia. Dile adónde fuiste. Después tu compañero(a) debe preguntarte:

- cuándo fueron
- quiénes fueron
- cómo fueron

A —*Fui a Los Ángeles.*
B —¿ . . . ?

El pretérito de los verbos *hacer, poder* y *tener*

You already know *hizo* and *hiciste.* Here are all the preterite forms of *hacer*.

(yo)	hice	(nosotros) (nosotras)	hicimos
(tú)	hiciste	(vosotros) (vosotras)	hicisteis
Ud. (él) (ella)	hizo	Uds. (ellos) (ellas)	hicieron

The preterite forms of *poder* and *tener* follow a similar pattern.

(yo)	pude tuve	(nosotros) (nosotras)	pudimos tuvimos
(tú)	pudiste tuviste	(vosotros) (vosotras)	pudisteis tuvisteis
Ud. (él) (ella)	pudo tuvo	Uds. (ellos) (ellas)	pudieron tuvieron

---

Options

Strategies for Reaching All Students

Students Needing Extra Help
Ex. 2: Some students don't take family trips. Suggest a place. Review months and means of transportation. Write the questions on the chalkboard. Model.
El pretérito de los verbos hacer, poder *y* tener: Review the present tense of each of these verbs. Point out that these preterite forms have no written accent marks.

Ex. 3: Review compound subjects. Provide a non-reflexive model.
Ex. 4: Have students do more than four subjects. Remind them that this is not a linear match for answers.

Enrichment
Ex. 4: Have students redo this exercise, giving far-fetched or obviously untrue excuses: *Tuve que lavar las ventanas del Empire State Building* or *Tuve que cuidar a la prima del Presidente de los Estados Unidos.*

3 El autobús que va al partido de tenis va a salir. Y nadie quiere llegar tarde. Con un(a) compañero(a) di qué no pudieron hacer estas personas antes de salir de sus casas.

A —¿Luz no tuvo tiempo de peinarse?
B —No, no pudo peinarse.

Luz

| a. Melba | b. (tú) | c. Sara y María |

| d. Tomás | e. Ud. | f. Enrique y tú |

4 ¿Por qué no pudieron hacerlo? Con un(a) compañero(a), contesta usando expresiones de cada lista.

A —¿No pudiste ir al desfile?
B —No, tuve que estudiar para un examen.

a. tú
b. (nombre)
c. (nombre) y tú
d. (dos nombres)

ver el partido de hockey
ir a la exposición de arte
ir a patinar sobre hielo
ir al concierto
jugar bolos
ir a la fiesta de disfraces
escuchar el disco compacto

hacer la tarea
ayudar en casa
escribir un informe
cuidar a mi hermana menor
salir con mi / su familia
hacer la cena
estudiar para un examen

Gramática en contexto 147

---

e. No, no pude cepillarme los dientes.
f. No, no pudimos desayunar.

4 ESTUDIANTE A
Questions will vary, but look for the correct preterite form of *poder* + an infinitive phrase from the second column.
a. ¿No pudiste . . .
b. ¿No pudo . . .
c. ¿No pudieron . . .
d. ¿No pudieron . . .

ESTUDIANTE B
Answers will vary, but look for the correct preterite form of *tener que* + an infinitive phrase from the third column.
a. No, tuve que . . .
b. No, tuvo que . . .
c. No, tuvimos que . . .
d. No, tuvieron que . . .

 Practice Wkbk. 4-7, 4-8

 Writing Activities 4-E, 4-F

 Prueba 4-6

 Comm. Act. BLM 4-2

Cultural Notes

Present & Practice

Answers

5 Answers will vary, but look for the correct forms of *saber* and a logical reason in the second sentence.

a. Mi madre sabe mucho sobre el arte.

b. Mis amigos *(dos nombres)* saben mucho sobre las bicicletas.

c. Tú y *(nombre)* saben mucho sobre los rompecabezas.

d. Mis hermanos y yo sabemos mucho sobre las pesas.

e. Tú sabes mucho sobre libros.

f. Yo sé mucho sobre películas.

g. Answers will vary.

 Prueba 4-7

Repaso: El verbo *saber*

We use *saber* to talk about knowing facts or information. Here are all of its present-tense forms.

(yo)	sé	(nosotros) (nosotras)	sabemos
(tú)	sabes	(vosotros) (vosotras)	sabéis
Ud. (él) (ella)	sabe	Uds. (ellos) (ellas)	saben

¡NO OLVIDES!

Remember that we can often omit the word "that" in English, but in Spanish we must always use *que*.

¿**Sabes** dónde juega hockey Javier?
¿**Saben** Uds. quién ganó el partido ayer?
Sabemos que ellos empataron.

- *Saber* followed by an infinitive means "to know how."

Yo **sé** jugar ajedrez.
¿**Sabe** Eduardo patinar sobre hielo?

- Both *saber* and *conocer* mean "to know." *Conocer* means "to know" in the sense of being acquainted or familiar with a person, place, or thing.

Jugando fútbol en Matapalo, Costa Rica

5 Túrnate con un(a) compañero(a) para decir sobre qué cosas saben mucho estas personas y por qué. Por ejemplo:

Mateo y Carmen / la moda — *Mateo y Carmen saben mucho sobre la moda. Trabajan en una tienda de ropa. (o: Leen mucho sobre ella / Les gusta mucho la ropa, etc.)*

a. Mi madre / el arte
b. Mis amigos *(dos nombres)* / las bicicletas
c. Tú y *(nombre)* / los rompecabezas
d. Mis hermanos y yo / las pesas
e. Tú / libros
f. Yo / películas
g. 🔆 / 🔆

148   Capítulo 4

Options

Strategies for Reaching All Students

Spanish-Speaking Students

 Un paso más Exs. 4-G, 4-H

Students Needing Extra Help
El verbo saber: Emphasize *sé.* Some students will insist on saying *sabo.* Remind them that this is the present tense. They have been doing preterite with the other verbs. They may interpret the note about *que* as meaning *que* always has to be used with *saber.* Give many examples to dispel that idea. In trying to show the distinction between *conocer* and *saber,* show students how *saber* is followed by question words or an infinitive. Students want to use *cómo* with *saber* in order to say *know how.* Tell them that "how" is included in the verb. Give examples of *conocer* and *saber.* See Level 2, Chap. 1 for examples of *conocer.*
Ex. 5: Brainstorm possible places of employment and activities associated with the *gustar* statement. Be careful not to let *saber* get lost in this exercise.
Ex. 6: Put both paradigms on the board or overhead. Have students decide first which verb to use. Point out the clues. Then conjugate and decide who the person is who does

148

6 Túrnate con un(a) compañero(a). Escojan el verbo *saber* o *conocer* para hacerse preguntas. Pueden usar estas u otras frases.

A —¿*Sabes dónde es el concierto de rock este sábado?*
B —*Yo no sé, pero creo que Mateo sabe.*
   o: *Sí sé. Es en el . . .*

a. ¿. . . dónde puedo comprar un casco de hockey?
b. ¿. . . a esa entrenadora?
c. ¿. . . quiénes juegan en el partido de tenis mañana?
d. ¿. . . a quién puedo pedirle prestado un bate de béisbol?
e. ¿. . . a los campeones de la liga escolar de béisbol?
f. ¿. . . cuántos goles metieron los jugadores de la escuela en el último partido?
g. ¿. . . quién ganó el campeonato de la Liga Nacional de Fútbol?
h. ¿. . . a algún entrenador de tenis?
i. ¿. . . dónde es el partido de bolos mañana por la noche?
j. 💡

El pretérito de los verbos reflexivos

Reflexive verbs have the same endings in the preterite as non-reflexive verbs.

7 Escoge verbos de la lista de la derecha para escribir lo que hiciste esta mañana antes de ir a la escuela.

Me desperté a las . . .

Luego, túrnate con tu compañero(a) para hacerse preguntas y contestar sobre lo que hicieron. Después, escriban un informe. Por ejemplo:

Nos despertamos a las . . . Ana se duchó en seguida, pero yo . . .

Ahora lo sabes

Can you:

■ talk about a person or an event in the past?
— Ayer Luis ___ el que metió todos los goles.

■ talk about what you did and why?
—Yo no ___ la tarea porque no ___ tiempo.

■ talk about things that happened to you?
—Me ___ la pierna jugando fútbol y me ___ en cama todo el día.

■ talk about someone you're acquainted with who knows a lot about a certain subject?
—(Yo) ___ a la madre de Luis. Ella ___ mucho sobre el arte.

¡NO OLVIDES!

Here are some of the reflexive verbs that you know:

aburrirse
acostarse (*o → ue*)
bañarse
cepillarse
despertarse (*e → ie*)
ducharse
lastimarse
lavarse
peinarse
probarse (*o → ue*)
quedarse
secarse

Gramática en contexto   149

6 ESTUDIANTE A
a. Sabes; b. Conoces; c. Sabes;
d. Sabes; e. Conoces; f. Sabes;
g. Sabes; h. Conoces; i. Sabes
j. Questions will vary, but look for the correct choice of *saber* or *conocer*.
ESTUDIANTE B
a.–j. Answers will vary, but look for logical responses.

 Practice Wkbk. 4-9

 Writing Activity 4-G

 Prueba 4-8

7 Answers will vary, but look for correct preterite forms and logical sequence.

Answers: Ahora lo sabes
• fue
• hice / tuve
• lastimé / quedé
• conozco / sabe

 Practice Wkbk. 4-10

 Audio Activities 4.4, 4.5

 Writing Activity 4-14

 Prueba 4-9

Cultural Notes ☀

know the information. Be sure students vary the "knower," using singular and plural.
El pretérito de los verbos reflexivos: Review the present tense of reflexives, especially the pronouns. Then review the preterite endings of *-ar* and *-ir* verbs. Remind students that there are no stem changes in the preterite of *-ar* verbs but there are in *-ir* verbs.

Ex. 7: The list is alphabetical. Separating it into *-ar* and *-ir* verbs can help students keep the endings straight. Give students a finite number of things to write about. Remind them that if two of them did the same thing, the response becomes *nosotros.* Brainstorm possible questions.
Ahora lo sabes: Have students write out this section so they can record what they have mastered.

(p. 148, photo)
Matapalo is part of the Osa Peninsula in the southeastern region of Costa Rica. Surfing and soccer are popular sports there, and after church on Sundays, many soccer clubs get together to play and socialize.

Apply

Using the Video

Episode 4 opens in the library, where Demetrio Alcocer is receiving a threatening phone call from don Silvestre Aguilar. Don Silvestre tells Demetrio never to reveal that Jamie is the real heir to La Catrina's fortune, which don Silvestre has acquired illegally. Moments later, Jamie arrives at the library looking for information about her great-grandmother. Demetrio offers to do what he can and instructs Jamie to return in a few days.

In the final scene, Jamie and María meet Felipe (Jamie's classmate from Los Angeles) in the recreational area of the university and decide to go swimming at the pool. María and Felipe have an especially good time together and

Para decir más

Aquí tienes vocabulario adicional que te puede servir para las actividades de esta sección.

recibir
to receive

montar a caballo
to ride a horse

manejar
to drive

el premio
prize

Actividades

Esta sección te ofrece la oportunidad de aumentar tus conocimientos de español al integrar lo que aprendiste en este capítulo con lo que aprendiste en capítulos anteriores.

1 Dile a un(a) compañero(a) qué crees que hizo el domingo pasado. Por ejemplo:

Creo que el domingo te despertaste muy tarde. Llamaste por teléfono a Lolita y saliste con ella. Uds. fueron a ...

Tu compañero(a) debe confirmar la información o corregir tus errores.

No, no me desperté muy tarde. Me desperté a las ...
No llamé por teléfono a Lolita. Y fui a la iglesia con ...

2 Cuéntale a un(a) compañero(a) cómo aprendiste a nadar, a cocinar, a montar en bicicleta o a hacer otra cosa. Usa estas u otras frases:

hace + *time expression*
aprender a / con
enseñarme a
ser difícil / fácil
cuando
una vez / dos (tres / muchas) veces
tener que
después de / antes de

Options

Strategies for Reaching All Students

Spanish-Speaking Students
Ex. 3: Have two Spanish-speaking students prepare the interview. One can be an athlete and the other a sports reporter. Videotape it to present to the class. Then, use it as a listening comprehension exercise. In addition to answering questions about the interview, other students can formulate questions they would like to ask the athlete.

 Un paso más Ex. 4-I

Students Needing Extra Help
Ex. 1: Use the vocabulary sections of the Organizers from this chapter and Chap. 2. If available, have students use the Organizers from Book 1, Chaps. 3 and 7. Point out why the *tú* form changes to *Uds.* Remind them to change back to *yo* for the response.
Ex. 2: If students need help, provide this model: *Hace diez años mi hermano mayor me enseñó a montar en bicicleta. Fue muy*

difícil. Tuve que practicar mucho tiempo. Pero, después de dos o tres meses aprendí, y ahora monto todos los días. Model several examples. Brainstorm other things students could learn to do.
Ex. 3: Model both questions and responses. Remind students they can do the exercise using a game they saw on TV. Review how the verb form will change in this report.

Una jugadora
de tenis mexicana

BICICLETA DE MONTAÑA DE MIGUEL INDURÁIN

DESCÚBRELA
EN BANESTO

Ha llegado el momento de
descubrirse ante una auténtica joya
del ciclismo: la bicicleta de montaña
de Miguel Induráin.
Un modelo tan extraordinario que
sólo nuestro campeón podía
darle nombre.
Ahora Banesto ofrece
a todos los
amantes
del

deporte un sueño hecho realidad:
la posibilidad de conseguir esta
magnífica bicicleta.
Acércate a la sucursal de
Banesto más cercana e
infórmate. Además, con
tu bicicleta te llevarás de
regalo el maillot
oficial del Equipo
Ciclista Banesto '93.
¡Es hora de descubrirse!

BICICLETA
BANESTO
INDURÁIN

B Banesto

3 Entrevista a tu compañero(a)
o a un(a) amigo(a) sobre el
último partido que vio o
en el cual *(in which)* participó.
Pregúntale, por ejemplo:

- qué tipo de partido fue
- quiénes jugaron
- cómo estuvo el partido
- quién ganó
- quién perdió
- si se lastimó alguien
- si alguien recibió
  un premio
- ¿...?

Prepara un informe para
la clase. Si quieres,
puedes incluir fotos o
dibujos en tu informe.

Actividades 151

she invites him to an upcoming
party for international students.
Meanwhile, Santana is spying on
them from his end of the pool.

 **La Catrina:
Capítulo 4**

Play

 Video Activity B

 **Para entender
mejor**

Play

 Video Activity C

 **Writing Activities
4-I, 4-J**

 **Comm. Act. BLMs
4-3, 4-4, 4-5**

Using Realia
Ask: *¿Por qué está Miguel
Induráin en este cartel?*

Enrichment
Ex 1: You may want to encourage students
to keep a tally of how many times they were
correct in their predictions.
Ex. 2: Another focus for this activity could
be other after-school activities, such as a
job or volunteer work.

Cooperative Learning
In groups of four, have students create a
"Who Is It?" game in which each group
writes out the clues to describe a famous
person or celebrity on an index card. Allow
about ten minutes for each group to write at
least five sentences. Then have each group
read its clues to another group and ask:
¿Quién soy yo?

Cultural Notes

(p. 151, realia)
Bicycling has increased in popularity during
the last decade and bicycle technology has
kept pace. This new mountain bike model
advertised in a Spanish magazine is named
for that country's cycling champion: Miguel
Induráin. Referred to as "Big Mig" by U.S.
sports writers, Induráin won his fourth suc-
cessive Tour de France in 1994. Cycling is
popular across Europe, and Induráin is
famous throughout the continent.

Apply

Process Reading
For a description of process reading, see p. 52.

Answers
Antes de leer
Answers will vary, but students may say that masks or whole-body costumes best conceal the wearer's identity.

Mira la lectura
Answers will vary.

¡Vamos a leer!

Antes de leer

STRATEGY Using prior knowledge

Have you ever been to a costume party? What did people wear? What kinds of costumes best conceal the wearer's identity?

Mira la lectura

STRATEGY Predicting the outcome

Read the first part of this story. Then ask yourself what comes next. See if you can predict what will happen.

Una fiesta curiosa

Había una fiesta de disfraces en la casa de los Márquez. Los invitados fueron al baile vestidos con muchos tipos de disfraces: de levantadora de pesas, de bailarina, de princesa, de astronauta, de médico, de Frankenstein y de torero. Pero, ¿por qué había tantas personas vestidas de fantasma? Una vez la señora Márquez vio a cuatro fantasmas cerca de la mesa de postres y tres cerca de la de ensaladas y sandwiches. ¿Y por qué entraban y salían tan frecuentemente del dormitorio de su hija Natalia?

La señora Márquez ya no pudo soportarlo. Se decidió a averiguar esta situación tan curiosa. Con mucho cuidado, sin hacer ningún ruido, fue al dormitorio de su hija. Se acercó a la puerta, escuchó por un momento el sonido alegre de mucha gente divirtiéndose, abrió la puerta y encontró . . .

152   Capítulo 4

Options

Strategies for Reaching All Students

Spanish-Speaking Students
Aplicación: ¿Te gustan las fiestas de disfraces? Si te invitaran a una fiesta de disfraces, ¿qué disfraz te gustaría llevar? Descríbelo y di por qué te gustaría llevarlo.

Students Needing Extra Help
Mira la lectura: Talk about context and picture clues. Call attention to the pictures.
Infórmate: Write word families on the chalkboard, drawing arrows to indicate the connection: *vestidas → el vestido.* Return to the text to see how the words are used in context. Give additional examples of word families.
Aplicación: You can prepare students for this activity by asking them to find the noun forms of *beber* and *comer* in the story and

to come up with the verb form of *disfraz.* Students know many more words. Have them keep a running list in their notebooks to be added to periodically. To avoid mention of inappropriate types of parties, suggest that the funny story be about a party students attended as a young child. Or have them model a "Once upon a time" story. Brainstorm as a class. Use the vocabulary section of the Organizer.

152

Infórmate

STRATEGY ➤ Recognizing word families

In the reading there are probably several unknown words that resemble words you already know. Use what you know about the meaning of the root (for example, *invit-*) and how the word is used in the sentence to help you figure it out. For example, *invitados* should remind you of *invitar*, "to invite." In the phrase *Los invitados fueron . . .* you see that the definite article *los* is used, that *invitados* is plural, and that it comes before a verb. So you probably figured out that *invitados* is a noun meaning "invited ones," or "guests."

1. Now try to figure out the meaning of these italicized words in the same way.

- *vestidos* con muchos tipos de disfraces
- de *levantadora* de pesas
- de *bailarina*
- con mucho *cuidado*
- *se acercó* a la puerta

What helped you figure out the new words?

2. Now turn the book upside down and read the ending to see if you predicted it correctly. If you did, or came close, what clues helped you? What happened in the first part of the story that led you to your prediction?

Aplicación

Use your knowledge of word families to complete this chart. Use a separate piece of paper.

dibujar	dibujo
	regalo
	entrevista
	lavadero

Find out if any of your classmates has a funny story about a party. Write a brief account of the story in Spanish.

. . . a Natalia y a una docena de sus amigos y amigas. Los más pequeños estaban sobre los hombros de los más grandes y se quitaban sus disfraces fantasmales, y en sus manos ¡llevaban platos de la comida deliciosa que servían los Márquez en su fiesta!

¡Vamos a leer! 153

Infórmate

1. *vestidos,* from *vestir* (dressed), *lavantadora,* from *levantar* (lifter), *bailarina,* from *bailar* (dancer), *cuidado,* from *cuidar* (care), *se acercó,* from *cerca* (she approached)

Aplicación

regalar, entrevistar, lavar

Enrichment

Aplicación: Additional activities: 1) Create a celebration that highlights something special about your school or your region's history, local culture, or a special natural feature. Decide on a name for the festival, the theme, and one or two events. Share your ideas with a classmate. 2) Describe seasonal festivals or celebrations in your area or in another area that you've visited or heard about. 3) Go to the library and research the kinds of festivals that used to be held in your area or state but that are no longer held. Try to find answers to these questions: What was celebrated at these festivals? What did people do? Why did the festivals die out? Would you like to have gone to one of these festivals? What has replaced them? Are there festivals in your area with a period or nostalgia theme? Have you gone or would you like to go to one of them?

Apply

Process Writing

For information regarding developing a writing portfolio, see p. 54.

see p. 54.

Todo junto

¡**V**amos a escribir!

Las reseñas (*reviews*) se publican en los periódicos y las revistas para informar al público sobre las películas, los programas de televisión y las obras de teatro. ¡Vamos a escribir una reseña!

1 Primero, escoge una obra para ver y describir en la reseña. Puede ser un programa de televisión, una película, una obra de teatro o un concierto. Después de ver la obra, escribe la reseña.

Para empezar, organiza tus ideas. Piensa en estas cosas:

- el nombre de la obra o del *show*
- cuándo y dónde lo (la) viste
- los artistas / actores / actrices
- lo que te gustó y por qué
- lo que no te gustó y por qué

Luego escribe el primer borrador. Sigue los pasos del proceso de escribir.

Los Lobos en concierto

Una exposición de arte en una plaza en México

154   Capítulo 4

Options

Strategies for Reaching All Students

Students Needing Extra Help

¡Vamos a escribir!: You may want to do these activities in groups or pairs.
Use the vocabulary section of the Organizer and, if available, the vocabulary section of the Organizer from Level 1, Chap. 11.
Ex. 1: Assign in advance. Students will need help with the descriptive vocabulary. Do a model based on a show or movie they saw.

Ex. 2: Brainstorm and model on the chalkboard or a transparency. Students may find it redundant to review a review. Have them start by critiquing the teacher's model.

2 Ahora escoge una reseña de un(a) compañero(a) y escribe tu opinión sobre ella. Escribe por qué estás o no estás de acuerdo. Puedes usar estas expresiones entre otras:

- creo que . . .
- por eso
- para mí
- por ejemplo
- porque
- además (*in addition*)

3 Para distribuir su trabajo, pueden:

- enviar las reseñas y las reacciones al periódico escolar
- incluirlas en un periódico publicado en su clase
- exhibirlas en la sala de clases
- ponerlas en su portafolio

El Ballet Folklórico de México es muy famoso por todo el mundo.

Cultural Notes

(p. 154, photo)
Los Lobos are a popular Mexican American rock group who count among their influences traditional *norteña,* or Tex-Mex *conjunto,* music. It is characterized by the accordion and the *bajo sexto,* a twelve-string guitar. *Norteña* music is basically a joining of the polka and mazurka rhythms of the German immigrants in Texas and the Latin rhythms brought by the Mexicans.

(p. 155, photo)
Supported in part by the Mexican Department of Tourism, the Ballet Folklórico de México is one of Mexico's premier cultural institutions. It was founded by choreographer Amalia Hernández in 1952 and had eight dancers. Now the company has two troupes: one which performs in Mexico and another which tours abroad.

You may want to assign parts of this section as homework or as an in-class writing activity prior to administering the *Examen de habilidades.*

Answers

Listening: *¿Francisco? Soy yo, Andrés. Francisco, ¿me prestas el casco, los patines de hielo y el palo? Me desperté tarde esta mañana y tuve que correr de casa. No tengo nada conmigo. Te puedo devolver todo esta noche. ¿Vas a estar en casa?*
Andrés has telephoned his friend Francisco in order to borrow his helmet, ice skates, and hockey stick. He is planning to play ice hockey.

Reading: 1. b; 2. a; 3. c

Writing: Notes will vary.

¿Lo sabes bien?

Esta sección te ayudará a prepararte para el examen de habilidades, donde tendrás que hacer tareas semejantes.

Listening
Can you understand when people talk about their leisure-time activities? Listen as your teacher reads a sample similar to what you will hear on the test. Why has Andrés telephoned his friend Francisco? What is Andrés planning to do?

Reading
Read the following excerpts from a teen magazine. Then match each excerpt with the right ending.

1. ¡Un desastre total! Nadie va a creer en estas aventuras de un niño que busca un jaguar grande que está amenazando a una comunidad pequeña del Amazonas. . . .
2. Por fin ganó el equipo de la secundaria Muñoz Marín. Y los ganadores defenderán el campeonato en un partido la semana que viene en el Estadio Bolívar. . . .

3. Las canciones incluyen la que cantó Ricky Gómez, "No me olvides." El grupo de jóvenes tiene mucho talento, pero todavía no encuentran su sonido especial. . . .

    a. . . . dijo el entrenador en un momento muy emocionante.
    b. . . . Seguramente va a salir en video pronto.
    c. . . . Quiero decir que todavía cantan como muchos otros.

Writing
Write a note to a friend to persuade him or her to accompany you to a special event. Here is a sample.

Querido Felipe,

¿Sabes que Patricia va a jugar en el campeonato de tenis de la liga escolar? El último partido va a ser el jueves. ¿Puedes ir conmigo? Va a ser muy emocionante porque las jugadoras de la Escuela Nacional también son muy buenas. Después podemos salir todos a celebrar—si gana Patricia. (No pude ir al partido el jueves pasado porque tuve que ir al dentista. Dicen que fue una ocasión muy alegre.)

Tu amigo,

Enrique

Culture
What do the paintings of Diego Rivera tell us about Mexican life? What do the paintings of Frida Kahlo tell us about her life?

Speaking
Work with a partner inviting him or her to join you in an activity. Here is a sample dialogue:

A —*¿Te gustaría ir a la exposición de obras de estudiantes en el Museo Universitario?*
B —*Ya la vi. Fui con mi hermana menor y me aburrí.*
A —*Pues, ¿sabes que hay un concierto en el parque el miércoles a la una?*
B —*¿Es de música clásica?*
A —*No. Es de jazz. Va a tocar Carlos Baker.*

156   Capítulo 4

Options

Strategies for Reaching All Students

Students Needing Extra Help
¿Lo sabes bien?: Remind students that this is just a sample, not the actual text.
Listening: Read the sample more than once. Remind students that they only need to listen for two pieces of information. Brainstorm what words they should listen for.
Reading: Tell students to watch for context clues. Because many tests have had narrations as opposed to excerpts, this format may cause confusion for some students.

Writing: Have students use the Organizer and write a sample note as pre-test practice. Brainstorm other special events and the corresponding vocabulary.
Culture: Have students review any notes they took during their first reading of the *Perspectiva cultural.*
Speaking: Brainstorm other places. Limit the number of lines of dialogue. You may want to have students accept or reject the invitation, not both, within one dialogue.

Resumen del capítulo 4

Usa el vocabulario de este capítulo para:

- talk about past and present activities
- extend, accept, or reject an invitation
- discuss and evaluate a leisure-time activity

to talk about sports
el bate
el guante (de béisbol)
la pelota (de béisbol, de tenis)
la raqueta (de tenis)
los bolos
el golf
el hockey
el palo (de golf, de hockey)
el disco de hockey
meter un gol
correr
levantar pesas
las pesas
montar en bicicleta
la bicicleta
el casco
el balón, *pl.* los balones
el patín, *pl.* los patines
patinar sobre hielo
el esquí, *pl.* los esquíes
el partido
la liga
el jugador, la jugadora
el campeón, *pl.* los campeones;
  la campeona
el campeonato
el entrenador, la entrenadora
empatar
ganar
perder *(e → ie)*

to discuss leisure activities
la diversión, *pl.* las diversiones
el desastre
el horror
el ajedrez
las damas
el desfile
la exposición, *pl.* las
  exposiciones (de arte)
(hacer) un crucigrama
(hacer) un picnic
(hacer) un rompecabezas
la música clásica
la música rock
la obra de teatro
la fiesta de disfraces
el casete
el disco compacto
el video musical
aburrirse
divertirse *(e → ie)*
pasarlo bien / mal
soportar

to describe people or things
alegre
último, -a

to discuss activities in the past
estuvo *(from:* estar)
fue *(from:* ser)
(yo) tuve que / (tú) tuviste que
  (from: tener que)

other useful words and expressions
bastante
prestar
pedir prestado, -a (a)
saber
tener tiempo de + *inf.*

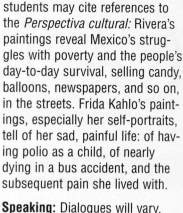

¿? Prueba cumulativa

¿? Examen de habilidades

Test Generator

CAPÍTULO 5
THEME: CHILDHOOD

SCOPE AND SEQUENCE Pages 158–189

COMMUNICATION

Topics
Toys
Animals
Playground equipment
Childhood activities

Objectives
To discuss the life and importance of José Martí

To talk about animals

To reminisce

To name toys

To discuss things you used to do

To talk about places children go

To talk about playground equipment

CULTURE

José Martí

GRAMMAR

El imperfecto de los verbos que terminan en -ar

El imperfecto de los verbos que terminan en -er e -ir

El imperfecto de los verbos ir y ser

Ancillaries available for use with Chapter 5

Multisensory/Technology

 Overhead Transparencies, 26–29

 Audio Tapes and CDs

 Vocabulary Art Blackline Masters for Hands-On Learning, pp. 28–32

 Classroom Crossword

 La Catrina

 CD-ROM

Print

 Practice Workbook, pp. 45–54

 Writing, Audio & Video Activities, pp. 29–34, 105–107, 159–160

 Communicative Activity Blackline Masters
  Pair and Small Group Activities, pp. 29–34
  Situation Cards, p. 35

 Un paso más: Actividades para ampliar tu español, pp. 25–30

Assessment

 Assessment Program
  Pruebas, pp. 71–80
  Examen de habilidades, pp. 81–84

 Test Generator

Video still from Chap. 5

Childhood in Spain and Latin America

As a general rule, children in Spain and Latin America are shown great verbal and physical affection. Adults are very tolerant of their behavior. However, children must show respect to adults, and are taught to treat their parents' friends courteously. They must address them as *usted*, and in some countries, such as Mexico, Nicaragua, and Colombia, are expected to address their parents formally as well. In these cases, the young child is addressed as *usted* as he or she is learning to speak. The difference between *usted* and *tú* is learned with the advent of increasing peer interaction.

When not in school, most children are cared for by parents, other family members, or maids, who either live with them or come to their homes on an almost daily basis. *Jardines de niños* (or *guarderías infantiles)* are common. They are similar to nursery schools where pre-kindergarteners learn social skills and have fun. Because many children attend private schools, and those who don't most likely spend their childhood in the same home, children who begin kindergarten together often remain classmates through high school. As a result, lifelong friendships begin at an early age, and there is much camaraderie.

In cities, small yards are the norm, even in upper-class neighborhoods. Children are often seen playing in the street, local parks, or *plazas.* They enjoy soccer, riding bicycles, flying kites, playing with marbles and tops, and jumping rope. Social interaction during play is much more important than possession of toys. Children in Spanish-speaking countries have dogs and cats for pets, but it is unusual for animals to be allowed in the house. They are generally not made members of the family, contrary to common practice in the U.S.

Birthdays and first communions are two important events in the lives of children throughout Spain and Latin America. First communion usually occurs around the age of ten. Although it is primarily a religious event, the child is often honored by his or her parents with a formal party that includes relatives, godparents, and family friends. A child celebrates a birthday with his or her peers, at parties that tend to be elaborate. Guests are expected to wear party clothes. In Mexico and Central America, one of the highlights of the birthday celebration is the breaking of the *piñata,* filled with candies the children scramble to pick up. Birthday party entertainment may also include a clown, magician, or puppet show. Each guest is presented with a party favor, which may be a beautifully sculpted piece of candy or another small but carefully chosen gift. The guests give the honoree presents, but unlike birthday parties in the U.S., they are usually not opened until all the guests have left.

Introduce

Re-entry of Concepts
The following list represents words, expressions, and grammar topics re-entered from Book 1 and Book 2 (Chaps. 1–4):

Book 1
numbers 0–31, *gustar* expressions, family members, places and buildings, household chores

Chapter 1
school subjects

Chapter 2
daily routine

Chapter 4
sports

Planning

Cross-Curricular Connections

Language Arts Connection *(pp. 162–163)*
Have students pretend that they are part of a large family from a Spanish-speaking country. Have them write a letter to Santa telling him what to give each member of the family and why they deserve their gift.

Sociology Connection *(pp. 166–167)*
As a homework assignment, have students interview their parents or an older relative about their childhood. Then have them write a brief composition about what their parents or other relatives did for fun, what they themselves did, and what they think their children will do in the future. Have students include any insights that they might have about the differences and similarities among the three groups.

Spanish in Your Community
Have students create bilingual posters for a daycare center or kindergarten in your community. Assign each one a color or a number (1–10). Provide a design format to ensure consistency. For the numbers, have them use simple shapes, such as circles, squares, and triangles for counting. For the colors, have them use easily identifiable objects, such as fruit or animals. Have a volunteer deliver the posters after you have made arrangements ahead of time.

CAPÍTULO 5

¿Qué te gustaba hacer de pequeño?

OBJECTIVES

At the end of this chapter, you will be able to:

- tell what you were like as a child
- tell what you used to like to do
- talk about what you learned to do
- understand how experiences in José Martí's early life affected his later life

Festival de cometas en Guatemala

159

Cultural Notes ☀

(p. 158, photo)
The skies over San Juan Sacatepequez just outside of Guatemala City are invaded once a year by giant flying animals, objects, people, and weird abstract forms swirling overhead! It is the *festival de barriletes* (Giant Kite Festival) held every November 1 to commemorate *el día de todos los santos* (All Saints' Day). People of all ages build kites and take part in the competition.

¡Piénsalo bien!

Mira las fotos. Los niños que vemos están haciendo sus actividades favoritas. ¿Qué te gustaba hacer cuando eras niño(a)?

"Aquí está mi nueva tarjeta de Juan González."

Cuando eras niño(a), ¿coleccionabas algo? ¿Tenías una colección grande? ¿Todavía la tienes?

Un niño de Caracas les muestra su colección de tarjetas de béisbol a unos amigos.

"¡Dos y dos son cuatro; cuatro y dos son seis; seis y dos son ocho y ocho dieciséis!"

¿Qué te gustaba jugar de niño(a)? Si saltabas a la cuerda, ¿cantabas canciones como ésta?

Niños hondureños saltando a la cuerda

160   Capítulo 5

Options

Strategies for Reaching All Students

Spanish-Speaking Students
Ask: *¿Sabes algunos trabalenguas o juegos infantiles? ¿Cómo son? Enséñale uno a un(a) compañero(a) de clase.*

 Un paso más Ex. 5-A

3 obediente
   A —*De pequeño(a), ¿eras* <u>*obediente*</u> *o no?*
   B —*Sí, era un(a) niño(a) (muy)* <u>*obediente*</u>.
      o: *No, era (muy)* <u>*desobediente*</u>.

Estudiante A

a. (bien) educado, -a   d. atrevido, -a
b. simpático, -a
c. ordenado, -a   e.

Estudiante B

4 jugabas con trenes
   A —*De pequeño(a), ¿*<u>*jugabas con trenes*</u>*?*
   B —<u>*No, yo no jugaba mucho con trenes.*</u>
      <u>*Jugaba con muñecos.*</u>
      o: *Sí,* <u>*yo jugaba con trenes.*</u>

Estudiante A

a. ibas al parque con (nombre)   d. tenías dinosaurios
b. te gustaba saltar a la cuerda   e. te gustaba montar en triciclo
c. tenías una silla alta para comer   f.

Estudiante B

Empecemos a escribir

Escribe tus respuestas en español.

5 De pequeño, ¿a qué lugares ibas a menudo? ¿Con quién? ¿Adónde te gustaba más ir?

6 ¿Cuántos años tenías cuando aprendiste a caminar? ¿Y a hablar? ¿Y a leer?

7 ¿Qué juguetes te gustaban más cuando eras pequeño(a)? ¿Por qué? ¿Tienes algunos todavía? ¿Cuáles?

8 ¿Te gustaba coleccionar cosas? ¿Qué colecciones tenías? ¿Qué coleccionas ahora?

También se dice

el velocípedo

los tarugos
los tacos

brincar a la cuerda

andar en triciclo

Vocabulario para conversar   165

4 ESTUDIANTE A
a. De pequeño(a), ¿ibas al parque con *(nombre)*?
b. . . . te gustaba saltar a la cuerda?
c. . . . tenías una silla alta para comer?
d. . . . tenías dinosaurios?
e. . . . te gustaba montar en triciclo?
f. Answers will vary, but look for the correct use of imperfect tense.
ESTUDIANTE B
a.–f. Questions will vary, but look for correct agreement of subject and verb.

Answers: Empecemos a escribir
5–8 Answers will vary, but look for correct tense of verbs.

 Practice Wkbk. 5-1, 5-2

 Audio Activity 5.1

 Pruebas 5-1, 5-2

 Comm. Act. BLM 5-1

Ex. 7: Provide necessary vocabulary for answering the *¿Por qué?* question. Ask why they still have the toys.
Ex. 8: Brainstorm types of collections. Review vocabulary for coins, stamps, photos, postcards, etc.

Enrichment
Ex. 2: As an additional assignment, students can describe other things they liked that they still like.
Ex. 5: Additional questions to expand responses: *¿Te gusta ir a esos lugares ahora? ¿Por qué sí o no?*
Ex. 8: Additional question to expand responses: *¿Por qué crees que la gente colecciona cosas?*

Present

Chapter Theme
Playground and behavior

Communicative Objectives
- To reminisce
- To talk about playground equipment
- To discuss things you used to do
- To talk about places children go

  Transparency 28

 Vocabulary Art BLMs

 Pronunciation Tape 5-2

Grammar Preview
Again, imperfect forms are presented here lexically. Encourage students to use them without explanation. If necessary, however, see pp. 175–177.

Teaching Suggestions
Preparing students to speak: Use one or two options from each of the categories of Comprehensible Input, Physical Response, or Limited Verbal Response. For a complete explanation of these categories and some sample activities, see pp. T16–T17.

Vocabulario para conversar

¿Cómo te portabas cuando eras pequeño(a)?

Aquí tienes el resto del vocabulario que necesitas en este capítulo para hablar de cuando eras pequeño(a).

el patio de recreo
el columpio
el tobogán, *pl.* los toboganes
el sube y baja
el carrusel
el cajón de arena, *pl.* los cajones de arena

166   Capítulo 5

Options

Strategies for Reaching All Students

Spanish-Speaking Students
 Un paso más Ex. 5-E

Students Needing Extra Help
También necesitas . . . : Present *portarse bien* and *portarse mal* separately. Avoid giving grammatical explanations until later on in the chapter. Review stem-changing verbs and their rules with *mentir.*

Because of the amount of vocabulary, you may want to organize the list into nouns, adjectives, and verbs. Divide the verbs by endings and / or reflexive vs. non-reflexive, etc.
Ex. 9: Review numbers. Discuss the ages at which these events usually occur.

También necesitas . . .

la guardería infantil	*day-care center*	llorar: (yo) lloraba	*to cry: I used to cry*
el vecino, la vecina	*neighbor*	pelearse: (yo) me	*to fight: I used to fight*
decir: (yo) decía	*I used to say / tell*	peleaba	
mentir *(e → ie):*	*to lie: I used to lie*	tímido, -a	*shy*
(yo) mentía		travieso, -a	*mischievous, naughty*
obedecer *(c → zc):**	*to obey: I used to obey*	consentido, -a	*spoiled*
(yo) obedecía		atrevido	
molestar:	*to bother, to annoy: I*		
(yo) molestaba	*used to bother, annoy*		
portarse (bien / mal):	*to behave (well / badly)*		
(yo) me portaba	*I / you used to behave*		
(tú) te portabas			
recordar *(o → ue)*	*to remember*		
preferir: (yo) prefería	*I preferred*		

> **¿Y qué quiere decir . . . ?**
> el kindergarten
> la escuela primaria
> la verdad
> desobedecer *(c → zc)*

Empecemos a conversar

9
jugar con
otros niños

A —*¿Cuántos años tenías cuando empezaste
a jugar con otros niños?*
B —*Tenía tres años.*
  o: *No recuerdo. Era muy pequeño(a).*

Estudiante A

a. **vestirte solo(a)**

b. **prestar tus juguetes a otros niños**

c. **ir a fiestas**

d. **estudiar español**

e. **ir a la escuela**

f.

Estudiante B

* Obedecer and *desobedecer* follow the pattern of *conocer: (yo) obedezco, (tú) obedeces,* etc.

Class Starter Review
On the day following the initial vocabulary presentation, begin the class with this activity:
In groups of three or four, have students survey each other by asking their classmates to name an event in their childhood when they behaved well; badly; were involved in a fight; cried a lot; were really spoiled; etc.

Re-enter / Recycle
Ex. 9: school subjects from Chap. 1, daily routine from Chap. 2

Answers: Empecemos a conversar
9 ESTUDIANTE A
a. ¿Cuántos años tenías cuando empezaste a vestirte solo(a)?
b. . . . prestar tus juguetes a otros niños?
c. . . . ir a fiestas?
d. . . . estudiar español?
e. . . . ir a la escuela?
f. Questions will vary.
ESTUDIANTE B
a.–f. Answers will vary.

Enrichment
Ex. 9: To extend the dialogue, students can ask each other: *¿Te gustaba más jugar con otros niños o solo(a)? ¿Por qué?*

Learning Spanish Through Action
STAGING VOCABULARY: *Pongan*
MATERIALS: pictures of playground equipment from the Vocabulary Art BLMs
DIRECTIONS: Direct students to place items in the "play area" of a nursery school as you describe them.

Practice & Apply

Answers: Empecemos a conversar

10 ESTUDIANTE A
a. ¿Cómo te portabas en el kindergarten?
b. ... en la escuela primaria?
c. ... en tu casa?
d. ... en la casa de (los vecinos)?
e. ... en el patio de recreo?
f. ... en el cine?

ESTUDIANTE B
a.–f. Answers will vary, but look for the suggested verbs in the imperfect.

11 ESTUDIANTE A
a. ¿Tus primos(as) son obedientes?
b. ... vecinos(as) son simpáticos(as)?
c. ... sobrinos(as) son consentidos(as)?
d. ... amigos(as) son tímidos(as)?
e. Questions will vary, but look for correct agreement of articles and adjectives.

ESTUDIANTE B
Answers will vary, but may include these opposite adjectives:
a. desobedientes
b. antipáticos(as)
c. no son consentidos(as)
d. sociables

Una familia hondureña

10 la guardería infantil

A —¿*Cómo te portabas en la guardería infantil?*
B —*Me portaba bien.*
    o: *No recuerdo (pero creo que me portaba mal).*

Estudiante A

a. el kindergarten
b. la escuela primaria
c. tu casa
d. la casa de (los vecinos)
e. el patio de recreo
f. el cine

Estudiante B

portarse bien / mal
molestar mucho a ___
llorar a menudo
ser muy (travieso, -a)

(nunca) obedecer a nadie
pelearse con los otros niños

168   Capítulo 5

Options

Strategies for Reaching All Students

Spanish-Speaking Students
Additional questions to expand responses:
Cuando eras pequeño(a), ¿tenías un(a) profesor(a) favorito(a)? ¿Cómo era? (Describe su apariencia física y su personalidad.)

 Un paso más Ex. 5-F

Students Needing Extra Help
Ex. 10: Remind students that the verbs in the responses for *Estudiante B* need to be conjugated: *ser* becomes *era*. Direct students to the *También necesitas...* list. Remind them to put a name in the blank for the *molestar mucho a ___* response. Brainstorm other possibilities for *ser muy (___).*
Ex. 11: Brainstorm possibilities for *e*. If available, use the Organizer for Book 1, Chap. 1.

Ex. 13: Students may need help with the structure of the responses to *¿Cuándo mentías?*.
Ex. 14: Point out that the last question is in the present tense; provide necessary vocabulary.
Ex. 15: Students may need help with the vocabulary for the *¿Por qué?* response.
Ex. 16: Show some possibilities for rewriting the sentences.

11 hermanos menores / educados

A —¿Tus *hermanos menores* son *educados*?
B —Sí, son *muy educados*.
  o: *No. Son muy maleducados y traviesos.*
  o: *No tengo hermanos menores.*

Estudiante A

a. primos(as) / obedientes

b. vecinos(as) / simpáticos(as)

c. sobrinos(as) / consentidos(as)

d. amigos(as) / tímidos(as)

e.

Estudiante B

Empecemos a escribir y a leer

Escribe tus respuestas en español.

12 Cuando eras pequeño(a), ¿ibas a una guardería infantil? ¿Te gustaba o no?

13 De pequeño(a), ¿decías siempre la verdad o mentías a menudo? ¿Cuándo mentías? Y ahora, ¿mientes a veces?

14 Cuando ibas al parque, ¿te gustaba jugar en el columpio, en el tobogán o en el sube y baja? ¿Te gustaba el carrusel? ¿O preferías el cajón de arena? ¿Por qué crees que a los niños les gusta tanto el cajón de arena?

15 De pequeño(a), ¿eras consentido(a)? ¿Y ahora? ¿Te gusta estar con los (las) niños(as) consentidos(as)? ¿Por qué?

16 Discute estas frases con un(a) compañero(a). Decidan si están de acuerdo o no. Si no están de acuerdo, cambien las frases y escríbanlas otra vez.

a. Los niños antipáticos suelen ser muy consentidos.
b. Es necesario portarse bien en la casa y en la escuela.
c. Los niños no deben jugar con pistolas de agua.
d. Los niños deben obedecer a todos los adultos.
e. Hay que decir la verdad siempre.

También se dice

el resbaladero
el deslizadero

el trapecio
la hamaca

el tiovivo
la calesita
los caballitos

ENSÉÑALES A PENSAR CON LAS MANOS.
MECCANO

Vocabulario para conversar 169

Practice

Answers
¡Comuniquemos!

1 Answers will vary for *Estudiante B*, but look for use of antonyms and correct adjective agreement.
a. antipático(a)
b. desobediente
c. desordenado(a)
d. divertido(a)
e. generoso(a)
f. impaciente
g. maleducado(a)
h. prudente
i. Answers will vary.

2–3 Answers will vary, but may include the following:
Rubén se pelea con los niños porque quiere el camión (de juguete). (La profesora debe poner el camión en el estante.) Anita tiene ropa sucia. (La profesora debe limpiarla.) Gabriel llora. (La profesora debe preguntarle por qué llora.) Patricia dibuja en las paredes. (La profesora debe ayudarle a limpiar las paredes.) Fernanda quiere un libro que está en el estante. (La profesora debe darle el libro.) Ignacio no puede ponerse la chaqueta. (La profesora debe ayudarle.)

¡Comuniquemos!

Aquí tienes otra oportunidad para usar el vocabulario de este capítulo.

1 Habla con un(a) compañero(a) de cómo eras antes y cómo eres ahora. Usa las características de la lista.

A —*Cuando eras niño(a), ¿eras (muy) perezoso(a)?*
B —*Sí, pero ahora soy (muy) trabajador(a).*
　　o: *No. Era (muy) trabajador(a).*

a. simpático(a)
b. obediente
c. ordenado(a)
d. serio(a)
e. tacaño(a)
f. paciente
g. educado(a)
h. atrevido(a)
i.

maleducado(a)
impaciente
desobediente
prudente
generoso(a)
antipático(a)
divertido(a)
desordenado(a)

2 Con un(a) compañero(a), habla de los juguetes para niños. ¿Cuáles son los mejores y por qué? Después, trabajen con otros dos estudiantes para hablar sobre lo que escogieron.

Options

Strategies for Reaching All Students

Spanish-Speaking Students
 Un paso más Exs. 5-G, 5-H

Students Needing Extra Help
Ex. 2: Model. Students may need help with the vocabulary needed to answer *¿Por qué?* Develop some questions for students to ask each other. The idea of choosing the "best" toys may be confusing.
Ex. 3: Remind students that there are two parts to this activity: identifying the problem and giving a solution.
¿Qué sabes ahora?: Have students write out this section so they can keep track of their progress.

Enrichment
Ex. 2: As an additional assignment, have students describe and draw a toy they would like to invent. Have them tell why they think this toy would be appealing to children.

170

3 La profesora de una guardería infantil no sabe qué hacer. Con un(a) compañero(a), describe los problemas que hay en la guardería.

Fernanda

Rubén

Patricia

Ignacio

Gabriel

Anita

Ahora decidan lo que debe hacer la profesora en cada situación. Pueden usar estos u otros verbos.

ayudar	lavar	poner
dar	limpiar	preguntar

¿Qué sabes ahora?

Can you:

■ tell what you were like when you were a child?
—De pequeño(a), yo era ___, y ___ mucho.

■ tell what you liked to play with?
—Me ___ jugar con ___.

■ talk about how old you were when you learned to do something?
—Aprendí a ___ cuando ___ años.

Answers: ¿Qué sabes ahora?

• Answers will vary, but the first blank should be an adjective and the second a verb in the imperfect tense.
• Answers will vary, but the first blank should be *gustaba* and the second a noun.
• Answers will vary, but the first blank should be an infinitive and the second *tenía* + number.

 Audio Activity 5.3

Ex. 3: The whole class may enjoy acting out the scene in the picture. Have students decide who will be the children and who will be the teacher (there may be more than one teacher). Suggest this plot line for the class to follow: The teachers have opposite attitudes as to how the situation should be handled; they get into an argument and end up acting like children.

Cooperative Learning
Divide the class into groups of three or four. Ask individuals in each group to prepare lists of toys and pets (from the vocabulary list) that would be appropriate gifts for each of the following types of children: *serio(a)*, *sociable*, and *travieso(a)*. Each person is responsible for one category. Have them provide brief reasons for their choices.

Groups should discuss the lists and choose one person to compile them. The remaining students from each group can report the results to the class.

Present & Apply

Cultural Objective
• To understand how childhood experiences affected José Martí's later life

Multicultural Perspectives
Gabriela Mistral was the first Latin American writer to be awarded the Nobel Prize for Literature. A native of Chile, Mistral loved children and wrote *Canciones de cuna,* a collection of lullabies. When the United Nations International Children's Emergency Fund (UNICEF) was created, Mistral said, *"Las Naciones Unidas son más que una Asamblea y una hechura política; ellas son la yema de una conciencia universal."* Make available a book of Mistral's poetry (or an equivalent in translation), and ask students to select a poem to present to the class.

Critical Thinking: Making Comparisons
Ask students if they know of anyone in U.S. history whose life or deeds paralleled those of Martí. Encourage discussions.

Answers
Answers to inductive questions will vary, but students may say that Martí participated in organizing Cuba's revolution while he lived in New York.

Perspectiva cultural

¿Por qué crees que hay una estatua de este héroe cubano en Nueva York? ¿Hay estatuas de héroes de otros países en tu ciudad? ¿Quiénes son?

EL CRIMEN: Incitar a la gente a rebelarse
EL VEREDICTO: Culpable
LA SENTENCIA: Seis años de trabajo forzad
EL ARMA CON QUE SE COMETIÓ EL CRIMEN: La pluma del poeta
LA EDAD DEL CRIMINAL: 16 años

Imagina que es el año 1870. Cuba es una colonia de España. Hay mucha intriga y mucha actividad política entre los españoles y los que están a favor de la independencia.

Tú tienes dieciséis años. Eres estudiante de secundaria. Escribes artículos políticos que se distribuyen no sólo en la escuela sino también en la ciudad. Y escribes poesía. Todo lo que escribes tiene el mismo tema: la independencia de Cuba.

Ahora estás en la corte en La Habana. Te dan una sentencia de seis años de trabajo forzado. ¿Por qué? Porque en una carta acusaste a un amigo de no ayudar a la revolución.

Ésta era la situación de un joven cubano, José Julián Martí y Pérez.

Martí pasó menos de un año en la prisión. Lo exiliaron a España en 1871 por sus actividades revolucionarias. En España, estudió y continuó su trabajo a favor de la independencia de Cuba. Escribió artículos, folletos, discursos y poesía.

En los años siguientes, Martí vivió y trabajó en México, Guatemala, los Estados Unidos y Venezuela. Escribía poemas y artículos, entre ellos, una columna en el periódico *La nación* de Buenos Aires. Era famoso en toda América Latina.

Cuando vivió en Nueva York, participó en la organización de la revolución cubana. Regresó a Cuba y murió en una batalla contra los españoles cerca de Dos Ríos en 1895. Siete años después, Cuba por fin obtuvo su independencia.

172 Capítulo 5

La cultura desde tu perspectiva

1 ¿Conoces a artistas de hoy que se dedican a una causa importante como hizo Martí? ¿Quiénes? ¿Qué hacen para la causa?

2 Imagina que José Martí vive hoy. ¿A qué causa se dedica? ¿Qué escribe?

Options

Strategies for Reaching All Students

Spanish-Speaking Students
Ask: *En la biblioteca de tu escuela o comunidad (o entre los estantes de libros en el salón de clase), busca información sobre la obra de un(a) poeta hispano(a). Puede ser Martí u otro(a) que te interese. Lee algunos de sus poemas, escoge uno que te guste y escribe tu interpretación del poema o tu reacción al leerlo.*

 Un paso más Ex. 5-I

Students Needing Extra Help
Have students take notes that can be reviewed in the *¿Lo sabes bien?* section. Read the questions from *La cultura desde tu perspectiva* first so that students can be looking for the information.
Ex. 1: Discuss the necessary qualities and then tie them in to people in the news. Students will tend to mention celebrities in sports and music.

Enrichment
Students can work in groups of three or four to research the name of a park, building, or street, and present their findings to the rest of the class.

Estatua de José Martí en el Central Park de Nueva York

Cultural Notes

(p. 172, photo)
Rubén Darío, the Nicaraguan poet, once said that José Martí did not "belong to Cuba alone, but to all of humanity." Martí, both through his writings and his actions, spoke out against the oppression and suffering of all people. When he was nine, Martí accompanied his father to work in a Matanzas sugar cane field. There he saw slaves for the first time and began to learn about the Caribbean plantation system. He was horrified, and the outrage he experienced at that moment guided his actions throughout his life. As an adult he wrote a poem describing himself in Matanzas and his determination to help end the cruelty and suffering of slavery and exploitation. These are the last two stanzas of that poem, *Versos sencillos:*

Rojo, como en el desierto,
Salió el sol al horizonte:
Y alumbró a un esclavo muerto,
Colgado a un ceibo del monte.

Un niño lo vió: tembló
De pasión por los que gimen:
¡Y, al pie del muerto, juró
Lavar con su vida el crimen!

(from José Martí: Revolutionary Democrat, 1986)

Preview

 Transparency 29

Teaching Suggestions
A: You may want to add another question: Which ending do you think goes with *Uds. / ellos / ellas?* Which one with *Ud. / él / ella?*

Answers:
A The ending *-aban* is found on the verbs *caminar, usar, jugar,* and *cantar.* The ending *-aba* is found on the verb *tocar.*

B The verb is *iban* from the infinitive *ir.*

C The verbs are *vivir, hacer, comer,* and *divertirse.*

Gramática en contexto

¿Cómo era la época colonial?

Mucha gente vivía en fincas. La gente hacía
su propia ropa y comía lo que la finca producía.

Los niños iban
a la escuela a pie.
Generalmente caminaban
largas distancias para llegar allí.

Los niños usaban juguetes hechos a mano y
jugaban con otros niños de la familia. Todos se divertían.

A menudo el padre o la madre le leía algo
a la familia por la noche. Muchas veces alguien
tocaba un instrumento y los otros cantaban o bailaban.

A When reading about what colonial families used to do, what endings do you find on the verbs *caminar, usar, jugar, tocar,* and *cantar?*

B Find the sentence that tells how children used to go to school. What is the verb? What is its infinitive form?

C The writer uses the words *vivía, hacía, comía,* and *se divertían.* What verbs do you think they come from?

174   Capítulo 5

Options

Strategies for Reaching All Students

174

El imperfecto de los verbos que terminan en *-ar*

You have already learned to talk about the past using the preterite tense for actions that began and ended at a definite time.

> Ana **cantó** en la fiesta anoche.
> *Ana **sang** at the party last night.*

The imperfect tense is another way to talk about the past. We use it to describe past actions without any indication of their beginning or end.

> Ana **cantaba**.
> *Ana **was singing**.*

Esta niña venezolana se divierte mucho durante el recreo.

• We use the imperfect to talk about actions that happened repeatedly in the past. In English we often say "used to" or "would" to express this idea.

> Generalmente **caminaban** mucho.
> *Generally **they would walk** a lot.*

> **Jugaban** con otros niños de la familia.
> ***They used to play** with other children in the family.*

• Expressions such as *generalmente, a menudo, muchas veces, todos los días, siempre,* and *nunca* can cue us to use the imperfect.

Here are all the forms of *-ar* verbs in the imperfect. Notice the accent mark on the *nosotros* form.

caminar

(yo)	camin**aba**	(nosotros) (nosotras)	camin**ábamos**
(tú)	camin**abas**	(vosotros) (vosotras)	camin**abais**
Ud. (él) (ella)	camin**aba**	Uds. (ellos) (ellas)	camin**aban**

• Since the *yo* and the *Ud. / él / ella* forms are the same, we often use the subject pronouns to avoid confusion.

Gramática en contexto   175

175

Present & Practice

Re-enter / Recycle

Ex. 1: sports from Chap. 4

Answers

1 ESTUDIANTE A

a ¿Qué deportes practicabas (tú) en la escuela primaria?

b. ...practicaba tu madre...

c. ...practicaban tú y tu hermano(a)...

d. ...practicaban tus hermanos(as) menores / mayores...

e. ...practicaba tu abuelo(a)...

f. ...practicaban tus amigos(as)...

g. Questions will vary, but look for the correct use of *practicar* in the imperfect.

ESTUDIANTE B

Answers will vary, but look for correct endings of *practicar* and a variety of appropriate sports.

a. Practicaba....

b. Practicaba....

c. Practicábamos....

d. Practicaban....

e. Practicaba....

f. Practicaban....

g. Answers will vary, but look for correct endings of *practicar*.

1 Con un(a) compañero(a), habla de los deportes que practicaban tú y otras personas en la escuela primaria.

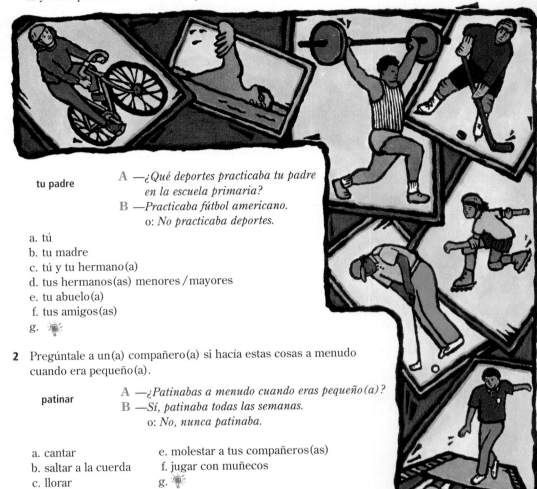

tu padre

A —*¿Qué deportes practicaba tu padre en la escuela primaria?*

B —*Practicaba fútbol americano.*
o: *No practicaba deportes.*

a. tú

b. tu madre

c. tú y tu hermano(a)

d. tus hermanos(as) menores / mayores

e. tu abuelo(a)

f. tus amigos(as)

g. 💡

2 Pregúntale a un(a) compañero(a) si hacía estas cosas a menudo cuando era pequeño(a).

patinar

A —*¿Patinabas a menudo cuando eras pequeño(a)?*

B —*Sí, patinaba todas las semanas.*
o: *No, nunca patinaba.*

a. cantar

b. saltar a la cuerda

c. llorar

d. montar en triciclo

e. molestar a tus compañeros(as)

f. jugar con muñecos

g. 💡

Ahora, dile a otro estudiante una o dos cosas que tu compañero(a) hacía a menudo.

—*Miguel patinaba todas las semanas y jugaba con muñecos todos los días.*

176   Capítulo 5

Options

Strategies for Reaching All Students

Students Needing Extra Help

Ex. 1: Ask students to determine the meaning of the question in order to cement in the idea of "used to." Review sports vocabulary. Let students guess what parents or other adults used to do.

Ex. 2: Ask students to identify the clue words in the directions. Point out that this exercise consists of two parts.

El imperfecto de los verbos que terminan en -er e -ir: Stress the simplicity of these endings.

Give more examples of *haber*. Give an example with *hay* and *había: Hay un gato en el sofá. Había un gato en el sofá.*

El imperfecto de los verbos que terminan en *-er* e *-ir*

Here are all the forms of *-er* and *-ir* verbs in the imperfect. Note that they have the same pattern of endings. Notice the accent mark on each ending.

comer / vivir

(yo)	comía vivía	(nosotros) (nosotras)	comíamos vivíamos
(tú)	comías vivías	(vosotros) (vosotras)	comíais vivíais
Ud. (él) (ella)	comía vivía	Uds. (ellos) (ellas)	comían vivían

• The verb *ver* is irregular in the imperfect only because the endings are added to the stem *ve-*:

(yo)	veía	(nosotros) (nosotras)	veíamos
(tú)	veías	(vosotros) (vosotras)	veíais
Ud. (él) (ella)	veía	Uds. (ellos) (ellas)	veían

• *Haber* is a special verb because it has only one form. You already know the present-tense form, *hay* ("there is / are"). The imperfect form is *había* ("there was / were, there used to be").

En la escuela **había** un patio de recreo muy grande.
En mi casa **había** dos baños.

Gramática en contexto   177

---

2 ESTUDIANTE A

a. ¿Cantabas a menudo cuando eras pequeño(a)?
b. ¿Saltabas a la cuerda...
c. ¿Llorabas...
d. ¿Montabas en triciclo...
e. ¿Molestabas a tus compañeros(as)...
f. ¿Jugabas con muñecos...
g. Questions will vary, but look for correct second person singular of the imperfect.

ESTUDIANTE B

a.–g. Answers will vary, but look for correct first person singular of the imperfect.

 Practice Wkbk. 5-5

 Writing Activity 5-D

 Prueba 5-5

Class Starter Review

On the day following the presentation of the imperfect of *-er* and *-ir* verbs, you might want to begin the class with this activity:
Have students create charts, with columns labeled *siempre, generalmente, a menudo,* and *nunca.* In each column, have students write three things they used to do with that frequency when they were five years old. Later, survey the class to find the most common activities for a five-year-old.

Present & Practice

Re-enter / Recycle

Ex. 4: daily routine from Chap. 2

Answers

3 ESTUDIANTE A

a. ¿Qué tenían tus tíos cuando tú eras pequeño(a)?

b. ¿Qué tenían tus primos...

c. ¿Qué tenías tú...

d. ¿Qué tenían tus hermanos y tú...

e. ¿Qué tenía tu vecino(a)...

f. Questions will vary.

ESTUDIANTE B

Answers will vary, but should include the following forms of *tener:*

a. Tenían...; b. Tenían...;
c. Tenía...; d. Teníamos...;
e. Tenía...; f. *Answers will vary.*

4 ESTUDIANTE A

a. ¿Uds. comían en la cafetería todos los días?

b. ...hacían fila antes de las clases?

c. ...veían videos en las clases?

d. ...leían libros en la biblioteca a menudo?

e. ...tenían tarea?

f. ...solían visitar museos?

g. ...escribían cartas a estudiantes de otras escuelas?

h. ...mentían mucho o siempre decían la verdad?

i. Answers will vary.

---

3 Túrnate con un(a) compañero(a) para hablar de lo que tenían estas personas cuando Uds. eran pequeños(as).

tus abuelos
A —*¿Qué tenían tus abuelos cuando eras pequeño(a)?*
B —*Tenían un proyector de diapositivas.*

a. tus tíos
b. tus primos
c. tú

d. tus hermanos y tú
e. tu vecino(a)
f. 💡

4 Pregúntale a dos compañeros(as) qué hacían ellos (ellas) en la escuela primaria.

obedecer siempre a sus padres
A —*¿Uds. obedecían siempre a sus padres?*
B —*Sí, obedecíamos siempre a nuestros padres.*
  o: *No, desobedecíamos a menudo.*

a. comer en la cafetería todos los días
b. hacer fila antes de las clases
c. ver videos en las clases
d. leer libros en la biblioteca a menudo
e. tener tarea
f. soler visitar museos
g. escribir cartas a estudiantes de otras escuelas
h. mentir mucho o siempre decir la verdad
i. 💡

Aquí hay un avión reactor, un Fórmula 1, un tren, una lancha motora, un camión, un robot y una nave espacial.

Aquí también.

MECCANO
El juguete de hacer juguetes

178   Capítulo 5

Options

Strategies for Reaching All Students

Students Needing Extra Help
Ex. 3: Review the model. Frame the exercise for students by saying: "When you were little, and you used to visit your grandparents, what things did they have that you used to play with or used to like to see?"
El imperfecto de los verbos ir *y* ser: Emphasize that the written accent mark is only on the *nosotros* form.

Have charts of all the different tenses of these two verbs posted around the room, with an example of usage.
Ex. 5: Review *al.*

Enrichment
Ex. 5: As an additional assignment to review location vocabulary, students can choose three of the places named in this exercise and describe where they were located and how they or the people named used to go there. Encourage use of expressions such as *quedaba cerca / lejos de, enfrente / detrás de, a la izquierda / derecha de,* etc.

El imperfecto de los verbos *ir* y *ser*

The verbs *ir* and *ser* are irregular in the imperfect. Here are all their imperfect forms:

ir

(yo)	iba	(nosotros) (nosotras)	íbamos
(tú)	ibas	(vosotros) (vosotras)	ibais
Ud. (él) (ella)	iba	Uds. (ellos) (ellas)	iban

ser

(yo)	era	(nosotros) (nosotras)	éramos
(tú)	eras	(vosotros) (vosotras)	erais
Ud. (él) (ella)	era	Uds. (ellos) (ellas)	eran

5 Usa las dos listas para decir adónde iban a menudo tú y otras personas cuando eran pequeños(as).

Cuando yo era pequeño(a), iba a menudo a la biblioteca.

a. yo	la biblioteca
b. mi hermano(a)	la escuela
c. mi hermano(a) y yo	la tienda cerca de mi casa
d. mi primo(a)	el centro comercial
e. mis primos(as)	el parque
f. mi vecino(a)	el cine
g. mis vecinos(as)	el supermercado
h.	

Algunas plazas tienen área de recreo, como ésta en San Sebastián, España.

Gramática en contexto   179

Cultural Notes

(p. 179, photo)
These children in San Sebastián, España, are enjoying the swings in a park playlot. San Sebastián, whose inhabitants are known as *donostiarras,* has substantial manufacturing, chemical and metalurgical industries. The city is famous for its beautiful bay and was one of Ernest Hemingway's favorite locations in Europe. San Sebastián is the capital of the province of Guipúzcoa.

Practice

Re-enter / Recycle

Ex. 7: daily routine from Chap. 2

Answers

6 Answers will vary, but should follow the format and include:
a. Mi . . . era muy maleducada, pero ahora es bastante educada.
b. . . . tímido(a) / sociable.
c. . . . antipático(a) / simpático(a).
d. . . . desobediente / obediente.
e. . . . gracioso(a) / serio(a).
f. Answers will vary, but look for agreement of adjectives.

7 Answers will vary, but may include the following verbs:
a. Cuando era pequeño(a) hacía la cama. Y ahora todavía hago la cama.
b. . . . sacaba / saco. . .
c. . . . lavaba / lavo. . .
d. . . . limpiaba / limpio. . .
e. . . . pasaba / paso. . .
f. . . . sacudía / sacudo. . .
g. Answers will vary.

8 Answers will vary, but should follow the format:
Ahora hay. . .
Cuando era pequeño(a) había. . .

---

6 Describe cómo han cambiado *(have changed)* tú, otras personas de tu familia, tus amigos(as) y tus vecinos(as). Por ejemplo:

travieso(a)

> *Mi vecino Jorge era muy travieso, pero ahora es bastante obediente.*
> o: *Mi vecino Jorge era muy travieso y todavía es bastante travieso.*

a. maleducado(a)
b. tímido(a)
c. antipático(a)
d. desobediente
e. gracioso(a)
f. 💡

7 Con un(a) compañero(a), compara lo que haces en casa ahora con lo que hacías en casa cuando eras pequeño(a). Puedes usar estas expresiones u otras:

poner la mesa

> *Cuando era pequeño(a) ponía la mesa. Y ahora todavía la pongo.*
> o: *Pero ahora debo pasar la aspiradora una vez por semana.*

a. hacer la cama
b. sacar la basura
c. lavar el suelo de la cocina
d. limpiar mi dormitorio
e. pasar la aspiradora
f. sacudir los muebles
g. 💡

8 Di qué hay en tu casa ahora que es diferente de lo que había antes. Por ejemplo:

Ahora hay un sofá blanco de cuero en mi casa. Cuando era pequeño(a) había un sofá negro de lona.

Un muchacho hondureño muestra a su hermanito cómo montar en bicicleta.

180   Capítulo 5

Options

Strategies for Reaching All Students

Students Needing Extra Help
Ex. 6: Brainstorm more possibilities. Have students make a list of who they will use as the subject of their sentences. Point out that in this exercise and in Ex. 7, each sentence contains a verb in the preterite and one in the present tense.

Ex. 8: Brainstorm things that might have been different in their homes when they were little: furniture, color of walls, etc. If available, use the Organizers from Book 1, Chap. 8.
Ahora lo sabes: Have students write out this list so that they can record what they have mastered.

Enrichment
Ex. 7: Students can also tell each other which chores they liked doing as children and why they enjoyed them.

Unas niñas españolas saltan a la cuerda delante de su casa en Andalucía.

Ahora lo sabes

Can you:

■ talk about your life as a child?

—De pequeño(a) ___ en un apartamento muy pequeño. Me ___ jugar con trenes.

■ tell what people used to do regularly?

—Los vecinos ___ de lunes a viernes. Y los fines de semana ___ de pesca.

■ compare what people used to do with what they do now?

—Cuando ___ pequeño(a), yo ___ los platos. Ahora ___ la comida.

Gramática en contexto   181

Answers: Ahora lo sabes
- vivía / gustaba
- trabajaban / iban
- era / lavaba / hago *or* preparo

 Practice Wkbk. 5-8, 5-9

 Audio Activities 5.4, 5.5

 Writing Activities 5-G, 5-H

 Prueba 5-7

 Comm. Act. BLM 5-2

Using Realia
Having students use reading strategies they've learned thus far, ask: *¿De qué se trata esta revista? ¿Cuáles son las palabras que te ayudaron a saberlo?*

Cultural Notes ☀

Cooperative Learning
Divide the class into groups of three of four. Have each group construct a composite diary that recalls the students' experiences as young children. Each group member should supply at least two entries for the diary. Entries shouldn't exceed one or two sentences and need not be real remembrances. Have a volunteer in each group record the entries. Afterward, the remaining group members can take turns reading their group's diary to the class.

(p. 181, photo)
These two girls are skipping rope on a cobblestone street in Casares, near Estepona, Andalucía, about 75 kilometers south of Málaga on the Costa del Sol. Brilliant white walls are a common sight in southern Spain, reflecting the intense Mediterranean sunlight. Residents whitewash *(blanquear)* the exterior walls of their homes using a solution of *cal* (lime) and water.

(p. 181, realia)
This monthly magazine published in Spain reflects contemporary interest in child care and child development. Directed toward new and prospective parents, this issue carries articles on such topics as inherited characteristics and how to interpret a child's artwork.

181

Pronunciation Tape 5-3

Answers: Actividades

1–3 Answers will vary, but look for the correct use of the imperfect.

¿Recuerdas?

Play

Video Activity A

Using the Video

Episode 5 opens at the Navarro family dinner table. Mr. Navarro becomes angry when Carlos wants to go to a party at the university instead of helping out at the restaurant that evening.
At the party, María and Felipe get to know each other, talking about their childhoods in their respective countries. Jamie shows up and they decide to leave and go to the Navarro family restaurant to keep Carlos company. Later, a fax arrives for Jamie from the library, telling her about a book on La Catrina.
Jamie goes to the library and finds the book, which describes La Catrina as a heroine of the Mexican Revolution. Traveling on horseback, La Catrina and her

Para decir más

Este vocabulario adicional te puede servir para las actividades de esta sección.

arar
to plow

cazar
to hunt

coser
to sew

cultivar
to grow

la calefacción
heating system

el maíz
corn

la vaca
cow

el caballo
horse

sembrar
to plant

tejer
to knit

182 Capítulo 5

Actividades

Esta sección te ofrece la oportunidad de aumentar tus conocimientos de español al integrar lo que aprendiste en este capítulo con lo que aprendiste en capítulos anteriores.

 Cada estudiante debe traer una foto de cuando era pequeño(a) o una foto de alguna revista. Pongan todas las fotos en una bolsa y escojan una. Según la foto van a inventar cómo era y qué hacía ese (esa) niño(a). Escriban un informe y léanlo en clase.

Este niño era muy... Lloraba...

Options

Strategies for Reaching All Students

Spanish-Speaking Students
Ex. 3: After this exercise, have students do this assignment: *Prepara una cápsula que se va a abrir en el futuro. ¿Qué te gustaría incluir en ella para indicar cómo era tu familia, cómo eras tú y cómo vivías? Explica por qué escogiste cada artículo.*

Students Needing Extra Help
Ex. 1: Using magazine pictures is a good alternative to having students bring in their own pictures: some may not have any or won't want to bring them in. Have extra magazine photos available.
Brainstorm possible characteristics and verbs that would apply to children.

Ex. 2: Divide the class into three groups and assign them specific areas. Have resources available or give them a few days to investigate.
Ex. 3: Brainstorm what things in your town could be considered ruins in the future: a statue in the park or an older school, for example. Do this exercise as a whole class.

2 ¿Cómo era tu comunidad hace 50 o 100 años? En grupo, investiguen sobre:

- las casas
- los trabajos
- la comida
- la ropa
- los pasatiempos
- los deportes
- el transporte

Preparen un informe para la clase. Pueden usar la selección de la página 174 como modelo e incluir dibujos o fotos de revistas. Por ejemplo:

En nuestra comunidad, había muy pocas casas . . .

3 Imagina que es el año 2999. Astronautas de otro planeta llegan a las ruinas de tu ciudad. ¿Qué encuentran? En grupo, hagan una lista. Por ejemplo:

- las ruinas de algún monumento
- muchos vasos de plástico con el nombre de un restaurante
- partes de computadoras
- discos compactos
- muchos tenis
- un oso de peluche
- una pistola de agua
- un carrusel

Ahora, escriban las conclusiones de los astronautas y presenten su informe a la clase. Por ejemplo:

En Nueva York había personas de metal muy grandes. La gente usaba zapatos bastante feos, pero muy cómodos.

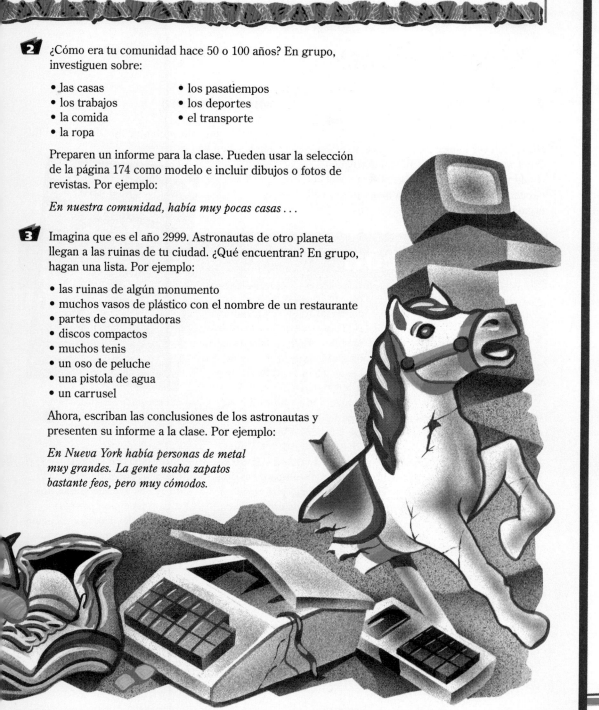

followers robbed from the rich to give to the poor, until she was betrayed and her property stolen from her.

 La Catrina: Capítulo 5

Play

 Video Activity B

 Para entender mejor

Play

 Video Activity C

 Writing Activities 5-I, 5-J

 Comm. Act. BLMs 5-3, 5-4, 5-5

Enrichment
Ex. 2: Additional topics to investigate:
¿Cómo eran las escuelas en tu comunidad?
¿Las tiendas? ¿Qué cosas no había en la biblioteca que sí hay ahora?

Apply

Process Reading
For a description of process reading, see p. 52.

Teaching Suggestions
You may want to set parameters and time limits for this activity. Each group could choose one or two topics and write two to three sentences about each. You could also assign a topic to each group to answer on a given day.

Multicultural Perspectives
Baseball is especially popular in the Caribbean countries of Cuba, the Dominican Republic, and Puerto Rico. Many players from these countries have become major leaguers in the U.S. The Dominican Republic has produced more professional major leaguers than any other Latin American country. Quisqueya Stadium in the capital of Santo Domingo is the national center of baseball. Young players aspire to be seen there by a scout from the U.S. Ask students if they can name any U.S. baseball players from the Dominican Republic.

¡Vamos a leer!

Antes de leer

STRATEGY Using prior knowledge

Have you ever known a really amazing athlete? What was he or she like? What information would you expect to find in the life story of an outstanding athlete? How is a biography usually organized?

Mira la lectura

Read the story through quickly. Did you find the information you expected?

Esta estatua de Roberto Clemente queda enfrente del estadio en Pittsburgh.

El campeón

—¡Roberto! ¡Roberto, ven! ¡Ya es hora de comer!

El pequeño Roberto no prestaba atención. Era un muchacho obediente, pero en ese momento, sólo pensaba en lo que hacía—jugar béisbol.

Roberto Clemente nació en 1934 en la pequeña comunidad de Carolina, Puerto Rico. Jugaba béisbol todos los días, pero también tenía que ir a la escuela y trabajar. Trabajaba porque quería comprarse una bicicleta. Después de trabajar tres años, tuvo bastante dinero para comprarse una. En la escuela secundaria, Roberto era un muchacho tímido, pero en el campo de béisbol su timidez desaparecía.

En 1953 representantes de los Brooklyn Dodgers fueron a Puerto Rico para observar y contratar a nuevos jugadores. —¡Tenía que contratarlo! Era el mejor atleta innato que había visto,— dijo el scout de los Dodgers cuando vio al joven Roberto jugar. Los Dodgers lo mandaron a su equipo de Montreal, Canadá. De allí pasó a los Piratas de Pittsburgh en 1955. Cinco años más tarde los Piratas ganaron el campeonato de la Liga Nacional y la Serie Mundial. Clemente fue nombrado el Jugador Más Valioso de la liga en 1966. El 24 de julio de 1970 se celebró la Noche de Roberto Clemente en el estadio Three Rivers de Pittsburgh para honrar al pelotero más famoso y más querido del equipo.

En diciembre de 1972, ocurrió un terrible terremoto en Nicaragua. En seguida Clemente organizó un vuelo de ayuda. Llevaba alimentos, ropa y medicina para las víctimas del desastre. El avión era viejo y pequeño y pesaba mucho, pero Clemente insistió en ir.

Cuando desapareció el avión en el mar poco antes de la medianoche del 31 de diciembre, murió no sólo un gran atleta sino un gran hombre.

184   Capítulo 5

Options

Strategies for Reaching All Students

Students Needing Extra Help
Antes de leer: As a class, generate a list of what students might expect to find in the life story of an outstanding athlete. Have them check off the items as they find them.
Infórmate: Students may have some difficulty recognizing the verb tense and making the connection with age and high school. After each entry on the list generated for *Antes de leer,* have students fill in Clemente's age.

Aplicación: Emphasize that the preterite is used for events in the past that have a definite beginning and end and that the imperfect is used to describe.
Have students form small groups to figure out the name of the person being described. Then have them list the person's accomplishments. They may need help putting the words into sentences.

Infórmate

STRATEGY ➤ Recognizing time expressions

Time expressions will help you understand writing that is organized chronologically, as a biography usually is. Some of the time expressions in this biography are:

- …en 1934…
- Cinco años más tarde…
- En diciembre de 1972…

Other expressions can help you to keep track of time by referring to activities associated with a certain stage of life. For example:

- …tenía que ir a la escuela…
- En la escuela secundaria, …

1. Now reread the biography. When you come to an expression that helps you fix the time, stop and quickly calculate how old Roberto was then.

2. Why is Roberto Clemente one of baseball's most honored players? Why is he considered a great humanitarian?

Managua, Nicaragua

La ciudad de Managua después del terremoto de 1972

BOB CLEMENTE — OUTFIELD PIRATES

Aplicación

Write three to five sentences with time expressions about a famous athlete or other famous person. Then read one sentence to a partner and ask him or her to guess who it is about. If your partner can't guess, read the next sentence, and so on. For example, these statements are about Nancy López.

1. Ganó el Torneo de Golf Femenino de Nuevo México cuando tenía 12 años.
2. En 1978 ganó nueve torneos de golf, entre ellos el de la Asociación de Mujeres Golfistas Profesionales (LPGA en inglés).
3. Siete años después, ganó cinco torneos, entre ellos el LPGA una vez más.

¡Vamos a leer! 185

Cultural Notes ☼

(p. 184, photo)
Artist Susan Wagner's 12-foot-high bronze sculpture of Roberto Clemente, located at Three Rivers Stadium in Pittsburgh, was dedicated at the start of the 1994 All Star Games hosted by the Pirates. 1994 would have marked Clemente's 60th birthday and is the 22nd year since his death. Clemente wears a sleeveless 1960s uniform and is rendered in an action pose, dropping his special knobless bat after a hit. The black

granite base of the statue reads "The Great One" and a baseball field design below his feet incorporates soil from Puerto Rico (first base), the old Forbes Field ball park (second base), and Three Rivers Stadium (third base). A timeline encircles the base with highlights from Clemente's career. However, the section between third base and home is left blank to symbolize the incompleteness of Clemente's life.

(p. 185, realia)
Roberto Clemente's early baseball cards remain a favorite among collectors. A 1955 Roberto Clemente "rookie" card in mint condition sells for about $2,000 on the market today. Clemente's second year (1956) card earns as much as $400. Clemente's cards are popular in part because of the star's reputation for generosity and kindness.

Apply

Process Writing
For information regarding developing a writing portfolio, see p. 54.

see p. 54.

Todo junto

¡Vamos a escribir!

Todos tenemos una persona especial en la vida. Puede ser un(a) pariente(a), un(a) amigo(a) o un(a) profesor(a). Vamos a escribir una biografía breve de una persona especial.

1 Primero entrevista a la persona o a alguien que la conoce. Contesta estas preguntas:

- ¿Cuándo y dónde nació?
- ¿Dónde vivía la familia cuando nació?
- ¿Cómo era de pequeño(a)?
- ¿Qué hacía de pequeño(a)? ¿De joven?
- ¿Cómo es ahora?
- ¿Qué hace ahora?

2 Organiza tus ideas en orden cronológico. Escribe el primer borrador. Sigue los pasos del proceso de escribir.

Ahora escribe una anécdota de la vida de la persona que escogiste. Debe ser una anécdota que revele algo de su carácter. Por ejemplo, ¿hizo alguna vez algo muy difícil? ¿Algo increíble?

3 Para distribuir las biografías y anécdotas, pueden:

- enviarlas a las personas de quienes escribieron
- enviarlas al periódico o a la revista literaria escolar
- incluirlas en un libro titulado *Personas especiales*
- ponerlas en sus portafolios

Un gaucho de San Antonio de Areco, Argentina

Entrevista con un gaucho

	ESTUDIANTE	¿Qué es un gaucho?
	GAUCHO	Somos vaqueros.
	ESTUDIANTE	¿La ropa que usa es típica?
	GAUCHO	Sí. El poncho, el sombrero negro, los pantalones flojos, el cinturón de plata y las botas son muy típicos.

186 Capítulo 5

Options

Strategies for Reaching All Students

Students Needing Extra Help
Ex. 1: Point out that three tenses are being used. Use the verb charts in the room, or if available, from Organizers from Book 1. Students will need help formulating sentences. Model, using yourself.
Ex. 2: Explain that an anecdote is a short account of an interesting or funny incident in someone's life. Some suggestions for topics: a friend who helped someone, a student who won an award, an athlete who scored the winning basket.

Enrichment
Point out that when speaking to their grandparents, many Spanish speakers use the *Ud.* form as a sign of respect.

Entrevista con mi abuela		
⚪	NIETA	¿Dónde vivía tu familia cuando naciste?
	ABUELA	Aquí en esta misma vecindad. Sólo a unas cuadras de donde vivo hoy.
⚪	NIETA	¿Qué hacías cuando eras niña?
	ABUELA	Recuerdo que iba a recoger flores y frutas con mis hermanos. A mi mamá—tu bisabuela—le encantaba tener flores frescas en la casa.
⚪		

Una niña en los brazos de su abuelita en Argentina

Un ecuatoriano en camino a su trabajo

Entrevista con un profesor de español		
⚪	ESTUDIANTE	¿Puede Ud. decirme cuándo y dónde nació?
	SR. ALLENDE	Nací en Ecuador. Ayer cumplí 30 años. ¡Tú puedes calcular el año!
	ESTUDIANTE	¿Qué hacía de pequeño?
⚪	SR. ALLENDE	A mi y a mis amigos nos encantaba montar en bicicleta. También pasábamos muchas horas

Cultural Notes

(p. 186, photo)
Gauchos are part of the national identity of Argentina. They represent freedom, independence, and strength. *Gauchos* are the cowboys who work on the *pampas,* herding cattle and doing other agricultural work. Some *gauchos* claim to have both Spanish and indigenous parentage and thus are among Argentina's small *mestizo* population. The modern *gaucho* in this photo leans on a pick-up truck instead of a horse.

(p. 187, top photo)
This girl and her grandmother are residents of Tucumán, a province in northern Argentina. The capital of the province, also called Tucumán, played a significant role in the history of Argentina. In 1816, members of the Congreso General Constituyente met there to proclaim their independence from Spain.

Assess & Summarize

Test Preparation
You may want to assign parts of this section as homework or as an in-class writing activity prior to administering the *Examen de habilidades*.

Answers
Listening: *De pequeña yo lloraba mucho y me peleaba con los otros niños. Era una niña muy traviesa y desobediente. Mi hermana, al contrario, se portaba bien y nunca se peleaba con nadie. Creo que es porque ella fue a una guardería infantil y yo no.*
Tina cried a lot and fought with other children; she was mischievous and disobedient. Her sister was polite and never fought with anyone. They were probably different because her sister went to a daycare center and Tina didn't.

Reading: d, a, c

Writing: Descriptions will vary.

Culture: Answers will vary.

Speaking: Dialogues will vary.

¿Lo sabes bien?

Esta sección te ayudará a preparte para el examen de habilidades.

Listening
Can you understand when people talk about what they were like as children? Listen as your teacher reads a sample similar to what you will hear on the test. How were Tina and her sister different? Why were they different?

Reading
Read the following fragment of an autobiography. Then complete the sentences with the right time expressions. (One choice will not be used.)

Cuando yo era niño, mi mamá me hacía animales de peluche. Mi papá me hacía juguetes de madera. ___ me hizo una casa de madera en un árbol. Yo no entendía por qué mis padres no me compraban juguetes de plástico, como los de mis compañeros. ___ por fin entendí. Estudiamos el medio ambiente y la importancia de reciclar los materiales. Mis padres estaban reciclando las cosas. ___ yo también hago juguetes de madera para mi hija.

Writing
Clara is going to spend a year in Guatemala as an exchange student. A Guatemala City newspaper has asked for a brief description of her as a child. This is what a long-time friend wrote. Write a similar description of *your* best friend.

> Recuerdo que Clara era una niña muy simpática y trabajadora. Cuando no conocía a la gente, era un poco tímida, pero después era sociable. Éramos vecinos. Íbamos a la misma escuela. Los fines de semana jugábamos en el parque. Yo sé que Clara va a tener muchos amigos en Guatemala.

Culture
If you had been a friend of José Martí, would you have helped him fight for Cuban independence? Why?

Speaking
With a partner, talk about your childhood. Ask one another some questions to find out what you were like as young children. Here is a sample dialogue.

A —*Cuando tenías cinco años, ¿cómo eras?*
B —*Obediente pero a veces un poco travieso. ¿Y tú?*
A —*Casi siempre me portaba bien, pero también era traviesa. ¿Con qué te gustaba jugar?*
B —*Me gustaban los bloques, los trenes eléctricos y las pistolas de agua. ¿Qué preferías tú?*
A —*A mí me encantaba montar en triciclo y saltar a la cuerda.*

a. cuando estaba en la escuela secundaria
b. el año pasado
c. ahora
d. cuando cumplí ocho años

Options

Strategies for Reaching All Students

Students Needing Extra Help
Have students write out this section so that they can check off what they have mastered. Remind students that this is just a sample of what will be on the test.
Listening: Read the listening sample more than once. Remind students that they only have to listen for two pieces of information. Brainstorm the words for which students should be listening.

Reading: Emphasize that one choice won't be used. Review the meanings of the choices. Put the choices in chronological order: eight years old, high school, last year, and now. This should help them as they try to connect the reading material to the time that it happened. See if students can recognize that one choice is a preterite.
Writing: Have students use the Organizer and write a sample description before the

test as practice. Brainstorm other description words. If available, use the Organizers from Book 1.
Culture: Have students review any notes they took during their reading of the *Perspectiva cultural*. Discuss the pros and cons of joining forces with Martí.
Speaking: Limit the number of lines of dialogue. Use the vocabulary section of the Organizer.

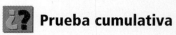

Resumen del capítulo 5

Usa el vocabulario de este capítulo para:

- tell what you were like as a child
- tell what you used to like to do
- talk about what you learned to do

to talk about animals
el animal, *pl.* los animales
el pájaro
el pez, *pl.* los peces
la tortuga

to talk about people
de pequeño, -a
el niño, la niña
el vecino, la vecina
obediente
desobediente
(bien) educado, -a
maleducado, -a
consentido, -a
tímido, -a
travieso, -a

to name toys
el juguete
la muñeca
el muñeco
el robot, *pl.* los robots
el animal de peluche, *pl.* los
    animales de peluche
el oso de peluche
el dinosaurio
el camión, *pl.* los camiones
el tren (de juguete)
el bloque
la pistola (de agua)

**to discuss things you used
to do**
ser: (yo) era, (tú) eras
caminar
montar en triciclo
el triciclo
saltar (a la cuerda)
la cuerda
ir: (yo) iba, (tú) ibas
recordar *(o → ue)*
coleccionar
la colección, *pl.* las colecciones
la verdad
mentir *(e → ie)*
obedecer *(c → zc)*
desobedecer *(c → zc)*
portarse (bien / mal)
molestar
pelearse (con)
llorar

**to talk about places
children go**
la guardería infantil
el kindergarten
la escuela primaria

**to talk about playground
equipment**
el patio de recreo
el cajón de arena, *pl.* los
    cajones de arena
el carrusel
el columpio
el sube y baja
el tobogán, *pl.* los toboganes

Resumen 189

CAPÍTULO 6

THEME: SPECIAL OCCASIONS

SCOPE AND SEQUENCE Pages 190–221

COMMUNICATION

Topics

Family celebrations

Extended family members

Holidays

Objectives

To discuss how one culture can influence another

To discuss celebrations

To identify family members

To talk about holidays

To greet people and say good-by

CULTURE

How cultures adopt, often in altered forms, aspects and traditions of other cultures

GRAMMAR

El pretérito de los verbos e → i

El pretérito del verbo dar

Otros usos del imperfecto

Los verbos reflexivos recíprocos

Ancillaries available for use with Chapter 6

Multisensory/Technology

 Overhead Transparencies, 30–34

 Audio Tapes and CDs

 Vocabulary Art Blackline Masters for Hands-On Learning, pp. 33–37

 Classroom Crossword

 La Catrina

 CD-ROM

Print

 Practice Workbook, pp. 55–65

 Writing, Audio & Video Activities, pp. 35–40, 108–110, 161–162

 Communicative Activity Blackline Masters

Pair and Small Group Activities, pp. 36–41

Situation Cards, p. 42

 Un paso más: Actividades para ampliar tu español, pp. 31–36

Assessment

 Assessment Program

Pruebas, pp. 85–95

Examen de habilidades, pp. 96–99

 Test Generator

Video still from Chap. 6

189A

Los días de fiesta

Some holidays are celebrated differently in Latin America and Spain than in the U.S. *La Nochebuena,* or Christmas Eve, is when most of the Spanish-speaking world celebrates Christmas. January 6, *el Día de los Reyes,* marks the formal end of the Christmas holidays because it is believed that on this date the three Wise Men arrived in Bethlehem. In Puerto Rico, it marks the last in a series of parties and is often held outdoors. *El Año Nuevo,* which falls in the summer in the southern hemisphere, is celebrated with fireworks in many parts of Latin America.

Unlike in the U.S., Mother's Day is always celebrated on May 10 in Spain and Latin America, regardless of the day of the week it falls on. Spanish-speaking countries also tend to celebrate *el Día de los Abuelos* and *el Día del Niño,* and the dates can vary from country to country.

Columbus Day is generally known as *el Día de la Raza.* The holiday honors the blending of the Spanish and indigenous cultures. In some Spanish-speaking countries it is also referred to as *el Día de la Hispanidad,* recognizing the impact of the Spanish culture on the American continent. In recent years, it has lost standing as a holiday in favor of holidays of greater national meaning: September 15 is *el Día de la Independencia* for Guatemala, Honduras, El Salvador, Nicaragua, and Costa Rica. Paraguay celebrates its independence from Spain on May 14; Venezuela, July 5; Argentina, July 9; Colombia, July 20; Peru, July 28; Bolivia, August 6; Ecuador, August 10; and Uruguay, August 25.

Extended families and close friends often get together during these *fiestas patrias.* In Chile, for example, Independence Day (September 18) may be celebrated with a *parrillada,* where a variety of grilled meats and *empanadas de pino* (turnovers of ground beef) are served.

In contrast, *Carnaval,* which corresponds somewhat to Mardi Gras, is a celebration that draws large crowds. Perhaps one of the most famous *Carnavales* is held in Oruro, Bolivia. Both indigenous and Spanish elements are present as throngs of spectators watch costumed dancers wind their way through the streets as a form of pilgrimage in honor of *la Virgen Morena.*

Introduce

Re-entry of Concepts

The following list represents words, expressions, and grammar topics re-entered from Book 1 and Book 2 (Chaps. 2–5):

Book 1
numbers 0–31, calendar terms, *gustar* expressions, foods, family members, clothing, formal clothing

Chapter 2
daily routine

Chapter 3
clothing

Chapter 4
leisure activities

Chapter 5
toys

Planning

Cross-Curricular Connections

Sociology Connection *(pp. 194–195)*
As homework, have students interview their own families to find out where their grandparents and great-grandparents came from, and where their aunts, uncles, cousins, nieces, or nephews live today. Have them share this information with the class.

Language Arts Connection *(pp. 198–199)*
Have students write a letter to a Spanish-speaking pen pal, describing how they celebrate Thanksgiving. Have them include which family members are present, which foods are served, and any traditional activities they participate in. When completed, have them seal the letter in an envelope and give it to you. The next day, pass out the envelopes at random. Have students read the letters and try to guess who wrote them.

Spanish in Your Community
Many shops offer greeting cards in Spanish. Have students visit stores in their community to see if they can find cards celebrating *cumpleaños, quinceañera, bautismo,* or other occasions. Encourage them to purchase a card to share with the class or place on a bulletin board.

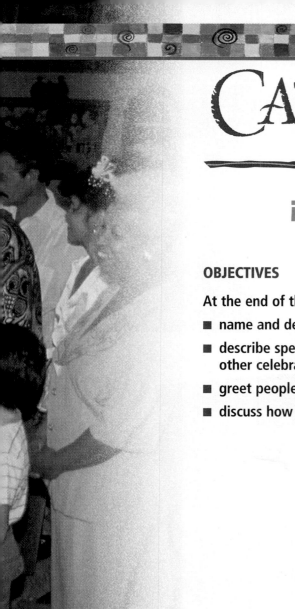

CAPÍTULO 6

¡Celebremos!

OBJECTIVES

At the end of this chapter, you will be able to:

■ name and describe members of an extended family

■ describe special family occasions, holidays, and other celebrations

■ greet people in several different ways

■ discuss how one culture can influence another

En el Palacio de los Matrimonios, La Habana, Cuba

191

Preview

Cultural Objective
• To discuss how holidays are celebrated in Spanish-speaking countries

Critical Thinking: Summarizing Information
Discuss with students similarities and / or differences they see between celebrations in the U.S. and those depicted in the photos.

¡Piénsalo bien!

Mira las pinturas. ¿Cómo son estas familias? ¿Qué diferencias ves en estas pinturas?

Una familia (1989), Fernando Botero

Carlos IV y su familia (1800), Francisco de Goya

192   Capítulo 6

Options

Strategies for Reaching All Students

Spanish-Speaking Students
Ask *¿Cuáles son los días de fiesta que celebra tu familia? ¿Y tu comunidad? ¿Se reúne mucha gente? ¿Por qué son tan importantes (y tan divertidas) estas celebraciones?*

 Un paso más 6-A

Cultural Notes

(p. 192, top photo)
Colombian painter and sculptor Fernando Botero (b. 1932), a native of Medellín, is famous for his gigantic, inflated-looking figures. Botero's early career was spent abroad, studying and traveling in Europe, Latin America, and the U.S. As his work matured, he turned to the daily life, religious myths, and folk art of Colombia. Here he depicts a middle-class family in a surrealistic setting with his typically humorous disregard of normal proportion.

Cultures develop unique ways of greeting each other—one kiss, two kisses, *un abrazo,* hand-shakes—or a touching of elbows. In Honduras, a woman and man may greet by facing each other and touching elbows. *Un abrazo fuerte* is a common greeting between men who know each other well in many Spanish-speaking countries. Ask students if they are familiar with the ways people greet each other in other cultures. Have them share this information with the class.

Answers: ¡Piénsalo bien!
Answers will vary.

Using Photos
Ask students: *¿Cómo se sienten las personas en este cuadro de Picasso? ¿Cómo lo sabes?*

Familia de saltimbancos (1905), Pablo Picasso

(p. 192, bottom photo)
Goya rendered this painting of Carlos IV (1748–1819), King of Spain (1788–1808) and his wife, Queen María Luisa, shown here surrounded by family members. The King's eldest son Ferdinand, in blue, stands to the left. The woman next to Ferdinand, with her face averted, represents his yet-to-be-chosen bride. María Luisa is flanked by her youngest children. Goya has included himself in the background, to the left of the painting, behind an easel.

(p. 193, photo)
Pablo Picasso (1881–1973) was born in Málaga. By the age of 20, he had developed a mature, personal style marked by melan-choly subject matter and a blue palette. The years 1901–1904 are referred to as his "blue period." In 1905 he began to paint portraits of circus performers, dancers, and acrobats in warmer, pink tones in what is referred to as his "rose period."
Picasso's inspiration for *Familia de saltimbancos* (acrobatic performers) was

the *Cirque Médrano* in Paris's Montmarte district. He attended the circus and made studies of acrobats and other performers. He combined these into a family portrait. Included in the painting are likenesses of the French poet Guillaume Apollinaire (the jester) and of the artist himself (the harle-quin at the far left).

Present

Chapter Theme
Family celebrations

Communicative Objectives
- To discuss celebrations
- To identify family members
- To greet people and say good-by

 Transparencies 30–31

 Vocabulary Art BLMs

 Pronunciation Tape 6-1

Grammar Preview
Reciprocal reflexive verbs are presented here lexically. Their explanation appears on p. 213. Allow students to practice these without explaining them at this point unless they express a need to understand the concept.

Teaching Suggestions
Preparing students to speak: Use one or two options from each of the categories of Comprehensible Input, Physical Response, or Limited Verbal Response. For a complete explanation of these categories and some sample activities, see pp. T16–T17.

Vocabulario para conversar

¿Cómo celebras tu cumpleaños?

Vas a necesitar estas palabras y expresiones para hablar sobre reuniones familiares y otras celebraciones. Después de leerlas varias veces, practícalas con un(a) compañero(a).

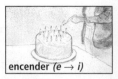
encender *(e → i)*

apagar

La fiesta de cumpleaños

la vela
el pastel

La graduación, *pl.* **las graduaciones**

graduarse

abrazarse

Options

Strategies for Reaching All Students

Spanish-Speaking Students

 Un paso más Ex. 6-B

Students Needing Extra Help
Begin the vocabulary section of the Organizer. Show word families with *abrazarse (brazo)* and *besarse (beso)*. Have a reflexive verb chart and a stem-change chart available. Help them see that these verbs are used only in the *nosotros(as)* and *Uds. / ellos / ellas* forms.
También necesitas . . . : Point out that *nacer* is rarely used in the present tense. Stress

how *nieto* looks like the English *niece* and shouldn't be confused with its true meaning. Stress the pronunciation and meaning of *familiar.*
¿Y qué quiere decir . . . ?: Review the paradigm of *estar.* Explain the difference between *el cumpleaños* and *cumplir años.* Again, emphasize word families.

La boda

casarse (con)

el esposo

la esposa

despedirse (e → i) (de)

darse la mano

decirse "¡Hola!"

besarse

También necesitas . . .

la reunión, *pl.* las reuniones	*gathering, get-together*	
saludar	*to greet*	
nacer	*to be born*	
(estar) casado, -a (con)	*(to be) married (to)*	
(estar) soltero, -a	*(to be) single*	
(estar) muerto, -a	*(to be) dead*	
el bisabuelo, la bisabuela	*great-grandfather /*	
	great-grandmother	
el nieto, la nieta	*grandchild*	
el cuñado, la cuñada	*brother-in-law / sister-in-law*	
el sobrino, la sobrina	*nephew, niece*	
familiar	*family (adj.)*	
de nuevo	*again*	

¿Y qué quiere decir . . . ?
el cumpleaños
cumplir años
el aniversario (de boda)
la celebración,
    pl. las celebraciones
celebrar
regalar
invitar
especial
(estar) divorciado, -a (de)
(estar) separado, -a (de)

Vocabulario para conversar   195

Practice & Apply

Reteach / Review: Vocabulary

Encourage students to use known vocabulary to vary their answers.
Ex. 1: *Sí, me encantan las fiestas de disfraces. / No, no me gusta nada ir a fiestas de disfraces.*

Re-enter/ Recycle

Ex. 1: leisure-time activities from Chap. 4

Answers: Empecemos a conversar

1 ESTUDIANTE A

a. ¿Sueles ir a fiestas de cumpleaños?
b. . . . a graduaciones?
c. . . . a conciertos?
d. . . . a obras de teatro?
e. . . . a bodas?
f. Questions will vary.

ESTUDIANTE B

a.–f. Answers will vary, but look for the correct forms: *me divierto, me aburro, lo paso bien / mal.*

2 ESTUDIANTE A

a. Generalmente, ¿cómo saludas a tus cuñados(as)?
b. . . . a tu madre / padre?
c. . . . a tu abuelo(a)?
d. . . . a tus amigos(as)?
e. . . . a tus bisabuelos(as)?
f. . . . al director (a la directora) de la escuela?
g. Questions will vary.

Empecemos a conversar

Túrnate con un(a) compañero(a) para ser *Estudiante A* y *Estudiante B*. Reemplacen las palabras subrayadas en el modelo con palabras representadas o escritas en los recuadros. Si ven pueden dar su propia respuesta.

1

A —¿*Sueles ir a fiestas de disfraces*?
B —*Sí, y me divierto bastante*.
   o: *No. Nunca voy a fiestas de disfraces.*
   o: *Sí, pero no las soporto.*

Estudiante A **Estudiante B**

divertirse
aburrirse
pasarlo bien / mal

2 tu tío(a)

A —*Generalmente, ¿cómo saludas a tu tío(a)*?
B —*Nos abrazamos*.
   o: *No tengo tíos.*

Estudiante A

a. tus cuñados(as)
b. tu madre / padre
c. tu abuelo(a)
d. tus amigos(as)
e. tus bisabuelos(as)
f. el director / la directora de la escuela
g.

Estudiante B

196   Capítulo 6

Options

Strategies for Reaching All Students

Spanish-Speaking Students

Exs. 1–4: Pair bilingual with non-bilingual students if possible.
After Ex. 5: *Piensa en cuando eras más joven y en tu fiesta de cumpleaños favorita. Descríbela. Di por qué te gustó. ¿Qué hicieron? ¿Qué regalos recibiste? ¿Quién fue a tu fiesta? ¿Qué comieron?*

 Un paso más Exs. 6-C, 6-D

Students Needing Extra Help

Ex. 1: Review reflexive verbs if necessary. With *pasarlo bien,* remind students to put the *lo* before the conjugated verb form. Discourage them from using *aburrirse* for every answer.
Ex. 3: Discourage students from always answering with *no recuerdo.* However, some students will not want to share the information requested in the question. Let them respond accordingly. Review the imperfect.

Previous activities have focused on the present tense.
Ex. 4: Some students will hesitate to discuss family celebrations. Don't obligate them to share their writing. Point out that this exercise uses three verb tenses. Review the preterite if necessary.
Ex. 5: Not all students have had joyous celebrations. Encourage them to come up with something imaginary if this seems more comfortable.

3

cumplir años

A —*Cuando eras pequeño(a), ¿qué hacía tu familia cuando alguien cumplía años?*
B —*Comprábamos un pastel.*
  o: *No recuerdo.*

Estudiante A

a. celebrar su aniversario de boda
b. graduarse
c. casarse
d. nacer

Estudiante B

comprar un pastel

invitar a ___

hacer una fiesta / cena / almuerzo

hacer una reunión familiar

no hacer nada

Empecemos a escribir

Escribe tus respuestas en español.

4 ¿Te diviertes cuando cumples años? ¿Cómo celebraste tu último cumpleaños? ¿A quiénes invitaste? ¿Qué te regalaron? ¿Había pastel? ¿Quién encendió las velas? ¿En qué pensaste cuando las apagaste?

5 ¿Qué ocasiones especiales celebra tu familia? ¿Cuándo fue la última vez que celebraron algo? ¿Cómo lo pasaste? Generalmente, ¿quiénes van a las reuniones familiares? ¿Qué haces tú en esas reuniones? ¿Qué hacías cuando eras pequeño(a)?

6 De tus actores o cantantes *(singers)* favoritos, ¿sabes quiénes están casados? ¿Quiénes están separados o divorciados? ¿Y solteros? ¿Quiénes están divorciados y casados de nuevo?

También se dice

el casamiento
el matrimonio

la colación

la torta   el ponqué
la tarta   el bizcocho
el queque

la candela

Vocabulario para conversar   197

Present

Chapter Theme
Holidays

Communicative Objectives
- To discuss celebrations
- To talk about holidays

 Transparencies 32–33

 Vocabulary Art BLMs

 Pronunciation Tape 6-2

Grammar Preview
Reflexive reciprocal verbs are presented here lexically. Their explanation appears on p. 213.

Vocabulario para conversar

¿Cómo celebras los días de fiesta?

Aquí tienes el resto del vocabulario que necesitas en este capítulo para hablar sobre reuniones familiares y otras celebraciones.

¡Una fiesta de sorpresa!
FECHA: _____
HORA: _____
LUGAR: _____

la invitación, *pl.* las invitaciones

la flor

el Día de la Madre (el segundo domingo de mayo)

los fuegos artificiales *(m.pl.)*

el Año Nuevo

el Día de los Enamorados

bailar

el Día del Padre (el tercer domingo de junio)

el baile

el Día de la Independencia

Options

Strategies for Reaching All Students

Spanish-Speaking Students

 Un paso más Ex. 6-E

Students Needing Extra Help
También necesitas . . . : Go over *encontrarse* for students who need to see all the verb forms. Help them see that this is used only in the *nosotros(as)* and *Uds. / ellos / ellas* forms. Give complete sentences for *desde* and *desde que.* Remind students that *pariente* is a false cognate, and that it means "relative."

Enrichment
Ask students to share information they know about two Mexican holidays that are widely celebrated in the U.S.: *Cinco de mayo* and Mexican Independence Day. You may also ask them if they know of other foreign holidays that are celebrated in the U.S. (Bastille Day, Chinese New Year). Have information ready about these holidays so that you can present it to the class.

una fiesta de sorpresa

Octubre

L	M	M	J	V	S	D
			1	2	3	4
⑫	6	7	8	9	10	11
19	13	14	15	16	17	18
26	20	21	22	23	24	25
	27	28	29	30	31	

el Día de la Raza

Noviembre

L	M	M	J	V	S	D
						1
2	3	4	5	6	7	8
9	10	11	12	13	14	15
16	17	18	19	20	21	22
23	24	25	㉖	27	28	29
30						

el pavo

el Día de (Acción de) Gracias
(el cuarto jueves de noviembre)

la Nochebuena

Diciembre

L	M	M	J	V	S	D
	1	2	3	4	5	6
7	8	9	10	11	12	13
14	15	16	17	18	19	20
21	22	23	㉔	㉕	26	27
28	29	30	㉛			

la Navidad

el fin de año

También necesitas . . .

charlar	to chat
encontrarse (o → ue)	to meet (each other)
felicitar	to congratulate
lanzar fuegos artificiales	to shoot / set off fireworks
¿a qué edad . . . ?	at what age . . . ?
a los ___ años	at the age of ___
desde (que + verb)	since, from
el pariente, la parienta	relative

¿Y qué quiere decir . . . ?
escribirse
hablarse
verse
el día de fiesta
la fiesta de fin de año
¡felicidades!

Teaching Suggestions
Preparing students to speak: Use one or two options from each of the categories of Comprehensible Input, Physical Response, or Limited Verbal Response. For a complete explanation of these categories and some sample activities, see pp. T16–T17.

Class Starter Review
On the day following the presentation of vocabulary, you might begin the class by asking students questions about their childhood: *¿A qué edad empezaste a ir a la escuela? ¿A qué edad empezaste a hablar?*

Learning Spanish Through Action
STAGING VOCABULARY: *Levanten*
MATERIALS: index cards with copies of Vocabulary Art BLMs mounted on them
DIRECTIONS: Hand out the cards to the class. Direct students to raise the card corresponding to the holiday you describe: *Este día lanzamos fuegos artificiales. En este día en mayo le regalo flores a mi mamá.*

Practice

Re-enter / Recycle
Ex. 9: clothing from Chap. 3

Answers: Empecemos a conversar

7 ESTUDIANTE A
a. ¿Cuándo es la Navidad?
b. ...el Año Nuevo?
c. ...el Día del Padre?
d. ...el Día de (Acción de) Gracias?
e. ...el Día de los Enamorados?
f. ...la Nochebuena?
g. Questions will vary.

ESTUDIANTE B
a. Es el veinticinco de diciembre.
b. ...primero de enero.
c. ...tercer domingo de junio.
d. ...cuarto jueves de noviembre.
e. ...catorce de febrero.
f. ...veinticuatro de diciembre.
g. Answers will vary.

Empecemos a conversar

7
A —¿Cuándo es *el Día de la Madre*?
B —Es *el segundo domingo de mayo*.

Estudiante A

a.
b.
c.

d.
e.
f.
g.

Estudiante B

200   Capítulo 6

Options

Strategies for Reaching All Students

Students Needing Extra Help
Ex. 7: Be sure that calendars are available. Provide a model using a date. *(Es el veinticinco de diciembre.)*
Ex. 8: Brainstorm the possibilities for celebrating these holidays.
Ex. 9: Review *desde que*.

8

tus amigos(as)

A —¿Cómo *celebran tus amigos(as) el Día de los Enamorados?*
B —*Envían tarjetas, regalan flores,* . . .
  o: *No hacen nada.*

Estudiante A

a. tu ciudad   b. tu familia   c. Uds.

d. tú   e. tú y tus amigos   f. tu familia   g.

Estudiante B

9

trabajar

A —*¿A qué edad vas a trabajar?*
B —*A los (18) años.*
  o: *Trabajo desde que tengo 12 años.*

Estudiante A

a. graduarte*   e. casarte

b. usar corbata / zapatos de   f. tener hijos
   tacón alto

c. comprar un coche   g.

d. vivir sólo(a)

Estudiante B

* When a reflexive verb is used in the infinitive *(graduarte, casarte),*
  the reflexive pronoun *(te)* agrees with the subject *(tú).*

Vocabulario para conversar   201

Practice & Apply

Re-enter / Recycle
Ex. 13: leisure-time activities from Chap. 4

Teaching Suggestions
Ex. 10: Explain to students that they can choose any family members they want in the question. Review reflexive verbs.

Answers: Empecemos a conversar

10 ESTUDIANTE A
a. ¿Se hablan por teléfono a menudo tú y ___?
b. ¿Se escriben a menudo tú y ___?
c. ¿Se encuentran a menudo tú y ___?
d. Questions will vary.

ESTUDIANTE B
a.–d. Answers will vary, but look for correct use of reflexive verbs *(nos hablamos / escribimos / encontramos)* and logical time expressions.

10

verse

A —*¿Se ven a menudo tú y tu bisabuelo(a)?*
B —*Nos vemos todos los días.*
    o: *Casi nunca nos vemos.*
    o: *Mis bisabuelos están muertos.*

Estudiante A

Estudiante B

a. hablarse por teléfono   b. escribirse

c. encontrarse   d.

una vez (dos veces) al mes / año

a veces

hace (3 meses) que no nos ___

El padre de la quinceañera baila el primer vals con su hija.

Una familia se reúne delante de una iglesia en la Ciudad de México después de un bautizo.

202   Capítulo 6

Options

Strategies for Reaching All Students

Spanish-Speaking Students
Exs. 10: Pair bilingual with non-bilingual students if possible.
After Ex. 14: *Escribe una nota de sociedad sobre una fiesta fabulosa. Puede ser una fiesta verdadera o una imaginaria ¿Qué tipo de fiesta fue? Cuándo y dónde fue? ¿Quiénes fueron a la fiesta? ¿Cómo se vistieron?*

 Un paso más Ex. 6-F

Students Needing Extra Help
Ex. 11: Encourage students to stay focused, as there are many questions that may seem redundant.
Ex. 12: Show students the difference between the third and fourth questions. One is indicating a specific day, while the other indicates when something occurs.
Ex. 13: Students will need help with the vocabulary to answer the first *¿por qué?*

Enrichment
As homework, have students write a newspaper article covering events mentioned in this letter. Have them invent details: How many people attended? What was the most interesting costume? What foods were served? What music was played? Or they can write tabloid-type articles: *¿De veras "perdió" su abrigo de piel la Srta. de la Luna en la fiesta de disfraces?* or *La Srta. de la Luna se lastima la pierna. ¡Algunos dicen que no fue accidente!*

Empecemos a escribir y a leer

11 ¿Cómo te gustaría celebrar tu próximo cumpleaños? ¿Piensas enviarles invitaciones a tus parientes y amigos? Generalmente, ¿qué haces de especial el día de tu cumpleaños? ¿Qué hacen tus parientes y amigos? ¿Cómo te saludan ese día? ¿Qué te dicen?

12 ¿Cuál es tu día de fiesta favorito? ¿Por qué? ¿En qué días de fiesta les dices "felicidades" a otras personas? ¿Cuándo felicitas a tus amigos(as) y a los miembros de tu familia? ¿En qué días de fiesta le envías tarjetas a la gente? ¿En qué días lanza la gente fuegos artificiales?

13 ¿Qué tipo de fiestas prefieres, las de sorpresa o las de disfraces? ¿Por qué? Cuando vas a un baile, ¿prefieres charlar o bailar? ¿Por qué?

14 ¿Cómo celebra tu familia el Día de Acción de Gracias?

15 Lee esta carta de agradecimiento *(thank you)*. En grupo, hablen de la visita de la señorita de la Luna. ¿Lo pasó bien o mal? ¿Cómo lo saben? Después, hagan una lista de las cosas positivas de su visita y otra lista de las cosas negativas.

Estimado Sr. Gastelotodo:

Gracias por su generosa invitación a La Vega durante el Primer Festival Internacional de Cine. Ya no recuerdo que llovió todos los días y que Ud. y yo sólo nos encontramos una vez. Recuerdo la fantástica fiesta de disfraces cuando bailé toda la noche con un hombre vestido de leopardo. Todavía pienso en el abrigo de piel que perdí. Lloré mucho, pero ahora ya no estoy tan triste. ¡Estaba un poco aburrida de llevar el mismo abrigo desde 1994! Y me compré uno más bonito y más caro.

¡Qué feliz me hizo ganar el plátano de oro para la mejor actriz del año! Pero la pierna que me lastimé cuando salía del escenario todavía me duele mucho.

Muchos besos y un abrazo fuerte,

Lucía de la Luna

También se dice

el Día de San Valentín

la Nochevieja

el guajolote
el chompipe

Vocabulario para conversar   203

Answers: Empecemos a escribir y a leer

11–14 Answers will vary.

15 *Lo pasó mal. Cosas positivas: la fantástica fiesta de disfraces, se compró un abrigo más bello y más caro, ganó el plátano de oro para la mejor actriz del año. Cosas negativas: llovió todos los días, ella perdió su abrigo de piel, la pierna que se lastimó todavía le duele mucho.*

 Practice Wkbk. 6-3, 6-4

 Audio Activity 6.2

 Writing Activity 6-C

 Pruebas 6-3, 6-4

Cultural Notes

(p. 202, left photo)
The *quinceañera*, a lavish fifteenth birthday party, is an important event in the life of a young woman in many Spanish-speaking countries and among families of Hispanic heritage in the U.S., such as this one in Novato, California. The celebration marks a young girl's passage into adulthood. The young woman dances first with her father and then with her *chambelán*, or escort.

(p. 202, right photo)
A baptism brings family and friends together to celebrate a baby's acceptance into the Church. Following a mass and the baptismal ceremony, the celebrants often meet at the parents' home for a reception. The child's parents and godparents are *compadres* in a relationship known as *compadrazgo*. *Compadres* (literally, "co-parents") help raise the child in the Church and provide legal guardianship if necessary.

Practice

Answers:
¡Comuniquemos!
1–3 Answers will vary, but look for correct use of present, preterite, and imperfect tenses.

¡Comuniquemos!

Aquí tienes otra oportunidad para usar el vocabulario de este capítulo.

1 Túrnate con un(a) compañero(a) para hablar de alguna fiesta a la que fue cada uno de ustedes. Pregunten:

- qué tipo de fiesta era y dónde fue
- qué celebraban
- quiénes fueron (¿parientes? ¿amigos?)
- qué hicieron
- 💡

Pueden usar las expresiones de la lista u otras para contestar las preguntas.

abrir los regalos
cantar "Feliz cumpleaños"
charlar
cortar / comer pastel
despedirse
encender / apagar las velas
felicitar
regalar
sacar fotos
saludar

Después, dile a otro(a) estudiante cómo fue la fiesta de tu compañero(a). Por ejemplo:

Miguel fue a una fiesta el sábado. Era el aniversario de boda de sus ... Fue en ... Había ...

Estas dos amigas en Montevideo, Uruguay, se saludan con un beso en la mejilla.

2 Hazle una entrevista a un(a) pariente(a) o a un(a) amigo(a). Luego, prepara su biografía. Puedes usar estas u otras preguntas:

- cuándo nació
- a qué edad empezó a ir a la escuela y cuándo se graduó
- a qué edad empezó a trabajar
- cuándo le pasó algo importante y qué le pasó

Luego, dile a tu compañero(a) lo que averiguaste *(found out)*:

Mi prima María Rosa nació el 7 de octubre de 1978 ...

Options

Strategies for Reaching All Students

Spanish-Speaking Students
Ex. 1: Pair Spanish-speaking students. Have them act out the conversation for the class. Use as a listening comprehension activity. To check comprehension, have other students write answers to the questions.
Ex. 2: Have Spanish-speaking students write out the biography of a relative: *Escribe una biografía de un(a) pariente(a) o de un(a) buen amigo(a). Usa las preguntas en el ejercicio 2 como guía.*

Students Needing Extra Help
¡Comuniquemos!: Have models ready for these activities.
Ex. 1: Tell students that they need not discuss the same party. Remind the person responding to the question to use the preterite. Explain that *fiesta* doesn't always have the same meaning we give it in English; it may imply a celebration such as an anniversary. Have pairs take notes so that they can give the information to someone else. Remind them to use a different form of the verb when reporting the celebration to a third student.
Ex. 2: Have students take notes before reporting the information.
Ex. 3: Help students choose the correct form of the verb when asking the second group of questions.
¿Qué sabes ahora?: Have students write out this section so they can record their progress.

3 Con un(a) compañero(a) inventa una conversación por teléfono. Él (Ella) te invita a una fiesta y te dice:

- la fecha
- la hora
- la dirección
- el tipo de fiesta que va a ser
- 💡

Tú le preguntas sobre:

- el regalo
- la ropa que debes llevar
- las personas que van a ir
- qué van a hacer
- si debes llevar algo de comida
- 💡

Pueden comenzar así:

A —¡Hola, Olga! Soy Luis. ¿Cómo estás?
B —Bien, gracias, Luis. ¿Y tú?
A —Muy bien. Yo quisiera invitarte a . . .

TARJETA TELEFÓNICA

Estas fiestas, más cerca.

Feliz 1994

Estas fiestas la TARJETA TELEFÓNICA tiene un regalo. Porque esta Navidad, la TARJETA TELEFÓNICA de 1000 pta sólo cuesta 800 pta. Un regalo de Telefónica para que esté más cerca de los suyos.
De venta en estancos, oficinas de correos y establecimientos autorizados.

Regalo de Navidad 200 pta

Telefónica

¿Qué sabes ahora?

Can you:

- talk about how your family celebrates certain occasions?
  —Mi familia celebra ____ todos los años. Hacemos un(a) ____ .
- talk about holiday celebrations?
  —El 4 de julio, día de ____ , la gente lanza ____ en la calle.
- talk about how you greet people?
  —Mi bisabuela y yo siempre nos ____ cuando nos ____ .

EN TU CUMPLEAÑOS
Casi no tenemos nada que decir, excepto que...

¡MUCHAS FELICIDADES!
¡SUPER ESPECIAL!
¡ERES UNA PERSONA FANTASTICA!
¡ERES LO MEJOR!
¡HOY Y SIEMPRE!
ERES SUPER
¡ERES SENSACIONAL!
¡ERES SIN IGUAL!
¡NADIE ES MEJOR QUE TU!

Vocabulario para conversar   205

Answers: ¿Qué sabes ahora?
- Answers will vary.
- la Independencia / fuegos artificiales
- Answers will vary, but both verbs should be in the *nosotros* form.

 Audio Activity 6.3

Cultural Notes ☀

Cooperative Learning
Divide the class into groups of four. Assign each group one of the holidays listed in the second *Vocabulario para conversar.* Tell students to plan a celebration for their holiday: one student will make a list of decorations needed, one will plan the menu, one will plan activities, and the fourth will design an invitation. After each group has planned their celebration, call on individuals from each group to share their results.

(p. 204, photo)
People in Spain and Latin America have unique ways of greeting each other. Women friends brush cheeks lightly and "kiss the air." *Adiós,* which literally means "good-by," is used to acknowledge someone in passing. In Guatemala, a kiss on the cheek combined with a gentle hug is a common greeting among women. In Puerto Rico, women grasp each other's shoulders and kiss each other on the cheek.

Present & Apply

Cultural Objective

• How cultures adopt, often in altered form, aspects and traditions of other cultures

Critical Thinking: Identifying Stereotypes

Celebrations represent only one aspect of the many diverse cultures in Latin America. Dispel any stereotypical ideas students might have that life in Latin America is one long string of parties.

Multicultural Perspectives

In Uruguay, groups perform for prize money in the month-long celebration for *Carnaval. Los parodistas*, wearing brightly colored clothes and painted faces, perform musical skits and parodies accompanied by electric guitar and keyboard. *Una revista* performs dances from the U.S. and Latin America, such as samba, salsa, and Charleston. A combo accompanies them, playing the music to special lyrics written by the group. *Los lubolos* paint their faces black and perform musical numbers of African origin, such as *milonga* and *candombe*. Ask students if they are famliar with Mardi Gras traditions in other parts of the world. (Those in New Orleans, Rio, and Nice, France, are proba-

Perspectiva cultural

¿Qué te dicen estas fotos sobre la religión en América Latina? ¿Qué influencias de diferentes culturas puedes observar en ellas?

La gente se disfraza con colores brillantes en un desfile de carnaval en Ponce, Puerto Rico.

Probablemente sabes que el catolicismo es la religión principal en los países hispanos. Es verdad, pero también se practican el protestantismo, el islamismo, el judaísmo, el budismo, la religión ortodoxa griega y las religiones indígenas. En el Caribe, mucha gente practica la santería, una combinación entre la religión yoruba africana y el catolicismo.

Hay celebraciones de origen religioso muy populares entre gente de todas las religiones. *Los carnavales*, por ejemplo, son desfiles con danza, música y disfraces que se celebran por toda América Latina. Empiezan en febrero, el fin de semana antes del Miércoles de Ceniza, que es el comienzo de los 40 días de la Cuaresma *(Lent)*.

Los carnavales se celebran de diferentes maneras. En Perú, Bolivia y el norte de Argentina, se ven las tradiciones incas. En la región del Caribe vemos símbolos cristianos mezclados con tradiciones africanas que llegaron a este hemisferio con los esclavos.

En los Estados Unidos también se ven tradiciones hispanas de origen religioso. Una de ellas es la tradición de las *luminarias*. Éstas son bolsas de papel con arena y una vela encendida adentro. Originalmente se usaban para iluminar la casa en la Nochebuena. Ahora se usan para iluminar la acera, una piscina o un patio cuando hay una fiesta.

206 Capítulo 6

Options

Strategies for Reaching All Students

Spanish-Speaking Students

Ask: *¿Cuáles son los días religiosos que celebra tu familia o tu comunidad? ¿Cómo los celebran? ¿Vas a continuar esas tradiciones? ¿Por qué?*

 Un paso más Ex. 6-G

Students Needing Extra Help

Explain Ash Wednesday and Lent.
Ex. 1: Direct students to paragraphs 3–4 if they are having difficulty.
Ex. 2. Explain the concept of the origin of holidays. Students probably haven't given much thought to how holidays began. Give an example as a model to help with a concept that may be difficult.

Cultural Notes

(pp. 206–207, photo)
In Ponce, Puerto Rico, *Carnaval* celebrants often wear brightly painted horned masks. Floats and parades are features of the festival, along with dancing to *plena* music, folk music with African roots. Slavery brought an African presence to Puerto Rico during the eighteenth and nineteenth centuries. In

Celebrando el carnaval
en Oruro, Bolivia

bly the best known.) Discuss the historical and present-day importance of *carnaval*. The etymology of the word is tied to the idea of abstaining from meat. *Carnaval* is the three-day period preceding Ash Wednesday and the 40 meatless days of Lent.

Answers

Answers to inductive questions will vary, but students may say that religion plays an important part in public celebrations in Latin America. It appears, too, as if African and Indian traditions and costumes are a part of these celebrations in regions where those groups represent a large percentage of the population. In the U.S. one can see the Hispanic influence in the use of traditional *luminarias* at Christmastime.

Answers: La cultura desde tu perspectiva

1 Answers will vary; students may say the celebration takes on aspects of the other culture: *Carnaval* in Bolivia, Peru, and Argentina shows Incan traditions, and in the Caribbean, African traditions.

2 Answers will vary, but may include Christmas and Chanukah, centering on gift-giving and decorations, and Easter, with its child-centered bunny and colored eggs. Have students research the origin of some of the more sectarian aspects of holidays that were once exclusively religious.

La cultura desde tu perspectiva

1 ¿De qué manera puede modificarse una costumbre religiosa cuando se encuentra con otra cultura? Da un ejemplo.

2 ¿Qué días de fiesta de origen religioso que tú celebras o conoces se celebran hoy de otra manera?

Casa de Nuevo México decorada con luminarias para la Navidad

207

---

addition, European influences came through immigration, mostly from Cataluña, Asturias, Galicia, and Mallorca. Although Puerto Rico had originally been populated by the Arawak people, only a very few traces of indigenous culture remain.

(p. 207, top photo)
Oruro, a small town on the high plateau of Bolivia, is famous for its *Carnaval*. Young Bolivians, members of *fraternidades,* travel from all parts of the country to dance during the celebration.

(p. 207, bottom photo)
Originally, *luminarias* were small fires of burning sticks, but today they are paper bags, weighted with sand, into which a lit candle is placed. *Luminarias* still have a religious significance in Mexico and parts of the U.S. Southwest. Placed along the sidewalks leading to a home, they provide a pathway for the Christchild.

Preview

 Transparency 34

Reteach / Review: Indirect object pronouns

You may want to review indirect object pronouns by asking who or what *le* refers to in the lower right-hand caption: *le di su comida favorita . . . .* (The dog Rex)

Answers

A Clues are described in the preterite: endings *-ió* and *-ieron*, and the words *pasado* and *ayer*.

B These are *e → i* stem-changing verbs.

C Preterite forms of *dar: dieron* and *di*. The preterite endings are like those of regular *-er* and *-ir* verbs.

Gramática en contexto

Mimi Abreu y su esposo Ricardo le dieron una fiesta de disfraces a su hija Juana el domingo, 22 de marzo. Roberto Calderón se vistió de pirata. Susana García Costa se vistió de astronauta.

Notas de sociedad

El sábado pasado el señor Pablo Rosas y la señora Matilde López de Rosas dieron una fiesta para celebrar el cincuenta aniversario de su boda. Sirvieron una espléndida cena.

El perro de Pedro Ramírez, Rex, con la medalla que ganó en el concurso que tuvo lugar ayer en el Estadio Central. Hablando de Rex, el señor Ramírez dijo, "Como siempre, no me pidió nada; pero yo le di su comida favorita: un hueso muy grande."

A Find the forms of *vestirse, servir,* and *pedir.* How can you tell that these events are described in the preterite tense?

B Compare the infinitives of these verbs to the forms used in the captions. What do you notice about the stem?

C In the captions, preterite forms of the verb *dar* are used. What are they? Are the endings of this *-ar* verb regular or irregular?

208 Capítulo 6

Options

Strategies for Reaching All Students

Students Needing Extra Help

Gramática en contexto: Begin the grammar section of the Organizer.

A: Use the grammar section from Chaps. 3 and 4 to review.

El pretérito de los verbos e → i: Give more examples using *vestirse* and *servir.* On the Organizer, have students highlight the irregular forms or write them in a different color.

El pretérito de los verbos con el cambio *e → i*

First, review the present-tense forms of *e → i* stem-changing verbs. Note that the change occurs in all except the *nosotros* and *vosotros* forms:

pedir

(yo)	**pido**	(nosotros) (nosotras)	pedimos
(tú)	**pides**	(vosotros) (vosotras)	pedís
Ud. (él) (ella)	**pide**	Uds. (ellos) (ellas)	**piden**

In the preterite, these verbs also have a stem change, but **only** in the *Ud./él/ella* and *Uds./ellos/ellas* forms:

(yo)	pedí	(nosotros) (nosotras)	pedimos
(tú)	pediste	(vosotros) (vosotras)	pedisteis
Ud. (él) (ella)	**pidió**	Uds. (ellos) (ellas)	**pidieron**

1 Imagina que Rosario, Luis, tu compañero(a) y tú son camareros en un restaurante donde van a celebrar una boda. Hay nueve mesas. Dile a tu compañero(a) qué mesas sirve cada uno.

> **Rosario /#8**   *Rosario sirve la mesa número 8.*

a. yo / #2
b. Luis y yo / #9
c. Rosario y Luis / #6
d. tú / #3
e. nosotros(as) dos / #7
f. Luis / #5
g.  /

Esta pareja argentina celebra su aniversario con una fiesta familiar en el campo.

209

Present & Practice

Class Starter Review
On the day following the presentation of the preterite of *-ir* verbs, you may want to begin the class with this activity:
Have students tell their classmates what they ordered the last time they went to a restaurant and what they served at their last family celebration. To practice the *-ieron* form, have students take notes on what three classmates ordered and served.

Answers
1 a. Yo sirvo la mesa número 2.
b. Luis y yo servimos la mesa número 9.
c. Rosario y Luis sirven la mesa número 6.
d. Tú sirves la mesa número 3.
e. Nosotros(as) dos servimos la mesa número 7.
f. Luis sirve la mesa número 5.
g. Statements will vary.

Present & Practice

Re-enter / Recycle

Ex. 4: Daily routine from Chap. 2

Answers

2 **ESTUDIANTE A**

¿Qué pidió la Sra. González?

¿Qué pidió la hermana del Sr. González?

¿Qué pidió el cuñado del Sr. González?

¿Qué pidieron los niños?

¿Qué pediste tú?

ESTUDIANTE B

El Sr. González pidió pavo y papas al horno.

La Sra. González pidió sopa de tomate y pollo.

La hermana del Sr. González pidió pavo y ensalada.

El cuñado del Sr. González pidió sopa de verduras y pescado.

Los niños pidieron hamburguesas y leche.

Yo pedí... *(Answers will vary.)*

3 El camarero le sirvió al Sr. González hamburguesas y papas fritas.

...le sirvió a la Sra. González café y sopa de verduras.

...le sirvió a la hermana del Sr. González pastel y un refresco.

...le sirvió al cuñado del Sr. González sopa de tomate y pollo.

...les sirvió a los niños pescado y papas al horno.

...me sirvió... *(Answers will vary.)*

2 Túrnate con un(a) compañero(a) para decir qué pidieron estas personas en la cena de fin de año.

A —*¿Qué pidió el señor González?*

B —*Pidió...*

3 Ahora, imagina que el camarero confundió lo que pidieron. Dile a tu compañero(a) lo que les sirvió el camarero.

El camarero le sirvió... al señor González.

210   Capítulo 6

¡NO OLVIDES!

Remember that we use indirect object pronouns to tell to whom or for whom an action is done.

me	nos
te	os
le	les

To make the meaning of *le* and *les* clear, we can add *a* + noun or pronoun. For example:

*El camarero **le** sirvió ensalada **al señor Rosas**.*

*Después **me** sirvió **a mí**.*

Options

Strategies for Reaching All Students

Students Needing Extra Help

Ex. 2: Remind students to use the definite article with *Sr. / Sra.* If available, use the vocabulary section of the Organizer from Book 1, Chap. 4.

¡No olvides!: Give additional examples of the use of *le* and *les* and ask students to help you do so.

Ex. 3: Remind students that *le* will change to *les* in some examples.

El pretérito del verbo dar: Stress that there are no written accents on these verb forms.

Ex. 5: Decide with students what the objects will be. They could use anything they might have with them, such as jewelry. Make sure they have three objects. Have extras on hand so that everyone doesn't use the same objects. Remind students that they have just reviewed indirect object pronouns. Model with three students so they can see the verbal exchange. Review *a mí, a ti,* etc. for this exercise and for Ex. 6.

4 Imagina que fuiste a la fiesta de disfraces de los Abreu. Cuéntale a tu compañero(a) de qué se vistieron tú y otras personas.

Pilar y Carlos se vistieron de astronautas.

a. yo

b. (nombre)

c. tú y (nombre)

d. (dos nombres)

e. las sobrinas del señor Abreu

f. la nieta de Ricardo Calderón

g.

¡NO OLVIDES!

Remember that we use *vestirse de* to mean "to be dressed as": *Me vestí de pirata.*

El pretérito del verbo *dar*

Dar is an *-ar* verb, but its preterite endings are the same as those of *-er* and *-ir* verbs.

(yo)	**di**	(nosotros) (nosotras)	**dimos**
(tú)	**diste**	(vosotros) (vosotras)	**disteis**
Ud. (él) (ella)	**dio**	Uds. (ellos) (ellas)	**dieron**

¡NO OLVIDES!

Do you remember the present-tense forms of *dar*?

doy	damos
das	dais
da	dan

5 Formen grupos de tres. Cada miembro del grupo debe tener tres objetos. Intercambien *(exchange)* esos objetos. Túrnense para decir lo que hicieron. Por ejemplo:

Yo te di un sujetapapeles a ti.
Tú le diste un sacapuntas a Francisco.
Y Francisco me dio una grapadora a mí.

Gramática en contexto   211

Teaching Suggestions

Ex. 5: Prepare for this exercise by practicing each sentence in isolation. For example, ask students to tell you one gift that they gave to someone recently *(Yo le di un suéter a mi hermana)*. In the same way, elicit sentences such as *Felipe le dio ___ a María, Roberto me dio ___ a mí.*

Answers

4 a. Yo me vestí de. . .

b. *(Nombre)* se vistió de. . .

c. Tú y *(nombre)* se vistieron de. . .

d. *(Dos nombres)* se vistieron de. . .

e. Las sobrinas del señor Abreu se vistieron de. . .

f. La nieta de Ricardo Calderón se vistió de. . .

g. Statements will vary.

5 Answers will vary, but look for correct use of indirect object pronouns and preterite forms of *dar*.

Present & Practice

Re-enter / Recycle

Ex. 6: clothing from Chap. 3, toys from Chap. 5

Answers

6 Answers will vary, but look for correct use of indirect object pronouns and preterite forms of *dar*.

🖊 **Practice Wkbk. 6-5, 6-6, 6-7, 6-8**

🖋 **Writing Activities 6-D, 6-E**

❓ **Pruebas 6-5, 6-6**

🗣 **Comm. Act. BLM 6-2**

7 imperfect: *vivían*
imperfect: *eran*
imperfect: *Iban*
imperfect: *se hablaban*
preterite: *tenían*
imperfect: *Jugaban*
imperfect: *tenían*
preterite: *se lastimó*
preterite: *corrió*
preterite: *pudo*
preterite: *fue*
preterite: *metió*
preterite: *ganó*

Students' paragraphs will vary, but look for correct imperfect and preterite forms.

---

6 Piensa en los regalos que tú y tu familia intercambiaron el año pasado para Navidad, Chanuka o alguna otra ocasión. Habla con un(a) compañero(a).

A —*Yo le di un bolso a mi mamá para su aniversario de boda.*
B —*¿Y qué le dio tu papá a ella?*
A —*Él le dio flores y un chaquetón de cuero.*
B — . . .

Otros usos del imperfecto

You know how to use the imperfect tense to talk about what someone **used to do** or **would do** in the past. We also use the imperfect tense:

• to describe people, places, or situations in the past.

   Era una casa muy grande.
   *It **was** a very big house.*

• to talk about a past action that was continuous or that kept on happening.

   Todavía **había** gente a las tres de la mañana.
   *People **were** still there at 3 A.M.*

7 Con un(a) compañero(a) termina de escribir la historia de Lola y Alba. Decidan si los verbos en paréntesis deben estar en el pretérito o en el imperfecto.

Lola y Alba *(vivir)* en la misma calle cuando *(ser)* pequeñas. *(Ir)* a la misma escuela y *(hablarse)* por teléfono casi todos los días. Las dos *(tener)* una gran pasión por el fútbol. *(Jugar)* desde que *(tener)* siete años. Un día, en un partido muy importante, Lola *(lastimarse)* una pierna. Alba *(correr)* a ayudarla y no *(poder)* jugar más. Pero no *(ser)* un día triste. El equipo *(meter)* tres goles y *(ganar)* el partido.

Ahora, escriban un párrafo similar.

LA NAVIDAD ES EL MEJOR REGALO

GUÍA DE SUGERENCIAS Y SERVICIOS DE El Corte Inglés

212   Capítulo 6

Options

Strategies for Reaching All Students

Students Needing Extra Help
Ex. 6: Brainstorm occasions and gifts.
Otros usos del imperfecto: Give additional examples.
Ex. 7: Brainstorm a storyline. Because of the number of tasks to be completed (creating a storyline, choosing the tense, conjugating the verb), do this as a class. Give help with the storyline and let students conjugate the verbs.

Los verbos reflexivos recíprocos: Compare this to regular reflexive verbs in which the action is done to oneself. Give examples.
Ex. 8: Remind students that this is the present tense. You may want to tell students to pretend rather than to use the *no tengo* response: it takes the focus away from the reflexive verbs.
Ahora lo sabes: Have students write out this section so they can keep track of their progress.

Enrichment
Ex. 7: After pairs of students have completed this exercise, you may want to go over it with the entire class sentence by sentence. Call on students to read a sentence and tell the rest of the class what their choice was for each verb and why they made that choice. Encourage students to discuss why the choices made are correct or not.

Los verbos reflexivos recíprocos

Sometimes we use the reflexive pronouns *se* and *nos* to express the idea of "(to) each other."

Los vecinos siempre **se saludan.**
*The neighbors always **greet each other.***

Mis amigos y yo **nos abrazamos** cuando **nos encontramos.**
*My friends and I **hug each other** when **we meet.***

8 Túrnate con un(a) compañero(a) para decir qué cosas hacen estas personas a menudo. Usa elementos de las tres listas. Por ejemplo:

A —*¿Tus padres y tíos se escriben a menudo?*
B —*No se escriben nunca, pero se hablan por teléfono a menudo.*
    o: *No tengo tíos.*

a. tus parientes	escribirse	algunas veces
b. tus amigos	ayudarse	a menudo
c. tus abuelos y tú	visitarse	todos los días
d. tus hermanas	verse	mucho
e. tu cuñado y tú	hablarse por teléfono	siempre
f. (nombre) y tú	saludarse	casi nunca
g.	pelearse	

Ahora lo sabes

Can you:

- talk about food that was ordered and served?

—Yo _____ pescado pero el camarero me _____ pollo.

- talk about gifts that someone gave?

—Mi mamá me _____ un violín para mi cumpleaños.

- describe something in the past?

—A las dos de la mañana José todavía no _____ sueño.

- talk about actions that refer to "each other"?

—Mi cuñada y yo _____ vemos todas las semanas.

Muchas familias mexicanas tienen un árbol de la vida.

213

Cultural Notes

Cooperative Learning
Divide the class into groups of three. Pass out magazine cutouts of animals and / or people. On one sheet of paper, using Ex. 8 as a model, the first student provides a descriptive noun about the cutout: *El pescado azul y la tortuga.* The second student continues with a reciprocal reflexive verb: *. . . se visitan.* The third student finishes the sentence: *El pescado azul y la tortuga se visitan en la piscina.* Poll students to see which sentences are logical.

(p. 213, photo)
The town of Metepec, located in the State of Mexico, is famous for its ceramic *artesanía.* The pieces produced by local craftspeople often reflect Biblical motifs. Based on the story of Adam and Eve, Metepec's "tree of life" *(árbol de la vida)* sculptures are especially famous and are found in many Mexican homes.

Apply

 Pronunciation Tape 6-3

Answers: Actividades
1–3 Answers will vary, but should include correct use of preterite and imperfect tenses.

 ¿Recuerdas?

Play

 **Video Activity A**

Using the Video

Episode 6 opens in a discotheque, where María and Susana, a girl from Spain, meet Felipe.
The next day, María and Jamie meet Carlos and Felipe in the university recreation area.
Afterwards, as the four of them are talking, they notice that Paco Aguilar (the son of Silvestre Aguilar) is staring at Jamie. Paco takes off in his new sports car, and the conversation turns to relationships. Carlos and María ask themselves what will happen after Jamie and Felipe go back to the U.S.
The next scene is set in the office of Operación Aztlán, the environmental organization where Carlos works. A girl arrives with a letter

Para decir más

Este vocabulario adicional te puede servir para las actividades de esta sección.

mientras
while

el padrastro, la madrastra
stepfather, stepmother

el hermanastro, la hermanastra
stepbrother, stepsister

odiar
to hate

adorar
to adore

Actividades

Esta sección te ofrece la oportunidad de aumentar tus conocimientos de español al integrar lo que aprendiste en este capítulo con lo que aprendiste en capítulos anteriores.

1 En grupo, miren el árbol genealógico de la familia de Rogelio y describan cómo están relacionadas las personas.

Después, escojan a una persona famosa e investiguen sobre su familia. Si prefieren, pueden escoger a alguien de sus familias. Preparen un árbol genealógico en un cartel con fotos de revistas o dibujos. Al final, presenten su cartel y explíquenlo. Pueden decir:

- quién es (o era) cada persona
- qué profesión tiene (o tenía)
- cuándo, y a qué edad, se graduó y se casó
- con quién está (o estaba) casado(a) o de quién está divorciado(a)
- cuántos hijos tiene (o tuvo)
- dónde vive (o vivía) o si está muerto(a)

[Family tree diagram]
Cecilia — Roberto
Marta — Bernardo   Elena — Patricio
Jorge   Mariana — Rodolfo   Silvia
Olga   Rogelio

214

Options

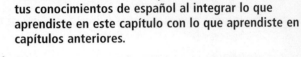
Strategies for Reaching All Students

Spanish-Speaking Students

 Un paso más Ex. 6-H

Students Needing Extra Help
Ex. 1: If available, use the grammar section of the Organizer from Book 1, Chap. 5. To save time, have students write about a friend's family instead of investigating. If students prefer, let them write about their whole family. Allow students to use notes when reporting to others.
Ex. 2: Use the vocabulary section of the Organizer. Brainstorm vocabulary used to

describe the party, food, clothing, etc. Have pictures available, because the magazines students know won't have this type of photo. Continue the model.
Ex. 3: Have extra photos on hand. Show students that three verb tenses are involved. Model a conversation. Have students take notes in order to report.

2 Trae fotos de eventos sociales de alguna revista. Formen un grupo y escriban comentarios sobre esos eventos. Al final, expliquen por qué les gustaría o no ir a cada evento. Sus comentarios pueden ser divertidos. Por ejemplo:

Era una cena muy aburrida en . . . La señora (nombre) llevaba . . . y el esposo de la señora (nombre) llevaba . . . Había . . .

A mí (no) me gustaría ir a esa fiesta porque . . .

Pueden poner sus fotos y comentarios en un cartel en la pared.

3 Trae una foto de una celebración familiar cuando tú eras pequeño(a) o trae una foto de revista. Intercámbiala *(exchange it)* con tu compañero(a). Túrnense para hablar sobre las circunstancias de la foto. Pregunten, por ejemplo:

- quiénes son las personas
- qué estaban celebrando
- cuándo y dónde fue la celebración
- qué sirvieron de comida

Luego, cada uno debe hablar con otro(a) estudiante sobre la foto de su compañero(a).

En esta foto Patricia tenía . . .

Actividades   215

from her mother, whose husband works at the hacienda La Jacaranda. The letter informs Carlos that the pesticides used on the produce grown there are affecting the health of the workers and putting consumers at risk. When Carlos discusses the matter with Silvia, another member of the organization, he remembers that La Jacaranda belongs to don Silvestre Aguilar.

 La Catrina: Capítulo 6

Play

 Video Activity B

 Para entender mejor

Play

 Video Activity C

 **Writing Activities 6-H, 6-I**

 Comm. Act. BLMs 6-3, 6-4, 6-5

Enrichment
Ex. 1: Some famous entertainers whose family backgrounds lend themselves particularly well to this exercise are Mexican Americans Linda Ronstadt, Emilio Estévez and his brother Charlie Sheen, and Panamanian singer Rubén Blades.
Ex. 3: As preparation for this exercise, bring in a poster or large book of photographs showing a celebration. Conduct a class discussion covering any of the questions listed that are applicable.

Apply

Process Reading
For a description of process reading, see p. 52.

Answers
Antes de leer
Answers will vary, but students may say *piñatas* are for children's birthday parties.

Mira la lectura
2. Un símbolo de alegría

¡Vamos a leer!

Antes de leer

STRATEGY ➤ Using prior knowledge

A *piñata* is often part of a Latin American family celebration. Have you ever seen a *piñata* for sale or been to a party where there was one? What are *piñatas* for?

Mira la lectura

STRATEGY ➤ Identifying the main idea

Read the following selection about *piñatas*. Then choose the best title from these choices:

a. La piñata en China
b. La piñata ayer y hoy
c. Cómo hacer una piñata

¡Crac! La piñata se rompe y cae una lluvia de dulces, monedas y juguetitos. Los niños corren para recoger todo lo que pueden. Saltan, gritan, se pelean y lloran, pero están contentos. Así terminan muchas fiestas en América Latina, sobre todo en México y el Caribe.

Una piñata es muchas cosas. Es una obra de arte. En una fiesta puede haber un concurso para ver quién hace la piñata más original. La piñata también es un juego. Los niños (¡o adultos!) tienen los ojos vendados y tratan de romper la piñata con un palo. También es un regalo, o mejor dicho, muchos regalitos que caen de la piñata cuando se rompe.

216   Capítulo 6

Options

Strategies for Reaching All Students

Spanish-Speaking Students
Aplicación: ¿Es verdad que la piñata es un símbolo de alegría? ¿Has recibido una piñata alguna vez? ¿Cuál fue la ocasión? ¿Qué hiciste con ella?

Students Needing Extra Help
Mira la lectura: Discuss the information that would be included in an article with each title.
Infórmate: Have students write down the supporting details.
Aplicación: Brainstorm the vocabulary needed to describe the shape, color, size, and contents of *piñatas*.

Algunos creen que la costumbre de la piñata es de origen chino. No sabemos si es verdad. Pero sí sabemos que la costumbre es muy antigua. En Italia, en el siglo dieciséis, ponían regalitos en una olla de barro que después rompían con un palo. De allí la costumbre llegó a España, y los españoles la llevaron al Nuevo Mundo. Ahora la piñata en forma de estrella, burro, tambor o tortuga ninja es un símbolo de fiesta y de alegría.

Vendedora de piñatas,
Ciudad de Guatemala

Infórmate

STRATEGY> Identifying supporting details

One way of organizing information is to give a general statement followed by supporting details. For example, after the general statement *Un perro puede ser más que una mascota* you would expect to find examples of the ways dogs can help us (as guard dogs, as seeing-eye dogs, etc.). These details explain or support the general statement. Reread the second paragraph and identify the details that support the general statement *Una piñata es muchas cosas.*

Aplicación

Which of the following supports the general statement *La costumbre de la piñata es muy antigua?*

a. A los adultos también les gustan las piñatas.
b. Una piñata no se puede usar más de una vez.
c. Nadie sabe el origen de la piñata.

Design a *piñata* for a holiday that you celebrate, and describe it in two or three sentences.

¡Vamos a leer! 217

Cultural Notes ☀

(p. 217, photo)
Piñatas are a form of folk art and some, such as these displayed in a Guatemala City shop, can be very elaborate. Originally made out of clay pots, they are now usually made by covering a blown-up balloon with papier-mâché, letting it dry for a few days, then popping the balloon. This makes for a safer *piñata* than the one made out of clay, which can shatter into dangerous shards when broken.

Apply

Process Writing
For information regarding developing a writing portfolio, see p. 54.

Todo junto

¡Vamos a escribir!

Piensa en las ocasiones especiales que celebras. ¿Hay otro día que te gustaría celebrar? Puedes honrar a alguien (como el Día del Niño que se celebra en Japón) o celebrar una fecha importante (el día que ganó el campeonato tu equipo de fútbol americano).

1 Escoge una ocasión y piensa en estas cosas:

- ¿Qué nombre le vas a dar al día de fiesta?
- ¿Cuándo se va a celebrar?
- ¿Cómo se va a celebrar? (¿Con ropa, comida o música especial? ¿Con eventos especiales?)

Organiza tus ideas y escribe el primer borrador. Sigue los pasos del proceso de escribir.

2 Ahora escribe una carta al editor de un periódico (nacional, local o escolar) y explícale por qué se debe celebrar ese día de fiesta. Puedes usar estas frases entre otras:

- celebrar / honrar
- el aniversario
- es necesario / importante

3 Al terminar la descripción y la carta, puedes:

- enviarlas a un periódico
- enviarlas a una organización relacionada con la ocasión
- exhibirlas en la sala de clases
- incluirlas en tu portafolio

Los incas de Cuzco, Perú, bailan vestidos con su ropa tradicional en la fiesta en que se celebra el solsticio de invierno.

218   Capítulo 6

Options

Strategies for Reaching All Students

Students Needing Extra Help
¡Vamos a escribir!: Do these activities in small groups or as a whole class. Students may have difficulty expressing why the day should be a holiday.
Give possibilities for the special day: the day Louis won the tennis match, the day Brian wasn't late, the day Tony received an A on his test, etc. Use the vocabulary section of the Chap. 4 Organizer.

Estudiantes jóvenes en Limón, Costa Rica, celebrando el Día de la Raza

Dos jóvenes españoles montan a caballo vestidos con ropa tradicional para un día de fiesta.

Cultural Notes

(p. 218, photo)
The winter solstice festival, or *festival Inti Raymi*, is celebrated in Cuzco, Peru, every June 24. Incan people come from all over the country to take part in the celebration, which takes place in the *Sacsayhuamán* ruins on the northern edge of Cuzco.

(p. 219, top photo)
Columbus Day in Limón is a time for dancing and street festivities. Groups of musicians and dancers called *comparsas* perform, each group distinguished by unique costumes and special dance steps. Many *limonenses* are descended from Jamaican immigrants who came to Costa Rica during the nineteenth century.

(p. 219, inset photo)
This young woman wears the *traje de flamenca* and the man the *traje de corto*, recalling the traditions of Andalucía, where horsemanship has long been valued. *Jerez de la Frontera* is home to one of the most important riding schools in Spain: the *Real Escuela Andaluza del Arte Ecuestre*.

Assess & Summarize

Test Preparation

You may want to assign parts of this section as written homework or as an in-class writing activity prior to administering the *Examen de habilidades*.

Answers

Listening: *Nosotros celebramos dos Días de Independencia, el de los Estados Unidos, que es el 4 de julio, y el de México, que es el 16 de septiembre. El 4 de julio toda la familia va al parque. Comemos hamburguesas y jugamos béisbol. Por la noche lanzamos fuegos artificiales. El 16 de septiembre vamos a la casa de mis abuelos. Comemos enchiladas y jugamos fútbol. Por la noche escuchamos música mexicana.*

Cristina is contrasting the celebration of Independence Day in the U.S. and in Mexico. On July 4 the whole family goes to the park, they eat hamburgers and play baseball, and at night they shoot fireworks. On September 16 they go to their grandparents' house, where they eat enchiladas and play soccer and listen to Mexican music.

Reading: 2. Algunas fiestas son para la familia.

Writing: Letters will vary.

¿Lo sabes bien?

Esta sección te ayudará a prepararte para el examen de habilidades, donde tendrás que hacer tareas semejantes.

Listening

Can you understand when people talk about a special occasion? What is Cristina contrasting? Name two differences between the two celebrations.

Reading

Read the following selection. Then choose the sentence that goes at the beginning.

... Parientes llegan de todas partes para estar con su familia en el Día de Acción de Gracias. Y mucha gente suele reunirse con su familia en la Navidad. ¿Y una boda? ¡Es muy importante ir a la boda de un hijo o un hermano!

1. Uno debe estar con los amigos en una fiesta de fin de año.
2. Algunas fiestas son para la familia.
3. Es fácil pasar tiempo con la familia.

Writing

Can you write a letter to a good friend describing a graduation party you gave or attended? Here is an example:

> Hola Ramón,
>
> Nuestro vecino Rodrigo se graduó el fin de semana pasado. (Le di una cartera de regalo.) Celebraron la graduación con una fiesta genial en que sirvieron comida fabulosa. Charlábamos y comíamos mucho cuando ocurrió algo muy divertido. Cuando llegó el cuñado de Rodrigo, ellos se abrazaron, pero Rodrigo olvidó que tenía el pastel en la mano. ¡Qué desastre! Su cuñado tuvo que pedir prestada una chaqueta al Sr. Ramírez. ¡Nunca vamos a olvidar esa fiesta!
>
> Un abrazo,
>
> Lorenzo

Culture

Can you explain why the celebration of the same holiday or festival can vary greatly from country to country in the Spanish-speaking world?

Speaking

Talk to a partner about a birthday party you attended recently. Discuss when and where the celebration took place and who attended. Here is a sample dialogue:

A —*¿Cuándo fue la fiesta de cumpleaños de Laura?*
B —*La semana pasada en casa de mis tíos.*
A —*¿Quiénes fueron?*
B —*Todas las amigas de Laura, ¡y ella tiene muchas amigas! También estuvieron sus hermanos y varios otros invitados que yo no conocía.*
A —*¿Cómo la celebraron?*
B —*Bailamos, encendimos las velas del pastel, le cantamos y todos comimos mucho.*

220 Capítulo 6

Options

Strategies for Reaching All Students

Students Needing Extra Help

Have students write out this section so that they can check off what they have mastered. *¿Lo sabes bien?:* Remind students that this is just a sample, not the actual test.
Listening: Read the sample more than once. Remind students that they only need to listen for two pieces of information. Brainstorm for which words they should be listening.

Reading: Familiarize students with the three choices, then read the article. If students still are having difficulty, have them read the paragraph, discuss the contents, and then choose the sentence.
Writing: Have students use the Organizer and write a sample letter before the test. Brainstorm other things that might happen at a party. Discuss some ordinary happenings (opened presents, went swimming,

etc.) so that students don't feel that they have to generate something unusual. But encourage creativity to the extent possible.
Culture: Have students review any notes they took during their reading of the *Perspectiva cultural.*
Speaking: Limit the number of lines of dialogue. Use the vocabulary section of the Organizer.

Resumen del capítulo 6

Usa el vocabulario de este capítulo para:

- name and describe members of an extended family
- describe special family occasions, holidays, and other celebrations
- greet people in several different ways

to discuss celebrations
invitar
la invitación, *pl.* las invitaciones
la reunión, *pl.* las reuniones
la celebración,
   pl. las celebraciones
celebrar
felicitar
¡felicidades!
la boda
casarse (con)
el aniversario (de boda)
la fiesta de sorpresa
la fiesta de cumpleaños
el cumpleaños
cumplir años
el pastel
la vela
encender
apagar
regalar
charlar
bailar
el baile
la graduación,
   pl. las graduaciones
graduarse

to describe family members
familiar
el bisabuelo, la bisabuela
el cuñado, la cuñada
el esposo, la esposa
el nieto, la nieta
el pariente, la parienta
el sobrino, la sobrina
(estar) casado, -a (con)
(estar) divorciado, -a (de)
(estar) separado, -a (de)
(estar) soltero, -a
nacer
(estar) muerto, -a

to talk about holidays
el día de fiesta
el Año Nuevo
el Día de los Enamorados
el Día de la Madre
la flor
el Día del Padre
el Día de la Independencia
los fuegos artificiales *(m.pl.)*
lanzar fuegos artificales
el Día de la Raza
el Día de (Acción de) Gracias
el pavo
la Nochebuena
la Navidad
el fin de año
la fiesta de fin de año

**to greet people
and say good-by**
abrazarse
besarse
darse la mano
decirse "¡Hola!"
despedirse *(e → i)*
encontrarse *(o → ue)*
hablarse
saludar

**other useful words
and expressions**
¿a qué edad ...?
a los ___ años
de nuevo
desde (que + *verb*)
especial
escribirse
verse

Resumen 221

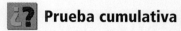
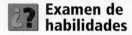

Enrichment
To help students organize their letter, encourage them to think of something outstanding or memorable about the graduation party, as in the model. You may also want to go over the model in class and ask students to help you list the information each sentence carries. Remind students that they do not have to follow the model exactly, but that they should try to convey equally pertinent information to make their letters substantial.

CAPÍTULO 7

THEME: LUXURIES AND NECESSITIES

SCOPE AND SEQUENCE Pages 222–255

COMMUNICATION

Topics

Personal possessions

Necessities and luxuries

Early American civilizations

Objectives

To discuss early American civilizations

To name and discuss personal possessions

To name home appliances and furnishings

To talk about emergencies

To talk about conservation

To express an opinion

CULTURE

Early American civilizations

GRAMMAR

Los adjetivos posesivos

Los pronombres posesivos

Repaso: Los usos del verbo ser

Ancillaries available for use with Chapter 7

| Multisensory/Technology | Print | Assessment |

 Overhead Transparencies, 35–38

 Audio Tapes and CDs

 Vocabulary Art Blackline Masters for Hands-On Learning, pp. 38–42

 Classroom Crossword

 La Catrina

 CD-ROM

 Practice Workbook, pp. 66–74

 Writing, Audio & Video Activities, pp. 41–46, 111–113, 163–166

 Communicative Activity Blackline Masters

Pair and Small Group Activities, pp. 43–48

Situation Cards, p. 49

 Un paso más: Actividades para ampliar tu español, pp. 37–42

 Assessment Program

Pruebas, pp. 100–109

Examen de habilidades, pp. 110–113

 Test Generator

Video still from Chap. 7

Possessions in Spanish-Speaking Countries

In many Spanish-speaking countries, wealthy families do not have as many items in their homes as middle class families in the U.S. do. Kitchen appliances, for example, are much less common; middle- and upper-class Hispanic families usually employ full-time maids and cooks. Because these people are paid to do domestic work, time-saving devices like electric can openers, food processors, or dishwashers are not necessary. In warm or dry climates, clothes are generally washed by hand and hung out to dry, so washing machines and dryers are rare. Most *electrodomésticos* are manufactured in other countries and imported, therefore making them too expensive for the general population.

Furniture is frequently more sparse in homes in Spanish-speaking countries than in the U.S., and it is rare to find a home with wall-to-wall carpeting, even among wealthy families. What is found, especially in countries with warmer climates, are courtyards filled with plants, and, in some cases, colorful caged birds. Hammocks and rocking chairs are plentiful, as people enjoy resting in them from the heat of the more tropical climates.

In Spain and Latin America, possessions which bring enjoyment or enrichment are prized. Music is highly valued in many Latin American countries; almost every home has a source of music, whether it is an inexpensive radio or a sophisticated stereo system. Dressing up is more common in Spanish-speaking countries than in the U.S. Stylish clothes are important: from hand-embroidered shirts and blouses in Central America to leather jackets and fur coats in South America. Hispanic women tend to wear more jewelry than American women. Most girls like to wear bracelets and earrings, and most have their ears pierced as infants.

Automobiles are considered a luxury in Spanish-speaking countries because of high import tariffs and high gasoline costs. They are not the necessity that they are in the U.S. because public transportation, taxis, and collective taxis (taxis that run the same routes repeatedly and carry four or five passengers) are so common.

Possessions can tell us about the way in which ancient peoples lived, including the Aztecs, Incas, and Mayas. The placement and types of objects found in undisturbed sites throughout Latin America have helped anthropologists deduce much of what is known about these indigenous cultures.

Introduce

The following list represents words, expressions, and grammar topics re-entered from Book 1 and Book 2 (Chaps. 1–6):

Book 1
calendar expressions, numbers 32–59, school supplies, time-telling, expressions of frequency, family, adjectives describing things, clothing, colors, household items, numbers 500–1,000, places in the community, *hay que* + inf., conservation, parties

Chapter 1
school subjects

Chapter 3
clothing

Chapter 4
sports
leisure-time activities

Chapter 6
special occasions

Planning

Cross-Curricular Connections

Art Connection *(pp. 230–231)*
Have students design an advertisement for a company that produces electrical appliances. Have them choose the items in the second *Vocabulario para conversar.* Encourage them to be as creative as possible. They should include a logo, the name of the item, its features, and the price. Display completed billboards around the classroom.

History Connection *(pp. 238–239)*
Have students choose an item from either *Vocabulario para conversar.* Have them think about the item's purpose and use today. What would the early American civilizations from the *Perspectiva cultural* have used instead? For example, instead of using a washing machine, they probably washed their clothes in a stream or a river.

Spanish in Your Community
Have students look for information in Spanish in the print material (instructions, warnings, etc.) that accompanies small appliances, make-up, and other personal products. Have them share this information with the class. Are students able to read and understand the information? Are the instructions in any other language besides Spanish and English? Do students think it is important to have these materials in many languages? Why?

CAPÍTULO 7

¿Es un lujo o una necesidad?

OBJECTIVES

At the end of this chapter, you will be able to:

■ name and describe personal possessions

■ tell to whom something belongs

■ state and defend opinions regarding necessities and luxuries

■ discuss aspects of early American civilizations

Apartamentos en Buenos Aires

223

Preview

Cultural Objective
• To discuss what personal belongings are important to Hispanic teens

Critical Thinking: Summarizing Information
Have students summarize the activities that are depicted in the photos on these pages. Discuss similarities and differences between the possessions shown here and what they have at home.

¡Piénsalo bien!

Mira las fotos. Los estudiantes que vemos están hablando de sus posesiones. ¿Qué tienes que es muy importante para ti?

"El equipo de sonido es una necesidad en nuestra vida. ¿Y en la tuya?"

¿Hay un tipo de música que les gusta a todos los miembros de tu familia?

Una familia de Santander, España, escuchando música en la sala

"Mi hermanito y yo no tenemos mucho en común, pero sí nos encantan los juegos de computadora."

¿Hay una computadora en tu casa? ¿Para qué la usas?

224   Capítulo 7

Estos hermanos de Santander usan la computadora para divertirse.

Options

Strategies for Reaching All Students

Spanish-Speaking Students
Ask: *¿Cuáles de estas posesiones son necesarias en tu vida? ¿Por qué?*

 Un paso más Exs. 7-A, 7-B

"**Sabemos tocar casi todas las canciones de los Beatles.**"

¿Tienes una guitarra o algún otro instrumento musical?
¿Es importante para ti? ¿Por qué?

Dos jóvenes españoles tocando la guitarra en Sevilla

225

Cultural Notes

(p. 224, top photo)
Famous international recording artists draw large followings everywhere. Young Spaniards, however, also listen to more traditional, regional music. The *cante hondo* of flamenco music, for example, continues to be popular. The Gipsy Kings combine the traditional forms of flamenco with rock, and they are popular throughout Spain and Latin America and the U.S.

(p. 225, photo)
The classical guitar, of Arabic and Greco-Roman ancestry, is central to Spanish and Latin American music. As Spanish explorers followed Columbus, they brought guitars and other stringed instruments with them. During the Conquest, their guitar music blended with the ancient flutes and pan-pipes of the indigenous American peoples and the drums of the African peoples brought to the continent as slaves.

Present

Chapter Theme
Personal possessions

Communicative Objectives
• To name personal possessions
• To discuss personal possessions
• To express an opinion

 Transparency 35

 Vocabulary Art BLMs

 Pronunciation Tape 7-1

Grammar Preview
Possessive pronouns are presented here lexically. Their explanation appears on p. 243.

Teaching Suggestions
Preparing students to speak: Use one or two options from each of the categories of Comprehensible Input, Physical Response, or Limited Verbal Response. For a complete explanation of these categories and some sample activities, see pp. T16–T17.

Vocabulario para conversar

¿Siempre llevas carnet de identidad?

Vas a necesitar estas palabras y expresiones para hablar sobre tus posesiones. Después de leerlas varias veces, practícalas con un(a) compañero(a).

la plata
el oro
el carnet de identidad
el televisor
el secador de pelo
el arete
el anillo (de plata)
el collar
la pulsera
el control remoto
el reloj (pulsera)
la moneda
el radio
el llavero
el peine
la llave
los lentes de contacto (m.pl.)
el tocacintas, pl. los tocacintas
los anteojos (m.pl.)
la cadena (de oro)

Options

Strategies for Reaching All Students

Spanish-Speaking Students
Vocabulario para conversar: ¿Usas otras palabras para los artículos que se ven aquí? ¿Cuáles? Haz una lista.
Ex. 1: Pair bilingual with non-bilingual students, if possible.

 Un paso más Ex. 7-C

Students Needing Extra Help
Begin to fill in the vocabulary section of the Organizer. Reorganize the list according to categories: jewelry and accessories; entertainment gadgets.
También necesitas . . . : Write out the *mostrar* paradigm for those students who need to see the whole chart. Give examples of *te parece* and *me parece*.

Learning Spanish Through Action
STAGING VOCABULARY: *Levanten*
MATERIALS: actual items from the vocabulary list (or vocabulary art BLMs)
DIRECTIONS: Hand out the props or BLMs. As you call out an item from the vocabulary list, have students hold up the item.

También necesitas . . .

mostrar *(o → ue)*	*to show*	(A mí) Me parece	*I think . . . ; it seems*
el lujo	*luxury*	que . . .	*to me (that) . . .*
propio, -a	*(one's) own*		
(yo) mismo, -a	*here: I myself*		
el mío, la mía	*mine*		
el tuyo, la tuya	*yours*	┌─────────────────────────┐	
de vez en cuando	*sometimes*	**¿Y qué quiere decir . . . ?**	
¿(A ti) Te parece	*Do you think*	la identificación	
que . . . ?	*(that) . . . ?*	la necesidad	

Empecemos a conversar

Túrnate con un(a) compañero(a) para ser *Estudiante A* y *Estudiante B*.
Reemplacen las palabras subrayadas en el modelo con palabras
representadas o escritas en los recuadros. Si ven 💡 pueden dar su
propia respuesta.

1

A —*¿Siempre llevas carnet de identidad?*
B —*Sí, siempre.*
   o: *No, nunca.*
   o: *Sólo de vez en cuando.*

Estudiante A   Estudiante B

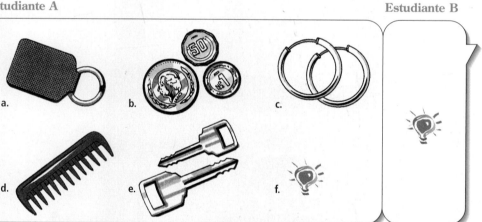

a.   b.   c.

d.   e.   f.

Reteach / Review: Vocabulary

Ex. 1: Remind students of other
expressions from Book 1: *a veces,
a menudo, de ninguna manera,
depende, ¡claro que sí (no)!*

Answers: Empecemos a conversar

1 ESTUDIANTE A
a. ¿Siempre llevas llavero?
b. . . . monedas?
c. . . . aretes?
d. . . . peine?
e. . . . llaves?
f. Questions will vary.
ESTUDIANTE B
a.–f. Answers will vary.

Class Starter Review

On the day following initial vocabulary presentation, you might
begin the class with either of
these activities:
1) Have students share with the
class one thing they always carry.
2) Have students ask a partner
about a possession, using *¿Te
parece que . . . ? (¿Te parece que
los collares caros de oro son un
lujo que no necesita nadie?)*
Partners answer using *Me parece
que . . . .*

Practice & Apply

Reteach / Review: Vocabulary

Ex. 2: Students can extend this dialogue by asking each other *¿Dónde compraste el tuyo (la tuya)? ¿Cuánto costó el tuyo (la tuya)?*

2 ESTUDIANTE A

a. Mi collar es de plata, ¿y el tuyo?

b. Mi pulsera es de oro, ¿y la tuya?

c. Mi reloj (pulsera) es de plástico, ¿y el tuyo?

d. Mi cartera es de cuero, ¿y la tuya?

e. Mi cadena es de plata, ¿y la tuya?

f. Questions will vary.

ESTUDIANTE B

a.–f. Answers will vary, but look for proper use of *el mío, la mía.*

2

A —Mi *anillo* es de *oro*, ¿y *el tuyo*?
B —*El mío* es de *plata*.
   o: *El mío* es de *oro* también.
   o: *Yo no tengo anillo*.

Estudiante A

Estudiante B

a.   b.   c.

d.   e.   f.

*L*A MIRADA ES LA EXPRESIÓN DEL DESEO.

MAJORICA

228   Capítulo 7

Options

Strategies for Reaching All Students

Spanish-Speaking Students
Exs. 2–3: Pair Spanish-speaking students, if possible.
Ex. 6: *¿Qué te gustaría tener en tu casa ideal? ¿Dónde puedes obtenerlo o comprarlo? ¿Por qué te gustaría tenerlo(la)?*

 Un paso más Ex. 7-D

Students Needing Extra Help
Ex. 2: Remind students that they have practiced *es de* with materials in Chap. 3.
Show students how *tuyo* in the question becomes *mío* in the answer.
For the first run-through, don't allow the *no tengo* response, as it doesn't provide practice of the possessive pronouns.
Encourage students to use responses involving more vocabulary and to use all the responses at least once.

Ex. 4: Model possible ways to answer question 2. Brainstorm possible responses to the *¿Por qué?* question. Remind students that *te parece* becomes *me parece*.
Ex. 5: Brainstorm possible responses to the *¿Por qué?* question.
Direct students to include household items.
Ex. 7: Brainstorm possible responses.
Students may need help with the vocabulary for all the questions.

228

3
A —*En tu casa, ¿tienes tu propio televisor?*
B —*Sí. Fue un regalo de (mi madre).*
   o: *No, sólo hay uno para toda la familia.*

Estudiante A

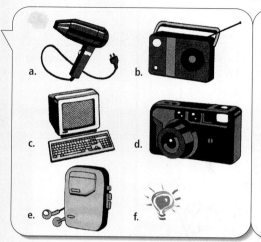
a.
b.
c.
d.
e.
f.

Estudiante B

No, sólo hay uno(a) para toda la familia.

Sí, lo (la) compré con mi propio dinero.

No, no tengo.

Sí, lo (la) compré yo mismo(a).

No, uso el (la) de ___.

Empecemos a escribir

Escribe tus respuestas en español.

4 ¿Quién usa anteojos o lentes de contacto en tu casa? ¿Desde cuándo los usan? Y tú, ¿necesitas anteojos? ¿A ti te parece necesario usar anteojos de sol? ¿Por qué?

5 ¿Qué haces para ganar dinero? ¿Te parece importante ganar tu propio dinero? Generalmente, ¿qué compras con tu propio dinero? ¿Y con el dinero de tus padres? ¿Por qué?

6 ¿Crees que un tocacintas es un lujo? ¿Y un control remoto? Haz una lista de cinco cosas que son necesidades y de cinco que son lujos. Compara tu lista con la de un(a) compañero(a).

7 ¿Por qué es importante llevar identificación? ¿Qué tipo de identificación tienes tú? ¿Dónde, a quiénes y para qué debes mostrarla?

También se dice

los lentes
las gafas
los espejuelos

las chapas
las pantallas
los zarcillos

Vocabulario para conversar   229

3 **ESTUDIANTE A**
a. En tu casa, ¿tienes tu propio secador de pelo?
b. ... propio radio?
c. ... propia computadora?
d. ... propia cámara?
e. ... propio tocacintas?
f. Questions will vary.
ESTUDIANTE B
a.–f. Answers will vary.

Answers: Empecemos a escribir

4–6 Answers will vary.

7 Answers will vary, but students may say that it is important to carry identification to provide vital information in case of an emergency. Some form of identification must be presented when making a purchase by check, when proof of age is required, and when requested by a police officer.

 Practice Wkbk. 7-1, 7-2

Audio Activity 7.1

Writing Activity 7-A

Pruebas 7-1, 7-2

For the last question, write out the three questions that are included in one: *¿Dónde debes mostrarla? ¿A quiénes debes mostrarla? ¿Para qué debes mostrarla?*

Enrichment
Ex. 6: Extend this exercise by asking about related possessions, such as *la video-casetera* and *el equipo de sonido*.

Cultural Notes

(p. 228, realia)
In Spain and Latin America, women are exposed to jewelry at a very early age. Tiny gold earrings are made for baby girls, many of whom have their ears pierced at birth. Several years later, gem-studded earrings replace those worn since birth. Rings and ID bracelets are also popular gifts for girls. *Medallas*, pendants depicting a religious figure, are usually given to a girl by her godparents at important religious ceremonies.

Present

Chapter Theme
Home appliances and furnishings

Communicative Objectives
- To name home appliances and furnishings
- To talk about emergencies
- To talk about conservation

 Transparencies 36–37

 Vocabulary Art BLMs

 Pronunciation Tape 7-2

Teaching Suggestions
Preparing students to speak: Use one or two options from each of the categories of Comprehensible Input, Physical Response, or Limited Verbal Response. For a complete explanation of these categories and some sample activities, see pp. T16–T17.

Vocabulario para conversar

¿Es necesario tener un detector de humo?

Aquí tienes el resto del vocabulario que necesitas en este capítulo para hablar sobre tus posesiones.

el bombillo

el detector de humo

el fregadero

el microondas

el ventilador

el incendio

el extinguidor de incendios

el tostador

el horno

el lavaplatos

el aire acondicionado

Options

Strategies for Reaching All Students

Spanish-Speaking Students
 Un paso más Ex. 7-E

Learning Spanish Through Action
STAGING VOCABULARY: *Apaguen, Enciendan, Pongan*
MATERIALS: flashlight, smoke detector, batteries, and items included in vocabulary that may be found in the classroom
DIRECTIONS: Direct students to turn off the heat, put dictionaries on the shelf, turn on the flashlight, etc.

el estante

la secadora

la lavadora

el calentador

la linterna

la pila

la mesa
de noche

la calefacción
central

También necesitas . . .

encender *(e → ie)*	here: *to turn on*
apagar	here: *to turn off*
funcionar	*to work, to function*
el aparato	*appliance, device*
ahorrar	*to save*

¿Y qué quiere decir . . . ?

la electricidad	conservar
eléctrico, -a	reparar
la emergencia	en caso de
la energía	suficiente
la posesión, *pl.* las posesiones	

Critical Thinking: Categorizing Information

Call on individuals to write in the name of an item under one of the following categories: *Aparatos grandes, Aparatos pequeños, Joyas, Objetos para emergencias.* Keep the chart on a bulletin board. Encourage students to add to the lists from time to time.

Reteach / Review: Vocabulary

También necesitas . . . : To review vocabulary appropriate to environmental conservation, refer to Book 1, Chap. 13.

Class Starter Review

On the day following initial vocabulary presentation, you might begin the class with one or both of these activities:

1) In pairs, have students say which of the vocabulary items is most essential in a house and explain why. Keep a class tally on the chalkboard.

2) Prepare a list of words from previous chapters associated with each vocabulary item. For example, *el pan (tostado)* for *el tostador.* Read the list aloud and have students respond with possible associated words.

Practice

Teaching Suggestions

Ex. 8: Encourage students to give a reason when answering positively: *Es necesario tener un microondas para cocinar más rápidamente cuando uno no tiene mucho tiempo.*

Answers: Empecemos a conversar

8 ESTUDIANTE A

a ¿Te parece que hay que tener aire acondicionado?

b. ...un lavaplatos?

c. ...calefacción central?

d. ...un tostador?

e. Questions will vary.

ESTUDIANTE B

Answers will vary, but negative responses may include the following:

a. A mí me parece que un ventilador es suficiente.

b. ...un fregadero...

c. ...un calentador...

d. ...un horno...

9 ESTUDIANTE A

a. ¿Crees que es necesario tener una linterna?

b. ...un extinguidor de incendios?

c. ...un radio?

d. ...un despertador?

e. ...pilas?

f. Questions will vary.

Empecemos a conversar

8

A —*¿Te parece que hay que tener <u>un microondas</u>?*

B —*<u>Claro que sí</u>. Ahorra mucha energía y mucho tiempo.*

o: *A mí me parece que <u>un horno</u> es suficiente.*

o: *¡No! ¡No soporto tantos aparatos!*

Estudiante A　　　　　　　　Estudiante B

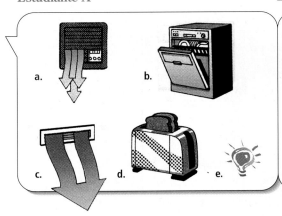

9

A —*¿Crees que es necesario tener <u>un detector de humo</u>?*

B —*¡Cómo no! Puedes <u>necesitarlo en caso de incendio</u>.*

Estudiante A　　　　　　　　Estudiante B

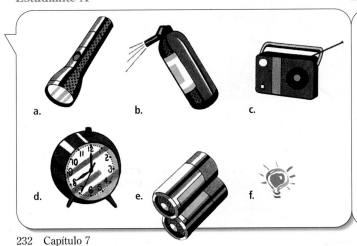

para despertarse por la mañana

en caso de incendio / emergencia

si no hay electricidad

para escuchar las noticias

para ver en la noche

No, no es necesario.

232　Capítulo 7

Options

Strategies for Reaching All Students

Spanish-Speaking Students

Exs. 8–11: Pair bilingual with non-bilingual students if possible.

Students Needing Extra Help

Ex. 8: For the first run-through, eliminate the *Claro que sí* and the *¡No! ¡No soporto...!* responses.

Help students with the association between air conditioner and fan, dishwasher and sink, etc.

Ex. 10: Brainstorm the possibilities for what may be found in their rooms. If available, use the vocabulary section of the Level 1, Chap. 9 Organizer.

Cooperative Learning

Have students form groups of three. Instruct groups to select one option from Ex. 10 for the question *¿Qué tienes en el / la ___ de tu dormitorio?* One student interviews the other members of the group, while the second one writes down the answers. The third student reports the results to the class: *Ana María tiene un espejo, perfume, y joyas en la cómoda de su dormitorio.*

10

A —¿Qué tienes en *la mesa de noche* de tu dormitorio?

B —Tengo *una lámpara, un radio y un despertador*.

o: *No tengo mesa de noche*.

¡NO OLVIDES!

Do you remember these words?
el cartel
la cómoda
el escritorio
el guardarropa

Estudiante A

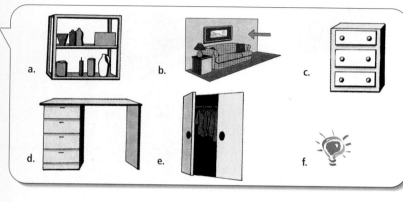

a.
b.
c.

d.
e.
f.

Estudiante B

¿Lujo o necesidad? Este joven de Madrid usa el lavaplatos.

Vocabulario para conversar   233

ESTUDIANTE B
Answers will vary, but may include the following:
a. ¡Como no! Puedes necesitarla para ver en la noche.
b. ...necesitarlo en caso de incendio.
c. ...necesitarlo para escuchar las noticias.
d. ...necesitarlo para despertarte por la mañana.
e. ...necesitarlas si no hay electricidad.
f. Answers will vary.

10 ESTUDIANTE A
a. ¿Qué tienes en los estantes de tu dormitorio?
b. ...la pared...
c. ...la cómoda...
d. ...el escritorio...
e. ...el guardarropa...
f. Questions will vary.

ESTUDIANTE B
a.–f. Answers will vary.

Cultural Notes

(p. 233, photo)
Spanish women have joined the workforce in large numbers in recent years, which means that other family members are increasingly called upon to do domestic work. Double incomes in a family and increased work hours outside the home make dishwashers not only affordable, but often necessary to keep up with chores.

Practice & Apply

11 ESTUDIANTE A

a. ¿Para qué sirve un lavaplatos?

b. . . . una cámara?

c. . . . una cartera?

d. . . . una secadora?

e. . . . un bombillo?

f. . . . una mesa de noche?

g. Questions will vary.

ESTUDIANTE B

Answers will vary, but may include the following:

a. Sirve para lavar platos.

b. . . . sacar fotos.

c. . . . llevar dinero.

d. . . . secar ropa.

e. . . . dar luz.

f. . . . poner el despertador.

g. Answers will vary.

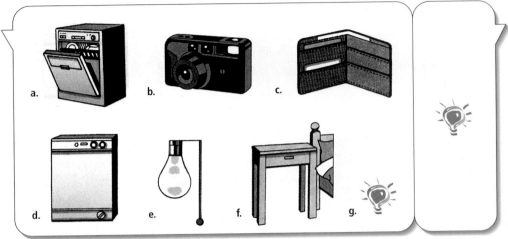

¿Es un lujo o una necesidad?

11

A —¿Para qué sirve _una lavadora_?

B —_Sirve para lavar ropa_.

Estudiante A

a. b. c.

d. e. f. g.

Estudiante B

Empecemos a escribir y a leer

Escribe tus respuestas en español.

12 ¿Qué podemos hacer todos los días para conservar energía? En tu casa, ¿encienden todas las luces por la noche? ¿Cómo podemos conservar agua? Tú mismo, ¿qué puedes hacer hoy para conservar energía y agua?

13 ¿Qué aparato eléctrico es el más necesario para ti? ¿Y para tus padres? Cuando no funciona un aparato, ¿te parece mejor repararlo o comprar uno nuevo? ¿Ahorras dinero si lo reparas? ¿Qué aparatos necesitan pilas?

14 Entre todas tus posesiones, ¿cuáles son las más importantes para ti? ¿Por qué? De esas posesiones, ¿hay cosas que ya no necesitas? ¿Cuáles?

15 En caso de incendio, ¿sabes qué hacer? ¿A qué número debes llamar? ¿Y en caso de alguna otra emergencia? ¿A quién le puedes pedir ayuda?

234   Capítulo 7

Options

Strategies for Reaching All Students

16 Aquí tienes una serie de reglas *(rules)* para conservar energía y agua. Con un(a) compañero(a), cámbienlas si no están de acuerdo con ellas. Después, escriban otras tres reglas.

Para conservar energía y agua es necesario:

- apagar los aparatos eléctricos por la mañana
- encender solamente las luces necesarias por la noche
- ducharse rápidamente
- usar la lavadora sólo cuando hay mucha ropa sucia
- usar el aire acondicionado sólo de vez en cuando
- reparar los aparatos que no funcionan bien

Pinnnn...

NOVEDAD MUNDIAL

...zassss

Toast Taurus, con pinzas. Para no quemarse.

La tostadora automática Toast Taurus tiene exterior frío. Cuenta, además, en exclusiva, con unas pinzas integradas que permiten coger las tostadas sin quemarse.
Por otra parte, está especialmente preparada para descongelar. La intensidad del tostado del pan se gradúa automáticamente. Su amplia abertura admite todo tipo de rebanadas, desde las de pan de molde hasta las de pan de hogaza.

taurus *crea*

También se dice

la tostadora

la batería

la bombilla
la bujía

el abanico

el lavatrastos
el lavatrastes

el foco

la repisa

la mesa de luz
la mesilla

Vocabulario para conversar   235

Cultural Notes

(p. 235, realia)
Pinzas, the selling point of this toaster, are used to create this onomatopeic ad:
Pinnnn... the toaster hums as it toasts the bread. Suddenly, ¡*...zassss!* The toast pops up and in one fell swoop, it is snatched up and placed on the plate. To facilitate this maneuver without burning oneself, this toaster comes equipped with *pinzas* (tongs).

Apply

Answers:
¡Comuniquemos!
1–3 Answers will vary.

Using Photos

Having students use what they've learned about word families (*dominical / domingo*), ask: *¿Cuándo van de compras estos jóvenes?*

¡Comuniquemos!

Aquí tienes otra oportunidad para usar el vocabulario de este capítulo.

1 Imagina que eres un(a) millonario(a). ¿Qué aparatos eléctricos te gustaría comprar? ¿Para quién? ¿Por qué? Trabaja con un(a) compañero(a).

para tu familia /
$1.500

A —*¿Qué aparato eléctrico te gustaría comprar para tu familia con $1.500?*
B —*Un televisor muy grande con control remoto.*
A —*¿Por qué?*
B — . . .

a. para ti /$250
b. para la escuela /$500
c. para tu mejor amigo(a) /$100
d. para tu familia /$1.000
e. para la guardería infantil a la cual ibas cuando eras niño(a) /$500
f. para tus vecinos /$50
g. para algún (alguna) niño(a) que conoces /$50
h. 💡

2 Hay un incendio en el horno eléctrico cuando tú y tu compañero(a) están cocinando. ¿Qué hacen? Escribe un diálogo con tu compañero(a).

A —*¡Aaaaay! ¡Mira, Luis, un incendio!*
B —*Hay que . . .*
A —*¡No! Trae . . .*
B — . . .

Unos jóvenes madrileños
en un mercado dominical

Options

Strategies for Reaching All Students

Students Needing Extra Help
Ex. 1: Students will need help with the response to *¿Por qué?* Use the vocabulary section of the Organizer.
Ex. 2: Discuss what to do during a kitchen fire (throw salt, not water). Model a complete dialogue. Students will most likely give the correct response first, not noticing that the third line of dialogue begins with *¡No! Trae . . .*

Ex. 3: If available, use the vocabulary section of Level 1, Chaps. 6 and 7 Organizers. *¿Qué sabes ahora?:* Have students write out this list so that they can keep track of their progress.

Enrichment
Have pairs of students embellish their dialogues and present them as skits to the rest of the class the next day. Encourage students to use real newspaper ads or mailings for props. Remind them that the shopping vocabulary from Chap. 3 would be helpful.

3 Túrnate con un(a) compañero(a). Van a ser el padre o la madre y su hijo(a). Quieres algo, pero tu padre o madre no quiere comprarlo. ¿Cómo puedes convencerlo(la)? Explícale:

- qué quieres
- por qué lo quieres
- dónde lo viste
- cómo es
- cuánto cuesta

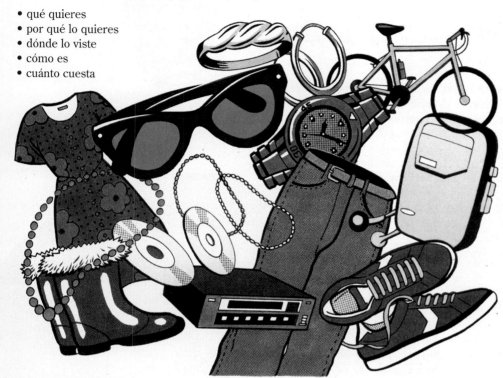

Answers: ¿Qué sabes ahora?
- Answers will vary, but each blank should contain a noun.
- Answers will vary, but the first blank should contain a material and the second a possessive pronoun.
- Answers will vary, but both blanks should contain nouns.

 Audio Activity 7.3

¿Qué sabes ahora?

Can you:

- **name some personal possessions?**

  —Tengo ___, ___ y ___ en mi dormitorio.

- **describe personal possessions and ask about those of other people?**

  —Mi anillo es de ___, ¿y el ___?

- **state and defend opinions regarding necessities and luxuries?**

  —Me parece que tener___ es una necesidad, pero tener ___ es un lujo.

Vocabulario para conversar   237

Cooperative Learning
Have students form groups of three. Two will act as though they are looking for an apartment; the third will be a landlord. Two apartments are available. One has a sink, an electric fan, and a refrigerator; it costs $450. The other has a microwave, a dishwasher, and central air conditioning; it costs $700. The renters have a combined monthly income of $1,000. The landlord must describe both apartments and try to convince the students to lease the more expensive one. The renters need to decide between themselves which one they will rent, and be prepared to explain their reasons to the class.

Cultural Notes

(p. 236, photo)
A Sunday morning excursion to *el Rastro,* Spain's famous flea market, is a Madrid tradition. Filled with surprises and discoveries, this market is not a destination for someone with a specific shopping list. Browsing is what brings real success. True flea markets such as this are disappearing from modern cities as malls, shopping centers, and discount malls grow more common.

Present & Apply

Cultural Objective
• To discuss early American civilizations

Critical Thinking: Synthesizing
Have small groups of students use encyclopedias or social studies texts to prepare maps showing the areas of the Aztec, Mayan, and Incan civilizations. Have them label each civilization's capital and important geographical features. In addition, they might illustrate their maps with drawings or descriptions of key accomplishments of each civilization.

Multicultural Perspectives
The Aztec description of the Spanish conquest of Tenochtitlán in the Codex Florentine reveals a difference in perceptions of what was considered valuable by the two cultures. The Spanish wanted gold and gold alone. The Aztecs were surprised when the Spanish tore off the *quetzal* feathers decorating the gold ornaments and burned them. For the Aztecs and the Maya, the *quetzal* was a spiritual protector, and its feathers were extremely valuable. Ask students if they know of any objects that are valued in one culture that are not necessarily valued in another.

Perspectiva cultural

¿Según las fotos, cómo se sabe que estas civilizaciones eran muy avanzadas en la agricultura? ¿En las ciencias? ¿En el arte?

Esta cabeza hecha de estuco está en una pared de la antigua ciudad maya de Comalcalco, México.

En el año 1500, los aztecas dominaban lo que hoy es México. La ciudad de Tenochtitlán, la capital azteca, tenía más o menos 200.000 habitantes, más que cualquier ciudad europea de ese tiempo. Esta ciudad tenía grandes templos y avenidas y un estadio para un deporte similar al básquetbol. Cultivaban maíz, verduras y flores en grandes jardines acuáticos. Hacían joyas de cobre, oro y plata. ¡Y hacían todo sin instrumentos de metal ni sistema alfabético de escribir!

El calendario azteca

238 Capítulo 7

Options

Strategies for Reaching All Students

Spanish-Speaking Students
After Ex. 2: *Haz una investigación sobre un aspecto de la vida diaria de una de estas civilizaciones indígenas. Luego, descríbelo en una composición breve. Puedes ilustrar tu informe y exhibirlo en la sala de clase.*

 Un paso más Ex. 7-H

Students Needing Extra Help
Have students take notes, as an aid in reviewing for the exam.
Have some background material on hand.
Ex. 1: Students will have very little knowledge of the Greeks and Romans. Be prepared to give them this information. You may want to invite the Latin teacher or someone from the history department to come to your class.
Ex. 2: Brainstorm possible solutions. Supply the vocabulary.

Cultural Notes

(p. 238, bottom photo)
The Calendar Stone was completed about 1479 A.D. From the center, the six circles contain 1) Tonatiuh, the Aztec sun god; 2) four ovals individually representing the previous stages of the world, and together representing our present world; 3) symbols for 20 days in the Aztec calendar; 4) symbols for jade or turquoise meaning "precious," referring to the sky's color; 5) glyphs for "star" penetrated by the sun's rays; 6) fire snakes symbolizing time.

Cuando el imperio romano estaba perdiendo su influencia en el año 200 d. C., en América Central crecía el imperio maya. Los mayas también tenían grandes ciudades. En el centro de Tikal, por ejemplo, había más de 300 edificios. Los mayas tenían observatorios astronómicos. Su calendario de 365 días era más preciso que el calendario europeo de esa época. Y todavía podemos admirar sus joyas, su cerámica y sus monumentos de piedra.

La civilización que dominaba la región de los Andes en el año 1500 era la de los incas. Construyeron caminos y puentes en las montañas. Hicieron edificios grandes y elegantes. Construyeron estos edificios tan bien que aun hoy no se puede poner un cuchillo entre las piedras de sus paredes.

"El Caracol," observatorio astronómico maya de Chichén Itzá, Yucatán, México

Vista de Machu Picchu, una ciudad incaica en los Andes peruanos

La cultura desde tu perspectiva

1 ¿Cuál de estas civilizaciones antiguas te parece más similar a la civilización romana o griega? ¿Por qué?

2 Imagina que tienes que hacer una pirámide como las de los aztecas o los mayas sin usar instrumentos de metal. ¿Qué problemas vas a tener? ¿Cómo los vas a solucionar?

Perspectiva cultural   239

(p. 238, top photo)
This stucco head is part of a wall relief in Comalcalco, a site in the Mexican state of Tabasco, at what was the western limit of the Mayan Civilization. Comalcalco flourished during the middle classic period (approximately 450–600 A.D.) The architecture and brick and stucco construction methods here are similar to those of Palenque.

(p. 239, left photo)
El Caracol (800–1000 A.D.) is believed to have had a purpose similar to that of an astronomical observatory. Through astronomy, the Mayas devised a calendar system more accurate than any except our Gregorian calendar. El Templo de los Guerreros *(right)* was built during the post-classic Maya period (1000–1200). The building features images of Quetzalcóatl, one of the legendary rulers of the Toltecs.

(p. 239, right photo)
Located in the Andes Mountains, at more than 8,000 feet above sea level, Machu Picchu is one of the best preserved archeological sites in South America. The ruins were rediscovered in 1911 by Hiram Bingham. These remains tell us many things about pre-Columbian Incan culture. The great stone temples and large above-ground cemeteries tell of the Incan belief in the afterlife and of the importance of religion to their civilization.

Preview

Answers

A He uses the word(s) *(los) míos.* If he were talking about *un disco compacto,* the word(s) would be *(el) mío.*

B The words used to describe characteristics of the robot are *(una) necesidad, (una) maravilla, fantástico, mágico,* and *resistente.* The verb used with the descriptions is *ser.*

Gramática en contexto

¡El último triunfo de la tecnología!

HACELOTODO funciona con electricidad o con pilas.

HACELOTODO da lecciones por computadora.

HACELOTODO juega video-juegos, damas y ajedrez.

HACELOTODO muestra video y toca discos compactos.

HACELOTODO envía mensajes por fax.

HACELOTODO es mucho mejor que una linterna. Tiene bombillos en las manos.

HACELOTODO tiene detector de humo y puede apagar incendios. ¡Y al final del día, cuando Ud. lo apaga, **HACELOTODO** no está cansado!

¿Qué dicen nuestros clientes?

❝**HACELOTODO** *no es un lujo, es una necesidad. ¡Es una maravilla! El mío ayuda a los niños en sus tareas.*❞
JUAN SOTO, MONTEREY PARK

❝**HACELOTODO** *es fantástico. Yo misma no puedo vivir sin él.*❞
CARLOTA SANTOS, LOMA LINDA

❝*Yo uso a* **HACELOTODO** *para escuchar música. Saco fácilmente los discos compactos de mis hijos y pongo los míos.*❞
FRANK ÁVALOS, MONTEBELLO

El mágico **HACELOTODO** *es de metal fuerte, no de plástico. Es resistente al calor y al frío.*
HACELOTODO *puede ser suyo por sólo $899. Reserve su propio* **HACELOTODO** *ahora mismo.*

A Frank Ávalos talks about "my children's CDs and mine." What word does he use for "mine"? If he were talking about *un disco compacto,* what form do you think that word would take?

B In this ad, users describe characteristics of the robot. What are they? At the bottom of the ad, other expressions tell what the robot is made of. What verb is used with both types of descriptions?

240 Capítulo 7

Options

Strategies for Reaching All Students

Students Needing Extra Help
Begin the grammar section of the Organizer.
Ex. A: On the chalkboard or overhead, write out *los discos compactos → los míos*
un disco compacto → _____.
Show the pattern that connects *los discos* and *los míos.*
Ex. B: Direct students to the words that describe characteristics.

Give examples of how these adjectives agree in number and, when applicable, in gender. You may now want to do Ex. 1 on p. 242. Give more examples using *su* and *sus* with *de.* Show how *my key* becomes *mine* (two words becoming one). Construct a chart in which you show students that you have really said the same thing in two different ways.

Enrichment
As an in-class written assignment, have students create more comments praising HACELOTODO, citing other things the robot has done for them. When students have finished, call on them to share their comments with the class.

Los adjetivos posesivos

You know that possessive adjectives agree in gender and number with the nouns they describe. They are always used before a noun.

mi, tu, su **nuestro**	televisor	**mis, tus, sus** **nuestros**	televisores
mi, tu, su **nuestra**	linterna	**mis, tus, sus** **nuestras**	linternas

- Since *su* and *sus* have many meanings, for clarity or emphasis we can use a prepositional phrase instead.

de	Ud. él ella	**de**	Uds. ellos ellas

—¡**Sus** zapatos son muy elegantes!   *(His /Her /Your /Their) shoes are very elegant!*

—¿Los zapatos **de ella**?   *Her shoes?*

—No, los **de Ud**.   *No, **yours**.*

- Like English, Spanish has another set of possessive adjectives that come *after* the noun. Compare these sentences.

Ésa es **mi** llave.   *That's **my** key.*

Esa llave es **mía**.   *That key is **mine**.*

Here are the possessive adjectives that follow a noun:

mío(s), mía(s)	*my, mine*	**nuestro(s), nuestra(s)**	*our, ours*
tuyo(s), tuya(s)	*your, yours*	**vuestro(s), vuestra(s)**	*your, yours*
suyo(s), suya(s)	*your, yours his her, hers*	**suyo(s), suya(s)**	*your, yours their, theirs*

Present

Class Starter Review

On the day following the presentation of possessive adjectives, you might begin the class with this activity:

Ask individual students about objects in the classroom: *¿De quién es ese suéter? (Es mío, es suyo.) ¿De quién es ese escritorio? (Es suyo, profesora.)*

Cooperative Learning

Tell students they will create a time capsule. In groups of three, using Vocabulary Art BLMs or magazine cutouts representing similar items, have each student mount a cutout on a sheet of paper, writing a description of the item underneath. When they are finished, students pass their papers to the left, and the receiving students write the use for the cutout item on their new paper. After passing their papers to the left again, students will write whether the item is a luxury or a necessity. Have each group collect the three papers and roll them into a "time capsule" tube, securing it with a rubber band or piece of yarn. Then each group passes its time capsule to another group.

The receiving group represents Aztecs from the year 1500. Each student will examine a paper from the previous group and answer in writing: What item do you use for the same purpose? How is it similar or different from this item? Is your item a luxury or a necessity for you? Call on students to report results.

Present & Practice

Multicultural Perspectives

Appliances such as refrigerators may be considered necessities in some places and luxuries in others. In some small towns in Latin America, for example, people who don't have refrigerators use other methods to preserve food. Raw meat is sometimes salted or smoked. In cold regions such as the Andes Mountains in South America, food may be frozen outside. Many people also buy the exact amount of food needed for that particular day, keeping perishable items cold in an ice-filled cooler. Ask students what appliances they use every day and how they would survive without these items.

Answers

1 ESTUDIANTE A
a. ¿Son tus llaveros?
b. ¿Es tu carnet de identidad?
c. ¿Son tus collares?
d. ¿Son tus lentes de contacto?
e. ¿Son tus pulseras?
f. Questions will vary.

ESTUDIANTE B
a. No, son los de ellos.
b. No, es el de Mauricio.
c. No, son los de Luz y Estela.
d. No, son los de nosotros.
e. No, son las de Uds.
f. Answers will vary.

- To clarify or emphasize, we can use *de* + pronoun instead of a form of *suyo*.

¿Es el ventilador **suyo**? *Is it (**his/her/your/their**) fan?*
Sí, es el ventilador **de ella**. *Yes, it's **her** fan.*

Note that the pronoun agrees in number and gender with the noun it refers to.

1 Pregúntale a un(a) compañero(a) si estas cosas son de él (ella).

A —¿*Es tu anillo?*
B —*No, es el de Mercedes.*

Mercedes

| a. ellos | b. Mauricio | c. Luz y Estela | d. nosotros | e. Uds. | f. |

2 ¿De quién son estos aparatos? Pregúntale a un(a) compañero(a).

A —*Éste es el calentador de Myriam, ¿verdad?*
B —*Sí, es el calentador suyo.*
    o: *No, no es el calentador suyo.*

Myriam

| a. ella | b. Carmina y Manuel | c. él |

| d. Uds. | e. ellas | f. Mateo | g. |

242   Capítulo 7

Options

Strategies for Reaching All Students

Students Needing Extra Help
Ex. 1: You may want to do this exercise right after reviewing the possessive adjectives that come before a noun (*mi, tu,* etc.) and the prepositional phrase using *de* (*de Ud., de él*).
Ex. 2: Review demonstrative pronouns. Point out that the possessive adjective agrees with the object, not the person.

Show on the board or overhead that students only need to eliminate the *de* phrase and replace it with the possessive adjective.

Los pronombres posesivos

A possessive pronoun takes the place of a noun and a possessive adjective.

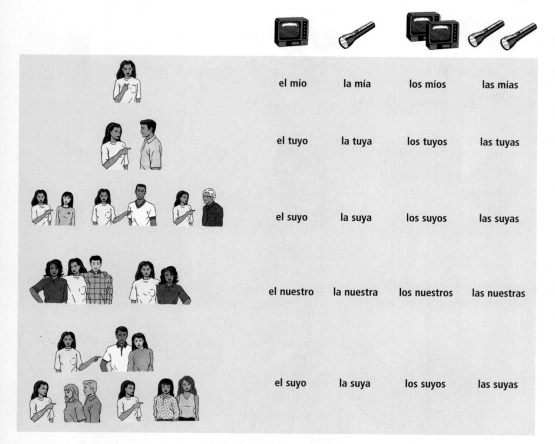

el mío	la mía	los míos	las mías
el tuyo	la tuya	los tuyos	las tuyas
el suyo	la suya	los suyos	las suyas
el nuestro	la nuestra	los nuestros	las nuestras
el suyo	la suya	los suyos	las suyas

- The possessive pronouns agree in number and gender with the nouns they replace. They are generally used with the appropriate definite article.

    Mi linterna está en el armario. ¿Dónde está **la tuya**?

- When possessive pronouns are used after the verb *ser,* we usually omit the definite article.

    —¿De quién es esta cartera?
    —Es **mía**.

Gramática en contexto   243

2 ESTUDIANTE A
a. Éste es el microondas de nosotros, ¿verdad?
b. ...el secador de pelo de Carmina y Manuel...
c. ...el tocacintas de él...
d. ...el tostador de Uds....
e. Éste es el radio de ellas...
f Éste es el extinguidor de incendios de Mateo...
g. Questions will vary.

ESTUDIANTE B
a. Sí, es (No, no es) el microondas nuestro *(or:* suyo).
b. ...el secador de pelo suyo.
c. ...el tocacintas suyo.
d. ...el tostador nuestro.
e. Sí, es (No, no es) el radio suyo.
f. Sí, es (No, no es) el extinguidor de incendios suyo.
g. Answers will vary.

Practice Wkbk. 7-5

Writing Activity 7-E

Prueba 7-5

Practice

Re-enter / Recycle

Exs. 3, 4, 6: clothing from Chap. 3
Ex. 4: school from Chap. 2
Ex. 6: sports from Chap. 4

Answers

3 ESTUDIANTE A

a. El anillo de plata, ¿es tuyo o de Rosa?

b. El reloj de plástico, ¿es tuyo o de Mario?

c. La mesa de noche de metal, ¿es tuya o de él?

d. La cartera negra, ¿es tuya o del profesor / de la profesora?

e. La camisa (blusa) a cuadros, ¿es tuya o de ella?

f. Questions will vary.

ESTUDIANTE B

Answers will vary.

a. Es suyo. El mío es de oro.

b. Es suyo. El mío es de cuero.

c. Es suya. La mía es de madera.

d. Es suya. La mía es marrón.

e. Es suya. La mía es a rayas.

f. Answers will vary.

4 Answers will vary.

5 ESTUDIANTE A

a. No encuentro mi champú. ¿Me prestas el tuyo?

b. ...mi pasta dentífrica. ...la tuya?

c. ...mis pesas. ...las tuyas?

d. ...mi tocacintas. ...el tuyo?

e. ...mi raqueta de tenis. ...la tuya?

f. ...mi radio. ...el tuyo?

g. ...mi secador de pelo. ...el tuyo?

---

3 Túrnate con un(a) compañero(a) para preguntar de quién es cada uno de estos objetos.

A —*El peine azul, ¿es tuyo o de Eva?*
B —*Es suyo. El mío es rojo.*

Eva

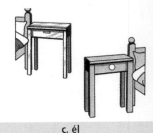

a. Rosa   b. Mario   c. él

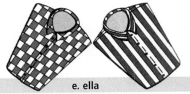

d. el (la) profesor(a)   e. ella   f.

4 Con un(a) compañero(a), hablen de sus posesiones. Por ejemplo:

A —*Mi cartera es negra. ¿Y la tuya?*
B —*La mía es verde. Es de plástico.*
     o: *La mía es negra también.*
     o: *No tengo cartera.*

244   Capítulo 7

Options

Strategies for Reaching All Students

Students Needing Extra Help

Ex. 3: Use vocabulary sections of Chap. 3. Do as a whole class, as this exercise involves multiple steps. Show students that a form of *tuyo, suyo,* and *mío* is used in each dialogue, just as in the model. One picture will be paired with a form of *tuyo.* Show how the *de* phrase becomes a form of *suyo.* Finally, show how the *tuyo* in statement A becomes the *el mío* in statement B. Provide more examples.

Ex. 4: Show students how *mi cartera* becomes *la tuya.* Demonstrate how a form of *tuyo* in the question becomes a form of *mío* in the answer. Do more examples using masculine, plurals, etc.

Ex. 5: You may want to have students answer only with the second response because it does not involve object pronouns. Remind students of the vocabulary they can use to excuse themselves if they do not have the item in question: *Lo siento (perdón), yo no tengo peine.*

Ex. 6: Use the vocabulary section of Chap. 3 Organizer. Remind students that the adjective in each sentence will be a form of *horrible.* Students may be confused to see *tu* and *tus* instead of *tuyo.* Explain.

Ex. 7: Practice the entire exercise, answering with only the first B response. This will help students stay focused on dropping the article before a form of *ser.* Then repeat, using the second response, reminding students of why *los* is present.

244

5 Estás con tu compañero(a) en el club deportivo y no encuentras tus cosas. Pídele las suyas.

peine

A —*No encuentro mi peine. ¿Me prestas el tuyo?*
B —*¿El mío? Aquí lo tienes.*
　　o: *¿El mío? Yo no tengo peine.*

a. champú
b. pasta dentífrica
c. pesas
d. tocacintas

e. raqueta de tenis
f. radio
g. secador de pelo
h. reloj

6 Rosita siempre prefiere las cosas de sus hermanas mayores. Con un(a) compañero(a), sigue el modelo.

A —*¿Por qué no usas tus propios anteojos de sol?*
B —*Porque los míos son horribles. Prefiero los suyos.*

7 Después de un incendio en un edificio de apartamentos, los bomberos preguntan de quién son estas cosas en la calle.

aparatos

A —*¿Son suyos estos aparatos?*
B —*Sí, señor, son nuestros.*
　　o: *No, señor, no sabemos dónde están los nuestros.*

a. estantes
b. mesas de noche
c. juguetes
d. lámparas

e. sillas
f. televisores
g. trajes
h. lavadora y secadora

Gramática en contexto　245

h. . . . mi reloj. . . . el tuyo?

ESTUDIANTE B
a. ¿El mío? Aquí lo tienes.
b. ¿La mía? . . . la . . .
c. ¿Las mías? . . . las . . .
d. ¿El mío? . . . lo . . .
e. ¿La mía? . . . la . . .
f. ¿El mío? . . . lo . . .
g. ¿El mío? . . . lo . . .
h. ¿El mío? . . . lo . . .

6 Answers will vary.

7 **ESTUDIANTE A**
a. ¿Son suyos estos estantes?
b. . . . suyas estas mesas de noche?
c. . . . suyos estos juguetes?
d. . . . suyas estas lámparas?
e. . . . suyas estas sillas?
f. . . . suyos estos televisores?
g. . . . suyos estos trajes?
h. . . . suyas esta lavadora y secadora?

ESTUDIANTE B
a. Sí, señor, son nuestros. / No, señor, no sabemos dónde están los nuestros.
b. . . . nuestras. / . . . las nuestras.
c. . . . nuestros. / . . . los nuestros.
d. . . . nuestras. / . . . las nuestras.
e. . . . nuestras. / . . . las nuestras.
f. . . . nuestros. / . . . los nuestros.
g. . . . nuestros. / . . . los nuestros.
h. . . . nuestras. / . . . las nuestras.

 Practice Wkbk. 7-6, 7-7

 Prueba 7-6

 Comm. Act. BLM 7-2

Present & Practice

Re-enter / Recycle
Ex. 9: school supplies from Chap. 2
Ex. 10: school subjects from Chap. 2, sports and leisure activities from Chap. 4, special occasions from Chap. 6

Class Starter Review
On the day following the review of *ser*, you might begin the class with this activity:
Using *nuestro* and *mi*, a vocabulary item from the chapter, and *ser* and *estar*, have students write a statement describing the item and where it is in their house.
(Nuestro tostador es bastante viejo; está en la cocina.)

Answers
8–9 Answers will vary.

10 ESTUDIANTE A
a. ¿Sabes cuándo (dónde) va a ser el partido de hockey?
b. ...la fiesta de cumpleaños de Teresa?
c. ...el desfile?
d. ...la graduación?
e. ...la boda de Luis y Pilar?
f. ...la reunión del coro?
g. ...la próxima prueba de química?
h. ...la exposición de arte?
i. Questions will vary.

Repaso: Los usos del verbo *ser*

Review the present-tense forms of *ser*.

soy	somos
eres	sois
es	son

Remember that we use *ser* to describe a characteristic that usually does not change from one minute to the next or over time.

> Carlos **es** alto y tiene pelo castaño.
> El helado **es** frío.

• We also use *ser* to indicate origin, material, or possession.

> Mi profesora **es** de Honduras.
> La linterna **es** de plástico.
> El llavero **es** del señor Durán.

• *Ser* is also used to tell where and when an event takes place.

> La reunión del consejo estudiantil **es** a las ocho.
> **Es** en el gimnasio.

8 Descríbele a tu compañero(a) tu posesión más importante. Debes decirle cómo es, pero no le digas qué es. Tu compañero(a) debe adivinarlo. Puedes decirle:

• el color, el tamaño
• de dónde es (si lo sabes)
• para qué sirve
• si lo (la) compraste tú o fue un regalo

Si tu compañero(a) no adivina, él o ella debe decirle la descripción a otro(a) estudiante. Por ejemplo:

Clara dice que su posesión más importante es bastante grande, verde, de cuero. La compró ...

9 Ahora túrnate con tu compañero(a) para describir dos salas diferentes de la escuela y lo que hay en ellas.

La sala de computadoras es grande, pero no hay ventanas.
Las computadoras son ... Hay ...

¡NO OLVIDES!
Do you remember the present-tense forms of *decir*?

digo	decimos
dices	decís
dice	dicen

246 Capítulo 7

Options

Strategies for Reaching All Students

Students Needing Extra Help
Ex. 8: Model a whole description (or more). Say it, but have copies of it ready to give to students so they can repeat it. Otherwise, they will have difficulty remembering the details and will lose the emphasis of the exercise, which is a review of *ser*.
Show how when repeating it to another classmate, the student must change the form of the verb. Review object pronouns. Do in small groups.

Brainstorm vocabulary to use in this section.
Ex. 10: Model an example using a place.
Ahora lo sabes: Have students write out this list so students can record their progress.

10 Túrnate con tu compañero(a) para decir dónde o cuándo van a ser estas actividades.

picnic / sábado /   **A**   —¿Sabes cuándo va a ser el picnic?
  10 A.M.   **B**   —Sí, el sábado a las 10 de la mañana.

a. el partido de hockey / jueves / gimnasio
b. la fiesta de cumpleaños de Teresa / viernes / 7 P.M.
c. el desfile / domingo / el parque
d. la graduación / martes / 4 P.M.
e. la boda de Luis y Pilar / sábado / 3 P.M.
f. la reunión del coro / miércoles / el auditorio
g. la próxima prueba de química / mañana / el laboratorio
h. la exposición de arte / la próxima semana / la biblioteca
i. 💡

Trajes de luces: Sólo los matadores pueden llevar trajes de oro. Los banderilleros—asistentes del matador—llevan los de plata.

Ahora lo sabes

Can you:

■ say what is yours and what belongs to someone else?
—Esa ___ es ___; la otra es de ___.

■ describe things?
—Mi reloj es de ___; no ___ de plata.

■ tell the time and place of an event?
—La graduación ___ el 23 de mayo.
Es ___ 5 de la tarde.

Gramática en contexto   247

a. Sí, el jueves en el gimnasio.
b. Sí, el viernes a las siete de la noche.
c. Sí, el domingo en el parque.
d. Sí, el martes a las cuatro de la tarde.
e. Sí, el sábado a las tres de la tarde.
f. Sí, el miércoles en el auditorio.
g. Sí, mañana en el laboratorio.
h. Sí, la próxima semana en la biblioteca.
i. Answers will vary.

Answers: Ahora lo sabes

• Answers will vary, but the first should be a feminine noun, the second *mía,* and the third a name or personal pronoun.
• Answers will vary, but the first blank should be a material, and the second *es.*
• es / a las

 Practice Wkbk. 7-8

 Audio Activities 7.4, 7.5

 Writing Activity 7-F

 Prueba 7-7

 Comm. Act. BLM 7-3

Cultural Notes ☀

(p. 247, photo)
In Spain and Latin America, the *matador's* outfit is a symbol of grace and courage. To earn the privilege of wearing the traditional gold-sequinned *traje de luces* (suit of lights), one must be given the title *matador de toros.* This is accomplished in a special ceremony known as *la alternativa.* Only the most skilled, experienced *matadores* are invited to participate. The *matador's* assistants, *los banderilleros,* wear silver to signify their desire to become a *matador.*

Apply

¿Recuerdas?

Play

Video Activity A

Using the Video

In Episode 7, Carlos calls up Jamie to go to the market to look for contaminated produce from the Hacienda la Jacaranda. Jamie finds corn which a local woman tells her is contaminated and is from La Jacaranda. In the background, Santana can be seen still spying on Jamie.

Carlos and Jamie take the corn to the university science laboratory. Carlos's former biology teacher offers to conduct pesticide tests and have the results ready in two days.

Next, Carlos and Jamie go to the city's health department, where they run into Roberto, an old friend of Carlos's who works there. Roberto locates a folder in which there are complaints of chemical abuse made against La Jacaranda. However, no action has been taken because the owner of the hacienda has not been located. When Jamie looks more closely at

Las figuras de madera hechas en Oaxaca se conocen por sus colores brillantes.

Actividades

Esta sección te ofrece la oportunidad de aumentar tus conocimientos de español al integrar lo que aprendiste en este capítulo con lo que aprendiste en capítulos anteriores.

1 En una hoja de papel haz dos listas de tus posesiones más importantes según el modelo.

Mis posesiones

Una necesidad	Un lujo

Escribe el nombre de tres objetos en cada columna. Compara tus listas con las de un(a) compañero(a). Luego, comparen sus listas con las de otros(as) compañeros(as). ¿Cuáles son los tres objetos que aparecen más en las listas de toda la clase? Discutan por qué cada objeto es un lujo o una necesidad.

Una artesana mexicana en Puerto Vallarta le da el toque final a un pájaro que hizo.

248   Capítulo 7

Options

Strategies for Reaching All Students

Spanish-Speaking Students
Ex. 2: Have Spanish-speaking students write out the second activity. Check for spelling, punctuation, and clarity of expression.
Ex. 3: *¿Qué cosas tenía que ya no tiene? ¿Qué cosas había que ya no hay? ¿Cuál es la cosa más importante que uno puede tener?*

Un paso más Ex. 7-1

Students Needing Extra Help
Ex. 1: Students will need help with the vocabulary in order to answer the *¿Por qué?* of the last statement.
Ex. 2: Be sensitive to students who may not want to do this exercise because of family issues. Have plenty of photos on hand. Brainstorm words to describe the family and the house. Give a specific number of sentences to create.

Ex. 3: Model. Review preterite and imperfect tenses. Use vocabulary section of the Organizer. Remind students that they can interview in English.

2 Busca en una revista dos fotos de familias y de las casas donde viven. Escoge a una persona de cada foto y compara sus familias y sus casas. Trae las fotos a la clase y haz tus comparaciones en grupo:

Ésta es la familia de ... Su familia no es tan grande como la de ... La suya es / tiene ...

Una familia mexicana en San Martín Tilcahete mostrando figuritas de madera que hicieron

3 Entrevista a una persona mayor. Puede ser un(a) pariente(a), amigo(a) de la familia o un(a) profesor(a) de la escuela. Pregúntale sobre las cosas que tenía cuando era joven y lo que tiene ahora. Toma notas. Pregúntale, por ejemplo:

- si tenía (aparatos eléctricos)
- si había (computadora, tocacintas, televisión, radio) cuando era niño(a)
- cuándo compró su primer (televisor, radio, coche)
- cuál era su posesión más importante, cómo era y si todavía la tiene
- si tenía animales y cómo se llamaban

Ahora, con tus notas, prepara un informe para la clase. Compara la vida de antes con la de hoy. Puedes empezar así:

Mi bisabuelo se llama Benjamín. Nació en 19 ... Cuando era pequeño no había ... Compró su ... en 19 ...

Actividades 249

the document, she finds that the owner's name is Josefa de González, La Catrina ... Jamie's great-grandmother.

 La Catrina: Capítulo 7

Play

 Video Activity B

 **Para entender mejor**

Play

 Video Activity C

 Writing Activities 7-G, 7-H

 Comm. Act. BLMs 7-4, 7-5

Cultural Notes

(p. 248, bottom right photo)
The artist, cradling her colorful parrot as she works, is one of thousands of Mexican *artesanas* (folk artists). Folk art *(el arte popular)* is born of human creativity and learned through experience and experimentation with little formal training. Skills are passed from generation to generation by family or community tradition. Having worked anonymously for many years, *artesanos(as)* in Mexico have begun to be recognized for their work in recent years.

(p. 249, photo)
Wood carving and painting are traditions in this family from San Martín Tilcajete in the state of Oaxaca, Mexico. Different municipalities in Mexico specialize in particular forms of folk art, such as ceramics, metal and leather work and woodworking. San Martín Tilcajete is well known for the animals and figures, made in white wood and painted with dyes, which are created by its townspeople.

Apply

Process Reading
For information regarding process reading, see p. 52.

Answers
Antes de leer
Answers will vary, but students may say they would expect to find information such as brand names, product features, and prices.

Mira la lectura
Answers will vary.

¡Vamos a leer!

Antes de leer
STRATEGY ➤ Using prior knowledge

This is an ad for electrical appliances from El Corte Inglés, a Spanish department store. What information would you expect to find?

Mira la lectura
STRATEGY ➤ Skimming

In advertisements, sentences are often short. Punctuation and capitalization may be unusual. Look over the selection to get the gist of it.

250   Capítulo 7

Options

Strategies for Reaching All Students

Students Needing Extra Help
Mira la lectura: Bring in an ad from an English language magazine to show how they also sometimes contain unusual punctuation, capitalization, or spelling.

Infórmate

$STRATEGIES$➤ Using cognates
Recognizing false cognates

You already know how to use cognates—for example, *sistemas*, *revolucionarios*, and *transporte*—to help you understand a selection. However, sometimes a Spanish word has a different meaning from that of the English word that it resembles.

When you come across a word that is important for understanding the selection, and the English meaning doesn't make sense, use the context to help you figure it out.

1 In the phrase *Además con la garantía y servicios que proporciona El Corte Inglés,* the word *proporciona* is similar to the English word "proportion." But the position of the word tells you that it probably is a verb. The ending tells you that it is an *él / ella* form. So *proporciona* is something that El Corte Inglés does. Ask yourself what verb best tells what a store does with regard to delivery, installation, etc.

2 The word *entrada* means "entrance," but it has another meaning here. Use the context to help you figure it out.

3 If you were going to buy an electrical appliance, would you go to El Corte Inglés? Why?

Aplicación

List as many words as you can that you learned from this selection. Underline the cognates. Then compare your list with a classmate's.

Infórmate

2. In the ad, *entrada* means "down payment."

Aplicación

Answers will vary, but the list of cognates may include: *presenta, exclusiva, tecnológicamente, garantía, instalación, especialistas*

¡Vamos a leer! 251

251

Apply

Process Writing
For information regarding
developing a writing portfolio,
see p. 54.

Using Realia
Remind students of *¡No olvides!*
What do they think that means?
Then ask: *¿Qué quiere decir
"inolvidable regalo"?*

¡Vamos a escribir!

Imagina que tu familia necesita hacer una lista de
sus posesiones para la compañía de seguros *(insurance
company)*. ¿Qué cosas tuyas quieres poner en la lista?

1 Primero, haz una lista de tres a cinco cosas
que son importantes para ti; por ejemplo, una
colección de monedas. Escribe una breve
descripción para cada una. Piensa en estas cosas:

- ¿Qué es el artículo?
- ¿Cómo es?
- ¿Cuánto tiempo hace
  que lo tienes?
- ¿Lo compraste o fue
  un regalo?
- ¿Cuánto costó?
- ¿Puedes comprar
  otro como éste?

Objetos del Museo
del Oro, Bogotá

252   Capítulo 7

Options

Strategies for Reaching All Students

Students Needing Extra Help
Ex. 1: Discuss the reasons why this list
would be made in reality. Most students will
not be familiar with this insurance concept.
Review *hace que* construction and the
preterite. Teacher should have one ready as
a model.
Ex. 2: Model. Brainstorm why their things
are important to them. Students will need
help with the vocabulary, particularly as to
why things are important to them.

Una familia viendo la televisión en Santander, España

2 Ahora imagina que tu familia va a mudarse *(to move)* y no puede
llevar todo. Tienes que dejar una de las cosas que describiste.
Escoge una cosa y la persona más apropiada para recibirla.
Escribe una carta breve a la persona y explícale:

- qué le vas a dar
- por qué vas a hacerlo
- qué importancia tiene la cosa para ti

3 Para distribuir tu trabajo, puedes:

- incluirlo en un libro titulado *Cosas preciosas*
- ofrecerlo a la revista literaria escolar
- exhibirlo en la sala de clases
- incluirlo en tu portafolio

Cultural Notes ☀

(p. 252, realia)
These specially minted gold and silver
Spanish coins honor the 500th anniversary
of Columbus' landing in the Americas. Each
coin is named for some aspect of Spanish
or Latin American history or culture and
struck in authentic denominations. *El real de
a ocho,* one type of coin produced for this
edition, was a common coin in seventeenth-
century Spain, and was minted in the New
World. The *pinzón,* also offered in this set,
is valued at about $400 U.S.

Assess & Summarize

Test Preparation

You may want to assign parts of this section as written homework or as an in-class writing activity prior to administering the *Examen de habilidades*.

Answers

Listening: —¿*Tenías dinero en la cartera?*
—*No tenía mucho dinero en efectivo, pero tenía mis tarjetas de crédito y el carnet de identidad. Menos mal que tenía mi llavero, anillo y cadena en el bolsillo de mi chaqueta.*
—*Ya viene el policía. Explícale lo que pasó.*
Horacio has lost his wallet, or it has been stolen.

Reading: Answers should be the modern counterparts to the items listed, for example, *el bombillo* for *la vela* and *el tocacintas* (or *el televisor*) for *el radio eléctrico.*

Writing: Thank you notes will vary.

¿Lo sabes bien?

Esta sección te ayudará a prepararte para el examen de habilidades, donde tendrás que hacer tareas semejantes.

Listening
Can you understand when people talk about their personal possessions? Listen as your teacher reads a sample similar to what you will hear on the test. What do you think Horacio's problem is?

Reading
Part of an advertisement for new appliances included comparisons between old and new. Add two modern items to complete the comparisons.

Antes	Ahora
el ventilador	el aire acondicionado
el fregadero	el lavaplatos
la vela	
el radio eléctrico	

Writing
Write a thank you note in which you explain to a relative how you used a gift of clothing. On the right is a sample.

Culture
How were the early American civilizations more advanced than those of Europe? How were they less advanced?

Speaking
In a discussion with your partner can you state and defend your opinion about some recent purchases you made?

A —¿*Te gusta el nuevo televisor que compré? Me encanta el control remoto.*

B —¡*Pero Uds. tienen muchos televisores! Me parece que es un lujo tener tantos aparatos.*

A —*Pues, a mí no me parece así. Somos una familia grande y todos tenemos nuestros programas favoritos. ¡Y lo compré con mi propio dinero!*

254   Capítulo 7

> Querida abuela,
>
> Muchas gracias por el abrigo de lana. Ya tenía un suéter y unos pantalones de lana, pero necesitaba un abrigo para el viaje a las montañas. (La familia de Maribel me invitó a su casa en Portillo.) ¡Olvidé llevar la bufanda y los guantes! Pero Maribel me prestó los suyos. Sí llevé una linterna y pilas en caso de emergencia, pero no las necesité. La casa tiene electricidad. También tiene calefacción central, una lavadora, una secadora ¡y un microondas!
>
> Un beso,
> Chelita

Options

Strategies for Reaching All Students

Students Needing Extra Help
Have students write out this section so they can check off what they have mastered. Remind students that this is just a sample of what the actual test will be like.
Listening: Read the sample more than once. Remind students that they only need to listen for one piece of information. Brainstorm for what words students should be listening.

Writing: Have students use the Organizer and write a sample note before the test as practice. Brainstorm other possibilities that are more low key for how a gift might be used. For example, the student could be simple and direct: the gift was worn to a party, was taken when he / she went skiing, has become his / her favorite sweater, etc. Give a required number of sentences to write.

Culture: Have students review the notes they took during their first reading of *Perspectiva cultural.*
Speaking: The statement "state and defend your opinion" may be confusing for students. Explain. Limit the number of lines of dialogue. Use the vocabulary section of the Organizer.

Resumen del capítulo 7

Usa el vocabulario de este capítulo para:

- name and describe personal possessions
- tell to whom something belongs
- state and defend opinions regarding necessities and luxuries

to name personal possessions

la posesión, *pl.* las posesiones
la necesidad
el lujo
el oro
la plata
el anillo
el arete
la cadena
el collar
la pulsera
el reloj (pulsera)
los anteojos *(m.pl.)*
los lentes de contacto *(m.pl.)*
la llave
el llavero
la moneda
el peine
el secador de pelo
la identificación
el carnet de identidad

to discuss personal possessions

propio, -a
mío, -a
tuyo, -a
suyo, -a
nuestro, -a
el mío, la mía; los míos,
    las mías

el tuyo, la tuya; los tuyos,
    las tuyas
el suyo, la suya; los suyos,
    las suyas
el nuestro, la nuestra; los
    nuestros, las nuestras

to name home appliances and furnishings

el aparato
la electricidad
eléctrico, -a
el bombillo
apagar
encender *(e → ie)*
funcionar
el horno
el lavaplatos
la lavadora
la secadora
el microondas
el tostador
el ventilador
el aire acondicionado
la calefacción central
el calentador
el fregadero
el estante
la mesa de noche
el radio
el televisor

el control remoto
el tocacintas, *pl.* los tocacintas

to talk about emergencies

el detector de humo
la emergencia
el incendio
el extinguidor de incendios
la linterna
la pila
en caso de

to talk about conservation

la energía
ahorrar
conservar
reparar

to express an opinion

¿(A ti) Te parece que ... ?
(A mí) Me parece que ...

other useful words and expressions

mostrar *(o → ue)*
suficiente
de vez en cuando
(yo) mismo, -a

Resumen 255

 Prueba cumulativa

 Examen de habilidades

 Test Generator

CAPÍTULO 8

THEME: SHOPPING

SCOPE AND SEQUENCE Pages 256–291

COMMUNICATION

Topics

Specialty shops

Asking for and giving directions

Places in a community

Pharmacy items

Departments in a store

Objectives

To compare bargaining in Guatemala and in the U.S.

To name things and places in a community

To name specialty shops

To ask for or give directions

To describe places

To identify personal hygiene items

To name and indicate departments in a store

To talk about shopping

CULTURE

Bargaining procedures in Guatemala

GRAMMAR

Repaso: Los usos de estar

Repaso: El presente progresivo

Construcciones negativas

El se impersonal

Ancillaries available for use with Chapter 8

Multisensory/Technology

 Overhead Transparencies, 39–43

 Audio Tapes and CDs

 Vocabulary Art Blackline Masters for Hands-On Learning, pp. 43–47

 Classroom Crossword

 La Catrina

 CD-ROM

Print

 Practice Workbook, pp. 75–84

 Writing, Audio & Video Activities, pp. 47–52, 114–116, 165–166

 Communicative Activity Blackline Masters

Pair and Small Group Activities, pp. 50–55

Situation Cards, p. 56

 Un paso más: Actividades para ampliar tu español, pp. 43–48

Assessment

 Assessment Program

Pruebas, pp. 114–124

Examen de habilidades, pp. 125–128

 Test Generator

Video still from Chap. 8

Resumen del capítulo 7

Usa el vocabulario de este capítulo para:

- name and describe personal possessions
- tell to whom something belongs
- state and defend opinions regarding necessities and luxuries

**to name personal
possessions**
la posesión, *pl.* las posesiones
la necesidad
el lujo
el oro
la plata
el anillo
el arete
la cadena
el collar
la pulsera
el reloj (pulsera)
los anteojos *(m.pl.)*
los lentes de contacto *(m.pl.)*
la llave
el llavero
la moneda
el peine
el secador de pelo
la identificación
el carnet de identidad

**to discuss personal
possessions**
propio, -a
mío, -a
tuyo, -a
suyo, -a
nuestro, -a
el mío, la mía; los míos,
    las mías

el tuyo, la tuya; los tuyos,
    las tuyas
el suyo, la suya; los suyos,
    las suyas
el nuestro, la nuestra; los
    nuestros, las nuestras

**to name home appliances
and furnishings**
el aparato
la electricidad
eléctrico, -a
el bombillo
apagar
encender *(e → ie)*
funcionar
el horno
el lavaplatos
la lavadora
la secadora
el microondas
el tostador
el ventilador
el aire acondicionado
la calefacción central
el calentador
el fregadero
el estante
la mesa de noche
el radio
el televisor

el control remoto
el tocacintas, *pl.* los tocacintas

to talk about emergencies
el detector de humo
la emergencia
el incendio
el extinguidor de incendios
la linterna
la pila
en caso de

to talk about conservation
la energía
ahorrar
conservar
reparar

to express an opinion
¿(A ti) Te parece que ...?
(A mí) Me parece que ...

**other useful words and
expressions**
mostrar *(o → ue)*
suficiente
de vez en cuando
(yo) mismo, -a

Culture: Answers will vary, but students may say that very early American civilizations were more advanced than ours because they were able to accomplish so much with limited resources. For example, the Aztecs built great temples and avenues without the use of metal instruments or a written means of communication.

Speaking: Dialogues will vary.

 Prueba cumulativa

Examen de habilidades

Test Generator

CAPÍTULO 8

THEME: SHOPPING

SCOPE AND SEQUENCE Pages 256–291

COMMUNICATION

Topics

Specialty shops

Asking for and giving directions

Places in a community

Pharmacy items

Departments in a store

Objectives

To compare bargaining in Guatemala and in the U.S.

To name things and places in a community

To name specialty shops

To ask for or give directions

To describe places

To identify personal hygiene items

To name and indicate departments in a store

To talk about shopping

CULTURE

Bargaining procedures in Guatemala

GRAMMAR

Repaso: Los usos de estar

Repaso: El presente progresivo

Construcciones negativas

El se impersonal

Ancillaries available for use with Chapter 8

| Multisensory/Technology | Print | Assessment |

Overhead Transparencies, 39–43

Practice Workbook, pp. 75–84

Assessment Program
Pruebas, pp. 114–124
Examen de habilidades, pp. 125–128

Audio Tapes and CDs

Writing, Audio & Video Activities, pp. 47–52, 114–116, 165–166

Test Generator

Vocabulary Art Blackline Masters for Hands-On Learning, pp. 43–47

Communicative Activity Blackline Masters
Pair and Small Group Activities, pp. 50–55
Situation Cards, p. 56

Classroom Crossword

Un paso más: Actividades para ampliar tu español, pp. 43–48

La Catrina

CD-ROM

Video still from Chap. 8

Running Errands

In Spain and Latin America, the downtown area is considered the hub of commercial activity. It usually features a main *plaza,* filled with shoeshine stands, newspaper kiosks, small candy stands, flower stands, and vendors selling everything from handcrafted jewelry to popcorn. Money exchange houses downtown provide foreign travelers a convenient way to exchange their currency. Another feature of the commercial area is the telephone company office, where local, long-distance, and international calls can be placed by those who do not have a telephone.

Larger cities may have several major commercial areas, with a large superstore as the anchor. *Supermercados* such as Comercial mexicana or Gigante are stocked with a variety of products. These stores offer the ultimate one-stop shopping experience: deli, bakery, dairy, hardware, electronics, books, clothing, CDs and cassettes—even carry-out buffets with such typical dishes as *mole poblano* and *nopalitos,* served hot and weighed at the checkout counter. Picnic tables outside the store offer a convenient place to enjoy lunch.

Some people, however, may go to specialty shops and open-air markets for their grocery shopping. A grocery run for the day's meal may include a stop at the *carnicería,* then to the *frutería* or *verdulería* and finally to the *tortillería.* Most towns have an open-air market, and if the market is especially large, it is divided into specialty sections. A characteristic of the marketplace is the custom of bargaining for the final price of an item. Vendors usually state their prices higher than they expect to receive, and shoppers often succeed in paying a lower price than the one originally offered. Bargaining is as much a part of the shopping experience in the marketplace as using cents-off coupons is in the U.S.

Introduce

Re-entry of Concepts

The following list represents words, expressions, and grammar topics re-entered from Book 1 and Book 2 (Chaps 2–4):

Book 1
numbers 0–31, physical sensations, leisure-time activities, family members, household chores, places in a community, personal hygiene items, directions

Chapter 2
daily routine

Chapter 3
greetings and leavetakings

Chapter 4
sports

Planning

Cross-Curricular Connections

Business Education Connection (pp. 260–261)
In groups of three, have students choose a type of shop from the given vocabulary, and create a poster to advertise it. They should include a name, logo, and slogan for the store, as well as a few special items for sale there. Display the posters, and have students tell why they would or would not shop there.

Geography Connection (pp. 278–279)
At a given hour in New York on Eastern Standard Time, it is two hours ahead in Buenos Aires, Argentina; eight hours ahead in Moscow, Russia; 12 hours ahead in Tokyo, Japan; and 15 hours ahead in Sydney, Australia. Create a transparency chart, adjusting the time differences for your local time zone. Ask students to write two responses for each city to the question: *¿Qué están haciendo ellos ahora?* Have them share their responses.

Spanish in Your Community
Have students name places in their community where they may have spotted the following items: a *piñata;* restrooms labeled for *damas* and *caballeros, bacalao* (salted, dried cod); chocolate disks for making Mexican hot chocolate; *piloncillo* (raw cone-shaped sugar); Spanish *chorizo* (sausage); yucca; a *panadería;* an exit sign labeled *salida.*

CAPÍTULO 8

¿Dónde sueles hacer tus compras?

OBJECTIVES

At the end of this chapter, you will be able to:

- name and describe the location of places in a community
- ask for and give directions
- locate items in a drugstore or department store
- describe bargaining procedures in a Latin American market

Vista de una calle en Madrid

257

Preview

Cultural Objective
• To compare specialty shops in Spain and Latin America with those in the U.S.

Critical Thinking: Summarizing Information
Have students summarize the activities depicted in the chapter opener photographs. Discuss any similarities and differences they may see between where they shop and the places shown here.

¡Piénsalo bien!

Mira las fotos. ¿Dónde compras tú estas cosas?

"Voy a llevar dos kilos de manzanas."

¿Prefieres las manzanas rojas o las amarillas? ¿Dónde compras las frutas? ¿Hay fruterías en tu ciudad?

Una frutería en Buenos Aires

258   Capítulo 8

Options

Strategies for Reaching All Students

Spanish-Speaking Students
Ask: *¿Cuáles de estos lugares hay en tu comunidad? ¿Prefiere tu familia comprar en tiendas grandes como almacenes y super-mercados, o en tiendas más pequeñas como fruterías, pescaderías, etc.? ¿Por qué?*

 Un paso más Ex. 8-A

Una carnicería en Santiago, Chile

¿Cuáles son las diferencias que ves en esta vitrina de lo que se ve en una carnicería típica en los Estados Unidos?

Una floristería en Las Ramblas, Barcelona

"Voy a llevarle rosas a mi mamá para su cumpleaños."

¿En qué ocasiones sueles comprar flores?

259

Cultural Notes ☀

(p. 259, top photo)
Sale banners entice passersby to buy some *queso cabeza* (head cheese), *lomito* (pork loin), or *panita* (beef liver). Specialty shops such as this *carnicería* are common in Latin America and Spain. They lend a personable atmosphere to even the largest cities, and serve as congenial meeting places where neighbors exchange greetings and keep abreast of local happenings.

(p. 259, bottom photo)
Newspaper kiosks, flower stalls, bird sellers, and *cafés* fill Las Ramblas, a boulevard linking Barcelona's port with Plaza Cataluña, the city's commercial and banking center. Las Ramblas is the nexus of community life for many *barceloneses*.

Present

Chapter Theme
Downtown

Communicative Objectives
- To name things and places in a community
- To name specialty shops
- To ask or give directions
- To talk about shopping

 Transparencies 39–40

 Vocabulary Art BLMs

 Pronunciation Tape 8-1

Teaching Suggestions
Preparing students to speak: Use one or two options from each of the categories of Comprehensible Input, Physical Response, or Limited Verbal Response. For a complete explanation of these categories and some sample activities, see pp. T16–T17.

Vocabulario para conversar

¿Podría indicarme dónde queda una floristería?

Vas a necesitar estas palabras y expresiones para hablar sobre dónde puedes encontrar ciertas cosas y lugares.

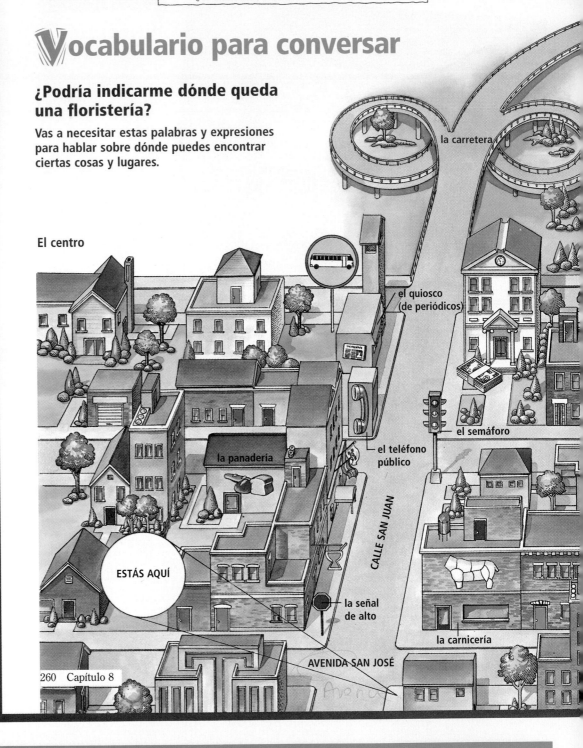

El centro

la carretera
el quiosco (de periódicos)
el semáforo
el teléfono público
la panadería
CALLE SAN JUAN
ESTÁS AQUÍ
la señal de alto
la carnicería
AVENIDA SAN JOSÉ

260   Capítulo 8

Options

Strategies for Reaching All Students

Spanish-Speaking Students
Have students list other words they might use for these places in the community.
¿Usas otras palabras para estos lugares en una comunidad? Haz una lista.

 Un paso más Exs. 8-B, 8-C

Students Needing Extra Help
Begin the vocabulary section of the Organizer.
Students may think *señal* sounds like signal, and make the assumption that it is a traffic light. Emphasize that it is a stop sign.
Present the shops (all of which end in *-ía*) as a group. Show the root words in this group: *carne → carnicería; fruta → frutería,* etc.
También necesitas . . . : Give examples of *por* + place.

Learning Spanish Through Action
STAGING VOCABULARY: *Pongan*
MATERIALS: transparency of a downtown area with squares and rectangles to indicate locations; cutouts of symbols for buildings, shops, etc.
DIRECTIONS: Direct students to place the symbols in the correct squares or rectangles as you give the location of each.

También necesitas . . .

seguir *(e → i)*: siga (Ud.)

doblar: doble (Ud.)
cruzar
¿Podría (Ud.) / Podrías (tú) + *inf.?*
el centro
el metro
la milla
por + *(place)*

to follow, to continue:
   follow! continue!
to turn: turn!
to cross
Could you . . . ?
downtown
here: *meter (measurement)*
mile
by, through, at

¿Y qué quiere decir . . . ?
indicar
hacer las compras   *to shop*
el transporte público
perdonar: perdone (Ud.)
el kilómetro
histórico, -a

¡NO OLVIDES!
Remember: *comprar* = to buy and
ir de compras = to go shopping.

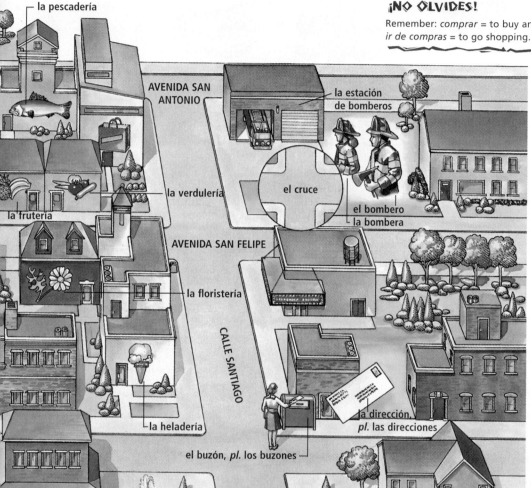

la pescadería
AVENIDA SAN ANTONIO
la estación de bomberos
la verdulería
el cruce
el bombero
la bombera
la frutería
AVENIDA SAN FELIPE
la floristería
CALLE SANTIAGO
la dirección, *pl.* las direcciones
la heladería
el buzón, *pl.* los buzones

Practice

Reteach / Review: Singular and Plural

Ex. 1: Remind students that, just as in English, when we talk about *flores* and *verduras,* we use the plural, and for *pan, pescado, carne,* and *helado,* we use the singular. Fruit takes either the singular or the plural.

Refer to vocabulary from Book 1, Chaps. 4 and 10 for a review of foods.

Answers: Empecemos a conversar

1 ESTUDIANTE A

a. Necesito comprar flores.

b. . . . verduras.

c. . . . pan.

d. . . . pescado.

e. . . . frutas.

f. . . . helado.

g. Statements will vary.

ESTUDIANTE B

a. Pues vamos, hay una floristería muy cerca.

b. . . . una verdulería . . .

c. . . . una panadería . . .

d. . . . una pescadería . . .

e. . . . una frutería . . .

f. . . . una heladería . . .

g. Answers will vary.

Empecemos a conversar

Túrnate con un(a) compañero(a) para ser *Estudiante A* y *Estudiante B.* Reemplacen las palabras subrayadas en el modelo con palabras representadas o escritas en los recuadros. Si ven 💡 pueden dar su propia respuesta.

1
A —*Necesito comprar <u>carne</u>.*
B —*Pues vamos, hay una <u>carnicería</u> muy cerca.*

Estudiante A **Estudiante B**

2
A —*Perdone, señor(ita), ¿sabe si hay <u>una farmacia</u> por aquí?*
B —*Sí. Hay <u>una a media cuadra</u>.*

¡NO OLVIDES!

Sabe is the *Ud.* form of *saber.* It is a regular *-er* verb except for its *yo* form: *sé.*

Estudiante A **Estudiante B**

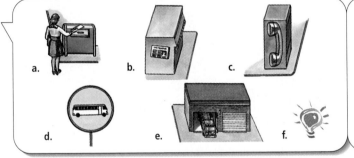

a (dos) cuadras

a media cuadra

enfrente de ____

en la esquina

262   Capítulo 8

Options

Strategies for Reaching All Students

Spanish-Speaking Students

Exs. 1–4: If possible, pair bilingual with non-biligual students.

Students Needing Extra Help

Ex. 2: Help students use the map.
Ex. 3: Review location words. If available, use the Organizer from Book 1, Chap. 10. Give several examples on the overhead so students don't start each one the same way.

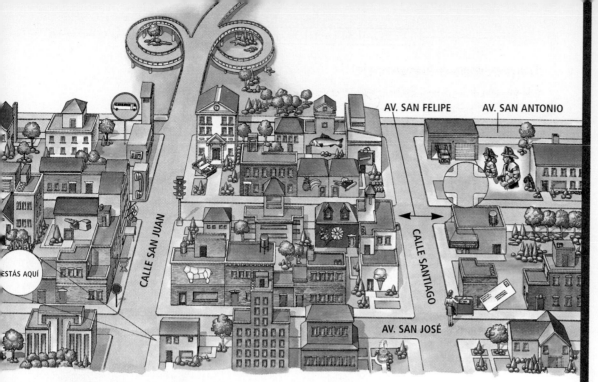

CALLE SAN JUAN

CALLE SANTIAGO

AV. SAN FELIPE

AV. SAN ANTONIO

AV. SAN JOSÉ

ESTÁS AQUÍ

3

A — ¿Podría indicarme dónde queda *una pescadería*?

B — Sí, señor(ita). *Siga por esta calle. En la segunda esquina, doble a la derecha.*

Estudiante A

Estudiante B

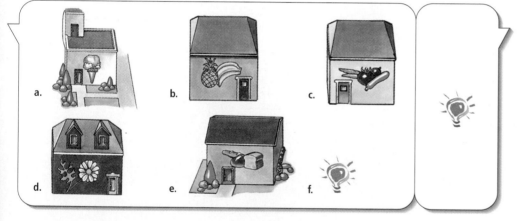

a.

b.

c.

d.

e.

f.

2 **ESTUDIANTE A**

a. Perdone, señor(ita), ¿sabe si hay un buzón por aquí?

b. ...un quiosco...

c. ...un teléfono público...

d. ...una parada del autobús...

e. ...una estación de bomberos...

f. Questions will vary.

ESTUDIANTE B

a. Sí. Hay uno a una cuadra.

b. ...uno a dos cuadras.

c. ...uno a una cuadra.

d. ...una a dos cuadras.

e. ...una a tres cuadras.

f. Answers will vary.

3 **ESTUDIANTE A**

a. ¿Podría indicarme dónde queda una heladería?

b. ...una frutería?

c. ...una verdulería?

d. ...una floristería?

e. ...una panadería?

f. Questions will vary.

ESTUDIANTE B

Directions will vary, but may include the following:

a. Sí, señor(ita). Siga por la avenida San José. En la primera esquina, doble a la izquierda.

b. ...En el semáforo, doble a la derecha.

c. ...En el semáforo, doble a la derecha. Está al lado de la frutería.

d. ...En el semáforo, doble a la derecha. Está enfrente de la frutería.

e. ...En el semáforo, doble a la izquierda.

f. Directions will vary.

Practice & Apply

Reteach / Review: Vocabulary

Review this additional location vocabulary from Book 1, Chap. 10 to help students vary their answers to the exercises that follow: *a la izquierda (de), al lado (de), detrás (de), entre.* Ask two volunteers to help you act out the different locations for the rest of the class.

Ex. 4: Encourage students to say more. For example, *cerca de ___, enfrente de ___, por ___.* You can extend the exercise by asking students to ask for a specific shop: *la panadería La Esperanza, la pescadería De Martino's,* etc.

Answers: Empecemos a conversar

4 ESTUDIANTE A

a. ¿Sabes si está lejos de aquí la estación de policía?

b. . . . la iglesia de ___?

c. . . . el templo de ___?

d. . . . el correo?

e. . . . el centro?

f. . . . (nombre de una comunidad)?

g. Questions will vary.

ESTUDIANTE B

a.–g. Answers will vary, but should reflect locations in your community.

---

4 Aquí hablamos de tu propia ciudad.

la estación de bomberos

A — ¿Sabes si está lejos de aquí *la estación de bomberos*?

B — *Un poco; está a dos millas de aquí, en la Calle Lincoln.*

o: *Lo siento, pero no lo sé.*

Estudiante A

a. la estación de policía

b. la iglesia de ___

c. el templo de ___

d. el correo

e. el centro

f. (nombre de una comunidad)

g.

Estudiante B

(número) kilómetros

(número) metros

(número) cuadras

(número) millas

medio kilómetro

media milla

Vista de una calle antigua al pie de las montañas en Quito, Ecuador

San Antonio de Oriente (1957), José Antonio Velásquez

264   Capítulo 8

Options

Strategies for Reaching All Students

Spanish-Speaking Students
Ex. 8: ¿*Cuál es tu lugar favorito en tu comunidad? ¿Se lo recomendarías a otras personas? ¿Por qué?*

 Un paso más Ex. 8-D

Students Needing Extra Help
Ex. 4: Discourage overuse of the second response. Using the classroom as a starting point gives everyone the same perspective. Give more than one example, so students don't always repeat the model dialogue.
Ex. 5: Refer students to the envelope in the visualized vocabulary section. Remind them that in Spanish the street name is written first, then the number.

Ex. 6: Students may need to sketch maps. Help them focus.
Ex. 7: Discuss the layout of the local market to help students think in terms of sections.
Ex. 8: Have students imagine they are in a new town. Discuss which places are important to know in case of emergency.

Empecemos a escribir

Escribe tus respuestas en español.

5 ¿Cuál es tu dirección? ¿Y la de la escuela? Escríbele una nota a un(a) amigo(a) explicándole cómo ir de la escuela a tu casa.

6 ¿Cuáles son las calles y carreteras más importantes de tu comunidad o ciudad? Para ir de tu casa al centro comercial, ¿qué calles o carreteras hay que tomar? ¿Más o menos cuántos cruces y señales de alto debes pasar? Y para ir al centro de la ciudad, ¿usas el transporte público o vas en coche?

7 ¿Dónde hace las compras tu familia? ¿Quién las hace? ¿Qué tiendas de comestibles hay cerca de tu casa? ¿Dónde quedan? ¿Qué tiene el supermercado (carnicería, panadería, etc.) donde hace las compras tu familia?

8 ¿Qué edificios históricos hay en tu comunidad o ciudad? ¿Los visitas de vez en cuando? En tu opinión, ¿qué lugares hay que conocer en una ciudad? ¿Por qué?

También se dice

la florería

el puesto de periódicos

la sorbetería
la nevería

el pare
el stop

Niños montando en bicicleta en Puerto Plata, República Dominicana

Vocabulario para conversar 265

Enrichment
Ex. 4: As a homework assignment, ask students to choose an item or place from the vocabulary list that they would like to have on the corner of their block and to give reasons for their choice. Example: *Me gustaría mucho tener un semáforo en la esquina. Siempre hay accidentes.*
Ex. 6: Additional questions: *¿Cuánto tiempo necesitas para ir al centro en coche? ¿Y en transporte público?*

Cooperative Learning
In pairs, one student is given a blank map of a *plaza* with four surrounding streets. Without letting his or her partner see the map, *Estudiante A* fills in eight symbols for the shop vocabulary. *Estudiante B* asks if a given shop is nearby. If the symbol is on the map, *Estudiante A* says where it is *(Está en la esquina)*. If not, he or she responds accordingly. *Estudiante B* records *Estudiante A*'s responses to read to the class, who checks responses against the map.

Cultural Notes

(p. 264, bottom left photo)
Honduran artist José Antonio Velásquez (1906–1983) created this painting of his native village. A self-taught artist who never learned to read or write, Velásquez achieved recognition as one of Latin America's leading artists. San Antonio de Oriente still retains much of the character captured in this painting.

265

Present

Chapter Theme
Store sections

Communicative Objectives
- To ask or give directions
- To identify personal hygiene items
- To name and indicate departments in a store
- To talk about shopping

 Transparencies 41–42

 Vocabulary Art BLMs

Pronunciation Tape 8-2

Grammar Preview
Se vende is presented here lexically. The explanation of impersonal *se* is on p. 282. Encourage its use without explanation.

Teaching Suggestions
Preparing students to speak: Use one or two options from each of the categories of Comprehensible Input, Physical Response, or Limited Verbal Response. For a complete explanation of these categories and some sample activities, see pp. T16–T17.

Vocabulario para conversar

¿Los ascensores están al fondo?

Aquí tienes el resto del vocabulario que necesitas en este capítulo para hablar sobre dónde puedes encontrar ciertas cosas y lugares.

La farmacia

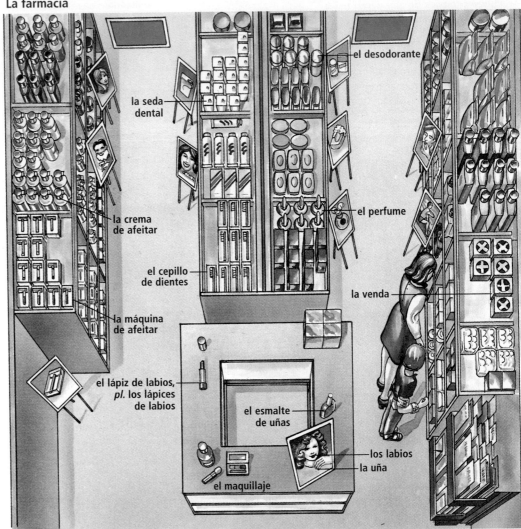

el desodorante

la seda dental

la crema de afeitar

el perfume

el cepillo de dientes

la venda

la máquina de afeitar

el lápiz de labios, *pl.* los lápices de labios

el esmalte de uñas

los labios

la uña

el maquillaje

Options

Strategies for Reaching All Students

Spanish-Speaking Students
 Un paso más Ex. 8-E

Students Needing Extra Help
Show root words and word families.

Learning Spanish Through Action
STAGING VOCABULARY: *Levanten*
MATERIALS: Vocabulary Art BLMs of vocabulary
DIRECTIONS: Distribute cutouts to students. Direct them to hold up the cutouts when they hear them named.

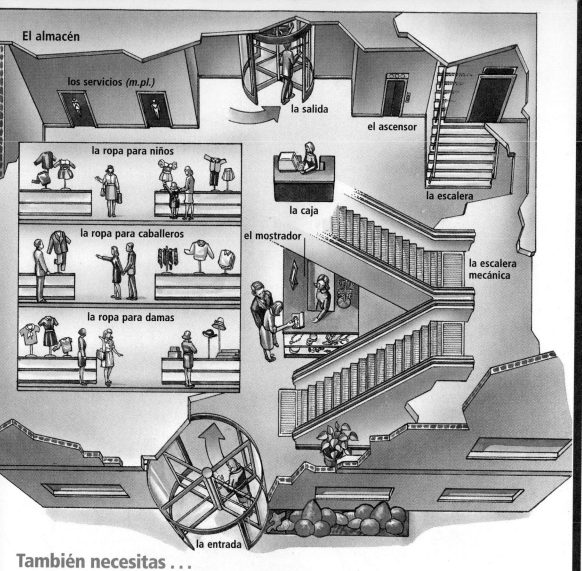

El almacén

los servicios (m.pl.)

la salida

el ascensor

la escalera

la ropa para niños

la caja

la ropa para caballeros

el mostrador

la escalera mecánica

la ropa para damas

la entrada

También necesitas . . .

al fondo	*in the back*
gastar	*to spend*
ponerse	*to put on (clothing, make-up, etc.)*
quitarse	*to take off (clothing, make-up, etc.)*
vender: se vende(n)	*to sell: is (are) sold*
mientras	*while*

¿Y qué quiere decir . . . ?
afeitarse
maquillarse
la distancia
la sección, *pl.* las secciones

Vocabulario para conversar   267

Practice

Reteach / Review: Vocabulary

Ex. 9: Note that there is more than one way to express location. Accept all appropriate answers. Tell students that in this context the plural forms *lápices de labios* and *perfumes* would be used. You may want to review vocabulary from Book 1, Chaps. 4 and 10.

Answers: Empecemos a conversar

9 ESTUDIANTE A

a. Por favor, ¿dónde puedo encontrar el desodorante?

b. ...los cepillos de dientes?

c. ...los perfumes?

d. ...los lápices de labios?

e. ...la crema de afeitar?

f. ...el esmalte de uñas?

g. ...las vendas?

h. Questions will vary.

ESTUDIANTE B

Answers will vary, but may include the following:

a. En la sección tres, enfrente de las pastillas para la garganta.

b. En la sección dos, al lado de la pasta dentífrica.

c. En la sección tres, al lado del jabón.

d. En la sección dos, al lado de los cepillos de dientes.

e. En la sección dos, enfrente de la pasta dentífrica.

f. En la sección tres, detrás de los lápices de labios.

Empecemos a conversar

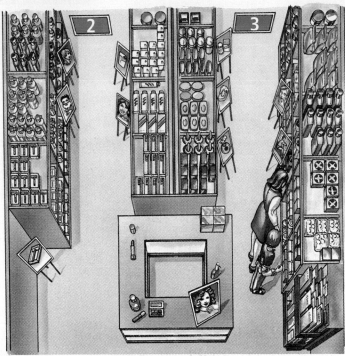

9

A — *Por favor, ¿dónde puedo encontrar la seda dental?*

B — *En la sección dos, enfrente de los champús.*

Estudiante A   Estudiante B

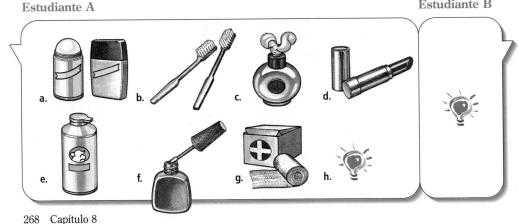

268   Capítulo 8

Options

Strategies for Reaching All Students

Spanish-Speaking Students
If possible, pair Spanish-speaking students for Ex. 9 and bilingual with non-bilingual students for Exs. 10–11.

Students Needing Extra Help
Ex. 9: Review location words.
Help students refer to the pharmacy layout. Use the Vocabulary section of the Organizer.
Ex. 10: If the answer is negative, have students complete the response by telling where these places are. Provide a model.

Enrichment
As an in-class written assignment, pairs of students can create a dialogue to present to the rest of the class. This dialogue will vary from the one in Ex. 9 in that *Estudiante B* tells *Estudiante A* that he or she has none of the items named. Encourage students to come up with a range of reactions on the part of *Estudiante A:* from ordinary questions regarding where else the item is sold

268

g. En la sección tres, al lado del algodón.

h. Answers will vary.

10 ESTUDIANTE A

a. ¿El mostrador está al fondo?

b. ¿La caja está . . .

c. ¿Los servicios están . . .

d. ¿La escalera mecánica está . . .

e. ¿La salida está . . .

f. ¿La escalera está . . .

ESTUDIANTE B

Answers will vary, but may include the following information:

a. No. Está al lado de la caja.

b. No. Está al lado del mostrador.

c. Sí, señor(ita).

d. No. Está cerca de la entrada.

e. Sí, señor(ita).

f. Sí, señor(ita).

10

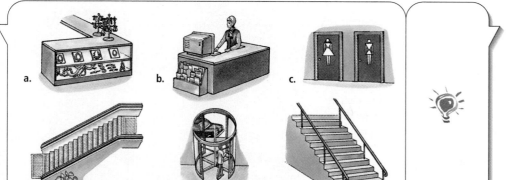

A — *¿Los ascensores están al fondo?*

B — *Sí, señor(ita), a la derecha de la salida.*
  o: *No, están . . .*

Estudiante A

a.

b.

c.

d.

e.

f.

Estudiante B

---

or when they are going to have it, to extraordinary, dramatic statements about how tired or sick he or she is, how badly he or she needs the item, etc.

Practice & Apply

Re-enter / Recycle
Ex. 16: daily routine from Chap. 2

Answers: Empecemos a conversar

11 ESTUDIANTE A

a. ¿Se venden sellos en una farmacia?

b. ¿Se venden revistas . . .

c. ¿Se vende ropa para damas . . .

d. ¿Se venden lápices de labios . . .

e. ¿Se venden verduras . . .

f. ¿Se vende crema de afeitar . . .

g. ¿Se vende perfume . . .

h. ¿Se venden flores . . .

i. ¿Se venden vendas . . .

j. Questions will vary.

ESTUDIANTE B

a.–j. Answers will vary, but should reflect your community.

---

11 periódicos

A —¿Se vende(n) _periódicos_ en una farmacia?

B —_En algunas sí._

o: _No sé, pero hay un quiosco en la esquina._

Estudiante A

a. sellos

b. revistas

c. ropa para damas

d. lápices de labios

e. verduras

f. crema de afeitar

g. perfume

h. flores

i. vendas

j.

Estudiante B

Claro que sí / no.

En algunas sí.

No sé.

El perfume que inspiró Carmen sólo se encuentra en Sevilla.

CARMEN
VICTORIO & LUCCHINO
SEVILLA

Empecemos a escribir y a leer

Escribe tus respuestas en español.

12 ¿A qué distancia de tu casa está la farmacia que queda más cerca? ¿Qué compras en la farmacia generalmente? ¿En qué tipo de tienda gastas más dinero?

13 ¿A qué edad empiezan a maquillarse las muchachas de tu comunidad? ¿Qué color de lápiz de labios está de moda ahora? ¿Y de esmalte de uñas? ¿Con qué se afeitan los hombres de tu familia?

Comprando lápices de labios
en El Corte Inglés, Madrid

270   Capítulo 8

Options

Strategies for Reaching All Students

Spanish-Speaking Students

Ex. 15: ¿_Te gusta ir a los centros comerciales con tus amigos(as)? ¿Cuándo van? ¿Van sólo a comprar? ¿Qué otras cosas hacen?_

 Un paso más Ex. 8-F

Students Needing Extra Help

Ex. 12: Refer students to the _Empecemos a conversar,_ Exs. 2 and 4 on pp. 262 and 264. Review types of stores. If available, use the Organizer from Book 1, Chap. 6.

Ex. 14: Students may need help with the ¿_por qué?_ response.

Ex. 15: Students may need help formulating the answer to the last question.

Ex. 16: Model the changes for a statement that students disagree with. Show which part of the statement changes.

14 Para ir al piso cinco de un almacén, ¿usas la escalera, el ascensor o la escalera mecánica? ¿Por qué?

15 Cuando vas de compras, ¿usas el transporte público? ¿Con quiénes sueles ir de compras? Cuando vas con un adulto, ¿qué haces tú mientras él o ella hace sus propias compras?

16 En grupo decidan si están de acuerdo con las siguientes frases. Si no están de acuerdo, escríbanlas de nuevo según su opinión y digan por qué.

a. La ropa para caballeros es más cara que la de damas.
b. La ropa para caballeros es más cómoda que la de damas.
c. Una mujer debe quitarse todo el maquillaje antes de acostarse.
d. Uno debe ponerse la camisa antes de peinarse.
e. Uno debe cepillarse los dientes antes de usar la seda dental.
f. Un hombre debe lavarse la cara antes de afeitarse.

También se dice

el hilo dental

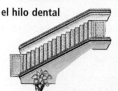
la escalera eléctrica

la pintura de uñas
el barniz de uñas

la pintura de labios
el crayón de labios
el lápiz labial

la máquina de rasurar
la rastrilla
la rasuradora

el elevador

Vocabulario para conversar   271

Cultural Notes

(p. 270, realia)
The opera *Carmen,* by Georges Bizet, is presumably the inspiration for this perfume. The ad implies that only a city like Sevilla would inspire such an opera or such a perfume.

(p. 271, realia)
The time of the year *(el tiempo)* when we are plagued with bad weather *(mal tiempo)* is time for Vitamin C. Using a play on words, this ad emphasizes the role of Vitamin C in preventing illnesses brought on by cold, wet weather. The product claims to replenish one's supply of Vitamin C with an effervescent tablet dissolved in water.

Practice

Teaching Suggestions

Ex. 2: Draw a simple map of your neighborhood or community on the chalkboard to help students do this activity. Include important landmarks such as *el correo, la estación de policía, la biblioteca pública, el parque,* etc. Students should give authentic answers. You may want to focus on school instead. Use *la cafetería, la oficina del director / de la directora, la enfermería, la biblioteca, el gimnasio,* and *el auditorio.* Be sure students know *el pasillo, el (segundo) piso, el patio de recreo,* if appropriate.

Ex. 3: You may want to have students use a guide from a store in your community.

Answers:
¡Comuniquemos!

1 Answers will vary, but may include the following:

ESTUDIANTE A

¿Cómo se llama el lugar donde se venden periódicos?

...el lugar donde se vende bronceador?

...la tienda donde se venden verduras?

...el lugar donde se venden vendas?

...el lugar donde hay un semáforo?

...el lugar donde se pagan las compras?

¡Comuniquemos!

Aquí tienes otra oportunidad para usar el vocabulario de este capítulo.

1 A veces uno no sabe la palabra correcta y necesita preguntar cómo se llama algo. Usa palabras como *lugar, cosa, tienda.* Túrnate con un(a) compañero(a). Puedes usar éstas u otras ideas. Por ejemplo:

A — *¿Cómo se llama el lugar donde se ponen las cartas?*

B — *Se llama un buzón.*

MARIBEL VERDÚ PRESENTA
LOS NUEVOS COLORES DE GIOVANNA

Giovanna se llena de color con la nueva línea de maquillaje Gio de Giovanna. Atrevida. Osada. Moderna. Para ponerte guapísima. Irresistible.
Con los lápices de labios más audaces que nunca hayas visto. Unas sombras de ojos arrebatadoras, para asombrarte... y asombrar. Y con unos rabiosos coloretes de auténtica locura. ¡Échale imaginación y ponte a la moda! ¡Te atreves? Gio, I nuovi colori di Giovanna.

Gio de Giovanna

Maribel Verdú

272 Capítulo 8

Options

Strategies for Reaching All Students

Spanish-Speaking Students
Exs. 1–3: If possible, pair bilingual with non-bilingual students.

 Un paso más Ex. 8-G

Students Needing Extra Help
Students may need help formulating the questions and retrieving the appropriate vocabulary. Do as a class or assign one example to each group.

Ex. 2: Give students time to make the map, or have a map ready. Do a complete model. Use the vocabulary section of the Organizer. *¿Qué sabes ahora?:* Have students write out this exercise so that they can record their progress.

Cooperative Learning
In groups of four, students will design a layout for a new department store having the following departments: *juguetes, aparatos eléctricos, cosméticos, muebles, ropa para niños,* and *zapatos.* Have two students decide where each department should go, and where the cash registers, elevators,

2 Túrnate con un(a) compañero(a) para ser el (la) policía y el (la) turista. Hagan un mapa de su comunidad y úsenlo para pedir y dar direcciones.

A —*Señor(ita), ¿me podría indicar dónde queda la biblioteca pública?*
B —*Claro que sí, . . .*

3 Túrnense para pedir y dar información. Uno de ustedes trabaja en el mostrador de información en el primer piso de un almacén. Usen la información en la tabla de la derecha.

A —*Perdone, señor(ita), ¿dónde están los perfumes?*
B —*Al fondo, señor(ita), cerca de la escalera mecánica.*

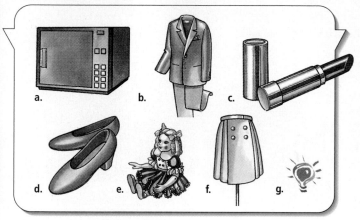

a. b. c.
d. e. f. g.

DIRECTORIO

administración	2
aparatos eléctricos	5
juguetes	6
maquillaje	1
muebles	4
perfumes	1
restaurante	sótano
ropa para caballeros	sótano
ropa para damas	2
ropa para niños	3
servicios	6
zapatos	3

¿Qué sabes ahora?

Can you:

■ name and describe the location of places in a community?
—Pon las cartas en ___. Está ___ el correo.

■ ask for and give directions?
—Perdone, señorita, ¿ ___ indicarme dónde ___ la estación de bomberos?
—Cruce ___, siga por ___ y ___ a la izquierda.

■ locate items in a drugstore or department store?
—¿La ropa de niños está en ___?
—No, señor, está en ___ .

escalators, and restrooms should be located. They should then tell a third student, so he or she can sketch out the layout of the store. As the group work proceeds, the fourth student should make a chart with the headings *Departamento, Lugar,* and *¿Por que?* and be prepared to present the data to the class.

Present & Apply

Cultural Objective
- To discuss bargaining procedures in Guatemala

Critical Thinking: Hypothesizing
Based on information in the *Perspectiva cultural* and students' general knowledge of U.S. history, what do they think might happen to the present-day Guatemalan system of buying goods in the next decade or so? Will bargaining become a thing of the past or will it remain a strong part of the Guatemalan economic system? Why? What is the likelihood of its becoming a part of our daily life?

Perspectiva cultural

¿Cómo sabe la gente los precios de las cosas en el mercado? ¿Crees que todos pagan el mismo precio? ¿Por qué crees eso? ¿Y en el almacén? ¿Por qué crees que sí o que no?

Options

Strategies for Reaching All Students

Spanish-Speaking Students
Ask: *¿Te gusta regatear, o prefieres comprar en un lugar con precios fijos? ¿Por qué? ¿Crees que los vendedores que tienen que regatear ganan mucho dinero? ¿Tienen un sueldo seguro? ¿Has regateado con un vendedor alguna vez? ¿Cómo te fue? ¿Qué compraste?*

 Un paso más Ex. 8-H

Students Needing Extra Help
Have students take notes to use when reviewing for the test. Discuss the idea of bargaining. Point out the differences in the photos, such as no price tags in the market, etc.
La cultura desde tu perspectiva: Students may need help defining yard sales, car purchases, etc.

Enrichment
Ex. 2: It might be helpful for students to make lists with the following headings to help them answer this question: *Aquí siempre se regatea, Aquí nunca se regatea, Aquí se regatea de vez en cuando.*
Additional questions: *¿Cómo debe ser una persona para poder regatear bien? ¿Qué tipo de personalidad debe tener? ¿Te gusta (gustaría) regatear? ¿Por qué sí o no?*

Roberto es un estudiante estadounidense que está viviendo con una familia guatemalteca en una comunidad pequeña. Hoy acompañó a doña* Francia, la madre de la familia, al mercado.

DOÑA FRANCIA	Buenos días, don Pancho.
VENDEDOR	Buenos días, doña Francia. ¿Cómo está?
DOÑA FRANCIA	Muy bien, gracias. ¿Y usted?
VENDEDOR	Bien, gracias a Dios.
DOÑA FRANCIA	Su hijo mayor es de la misma edad que Roberto, ¿verdad? ¿Ya se graduó?
VENDEDOR	No, todavía no. Se gradúa el año que viene, si Dios quiere. Está sacando buenas notas.
DOÑA FRANCIA	Me alegro.
VENDEDOR	Las manzanas están muy buenas hoy. Están a 75 centavos el kilo.
DOÑA FRANCIA	(inspeccionando las manzanas) Mmmm.
VENDEDOR	(en voz baja) Sesenta centavos.
DOÑA FRANCIA	Me da dos kilos, don Pancho. (Don Pancho le entrega las manzanas, y doña Francia le paga.) Gracias, don Pancho. Hasta la próxima vez. Salúdeme a su señora.
VENDEDOR	¡Cómo no, doña Francia! Que estén bien por su casa.

*Don and doña are titles of respect used with a person's first name.

Doña Francia y don Pancho charlan un poco antes de hablar de lo que ella va a comprar porque las relaciones personales son muy importantes en su cultura. Es necesario confirmarlas antes de negociar.

Más tarde Roberto va a un mercado turístico para comprar unos recuerdos.

ROBERTO	Buenas tardes, señor.
VENDEDOR	Buenas tardes, joven.
ROBERTO	¿A cuánto están estas bolsas?
VENDEDOR	A cien quetzales cada una. Son de pura lana y de colores firmes.
ROBERTO	¿No me puede dar una por ochenta quetzales?
VENDEDOR	No, lo siento. Pero sí por noventa.

La cultura desde tu perspectiva

1 Compara los dos diálogos según estas preguntas: ¿Se conocen el cliente y el vendedor? ¿Cómo lo sabes? ¿De qué hablan? ¿Quién menciona el precio primero? ¿Cambia mucho el precio?

2 ¿Cuándo y dónde se regatea (bargain) en los Estados Unidos? Compara la manera de regatear en los Estados Unidos y en Guatemala.

De compras en el mercado de Momostenango, Guatemala

Unas mujeres admiran una blusa en el mercado de Chichicastenango, Guatemala.

Cultural Notes

(p. 274, photo)
Chichicastenango, in the Department of Quiché, Guatemala, is known for its market, held every Sunday and Thursday. The colorful huipil (embroidered blouse made of handwoven fabric) worn by the woman in this photo identifies her as a member of a particular community. Each village designs a signature pattern into its huipil. Also situated on the plaza is Santo Tomás, the church where the Popol Vuh, a book written in Maya-Quiché about the indigenous peoples of Guatemala, was first translated into Spanish.

(p. 275, photo)
Momostenango is a small town in the Department of Huehuetenango, one of the most mountainous regions of Guatemala. Temperatures range from 40–70° F. Momostenango is known for its production of heavy wool blankets, called ponchos, which typically feature the design of two quetzales facing each other.

Preview

Teaching Suggestions

A: Have students predict what the present participle of *servir* would be. Then ask them to find that form in the text to see if their prediction is correct. *75 años sirviendo a nuestros clientes.*

B: Ask students to guess what *Se prohibe fumar* means. ("Smoking is prohibited" or "No smoking.")

Answers

A The line is *¡Aprenda español mientras está durmiendo!* The form of *dormir* is *durmiendo.* The stem of the present participle contains the stem change (o → u). The present participle of *pedir* is *está pidiendo;* the present participle of *servir* is *está sirviendo.*

B People in general (also expressed as "we") perform the action. The word that follows the verb (in this case, the subject of the sentence) determines whether the verb is singular or plural.

C The expression is *Ud. no paga nada.* Two negative words *(no* and *nada)* are used. *No* comes before the verb, and *nada* comes after. "I don't see anything" is said *(Yo) no veo nada.*

Gramática en contexto

¡Aprenda español mientras está durmiendo!

¿Imposible? ¡Sí es posible con el fabuloso y nuevo

método Dormex!

Llame hoy al 555-7777 y ¡ábrale las puertas a un nuevo futuro!

Librería El Quijote
Paseo de la Reforma 327

Se venden libros, revistas, periódicos, mapas y guías turísticas

75 años sirviendo a nuestros clientes

— Se habla inglés. —

Taller Hermanos Gómez

Se vende gasolina.

Se reparan coches y camiones.

Si su vehículo no queda en perfectas condiciones, ¡Ud. no paga nada!

A You know that we use *estar* + present participle to talk about something that is happening right now. Find the sentence that talks about sleeping in the first ad. How is the stem different from *dormir?* What do you think the present participle of *pedir* and *servir* might be?

B In these ads, *se habla, se reparan,* and *se vende(n)* are used. In these sentences, who do you think performs the action? In some cases the verb is singular; in others, plural. What do you think determines this?

C Find the expression that means "you pay nothing." How many negative words are used? Where do they appear in relation to the verb? How would you say "I don't see anything"?

276   Capítulo 8

Options

Strategies for Reaching All Students

Students Needing Extra Help
Begin the grammar section of the Organizer.
B: Students may have difficulty explaining the impersonal *se* in these sentences. Give more examples (in columns) to help them determine when the verb is singular and when it is plural.
Repaso: Los usos de estar: Give additional examples. If available, use the Organizer from Book 1, Chap. 3.
Ex. 1: Create additional examples to include the points made in the *estar* explanation.

276

Repaso: Los usos de *estar*

Review the present-tense forms of *estar*.

(yo)	**estoy**	(nosotros) (nosotras)	**estamos**
(tú)	**estás**	(vosotros) (vosotras)	**estáis**
Ud. (él) (ella)	**está**	Uds. (ellos) (ellas)	**están**

• Remember that we use *estar* to indicate location.

> Los servicios **están** al fondo.

• We also use *estar* to talk about conditions and characteristics that are not always associated with that person or thing.

> La venda **está** limpia.
> La máquina de afeitar **está** sucia.

Compare this use of *estar* with the use of *ser* for conditions and characteristics that usually *are* associated with a person or thing.

> Juan **es** guapo.   *Juan **is** good-looking.*
> ¡Qué guapo **estás** hoy!   *How nice you **look** today!*

• *Estar* is also used to form the present progressive tense.

> Patricia **está cruzando** la calle.

1 Tu equipo ganó el partido de fútbol. Túrnate con un(a) compañero(a) para decir cómo están estas personas.

> **yo**   *Estoy (muy) cansado.*

a. el entrenador de tu equipo   alegre
b. el entrenador del otro equipo   triste
c. los jugadores de tu equipo   de buen / mal humor
d. los jugadores del otro equipo   cansado(a)
e. algunos amigos tuyos   callado(a)
f. Uds.
g. la esposa de tu entrenador

Present & Practice

Reteach / Review: Uses of *estar*
After reviewing the examples, call on students to give other sentences illustrating uses of *estar*.

Re-enter / Recycle
Ex. 1: sports from Chap. 4

Answers
1 Answers will vary, but may include:
a. Está (muy) alegre.
b. Está de mal humor.
c. Están (muy) cansados.
d. Están (muy) callados.
e. Están de buen humor.
f. Están (muy) alegres.
g. Está alegre.

 Practice Wkbk. 8-5

 Prueba 8-5

Present & Practice

Re-enter / Recycle

Ex. 3: greetings and leavetakings from Chap. 6
Ex. 5: daily routine from Chap. 2

Answers

2 a. Está bebiendo (un vaso de) agua.

b. Están escribiendo en la pizarra.

c. Están sacando la basura.

d. Están encendiendo las velas.

e. Está tocando la trompeta.

f. Está patinando (en la acera).

3 a. Carla está durmiendo.

b. Yo estoy vistiendo al niño.

c. Él está pidiendo una venda.

d. Ellas se están diciendo "¡Hola!" / Ellas están diciéndose "¡Hola!"

e. Uds. se están divirtiendo. / Uds. están divirtiéndose.

f. (Nosotros) nos estamos despidiendo. / (Nosotros) estamos despidiéndonos.

4 ESTUDIANTE A

a. ¿Quién está haciendo las compras?

b. ... está reparando la escalera mecánica?

c. ... (es) está(n) buscando la verdulería?

d. ... está comprando la crema de afeitar?

e. ... (es) está(n) apagando el incendio?

f. ... está colgando la ropa?

g. ... está enviando las cartas?

Repaso: El presente progresivo

You know that when we want to express that an action is happening right now, we use the present progressive tense. We form it using the present tense of *estar* + the present participle of another verb. To form the present participle, we add *-ando* to the stem of *-ar* verbs and *-iendo* to the stem of *-er* and *-ir* verbs.

habl**ar**	**estoy** habl**ando**
com**er**	**estamos** com**iendo**
escrib**ir**	**están** escrib**iendo**

- Verbs that have the stem change $o \rightarrow u$ or $e \rightarrow i$ in the preterite have the same change in the present participle. For example:

INFINITIVE	PRETERITE	PRESENT PARTICIPLE
dormir *(o → u)*	**durm**ieron	**durm**iendo
servir *(e → i)*	**sirv**ieron	**sirv**iendo

Juan todavía **está durmiendo**.
El camarero **está sirviendo** la comida.

- Reflexive or object pronouns can be placed before the form of *estar*, or they can be attached to the end of the present participle. If they are attached to the present participle, a written accent is needed.

Ahora **me** estoy **divirtiendo**.	Ahora estoy **divirtiéndome**.
Lo está **haciendo** ahora.	Está **haciéndolo** ahora.

2 Mira los dibujos y di qué están haciendo estas personas.

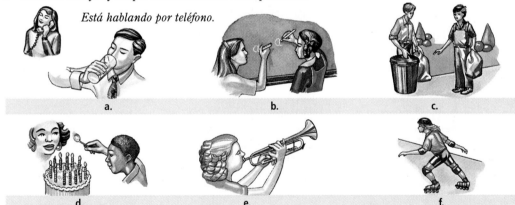

Está hablando por teléfono.

a.   b.   c.

d.   e.   f.

Options

Strategies for Reaching All Students

Students Needing Extra Help
Repaso: El presente progresivo: If available, use the Organizer from Book 1, Chap. 14. Review all the verbs having the stem change: *vestirse, conseguir, despedirse, pedir.* Write them on the chalkboard and have students copy the list. Give more examples of the reflexive and object pronoun construction. If students are having

difficulty, review indirect object pronouns with infinitives. Encourage students to use the construction that is most comfortable for them.
Ex. 2: Remind students that this exercise contains *-ar, -er,* and *-ir* verbs.
Ex. 3: Point out that this exercise uses stem-changing verbs.

Ex. 4: Point out where the *lo* came from. Model with a feminine object pronoun. Go through the exercise, using the first response, then again using the second response.
Ex. 5: If available, use the vocabulary section of the Organizer from Chap. 2.

3 ¿Y qué están haciendo estas otras personas?

Ramón / servir los refrescos   *Ramón está sirviendo los refrescos.*

a. Carla / dormir
b. yo / vestir al niño
c. él / pedir una venda

d. ellas / decirse "¡Hola!"
e. Uds. / divertirse
f. nosotros / despedirse

4 ¿Quién está haciendo estas cosas? Túrnate con otro(a) compañero(a).

lavar el coche / Jorge
   A — *¿Quién está lavando el coche?*
   B — *Jorge está lavándolo.*
       o: *Jorge lo está lavando.*

a. hacer las compras / Rafael
b. reparar la escalera mecánica / Patricia
c. buscar la verdulería / ellos
d. comprar la crema de afeitar / Mario
e. apagar el incendio / los bomberos
f. colgar la ropa / Juana
g. enviar las cartas / Marco

5 Son las siete de la mañana. ¿Qué está haciendo la familia de Javier? Túrnate con otro(a) compañero(a).

Su padre está afeitándose.

su padre

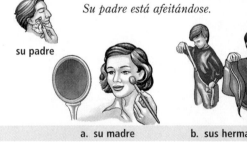

a. su madre   b. sus hermanos menores   c. su hermana mayor

d. Javier   e. su bisabuela   f. su hermana menor

Gramática en contexto   279

Enrichment
Use the examples showing the placement of reflexive or object pronouns for a quick review. Write these sentences on the chalkboard and call on students to change them according to your cue for a different reflexive verb or pronoun: *Ahora Javier se está divirtiendo. Ahora está divirtiéndose. (nosotros / aburrirnos; yo / quedarme en cama; tú / sentirte mal)*

279

Present & Practice

Reteach / Review: Negative constructions

To reinforce affirmative and negative words, call out a word and have students call out the antonym.

Re-enter / Recycle

Ex. 9: daily routine from Chap. 2

Answers

6 Answers will vary, but look for the correct forms of *estar* + present participle.

7 ESTUDIANTE A

a. ¿Celebraste algo especial esta semana?

b. ¿Compraste . . .

c. ¿Encontraste . . .

d. ¿Escribiste . . .

e. ¿Viste . . .

f. ¿Hiciste . . .

ESTUDIANTE B

Answers will vary; look for correct first-person preterite forms.

a. (No) Celebré . . .

b. (No) Compré . . .

c. (No) Encontré . . .

d. (No) Escribí . . .

e. (No) Vi . . .

f. (No) Hice . . .

8 ESTUDIANTE A

a. ¿Ves alguna máquina de afeitar por aquí?

b. . . . algún perfume . . .

c. . . . algún desodorante . . .

6 Imagina qué están haciendo varias personas (el presidente de los Estados Unidos, el (la) director(a) de la escuela, etc.) en este momento. Túrnate con un(a) compañero(a).

A — ¿Qué está haciendo ___?

B — Creo que está ___.

Construcciones negativas

Here are some affirmative and negative words that you already know. Remember that they are antonyms.

AFFIRMATIVE	NEGATIVE
alguien	nadie
algo	nada
alguno, alguna *(pronoun)*	ninguno, ninguna *(pronoun)*
algún, alguna *(adj.)*	ningún, ninguna *(adj.)*
siempre	nunca
también	tampoco

Algún and *ningún* are always written with an accent.

- Affirmative words usually come before the main verb of the sentence. In a question they may come after the verb.

  Ella **también** lo recuerda.   ¿Se repartió **algo**?
  ¿**Alguien** cumplió años?   ¿**Siempre** vas a la panadería?

- Negative words may come before or after the verb. But if they come after, we must use *no* before the verb.

  Nadie fue a la reunión.   **No** fue **nadie** a la reunión.
  Nunca llora.   **No** llora **nunca**.
  Ninguno de ellos se quitó el abrigo.   **No** se quitó el abrigo **ninguno** de ellos.

7 Túrnate con un(a) compañero(a) para contestar las preguntas.

comer
A — ¿Comiste algo especial esta semana?
B — Sí, comí ___.
o: No, no comí nada especial.

a. celebrar   c. encontrar   e. ver

b. comprar   d. escribir   f. hacer

280   Capítulo 8

Options

Strategies for Reaching All Students

Students Needing Extra Help

Ex. 6: Brainstorm people and their activities as a whole class.

Construcciones negativas: continuación: Help pairs of students read the chart. Give additional examples of the placement of affirmative words. If available, refer to the grammar section of the Organizer for Book 1, Chap. 14.

Give additional examples of negative constructions using *no,* emphasizing that this is just another way of saying the same thing.

Ex. 7: Model more of these responses, especially a positive response. Brainstorm possible responses.

Ex. 8: Remind students that *alguno(a)* and *ninguno(a)* must agree with the nouns they

replace. Point out the artwork, and remind students that their response depends on it. Give an example using the second response.

Ex. 9: Do the exercise twice, as an oral and as a written exercise, using the two negative responses separately. Remind students that this practices two ways of saying the same thing.

8 Con un(a) compañero(a) contesta las preguntas.
Por ejemplo:

pasta dentífrica

A —¿Ves alguna pasta dentífrica
   por aquí?
B —No, no veo ninguna.
   o: Sí, aquí está.

a. máquina de afeitar   e. lápiz de labios
b. perfume   f. jabón
c. desodorante   g.
d. cepillo de dientes

9 ¿Qué haces todas las mañanas? Con un(a)
compañero(a) contesta las preguntas.

A —¿Siempre te bañas por la mañana?
B —No, nunca me baño por la mañana.
   o: No, no me baño nunca por la mañana.
   o: Sí, siempre./Sólo de vez en cuando.

a.

b.

c.

d.

e.

f.

d. ...algún cepillo de dientes ...
e. ...algún lápiz de labios ...
f. ...algún jabón ...
g. Questions will vary.
ESTUDIANTE B
a. No, no veo ninguna.
b. Sí, aquí está.
c. No, no veo ninguno.
d. Sí, aquí está.
e. Sí, aquí está.
f. No, no veo ninguno.
g. Answers will vary.

9 **ESTUDIANTE A**
a. ¿Siempre te maquillas por la
mañana?
b. ...te cepillas los dientes ...?
c. ...te duchas ...?
d. ...te peinas ...?
e. ...te lavas la cara ...?
f. ...te secas el pelo ...?
ESTUDIANTE B
Answers will vary, but should
include the following:
a. ...me maquillo ...
b. ...me cepillo ...
c. ...me ducho ...
d. ...me peino ...
e. ...me lavo ...
f. ...me seco ...

**Practice Wkbk. 8-6,
8-7, 8-8**

Pruebas 8-6, 8-7

Comm. Act. BLM 8-3

Enrichment
Construcciones negativas: As a homework
assignment, have students write on the following topic, using as many appropriate
affirmative and negative words as possible:
*Rodrigo perdió su carnet de identidad. ¿Qué
le dice un optimista? ¿Qué le dice un pes-
imista?*

Ex. 9: You may want to do this exercise with
the entire class, with you posing the same
question four times and eliciting from students the four different responses provided
in the example. Remind students that they
can use other time expressions such as *a
veces, muchas veces, a menudo, casi siempre,* and *casi nunca.*

281

Present & Practice

Answers

10 ESTUDIANTE A

a. ¿Aquí se bailan bailes latinos o americanos?

b. ...se sirve comida o sand-wiches?

c. ...se permite sacar fotos o no?

d. ...se ve gente famosa o no?

e. ...se lleva ropa elegante o deportiva?

ESTUDIANTE B

a. Aquí se bailan bailes ameri-canos.

b. ...se sirven sandwiches.

c. ...se permite sacar fotos.

d. ...se ve gente famosa.

e. ...se lleva ropa deportiva.

Class Starter Review

On the day following the presenta-tion of the impersonal *se,* you might begin the class with this activity:

In pairs, have students prepare to share with the class one thing that is permitted in school *(se permite llevar pantalones cortos)* and one that isn't *(no se permite maqui-llarse en la sala de clase).*

El *se* impersonal

In English we often use *they, you, one,* or *people* in an impersonal or indefinite sense meaning "people in general." In Spanish we use *se* + the *Ud. / él / ella* or the *Uds. / ellos / ellas* form of the verb.

Se habla español.	*Spanish is spoken (here).*
Se venden perfumes en esa tienda.	*They sell perfume in that store.*
¿**Se permite** sacar fotos?	*Can you take pictures?*

10 Con un(a) compañero(a), habla de un club nuevo. Por ejemplo:

tocar música   A —¿Aquí se toca música rock o clásica?
rock o clásica   B —Aquí se toca música rock.

a. bailar bailes latinos o americanos
b. servir comida o sandwiches
c. permitir sacar fotos o no
d. ver gente famosa o no
e. llevar ropa elegante o deportiva

Options

Strategies for Reaching All Students

Students Needing Extra Help

El se *impersonal:* Give more examples. Point out which verbs can be used with the imper-sonal *se.* Review Ex. 11 from p. 270.
Ex. 10: Remind students to conjugate the verbs. Give a model using the plural.

Ex. 11: Give an example using the singular. Help students make the correct association: ice cream with soda fountain, money with bank, etc.
Ahora lo sabes: Have students write out this exercise so they can keep track of their progress.

11 Pregúntale a un(a) compañero(a) qué se hace en estos lugares.

A —¿*Qué se repara aquí?*
B —*Se reparan zapatos.*

reparar

a. vender

b. servir

c. hacer

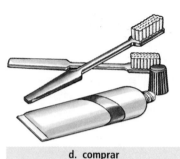

d. comprar

e. pedir prestado

f. practicar

Ahora lo sabes

Can you:

■ talk about actions that are happening right now?

—¡Silencio! Pablo está ___.

■ use negative words?

—___ compré ___ revista porque no encontré el quiosco.

■ talk about actions without specifying who does them?

—En una estación de servicio, se ___ gasolina y algunas veces ___ reparan coches.

Gramática en contexto   283

11 ESTUDIANTE A
a. ¿Qué se vende aquí?
b. . . . se sirve . . .
c. . . . se hace . . .
d. . . . se compra . . .
e. . . . se pide prestado . . .
f. . . . se practica . . .

ESTUDIANTE B
a. Se vende maquillaje.
b. Se sirve(n) helado (refrescos).
c. Se hacen llaves.
d. Se compran pasta dentífrica y cepillos de dientes.
e. Se pide prestado dinero.
f. Se practica básquetbol.

Answers: Ahora lo sabes
• Answers will vary, but should be a present participle.
• No / ninguna
• vende / se

Practice Wkbk. 8-9

Audio Activities 8.4, 8.5

Prueba 8-8

Apply

Pronunciation Tape 8-3

Teaching Suggestions

Ex. 2: You may want to use different settings, such as a classroom, a department store, a drugstore, etc.

Answers: Actividades

1–3 Answers will vary.

¿Recuerdas?

Play

Video Activity A

Using the Video

In Episode 8, Jamie and Carlos drop off the vegetables they bought for Sr. Navarro, who tells them that the produce from La Jacaranda is overpriced and of inferior quality.

The next day, Jamie, Carlos, María and Felipe go shopping together. There is tension between Felipe and Carlos over María, and the two young men get into an argument. Felipe is not convinced that Carlos is not still interested in María until he arrives that night at María's house to find Carlos and an *estudiantina* (a musical band formed by students) singing a serenade to Jamie.

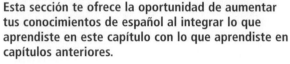

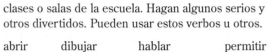

Actividades

Esta sección te ofrece la oportunidad de aumentar tus conocimientos de español al integrar lo que aprendiste en este capítulo con lo que aprendiste en capítulos anteriores.

1 Hagan varios carteles para la clase de español y otras clases o salas de la escuela. Hagan algunos serios y otros divertidos. Pueden usar estos verbos u otros.

abrir	dibujar	hablar	permitir
beber	entregar	jugar	prohibir
cerrar	escribir	maquillarse	reparar
correr	explicar	nadar	vender

Mapa de la ciudad de Cuzco, Perú

284   Capítulo 8

Options

Strategies for Reaching All Students

Students Needing Extra Help

Ex. 1: Give examples of how *deber, permitir,* and *prohibir* are used with infinitives. Review the impersonal *se*. Give additional examples using the negative. Point out that students do not need to make two sentences for each sign. Brainstorm the possibilities for each infinitive. Assign a few infinitives to each pair of students to ensure that everyone contributes.

Ex. 2: Limit the possibilities to things that students can clearly see: for example,

objects in the classroom or playground. Review the present progressive, the uses of *estar,* and the impersonal *se*. Brainstorm possible questions. If, for example, the objects are all in the classroom, necessary vocabulary would deal with size, shape, color, material, usage, etc.

Ex. 3: Use the vocabulary section of the Organizer. Review location words and words such as *caminar, doblar, quedar,* etc. Give students a place on the map from which to begin.

Enrichment

Ex. 2: Pairs of students can play a guessing game in which one student can give hints about a famous person or date in history and the other can try to name it. Example: *Estoy pensando en el jugador de básquetbol que después jugó béisbol. / Estoy pensando en algo que pasó en la luna el 20 de julio de 1969. / Estoy pensando en la persona que dijo, "Un paso pequeño para un hombre, un salto gigante para la humanidad."*

284

2 En grupo, van a jugar *Veinte Preguntas*. Una persona piensa en un objeto. Las otras le hacen preguntas. Ella sólo puede contestar sí o no. Por ejemplo:

    A —*Estoy pensando en algo que está en la esquina de una calle.*
    B —*¿Se ponen cartas allí?*
    A —*No.*
    B —*¿Se venden . . . ?*

3 Túrnate con un(a) compañero(a) para darle direcciones. Tu compañero(a) tiene que adivinar adónde lo llevas. Puedes usar lugares del mapa de las páginas 260–261, de la escuela o de tu comunidad. Por ejemplo:

Estás en la pescadería. Camina media cuadra hasta llegar al banco. Allí, dobla a la izquierda y camina una cuadra. Ahora, dobla a la izquierda de nuevo. El lugar queda al lado de la verdulería. ¿Dónde estás?

Parc Güell en Barcelona

Estas señales indican lugares de interés en una sección histórica de Colonia del Sacramento, Uruguay.

Later, Jamie and Carlos visit the offices of Operación Aztlán and report the results of the tests: the pesticides used at the hacienda La Jacaranda are illegal.
In the final scene, Jamie and Carlos are in Carlos's *yip* (all-terrain vehicle) admiring the view and talking about the future.

 La Catrina: Capítulo 8

Play

 Video Activity B

 Para entender mejor

Play

 Video Activity C

 Comm. Act. BLMs 8-4, 8-5

Cultural Notes

Cooperative Learning
Divide students into groups of four. Tell each group that they are going on a picnic. Assign each student a responsibility: planning the menu, organizing sports and activities, listing paper goods, and planning musical entertainment. Ask: *¿Qué llevaste al picnic? ¿Dónde lo (la) compraste? ¿Cuánto costó? ¿Qué hiciste en el picnic?* Have one student from each group compile the data and another present it to the class.

(p. 285, left photo)
The style of Catalan architect Antonio Gaudí (1852–1926) remains unique. Parc Güell in Barcelona is one of Gaudí's most famous works. Planned as a hillside garden suburb, the never-finished project contains two houses, undulating benches, tiled lizards guarding a grotto, and a pagoda.

(p. 285, right photo)
Colonia del Sacramento, Uruguay, originally a seventeenth-century Portuguese settlement, still retains a colonial atmosphere. Narrow cobblestone streets and ornate wrought-iron work decorate residential buildings in the vicinity. (Note that the word *pulpería* is a regionalism for "general store.") A hydrofoil crosses the Río de la Plata three times daily, connecting Colonia del Sacramento and nearby Buenos Aires.

Apply

Process Reading
For a description of process reading, see p. 52.

Teaching Suggestions
Aplicación: The flags of Puerto Rico (No. 3), Argentina (No. 5), and Panamá (No. 6) are not described in the text. You may want to have groups of three work together, with one student giving the description and the other two guessing.

Answers
Antes de leer
Answers will vary, but students may say that they will find information about Central and South American countries and their flags.

¡Vamos a leer!

Antes de leer

STRATEGY Using prior knowledge

These are excerpts from a geography textbook. Look at the map and flags. What kind of information do you think will be in the text?

Mira la lectura

STRATEGY Skimming

Now skim the text to get a general idea of what it says. Was your guess correct?

¿DE QUÉ PAÍS ES ESTA BANDERA?

286   Capítulo 8

Options

Strategies for Reaching All Students

Spanish-Speaking Students
Aplicación: Have students research the history of one of the flags shown on p. 287: *Haz una investigación sobre la historia de una bandera en la página 287.*

 Un paso más Ex. 8-I

Students Needing Extra Help
Mira la lectura: Go over each description carefully after the answer has been given to ensure that students understand it. You may want to use a large wall map and have one student point as you read aloud.
Aplicación: Have students describe the location and flag of the U.S. Let them use this and other models to write their own descriptions.

Cultural Notes

Flags of Spain and Latin America

Argentina: (1818) Sun represents independence. Blue and white worn by patriots who fought off British invaders in 1806 and 1807.
Bolivia: (1888) Coat of arms has a breadfruit tree, a bundle of wheat, and a mountain. Also pictures a condor and an alpaca.
Chile: White star, progress and honor; red, blood of heroes; white, snow of Andes; blue, sky.
Colombia: (1861) Yellow represents New World; red, the blood of heroes; blue, the ocean.
Costa Rica: (1848) Coat of arms shows three volcanoes, the Caribbean, and seven stars, each representing a province.

Este país está situado en el norte de América del Sur y al este de Colombia. La bandera tiene una franja central azul con siete estrellas blancas. La primera franja es amarilla y la última roja.

Este país está situado en América Central y está al norte de Nicaragua. La bandera tiene una franja central blanca con cinco estrellas azules. Las otras dos franjas también son azules.

Este país está situado al sur de Brasil y es un país pequeño bañado por el Océano Atlántico. La bandera tiene cinco franjas blancas, cuatro azules y un sol amarillo.

Este país está situado en el sur de América del Sur, está bañado por el Océano Pacífico y limita con Perú, Bolivia y Argentina. La bandera tiene una franja superior blanca y otra roja. También tiene una estrella blanca en un cuadrado azul.

Infórmate

STRATEGY➤ Coping with unknown words

You already know that some words are essential to understanding and some aren't. In this selection, the word *franja* occurs often, and it is important for understanding the text. What do you think it means?

Here are some clues. Look at the flags and name some features they have in common. Then look at the text and the color adjectives used with the word *franja*. Can you guess the meaning? Now do the same with the word *estrella*. Verify your guesses by consulting a dictionary.

Which flag goes with each of the four countries and descriptions?

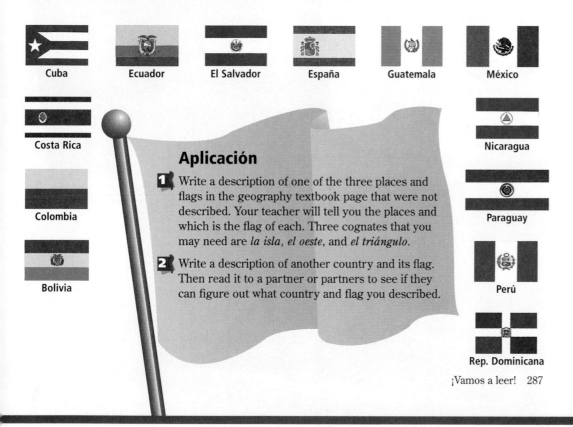

Cuba
Ecuador
El Salvador
España
Guatemala
México
Costa Rica
Colombia
Bolivia
Nicaragua
Paraguay
Perú
Rep. Dominicana

Aplicación

1 Write a description of one of the three places and flags in the geography textbook page that were not described. Your teacher will tell you the places and which is the flag of each. Three cognates that you may need are *la isla, el oeste*, and *el triángulo*.

2 Write a description of another country and its flag. Then read it to a partner or partners to see if they can figure out what country and flag you described.

¡Vamos a leer!   287

Mira la lectura
Answers will vary.

Infórmate
Franja means "stripe." *Estrella* means "star."
Venezuela (No. 2)
Honduras (No. 4)
Uruguay (No. 7)
Chile (No. 1)

Aplicación
Answers will vary.

Flags of Spain and Latin America cont'd.

Cuba: (1902) Star represents independence.
Dominican Republic: Blue, liberty; white, salvation; red, blood of heroes.
Ecuador: Coat of arms has a condor, Chimborazo mountain, and the first steamboat built in Ecuador.
El Salvador: (1912) Blue stripes represent unity; white, peace.
Guatemala: (1971) Blue stripes represent the Atlantic and Pacific; coat of arms has quetzal with scroll bearing date of independence.
Honduras: (1866) Stars represent the five Central American republics that formed a union in early 1880s.

Mexico: (1821) Coat of arms in the center. Green, independence; white, religion; red, union.
Nicaragua: (1908) Coat of arms features volcanoes representing Central American union; triangle, equality; rainbow, peace; cap, liberty.
Panama: (1903) Blue star, honesty and purity; red star, authority and law.
Paraguay: Red, white, and blue stripes honor French ideals. Coat of arms on front; treasury seal with a lion and liberty cap on back.
Peru: (1825) Symbols represent abundant animal, plant, and mineral resources.

Puerto Rico: (1952) Resembles Cuban flag recalling 1890s when both countries opposed Spanish rule.
Spain: (1981) Shield represents Aragón, Castilla, and other historic kingdoms of Spain.
Uruguay: Stripes represent political division at time of independence. The sun represents independence.
Venezuela: (1954) Red, blood of heroes; blue, Atlantic; yellow, prosperity. Stars represent original states that united to proclaim independence.

Apply

Process Writing

For information regarding developing a writing portfolio, see page 54.

Teaching Suggestions

Students may need help identifying local landmarks. Use this as an opportunity to instill pride in their hometown. Have students contact The Chamber of Commerce, the Visitors' Bureau if there is one, or the public library to learn more about local history and any places of interest that they may be unaware of.

¡Vamos a escribir!

¿Qué lugares de interés hay en tu comunidad, ciudad o estado? Vamos a preparar una guía turística con descripciones de los lugares de más interés.

1 Primero, identifiquen los lugares históricos, famosos o importantes de su comunidad. Piensen en estas cosas:

- cómo se llama el lugar
- dónde queda
- cuál es su historia o qué importancia tiene
- cómo se llega a él
- el horario y el precio de la entrada

Cada estudiante o grupo pequeño debe escoger un lugar y escribir el primer borrador. Consulten con un(a) compañero(a), y sigan los otros pasos del proceso de escribir. Escriban la versión final en un procesador de texto si es posible. Usen dibujos o fotos para ilustrar la guía.

Vista de Toledo (c. 1600), El Greco (Domenicos Theotokopoulos)

Vista moderna de Toledo

Options

Strategies for Reaching All Students

Students Needing Extra Help

After discussing your community, divide the class into two groups: one to work on places of interest, one for the community as a whole. Have tourist guides and community information available. Show how tourist guides keep descriptions short.

As a class, brainstorm places to include in the guide. Model one description, using the vocabulary section of the Organizer. If available, use the Organizer from Book 1, Chap. 10. Remind students that they may have to contact these places for more information. Limit paragraph length. Review the preterite and imperfect tenses and their uses. Give students time to research. They may also need help with the vocabulary and the structure of the sentences. Assign four or five areas to cover: population, number of schools, etc.

2 Ahora, en grupo escriban uno o dos párrafos sobre su comunidad, ciudad o estado para incluir en la guía. Piensen en estas cosas:

- de dónde viene el nombre de la comunidad
- quiénes eran los primeros habitantes del área
- cuándo llegaron los europeos
- qué se cultivaba o qué industria había
- cómo es la comunidad hoy

3 Para distribuir su trabajo, pueden:

- enviarlo a los hoteles o moteles de la comunidad
- enviarlo a la cámara de comercio (*chamber of commerce*) de la comunidad
- exhibirlo en la biblioteca escolar
- ofrecerlo a una revista o un periódico hispano
- exhibirlo en la sala de clases
- incluirlo en su portafolio

Greetings from Toledo, Ohio!

Cultural Notes

(p. 288, top photo)
Domenikos Theotokopoulos, El Greco (1541–1614), was born in Crete. Around 1560, he left to study in Venice, where he began to experiment with the style of painting called "mannerism," characterized by graceful linés, elongated figures, and unusual perspectives. Seeking patronage, he went to Toledo in 1577, where he settled permanently and completed many paintings of its landscape.

(p. 288, bottom photo)
Toledo has long been a crossroads of culture and religion. The Romans entered the already existing city in 193 B.C. The Visigoths and the Moors occupied Toledo in later centuries. In 1085 King Alfonso I took the city from the Moors during the Reconquest and established the political center of Castilla there. During the middle ages, Toledo was an intellectual and artistic center, home to a multicultural citizenry of large numbers of Jews, Muslims, and Christians. The Alcázar, a fortress built in the Moorish style in 1531, dominates this view on the right.

Assess & Summarize

Test Preparation

You may want to assign parts of this section as homework or as an in-class writing activity prior to administering the *Examen de habilidades*.

Answers

Listening: —*Sí, señor. Hay uno muy cerca, a tres cuadras de aquí. Siga por esta calle dos cuadras. En el semáforo, doble a la derecha. Siga por esa calle y el quiosco de periódicos está al final de la cuadra, enfrente de una estación de metro.*
Answers will vary, but may include *¿Hay un quiosco (de periódicos) cerca de aquí?*

Reading: *Rebaja* means "reduction" or "discount."
Answers will vary, but students may say the use of "50 percent" or that they could not be combined with any other discount clued them in to its meaning.

Writing: Directions should be accurate for your community.

Culture: Answers will vary, but students may mention that if the buyer and seller know each other, the bargaining process is subtle. The seller is the first to mention the price of an item, and the buyer then offers a lower amount.

¿Lo sabes bien?

Esta sección te ayudará a prepararte para el examen de habilidades, donde tendrás que hacer tareas semejantes.

Listening

Can you understand when someone gives directions? Listen as your teacher reads a sample similar to what you will hear on the test. What question is this the response to?

Reading

Can you understand a written advertisement describing a department store sale? What do you think *rebaja* means? How do you know?

¡Gran Liquidación— Sólo Hoy!

En los Almacenes Flores, donde las rebajas son fantásticas

♦ ropa para damas, caballeros y niños ♦
♦ maquillaje y productos personales ♦
♦ muebles ♦

Rebajas especiales de hasta 50% en todas las secciones.*

*Estas rebajas especiales no se pueden combinar con ningún otro descuento.

Writing

Can you write a note giving directions to a friend who is going to the public library? This is an example.

Carlos,
Es muy fácil ir a la biblioteca desde la parada del autobús en la Calle Franklin. Primero, dobla a la izquierda en la Calle Monroe. Camina dos cuadras. (Hay una señal de alto en la esquina y una heladería cerca.) Dobla a la derecha. Camina por seis cuadras. La biblioteca está en esa esquina. No hay ningún otro edificio grande allí. (En la biblioteca se están vendiendo bolsos muy bonitos esta semana.)
Anabel

Culture

Can you explain how a price is usually negotiated while bargaining in Guatemala?

Speaking

Create a dialogue with your partner about a customer trying to find some things in a department store.

A —*Por favor, ¿dónde puedo encontrar la ropa para damas?*
B —*Está en el tercer piso.*
A —*¿Y dónde están los ascensores? ¿Están al fondo?*
B —*No. Están cerca de la entrada. Siga por aquí. Doble a la derecha en la sección de perfumes. Están enfrente de la caja.*
A —*Muchas gracias. Usted es muy amable.*

290 Capítulo 8

Options

Strategies for Reaching All Students

Students Needing Extra Help
Have students write out this exercise so that they can check off what they have mastered. Remind students that this is just a sample of what the test will be like.
Listening: Read more than once. Remind students they only need to listen for one piece of information. Brainstorm for what words they should be listening.
Reading: Remind students of context clues.

Writing: Have students use the Organizer and write a sample note as practice. Give students a common starting point. Remind them to give clues, such as buildings, street names, etc. Allow them to use a map as they write their directions, and give a required number of sentences to write.
Culture: Have students review the notes they took during their first reading of the *Perspectiva cultural*. Role play a bargaining scene with a student, or videotape one with a colleague before-

hand. Review the *Perspectiva cultural*.
Speaking: Choose a store that everyone in the class is familiar with. Discuss the layout of the store, and get students to think in terms of sections. Draw a layout on the chalkboard that students can refer to while speaking. Remind them to give clues such as floor numbers, front, entrance, etc. Use the vocabulary section of the Organizer. Limit the number of lines of the dialogue.

Resumen del capítulo 8

Usa el vocabulario de este capítulo para:

- name and describe the location of places in a community
- ask for and give directions
- locate items in a drugstore or department store

to name things and places in a community
el centro
el semáforo
la señal de alto
el cruce
la carretera
el buzón, *pl.* los buzones
el teléfono público
el transporte público
la estación de bomberos
el bombero, la bombera

to name places where you shop
la carnicería
la floristería
la frutería
la heladería
la panadería
la pescadería
el quiosco (de periódicos)
la verdulería

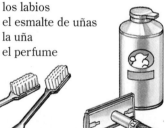

to ask or give directions
la dirección, *pl.* las direcciones
indicar
perdonar: perdone (Ud.)
¿Podría (Ud.) /
   Podrías (tú) + *inf.?*
seguir *(e → i)*: siga (Ud.)
por + *(place)*
doblar: doble (Ud.)

cruzar
la distancia
la milla
el kilómetro
el metro

to describe places
histórico, -a

to talk about personal care
el cepillo de dientes
la seda dental
el desodorante
la crema de afeitar
la máquina de afeitar
afeitarse
la venda
ponerse
quitarse
maquillarse
el maquillaje
el lápiz de labios,
   pl. los lápices de labios
los labios
el esmalte de uñas
la uña
el perfume

to name and indicate places in a store
el ascensor
la escalera
la escalera mecánica
la caja
el mostrador
la entrada
la salida
al fondo
los servicios
la ropa para caballeros
la ropa para damas
la ropa para niños
la sección, *pl.* las secciones

to talk about shopping
vender: se vende(n)
hacer las compras
gastar

other useful words
mientras

Resumen 291

CAPÍTULO 9

THEME: ACCIDENTS AND ILLNESS

SCOPE AND SEQUENCE   Pages 292–325

COMMUNICATION

Topics

Parts of the body

Medical procedures

Medicines

Allergies

Objectives

To compare pharmacies in Spanish-speaking countries with those in the U.S.

To identify parts of the body

To discuss an illness

To talk about allergies

To talk about treatment for medical conditions

To describe how an accident occurred

To indicate time

CULTURE

Medical care

GRAMMAR

El imperfecto progresivo

El uso del pretérito y del imperfecto progresivo

El pretérito de caerse

El pretérito de poner

Ancillaries available for use with Chapter 9

Multisensory/Technology

 Overhead Transparencies, 44–47

 Audio Tapes and CDs

 Vocabulary Art Blackline Masters for Hands-On Learning, pp. 48–52

Classroom Crossword

La Catrina

 CD-ROM

Print

 Practice Workbook, pp. 85–94

 Writing, Audio & Video Activities, pp. 53–58, 117–119, 167–168

 Communicative Activity Blackline Masters

   Pair and Small Group Activities, pp. 57–62

   Situation Cards, p. 63

 Un paso más: Actividades para ampliar tu español, pp. 49–54

Assessment

 Assessment Program

   Pruebas, pp. 129–139

   Examen de habilidades, pp. 140–143

 Test Generator

Video still from Chap. 9

291A

Medical Care in Latin America

Latin Americans rely on many different forms of health care, depending on the resources available to them. Doctors and nurses trained in Latin America and abroad work in private practice, clinics, and hospitals in every country. In rural areas where hospitals are not accessible, women often rely on the wisdom and experience of midwives *(parteras)*. Some people go to holistic healers known as *curanderos,* who use traditional spiritual, herbal, and other remedies.

A visit to a Latin American doctor's office can be both similar to and different from a typical visit in the U.S. The office is frequently in the doctor's home, and he or she will often take the time to discuss the patient's problems at length. Although advanced medical training and technology may not be readily available to them, many doctors have a reading knowledge of one or more foreign languages and stay aware of the latest developments in their fields through medical journals from all over the world. In the specialized fields of rural medicine and parasitic diseases, Latin American doctors often have more expertise than their counterparts in other countries. Cuba, in fact, is a world leader in rural medicine.

Conventional pharmacies abound in Latin America. They often do not require a prescription for dispensing medication. In this case, if a person is fairly certain of his or her ailment, a simple description of the symptoms will enable the patient to obtain the necessary medicine. In some Spanish-speaking countries, homeopathic pharmacies specializing in remedies based on natural foods and plants are commonplace. They carry products similar to those found in U.S. health food stores. In addition, roots and herbs are popular for healing many illnesses, from liver ailments to insomnia. An impressive variety of these natural medicines is displayed in small packages on sidewalks and in marketplaces. Herbal teas *(agüitas)* are also popular, especially chamomile *(té de manzanilla)* for soothing stomach upsets. (See the reading selection, p. 320.)

In many small villages, doctors, nurses, and modern medicines are scarce. In these areas, *curanderos* and *parteras* have long been able to help and heal with their detailed knowledge of natural remedies. Health projects that provide additional resources are frequently organized by national governments in conjunction with local volunteers and international health organizations.

Introduce

Re-entry of Concepts

The following list represents words, expressions, and grammar topics re-entered from Book 1 and Book 2 (Chaps. 2–7):

Book 1
numbers 0–31, calendar expressions, leisure-time activities, family members, vacation items and activities, household chores, parts of the body, physical symptoms

Chapter 2
daily routine

Chapter 4
sports

Chapter 7
pharmacy items

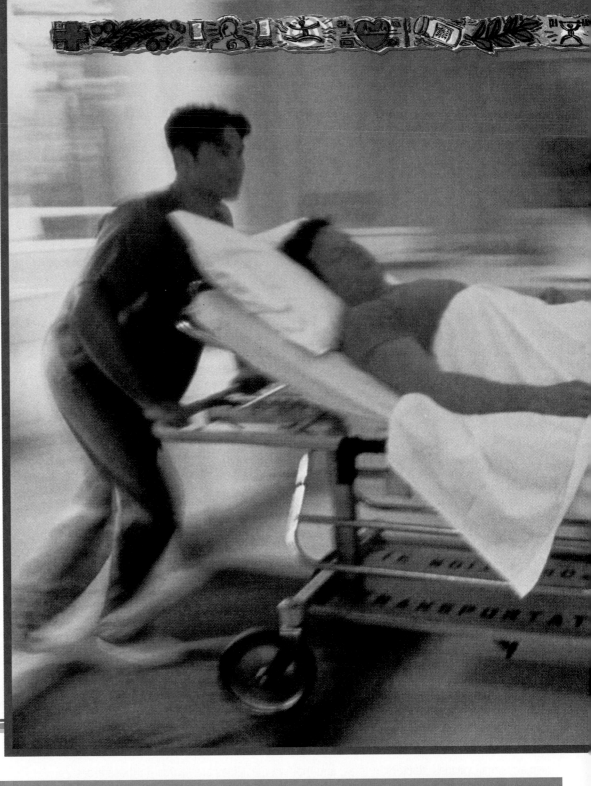

Planning

Cross-Curricular Connections

Health Connection (pp. 296–297)
Divide the class into three groups, giving each group one of the following situations: *Se rompieron el codo; Se quemaron la mano; Se cortaron el dedo.* Within each group, students should divide into three groups, each group creating three sentences. One group should discuss how the injury occurred, another what type of treatment they need, and the third should tell how long they will be injured, and what they won't be able to do because of the injury. Have groups present their scenarios to the class.

History/Science Connection (pp. 308–309)
The use of medicinal herbs was common in early American civilizations. These herbs were complemented with other natural elements, such as mud for healing open wounds and rocks used as surgical instruments. Have students investigate other natural healing methods used by any of the early American civilizations they have studied.

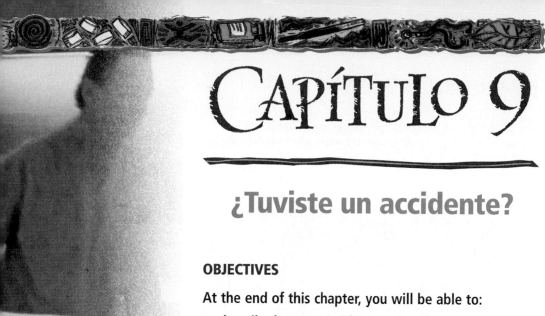

CAPÍTULO 9

¿Tuviste un accidente?

OBJECTIVES

At the end of this chapter, you will be able to:

- describe how an accident occurred
- discuss an injury or illness
- describe treatment for an injury or illness
- compare pharmacies in Latin America and the United States

En un hospital en Miami, Florida

293

Spanish in Your Community
Have students go to their local pharmacy to look for over-the-counter medical supplies (aspirin, bandages, etc.) that are either imported from Spanish-speaking countries or have an extra set of instructions in Spanish. Tell them to make a list of the products they find, including: pharmacy name, product name, product type, price, and whether or not it was imported.

Preview

Cultural Objective

• To discuss health care in Spanish-speaking countries and in the U.S.

Critical Thinking: Summarizing Information

Have students summarize what they see in the photographs. Discuss student summaries as a whole class. Ask students what clues in the photos led them to their conclusions.

Answers: ¡Piénsalo bien!

Answers will vary.

¡Piénsalo bien!

Mira las fotos. Las personas que vemos están hablando de sus enfermedades y de lo que les pasó. ¿Te rompiste alguna vez la pierna o el brazo? ¿Qué ocurrió?

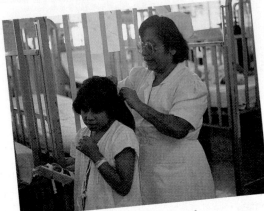

"Me lastimé el brazo. Por eso la enfermera tuvo que cepillarme el pelo."

¿Sabes cómo son los hospitales de tu ciudad? ¿Son los enfermeros y las enfermeras tan amables como ésta?

En el Hospital Benjamín Bloom, San Salvador, El Salvador

"¿Cómo te rompiste la pierna?" "Aprendiendo a esquiar."

¿Alguien en tu clase lleva un yeso? ¿Por cuánto tiempo tiene que llevarlo? ¿Qué hueso se rompió? ¿Cómo se lo rompió?

Unas jóvenes charlando en Santiago, Chile

294   Capítulo 9

Options

Strategies for Reaching All Students

Spanish-Speaking Students

Ask: *¿Has estado en una sala de emergencia? ¿Estabas herido o enfermo? ¿Quién te ayudó y cómo? ¿Qué más viste allí? ¿Quiénes deben ir a salas de emergencia? ¿Cuándo debes ir al médico? ¿Cuándo usas remedios caseros en vez de ir al médico? ¿Cuáles son algunos de esos remedios?*

 Un paso más Ex. 9-A

"Perdone. ¿Podría indicarme dónde puedo ir para donar sangre?"

Letreros en un hospital en Madrid

295

Cultural Notes

(p. 294, left photo)
Hospital Benjamín Bloom, named for its benefactor, is a large, modern facility located in the center of San Salvador. A private hospital serving the city's health care needs, it has a well-known pediatric department with notable diagnostic capabilities.

(p. 295, photo)
City hospitals in Spain are often large, multi-purpose facilities engaged in medical research and teaching as well as healing. These medical centers may offer less personalized service, but they provide state-of-the-art medical technology for precise diagnosis and specialized treatment. As in most countries, rural areas in Spain often have limited access to the advanced facilities located in the more populated areas.

Present

Chapter Theme
In the emergency room

Communicative Objectives
- To identify parts of the body
- To talk about treatment for medical conditions
- To describe how an accident occurred
- To indicate time

 Transparency 44

 Vocabulary Art BLMs

 Pronunciation Tape 9-1

Grammar Preview
(*Yo) me caí* and *(usted / él / ella) puso* are presented here lexically. The preterite forms of *caerse* and *poner* are on pp. 314 and 316, respectively.

Teaching Suggestions
Preparing students to speak: Use one or two options from each of the categories of Comprehensible Input, Physical Response, or Limited Verbal Response. For a complete explanation of these categories and some sample activities, see pp. T16–T17.

Vocabulario para conversar

¿Te rompiste el tobillo?

Vas a necesitar estas palabras y expresiones para hablar sobre ciertos accidentes y enfermedades. Después de leerlas varias veces, practícalas con un(a) compañero(a).

la sala de emergencia

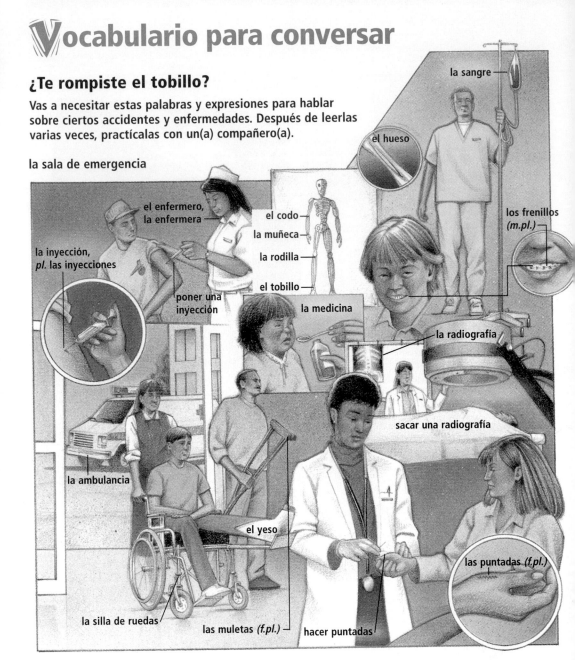

la sangre

el hueso

el enfermero, la enfermera

el codo

la muñeca

la rodilla

el tobillo

los frenillos *(m.pl.)*

la inyección, *pl.* las inyecciones

poner una inyección

la medicina

la radiografía

sacar una radiografía

la ambulancia

el yeso

las puntadas *(f.pl.)*

la silla de ruedas

las muletas *(f.pl.)*

hacer puntadas

296   Capítulo 9

Options

Strategies for Reaching All Students

Spanish-Speaking Students
Ask: *¿Sabes otras palabras que se pueden incluir aquí? Haz una lista.*

 Un paso más Ex. 9-B

Students Needing Extra Help
Begin the vocabulary section of the Organizer.
Show students that *la muñeca* has two meanings (they saw it in Chap. 5 as "doll"). Point out the cognates.
También necesitas . . . : Show examples of the reflexives.

Give examples of *por* + time expression.
Ex. 1: If available, refer to the Organizer from Book 1, Chap. 9.
Review reflexive verbs in the preterite.
Encourage students to use both positive and negative responses.
Remind students that in Spanish "the leg" is used as opposed to "my leg."

También necesitas . . .

el análisis, *pl.* los análisis	*medical test*	¿Qué te pasó?	*What happened to you?*
caerse: (yo) me caí	*to fall down: I fell down*	por + *time expression*	*for*
		además	*in addition, besides*
poner: (Ud. /él /ella) puso	*you /he /she put*		
cortarse	*to cut oneself*		
quemarse	*to burn oneself*		
romperse (un hueso)	*to break (a bone)*		
roto, -a	*broken*		

> **¿Y qué quiere decir . . . ?**
> el accidente
> el antibiótico
> el músculo
> la operación, *pl.* las operaciones

Empecemos a conversar

Túrnate con un(a) compañero(a) para ser *Estudiante A*
y *Estudiante B*. Reemplacen las palabras subrayadas
en el modelo con palabras representadas o escritas en los
recuadros. Si ven 💡 pueden dar su propia respuesta.

1

A —¿Te rompiste *el brazo*?
B —Sí, me rompí *el brazo*.
    o: No. Me rompí el codo.

¡NO OLVIDES!

Do you remember these body parts?
  el brazo
  la mano
  el dedo
  la espalda
  la pierna
  el pie
  el dedo del pie

Estudiante A

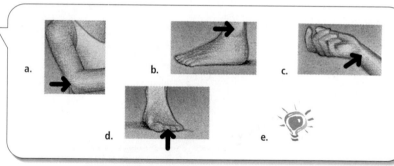

a.　　b.　　c.

d.　　e. 💡

Estudiante B

💡

Vocabulario para conversar　297

Practice & Apply

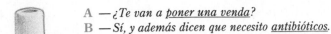

Reteach / Review: Vocabulary

Ex. 2: *Estudiante A* can ask *Estudiante B*: *¿Y qué te parece?* regarding the treatment he or she is being told to follow. Encourage *Estudiante B* to express a range of emotions, including agreement, disagreement, fear, impatience, boredom, or anger.

Answers: Empecemos a conversar

2 ESTUDIANTE A

a. ¿Te van a poner un yeso?

b. . . . sacar una radiografía?

c. . . . dar una medicina?

d. . . . poner sangre?

e. . . . poner una inyección?

ESTUDIANTE B

Answers will vary, but may include:

a. Sí, y además dicen que necesi-to usar muletas.

b. . . . más análisis.

c. . . . quedarme en cama.

d. . . . una operación.

e. . . . antibióticos.

3 ESTUDIANTE A

a. ¿Qué te pasó en el brazo? ¿Te quemaste?

b. . . . el codo? ¿Te caíste?

c. . . . la espalda? ¿Te lastimaste?

d. . . . la rodilla? ¿Te lastimaste?

e. . . . el dedo? ¿Te cortaste?

f. . . . la mano? ¿Te cortaste?

2

poner

A — ¿Te van a *poner una venda*?

B — *Sí, y además dicen que necesito antibióticos.*

Estudiante A

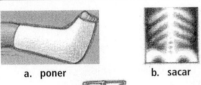

a. poner   b. sacar   c. dar

d. poner   e. poner

Estudiante B

antibióticos

más análisis

una operación

quedarme en cama

usar muletas

3

caerse

A — ¿Qué te pasó en *la pierna*? ¿*Te caíste*?

B — Sí, *me caí* cuando estaba *subiendo una escalera*.

Estudiante A

a. quemarse   b. caerse   c. lastimarse

d. lastimarse   e. cortarse   f. cortarse

Estudiante B

preparar la ensalada

reparar la bicicleta

patinar

levantar pesas

encender el horno

jugar____

Options

Strategies for Reaching All Students

Spanish-Speaking Students

Exs. 1–3: Pair bilingual with non-bilingual students if possible.

Ex. 8: Ask: *¿Por qué son necesarios los frenillos?*

 Un paso más Ex. 9-C

Students Needing Extra Help

Ex. 2: Help students make the correct association between the two parts of the answers. Show them what changes and what does not.

Ex. 3: Remind them that these are all -*ar* reflexive verbs except for *caerse*.

Remind students there are two tenses here: the preterite and the imperfect progressive.

Remind them to fill in the blank after *jugar*.

Provide students with the following steps:

a.) identify the body part, b.) form the question in the preterite, c.) answer using the preterite, d.) make the association, and e.) form the imperfect progressive.

Ex. 4: Brainstorm the time frames. Review calendar expressions.

Ex. 6: Use the vocabulary section of the Organizer.

Ex. 7: Help students stay focused.

Ex. 9: Summarize treatment of burn victims.

4

llevar

A —*Doctor(a), ¿por cuánto tiempo tengo que llevar el yeso?*
B —*Por seis semanas.*

Estudiante A

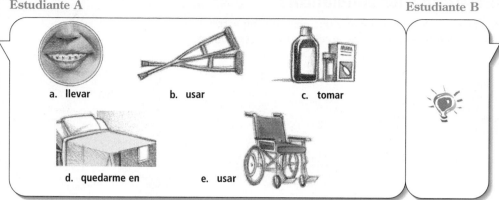

a. llevar

b. usar

c. tomar

d. quedarme en

e. usar

Estudiante B

Empecemos a escribir

Escribe tus respuestas en español.

5 Piensa en alguien que conoces que se rompió un hueso. ¿Le sacaron radiografías? ¿Tuvo que llevar un yeso? ¿Tuvo que usar una silla de ruedas o muletas? ¿Por cuánto tiempo?

6 ¿Cuándo te lastimaste la última vez? ¿Qué te pasó? ¿Fuiste al (a la) médico(a)? ¿Qué te dio? ¿Qué te puso?

7 Piensa en alguien que conoces que estuvo en un hospital. ¿Tuvo un accidente o le hicieron una operación? ¿Lo (la) tuvieron que llevar en ambulancia o fue en coche? ¿Le tuvieron que poner sangre? ¿Le hicieron muchos análisis? ¿Le hicieron puntadas? ¿Por cuánto tiempo se quedó en el hospital?

8 Generalmente, ¿por cuánto tiempo tiene uno que llevar los frenillos?

9 ¿Dónde está la sala de emergencia más cerca de la escuela? ¿Y de tu casa? Generalmente, ¿qué le hacen a una persona que tiene un hueso roto? ¿Qué le hacen a una persona que se corta? ¿Y a una persona que se quema?

También se dice

la sala de urgencia
el servicio de emergencia

los frenos
los aparatos (para los dientes)

la escayola

el medicamento

Vocabulario para conversar 299

Present

Chapter Theme
Allergies

Communicative Objectives
- To discuss an illness
- To talk about allergies
- To talk about treatment for medical conditions
- To describe how an accident occurred

 Transparencies 45–46

 Vocabulary Art BLMs

 Pronunciation Tape 9-2

Teaching Suggestions
Preparing students to speak: Use one or two options from each of the categories of Comprehensible Input, Physical Response, or Limited Verbal Response. For a complete explanation of these categories and some sample activities, see pp. T16–T17.

Vocabulario para conversar

¿Eres alérgico a los antibióticos?

Aquí tienes el resto del vocabulario que necesitas en este capítulo para hablar sobre ciertos accidentes y enfermedades.

"¡Ajem!"

la tos
toser

"¡Hachís!"

la pastilla

estornudar

el jarabe
(para la tos)

las gotas
(para los ojos)

la receta

300   Capítulo 9

Options

Strategies for Reaching All Students

Spanish-Speaking Students

 Un paso más Ex. 9-D

Students Needing Extra Help
Show the connection of *tos* to *toser*.
Point out that *tos* is singular, even though it ends in *s*.
Show word families: *picar, picadura; insecto, insecticida;* etc.
Tambien necesitas . . . : Write out the whole verb chart in the present tense for *sentirse* and *protegerse*.

Learning Spanish Through Action
STAGING VOCABULARY: *Dibujen*
MATERIALS: paper and pencil
DIRECTIONS: Describe a walk that you took in the woods. Tell students to draw what you saw. Include insects and known vocabulary for nature and animals.

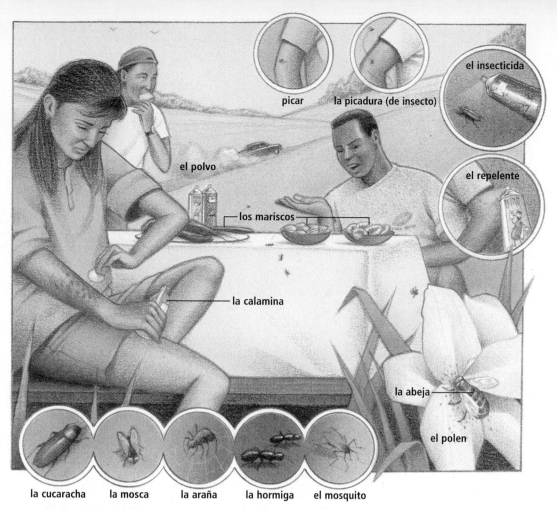

picar

la picadura (de insecto)

el insecticida

el polvo

el repelente

los mariscos

la calamina

la abeja

el polen

la cucaracha   la mosca   la araña   la hormiga   el mosquito

También necesitas . . .

proteger(se) (g → j)*	to protect (oneself)
sentirse (e → ie)	to feel
la enfermedad	illness
antialérgico, -a	nonallergenic
fuerte	strong
leve	light, minor

¿Y qué quiere decir . . . ?

la alergia	el síntoma
la infección,	el virus
pl. las infecciones	(ser) alérgico, -a (a)
la reacción,	recetar
pl. las reacciones	vomitar

*Infinitives that end in -ger change the g to a j in the yo form of the present tense: proteger: (yo) protejo.

Vocabulario para conversar   301

Practice

Answers: Empecemos a conversar

10 ESTUDIANTE A
a. ¿Te dan miedo los mosquitos?
b. ...las arañas?
c. ...las hormigas?
d. ...las cucarachas?
e. ...las moscas?
f. Questions will vary.

ESTUDIANTE B
Answers will vary, but may include the following:
a. Sí, porque pican.
b. Sí, porque son feas.
c. No. No me dan miedo.
d. Sí, porque son sucias.
e. Sí, porque traen enfermedades.
f. Answers will vary.

11 ESTUDIANTE A
a. ¿Eres alérgico(a) al polen?
b. ...a los mariscos?
c. ...a las picaduras de insecto?
d. ...al bronceador?
e. ...al polvo?
f. Questions will vary.

ESTUDIANTE B
a.–f. Answers will vary.

Empecemos a conversar

10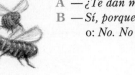

A —¿Te dan miedo _las abejas_?
B —Sí, porque _pican_.
  o: _No. No me dan miedo._

Estudiante A   Estudiante B

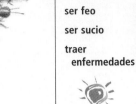

picar
ser feo
ser sucio
traer enfermedades

11

A —¿Eres alérgico(a) a _los gatos_?
B —Sí, y me dan una reacción (muy) _fuerte_.
  o: _Sí, pero sólo me dan una reacción leve._
  o: _No, no tengo ninguna reacción._

Estudiante A   Estudiante B

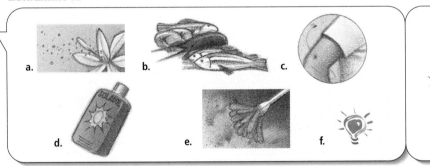

302   Capítulo 9

Options

Strategies for Reaching All Students

Spanish-Speaking Students
Exs. 10–12: Pair bilingual with non-bilingual students if possible.

Students Needing Extra Help
Ex. 10: Encourage students not to use the negative response.
Ex. 11: Brainstorm possible responses.
Ex. 12: Brainstorm possibilities for the blanks in the _Estudiante A_ choices and for additions to the _Estudiante B_ responses: _Me siento mejor, pero necesito antibióticos._

Enrichment
Ex. 12: To extend this dialogue, _Estudiante A_ can ask _Estudiante B_ what he or she took or did to feel better.

302

12 el resfriado

A —*¿Cómo estás del resfriado?*
B —*Me siento (mucho) mejor, gracias.*

Estudiante A

a. la infección en ___

b. la alergia

c. el virus

d. el dolor de ___

e. el tobillo

f. la gripe

g.

Estudiante B

(mucho) mejor

(mucho) peor

¡NO OLVIDES!

Do you remember these words related to health?
dolor de cabeza
            estómago
            garganta
            oído
            muelas
tengo fiebre
            gripe
            resfriado
las pastillas para la garganta

Vocabulario para conversar   303

---

12 ESTUDIANTE A

a. ¿Cómo estás de la infección en (el oído / el ojo / la garganta)?

b. ... de la alergia?

c. ... del virus?

d. ... del dolor de (cabeza / estómago / muelas)?

e. ... del tobillo?

f. ... de la gripe?

g. Questions will vary.

ESTUDIANTE B

a.–g. Answers will vary.

Using Realia
Refer students to the heading on the ad. Ask: *¿A qué se refiere el verbo "piquen"? (a los mosquitos) ¿Y "pica"? (a la medicina)*

Cooperative Learning
Brainstorm with students three things they might be afraid of in addition to those listed in Ex. 10 *(los perros, los pájaros, los exámenes,* etc.). In groups of four, have each student list the insects from Ex. 10, plus any brainstormed items, in order of how they fear them: from the most to the least. Have two students from each group combine the lists and determine which three things the group fears most. Another student can report the findings to the class. Write each group's findings on the chalkboard, and tabulate which three things the class fears most.

303

Practice & Apply

Re-enter / Recycle

Ex. 13: pharmacy items from Chap. 7

Answers: Empecemos a conversar

13 ESTUDIANTE A

a. ¿Estás tomando las pastillas?
b. . . . poniéndote las gotas para los ojos?
c. . . . tomando el jarabe?
d. . . . poniéndote una venda?
e. . . . poniéndote la calamina?
f. . . . tomando la receta?
g. Questions will vary.

ESTUDIANTE B

Answers will vary, but may include the following:
a. Sí, porque todavía tengo fiebre.
b. . . . una leve infección.
c. . . . tos.
d. . . . puntadas.
e. . . . muchas picaduras.
f. . . . un dolor fuerte en el músculo.
g. Answers will vary.

Answers: Empecemos a escribir y a leer

14–17 Answers will vary, but look for correct use of present, preterite, and imperfect tenses.

13

tomar

A — ¿Estás *tomando las pastillas para la garganta*?
B — Sí, porque tengo *dolor de garganta*.

Estudiante A

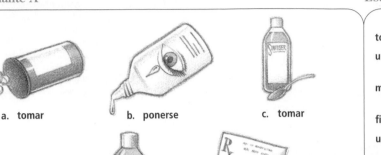

a. tomar b. ponerse c. tomar

d. ponerse e. ponerse f. tomar g.

Estudiante B

tos

una leve infección

muchas picaduras

fiebre

un dolor fuerte en el músculo

puntadas

Empecemos a escribir y a leer

Escribe tus respuestas en español.

14 ¿Qué haces cuando no te sientes bien? Y después, ¿generalmente te sientes mejor?

15 ¿Qué síntomas tienes cuando tienes gripe? ¿Estornudas? ¿Vomitas? ¿Qué te duele? Generalmente, ¿qué te receta el (la) médico(a) cuando tienes tos o gripe? ¿Y cuando tienes una infección fuerte?

16 ¿Cuándo fue la última vez que te pusiste gotas en los ojos? ¿Qué tenías?

Una joven busca un libro en un quiosco en la Ciudad de México.

304   Capítulo 9

Options

Strategies for Reaching All Students

Spanish-Speaking Students
Ex. 13: Pair bilingual with non-bilingual students if possible.
After Ex. 18, Have Spanish-speaking students take a class survey.
Pregúntales a tus compañeros(as) sobre las alergias: ¿Tienen alergias? ¿A qué son alérgicos(as)? ¿Cuáles son los síntomas? ¿Qué remedios o medicinas usan o prefieren?

Un paso más Ex. 9-E

¿Cuáles son los alergias más comunes entre tus compañeros(as)? Escoge cuatro o cinco y prepara una hoja en tres columnas con esta información: Alergia, Síntomas, Remedio preferido. Exhíbela en el salón de clase o en la oficina de la enfermera o del enfermero de la escuela.

Students Needing Extra Help
Ex. 13: Students may need help associating the ailment with the cure.
Review the present progessive tense.
Ex. 14: Use the vocabulary section of the Organizer.
Ex. 17: Students will need help with the vocabulary for answering the fourth question about how to protect oneself from allergies.
Ex. 18: Students may need help with the vocabulary.

17 ¿A qué eres alérgico(a)? ¿Y los otros miembros de tu familia? ¿La reacción es fuerte o leve? ¿Qué se puede hacer para protegerse de las alergias? ¿Qué le recetan a uno cuando tiene alergia?

18 ¿Cómo puede uno protegerse de las cucarachas? ¿Y de las picaduras de insecto? Aquí tienes algunas ideas. Con un(a) compañero(a), escribe otras dos ideas para cada categoría.

Uno puede protegerse de las cucarachas
• limpiando la cocina todas las noches
• poniendo insecticida en el sótano

Uno puede protegerse de las picaduras de insecto
• usando repelente en la cara, en los brazos y en las manos
• poniéndose guantes para trabajar en el patio

También se dice

la píldora

el piquete

el zancudo

la avispa

Vocabulario para conversar   305

Cooperative Learning
Divide the class into groups of three. Within each group, students will decide on an allergy they have, and write a list of three symptoms of that allergy. They then exchange lists with another group, who will act as doctors. The doctors must diagnose the allergy and prescribe a treatment in writing. After papers are returned to the original groups, call on students to tell the class their allergy and the prescription, letting the class decide if the treatment was appropriate.

Cultural Notes ☼

(p. 305, photo)
Browsing for books is easy in many of Mexico City's *colonias* (neighborhoods). Open-air *librerías* display numerous popular titles, magazines, and other printed materials. Some sell school books, for most students in Mexico must purchase their own texts. This stall displays packets of study sheets illustrating the human anatomy.

Practice

Re-enter / Recycle:
Ex. 2: sports from Chap. 4

Answers:
¡Comuniquemos!
1 Answers will vary.

2 ESTUDIANTE A
¿Cómo puedes protegerte de los accidentes cuando cambias un bombillo?
...cuando corres?
...cuando cocinas?
...cuando paseas en bote?
...cuando montas en bicicleta?
...cuando levantas pesas?
...cuando cruzas la calle?

ESTUDIANTE B
Answers will vary, but may include:
Puedo protegerme apagando la lámpara.
Puedo protegerme corriendo con un amigo.
Puedo tener un extinguidor de incendios cerca de la estufa.
Puedo protegerme no paseando cuando hace mal tiempo.
Puedo protegerme usando casco.
Puedo protegerme usando un cinturón.
Puedo protegerme mirando el semáforo.

3 Answers will vary, but look for correct use of the preterite and imperfect tenses.

¡Comuniquemos!

Aquí tienes otra oportunidad para usar el vocabulario de este capítulo.

1 Túrnate con un(a) compañero(a). Pregúntale sobre la última vez que estuvo enfermo(a).

A —¿Qué tenías la última vez que estuviste enfermo(a)?
B —Tenía una infección en...
A —¿Y qué síntomas tenías?
B —Me dolía mucho...

2 Túrnate con otro(a) compañero(a). Habla de cómo protegerse de los accidentes al hacer estas actividades.

A —¿Cómo puedes protegerte de los accidentes cuando montas en bicicleta?
B —Puedo protegerme usando...

Options

Strategies for Reaching All Students

Spanish-Speaking Students
Exs. 1–3: Pair Spanish-speaking students to prepare these dialogues and present them orally or on tape. Use as listening comprehension exercises with true / false statements.

Students Needing Extra Help
Ex. 1: Review *doler* and point out that *dolía* is the imperfect tense.
Use the vocabulary section of the Organizer.
Ex. 2: Brainstorm the possibilities for protecting yourself. Help students with the vocabulary.
Ex. 3: Refer to Ex. 3 in the *Vocabulario para conversar.*
Present a complete model.

Help students with the *Pues* response: Brainstorm situations that would lead to each outcome listed.
¿Qué sabes ahora?: Have students write out this list so that they can record their progress.

3 Escoge dos de las siguientes ideas. Pregúntale a tu compañero(a) si alguna vez tuvo que:

llevar un yeso   tomar medicina antialérgica
llevar una venda grande   usar muletas
ponerse gotas para los ojos   usar una silla de ruedas

A —¿Tuviste que usar muletas alguna vez?
B —Sí, cuando . . .
A —¿Y qué te pasó después?
B —Pues, . . .

¿Qué sabes ahora?

Can you:

■ **describe how an accident occurred?**

—Anita se ___ el brazo cuando estaba ___ básquetbol.

■ **tell the cause of an accident?**

—Estaba ___ una escalera cuando me ___.

■ **talk about someone's health?**

—Él se ___ mejor pero todavía tiene ___.

Vocabulario para conversar   307

Answers: ¿Qué sabes ahora?
• rompió / jugando
• subiendo / caí
• siente / *Answers will vary, but may include:* infección, virus, tos

 Audio Activity 9.3

Enrichment
Ex. 2: Students can also talk about hazards for children and how they can be protected in the following situations: at a picnic, at a pool, on the playground, in the kitchen, in the bathroom.

Cooperative Learning
Brainstorm with students other situations in which one might want to protect oneself (at the beach, preparing food, etc.). Instruct groups of three to select one topic and develop two protection strategies. Exchange strategies with another group, who will edit the work for clarity and gramatical correctness and prepare a poster with slogans and pictures describing the methods of protection. Posters should be displayed so the original group can see how their ideas evolved.

Apply

Cultural Objective
• To discuss pharmacies in Spanish-speaking countries

Critical Thinking: Formulating Questions
After reading the *Perspectiva cultural,* have small groups formulate questions that they might have. Collect the questions and read them to the class. Encourage students familiar with Latin American pharmacies to provide answers and additional information.

Answers
Answers to inductive questions will vary, but students may say that they knew they were pharmacies by the merchandise displayed. *Una inyectología* is a place where injections or shots are given. *Una farmacia de turno* is a pharmacy whose turn it is to stay open overnight.

Perspectiva cultural

¿Qué tiendas son éstas? ¿Cómo lo sabes? ¿Qué lugar crees que es una *inyectología*? ¿Qué crees que significa *farmacia de turno*?

En América Latina, para ciertas enfermedades uno puede decidir ir a un médico o a un curandero. Mucha gente cree que los dos sistemas, uno basado en la ciencia y la medicina moderna y el otro en las hierbas y la tradición, son igualmente válidos.

Imagina que estás viajando en un país latinoamericano. Ya no tienes el antibiótico que te recetó tu médico. Decides ir a una farmacia.

Encuentras una muy pequeña. Las medicinas están detrás del mostrador y hay que pedir lo que quieres comprar. Le explicas al farmacéutico el problema, y él te vende la medicina en seguida.

En algunas farmacias, también ponen inyecciones. Si te enfermas y sabes lo que necesitas, puedes ir a una farmacia donde se ve el letrero *inyectología* y allí te ponen la inyección.

Ahora imagina que despiertas con un ataque fuerte de asma y no tienes medicina. ¿Qué haces? Puedes ir a la sala de emergencia de un hospital. Pero si sólo necesitas medicina, puedes ir a una farmacia. Las farmacias de una comunidad se turnan para quedar abiertas por la noche. El horario se publica en el periódico, y en la vitrina se ve el letrero *farmacia de turno*. Así se pueden obtener medicinas en caso de emergencia.

La cultura desde tu perspectiva

1 Compara lo que puede hacer un farmacéutico en América Latina con lo que puede hacer uno en los Estados Unidos.

2 ¿Cuáles son las ventajas y las desventajas de vender medicinas sin receta, como, por ejemplo, los antibióticos? En caso de urgencia médica, ¿qué hay que hacer en los Estados Unidos?

"Dicen que estas hierbas pueden curar muchas enfermedades."

308 Capítulo 9

Options

Strategies for Reaching All Students

Spanish-Speaking Students
Ask: *¿Conoces a una persona que sepa utilizar hierbas y plantas para curar o aliviar a alguien? ¿Quién es? ¿Dónde aprendió estos remedios? ¿Se pueden encontrar hierbas medicinales en tu comunidad? ¿Dónde?*

 Un paso más Ex. 9-F

Students Needing Extra Help
Have students take notes for use in reviewing for the test.
Discuss the idea of alternative medicine versus standard medical practices.
Ex. 2: Encourage discussion, emphasizing the dangers of misusing medicine.

Enrichment
Additional question: *Pregunta a tus padres u otras personas mayores cómo eran las farmacias cuando eran pequeños.*

Una farmacia en Buenos Aires

Hierbas medicinales de venta en el mercado San Juan de Dios, Guadalajara, México

Cultural Notes

(p. 308, photo)
Very common in Mexican markets is a section of *botánicas* selling medicinal herbs used to treat ailments ranging from a stomachache to a "broken heart." El Mercado San Juan de Dios, el Mercado Corona and el Mercado Libertad are three well-known Guadalajaran markets having large *botánicas*.

(p. 309, top photo)
Although large chain stores are becoming more common in Latin America, smaller *farmacias* are still prevalent. These privately owned businesses typically sell only medical supplies, vitamins, and personal hygiene and beauty products.

(p. 309, bottom photo)
Many people learn from their elders how to use traditional healing methods. Chamomile (*manzanilla*), for example, reduces fever. *Té de canela* treats a stomachache. *Té de orégano* soothes a colicky baby. *Flor de tilo* (lime blossom), *flor de valeriana* (valerian blossom), and *flor de azahar* (orange blossom) relax the nerves. *Gordolobo* (mullein) is used to treat a cough and *té de linaza* (linseed) works as a laxative.

Preview

Answers

A The similar form is *estaba limpiando*. The action takes place in the past. The meaning is "was cleaning."

B *Sonó* and *corrí* tell what happened at a specific moment. *Estaba limpiando* and *estaba jugando* tell what was going on when the phone rang.

The other verbs that tell what happened are *regresé, fui, vi,* and *(no le) pasó (nada)*.

C The verb is *se cae*. The stem of *caer* is *ca-*. The ending is *-e*. The preterite form is *se cayó*. The stem is *ca-*. The ending is *-yó*. It is different in that the *i* of the *ió* ending changes to *y*.

Gramática en contexto

¡Niño Se Cae de Tercer Piso y Vive!

Ayer, en un accidente casi mortal, un niño de dos años y medio se cayó del tercer piso de su casa y ¡salió con vida! El accidente ocurrió cuando la madre, la Sra. Luz María López de Chávez, estaba limpiando las ventanas. La señora Chávez dice que el niño estaba

jugando en el suelo. "Sonó el teléfono y corrí al otro cuarto a contestarlo. Cuando regresé, ¡el niño ya no estaba! Fui a la ventana y lo vi tres pisos más abajo en la nieve. ¡Mi pobre niño! Había tanta nieve que, milagrosamente, no le pasó nada."

A You know the present progressive form *está limpiando*. What similar form is used in this article? Does the action take place in the present or in the past? What do you think this verb form means?

B When Sra. Chávez describes the accident, she uses the verbs *sonó (el teléfono)* and *corrí*. The reporter uses the verbs *estaba limpiando* and *estaba jugando*. Which pair of verbs tells what happened at a specific moment, and which pair tells what was going on when that happened?

What other verbs tell what happened at a specific moment?

C In the headline, what verb is used to say "child falls"? What is the stem, and what is the ending?

Now look for the corresponding preterite form ("fell") at the beginning of the article. What is the stem, and what is the ending? How is this preterite form different from the preterite form of other *-er* verbs?

310   Capítulo 9

Options

Strategies for Reaching All Students

Spanish-Speaking Students

 Un paso más Ex. 9-G

Students Needing Extra Help
Begin the grammar section of the Organizer.
A: Review the meaning of *está limpiando* before contrasting it with *estaba limpiando*.
B: In a two-column chart headed *¿Qué ocurrió?* and *¿Qué estaba pasando?,* have students write the correct words in the appropriate columns.
C: Write the answers *(se cae* and *se cayó)* on the chalkboard.

El imperfecto progresivo: Model the present progressive to help students remember. Have students add additional examples. If available, use the Organizer from Book 1, Chap. 14.
Review *estar* in the imperfect, and how to form present participles.
Ex. 1: Have students list the infinitive expressions, then conjugate the verbs according to the pictures. If available, use the Organizers from Book 1.

El imperfecto progresivo

You have learned to use the present progressive tense to describe an action or event that is taking place right now. To describe something that was taking place at a certain time in the past, we use the imperfect progressive. We form this tense by using the imperfect forms of *estar* + the present participle.

> Cuando el niño se cayó, la señora Chávez **estaba hablando** por teléfono.
> Sus otros hijos **estaban haciendo** la tarea.
> Su esposo **estaba preparando** la cena.

1 ¿Qué estaban haciendo estas personas cuando ocurrió el accidente?

Cuando ocurrió el accidente, una mujer estaba cortando el césped. Una muchacha . . .

Present & Practice

Reteach / Review: Vocabulary
Ex. 1: As an extension of this exercise, have students play the role of reporters writing an article describing an accident at one of the following places: *un restaurante, una estación de servicio, un centro comercial, un parque de atracciones, una parada de autobús.* Tell students to include the time of the accident, what happened, people who were witnesses, and the outcome (people who went to the hospital, etc.).

Answers
1 Order of answers will vary, but should include:
Una muchacha estaba montando en bicicleta.
Un cartero estaba repartiendo cartas.
Unos niños estaban jugando béisbol.
Un hombre estaba poniéndose bronceador.
Una señora estaba cruzando la calle.
Una mujer estaba hablando por teléfono.
Un muchacho estaba estornudando.
Dos hombres estaban comprando flores.
Una mujer estaba cortando el césped.

Present & Practice

Reteach / Review: Indirect object pronouns

Ex. 2: Remind students that some of these verbs, like *sacar una radiografía, poner una inyección,* and *dar medicina* take the indirect object pronoun *le(s)* and the preposition *a.*

Have students also tell what each person was doing by using the construction that attaches the object pronoun to the participle. *Cuando llegó la ambulancia, el médico estaba poniéndole un yeso a Luisa. La enfermera estaba . . .*

Re-enter / Recycle

Exs. 3–4: daily routine from Chap. 2

Answers

2 La enfermera le estaba dando el jarabe a Angélica.
Gloria estaba poniéndose una venda en el tobillo.
El enfermero le estaba poniendo una inyección a Mateo.
La médica le estaba haciendo puntadas a Fernando en el codo.
La médica estaba mirando una radiografía.

2 Di qué estaban haciendo estas personas cuando llegó la ambulancia. Usa los dibujos.

Cuando llegó la ambulancia, el médico le estaba poniendo un yeso a Luisa. La enfermera le . . .

Angélica
Gloria
Fernando
Luisa
Carmen
Mateo

¡NO OLVIDES!

Remember that object pronouns can be placed before the form of *estar* or attached to the end of the present participle. If they are attached to the present participle, a written accent is needed:

El enfermero le estaba poniendo (estaba poniéndole) una inyección a Martín.

312   Capítulo 9

Options

Strategies for Reaching All Students

Students Needing Extra Help
Ex. 2: Write the sentence included in *¡No olvides!* and the model sentence for Ex. 2 on the chalkboard. With as much help as students can give, write the second clause of the model sentence again, attaching the *le* to the present participle as in the *¡No olvides!* Help them see the need for the added accent mark. Remind students that both structures mean the same thing.

Show students they are doing the same thing as they did in Ex. 1, except that the scene has changed.
Use the vocabulary section of the Organizers.
El uso del pretérito y del imperfecto: In the two examples, have students show which actions have a beginning and an end, and which are ongoing. Using the same examples, reverse the order of the verbs to show

students that the *cuando* clause does not always come first. Give additional examples.
Ex. 3: Present another model that does not use a reflexive verb. Remind students that the imperfect phrase stays in the *yo* form. Review *estar* in the imperfect tense. Review the preterite endings using the grammar section of the Chap. 3 Organizer. Create further examples to accustom students to the structure.

El uso del pretérito y del imperfecto progresivo

The preterite tense is used to tell that something began and ended in the past, and the imperfect progressive describes something that was taking place. They are often used together.

Cuando **llegó** la ambulancia, el niño **estaba llorando**.
*When the ambulance **arrived**, the child **was crying**.*

Cuando **sacamos** esta foto, la señora Chávez **estaba hablando** con la periodista.
*When we **took** this photograph, Mrs. Chávez **was talking** to the reporter.*

Un cartel en La Paz motiva a los padres a mantener la salud de sus hijos.

3 Di lo que estabas haciendo cuando pasaron estas cosas. Por ejemplo:

ponerse las gotas / alguien / llamarme por teléfono	*Yo estaba poniéndome las gotas cuando alguien me llamó por teléfono.*

a. tomar el jarabe / tú / estornudar
b. dormir / mi mamá / caerse de la escalera
c. comer / (nombre) / quemarse la mano
d. peinarse / mi hermano menor / vomitar
e. ponerse la venda / mi padre / despertarse
f.

4 Di qué estaban haciendo algunas personas que conoces ayer cuando ocurrió otro evento.

afeitarse	encontrar(se)	pelearse
buscar	escoger	ponerse
comprar	escuchar	probarse
cortar(se)	estornudar	quemar(se)
desayunar	hacer	reparar
despertarse	levantarse	romperse
empezar	maquillarse	toser

Freddy y Paula estaban comprando pastillas cuando empezaron a estornudar.

Gramática en contexto   313

Present & Practice

Re-enter / Recycle
Ex. 5: sports from Chap. 4

El pretérito del verbo *caerse*

Here are the preterite forms of *caerse*.

(yo)	me **caí**	(nosotros) (nosotras)	nos **caímos**
(tú)	te **caíste**	(vosotros) (vosotras)	os **caísteis**
Ud. (él) (ella)	se **cayó**	Uds. (ellos) (ellas)	se **cayeron**

¡NO OLVIDES!

Remember that in the present tense *caerse* follows the same pattern as *traer*. It is a regular -*er* verb except in the *yo* form.

me caigo	nos caemos
te caes	os caéis
se cae	se caen

We add *y* to the stem in the *Ud. / él / ella* and *Uds. / ellos / ellas* forms. We use an accent over the *i* in all the other forms.

• *Creer* and *leer* follow the same pattern in the preterite.

creí	creímos	leí	leímos
creíste	creísteis	leíste	leísteis
creyó	creyeron	leyó	leyeron

Esta gente de Santander, España, mantiene su salud montando en bicicleta.

314   Capítulo 9

Options

Strategies for Reaching All Students

Students Needing Extra Help
El préterito de caerse: Use the grammar section of the Chap. 1 Organizer to review *traer*.
Emphasize that all the forms have written accent marks, except the *Uds. / ellos / ellas* form.
Remind students of the spelling change in both singular and plural third person forms.

Ex. 5: Present a model with a non-reflexive verb.
Have students go through the exercise in two steps, the first time giving the imperfect progressive of the verb represented by the art, the second time putting both verb phrases together.

5 Di qué estaban haciendo estas personas cuando se cayeron.

Mateo estaba duchándose cuando se cayó.

Mateo

a. (yo)

b. el señor Soto

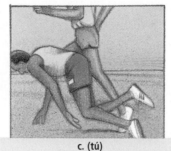

c. (tú)

d. Teresa y Lourdes

e. mi amigo y yo

f. Uds.

Estudiantes españolas
haciendo un examen de
educación física en Mallorca

Gramática en contexto   315

Cultural Notes

(p. 314, bottom photo)
Europeans love bicycle racing, and some of the most competitive races are held in Spain. The *Semana catalana* race takes place in March. *La Vuelta del país vasco* is held in April and is considered a preliminary for the April–May Tour of Spain, or, simply, *La Vuelta.* Each cycle of *la Vuelta* is held in a different location in Spain. Spain's racing season concludes with the *Clásica de San Sebastián* in August.

(p. 315, photo)
These young people are taking their high-school physical fitness test. A program of exercise begun in childhood has lifelong benefits. Schools around the world try to generate positive attitudes toward exercise by teaching fitness to young students.

Practice

Re-enter / Recycle
Ex. 6: pharmacy items from Chap. 7

Answers

6 a. (Tú) te pusiste gotas para los ojos.
b. Tomás se puso calamina.
c. Ellos se pusieron crema de afeitar.
d. Nosotros nos pusimos bronceador.
e. (Yo) me puse repelente.
f. La señora Bonilla se puso perfume.
g. Juan y Víctor se pusieron desodorante.

7 ESTUDIANTE A
a. ¿Dónde pusieron Miguel y Carlota los platos sucios?
b. ... pusieron Uds. la ropa sucia?
c. ... pusiste el libro?
d. ... puso Carolina el video?
e. ... puso tu padre la carta?
f. ... puse la leche?
g. Questions will vary.

ESTUDIANTE B
a. Los pusieron en el lavaplatos, ¡por supuesto!
b. La pusimos en el cesto de la ropa sucia ...
c. Lo puse en el estante ...
d. Lo puso en la videocasetera ...
e. La puso en el escritorio ...
f. La pusiste en el refrigerador ...
g. Answers will vary, but should be in the preterite.

El pretérito del verbo *poner*

Here are the preterite forms of *poner*.

(yo)	**puse**	(nosotros) (nosotras)	**pusimos**
(tú)	**pusiste**	(vosotros) (vosotras)	**pusisteis**
Ud. (él) (ella)	**puso**	Uds. (ellos) (ellas)	**pusieron**

6 Di qué se pusieron estas personas.

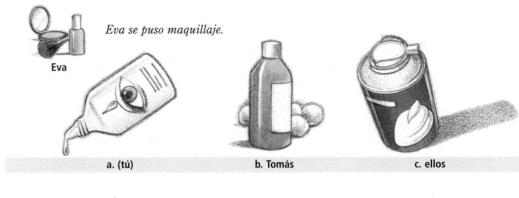

Eva se puso maquillaje.

Eva

a. (tú) b. Tomás c. ellos

d. nosotros e. (yo) f. la señora Bonilla g. Juan y Víctor

316 Capítulo 9

Options

Strategies for Reaching All Students

Students Needing Extra Help
El pretérito de poner: Emphasize that *poner* is irregular in the preterite.
Write the *ponerse* chart on the chalkboard.
Ex. 6: Use the vocabulary section of the Organizer.
Ex. 7: Review direct object pronouns.
Remind students to fill in the blank after *el cesto de (la ropa sucia).*
Remind students that the verb changes from the question to the answer.

Ahora lo sabes: Have students write these out so they can keep track of their progress.

7 No puedes encontrar nada, pero todos te dicen que pusieron
las cosas en un lugar lógico. Con un(a) compañero(a),
pregunta y contesta.

(tú) / el pastel
    A — *¿Dónde pusiste el pastel?*
    B — *Lo puse en el horno, ¡por supuesto!*

a. Miguel y Carlota / los
   platos sucios

b. Uds. / la ropa sucia

c. (tú) / el libro

d. Carolina / el video

e. tu padre / la carta

f. (yo) / la leche

g.

el escritorio

el lavaplatos

la videocasetera

el cesto de ___

el refrigerador

el estante

Un letrero bonito de una farmacia en Pamplona, España

Ahora lo sabes

Can you:

- talk about conditions or situations in the past?
  —Antes de la clase, los estudiantes estaban charlando y ___.
- talk about what was going on when something happened?
  —Yo estaba ___ cuando alguien me ___.
- talk about an accident?
  —María se ___ y se ___ un músculo.

Apply

Teaching Suggestions

Ex. 2: You may want to extend this exercise by having groups create an emergency room drama for a TV show.

Answers: Actividades

1–3 Look for correct usage of present, preterite, and imperfect tenses.

 ¿Recuerdas?

Play

Using the Video

Episode 9 begins as Jamie and María are waiting in the doctor's office. They listen as an agricultural worker tells his wife the doctor's diagnosis: that his illness was caused by pesticides (from working at La Jacaranda). María then sees the doctor and returns to report that she has a cold. Meanwhile, Santana has been spying on Jamie from a wheelchair. As Jamie and María are walking home, Felipe shows up and excitedly tells María that he wants to see her soon.

At María's house, Jamie listens to a phone message from Rogelio

Para decir más

Aquí tienes vocabulario adicional que te puede servir para hacer las actividades de esta sección.

el paramédico, la paramédica
paramedic

la bolsa de hielo
ice pack

la camilla
stretcher

el tanque de oxígeno
oxygen tank

la cortada
cut

la quemadura
burn

el remedio
remedy

grave
serious

esperar
to wait

tomar la temperatura
to take someone's temperature

318 Capítulo 9

Actividades

Esta sección te ofrece la oportunidad de aumentar tus conocimientos de español al integrar lo que aprendiste en este capítulo con lo que aprendiste en capítulos anteriores.

1 ¡Tantos pacientes y cada uno con su historia! En grupo, inventen diálogos entre un(a) enfermero(a) y los pacientes en la sala de espera *(waiting room)*. El (la) enfermero(a) va a preguntar:

- tu nombre
- tu edad y fecha de nacimiento
- tu dirección y número de teléfono
- por qué quieres ver al (a la) médico(a)
- cuáles son tus síntomas
- hace cuánto tiempo que los tienes

Después, el (la) médico(a) va a decirte lo que debes hacer.

Vas a quedarte en . . .

Options

Strategies for Reaching All Students

Spanish-Speaking Students
Ex. 3: Have students write out what they learned from the person they interviewed. Since others will most likely conduct their interviews in English, Spanish speakers might be enlisted to help them put their interviews into the target language.

Students Needing Extra Help
Ex. 1: Use the vocabulary section of the Organizer.
Help students brainstorm and formulate the structure of the questions as a class. Brainstorm possible remedies.
Model possible dialogues.
Ex. 2: Help students with the vocabulary and the structure of the sentences.
Remind them to use the *Para decir más* list in this exercise, and the vocabulary section of the Organizer.

Ex. 3: Remind students to conduct the interviews in English.
Students should already have the questions written before the interview with space between them so they can take complete notes.
Help them translate their notes into Spanish, and decide what information should be included in the report.

2 ¿Estuviste alguna vez en una sala de emergencia? (Si no, describe la sala de emergencia de una película o un programa de televisión.) En grupo, hablen sobre esa sala. Digan:

- cómo era
- qué había en la sala
- quiénes estaban allí
- cómo llegaron
- qué problemas tenían
- cómo se sentían
- qué hacían mientras esperaban

3 Entrevista a uno de tus abuelos o a una persona de 60 ó 70 años. Pregúntale cómo eran los servicios médicos cuando él (ella) era joven. Luego, haz un informe. Habla sobre:

- cómo eran los médicos y los dentistas
- las medicinas y los remedios
- los hospitales
- las farmacias
- cuánto costaba ir al médico

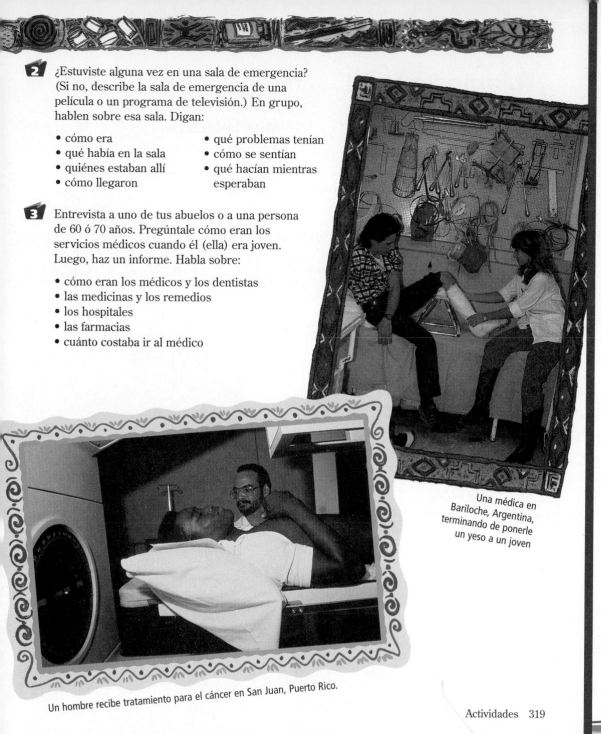
Un hombre recibe tratamiento para el cáncer en San Juan, Puerto Rico.

Una médica en Bariloche, Argentina, terminando de ponerle un yeso a un joven

Salazar, the library assistant, who wants to talk to Jamie.

The next evening, Jamie, Carlos, María and Felipe attend a conference at the university on environmental pollution.

Rogelio is also in attendance, as well as Paco Aguilar (son of Silvestre). After the conference, Rogelio explains to Jamie that Demetrio Alcocer wants to help her but is afraid of don Silvestre. Rogelio suggests that Jamie visit Demetrio. At the same moment, another scene shows an ambulance arriving at the library.

 Video Activity A

 La Catrina: Capítulo 9

Play

 Video Activity B

 Para entender mejor

Play

 Video Activity C

 Comm. Act. BLMs 9-4, 9-5

Actividades   319

Cooperative Learning
Tell pairs of students they are preparing a scene for an upcoming live episode of a popular TV hospital drama, but they should not discuss the scene beforehand. Each student will be responsible for four lines of dialogue. On one sheet of paper, have *Estudiante A* write the first line of the dialogue. *Estudiante B* should read the line and write the next one. When they have completed the eight-line dialogue, they should practice it before presenting it to the class.

Apply

Process Reading
For a description of process reading, see p. 52.

Answers
Antes de leer
Students may say that the child would become ill and have to go to the hospital. The child would receive medicine there, and would probably not eat that much again.

Mira la lectura
Ask at random what students think the poem is about. Avoid correcting misunderstandings.

¡Vamos a leer!

Antes de leer

STRATEGY ➤ Using prior knowledge

What would happen if a child ate too much of something? Where might a parent take the child, and what might happen there? Do you think he or she would ever do it again?

Mira la lectura

STRATEGY ➤ Skimming

Skim this poem to get a general idea of what happens.

Chana y su rana

—Cecilia Ávalos

Doña Chana tenía una rana
que le gustaba comer manzana.
Cien manzanas se comió.
Y la rana se empachó.

Doña Chana llevó a su rana
con la curandera Doña Sana.
Una sobada Doña Sana le dio,
y té de manzanilla le recetó.

Doña Chana, con su rana,
a su casita regresó.
Tomando té de manzanilla cada día
del empacho la rana sanó.

Doña Chana le dijo a su rana:
—¡Ya NO vuelvas a comer manzana!
Y triste su rana suspiró:
—¡Ay, mamita, yo creo que NO!

320   Capítulo 9

Options

Strategies for Reaching All Students

Spanish-Speaking Students
Ask: *¿Crees que cuentitos de este tipo impresionan a los niños más que las advertencias de sus padres? ¿Por qué?*

Students Needing Extra Help
Mira la lectura: Read the poem aloud so students can hear the rhyme and rhythm. Remind them to look at the pictures carefully for clues.
Students may think *manzanilla* means some type of apple. Explain that it is chamomile tea.

Infórmate: For point 3 write the last two lines of the third stanza on the chalkboard. Then, insert *se* before *sanó*. Give students choices of meaning: became sane, was clean, was cured.
Review the meaning of "idiom" in point 4.
Aplicación: Encourage students to use words directly from the poem in the new title.

320

Infórmate

STRATEGY ➤ Using context to get meaning

1 Sometimes *se* is used to make the meaning of a verb stronger; for example, *caer* = "to fall," *caerse* = "to fall down" and *beber* = "to drink," *beberse* = "to drink (something) up." Given this information, what do you think *comerse* means?

2 In this poem, what is another way to say *se empachó*?

a. comió mucho
b. le dolió el estómago porque comió demasiado
c. tenía hambre

3 Sometimes *se* is left out so that a line will "flow" better. For example, line 4 of stanza 3 could read, *del empacho la rana se sanó*. Does that help you understand the meaning of *sanó*? What do you think it means?

4 *Volver a* + infinitive is an idiom. Which phrase comes closest to expressing the meaning of *no vuelvas a comer manzana*?

a. no vas a comer tantas manzanas otra vez
b. no tienes que comer manzanas
c. no te gustan las manzanas

Infórmate
1. to eat (something) up
2. b
3. was cured
4. a

Aplicación

Titles will vary. Some possibilities: *La rana que comió demasiado, La rana que nunca va a comer demasiado.*

Names of stories will vary, but students may mention *Charlotte's Web,* or *The Wind in the Willows,* or Aesop's fables. *Chana y su rana* is the same as these stories in that the animals act like children, and there is a moral.

Aplicación

1 Choose another title for this story that gives a clue to what happens in it.

2 Do you know other stories in which animals behave like people? How is this story similar or different?

Apply

Process Writing
For information regarding developing a writing portfolio, see p. 54.

see p. 54.

¡Vamos a escribir!

Vamos a escribir una entrevista divertida sobre el tema de la salud.

 Primero, piensa en un insecto u otro animalito que causa enfermedades. Piensa en lo que hace y por qué. ¿Qué va a decir el insecto en una entrevista? Por ejemplo, una entrevista con un mosquito puede empezar así:

> **REPORTERO** Buenos días, señor Mosquito. En su opinión, ¿cuál es el problema entre los mosquitos y las personas?
>
> **SR. MOSQUITO** Pues, yo no sé por qué no le gustamos a la gente. No somos malos. Somos muy simpáticos y trabajadores.

Escribe el primer borrador y consulta con un(a) compañero(a). Sigue los otros pasos del proceso de escribir. Puedes usar estas palabras u otras:

- picar / picadura
- sangre
- piel (*skin*)
- brazo / mano
- protegerse
- repelente / insecticida
- calamina
- enfermedad
- dolerle a uno
- tener razón

 Ahora, imagina que lees en una revista una de las entrevistas que escribieron tus compañeros. Escribe tu opinión en una carta al redactor *(editor)*. Debes atacar o defender el punto de vista del insecto. Puedes hacer sugerencias *(suggestions)* para resolver el problema. Usa estas frases u otras:

- a mí me parece que
- creo que
- para mí
- es verdad que
- (no) estoy de acuerdo
- además
- por ejemplo

322   Capítulo 9

Options

Strategies for Reaching All Students

Students Needing Extra Help
Ex. 1: Brainstorm insects or small animals that might provide possibilities for this exercise.
Assign a specific number of lines, perhaps three for each character. Have students work in pairs.
Help students with sentence structure.

Ex. 2: Use your local paper to review the idea behind letters to the editor. Why might they write a letter to the editor? Emphasize the idea of freedom of thought, opinion, and speech.
Have students use as much vocabulary from the interview as they can when writing the letter.
Help students incorporate their opinions using the phrases listed in section 2.

3 Para compartir tu trabajo, puedes:

- presentar las entrevistas como obras de teatro
- grabarlas en audio o video
- enviar las entrevistas y las cartas
  al periódico o revista escolar
- enviarlas a un periódico local
- incluirlas en tu portafolio

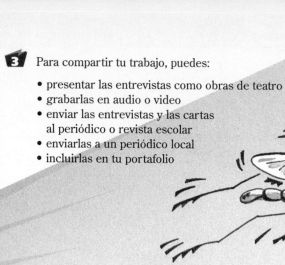

Assess & Summarize

Test Preparation

You may want to assign parts of this section as written homework or as an in-class writing activity prior to administering the *Examen de habilidades.*

Answers

Listening: *—Nuestro gato estaba en un árbol y yo subí para sacarlo. Yo me caí y me lastimé el tobillo. El gato está bien, pero yo tengo que llevar una venda y usar muletas por tres semanas. ¡Caramba!* Students may say the cause of the accident was either the cat or loss of footing. The person speaking has to wear a bandage and use crutches for three weeks.

Reading: Answers will vary, but may include the following:
mal
cabeza
Usted puede ser
Debe comprar
Salud

Writing: Questions will vary, but should include a variety of chapter vocabulary.

¿Lo sabes bien?

Esta sección te ayudará a prepararte para el examen de habilidades, donde tendrás que hacer tareas semejantes.

Listening

Can you understand when someone describes an accident? Listen as your teacher reads a sample similar to what you will hear on the test. What caused the accident? What treatment did the person speaking receive?

Reading

Alicia read the following advertisement on the side of a bus. But she couldn't remember all of it. Supply the missing text in the blanks so that the ad makes sense.

Writing

Can you write questions for a health-services survey in a Spanish-speaking community? Add three more to these.

1. ¿Va a un(a) médico(a) por lo menos una vez al año?
2. ¿Dónde queda la sala de emergencia más cerca?

Culture

Can you explain how to find a pharmacy late at night in Latin America? What kind of medicine can you buy there that you would not be able to buy without a prescription in the United States?

Speaking

Create a dialogue with your partner in which you discuss an injury with a doctor.

A —*¿Qué te pasó? ¿Tuviste un accidente?*
B —*Sí, doctor(a). Estaba corriendo por el parque con mis amigos cuando me caí.*
A —*¿Te duele mucho la rodilla?*
B —*Sí.*
A —*Mmmm. Necesito sacarte una radiografía y hacer algunos análisis.*

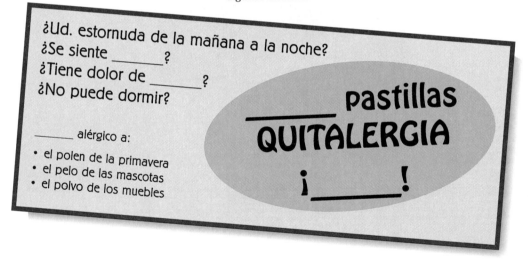

¿Ud. estornuda de la mañana a la noche?
¿Se siente _____?
¿Tiene dolor de _____?
¿No puede dormir?

_____ alérgico a:
• el polen de la primavera
• el pelo de las mascotas
• el polvo de los muebles

_____ pastillas
QUITALERGIA
¡_____!

Options

Strategies for Reaching All Students

Students Needing Extra Help
Have students write out this section so that they can check off what they have mastered. Remind students that this is just a sample of what the actual test will be like.
Listening: Read more than once. Remind students that they need only listen for two pieces of information. Brainstorm for what words they should listen.
Reading: Review commands. Point out that some blanks can be filled in with verbs.

Bring in magazine ads for allergy medications to use as a model.
Writing: Have students use the Organizer and write a sample survey as practice. Discuss health surveys, pointing out that they are taken to improve local services. Brainstorm what other questions might be important.
Culture: Have students review any notes they may have taken during their reading of the *Perspectiva cultural.*

Speaking: Use the vocabulary section of the Organizer.
Limit the number of lines of dialogue.
Remind students to use the preterite and the imperfect progressive.

Resumen del capítulo 9

Usa el vocabulario de este capítulo para:

- describe how an accident occurred
- discuss an injury or illness
- describe treatment for an injury or illness

to identify parts of the body
el codo
el hueso
la muñeca
el músculo
la rodilla
el tobillo

to discuss an illness
la enfermedad
la infección, *pl.* las infecciones
el síntoma
la tos
el virus
estornudar
sentirse *(e →ie)*
toser
vomitar

to talk about allergies
la alergia
(ser) alérgico, -a (a)
antialérgico, -a
la abeja
la araña
la cucaracha
la hormiga
el insecticida
los mariscos
la mosca

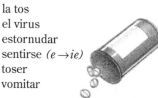

el mosquito
la picadura (de insecto)
picar
el polen
el polvo
la reacción,
    pl. las reacciones
el repelente

to talk about treatment for medical conditions
la ambulancia
el análisis, *pl.* los análisis
el antibiótico
la calamina
el enfermero, la enfermera
los frenillos *(m.pl.)*
las gotas (para los ojos)
la inyección, *pl.* las inyecciones
poner una inyección
el jarabe (para la tos)
la medicina
las muletas *(f.pl.)*
la operación, *pl.* las
    operaciones
la pastilla
las puntadas *(f.pl.)*
hacer puntadas
la radiografía
sacar una radiografía

la receta
recetar
la sala de emergencia
la sangre
la silla de ruedas
el yeso

to describe how an accident occurred
el accidente
caerse: (yo) me caí
cortarse
proteger(se) *(g →j)*
quemarse
romperse (un hueso)
roto, -a

to indicate time
por + *time expression*

other useful words and expressions
poner: (Ud. /él /ella) puso
además
fuerte
leve
¿Qué te pasó?

Resumen 325

Enrichment
Pairs of students can also create a dialogue in which one person is trying to persuade the other to seek medical care for an ailment that clearly needs professional attention. The reluctant person can be a child, friend, relative, or older person.

CAPÍTULO 10

THEME: MOVIES AND TELEVISION

SCOPE AND SEQUENCE   Pages 326–359

COMMUNICATION

Topics

Movie character types

Television shows

Natural disasters

Objectives

To compare soap operas in Spanish-speaking countries with those in the U.S.

To talk about movie-making

To talk about various kinds of films

To talk about natural disasters

To summarize movies and TV programs

To talk about TV programs

CULTURE

Soap operas in Latin America

GRAMMAR

El pretérito y el imperfecto

El pretérito del verbo decir

Ancillaries available for use with Chapter 10

Multisensory/Technology

 Overhead Transparencies, 48–51

 Audio Tapes and CDs

 Vocabulary Art Blackline Masters for Hands-On Learning, pp. 53–57

 Classroom Crossword

 La Catrina

 CD-ROM

Print

 Practice Workbook, pp. 95–104

 Writing, Audio & Video Activities, pp. 59–64, 120–122, 169–170

 Communicative Activity Blackline Masters

Pair and Small Group Activities, pp. 64–69

Situation Cards, p. 70

 Un paso más: Actividades para ampliar tu español, pp. 55–60

Assessment

 Assessment Program

Pruebas, pp. 144–154

Examen de habilidades, pp. 155–158

 Test Generator

Video still from Chap. 10

¿Qué prefieres, el cine o la televisión?

Movies, television, and VCRs are all part of the growing entertainment industry in Spain and Latin America. In theaters, movies are shown from one month to a year, depending on the success of the film. Then, they go to video rental stores and to cable systems. Movies made in the U.S. are the most popular. *Jurassic Park (Parque jurásico)* or *Schindler's List (La lista de Schindler)* were as successful in Latin America as they were in the U.S. Movies such as *La belle époque,* from Spain, and *Como agua para chocolate (Like Water for Chocolate),* from Mexico, have also won recognition in film festivals around the world. The former won the Academy Award for the best foreign film in 1993; the latter broke the record for box office sales in New York. These films are becoming more and more popular in Spain and Latin America.

There is a long tradition of movies and filmmaking in Spanish-speaking countries. *Un perro andaluz (An Andalusian Dog),* 1928, and *Los olvidados (The Forgotten Ones),* 1950, both by the great Spanish director Luis Buñuel, are still shown in universities and video clubs. Also, any new film by Pedro Almodóvar, creator of *Matador* and *Mujeres al borde de un ataque de nervios (Women on the Verge of a Nervous Breakdown),* is received with as much excitement in Spain and Latin America as in the U.S.

Just as in the U.S., TV talk shows, sports programs, news broadcasts, educational TV, and music videos are offered in Spanish-speaking countries. Two of the most popular variety shows are also broadcast in the U.S.: *Sábado gigante* from Miami and Chile, and *Siempre en domingo* from Mexico. Soap operas are normally broadcast in the evening in Latin America, running a few months at a time. News programs always cover other Spanish-speaking countries as well as major news stories from the U.S. and other countries. Television programs from the U.S. are frequently shown in Latin America, almost invariably dubbed into Spanish.

The Spanish and Latin American TV industry is also expanding. For example, the Mexican news channel ECO (Echo) broadcasts 24 hours a day in more than 20 countries. Soap operas from Latin America are not only shown in Venezuela and Peru, but also in the Soviet Union and Poland.

Introduce

Re-entry of Concepts

The following list represents words, expressions, and grammar topics re-entered from Book 1 and Book 2 (Chaps. 2 and 4):

Book 1
numbers 0–31, time-telling, expressing likes or preferences, indicating hunger, weather expressions, rooms in a house, household chores, making comparisons, expressing opinions

Chapter 2
daily routine

Chapter 4
leisure-time activities

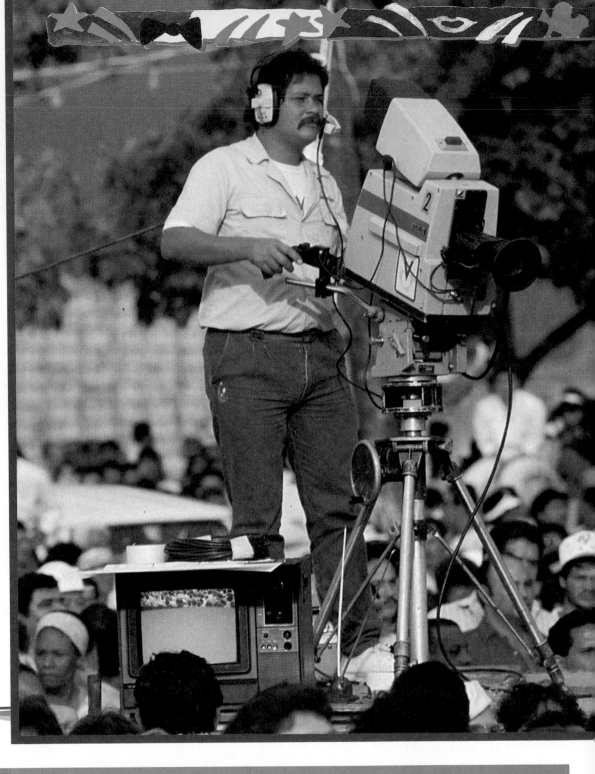

Planning

Cross-Curricular Connections

Language Arts Connection *(pp. 346–347)*
In pairs, have students choose a famous fairy tale and retell it from the point of view of the villain or anti-hero, using the preterite and imperfect tenses. Students may follow up with a book cover or an oral presentation to the class.

Drama Connection *(pp. 352–353)*
In groups of four, have students choose a current event or controversial situation in the news. They then create a soap opera title and a short (three-minute) scene depicting the events or issues involved. Encourage satire, comedy, and exaggeration. Have students present their skits in class or videotape them.

Spanish in Your Community
Assign pairs of students to watch one game show on Spanish-language TV and one on English-language TV. Have them take notes during the broadcasts in order to create a two-column table headed "English-language" and "Spanish-language." Have them write about what they see (similarities and differences) in the types of games played and prizes awarded.

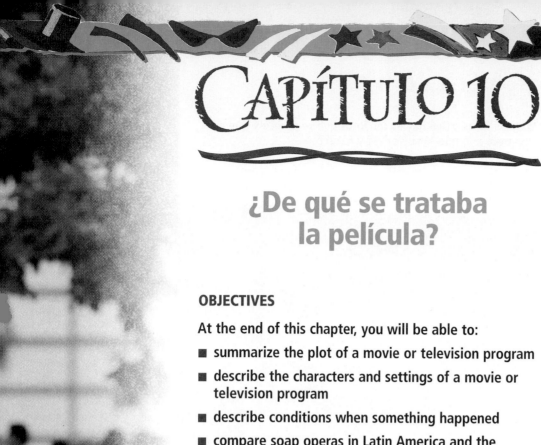

CAPÍTULO 10

¿De qué se trataba la película?

OBJECTIVES

At the end of this chapter, you will be able to:

- summarize the plot of a movie or television program
- describe the characters and settings of a movie or television program
- describe conditions when something happened
- compare soap operas in Latin America and the United States

Filmando en Caracas, Venezuela

327

(p. 326, photo)
Venezuela is a center of television production in Latin America. Both government-owned and private Venezuelan television broadcasting companies produce programs to be seen all over the world. Venezuelan productions are exported and dubbed into many languages. Venezuela is especially well known for its production of *telenovelas*.

Preview

Cultural Objective

• To discuss movies and television in Spanish-speaking countries

Multicultural Perspectives

Como agua para chocolate, one of the greatest international successes in Mexican cinematic history, is based on the popular novel of the same name by Laura Esquivel, who also wrote the screenplay. Her husband, Alfonso Arau, directed the film which was nominated for the Best Foreign Film Oscar in 1992, and in the same year won 10 *Arieles,* the Mexican equivalent of the Oscar. The story is set in the early 1900s in Texas and Coahuila, Mexico. Tita, the protagonist, is forced to give up the man she loves (Pedro) in order to care for her domineering mother. Pedro then marries her older sister so as to be near his true love. This situation proves to be very difficult, but all Tita can do is take out her frustrations through cooking. Ask students if they are familiar with it, or with other Spanish-language films. Have students research what Spanish-language films are available in their local video store.

¡Piénsalo bien!

Mira las fotos. ¿Qué hay en las fotos que se parece y que no se parece a lo que tú sueles ver y hacer?

"A toda la familia le gusta este programa. No se aburre nadie."

Una familia maya viendo la televisión en Chamula, México

328   Capítulo 10

Options

Strategies for Reaching All Students

Spanish-Speaking Students

Ask: *¿Has visto películas en español? ¿Cuál te gustó más? ¿Qué clases de programas en la televisión te gustan más? ¿Por qué?*

 Un paso más Ex. 10-A

"Pedro estaba saliendo y Lucía llorando cuando terminó el capítulo del viernes pasado."

¿Te gustan las telenovelas? ¿Cuál es tu favorita?

Unas hermanas en Bogotá viendo la televisión en el dormitorio de sus padres

"Yo veía muchos dibujos animados cuando era pequeño, pero ahora los programas de concursos son mis favoritos."

¿Qué tipo de programa de televisión te gusta más? ¿Te gustaría participar en algún programa de concursos? ¿Cuál es tu favorito, o no los ves nunca?

Filmando el programa de concursos 1, 2, 3 en España

329

Cultural Notes

(p. 328, photo)
Traditional life and modern technology are juxtaposed in this Mayan home in San Juan Chamula, a village in the Chiapas highlands, near the colonial city of San Cristóbal de las Casas. The Chamula church, famous for its fusion of Mayan and Catholic rituals, is a major cultural and ceremonial center for the people of this area.

(p. 329, bottom photo)
The game show *1, 2, 3* is very popular in Spain. To play, three contestants are asked trivia questions and awarded points for answering correctly. The winner goes on to the next phase in which he or she must choose between prizes concealed behind doors, in boxes, or behind curtains, in the hope of finding the grand prize—a car, a condo, or cash. However, they may be asked to perform a stunt, or they may go home with a pumpkin or a lump of coal.

Present

Chapter Theme
Movies and movie characters

Communicative Objectives
- To talk about movie-making
- To talk about various kinds of films
- To summarize movies and TV programs

 Transparencies 48–49

 Vocabulary Art BLMs

 Pronunciation Tape 10-1

Teaching Suggestions
Preparing students to speak: Use one or two options from each of the categories of Comprehensible Input, Physical Response, or Limited Verbal Response. For a complete explanation of these categories and some sample activities, see pp. T16–T17.

Inform students that the word for "victim" (*la víctima*) is always feminine.

¿De qué se trataba la película?

Vocabulario para conversar

¿De qué se trata tu película favorita?

Vas a necesitar estas palabras y expresiones para hablar sobre películas y programas de televisión. Después de leerlas varias veces, practícalas con un(a) compañero(a).

el director
dirigir (g → j)

la científica

el monstruo

el científico

el vaquero /la vaquera

el /la extraterrestre

el caballo

montar a caballo

el galán, pl. los galanes

la heroína

Options

Strategies for Reaching All Students

Spanish-Speaking Students
Haz una lista de otras palabras que tú sabes que se relacionan a este tema.

 Un paso más Exs. 10-B, 10-C

Students Needing Extra Help
Vocabulario para conversar: Begin the vocabulary section of the Organizer.
Write out the *dirigir* paradigm for those students who need to see it completed.
Point out how similar these words are to the English.
También necesitas . . . : Give some examples with *enamorarse de, tratarse de,* and *¿Qué tal es . . . ?*
¿Y qué quiere decir . . . ?: Give examples of *esconder* and *esconderse.*

Enrichment
Ask students to name recent or older television programs in which various types of characters appear. For example: *¿Cuáles son algunas películas en que vemos extraterrestres?* As a homework assignment, students can make up the names of television programs or movies in which these characters would appear, and write a brief description of what the program or movie would be about.

la ladrona
esconder
la víctima
robar
el ladrón, *pl.* los ladrones
el criminal
matar
la policía
la criminal
el /la detective
la directora
el policía
arrestar

También necesitas . . .

actuar*	to act	
la actuación	acting	
enamorarse (de)	to fall in love (with)	
hacer el papel (de)	to play the part / role (of)	
el papel	here: part, role	
tratarse de	to be about	
el argumento	plot	
el crimen	crime	
la escena	scene	
el guión, *pl.* los guiones	script	
el personaje	character	
¿Qué tal es . . . ?	How is . . . ?	

¿Y qué quiere decir . . . ?
la ayuda
la dirección
los efectos especiales
la fotografía
la película de acción
esconderse
investigar
excelente
principal
típico, -a

* *Actuar* has an accent on the *u* in all present-tense forms except the *nosotros* and *vosotros* forms: *actúo, actúas, actúa, . . . actúan.*

Vocabulario para conversar   331

Class Starter Review
On the day following initial presentation of vocabulary, you might begin the class with this activity: On a transparency, have a list of Spanish movie titles and their English counterparts. Have students match the titles.

Reteach / Review: Vocabulary
También necesitas . . . : Review Book 1, Chap. 11 vocabulary.

Learning Spanish Through Action
STAGING VOCABULARY: *Actúen, Levanten*
MATERIALS: flashcards for the types of movies listed in Book 1, Chap. 11; cards of current vocabulary, including items from *También necesitas . . .*
DIRECTIONS: Direct students to form groups of three and pantomime the kind of program they see on the card.

Practice

Answers: Empecemos a conversar

1 ESTUDIANTE A

a. ¿Qué personaje es típico en una película romántica?

b. ...de acción?

c. ...de aventuras?

d. ...del oeste?

e. ...de ciencia ficción?

ESTUDIANTE B

a. Un galán.

b. Una detective.

c. Un ladrón.

d. Un vaquero.

e. Un extraterrestre.

Empecemos a conversar

Túrnate con un(a) compañero(a) para ser *Estudiante A* y *Estudiante B*. Reemplacen las palabras subrayadas en el modelo con palabras representadas o escritas en los recuadros. Si ven 💡 pueden dar su propia respuesta.

1   de terror   A —¿Qué personaje es típico en una película *de terror*?
                     B — *Un monstruo.*

Estudiante A

a. romántica

b. de acción

c. de aventuras

d. del oeste

e. de ciencia ficción

Estudiante B

Options

Strategies for Reaching All Students

Spanish-Speaking Students
Exs. 1–3: Pair bilingual with non-bilingual students, if possible.

Students Needing Extra Help
Ex. 2: Show how the relationship in the question is incorrect, and that it is corrected in the response.
Ex. 3: Help students understand how to judge a film's script and direction. Brainstorm the titles of films. Encourage them to vary their responses.

Enrichment
Ex. 2: To extend this exercise, you may want to elicit the titles of some current movies. Have students apply the questions in this exercise to those movies.

2

investigar el crimen

A —*Generalmente, ¿investiga el crimen el galán?*
B —*No. El detective investiga el crimen.*

Estudiante A

Estudiante B

a. **enamorarse**

b. **montar a caballo**

c. **matar a la gente**

d. **arrestar al criminal**

e. **pedir ayuda**

f. **robar el banco**

g. **esconderse de la policía**

3 el argumento

A —*¿Qué tal es el argumento en (nombre de película)?*
B —*(Es) excelente.*

Estudiante A

a. la dirección	d. el guión
b. la actuación	e. la fotografía
c. los efectos especiales	f. la música

Estudiante B

excelente	terrible
un desastre	
así, así	

Vocabulario para conversar   333

---

2 ESTUDIANTE A
a. Generalmente, ¿se enamora la criminal?
b. ... monta a caballo la extraterrestre?
c. ... mata a la gente la policía?
d. ... arresta al criminal el científico?
e. ... pide ayuda el monstruo?
f. ... roba el banco el detective?
g. ... se esconde de la policía la víctima?

ESTUDIANTE B
Answers will vary, but may include the following:
a. No. El galán y la heroína se enamoran.
b. ... El vaquero monta a caballo.
c. ... El criminal mata a la gente.
d. ... El detective o la policía arrestan al criminal.
e. ... La víctima pide ayuda.
f. ... El ladrón (la ladrona) roba el banco.
g. ... El criminal o el ladrón (la ladrona) se esconde de la policía.

3 ESTUDIANTE A
If possible, provide Spanish titles of recent films students will know.
a. ¿Qué tal es la dirección en (nombre de película)?
b. ... es la actuación ...
c. ... son los efectos especiales ...
d. ... es el guión ...
e. ... es la fotografía ...
f. ... es la música ...

ESTUDIANTE B
a.–f. Answers will vary.

Practice & Apply

Una escena de la película
El Norte

Answers: Empecemos a conversar

4 ESTUDIANTE A

a. ¿De qué se trata *Frankenstein*?
b. ... *Parque Jurásico*?
c. ... *La bella y la bestia*?
d. ... *Ricitos de oro*?
e. ... *La bella durmiente*?
f. ... *E.T.*?
g. Questions will vary.

ESTUDIANTE B

a. Se trata de un científico que hace un monstruo.
b. ... unos dinosaurios que viven en una isla.
c. ... un monstruo que se enamora de la heroína.
d. ... una niña que encuentra la casa de unos osos.
e. ... una muchacha que duerme por muchos años y un galán que la despierta.
f. ... un extraterrestre que llega a los Estados Unidos y un niño que lo protege.
g. Answers will vary.

Answers: Empecemos a escribir

5–7 Answers will vary, but should include a variety of chapter vocabulary.

---

4 *Romeo y Julieta*

A —¿De qué se trata <u>Romeo y Julieta</u>?
B —Se trata de <u>una muchacha y un muchacho que se enamoran</u>.

Estudiante A

a. *Frankenstein*
b. *Parque Jurásico*
c. *La bella y la bestia*
d. *Ricitos de oro* (Goldilocks)
e. *La bella durmiente*
f. *E.T.*
g.

Estudiante B

una muchacha que duerme por muchos años y un galán que la despierta

un científico que hace un monstruo

un extraterrestre que llega a los Estados Unidos y un niño que lo protege

un monstruo que se enamora de la heroína

unos dinosaurios que viven en una isla

una niña que encuentra la casa de unos osos

334   Capítulo 10

Options

Strategies for Reaching All Students

Spanish-Speaking Students
Ask: *¿Quién es tu actor favorito o tu actriz favorita? ¿En qué película o programa de televisión ha actuado? ¿Por qué te gusta?*

 Un paso más Ex. 10-D

Students Needing Extra Help
Ex. 4: Have students create more examples.
Ex. 5: If available, use the vocabulary section of the Organizer from Book 1, Chap. 11. Point out that the first question is similar to those in Ex. 4. Review *¿Qué tal es?* so that students do not confuse it with *¿Qué tal?* Model the answers for questions regarding photography, script, and favorite scene.
Ex. 6: Students may have difficulty articulating their thoughts regarding their choices. Brainstorm possible answers.

Cooperative Learning
In groups of four, have students decide who will interview and who will play three famous actors from three different types of films. In front of the class, the interviewer will ask each person three questions designed to reveal his or her identity without revealing the name. The actors must answer truthfully according to their characters, and when all three have finished, the class must try to guess the identity of each.

Empecemos a escribir

Escribe tus respuestas en español.

5 ¿De qué se trata tu película favorita? ¿Qué tipo de película es? ¿Qué actor y actriz hacen los papeles principales? ¿Qué tal es la actuación? ¿La fotografía? ¿El guión? Describe tu escena favorita.

6 ¿Qué es más importante en una película, un buen director o buenos actores? ¿Un buen argumento o efectos especiales? Explica por qué. ¿Hay tipos de películas en que la fotografía es mejor en blanco y negro que en colores? ¿Cuáles? ¿Por qué piensas eso?

7 ¿Qué tipo de película te gustaría dirigir? ¿O en qué tipo te gustaría actuar? ¿Qué tipo de papel te gustaría hacer? ¿Por qué? ¿Qué te gustaría más, escribir un guión o hacer los efectos especiales? ¿Por qué?

También se dice

el marciano / la marciana

el héroe

el bandido
el villano
el malo
el maleante

¿En Qué Se Parece Cristina A La Mona Lisa?

La Mona Lisa es trigueña, Cristina es rubia.
La Mona Lisa es Europea, Cristina es Latina.
La Mona Lisa es antigua, Cristina es moderna.
¿En qué se parece La Mona Lisa a Cristina?
En que las dos son únicas.

Cristina: Lunes a viernes 4pm/3pm Centro.
Cristina Edición Especial: Lunes 10pm/9pm Centro.

Univisión

Una escena de la película
argentina *La historia oficial*

Vocabulario para conversar   335

Multicultural Perspectives

El Show de Cristina is becoming the most popular television talk show for Spanish-speaking audiences in the U.S., as well as in Puerto Rico and Latin America. The show follows the same format with the same controversial topics as many of the popular daytime talk shows for English-speaking audiences. Cristina is also heard on radio. Ask students to compile a list of topics for a talk show. Have them write questions in Spanish for their panel of guests.

Practice Wkbk. 10-1, 10-2

Audio Activity 10.1

Writing Activity 10-A

Pruebas 10-1, 10-2

Cultural Notes

(p. 334, photo)
The events in *El Norte* take place in three locations: the Guatemalan highlands, Mexico, and California. Characters may speak Maya Quiché, Spanish, or English. The Guatemalan Spanish used includes the *voseo* (for example: *vos sos, vos sabés, vos salís*) of Central America. The plot revolves around the journey of a brother and sister, Rosa and Enrique, to the U.S., upon the death of their father and disappearance of their mother.

(p. 335, realia)
Cristina Saralegui is well known for her forthright interview style. In 1989 she became executive producer and host of Univisión's *El show de Cristina,* now ranked among the top ten Spanish-language programs in the U.S. In 1992 Saralegui became executive producer and host of "Cristina," an English-language version of her talk show, making her the first person to host daily programs in two languages.

(p. 335, photo)
The 1985 Academy Award winner for Best Foreign Film was *The Official Story.* Produced in Argentina and based on a true story, the film tells of a young couple's search for the natural father of their adopted daughter. They discover that he has been imprisoned for political reasons, and become involved in trying to secure his release.

Present

Chapter Theme
Television

Communicative Objectives
• To talk about natural disasters
• To summarize movies and TV programs
• To talk about TV programs

 Transparency 50

 Vocabulary Art BLMs

 Pronunciation Tape 10-2

Teaching Suggestions
Preparing students to speak: Use one or two options from each of the categories of Comprehensible Input, Physical Response, or Limited Verbal Response. For a complete explanation of these categories and some sample activities, see pp. T16–T17.

Vocabulario para conversar

¿No te parecen exageradas las telenovelas?

Aquí tienes el resto del vocabulario que necesitas en este capítulo para hablar sobre películas y programas de televisión.

la erupción, pl. las erupciones

el huracán, pl. los huracanes

el terremoto

la tormenta

el derrumbe

la inundación, pl. las inundaciones

la locutora

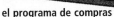
el locutor

Anillo de oro
$499
$449
1-800-555-2345

el programa de compras

$1.500 $900

el programa de concursos

336   Capítulo 10

Options

Strategies for Reaching All Students

Spanish-Speaking Students
Tell students: *Agrega otras palabras relacionadas con el tiempo a tu lista de vocabulario.*

 Un paso más Ex. 10-E

Students Needing Extra Help
Tambien necesitas . . . : Give examples of *el comentario (sobre).*
Review *hay* and *había.* Call students' attention to the footnote.
¿Y qué quiere decir . . . ?: Create some examples for *(estar) basado, -a (en).*
Ex. 8: Review time expressions.

Enrichment
Ex. 8: To extend this exercise, you may want to ask: *¿Qué hubo en la televisión ayer a las . . . ?*

También necesitas . . .

el comentario (sobre)	*review (of)*	sensacionalista*	*sensational*
el fracaso	*failure*		
el hecho	*fact*		
dañar	*to damage*		
destruir:	*to destroy:*		
Ud. /él /ella	*you /he /she*		
destruyó	*destroyed*		
hubo *(preterite of* haber)	*there was /were*		
tener éxito	*to be successful*		

¿Y qué quiere decir . . . ?

la entrevista	ocurrir
la información	(estar) basado, -a (en)
la violencia	exagerado, -a
violento, -a	internacional
cambiar	local

Empecemos a conversar

8

A —*Generalmente, ¿qué hay en la televisión a <u>las seis de la tarde</u>?*

B —<u>*Las noticias.*</u>

Estudiante A

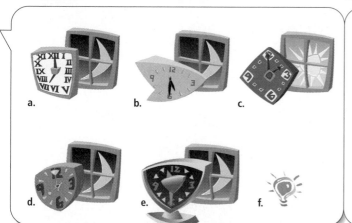

a.   b.   c.

d.   e.   f.

Estudiante B

las noticias

telenovelas

programas de concursos

programas de acción
  y comedias

programas de entrevistas

programas de compras

dibujos animados

documentales

---

*Sensacionalista is used with both masculine and feminine singular nouns: un programa
de televisión sensacionalista; una noticia sensacionalista.*

Vocabulario para conversar   337

Practice & Apply

Answers: Empecemos a conversar

9 ESTUDIANTE A
a. ¿Viste las noticias locales?
b. ...la información deportiva?
c. ...el anuncio de perfume?
d. ...el comentario sobre (nombre de película)?
e. ...la entrevista con (nombre)?
f. ...las noticias internacionales?

ESTUDIANTE B
a. Sí. Robaron un banco en el centro.
b. ...Nuestro equipo perdió.
c. ...Lo venden en muchas farmacias.
d. ...Dicen que la actuación es excelente.
e. ...La locutora dijo que estaba haciendo otro video.
f. ...Dicen que hubo un derrumbe en Guatemala.

10 ESTUDIANTE A
a. ¿Viste que hubo un terremoto en Costa Rica?
b. ...una erupción en Perú?
c. ...una tormenta en Cuba?
d. ...una inundación en Argentina?
e. ...un derrumbe en Chile?
f. Questions will vary.

ESTUDIANTE B
a.–f. Answers will vary, but should include correct use of the preterite tense.

¿De qué se trataba la película?

9 el pronóstico del tiempo

A — ¿Viste *el pronóstico del tiempo*?
B — Sí. *Va a llover este fin de semana.*

Estudiante A

a. las noticias locales
b. la información deportiva
c. el anuncio de perfume
d. el comentario sobre (nombre de película)
e. la entrevista con (nombre)
f. las noticias internacionales

Estudiante B

Dicen que la actuación es excelente.
La locutora dijo que estaba haciendo otro video.
Nuestro equipo perdió.
Dicen que hubo un derrumbe en Guatemala.
Lo venden en muchas farmacias.
Robaron un banco en el centro.

10

Puerto Rico

A — ¿Viste que hubo *un huracán* en *Puerto Rico*?
B — Sí. *Destruyó muchos edificios.*

Estudiante A

a. Costa Rica
b. Perú

c. Cuba
d. Argentina
e. Chile
f.

Estudiante B

destruir ___
dañar ___
matar a ___

338   Capítulo 10

Options

Strategies for Reaching All Students

Spanish-Speaking Students
Exs. 9–11: Pair Spanish-speaking students, if possible.
Ex. 16: *Trata de convencer a un compañero que el programa que quieres ver es el mejor. Haz una lista de las razones que le vas a dar.*

 Un paso más Ex. 10-F

Students Needing Extra Help
Ex. 9: Show students that they need to provide additional information for *d* and *e*.
Ex. 10: Brainstorm the information that will go in the blanks for *Estudiante B*.
Remind students to use the preterite.
Review the *a personal*.
Ex. 11: Review the *Estudiante A* list with the class, choosing the correct endings for the adjectives before students begin the exercise.

Ex. 12: Students may need help with the *¿Por qué?* questions.
Ex. 13: Students may need help with the vocabulary for the first question.
Ex. 14: Brainstorm book titles that were made into movies. Have background information available in order to discuss the last question.
Ex. 15: Students may need help with the vocabulary for the last question.

11 exagerado(a) /
las telenovelas

A — ¿*No te parecen exageradas las telenovelas?*

B — *Sí, no las soporto.*

Estudiante A

a. tonto(a) / los dibujos animados

b. sensacionalista / los programas de entrevistas

c. exagerado(a) / las comedias

d. aburrido(a) / los programas de compras

e. violento(a) / los programas de detectives

Estudiante B

Sí, no los (las) soporto.

Sí, pero me fascinan.

No. Me encantan.

También se dice

el presentador / la presentadora

Empecemos a escribir y a leer

Escribe tus respuestas en español.

12 En tu opinión, ¿qué programa de televisión tiene más éxito? ¿Por qué tiene éxito? ¿Qué personajes son populares hoy? ¿Quiénes hacen esos papeles? ¿Qué programa es un fracaso? ¿Por qué?

13 ¿Cómo se debe preparar alguien para participar en un programa de concursos?

14 ¿Conoces alguna película que está basada en un libro? ¿Leíste el libro? ¿Viste la película? ¿Cuál te gustó más? ¿Por qué? ¿Conoces alguna película basada en un hecho de la vida real? ¿Cuál? ¿Ocurre en la película lo mismo que en la realidad?

15 ¿Qué piensas de la violencia en la tele? ¿Crees que se debe hacer algo?

16 Lee esta lista de programas de televisión. Sólo puedes ver la tele por dos horas. Escoge lo que quieres ver. Compara tus programas con los de un(a) compañero(a). Imaginen que hay un sólo televisor y que necesitan ponerse de acuerdo.

	Canal 2	Canal 4	Canal 6
6:00	Moda: La chica de hoy	Noticias locales	Busca tu fortuna
7:00	Información deportiva	Telenovela: Marianela	Música de hoy
8:00	Película: Batman	Telenovela: Corazones tristes	Palabra de Dios
9:00	El chef francés: pasteles	Telenovela: Vidas exageradas	¡Bailemos!
10:00	Cine 2: El otoño de un vaquero	Noticias locales	Película: Derrumbe de noche
11:00		Noticias latinoamericanas	Noticias internacionales

Vocabulario para conversar 339

Practice

Teaching Suggestions
Ex. 1: Encourage students to watch the news the day before doing this exercise.

Answers:
¡Comuniquemos!
1–3 Answers will vary, but should include a variety of chapter vocabulary.

¡Comuniquemos!

Aquí tienes otra oportunidad para usar el vocabulario de este capítulo.

1 Con un(a) compañero(a), habla de las noticias en la televisión.

A —¿Viste las noticias ayer?
B —Sí. Me interesaron mucho.
A —¿Y qué piensas de lo que dijo el locutor sobre . . . ?
B — . . .

2 Con un(a) compañero(a), compara dos programas de televisión.

A —¿Qué programa de televisión te gusta más, *(nombre)* o *(nombre)*?
B —A mí . . .
A —¿Por qué?
B —Porque los personajes son . . .
A — . . .

3 Habla con un(a) compañero(a) sobre la película que tiene más éxito en estos días. Discutan por qué tiene éxito. Hablen de estas cosas:

• el nombre de la película
• el tipo de película
• el argumento
• los personajes
• la actuación y los actores
• la fotografía
• el guión
• la dirección

340   Capítulo 10

Options

Strategies for Reaching All Students

Spanish-Speaking Students
Ex. 3: Have students write out this exercise.

 Un paso más Ex. 10-G

Students Needing Extra Help
Ex. 1: Encourage students to create a news story using the vocabulary section of the Organizer. Do a complete model. Assign this a day in advance so that students will watch the news and take notes.
Ex. 3: Model. Students may have difficulty with the concept of judging the script, photography, and acting.
¿Qué sabes ahora?: Have students write out this section so that they are able to record their progress.

Cooperative Learning
Instruct students in groups of four to create a newscast. Each person will be responsible for three sentences on one of the following topics: national news, international news, weather, or sports. Students should read aloud within the group to check for clarity and correctness. Each group should then present its newscast to the class. You may want to videotape these presentations.

Esta joven puertorriqueña aprende sobre la televisión en la Universidad de San Juan.

Una locutora de un canal hispanohablante en Chicago

PIDE AYUDA

41

CARLA SANCHEZ

Answers: ¿Qué sabes ahora?
• Answers will vary.
• Answers will vary, but will probably be in present tense.
• name of a country / *hubo*

Audio Activity 10.3

¿Qué sabes ahora?

Can you:

■ discuss a film?

—Lo que más me gustó de la película fue el ___ y la ___.

■ summarize the plot of a movie or television program?

—(Nombre) se trata de un(a) ___ que ___.

■ discuss a major news story?

—El terremoto en ___ fue horrible, pero no ___ muchas víctimas.

Vocabulario para conversar   341

Cultural Notes ☼

(p. 340, realia)
The pop art style of Roy Lichtenstein plays a prominent role in this *telenovela* ad. His distinctive work often uses arrangements of large, colored dots to create cartoonlike images. This exaggeration adds to the "larger-than-life" appeal of the *novela*.

(p.341, top photo)
Students learn to direct their own television productions as they pursue degrees in telecommunications at the University of Puerto Rico. Courses leading to this degree include film and video production techniques and processes, writing for film and television, and the role of media in contemporary culture and society. The University of Puerto Rico in San Juan is well known for its classes in radio production.

(p. 341, bottom photo)
Carla Sánchez, reporter and anchorperson for TV Channel 44 in Chicago, was born in Blue Island, Illinois, but moved to Guadalajara, when she was in fourth grade. She finished *primaria* and *secundaria* there, and returned to Chicago to attend Columbia College where she majored in radio. She began working as a part-time DJ on Chicago's WIND radio, and later became the first Hispanic airborne traffic reporter in the city.

Present & Apply

Cultural Objective

• To compare soap operas in Spanish-speaking countries with those in the U.S.

Multicultural Perspectives

Telenovelas were originally adaptations of great literary works, broadcast over the radio as *radionovelas.* A few *telenovelas* have remained true to the meaning of the word *novela,* with complex characters and quality production. *Escalona* is one such *novela de época* (thus called because it takes place in the 1940s) that stars the popular singer Carlos Vives as Rafael Escalona, a young student dedicated to composing songs, romancing women, and enjoying life. This *novela* makes several literary allusions: in one episode Escalona refers to a woman as a *... diosa coronada de mi compadre Leandro Díaz* (Leandro Díaz is a popular Colombian composer; "La Diosa Coronada" is one of his songs. Gabriel García Márquez, in the epigraph of his novel, *Amor en los tiempos de cólera,* also mentions this *diosa coronada.*). This *novela* has been compared to the MGM musicals of the '40s, with Carlos Vives bursting into song at any moment. You may

Perspectiva cultural

Según lo que ves en estas escenas de telenovelas venezolanas, ¿serían *(would be)* estos programas muy diferentes de las telenovelas estadounidenses?

Options

Strategies for Reaching All Students

Spanish-Speaking Students

Have students answer either orally or in writing: *¿Ves telenovelas o las ve alguien en tu familia? Di por qué te gustan a ti o por qué le gustan a los miembros de tu familia.*

 Un paso más Ex. 10-H

Students Needing Extra Help

Perspectiva cultural: Have students take notes to use later in the *¿Lo sabes bien?* section.

La cultura desde tu perspectiva, Ex. 1: Make a two-column chart in which students list a feature of the *telenovela* in one column and, in the second column, write how it would be different in the English version.

Ex. 2: Videotape a *telenovela* presented on your local channel.

Enrichment

If possible, videotape an episode of a U.S. soap opera. Show parts of it to generate class discussion in Spanish about how American cultural values are represented in the episode. Ask students to compare these with what they know about Hispanic cultural values.

Las telenovelas en español son muy populares. Generalmente se dan episodios todos los días por dos o tres meses. El episodio final tiene una audiencia muy grande y mucha gente se reúne con su familia y amigos para verlo. Éstas son dos escenas de la telenovela *Ladrón de corazones*.

La hermana mayor de la familia se divorció y regresó a vivir con sus padres. La hermana menor, Claudia, quiere tener su propio apartamento.

> **CLAUDIA:** Pero, papá, ahora no hay espacio para mí en el dormitorio.
>
> **PAPÁ:** Hija, tú eres el sol de esta casa. No lo olvides. Mientras este viejo cuerpo tenga vida, ¡no te voy a permitir vivir sola!

El presidente de Aerolíneas del Caribe, el señor Bastos, está hablando con su hijo David.

> **DAVID:** Pero, papá, yo quiero ser músico. No me gusta el negocio, y me da miedo volar.
>
> **SR. BASTOS:** ¡Eso no importa! Toma. *(Le da su carnet de identidad de las aerolíneas y lo besa.)* No te olvides de quién eres y de tus responsabilidades como el nuevo presidente de la línea aérea más grande del Caribe.

En todas las telenovelas, tanto en inglés como en español, la manera de hablar es exagerada porque se trata de situaciones exageradas. Pero en las culturas latinoamericanas, palabras y expresiones poéticas como "tú eres el sol de esta casa" y "mientras este viejo cuerpo tenga vida" se usan en la vida diaria y no son exageraciones.

María Conchita Alonso y Jorge Schubert hacen el papel de médicos en la telenovela venezolana *Alejandra*.

Inset: Flavio Caballero y Ruddy Rodríguez, el galán y la heroína de la telenovela venezolana *Volver a ti*

En las telenovelas en español también se expresa muy abiertamente el cariño (*affection*) entre parientes y amigos. En las telenovelas, como en la vida real, la gente se abraza y se besa con frecuencia. También los hombres expresan sus emociones más abiertamente. Por ejemplo, el papá besa a su hijo para felicitarlo en *Ladrón de corazones*.

Las telenovelas tienen argumentos, personajes y guiones muy exagerados, pero también pueden indicar cosas importantes sobre la cultura.

La cultura desde tu perspectiva

1 Imagina que hay una telenovela en inglés con el mismo argumento que *Ladrón de corazones*. ¿En qué sería diferente? ¿Qué nos dicen las diferencias sobre las dos culturas?

2 Si puedes ver telenovelas en español, ve un episodio. Haz una lista de por lo menos tres cosas que te parecen diferentes de las telenovelas en inglés.

Claudia Venturini actúa en la telenovela venezolana *Inocente en línea*.

Perspectiva cultural 343

Cultural Notes

Preview

Transparency 51

Answers

A The expression is *Había una vez.* The verb *había* is in the imperfect tense. The other verb is *vivían.*

B The verb *estaba caminando* tells what was going on. It is in the imperfect progressive. The verb *encontró* tells what happened. It is in the preterite.

C *Dijo* is used to tell what Ricitos de oro said. The verb ending has no *i* and ends in an unaccented *o*, unlike the verb *vivió,* for example.

D The expression *tenía mucha hambre* tells what Ricitos de oro was feeling. The verb *(tenía)* is in the imperfect. The verbs that tell what she did are *entró, vio,* and *decidió.* They are in the preterite.

Gramática en contexto

Ricitos de oro y los tres osos

Había una vez una familia de tres osos: El papá oso, la mamá osa y el bebé oso. Vivían en el bosque.

Un día la mamá osa preparó tres platos de avena. La familia decidió dar un paseo porque la avena estaba muy caliente.

Una niña estaba caminando en el bosque cuando encontró la casa de los osos. "¡Qué casita tan bonita!" dijo ella. La niña se llamaba Ricitos de oro.

Entró en la casa y vio los tres platos de avena. Ricitos de oro tenía mucha hambre y decidió probar la avena.

A In caption 1, what expression corresponds to "Once upon a time there was"? What is the verb? What tense is it in? What is the other verb in caption 1?

B In caption 3, which verb tells what action was going on when something happened? Which verb tells what happened? What tense is each verb in?

C In caption 3, which verb is used to tell what Ricitos de oro said? How is this form different from the equivalent preterite form of other *-ir* verbs?

D In caption 4, what expression tells what Ricitos de oro was feeling? What tense is the verb in? Find the verbs that tell what she did. What tense are they in?

344 Capítulo 10

Options

Strategies for Reaching All Students

Students Needing Extra Help
B: Caption 2 offers another example of a contrast between a condition *(estaba muy caliente)* and an action *(decidió dar un paseo).*
C: Point out that the unaccented *o* ending in *dijo* is like the *Ud. / él / ella* form of *hacer, poder,* and *tener* in the preterite.

Students may have to refer to the *decir* chart to see that there are no written accents in the preterite paradigm.
El pretérito y el imperfecto: Give additional examples.

El pretérito y el imperfecto

We often use the preterite and the imperfect together. The imperfect may be used to put an action in the context of what time it was or what the weather was like.

> **Eran** las seis de la mañana cuando Ricitos de oro **se despertó.**
> El día **estaba** muy bonito. **Hacía** sol. No **hacía** frío.

1 ¿Qué tiempo hacía en España la semana pasada? Usa este pronóstico del tiempo y haz una frase por cada ciudad. Por ejemplo:

En Sevilla hacía mucho sol y viento. Hacía fresco.

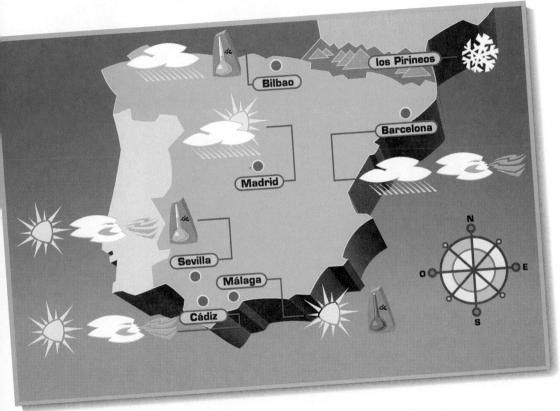

Gramática en contexto   345

Present & Practice

Answers

1 En Madrid llovía y también hacía (un poco de) sol.
En Barcelona llovía y hacía viento.
En Bilbao llovía (mucho) y hacía (mucho) frío.
En Cádiz hacía sol y viento.
En Málaga hacía sol y (mucho) calor.
En los Pirineos nevaba.

 Writing Activities 10-D, 10-E

Present & Practice

Teaching Suggestions

El pretérito y el imperfecto 2:
Have students identify the verbs
in the examples that describe
Goldilocks' feelings. Ask: What
tense is each of the verbs in?
Then have students locate the
sentences and verbs that express
action. Ask: What tense is each of
those verbs in?

Re-enter / Recycle

Ex. 3: daily routine from Chap. 2

Answers

2 Answers will vary, but look for
the correct form of *ser* in the
imperfect with the expressions of
time and the correct form of the
preterite in the second part of the
sentence.

2 Aquí tienes posibles situaciones en las noticias del día. Con un(a) compañero(a), túrnense haciendo preguntas y contestando.

A — *¿Cuándo empezó la tormenta?*
B — *Eran las 9:45 de la noche cuando empezó.*

la tormenta / empezar

a. la víctima / subir a la ambulancia   b. el incendio / empezar   c. el ladrón / robar el banco

d. el niño / caerse del segundo piso   e. el ascensor / romperse   f. el científico / quemarse las manos

g. el derrumbe / ocurrir   h. la policía / arrestar a los criminales

El pretérito y el imperfecto 2

Sometimes we use the preterite and imperfect tenses to contrast
a physical, mental, or emotional state with an action.

Ricitos de oro **vio** la avena. **Tenía** mucha hambre.
Ricitos de oro **quería** comerla. No **sabía** qué hacer.
Tomó la cuchara y **empezó** a comer.

346   Capítulo 10

Options

Strategies for Reaching All Students

Students Needing Extra Help

Ex. 2: Review preterite endings and time-telling.
Point out that *d.–f.* include reflexive verbs.
El pretérito y el imperfecto 2: Have students
decide which verb in each example indicates
the physical state. Then repeat separately
for the mental and emotional states. Give
further examples.

Ex. 3: Have students identify which answers
contain examples of the physical, mental,
and emotional states.
Ex. 4: Brainstorm possible excuses.

3 Dí por qué están pasando estas cosas en un estudio de cine.

la heroína /
ir al baño /   *La heroína fue al baño porque se sentía mal.*
sentirse mal

a. el niño / esconderse / darle miedo el monstruo
b. el director y el galán / pelearse / estar de mal humor
c. el vaquero / acostarse / estar muy cansado
d. el caballo / comer las flores / tener hambre
e. el extraterrestre / quitarse el disfraz / tener calor
f. los músicos / salir de la escena / aburrirse

4 Con un(a) compañero(a), termina estas excusas diciendo por qué. Puedes usar estos u otros verbos: *tener (que), querer, estar, poder* y *hacer.*

no ir a   A — *¿Por qué no fuiste a la escuela?*
la escuela   B — *No fui a la escuela porque tenía fiebre.*

a. no hacer la tarea
b. no ir al partido de fútbol
c. levantarse tarde
d. no ayudar a limpiar la casa
e. no tomar la medicina
f. no llamar a nadie

Este cartel en Madrid anuncia una película de ciencia ficción.

Esta película tuvo éxito internacional.

347

3 You might want to ask students to draw these situations for extra credit.
a. El niño se escondió porque le daba miedo el monstruo.
b. El director y el galán se pelearon porque estaban de mal humor.
c. El vaquero se acostó porque estaba muy cansado.
d. El caballo comió las flores porque tenía hambre.
e. El extraterrestre se quitó el disfraz porque tenía calor.
f. Los músicos salieron de la escena porque se aburrían.

4 ESTUDIANTE A
a. ¿Por qué no hiciste la tarea?
b. ...no fuiste al partido de fútbol?
c. ...te levantaste tarde?
d. ...no ayudaste a limpiar la casa?
e. ...no tomaste la medicina?
f. ...no llamaste a nadie?
ESTUDIANTE B
a.–f. Answers will vary, but look for the correct forms of the preterite and imperfect and logical responses.

**Practice Wkbk.
10-5, 10-6, 10-7**

**Writing Activity
10-F**

Pruebas 10-5, 10-6

Cultural Notes

(p. 347, top photo)
The U.S. film market in Spain is very successful. Hollywood blockbuster films often appear soon after their U.S. release dates. Spain has a well-developed dubbing industry that produces high quality Spanish-language sound tracks. Some films rely on subtitles, which especially appeal to viewers who enjoy listening to English.

(p. 347, photo)
Steven Spielberg's 1993 Oscar-winning *Schindler's List* is based on Thomas Keneally's book of the same name. This true story of the Holocaust describes industrialist Oskar Schindler's efforts to save more than 1,000 Polish Jews, some of whom are still alive today.

Present & Practice

Class Starter Review

On the day following the presentation of the preterite and imperfect 3, you might begin the class with the following activity:
Compile a list of 20 basic action verbs *(bailar, comer, nadar,* etc.) and write them on the chalkboard. Have students stand and pantomime a verb from the list, while watching a classmate at the same time. When you say *alto,* all students write what the student they were watching was doing *(Cuando el profesor / la profesora dijo "alto," Andrés estaba llorando).*

Re-enter / Recycle

Ex. 5: daily routine from Chap. 2

Answers

5 Answers will vary, but may include:
En el 1-A un señor estaba viendo la televisión y unos jóvenes estaban lavando los platos.
En el 1-B una niña y su mamá estaban saludándose en el comedor.
En el 2-A unos muchachos estaban tocando música y otro estaba cantando. Un niño estaba cepillándose los dientes.

El pretérito y el imperfecto 3

Sometimes the preterite and the imperfect (or the imperfect progressive) contrast a continuing action with an action that has a definite beginning and end.

> Una niña **estaba caminando** por el bosque cuando **vio** la casa de los osos.

5 Con un(a) compañero(a), di qué estaba pasando en los apartamentos del dibujo cuando ocurrió el terremoto. Escoge por lo menos seis situaciones.

A —¿*Qué estaba pasando en el apartamento 3-A cuando ocurrió el terremoto?*
B —*En el 3-A un señor estaba afeitándose en el baño.*

6 Inventa tres escenas divertidas para una película. Usa una sola frase para cada descripción.

Una señora estaba desayunando cuando el gato saltó y se cayó en el plato de cereal.

Después, formen un grupo para escoger las tres escenas más divertidas.

348 Capítulo 10

Options

Strategies for Reaching All Students

Students Needing Extra Help

El pretérito y el imperfecto 3: Give additional examples.
Ex. 5: Have students decide on the vocabulary before conjugating the verbs. Point out that in some apartments, more than one action is taking place.
Ex. 6: Do as a whole class. Help students by giving them the beginning phrase (the setting). Encourage them to create the *cuando* phrase.

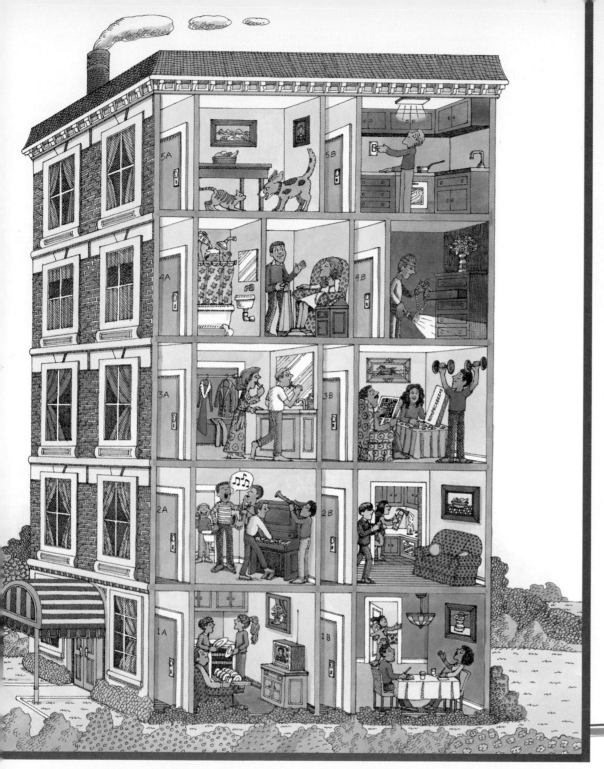

En el 2-B un hombre estaba poniéndose la corbata y una mujer estaba usando un extinguidor de incendios en la cocina.

En el 3-A una mujer estaba maquillándose en el baño.

En el 3-B un hombre estaba haciendo un crucigrama, una muchacha estaba haciendo un rompecabezas y un muchacho estaba levantando pesas.

En el 4-A un muchacho estaba bañándose mientras alguien estaba pasando la aspiradora y otra persona estaba hablando por teléfono.

En el 4-B un ladrón estaba robando unas joyas.

En el 5-A un perro y un gato estaban peleándose.

En el 5-B un hombre estaba encendiendo la luz.

6 Answers will vary, but look for the correct use and forms of the imperfect progressive and the preterite.

 Practice Wkbk. 10-8

 Writing Activity 10-G

 Prueba 10-7

Present & Practice

Answers

7 ESTUDIANTE A

a. ¿Qué dijeron tú y *(nombre)* de la película de aventuras?

b. ...dijeron Felipe y Susana de la película romántica?

c. ...dijo Ramón de la película de ciencia ficción?

d. ...dijeron Roberto y Marina de la película del oeste?

e. ...dijiste (tú) de la película de acción?

f. Questions will vary.

ESTUDIANTE B

Answers will vary, but should begin as follows:

a. (Nosotros) dijimos ...

b. (Ellos) dijeron ...

c. (Él) dijo ...

d. (Ellos) dijeron ...

e. (Yo) dije ...

f. Answers will vary.

El pretérito del verbo *decir*

In the preterite tense, the stem of *decir* is *dij-*, and the endings follow the pattern of *hacer, poder,* and *tener*. Notice that the Uds. / ellos / ellas form does not have an *i* in the ending.

(yo)	**dije**	(nosotros)(nosotras)	**dijimos**
(tú)	**dijiste**	(vosotros)(vosotras)	**dijisteis**
Ud.(él)(ella)	**dijo**	Uds.(ellos)(ellas)	**dijeron**

7 ¿Qué tal fueron los comentarios de estas personas sobre la última película que vieron? Con un(a) compañero(a), usa los dibujos para preguntar y contestar. Por ejemplo:

A —¿*Qué dijo Marta de la película de terror?*
B —*Dijo que era un fracaso.*

Marta

Estudiante A — Estudiante B

a. (nombre) y tú

b. Felipe y Susana

c. Ramón

d. Roberto y Marina

e. (tú)

f.

350 Capítulo 10

Options

Strategies for Reaching All Students

Students Needing Extra Help
El pretérito del verbo decir: Review the preterite forms of *hacer, poder,* and *tener* by writing them on the chalkboard. Stress that there is no *i* in the third person plural ending. Ex. 7: Brainstorm the possible reactions. Remind students that they need to adjust the verb endings. If available, use the vocabulary section of the Book 1, Chap. 11 Organizer.

Ahora lo sabes: Have students write this so that they can record their progress.

Enrichment
To extend this exercise, name a movie or television show that students can question each other about. In groups of three, have students ask questions and take notes about what their group members answer. Students will report the comments to the rest of the class when called on to answer the following question: *En tu grupo, ¿qué dijeron las personas de* (name of movie or TV program)? *Explica por qué dijeron eso.*

WILLOW

LOS INTOCABLES DE ELLIOT NESS

ENTRE PILLOS ANDA EL JUEGO

ROBOCOP

CORTOCIRCUITO II

LOS FANTASMAS ATACAN AL JEFE

NOSOTROS PONEMOS EL CINE DE TU VIDA. TU, LAS PALOMITAS

Estas Navidades no tendrás que salir de casa para ver el mejor cine. Sólo tienes que comprarte palomitas y enchufarte a TELECINCO. Porque hemos preparado para estas fiestas, unas películas que te dejarán pegado al sillón.

Una selección especial para todos los gustos. Para toda la familia: humor, intriga, acción, fantasía... Cómprate las palomitas y ponte cómodo. Porque las películas de tu vida están en TELECINCO.

TELE 5

La Navidad De Tu Vida

Answers: Ahora lo sabes
- hacía
- tuvo / eran
- dijo / dije

 Practice Wkbk. 10-9

 Audio Activities 10.4, 10.5

 Writing Activity 10-H

 Prueba 10-8

 Comm. Act. BLM 10-2

Ahora lo sabes

Can you:

■ describe the conditions when something happened?
—Cuando el incendio empezó, ___ mucho viento.

■ tell what happened and why?
—La película ___ éxito porque los actores principales ___ excelentes.

■ report what someone said?
—Felipe ___ que quería ver una película de acción, pero yo ___ que no.

Gramática en contexto   351

Cultural Notes

(p. 351, realia)
According to this ad for a local television station's Christmas programming, viewers can "stay home, make popcorn, and get comfortable" to watch such popular U.S. films as *The Untouchables, Willow,* and *Short Circuit II.* They won't need to be fluent English-speakers either. Most U.S. movies shown on Spanish-speaking television are dubbed rather than subtitled.

Apply

Using the Video

In Episode 10, Jamie goes to the library and finds police and reporters there. Demetrio Alcocer has injured himself trying to catch a thief attempting to steal La Catrina's will.

Demetrio tells Jamie that Silvestre Aguilar's grandfather was the lawyer in charge of La Catrina's will. Instead of finding an heir to La Catrina's estate, Silvestre's grandfather kept the estate for himself. Demetrio then gives Jamie La Catrina's will.

On the way to the Hacienda la Jacaranda, Jamie tells Carlos about her talk with Demetrio. At the hacienda, Jamie and Carlos talk to a worker about the pesticides used on the corn.

At home with María, Jamie watches a TV program about *El día de los muertos.* That night, she dreams that don Silvestre appears to her on the Day of the Dead, threatening to harm her if she claims the estate. Then La Catrina

Para decir más

Este vocabulario adicional te puede servir para las actividades de esta sección.

el planeta
planet

la Tierra
Earth

la vida
life

el volcán
volcano

los primeros auxilios
first aid

disparar
to shoot

morir *(o → ue)*
to die

moverse *(o → ue)*
to move

herido, -a
wounded

(estar) nervioso, -a
(to be) nervous

352   Capítulo 10

Actividades

Esta sección te ofrece la oportunidad de aumentar tus conocimientos de español al integrar lo que aprendiste en este capítulo con lo que aprendiste en capítulos anteriores.

 Describe una ocasión cuando tuviste que:

- hacer un informe oral
- asistir a una boda (o a algún otro evento importante)
- recibir un premio (o un diploma)
- actuar, cantar, bailar o tocar un instrumento

En dos o tres frases dile a un(a) compañero(a) qué día era, qué tiempo hacía, cómo te sentías y por qué. Luego, formen grupos. Tu compañero(a) debe contarle al grupo lo que le dijiste.

Un día tuve que ... Era ...

Este locutor espera a sus invitados para hacer un programa de entrevistas durante el festival de películas en San Sebastián, España.

Options

Strategies for Reaching All Students

Spanish-Speaking Students
Ex. 1: Have students write out this activity, choosing two of the options and giving more details.

Students Needing Extra Help
Todo junto: If there are time constraints, choose Ex. 2 or 3.
Ex. 1: Do a complete model. Remind students to change the verb form to third person when reporting. Review uses of preterite and imperfect.
Ex. 2: Do a complete model. Remind students not to use the entire list.
Ex. 3: Review indirect object pronouns. Have students refer to the vocabulary section of the Organizer.

Cooperative Learning
Divide the class into groups of five. One student from each group writes a sentence about his or her favorite movie or TV program as a child, using the imperfect tense. He or she then gives that paper to you. Each group forms a circle. *Estudiante A* whispers that sentence to *Estudiante B,* who then whispers *Él / ella me dijo que ...* and the rest of the message as he / she heard it. This repeats to the right until *Estudiante E* receives the message. He / she must report

2 Piensa en algún crimen o desastre natural reciente. Habla con un(a) compañero(a) sobre:

- qué pasó
- cuándo
- dónde

Usen palabras y expresiones como las siguientes:

(No) había...
ayudar
pedir ayuda
la ambulancia
los bomberos
la policía
la emergencia
estar muerto(a)
matar a
quedarse sin casa / ropa / comida
las víctimas
la vida

EL 23 DE JUNIO VERÁ...
EL LIBRO 3 DE

Aunque Ud. No Lo Crea
de Ripley

EXTRAÑOS CRÍMENES Y MUERTES

LA "BOLA DE FOUL" QUE MATÓ A UN AFICIONADO

SÓLO N$ 5.00 EJEMPLAR

¡INCREÍBLES LIBROS DE BOLSILLO!

3 ¿Quién crees que dijo las siguientes frases y a quién? Díselo a un(a) compañero(a).

"¡Luces! ¡Cámara! ¡Acción!"

El director les dijo a los actores, "¡Luces! ¡Cámara! ¡Acción!"

a. "¡Estoy dirigiendo esta película! Y ni tú ni ese galán tonto pueden sugerir nada."
b. "¡Manos arriba! ¡Si te mueves, disparo!"
c. "Me gusta mucho el guión, pero el papel de la heroína es más importante que el mío."
d. "¡Encontré una fórmula que va a destruir la Tierra! ¡Ja! ¡Ja! ¡Ja!"
e. "¡Ayúdenme! ¡Me robaron las botas, las pistolas y el caballo!"
f. "Me enamoré de ti, pero tengo que regresar a mi planeta."

Ahora inventa otras frases y pregúntale a tu compañero(a) quién las dijo.

Actividades 353

---

appears and confirms that Jamie is her true heir.

 La Catrina: Capítulo 10

Play

 Video Activity B

 Para entender mejor

Play

 Video Activity C

Answers: Actividades
1–2 Answers will vary.

3 a. El (La) director(a) le dijo a la heroína, "¡Estoy dirigiendo esta película! ¡Y ni tú ni ese galán tonto pueden sugerir nada!"
b. El / la detective le dijo al criminal...
c. El galán le dijo al director...
d. El (La) científico(a) loco(a) le dijo al (a la) locutor(a)...
e. El (La) vaquero(a) le dijo al (a la) policía...
f. El (La) extraterrestre le dijo a la heroína (al galán)...

 Writing Activities 10-I, 10-J

Comm. Act. BLMs 10-3, 10-4, 10-5

Cultural Notes

the message to the class. You will report the original message.

(p. 352, photo)
Spain is the eighth-largest market for Hollywood films, many of which are shown at the San Sebastián film festival each September. The festival attracts tourists from all over the world, as well as film distributors in search of new successes. Film critics and students also attend, to critique and study motion pictures from diverse cultures.

(p. 353, photo)
The collection of *Believe It or Not* stories by American cartoonist Robert Ripley continues to have new books published in ten languages around the world. Originally published in 1918 as single-panel newspaper cartoons, they once had a peak daily readership of 80 million.

Apply

Process Reading
For a description of process reading, see p. 52.

Answers
Antes de leer
Answers will vary, but will most likely include: 1, 2, 3, 5, 8, 10.

Mira la lectura
Students should skim the story to get a general idea of what happens.

¡Vamos a leer!

Antes de leer

STRATEGY➤ Using prior knowledge

Decide which of the following events is likely to occur in a soap opera. Write down the numbers of those that are likely to occur, then compare your choices with those of a partner.

1. Alguien tiene un accidente grave.
2. Dos jóvenes se enamoran a primera vista.
3. Unos criminales roban una joyería.
4. Un joven va a clases todos los días y estudia mucho.
5. Alguien pierde la memoria.
6. Una joven monta a caballo.
7. Un hombre y una mujer se casan y no tienen ningún problema.
8. Madre e hijo se separan.
9. Un consejero de campamento se cae de un árbol.
10. La gente cree que la heroína mató a alguien.

Mira la lectura

STRATEGY➤ Skimming

Read the selection once through to get the gist of it.

Cómo escribir una telenovela

Las telenovelas latinas no son tan complicadas como parecen. Todas están hechas con la misma fórmula.

La heroína es, por lo general, joven, linda e inocente. Es pobre y sufre mucho para pagar sus estudios.

Se cree todo lo que le dicen y por eso tiene tantos problemas. No es raro que, en un momento u otro, termine en la cárcel, acusada de un crimen que no cometió. Si tiene un hijo, no le permiten verlo y pasa mucho tiempo buscándolo. Últimamente, las pobres heroínas están perdiendo la memoria con frecuencia. Al final siempre recibe una gran fortuna y entonces puede vengarse.

Y, por supuesto, hay un galán. Es muy guapo, rico y se enamora de la heroína a primera vista. Pero es un muñeco en las manos de su mamá, que es un monstruo. Él también se cree todo lo que le dicen, sobre todo si es algo malo sobre la heroína. Es terrible ver cómo el galán trata a la heroína en el período en que la cree mala: la humilla y la maltrata delante de la gente. Al final, por supuesto, comprende que ella es buena y que la quiere de veras.

Si usted quiere escribir una telenovela, tiene que incluir estos personajes, y nunca olvide que todo es fórmula y repetición.

354   Capítulo 10

Options

Strategies for Reaching All Students

Spanish-Speaking Students
Have students write out a short scene from one of the types of TV programs or movies listed. *Escribe una escena de uno de los tipos de obra mencionados. Luego, con unos compañeros, puedes presentarla en clase.*

Students Needing Extra Help
Mira la lectura: Remind students that they don't have to understand every word, that they are just looking for the main idea of each paragraph.
Infórmate: Explain the reason for reading the selection more than once. Read aloud as students follow along. Read aloud again, one sentence at a time, giving students an opportunity to write down the unfamiliar words.

Have students work in pairs or small groups in order to share their knowledge of the vocabulary. Collect their lists and combine them into one for the next day's class. Put this list on the chalkboard (or have it copied for each student). As a class, decide which words are not important for an understanding of the reading.

Infórmate

$STRATEGIES➤$ Distinguishing essential from nonessential words
Identifying supporting details

1 Now read the selection more carefully, and make a list of those words you don't know. Read the selection a third time, and cross out on your list the words that are not important for understanding the selection.

2 Were any of the events that you identified in *Antes de leer* mentioned in the selection? Read aloud to your partner the places in the selection where they are mentioned.

3 List at least four events that are part of the formula for soap operas in Spanish.

DE LUNES A SÁBADO
A LAS 9 DE LA NOCHE

Manuela
Un Apasionante Romance Para Tus Noches De Amor

Ahora, Grecia Colmenares te invita a vivir nuevas y fuertes emociones. Con "Manuela". La dramática historia de dos hermanas, Isabel y Manuela, enfrentadas por el amor de un mismo hombre: Fernando. Intrigas, celos, pasiones y odios. "Manuela". La nueva telenovela de TELECINCO que mantendrá tu corazón en vilo desde el primer al último capítulo. ¡Vívela todas las noches en tu pantalla amiga!

Enchúfate a
TELE5

Aplicación

Many kinds of books, movies, and television shows have their own formulas. List at least four events that are likely to occur in one of these: a teen romance, a western, a situation comedy, a detective story.

¡Vamos a leer!   355

Infórmate

1.–2. Answers will vary.

3. Answers will vary, but may include the following:
La heroína busca a su hijo.
La heroína termina en la cárcel.
La heroína pierde la memoria.
La heroína consigue una gran fortuna y puede vengarse.
El galán maltrata a la heroína.
El galán comprende que quiere a la heroína de veras.

Aplicación

Answers will vary, but may include the following:
Teen romance: Dos jóvenes se enamoran, pero los padres de la muchacha no están de acuerdo con el romance. El jóven tiene que mostrarles que él es un buen muchacho.
Western: Hay un nuevo sheriff. El hombre que mató al antiguo sheriff regresa; se pelean; el asesino muere y el sheriff es un héroe.
Sit-com: Un niño saca mala nota, y la cambia con un marcador. La profesora, los padres y el niño se encuentran en el supermercado, y hablan sobre las notas del niño.
Detective story: El detective habla con la persona que vio el robo de una joyería. El detective encuentra al ladrón, y devuelve las joyas a la joyería.

Cultural Notes

Aplicación: The idea of "formula" may be unfamiliar to students. As a whole class, brainstorm the elements that you always expect to see in certain types of shows.

Enrichment
As a homework assignment, have students write *diálogos típicos* between characters in a soap opera. Explain that what each character says should reveal how his or her personality follows the formula described in the selection (for example, the heroine should say something that shows she is gullible, or that she has lost her memory; the mother of the rich young man should say something that shows how manipulative or evil she is, etc.).

(p. 355, realia)
Manuela is a *telenovela* about two half-sisters, Manuela and Isabel, who do not know of each other's existence. However, they both love the same man, Fernando (Jorge Martínez). After Isabel disappears in a drowning accident Manuela innocently takes her place and the mystery about the sisters' past begins to unfold. Grecia Colmenares plays both Isabel and Manuela. This *novela* was filmed in Italy, Los Angeles, and Argentina.

Apply

Process Writing
For information regarding developing a writing portfolio, see p. 54.

 # ¡**V**amos a escribir!

A veces tenemos una buena idea para una película. Vamos a inventar una película y a hacer un cartel para anunciarla al público.

1 Piensa en estas cosas:

- qué tipo de película es
- quiénes son los personajes principales
- de qué se trata
- los comentarios que van a escribir los críticos

Escribe el primer borrador y consulta con un(a) compañero(a). Sigue los otros pasos del proceso de escribir.

Options

Strategies for Reaching All Students

Students Needing Extra Help
Bring in the movie section of the weekend paper so that students can see how a movie they are familiar with is publicized. Compare one of the full-page ads to the model in the book, pointing out that students don't have to create something as sophisticated as the one in the paper. Remind students that they are creating a new movie, not translating a current ad into Spanish. Use the vocabulary section of the Organizer.

Enrichment
Have students create posters for real movies. Discuss how English movie titles translated into Spanish can sometimes be quite different from the original.

2 Ahora escoge el cartel que más te guste. Quieres que una compañía de cine filme esta película. Escribe una descripción de la película según este modelo.

nombre:	La Tierra en ruinas
personajes:	una científica y un policía
lugar:	Caracas en el año 2050
argumento:	Los extraterrestres necesitan agua. Llegan a la Tierra y empiezan a destruir las grandes ciudades.
audiencia:	jóvenes de 12 a 18 años

3 Para distribuir su trabajo, pueden:

- exhibir los carteles en la sala de clases
- exhibirlos en el vestíbulo o en la biblioteca escolar
- enviar las descripciones al periódico o a la revista escolar
- enviarlas a un periódico local
- escoger la mejor descripción, escribir el guión para una escena y presentarla a otras clases de español
- incluir todo en sus portafolios

¡Vamos a escribir! 357

Assess & Summarize

Test Preparation

You may want to assign parts of this section as written homework or as an in-class writing activity prior to administering the *Examen de habilidades*.

Answers

Listening: —*Era muy interesante. Se trataba de un vaquero que llega a una comunidad pequeña y se pelea con algunos criminales. La heroína tiene un rancho. El vaquero se enamora de ella. Hay una pelea terrible, y el vaquero mata a los criminales. Luego se monta a caballo y se va. La heroína se queda llorando. La película estuvo muy buena.*
A western movie is being discussed. The speaker likes the film.

Reading: 1. No vale la pena verla.
2. La recomiendo.
Words that one would *not* need to know will vary, but may include: *varios, anciano, sucesos.*

Writing: Summaries will vary.

Culture: Answers will vary, but may include the following: The expression of affection is frequent. Men express emotion openly. Language and actions are often exaggerated.

Speaking: Dialogues will vary.

¿Lo sabes bien?

Esta sección te ayudará a prepararte para el examen de habilidades, donde tendrás que hacer tareas semejantes.

Listening

Can you understand when people talk about a movie or TV program? Listen as your teacher reads a sample similar to what you will hear on the test. What kind of movie is being discussed? Did the speaker like it or not?

Reading

Read what two critics have written about a film. List at least three words that you *would not* need to know in order to understand these reviews. Then assign the correct last sentence to each review.

1 En Tijuana, un detective investiga un crimen que se cometió hace varios años. El argumento es muy complicado, y nunca se explica el crimen. Después de muchas aventuras exageradas, escenas sensacionalistas y un derrumbe que casi no daña nada, termina la película....

2 Un detective descubre un crimen horrible en Tijuana. Conoce a un anciano que puede ser el criminal y a su hija, de quien se enamora. Tienen muchas aventuras. Casi los mata un derrumbe. No comprendemos muy bien los sucesos, pero la película es divertida....

a. No vale la pena verla.
b. La recomiendo.

Writing

Can you write a summary of a television drama or comedy? Here is an example for a teen drama.

Culture

Can you give three characteristics of a Spanish-language soap opera?

Speaking

Talk to your partner about your favorite actor. Discuss the actor's movies and / or television shows.

A —*¿Qué actor o actriz te gusta más?*
B —*Arnold Schwarzenegger.*
A —*¿Por qué?*
B —*Porque hace películas de acción y comedias muy buenas.*
A —*¿Te gustó su actuación en (nombre de película)?*
B — ...

Se trata de unos jóvenes que van a la misma escuela secundaria. Los muchachos son muy guapos y las muchachas muy bonitas. La semana pasada, uno de los muchachos se enamoró de una chica pobre. Los jóvenes se querían mucho y querían casarse, pero sus padres no lo permitieron y el joven se peleó con ellos.

358 Capítulo 10

Options

Students Needing Extra Help
Have students write out this exercise so that they can check off what they have mastered. *¿Lo sabes bien?:* Remind students that this is just a sample of what the test will be like.
Listening: Read more than once. Remind students that they only need to listen for two pieces of information. Brainstorm for which words they should be listening.

Reading: Show students where the choices are located on the page. They may have difficulty distinguishing which words are unimportant. They will probably choose smaller words, such as *en, un, a,* etc.
Writing: Have students use the Organizer and write a sample summary before the test as practice. Limit the number of required sentences. Brainstorm possible plot lines. Create with students the first sentence or two.

Culture: Have students review the notes they took during their first reading of the *Perspectiva cultural*. Also, review the reading in *¡Vamos a leer!*
Speaking: Use the vocabulary section of the Organizer. Limit the number of lines of dialogue. Do a complete model. Remind students to think about which tenses they need to use.

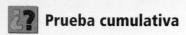

Resumen del capítulo 10

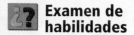

¿? Prueba cumulativa

¿? Examen de habilidades

Test Generator

Usa el vocabulario de este capítulo para:

■ summarize the plot of a movie or television program
■ describe the characters and settings of a movie or television program
■ describe conditions when something happened

to talk about moviemaking
actuar
la actuación
dirigir *(g → j)*
el director, la directora
la dirección
los efectos especiales
la escena
la fotografía
el guión, *pl.* los guiones

el /la criminal
el crimen
el /la detective
el ladrón, *pl.* los
   ladrones; la ladrona
el /la policía
la víctima
el científico, la científica
el /la extraterrestre
el monstruo

el personaje
principal
tener éxito
el fracaso
ocurrir
el hecho
la información
la violencia
violento, -a
exagerado, -a
excelente
sensacionalista
típico, -a

to talk about various kinds of films
la película de acción
montar a caballo
el caballo
el vaquero, la vaquera
enamorarse (de)
el galán, *pl.* los galanes
la heroína
arrestar
investigar
matar
robar

to talk about natural disasters

dañar
destruyó *(from:* destruir)
el derrumbe
la erupción, *pl.* las erupciones
el huracán, *pl.* los huracanes
la inundación, *pl.* las
   inundaciones
el terremoto
la tormenta

to talk about TV programs
el comentario (sobre)
la entrevista
el locutor, la locutora
el programa de compras
el programa de concursos
internacional
local

to summarize movies and TV programs
(estar) basado, -a (en)
tratarse de
el argumento
hacer el papel (de)
el papel

other useful words and expressions
la ayuda
cambiar
esconder(se)
hubo *(from:* haber)
¿Qué tal es...?

Resumen 359

CAPÍTULO 11

THEME: THE FUTURE

COMMUNICATION

Topics
Professions
Space
Environment
Recyclables

Objectives
To compare Latin American and U. S. attitudes toward the future

To discuss professions

To discuss career education

To describe homes of the future

To describe the world of the future

To discuss the environment

CULTURE

Latin American attitudes toward the future

GRAMMAR

El futuro

Ancillaries available for use with Chapter 11

Multisensory/Technology

 Overhead Transparencies, 52–56

 Audio Tapes and CDs

 Vocabulary Art Blackline Masters for Hands-On Learning, pp. 58–62

Classroom Crossword

 La Catrina

 CD-ROM

Print

 Practice Workbook, pp. 105–114

 Writing, Audio & Video Activities, pp. 65–70, 123–125, 171–172

 Communicative Activity Blackline Masters
  Pair and Small Group Activities, pp. 71–76
  Situation Cards, p. 77

 Un paso más: Actividades para ampliar tu español, pp. 61–66

Assessment

 Assessment Program
  Pruebas, pp. 159–169
  Examen de habilidades, pp. 170–173

 Test Generator

Video still from Chap. 11

El año 2000 comienza en febrero

Education is an investment for the future, and many Latin American countries, such as Mexico, have made changes in their educational systems.

The government of Mexico emphasized the connection between education and the future by encouraging parents to register their children in February for the upcoming elementary school year. The 1982 slogan for this campaign was *El año 2000 comienza en febrero.* Prior to this time, students were registered just before the school year, in September. From their first year on, these students will study a comprehensive variety of subjects, including English, which are important to Mexico's success in the areas of technology, health care, tourism, and trade.

During the Salinas de Gortari administration (1988–1994), the country experienced a sweeping educational reform. Course curriculum was updated and the role of the teacher was re-evaluated, along with the relationship of families and school authorities. Another change during this time was the decentralization of the educational system, which gave the individual states more control of the schools.

Science and technology are key to building a competitive economy, and the budget allocated to these areas has increased each year since 1989. More resources have been allocated to the development of public universities and technological institutes. In 1994, 114 technological high schools and 16 higher education institutes were created. CONALEP (Colegio Nacional de Educación Profesional), ITESM (Instituto Tecnológico de Estudios Superiores de Monterrey), and CBTIS (Centro de Bachillerato Técnico Industrial y de Servicios) are a few examples of technological schools. A new alternative, the technological university, is being offered in seven Mexican states.

Although Mexico faces a challenge in providing enough schools to keep up with its population growth, the reform of Mexico's educational system offers hope for the future.

Introduce

Re-entry of Concepts
The following list represents words, expressions, and grammar topics re-entered from Book 1 and Book 2 (Chaps. 2 and 10):

Book 1
school subjects, conservation, recyclable items, environment

Chapter 2
school subjects

Chapter 10
TV and movie character types

Planning

Cross-Curricular Connections

Vocational Education Connection
(pp. 364–365)
In pairs, have students develop a job interview for one of the careers shown. They should include a cover sheet with the preferred educational, professional, and personal qualifications. These can be passed to another pair, who can conduct a mock interview or write a letter of introduction for the job. As follow-up, have each pair write a classified ad for the Classified section. Compile these for use in class review and questioning.

Industrial Arts Connection *(pp. 370–371)*
Have students individually design a poster of a house of the future and label it using vocabulary from Chaps. 8 and 11. They should then write a paragraph describing one room of the house in detail. Both posters and paragraphs could be displayed.

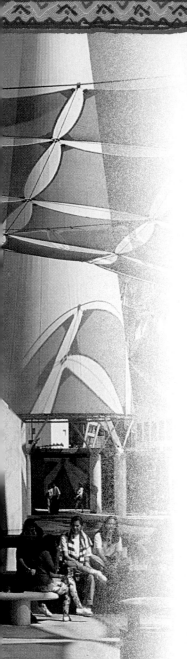

CAPÍTULO 11

¿Cómo será el futuro?

OBJECTIVES

At the end of this chapter, you will be able to:

- discuss various professions
- say what you think the world will be like in the future
- discuss how to protect the environment
- compare attitudes toward the future in Latin America and the United States

Pabellón de la Comunidad Económica Europea en la Expo '92, Sevilla

361

Cultural Notes

Spanish in Your Community
In pairs, have students choose a profession and create a strategy to attract Spanish-speaking customers or clients. They should list five things that they think will influence the local Hispanic communities. Ask local Spanish-speaking merchants or business-people to comment on students' lists.

(p. 360, photo)
Expo 92, the Age of Discovery, ran from April 20 to October 12, coinciding with the 500th anniversary of Columbus's first voyage of exploration. Several corporations, 111 countries and 23 international organizations, such as the Red Cross and the United Nations, exhibited. The expo site, built on Cartuja Island in the Guadalquivir River, has been converted to a park and scientific research center. In the future, an amusement park may also be created there.

Preview

Cultural Objective
• To discuss possible future professions in Spanish-speaking countries

Critical Thinking: Paraphrasing
Have students write a description of the activities in the photographs. As a class, brainstorm ways to describe things for which students have not yet learned the vocabulary. For example, students have not learned the Spanish word for "test tube," but they could paraphrase using *botella larga de vidrio*.

¡Piénsalo bien!

Mira las fotos. ¿A qué piensas dedicarte en el futuro, o piensas raramente en eso? ¿Te interesa lo que hacen estas personas?

En Cancún, un paramédico habla con unos jóvenes sobre su profesión.

"Después de las clases trabajamos como voluntarios de la Cruz Roja."

¿Qué te gustaría ser de mayor? ¿Haces algo como voluntario? ¿Puede ayudarte ese trabajo en alguna profesión? ¿En cuál?

"Todavía no sabemos todos los usos que este aceite puede tener."

¿Te interesan las ciencias? ¿Te gustaría ser médico(a), enfermero(a) o científico(a)? ¿Por qué?

Científicos españoles investigando los usos del aceite de oliva

362   Capítulo 11

Options

Strategies for Reaching All Students

Spanish-Speaking Students
Ask: *¿Cuál(es) de estas profesiones te interesa(n)? ¿Por qué?*

 Un paso más 11-A

"¿En qué puedo servirle?"

¿Te interesa algún trabajo de servicio público, como por ejemplo, el de policía, bombero(a) o paramédico(a)? ¿Por qué?

Esta policía mexicana patrulla las calles en su carrito.

363

Cultural Notes ☼

(p. 362, top photo)
Paramedics in Mexico often volunteer through the Mexican Red Cross *(la Cruz Roja),* founded in 1910. Its greatest crisis by far came in the aftermath of the 1986 earthquake, when *la Cruz Roja* participated in rescue operations and provided emergency medical care, water, food, counseling, and shelter to tens of thousands of victims. *La Cruz Roja* also sponsors first-aid training and health education classes.

(p. 362, bottom photo)
Olives *(las aceitunas),* so important to Mediterranean culture, have been cultivated since approximately 3500 B.C. Olive oil *(el aceite de oliva)* has multiple uses and is classified by grade, from cooking to industrial quality. Diamond cutters use an abrasive paste of diamond dust and olive oil to polish the facets of newly cut stones. Coin collectors clean rare copper coins by rubbing them with olive oil. Olive trees *(los olivos)* may live as long as 1,500 years.

(p. 363, photo)
The Mexican judicial system oversees the country's police agencies. The *policía preventativa* directs traffic during rush hours, tickets speeders, and assists motorists. The *policía judicial* investigates crimes and makes arrests. The newest branch of the Mexican police force, the *policía ecológica,* enforces the *Hoy no circula* program, which attempts to reduce air pollution by limiting the number of vehicles in circulation each day.

Present

Chapter Theme
Professions

Communicative Objectives
• To discuss professions
• To discuss career education

 Transparencies 52–53

 Vocabulary Art BLMs

 Pronunciation Tape 11-1

Teaching Suggestions

Preparing students to speak: Use one or two options from each of the categories of Comprehensible Input, Physical Response, or Limited Verbal Response. For a complete explanation of these categories and some sample activities, see pp. T16–T17.

Vocabulario para conversar

¿A qué vas a dedicarte?

Vas a necesitar estas palabras y expresiones para hablar sobre el futuro. Después de leerlas varias veces, practícalas con un(a) compañero(a).

el /la astronauta

el /la deportista

el mecánico, la mecánica

el técnico, la técnica (de computadoras)

el obrero, la obrera

el político, la política

el veterinario, la veterinaria

el escritor, la escritora

la novela

364   Capítulo 11

Options

Strategies for Reaching All Students

Spanish-Speaking Students
Haz una lista de otras profesiones que puedes nombrar.

 Un paso más Ex. 11-B

Students Needing Extra Help
Have students begin to fill in the Vocabulary section of the Organizer. Group the vocabulary by spelling. Put the words that remain the same for both masculine and feminine in one group, those that follow the regular pattern in another group, those that end in a

consonant for masculine and *-a* for feminine in another, etc.
Keep *novela* separate from the occupations. Point out the change in the plural form of *juez.*
También necesitas . . . : Give examples of *dedicarse a.*

la abogada

el abogado

el juez, *pl.* los jueces

la juez, *pl.* las jueces

el músico, la música

el /la cantante

el bailarín   la bailarina

el pintor, la pintora

el hombre de negocios   el secretario

la mujer de negocios   la secretaria

También necesitas . . .

la ventaja — *advantage*
querer: (yo) quisiera / — *I'd like; you'd like*
    (tú) quisieras
dedicarse (a) — *to be involved in*

¿Y qué quiere decir . . . ?
la desventaja   la profesión, *pl.*
la educación   las profesiones
el futuro   la tecnología
los negocios   la universidad
la política   ganarse la vida

Vocabulario para conversar   365

Practice

Re-enter / Recycle
Ex. 2: TV and movie character types from Chap. 10

Answers: Empecemos a conversar

1 ESTUDIANTE A

a. ¿Conoces a algún cantante?

b. ...algún bailarín?

c. ...algún veterinario?

d. ...algún obrero?

e. ...algún técnico?

f. ...algún hombre de negocios?

g. Questions will vary.

ESTUDIANTE B

a.–g. Answers will vary, but should include *(No) conozco a* ....

Empecemos a conversar

Túrnate con un(a) compañero(a) para ser *Estudiante A* y *Estudiante B*. Reemplacen las palabras subrayadas en el modelo con palabras representadas o escritas en los recuadros. Si ven pueden dar su propia respuesta.

¡NO OLVIDES!

Do you remember these words for professions?

el actor, la actriz

el bombero, la bombera

el / la dentista

el / la detective

el director, la directora (de cine, de orquesta, de una escuela)

el locutor, la locutora (de radio, de televisión)

el enfermero, la enfermera

el médico, la médica

el / la policía

el profesor, la profesora

1   A — *¿Conoces a algún dentista?**
     B — *Sí, conozco a uno(a) / muchos(as).*
         o: *No, no conozco a ninguno.*

Estudiante A   **Estudiante B**

a.   b.   c.

d.   e.   f.   g.

*Note that whenever we make a general statement about a profession we use a masculine singular noun.

Options

Strategies for Reaching All Students

Spanish-Speaking Students
Exs. 1–4: Pair bilingual with non-bilingual students, if possible.

Students Needing Extra Help
Ex. 1: Give additional examples of the footnote. Remind students that the asterisk is not part of the spelling. Review *ninguno* and the *a personal*.
Ex. 2: Give students time to pair the appropriate responses and fill in the *jugar* blank. Remind them to use the appropriate form, depending on the gender of the person with whom they are speaking, when they see the male and the female writer.

Enrichment
Ex. 1: You may want students to expand on this exercise by giving a person's name: *¿Conoces a algún dentista? Sí, conozco a uno, el doctor Fernández; trabaja en ... Sí, conozco a una, la doctora Gómez; trabaja en ....*

2

A —¡Ah! ¿Entonces eres *escritor(a)*?
B —Sí, me dedico a *escribir novelas*.

Estudiante A

a.

b.

c.

d.

e.

f.

g.

Estudiante B

dar las noticias en
el canal 7

enseñar física en la
universidad

escribir novelas

hacer negocios en
un banco

investigar crímenes

jugar ___

reparar coches

2 ESTUDIANTE A
a. ¡Ah! ¿Entonces eres
deportista?
b. . . . detective?
c. . . . mujer / hombre de
negocios?
d. . . . mecánico(a)?
e. . . . científico(a)?
f. . . . locutor(a)?
g. Questions will vary.
ESTUDIANTE B
a. Sí, me dedico a jugar ___.
b. . . . investigar crímenes.
c. . . . hacer negocios en un
banco.
d. . . . reparar coches.
e. . . . enseñar física en la universidad.
f. . . . dar las noticias en el
canal 7.
g. Answers will vary.

Ex. 3: As a follow-up to this exercise, write
the following sentences on the chalkboard,
calling on students to complete them: *Para
ser científico(a) es necesario ser muy ___.
También hay que sacar buenas notas, especialmente en estas materias: ___.*
Point out that students should name personality traits for the first sentence.

367

Practice & Apply

Re-enter / Recycle

Ex. 4: TV and movie character types from Chap. 10
Ex. 5: school subjects from Chap. 2

Answers: Empecemos a conversar

3 ESTUDIANTE A

a. ¿Te interesan los negocios?

b. ...interesa la música?

c. ...interesa la tecnología?

d. ...interesa la medicina?

e. ...interesa la educación?

f. Questions will vary.

ESTUDIANTE B

a. Sí, quisiera ser hombre / mujer de negocios / trabajar en una oficina; *or* no me interesan los negocios.

b. ...ser músico(a) / bailarín (bailarina) / cantante *or* no me interesa la música.

c. ...ser técnico(a) *or* no me interesa la tecnología.

d. ...ser médico(a) / enfermero(a) / trabajar en un hospital; *or* no me interesa la medicina.

e. ...ser profesor(a) / trabajar en una escuela / universidad; *or* no me interesa la educación.

f. Answers will vary.

3 las ciencias

A — ¿*Te interesan las ciencias*?

B — *Sí, quisiera ser científico(a)*.
   o: *No, no me interesan. Prefiero . . .*

Options

Strategies for Reaching All Students

Spanish-Speaking Students
Ex. 7: *¿Qué profesiones crees que no se necesitarán en el futuro? ¿Por qué?*

 Un paso más Ex. 11-C

Students Needing Extra Help
Ex. 3: Model using a singular subject. Complete the blanks in the *Estudiante B* response. Do the exercise once using the affirmative response, then again using the negative response after modeling a completed *Prefiero* statement.
Ex. 4: Brainstorm the vocabulary for the *Estudiante B* responses and why people choose the careers they do.
Ex. 5: Review *escolares* and *mejores*.

If available, use the vocabulary section of the Book 2, Chap. 1 Organizer.
Ex. 6: Point out the connections between students' interests and a career. Brainstorm possible answers to the *¿Por qué?* question.
Ex. 7: Use the vocabulary section of the Organizer. Brainstorm with students which professions will be important in the future, and the advantages and disadvantages of each. Model possible answers for the *¿Por qué?* question.

4   detective /   A —¿Te gustaría ser _detective_ o _bombero(a)_?
   bombero(a)   B —_Bombero(a)_ porque quiero dedicarme a
          ayudar a la gente.
          o: _Ni detective ni bombero(a). Quisiera ser ..._

Estudiante A   **Estudiante B**

a. **mecánico(a) / técnico(a)**   e. **político(a) / juez**
   de computadoras
                    f. **actor (actriz) / locutor(a)**
b. **astronauta / científico(a)**
                    g. **cantante / bailarín (bailarina)**
c. **hombre (mujer) de negocios /**
   abogado(a)   h.

d. **enfermero(a) / médico(a)**

Empecemos a escribir

Escribe tus respuestas en español.

5 ¿Cuáles son tus actividades favoritas? ¿Qué materias escolares
   te gustan más? ¿En qué materias sacas las mejores notas?

6 ¿En qué profesiones podrías hacer lo que más te interesa?
   ¿Qué es más importante para ti, una profesión que te gusta
   mucho o una en que ganas mucho dinero? ¿Por qué? ¿Te
   gustaría ir a la universidad o a una escuela técnica? ¿Qué
   quisieras estudiar? ¿Cómo te gustaría ganarte la vida?

7 En tú opinión, ¿qué profesiones son mejores para el futuro? ¿Por
   qué? ¿Cuáles son las ventajas y desventajas de esas profesiones?

¿A ti te gustaría diseñar juguetes para niños?

La Nave, centro de diseño en Valencia, España

También se dice

el trabajador, la trabajadora

el bailador, la bailadora
el / la danzante

el cantador, la cantadora

Vocabulario para conversar   369

Present

Chapter Theme
Changes in the future

Communicative Objectives
- To describe homes of the future
- To describe the world of the future
- To discuss the environment

 Transparencies 54–55

 Vocabulary Art BLMs

 Pronunciation Tape 11-2

Grammar Preview
Habrá, tendrán, and *será* are presented here lexically. The paradigm of future-tense verbs is on p. 379.

Teaching Suggestions
Preparing students to speak: Use one or two options from each of the categories of Comprehensible Input, Physical Response, and Limited Verbal Response. For a complete explanation of these categories and some sample activities, see pp. T16–T17.

Vocabulario para conversar

¿Qué cambios habrá en el futuro?

Aquí tienes el resto del vocabulario que necesitas en este capítulo para hablar sobre el futuro.

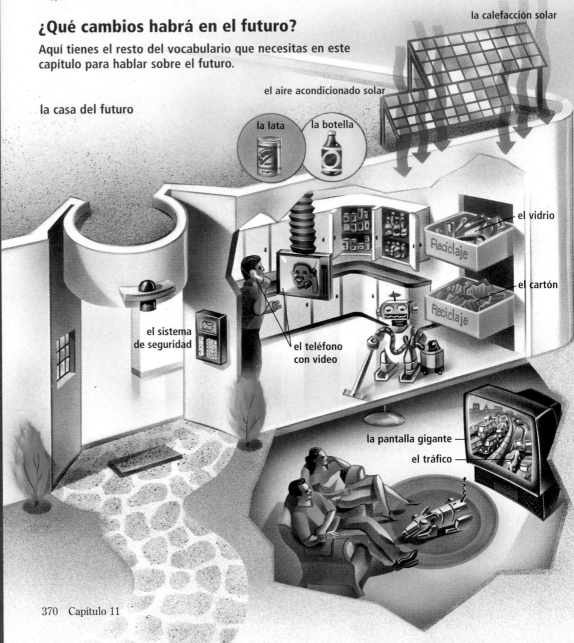

la calefacción solar

el aire acondicionado solar

la casa del futuro

la lata

la botella

el vidrio

el cartón

el sistema de seguridad

el teléfono con video

la pantalla gigante

el tráfico

370   Capítulo 11

Options

Strategies for Reaching All Students

Spanish-Speaking Students
Añade otras palabras relacionadas a este tema a tu vocabulario personal. Mira la casa del futuro. ¿Qué te gustaría tener en tu propia casa? ¿Por qué? ¿En cuál de las actividades para proteger el medio ambiente crees que debemos todos participar? ¿Por qué?

 Un paso más Ex. 11-D

Students Needing Extra Help
Remind students who used Book 1 that they have seen some of these words before. *También necesitas . . . :* Review the present, preterite, and imperfect forms of *haber.*

Learning Spanish Through Action
STAGING VOCABULARY: *Levanten*
MATERIALS: Vocabulary Art BLMs
DIRECTIONS: After copying and cutting the appropriate Vocabulary Art BLMs, distribute to students. Give a message to transmit to outer space describing life on Earth. Have students hold up pictures of the items as you mention them in the message.

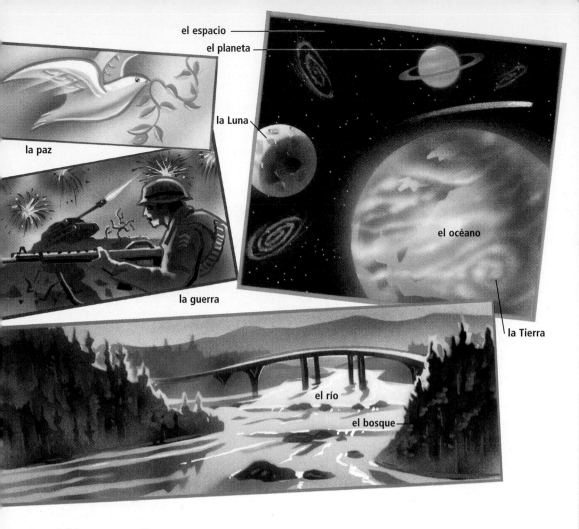

la paz

el espacio

el planeta

la Luna

el océano

la guerra

la Tierra

el río

el bosque

También necesitas . . .

el medio ambiente	*environment*	
por supuesto	*of course*	
echar	*to throw out; to dump*	
gastar	*here: to waste*	
haber: habrá	*there will be*	
ser: (él / ella) será	*he / she / it will be*	
tener: (Uds. / ellos / ellas) tendrán	*you / they will have*	

¿Y qué quiere decir . . . ?

automático, -a	el ser humano
económico, -a	contaminar
eficiente	explorar
gigante	reciclar
solar	reducir *(c →zc)*
el cambio	separar

Vocabulario para conversar   371

Practice & Apply

Answers: Empecemos a conversar

8 ESTUDIANTE A

a. ¿Te parece que en todas las casas del futuro habrá teléfonos con video?

b. . . . habrá sistemas de seguridad?

c. . . . habrá robots?

d. . . . habrá aire acondicionado solar?

e. . . . habrá pantallas gigantes?

f. . . . habrá microondas?

g. Questions will vary.

ESTUDIANTE B

a.–g. Answers will vary.

9 ESTUDIANTE A

a. ¿Crees que es importante explorar los planetas?

b. . . . el espacio?

c. . . . el océano?

d. . . . las ruinas?

e. . . . la selva?

ESTUDIANTE B

a.–e. Answers will vary.

Empecemos a conversar

8

A —¿Te parece que en todas las casas del futuro habrá <u>calefacción solar</u>?

B —¡Por supuesto, <u>es mucho más económico</u>!
o: Creo que no, pero . . .

Estudiante A   **Estudiante B**

es mucho más económico

es mucho más eficiente

será mejor para el medio ambiente

será más divertido

es necesario protegerse de los ladrones

9

A —¿Crees que es importante explorar <u>la Luna</u>?

B —<u>Sí, por supuesto</u>.
o: No. Pienso que hay cosas más importantes. Por ejemplo, debemos . . .

Estudiante A   **Estudiante B**

Options

Strategies for Reaching All Students

Spanish-Speaking Students

Exs. 8–9: Pair Spanish-speaking students if possible.

Ex. 10: Have students write out this exercise using declarative statements instead of questions and answers: *Para reducir la basura, podemos reciclar las botellas.*

Ex. 13: *¿Te gustaría explorar el espacio? ¿Por qué? ¿Adónde te gustaría ir?*

 Un paso más Ex. 11-E

Students Needing Extra Help

Ex. 8: Help students recall *calefacción central* from Chap. 7 with the given artwork. Encourage them to use a response from the *Estudiante B* list rather than *Creo que no.*

Ex. 9: Brainstorm possible responses. Discourage use of the *por supuesto* response.

Ex. 10: Explain why the participle is not paired with a form of *estar.*

Ex. 12: Brainstorm possible vocabulary.

Ex. 13: Emphasize that *humano* is a part of *el ser humano*. Point out the meaning of *enviar* in this context. Brainstorm possible responses to the *¿Por qué?* question.

Ex. 14: Do this exercise as a whole class, emphasizing the vocabulary used.

Ex. 15: If available, use the vocabulary section of the Book 1, Chap. 13 Organizer, as well as the Organizer from this chapter. Refer to Ex. 10.

10 reducir la basura

A — ¿*Cómo podemos reducir la basura*?
B — *Reciclando las botellas.*

Estudiante A

a. reducir el tráfico
b. no gastar agua
c. conservar energía
d. no contaminar el aire

e. proteger el océano
f. no dañar la selva

g.

Estudiante B

¡NO OLVIDES!

Do you remember these words for talking about the environment?
el agua
la energía
la luz, *pl.* las luces
ahorrar
conservar
la electricidad
eléctrico, -a

Empecemos a escribir y a leer

Escribe tus respuestas en español.

11 ¿Qué profesión te gustaría tener? ¿Una profesión tradicional o una más moderna? ¿Cuál?

12 ¿Es más importante resolver los problemas de la Tierra o explorar el espacio? ¿Por qué piensas así?

13 ¿Debemos enviar a seres humanos o a robots a explorar los planetas? ¿Por qué?

14 ¿Crees que siempre habrá guerra en la Tierra? ¿Es posible tener paz en el futuro? En grupos pequeños, hagan una lista de lo que podemos hacer para tener paz. Después, todos juntos, hablen de las listas que hicieron.

15 Aquí tienes unas reglas *(rules)* para proteger el medio ambiente. Con un(a) compañero(a), léelas y escribe otras dos en cada categoría.

Para proteger el medio ambiente en la Tierra, debemos:
• hacer más bosques
• ir a pie o usar bicicletas

No debemos:
• usar tanto papel
• echar basura en los ríos, lagos y océanos

Después, todos juntos, hagan un cartel para la sala de clases. Pueden ponerle fotos y dibujos.

También se dice

el tránsito

10 **ESTUDIANTE A**
a. ¿Cómo podemos reducir el tráfico?
b. ...no gastar agua?
c. ...conservar energía?
d. ...no contaminar el aire?
e. ...proteger el océano?
f. ...no dañar la selva?
g. Questions will vary.
ESTUDIANTE B
a.–g. Answers will vary.

Answers: Empecemos a escribir y a leer
11–14 Answers will vary.

15 Answers will vary, but may include:
Debemos reducir la basura y reciclar el vidrio.
No debemos usar tanta electricidad ni contaminar el aire.

 Practice Wkbk.
11-3, 11-4

 Audio Activity 11.2

 Writing Activities
11-B, 11-C

 Pruebas 11-3, 11-4

Enrichment
Ex. 8: In groups of three, have students discuss the following question and report their findings to the class. *¿Te parece que el ser humano será muy diferente en el futuro? ¿Cómo cambiará?* Guide students to consider changes that medical or technological advances may bring.
Ex. 10: As a homework assignment, have students write about their community's

effort to protect the environment. Suggest the following questions to help them get started: *¿Hay camiones en tu comunidad que recojan cosas que se pueden reciclar? ¿Qué hace tu comunidad para reducir el tráfico? ¿Qué hace para proteger el medio ambiente? ¿Qué problemas están causando las fábricas de los Estados Unidos y de otros países en el norte de México?*

Ex. 13: Additional questions: *¿Para qué trabajos crees que un robot sirve mejor que un ser humano? ¿Por qué piensas así? ¿Qué trabajos crees que un robot nunca podrá hacer? ¿Por qué piensas así?*

Practice

Answers:
¡Comuniquemos!
1–3 Answers will vary, but look for a wide variety of appropriate vocabulary.

¡Comuniquemos!

Aquí tienes otra oportunidad para usar el vocabulario de este capítulo.

1 Dile a un(a) compañero(a) qué profesión crees que debe tener él o ella en el futuro. Dile también por qué piensas así.

A —*Yo creo que debes ser . . .*
B —*¿ ___ ? ¿Yo? ¡Nunca! ¿Por qué lo dices?*
A —*Pues, porque . . .*
B — *. . .*

2 Con un(a) compañero(a), hablen de las ventajas y desventajas de varias profesiones. Hablen de:

- cuánto tiempo hay que estudiar
- en qué y cuánto hay que trabajar
- cuánto dinero se puede ganar
- si es interestante o no y por qué
- si sirve para el futuro y por qué

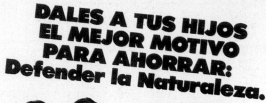

CUENTA AHORRO INFANTIL.

El Banco Santander te propone el mejor de los motivos: Colaborar en la defensa de la Naturaleza. Porque gracias a la Cuenta Ahorro Infantil, el Banco Santander destinará una importante cantidad a ADENA/WWF, sociedad dedicada a proteger y defender nuestro medio ambiente. Además, tus hijos contarán con todas las ventajas de esta Cuenta Ahorro Infantil: **8%** * en saldos iguales o superiores a 15.000 ptas., regalo seguro por apertura de cuenta y por aumento de saldo mensual. Invítales a ahorrar mientras defienden la Naturaleza.

Banco Santander

Estamos de acuerdo con la Naturaleza.

Si desea recibir más información sobre la Cuenta Ahorro Infantil Banco Santander, llámenos gratuitamente al teléfono:

900-17 17 17

o envíenos cumplimentado el cupón que le adjuntamos, al Apartado de Correos n.º 668. 28028 MADRID.

Nombre: _____
Apellidos: _____
Domicilio: _____ N.º: ___
Población: _____
Provincia: _____ C.P.: ___
Tel.: ( )

T.A.E.: 8,16%.

374   Capítulo 11

Options

Strategies for Reaching All Students

Spanish-Speaking Students
Ex. 3: Have students write out this exercise. Afterwards, have them conduct a survey. *Haz una encuesta. Pregúntales a tus compañeros sobre la profesión que quieren seguir después de terminar sus estudios. Luego, en un cartel, indica qué profesiones escogen y cuántos las escogen. Presenta tu información a la clase.*

Students Needing Extra Help
Ex. 1: As a class, generate a list of careers and the qualities, interests, and talents needed to succeed in them. Model an example.
Ex. 2: Limit the number of professions to five. You might divide the class into five groups and have each discuss one profession. Have materials available that will help students complete this activity. Or you might just choose one profession and do as a whole class.

Ex. 3: Brainstorm in order to develop two ideas about each topic. Do a complete model. Students may need help articulating their ideas.
¿Qué sabes ahora?: Have students write this so they can record their progress.

3 Con un(a) compañero(a), imaginen que tienen un millón de dólares. Discutan estas dos alternativas para gastarlo:

**la tecnología y el espacio
o la educación y el medio ambiente**

A — *Creo que explorar el espacio es . . .*
B —*Pues, yo pienso que aquí se necesitan más escuelas y . . .*

¿Qué sabes ahora?

Can you:

- discuss professions?
  —Me gustaría ser ___ y trabajar en ___.
- say what you think the world will be like in the future?
  —Creo que en las casas del futuro habrá ___ y ___.
- talk about protecting the environment?
  —Creo que debemos ___ todos los (todas las) ___.

En la selva del Río Napo, Ecuador

Vocabulario para conversar   375

Cultural Notes

Cooperative Learning
In groups of four, have students create a brochure for a recycling center. Each student is responsible for a paragraph about one recyclable: *el papel, el cartón, las latas,* or *el vidrio*. Students should include the following information: advantages of recycling that item, how much money the recycled item is worth, and how the recycled material will be used afterwards. Display the finished brochures.

(p. 375, photo)
The greatest diversity of plant and animal life exists in rain forests, found in tropic and subtropic regions. Over 2,000 species of trees, including hardwoods such as rosewood, mahogany, ebony, and teak, are found in the rain forests of Latin America. Some of these trees may reach heights of 150 feet or more. Some plants common to rain forests are bromeliads, orchids, and ferns.

(p. 374, realia)
Banco Santander, Spain's largest banking group, has branches throughout Europe. The bank offers the *Cuenta ahorro infantil* for children from birth to 18 years of age. These accounts feature high interest, a monthly gift of age-appropriate books, and donations to the Spanish affiliate of the World Wildlife Fund. After age 18 until age 26, the account may be converted to a *Cuenta ahorro joven* for continued special savings.

375

Present & Apply

Cultural Objective
• To compare Latin American and U.S. attitudes toward the future

Answers
Answers to inductive questions will vary, but students may say that it is important to make plans for the future to ensure that it turns out well. Students may say that the young people in the photos may choose to continue studying in the respective fields pictured, and that the parade queen may do community work.

Perspectiva cultural

¿Crees que es importante hacer planes para el futuro? ¿Qué crees que los jóvenes en estas fotos piensan hacer después de terminar la escuela secundaria?

Aprendiendo a tocar la trompeta en una escuela en España

Rubén, un joven norteamericano, está hablando con Ricardo, un costarricense.

RUBÉN   Estudiar en la universidad es muy caro. Por eso, cuando nací, mis padres abrieron una cuenta de ahorros para mis gastos universitarios.

RICARDO   Los míos tienen algunos ahorros, pero no tienen ninguna cuenta bancaria especial para mis estudios. Yo no sé si estudiaré en los Estados Unidos o en Costa Rica.

(Los latinoamericanos hacen planes para el futuro, pero generalmente no para un futuro lejano. Por ejemplo, normalmente no hacen planes especiales para los gastos universitarios.)

Una estudiante de arquitectura en Guadalajara

RUBÉN   Además, mis padres no me permiten gastar todo lo que gano cortando céspedes cada verano. Una gran parte de ese dinero es para pagar mis estudios.

RICARDO   ¿Ahorras dinero para tus estudios?

RUBÉN   Sí. ¿En Costa Rica no lo hacen?

RICARDO   No es muy común. No cuesta mucho ir a la universidad allá. ¿Sabes ya lo que vas a estudiar?

RUBÉN   Sí, química. Pienso ser ingeniero químico. ¿Y tú?

RICARDO   Quizás estudiaré derecho.

RUBÉN   ¿Quieres ser abogado?

RICARDO   Realmente no, pero en Costa Rica es más fácil ser ejecutivo en una gran compañía si eres abogado.

376 Capítulo 11

Las universidades latinoamericanas dan mucha importancia a los estudios humanísticos, como la filosofía, la literatura y el arte. También dan importancia a las profesiones tradicionales, como el derecho y la medicina. Por eso, muchas veces un graduado no practica la profesión que estudió.

La cultura desde tu perspectiva

1   ¿Cómo crees que muchos norteamericanos ven el futuro?

2   ¿Qué ventajas y desventajas ves en la manera que tienen los latinoamericanos de ver el futuro?

En Nueva York, una locutora entrevista a la reina del desfile dominicano.
(inset) Este joven de Málaga, España, quizás será locutor.

Options

Strategies for Reaching All Students

Spanish-Speaking Students
Ask: ¿Cómo piensas prepararte para el futuro? ¿Vas a seguir estudiando? ¿Cómo pagarás los gastos? ¿Crees que es importante hacer planes para el futuro? ¿Por qué?

 Un paso más Ex. 11-F

Students Needing Extra Help
Have students take notes for use in the ¿Lo sabes bien? section.
Ex. 1: Discuss in depth the cultural differences in terms of saving money for college, knowing what you want to study, and actually working in that field.
Ex. 2: Brainstorm the advantages and disadvantages with the whole class. Write two lists on the chalkboard.

Enrichment
Ex. 1: Additional questions: ¿Por qué crees que los norteamericanos ven el futuro de esa manera? ¿Qué ideas hay en la cultura norteamericana que influyen ese punto de vista?

Cultural Notes

(p. 376, top photo)
Originally from the U.S., jazz music is becoming increasingly popular in Spain. Two major jazz festivals, both held in July, are in Vitoria and San Sebastián. Artists from all over the world perform for thousands of fans in concert halls and on the streets. The festivals are supported by the government and the private sector, and there are radio and television transmissions of the concerts.

(p. 376, bottom photo)
Increasingly, women are entering such previously male-dominated fields as architecture. At the Universidad de Guadalajara, for example, 30 percent of the students in *la facultad de arquitectura* are women.

(p. 377, photo)
Every summer, floats and marchers stream along Madison from 38th St. to 55nd St. in the annual Dominican parade. Many of New York's 350,000 Dominicans live in the Washington Heights neighborhood between 168th St. and 190th St. Dominican immigration to New York began in the early 1960s and increased during the 1970s and 1980s. Dominicans are the second-largest Hispanic group in New York City after Puerto Ricans.

Preview

Teaching Suggestions

B: You may want to point out the verb forms *será, harán,* and *habrán.* Help students figure out that they come from the infinitives *ser, hacer,* and *haber.*

Answers

A The Spanish infinitives are *vivir(emos), vivir(án), estudiar(á), dormir(án), trabajar(án).* / The endings *-emos, -án, -á* have been added to the infinitives. The future is being talked about. / *Comerán.*

B The infinitive is *tener que.* The word that follows it is *dirigir.* The infinitive is *poder.*

Gramática en contexto

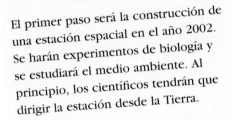

Una estación espacial en el año 2002

¿Viviremos en el espacio algún día? ¿Podremos viajar a las estrellas fácilmente? Algunos científicos norteamericanos dicen que el espacio será nuestro.

Diseño de una estación espacial (1994)

El primer paso será la construcción de una estación espacial en el año 2002. Se harán experimentos de biología y se estudiará el medio ambiente. Al principio, los científicos tendrán que dirigir la estación desde la Tierra.

Pero luego, seis astronautas vivirán allí. Dormirán en la nave y trabajarán en la estación. El proyecto costará mucho dinero, pero si tiene éxito, habrá bases en la Luna y, más tarde, se harán viajes a Marte.

A Some of the verb forms in this article contain an infinitive. Can you find the Spanish infinitives for *live, study, sleep,* and *work?* Now look at the complete forms. What has been added to the infinitive? What period of time is being talked about? What verb form do you think you would use to tell what the astronauts will eat?

B Now look for the expression *tendrán que.* What do you think the infinitive is? What word follows it? Look for the verb *podremos.* What do you think the infinitive is?

378   Capítulo 11

Options

Strategies for Reaching All Students

Students Needing Extra Help
Begin the grammar section of the Organizer.
A: Emphasize that the infinitive is contained within another verb form. Review subject pronouns.
B: Tell students that *tendrán* and *podremos* are irregular, and to look at the first three letters of the words to find a clue to the infinitive.

El futuro: Point out to students that this is the first time they are adding something to the infinitive, rather than taking something away. Give further examples of the two ways students already know to express future tense. Stress the written accents. Write some regular infinitives on the chalkboard and have students conjugate them in the future tense.

El futuro

You have learned two ways to talk about future events. One way is by using the present tense with a time expression.

El tren **sale** a las dos.

The other way is by using *ir a* + infinitive.

Este sábado **voy a reciclar** todas las botellas.

A third way is to use the future tense. For most verbs, the stem for the future tense is the infinitive, so learning this tense is easy.

En el futuro, la gente **vivirá** en la Luna.

Here are all the forms of *hablar, aprender,* and *vivir* in the future tense. Note that all three kinds of verbs have the same endings.

hablar

hablar**é**	hablar**emos**
hablar**ás**	hablar**éis**
hablar**á**	hablar**án**

aprender

aprender**é**	aprender**emos**
aprender**ás**	aprender**éis**
aprender**á**	aprender**án**

vivir

vivir**é**	vivir**emos**
vivir**ás**	vivir**éis**
vivir**á**	vivir**án**

- Note that all the forms need a written accent except the *nosotros / nosotras* form.

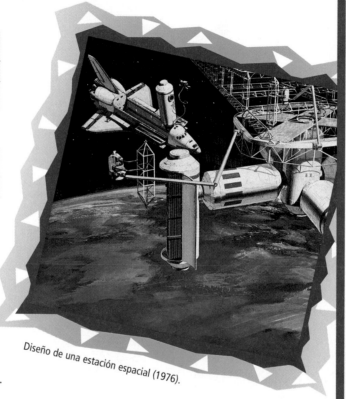

Diseño de una estación espacial (1976).

Gramática en contexto   379

Present

Class Starter Review

On the day following presentation of the future tense, you might begin the class with this activity: In pairs, students take turns saying what they will do next summer. Have them continue until they find three things they both plan to do, and three they both plan not to do. Have students write their sentences out and share them with the class.

Present & Practice

Answers

1 ESTUDIANTE A

a. ¿Vivirás solo(a) después de la escuela secundaria?
b. ¿Irás a la universidad . . .
c. ¿Te dedicarás a . . .
d. ¿Serás . . .
e. ¿Aprenderás a . . .
f. ¿Ganarás . . .
g. ¿Te casarás . . .
h. ¿Echarás . . .
i. Questions will vary.

ESTUDIANTE B

a.–i. Answers will vary, but should include the correct *yo* form in the future tense.

2 ESTUDIANTE A

a. ¿Qué será Andrés en el futuro?
b. . . . seremos Miguel y yo . . .
c. . . . serán tus hermanas . . .
d. . . . serás (tú) . . .
e. . . . serán Uds. . . .
f. . . . será Claudia . . .
g. . . . será tu hermano . . .
h. . . . seré (yo) . . .

ESTUDIANTE B

a. Creo que será veterinario. Trabajará en una clínica de animales.
b. Creo que seremos escritores. Escribiremos una novela.
c. Creo que serán deportistas. Correrán en los Juegos Olímpicos.
d. Creo que seré astronauta. Exploraré nuevos planetas.

---

1 ¿Qué vas a hacer después de la escuela secundaria? Pregunta y contesta según lo que piensas hacer.

trabajar

A —¿*Trabajarás después de la escuela secundaria?*
B —*Sí, trabajaré en un banco.*
  o: *No. Pienso . . .*

a. vivir solo(a)
b. ir a la universidad
c. dedicarse a . . .
d. ser . . .
e. aprender (a) . . .

f. ganar tu propio dinero
g. casarse
h. echar en la basura todos los cuadernos escolares
i.

2 Di qué serán estas personas en el futuro. Después, escoge elementos de la lista y di lo que harán. Pregunta y contesta según el modelo.

Sonia

A —¿*Qué será Sonia en el futuro?*
B —*Creo que será música. Tocará en una orquesta.*

proteger a las víctimas de crímenes
trabajar en una clínica de animales
dirigir un banco
correr en los Juegos Olímpicos

explorar nuevos planetas
reparar calefacciones solares
escribir una novela
servir al país

a. Andrés

b. Miguel y yo

c. tus hermanas

d. (tú)

e. Uds.

f. Claudia

g. tu hermano

h. (yo)

Options

Strategies for Reaching All Students

Students Needing Extra Help

Ex. 1: Give another model using a reflexive verb. Remind students to change the verb form when answering questions. Brainstorm possibilities for the blanks in *c, d,* and *e.* Have students vary their answers, and discourage use of the negative response.

Ex. 2: You may want to write the paradigm of *ser* in the future tense. Point out that in the future it is completely regular. Review future endings. Use the vocabulary section of the Organizer. Allow time for students to match the columns before they start the exercise.

Ex. 3: Brainstorm possible resolutions. Point out that each statement is in the *yo* form and should reflect their own thinking.

El futuro: continuación: Students may need to see the complete paradigms of these irregular verbs. Give additional examples of *si* + a regular verb in the present tense.

Ex. 4: Model using a non-reflexive verb. Have students do all except *g,* which you can do as a whole-class activity.

3 Es el fin de año. ¿Qué resoluciones vas a hacer para el año nuevo? Dile por lo menos cinco resoluciones a un(a) compañero(a). Por ejemplo:

Estudiaré por lo menos una hora y media todos los días.

El futuro: continuación

The verbs *tener, poder, saber,* and *hacer* have irregular stems in the future tense: *tendr-, podr-, sabr-, har-.* The endings, however, are the same as for regular verbs.

Si viajas al espacio, **¿tendrás que** llevar un traje especial? Claro, **tendré que** llevar un traje de astronauta.

¿Podrás ver la Tierra desde la Luna? Sí, creo que **podré** verla.

¿Sabrás qué hacer en caso de emergencia? Sí, me parece que **sabré.**

¿Harás informes todos los días? Pienso que **haré** muchos informes.

• *Habrá* is the future of *haber.* The future stem is *habr-.*

¿Crees que en el futuro **habrá** una comunidad de seres humanos en el espacio?

• The future is often used with *si* + a verb in the present tense.

Si viajas al espacio, **¿tendrás que** comer comida especial?

¡NO OLVIDES!

Like *hay, había,* and *hubo, habrá* is used only in the singular.

4 ¿Cómo será el futuro? Forma frases con los siguientes elementos.

(nosotros) /   *En el futuro, podremos vernos en los teléfonos con video.*
poder verse en los teléfonos con video

a. (tú y yo) / poder vivir debajo del océano
b. las familias / hacer viajes en coches solares
c. los científicos / saber más sobre los otros planetas
d. un robot / hacer todos nuestros quehaceres
e. nuestro planeta / no tener bastante comida para todos
f. nuestros océanos / tener menos contaminación
g. haber ciudades en el espacio

e. Creo que seremos mécanicos. Repararemos calefacciones solares.
f. Creo que será mujer de negocios. Dirigirá un banco.
g. Creo que será político. Servirá al país.
h. Creo que serás abogado(a). Protegerás a las víctimas de crímenes.

3 Answers will vary, but should include the future tense.

4 a. En el futuro, (tú y yo) podremos vivir debajo del océano.
b. ...las familias harán viajes en coches solares.
c. ...los científicos sabrán más sobre los otros planetas.
d. ...un robot hará todos nuestros quehaceres.
e. ...nuestro planeta no tendrá bastante comida para todos.
f. ...nuestros océanos tendrán menos contaminación.
g. ...habrá ciudades en el espacio.

Practice Wkbk. 11-5, 11-6

Writing Activities 11-D, 11-E

Pruebas 11-5, 11-6

Enrichment

Ex. 1: In groups of four, have students interview one another on aspects of their daily routine tomorrow. Tell students to ask the following questions and write down the answers to report to the rest of the class: *¿A qué hora te levantarás mañana? ¿A qué hora te ducharás o bañarás? ¿A qué hora te acostarás?* Call on representatives to report each group's responses.

Ex. 4: As a homework assignment, have students write five other ways in which the future will be different, using the verbs *tener, poder, saber,* and *hacer.* Encourage students to be creative and to use as much of their vocabulary as possible.

Practice

Answers

5 Questions will vary, but should include the future tense and an interrogative word.

6 Answers will vary, but should include the present tense in the first part and the future tense in the second part of the sentence.

Multicultural Perspectives

According to data from the U.S. Census Bureau, the Hispanic population grew by 53 percent between 1980 and 1990, to a total of over 22 million. At its current rate of growth, it will double by the year 2020—making it the single largest minority group in the U.S. Because it is increasing faster than any other ethnic group, it affects the educational programs in such large states as California, Texas, and Florida, as well as in such cities as New York and Chicago. Bilingual and bicultural programs are in great demand. Teachers who study how LEP (Limited English Proficient) students learn in a second-language classroom, in addition to their chosen field of education, often earn significantly higher salaries and have an easier time finding work after graduation. Ask students how they think knowing Spanish will help them in their chosen career.

5 Con un(a) compañero(a), hagan los papeles de un escritor y un científico en una entrevista sobre el futuro. Escojan un elemento de cada columna para hacer por lo menos siete preguntas. Por ejemplo:

ESCRITOR — *¿Dónde podremos echar la basura?*
CIENTÍFICO — *No tendremos basura, por supuesto. La reciclaremos.*

¿Quién?	hacer
¿Qué?	tener
¿Cómo?	haber
¿Cuándo?	poder
¿Dónde?	saber

En el parque de Chapultepec piden a la gente que recicle.

6 Combina elementos de las dos columnas para hacer frases como la siguiente.

si mi papá me presta el coche   *Si mi papá me presta el coche, tú y yo iremos* (o: *podremos ir*) *a la playa mañana.*

a. si te interesa la tecnología   tú
b. si compro un sistema   tú y yo
    de seguridad   yo
c. si hay seres extraterrestres   nosotros / nosotras
d. si trabajo todo el verano   (nombre)
e. si viajas al espacio   (dos nombres)
f. si hay paz en la Tierra
g. si se puede vivir en la Luna
h. si pensamos en el medio ambiente
i. si reducimos la contaminación
j. 💡

También piden que la gente proteja el parque.

382   Capítulo 11

Options

Strategies for Reaching All Students

Students Needing Extra Help
Ex. 5: Brainstorm possible phrases to link with the infinitives. Do as a whole class activity.
Ex. 6: Brainstorm possible responses to the *si* clauses. Do as a whole class activity.
Ahora lo sabes: Have students write this so that they can record their progress.

En un mundo de revistas, sólo hay una··· Dinámica, Apasionante, Excepcional y ¡DI-FE-REN-TE!

MUNDO 21
¡EL MUNDO DEL MAÑANA YA ESTÁ AQUÍ!

Ahora lo sabes

Can you:

- say what will happen in the future?
  —El próximo año (yo) ___ química.
- say what you and your friends will be in the future?
  —Yo ___ médico(a) y dos de nosotros(as) ___ abogados(as).
- talk about possibilities in the future?
  —Si tengo tiempo mañana, ___ al centro comercial.

Gramática en contexto   383

Cultural Notes ☼

(p. 383, realia)
The magazine *Mundo 21* presents contemporary science-related news with an eye to possible future changes in such social institutions as food production, health care, family life, education, transportation, ecology, and communications.

Apply

Pronunciation Tape 11-3

¿Recuerdas?

Play

Video Activity A

Using the Video

Episode 11 begins in Silvestre Aguilar's office at La Jacaranda. His lawyer, who has read La Catrina's will, tells him that Jamie probably has legal rights to the inheritance. Silvestre responds angrily and sends his bodyguards to Jamie's house to look for the will. Santana can be seen outside Silvestre's office, listening.
In the next scene, Felipe and María choose a movie and watch it at María's house. After the movie, they talk about their future.
Later, as María and Jamie are getting ready for bed, one of Silvestre's bodyguards enters the house and rummages through the drawers of a desk. María and Jamie drive him out of the house and Santana helps chase him away. The will is still safe because Jamie had hidden it.

Para decir más

Este vocabulario adicional te puede servir para las actividades de esta sección.

las armas
weapons

la delincuencia
delinquency

el desempleo
unemployment

las drogas
drugs

la pobreza
poverty

el racismo
racism

Actividades

Esta sección te ofrece la oportunidad de aumentar tus conocimientos de español al integrar lo que aprendiste en este capítulo con lo que aprendiste en capítulos anteriores.

 Formen grupos. Díganle a su grupo lo que quisieran ser en el futuro. Cada miembro les dará un consejo *(advice)*.

   A — *Quisiera ser . . .*
   B — *Si quieres ser . . . tendrás que . . .*
   C — *Para ser . . . , habrá que estudiar . . .*
   D — *Podrás . . .*

Options

Strategies for Reaching All Students

Spanish-Speaking Students
Exs. 1–2: If possible, have one Spanish-speaking student in each group.
Ex. 3: If possible, group Spanish-speaking students together.

 Un paso más Ex. 11-G

Students Needing Extra Help
Ex. 1: Give a complete model. As a class, generate a list of careers and the qualities, interests, and talents needed to succeed in them.
Ex. 2: Brainstorm phrases and write them on the chalkboard. Let students match them up with their classmates. Encourage creativity.
Ex. 3: Brainstorm some *si* clauses. Students may need help articulating their thoughts about the future.

Enrichment
As a homework assignment, have students write about one of the following topics: *Para eliminar el racismo (las armas, la delincuencia, el desempleo, las drogas, la pobreza), tendremos que . . .*

2 ¿Cómo será el futuro de tus compañeros(as) de clase? Dividan la clase en cuatro grupos. Cada grupo va a predecir el futuro de los miembros de otro grupo.

Juan escribirá una novela.
Julia será veterinaria, por supuesto.

3 ¿Qué cambios crees que son necesarios para tener un futuro mejor? En grupo, escriban frases como la siguiente:

Si el sistema escolar tiene más dinero, tendremos mejor educación
Si hay paz en la Tierra, . . .
Si vamos a la Luna, . . .
Si. . .

385

La Catrina: Capítulo 11

Play

Video Activity B

Para entender mejor

Play

Video Activity C

Answers: Actividades
1–3 Answers will vary, but should include a wide variety of chapter vocabulary and correct use of the present and future tenses where appropriate.

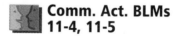
Writing Activity 11-H

Comm. Act. BLMs 11-4, 11-5

Cooperative Learning
In groups of five, have students envision their community in the year 2200. Each student gives three predictions about one of the following areas: housing, schools, transportation, environment, and energy. Have them make a captioned poster illustrating how they predict their community will look.

Apply

Process Reading
For a description of process reading, see p. 52.

Answers
Antes de leer
Answers will vary, but may include: the use of lightweight materials, an aerodynamic front, a solar panel that can be adjusted to best capture the sun's rays, rear-wheel drive, and a weight of 180 kilograms.

Mira la lectura
Answers will vary, but may include the following cognates: *materiales, aerodinámica, panel solar orientable, tracción, kilogramos*

¡Vamos a leer!

Antes de leer

STRATEGY ➤ Using prior knowledge

Look at the photo of this energy-efficient solar-powered car. List in English four or five features relating to energy sources and body design that it might have.

Mira la lectura

STRATEGY ➤ Scanning

Now scan the selection to see if you can find Spanish cognates of the features you listed. Write them next to the corresponding English terms on your list.

Tonatiuh, el hijo del Sol para los aztecas, dio su nombre al primer automóvil solar mexicano. El coche Tonatiuh fue diseñado por un grupo de jóvenes universitarios que querían ayudar a controlar el alto nivel de contaminación de muchos lugares en México. El proyecto está basado en la alta eficiencia y en el uso de fuentes renovables de energía. Por eso se usaron materiales ligeros y se diseñó un área frontal aerodinámica que ofrece muy poca resistencia al viento.

El chasis está hecho de fibras compuestas que pueden soportar un conjunto pesado de baterías y toda la electrónica. Tiene un panel solar orientable, es decir, que se puede mover para recibir los rayos del Sol. Tiene tres ruedas y tracción en la de atrás. Pesa alrededor de 180 kilogramos. El proyecto costó aproximadamente 150 mil dólares.

Tonatiuh: AUTOMÓVIL SOLAR

386   Capítulo 11

Options

Strategies for Reaching All Students

Spanish-Speaking Students
Aplicación: ¿Crees que un coche solar será práctico? ¿Por qué? ¿Qué te gustaría cambiar en el coche que se describe aquí para hacerlo más práctico? Explica.

Students Needing Extra Help
Discuss car model names (Bronco, Pinto, Mustang, etc.). Brainstorm why manufacturers name their cars this way. Background knowledge will be very limited for some students. Discuss some basic background material before the actual reading.
Infórmate: Students may be unfamiliar with the English word "to orient." Model its use and give synonyms.

Infórmate

STRATEGIES — Using cognates
Understanding suffixes

1 There are many cognates in this selection that will help you understand it. Among them are the words *renovables* and *orientable*. *Renovable* is formed from the verb *renovar*. It has the same Latin root as the adjective *nuevo*. Given what you know of prefixes (*re-*) and suffixes (*-able*), what do you think *renovable* means?

In the same way, *orientable* is formed from the verb *orientar*. What do you think it means?

2 Now list in Spanish the three most important features of the solar car. Compare your list with that of a partner. Discuss any differences in your lists and agree on one set of the most important features.

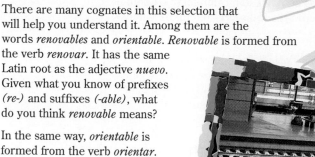
Tren de alta velocidad española

Aplicación

Think about the features of the car described in this selection and, with a partner, compare them to corresponding features of cars you are familiar with.

Infórmate

1. renewable, movable (can be positioned to capture the sun's rays)
2. Answers will vary, but may include the following:
Usa materiales ligeros.
El chasis está hecho de fibras compuestas.
El coche tiene un panel solar orientable.

Aplicación

Answers will vary.

Cultural Notes ☀

(p. 387, photo)
The inauguration of *el tren de alta velocidad española* (AVE) coincided with the opening of the Expo 92 in Sevilla. These trains, run by RENFE, the Spanish national railroad, make 12 trips daily from Madrid's Estación Atocha to Sevilla's Estación Santa Justa in less than 3 hours, with one stop en route in Córdoba. The state-of-the-art AVE is similar to Japan's Shinkansen Supertrains and France's TGV.

Apply

Teaching Suggestions

Ex. 1: Be sure to display all the descriptions on a bulletin board so that students who are doing the second writing task can choose one.

Process Writing

For information regarding developing a writing portfolio, see p. 54.

¡Vamos a escribir!

Los aparatos electrónicos de hoy están cambiando. ¿Cómo será el televisor del futuro? ¿La radio? ¿El teléfono? Vamos a describirlos.

1 Primero, escoge un aparato y piensa en cómo será en el futuro. Dibuja el aparato. Luego, escribe una breve descripción según este modelo. Pídele comentarios a un(a) compañero(a) y sigue los otros pasos del proceso de escribir. Por ejemplo:

APARATO: teléfono con video de bolsillo

DESCRIPCIÓN: un teléfono celular con una pantalla pequeña

VENTAJAS: las personas que hablan se pueden ver; tamaño de bolsillo; no daña el medio ambiente

COSTO: 30 dólares

388 Capítulo 11

Options

Strategies for Reaching All Students

Students Needing Extra Help
Have students use the vocabulary section of the Organizer from Chap. 7. Brainstorm ways that some of these appliances could be modified in the future. Do the exercise in pairs or small groups. Try to group an artistic student, a mechanically inclined student, and a strong language student together.

Ex. 2: Students may need help with the vocabulary. Present a paragraph based on the information given in the model. Discourage students from keeping their ideas in list form, rather than a paragraph.

Enrichment
Have students list *aparatos electrónicos* that are common in homes today, but that were rare or nonexistant twenty years ago *(video-caseteras, hornos microondas, teléfonos celulares,* etc.).

2 Ahora lee todas las descripciones y escoge uno de los aparatos del futuro. Piensa en los cambios sociales que traerá. Por ejemplo, el videoteléfono traerá los siguientes cambios:

- Las personas que se conocen no necesitarán identificarse.
- Será necesario peinarse y maquillarse antes de hablar con alguien que no conoces.
- Las familias se sentirán más unidas.

Escribe un párrafo breve sobre los cambios que traerá el aparato.

3 Para distribuir su trabajo, pueden:

- enviar las descripciones y los ensayos al periódico o a la revista escolar
- coleccionarlos en un libro titulado *Nuestro futuro electrónico*
- exhibirlos en la sala de clases
- incluirlos en sus portafolios

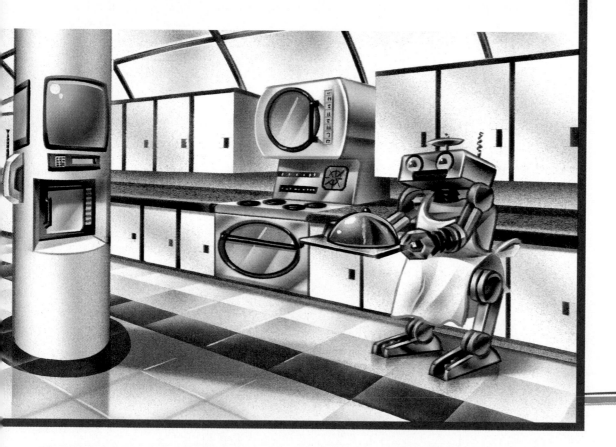

Assess & Summarize

Test Preparation

You may want to assign parts of this section as written homework or as an in-class writing activity prior to administering the *Examen de habilidades.*

Answers

Listening: *No sé a qué profesión me dedicaré. Me gusta escribir, pero los escritores no ganan mucho. También me gusta cantar y bailar, pero la vida de una cantante o bailarina no será fácil. Mi hermana prefiere las ciencias. Le gustan los animales. Ella será médica o veterinaria.*
High-school courses recommended for the speaker: creative writing, English, literature, chorus, dancing; courses recommended for the speaker's sister: science courses, especially biology.

Reading: The ad is for a large-screen TV; *combinar, adaptar;* to combine, to adapt

Writing: Interviews will vary.

Culture: Answers will vary, but should include the information that a Latin American is less likely than a North American to make long-range plans.

Speaking: Dialogues will vary.

¿Lo sabes bien?

Esta sección te ayudará a prepararte para el examen de habilidades, donde tendrás que hacer tareas semejantes.

Listening

Can you understand when people talk about professions? Listen as your teacher reads a sample similar to what you will hear on the test. What high-school courses would you recommend to the speaker? And to her sister?

Reading

Óscar is reading an ad in his favorite magazine. What is the ad for? What verbs do *combinable* and *adaptable* come from? What do the verbs mean?

El futuro ya llegó.

Tiene una pantalla gigante de 41 pulgadas.

Tiene control remoto.

Tiene ajuste automático de color y de sonido.

Combinable con sus videojuegos y adaptable al cable.

La pantalla se puede colgar de la pared o montarse en el aparato.

¡Llévese el futuro a casa por sólo 725 dólares!

390 Capítulo 11

Writing

Can you interview a scientist about the planet Earth in the year 3000? Write three more questions like the following one. Then write a logical answer to each.

1. ¿En qué tipo de casa vivirá la gente en el año 3000?

Culture

Can you compare how a North American and a Latin American might plan for the future?

Speaking

Create a dialogue in which you talk to your partner about a possible future career.

A — *¿A qué piensas dedicarte?*
B — *Pienso estudiar para ser abogado.*
A — *Necesitarás estudiar por muchos años, ¿no?*
B — *Sí, pero trabajaré mientras estudio. Y tú, ¿cómo te ganarás la vida?*
A — ...

Options

Strategies for Reaching All Students

Students Needing Extra Help
Have students write out this exercise so that they can check off what they have mastered. *Lo sabes bien:* Remind students that this is only a sample of the actual test.
Listening: Read more than once. Remind students that they did something similar to this in *Todo junto,* Ex. 1. Brainstorm for what words students should be listening.

Reading: Review cognates. Remind students that they did something similar in *Infórmate* in the *¡Vamos a leer!* section.
Writing: Have students use the Organizer to write a sample interview before the test. Point out that they have to answer the questions they create. Remind them that they did something similar in Exs. 4–5, pp. 381–382.

Culture: Have students review the notes they took during the first reading of the *Perspectiva cultural.* Give them time to gather their ideas.
Speaking: Use the vocabulary section of the Organizer. Limit the number of lines of dialogue. Give a complete model. Remind students to think about which tenses they need to use.

Resumen del capítulo 11

Usa el vocabulario de este capítulo para:

- discuss various professions
- say what you think the world will be like in the future
- discuss how to protect the environment

to discuss professions
la profesión, *pl.* las profesiones
el abogado, la abogada
el / la juez, *pl.* los / las jueces
el político, la política
la política
el / la astronauta
el bailarín, la bailarina
el / la cantante
el músico, la música
el escritor, la escritora
la novela
el pintor, la pintora
el / la deportista
el mecánico, la mecánica
el obrero, la obrera
el técnico, la técnica
  (de computadoras)
la tecnología
el hombre de negocios,
  la mujer de negocios
los negocios
el secretario, la secretaria
el veterinario, la veterinaria

to talk about career education
la educación
la universidad
la ventaja
la desventaja
dedicarse (a)
ganarse la vida

to describe homes of the future
la pantalla gigante
el sistema de seguridad
el teléfono con video
automático, -a
económico, -a
eficiente
gigante
solar

to describe the world of the future
el cambio
el futuro
la guerra
la paz
el espacio
la Luna
el planeta

el ser humano
la Tierra
explorar

to discuss the environment
el medio ambiente
el bosque
el océano
el río
la botella
el cartón
la lata
el tráfico
el vidrio
contaminar
echar
gastar
reciclar
reducir *(c → zc)*
separar

other useful words and expressions
querer: (yo) quisiera,
  (tú) quisieras
por supuesto

Resumen 391

CAPÍTULO 12

THEME: TRAVEL

SCOPE AND SEQUENCE   Pages 392–423

COMMUNICATION

Topics

Tourism

Customs

Air travel

Places in an airport

Objectives

To compare accommodations in Spain with those in the U.S.

To discuss travel arrangements

To describe a plane trip

To discuss tourist accommodations

To discuss tourist activities

CULTURE

Accommodations in Spain

GRAMMAR

Repaso: Los mandatos afirmativos con tú

Los mandatos negativos con tú

Los mandatos negativos: continuación

Ancillaries available for use with Chapter 12

Multisensory/Technology

Overhead Transparencies, 57–61

Audio Tapes and CDs

Vocabulary Art Blackline Masters for Hands-On Learning, pp. 63–67

Classroom Crossword

La Catrina

CD-ROM

Print

Practice Workbook, pp. 115–124

Writing, Audio & Video Activities, pp. 71–76, 126–128, 173–174

Communicative Activity Blackline Masters

   Pair and Small Group Activities, pp. 78–83

   Situation Cards, p. 84

Un paso más: Actividades para ampliar tu español, pp. 67–72

Assessment

Assessment Program

   Pruebas, pp. 174–183

   Examen de habilidades, pp. 184–187

Test Generator

Video still from Chap. 12

International Travel

When planning a trip to a foreign country, it is important to know what documentation is needed. Most countries require travelers to present their passports in order to obtain a tourist visa, which authorizes visits lasting from a few weeks to several months. Some span a period of several years, and allow multiple entries with the same visa. Some countries require the visa to be secured before departure, while others allow tourists to obtain one at the port of entry. It is always best to check with a travel consultant, airline representative, or consulate agent to verify entrance requirements to a particular country.

Once the destination has been decided and the entrance requirements fulfilled, the next step is to determine how to actually travel to that country. Many Spanish-speaking countries have their own international airlines which provide direct service from major U.S. cities like New York, Chicago, Los Angeles, Houston, or Miami. More flights to Latin America leave from Miami than any other U.S. city. The only major difference between airports in the U.S. and those in Latin America is that when the plane lands, passengers usually disembark on the runway and walk or take a shuttle bus to the customs area.

Spain and Latin America offer an impressive variety of places to visit. Spain presents historical sites and artifacts dating back to before the Roman Empire. Some of the most notable buldings are the *alcázares,* palaces built by the Arabs who occupied Spain for nearly 800 years. Aside from these historical treasures, some of the most popular beaches in Europe are found along Spain's Costa del Sol, as well as fine ski resorts in the Sierra Nevada and Pyrenees. Locations to visit in Latin America include complex pre-Columbian archeological sites such as Chichén Itzá in Mexico, Tikal in Guatemala, and Machu Picchu in Peru. Many of the objects originally found at these sites are now displayed in museums in Mexico City, San José, Costa Rica, Bogotá, and Lima. Colorful marketplaces, particularly Chichicastenango in Guatemala and Otavalo in Ecuador, are popular with tourists looking for authentic native crafts. Beautiful colonial architecture, blending the seventeenth and eighteenth century Spanish styles with that of the indigenous people, appears throughout Central and South America. Two of the best examples are found in Guadalajara, Mexico: the Palacio de Gobierno and the Templo de Aranzazú. For the sports enthusiast, ski resorts in the southern Andes are open from June through August, and scuba-diving off the coast of Mexico's Yucatán peninsula and Honduras' Roatán Island is available year-round.

Tourism is a major industry in Spain and Latin America. Both government and private agencies can provide information and tours to accommodate anyone's travel interests.

Introduce

Re-entry of Concepts
The following list represents words, expressions, and grammar topics re-entered from Book 1 and Book 2 (Chaps. 8 and 11):

Book 1
time-telling, leisure-time activities, nature items, recyclables

Chapter 8
places in a community

Chapter 11
nature
recycleables

Planning

Cross-Curricular Connections

Mathematics and Geography Connection *(pp. 406–407)*
In pairs, have students choose one Latin American country. They are to make a train or plane schedule listing trips between the capital and five major cities. The schedule should include the cities, their distances from the capital in kilometers, arrival and departure times using the 24-hour clock, and the fare amount in the currency of that country. These can be passed to other groups or photocopied for the whole class to use in question-and-answer sessions or to practice travel vocabulary.

Geography Connection *(pp. 410–411)*
In pairs, have students choose a favorite monument, either in the U.S. or in another country. They will prepare a travel guide, either in poster or brochure form. This should include a short tour, which takes the tourists through the monument's different rooms or points out its features and tells of its historical or cultural significance. Students should use command forms and preterite and imperfect tenses as needed.

CAPÍTULO 12

¡El pasaporte, por favor!

OBJECTIVES

At the end of this chapter, you will be able to:

- give advice
- discuss travel arrangements
- make recommendations about what to do and see in your community
- discuss the variety of travel accommodations in Spain

Machu Picchu, Perú

393

Preview

Cultural Objective

• To discuss travel in Spain

Multicultural Perspectives

By A.D. 718, the Moors had conquered nearly all of the Iberian Peninsula, and would occupy it for 700 years. As a result, Moorish culture greatly affected that of Spain. For example, Arabic-language influences are present in place names, such as the Andalusian (Al-Andaluz) towns of Almería, Alicante, and Algeciras. Many Spanish agricultural, architectural, administrative, and commercial terms also come from Arabic because of their heavy involvement in these areas during the occupation. Examples include *café* (coffee), *algarroba* (carob), *tamarindo* (tamarind), *alcázar* (palace), *alcantarilla* (sewer or underground aqueduct), *jabega* (fishing net), *álgebra* (algebra), *azumbre* ("azumbre" or a liquid measurement approximately equal to two liters). If available, have students research the different languages that influence Spanish by looking up five words in a standard dictionary and finding their origins. If no standard Spanish dictionary is available, have students research word origins in English using standard English dictionaries.

¡Piénsalo bien!

Mira las fotos. Los estudiantes que vemos están hablando de viajes. ¿Hiciste un viaje alguna vez? ¿Adónde fuiste? ¿Crees que hiciste lo mismo que estos jóvenes?

"¡Mira, Jorge! Aquí estamos tratando de regatear en el mercado. Pero no tuvimos éxito."

¿Fuiste alguna vez a un mercado? ¿Compraste algo? ¿Pagaste lo que pidió el (la) vendedor(a) o regateaste? Si regateaste, ¿tuviste éxito? ¿Pudiste comprar algo muy barato?

Jóvenes madrileños mirando fotos de su viaje

"No compraré ningún recuerdo turístico en Barcelona. Iré a las Ramblas para buscar gangas."

Cuando haces un viaje, ¿qué te gusta comprar? ¿Recuerdos o artesanía típica del lugar, o cosas como las que compra la gente que vive allí?

Options

Strategies for Reaching All Students

Spanish-Speaking Students

Ask: *¿Has viajado en avión? ¿Adónde ibas? ¿Te gustaría viajar a otro país? ¿Qué necesitas para viajar de un país a otro?*

 Un paso más Ex. 12-A

"Nuestra guía nos dijo que Antonio Gaudí fue un arquitecto muy importante. Yo sé que nunca vi nada parecido al Parc Güell."

Cuando viajas, ¿a veces vas a ver edificios o monumentos importantes? Por ejemplo, ¿vas a museos?

Un grupo escolar visita el Parc Güell en Barcelona.

395

Cultural Notes

(p. 394, bottom photo)
For visitors to Barcelona, a stroll along Las Ramblas is an excellent way to see many of the city's architectural highlights. The Museu Marítim (Maritime Museum) is located in the Royal Dockyards (Drassanes Reials) dating from the thirteenth century. Palau Güell is a decorative modernist house built by Antonio Gaudí. Paving stones along Las Ramblas were designed by Catalan artist Joan Miró.

(p. 395, photo)
Antonio Gaudí's Parc Güell, with its organic, asymmetrical forms and brilliantly patterned surfaces, is representative of the architect's eclectic style combining elements of *mudéjar* (Spain's characteristic Christian-Muslim amalgam), Gothic, and baroque architecture. Gaudí declared that his build-

ings should "stand as trees stand" and designed them without any internal bracing or external buttressing. He often used tilted piers and columns to transmit the construction's diagonal thrusts. Gaudí was a major figure in the Catalan *Renaixensa,* or artistic and political revival.

Present

Chapter Theme
At the airport

Communicative Objectives
• To discuss travel arrangements
• To describe a plane trip

 Transparencies 57–58

 Vocabulary Art BLMs

 Pronunciation Tape 12-1

Teaching Suggestions

Preparing students to speak: Use one or two options from each of the categories of Comprehensible Input, Physical Response, or Limited Verbal Response. For a complete explanation of these categories and some sample activities, see pp. T16–T17.

If there are any students who have been through customs, ask them to describe the experience.

Vocabulario para conversar

¿Compraste un boleto de ida y vuelta?

Vas a necesitar estas palabras y expresiones para hablar sobre viajes. Después de leerlas varias veces, practícalas con un(a) compañero(a).

el aeropuerto

despegar

la empleada

el empleado
(de la línea aérea)

el avión,
pl. los aviones

la ventanilla

aterrizar

la puerta

C3

VUELOS
709 ... Quito
1214 ... La Paz

la terminal de equipaje

el equipaje

la aduana
el aduanero   la aduanera

Options

Strategies for Reaching All Students

Spanish-Speaking Students
Ask: *¿Sabes otras palabras relacionadas al tema? Escríbelas en tu vocabulario personal.*

 Un paso más Exs. 12-B, 12-C

Students Needing Extra Help
Begin the vocabulary section of the Organizer. Point out that *piloto* is spelled the same, for both men and women. Point out that *avión* loses its accent in the plural. Show the word family of *ventanilla*. *También necesitas . . . :* Explain the "going and returning" concept of *de ida y vuelta*. Show the complete paradigm of *conseguir* for those students who need to see it. Explain the steps involved in going through customs in the U.S. and abroad.

Enrichment
As homework, have students rank the travel-related professions according to how much they would like to be in them. Ask them to explain their choices for the top and bottom of the list.

la auxiliar de vuelo
el pasillo
abrocharse
desabrocharse*
el piloto   la piloto
el pasajero   la pasajera
el auxiliar de vuelo
el cinturón (de seguridad)

la agencia de viajes
CASTILLOS en España
¡No te aburras! Disfruta de la vida venezolana.
hacer la maleta
el /la agente (de viajes)
deshacer* la maleta

También necesitas . . .

el boleto (de ida y vuelta)	(round-trip) ticket	con destino a	going to
la escala	stopover	procedente de	arriving from
el retraso	delay		
la tarjeta de embarque	boarding pass		
el vuelo	flight		
facturar	to check (baggage)		
conseguir (e → i)	to get, to obtain		
pasar por	to pass /go through		
registrar	to inspect, to search		
viajar	to travel		
a mano	by hand		

¿Y qué quiere decir . . . ?
el cheque de viajero
el viajero, la viajera
la línea aérea
la reservación,
    pl. las reservaciones
sin escala
sólo de ida

* Notice that *des-* is the equivalent of *un-* in English.

Vocabulario para conversar   397

Learning Spanish Through Action
STAGING VOCABULARY: *Levanten*
MATERIALS: envelope containing copies of items from the Vocabulary Art BLMs to remember before leaving for the airport
DIRECTIONS: Play the part of a parent checking to see if a child has everything ready for the departure. Give each student one picture, then direct them to hold up the appropriate picture as you ask who has that item.

Practice

Empecemos a conversar

Túrnate con un(a) compañero(a) para ser *Estudiante A* y *Estudiante B*. Reemplacen las palabras subrayadas en el modelo con palabras representadas o escritas en los recuadros. Si ven 💡 pueden dar su propia respuesta.

1 necesitar tarjetas de embarque

A —¿Quiénes *necesitan tarjetas de embarque*?
B —*Los pasajeros*.

Estudiante A

a. servir la comida en el avión

b. facturarles el equipaje a los pasajeros

c. abrocharse el cinturón

d. mostrar la tarjeta de embarque

e. registrar las maletas

f. pasar por la aduana

g. decir que hay que abrocharse los cinturones

h. vender boletos

Estudiante B

Options

Strategies for Reaching All Students

Spanish-Speaking Students
Exs. 1–2: Pair bilingual with non-bilingual students, if possible.
Ex. 3: Pair Spanish-speaking students if possible.

Students Needing Extra Help
Ex. 1: Review stem-changing and reflexive verbs, and the present-tense forms of *decir*. Point out that the *Estudiante B* responses can be used more than once if appropriate.
Ex. 2: Read through the schedule as a class. Model a response without using the *retraso* phrase. You may want to review time-telling before beginning this exercise. Point out that all of these cities are in Colombia.
Ex. 3: Point out that this is not a linear match for answers.

Enrichment
Ex. 3: To extend this exercise, call on the entire class to suggest things the people named usually say. You may want to make a chart with the following headings: *Lo que dice un(a) piloto, Lo que dice un(a) auxiliar de vuelo, Lo que dice un(a) agente de viajes,* etc.

2 salir / el avión para Pasto

A —*Perdone, señor (señora / señorita), ¿a qué hora* *sale el avión para Pasto?*

B —*A las 9:25. Tiene un retraso de 25 minutos.*

Estudiante A

a. llegar / el vuelo número 115 procedente de Medellín

b. aterrizar / el vuelo 093 de Bogotá

c. salir / el vuelo con destino a Cali

d. llegar / el vuelo de Cartagena

e. aterrizar / el avión procedente de Barranquilla

f. despegar / el vuelo con destino a Santa Marta

Estudiante B

Vuelo	Ciudad	Llegada	Salida
353	Cali		8:30 (retraso de 30 min.)
297	Cartagena	9:20	
116	Pasto		9:25 (retraso de 25 min.)
093	Bogotá	10:50	
115	Medellín	11:10	
193	Santa Marta		3:00 (retraso de 15 min.)
245	Barranquilla	5:45	

3 el piloto

A —*¿Qué dijo el piloto?*

B —*Dijo que íbamos a aterrizar en 20 minutos.*

Estudiante A

a. el empleado de la línea aérea

b. la auxiliar de vuelo

c. ese mecánico

d. el agente de viajes

e. esa pasajera

f. el aduanero

g.

Estudiante B

íbamos a aterrizar en (20) minutos

íbamos a salir por la puerta número 3

quería un asiento cerca de la ventanilla

había que registrar todas las maletas

había que comprar los boletos en seguida

tenía que reparar algo en el avión

debíamos abrocharnos el cinturón

ESTUDIANTE B

a. A las 11:10.

b. …10:50.

c. …8:30. Tiene un retraso de 30 minutos.

d. …9:20.

e. …5:45.

f. …3:00. Tiene un retraso de 15 minutos.

3 **ESTUDIANTE A**

a. ¿Qué dijo el empleado de la línea aérea?

b. … la auxiliar de vuelo?

c. … ese mecánico?

d. … el agente de viajes?

e. … esa pasajera?

f. … el aduanero?

g. Questions will vary.

ESTUDIANTE B

a. Dijo que íbamos a salir por la puerta número tres.

b. … debíamos abrocharnos el cinturón.

c. … tenía que reparar algo en el avión.

d. … había que comprar los boletos en seguida.

e. … quería un asiento cerca de la ventanilla.

f. … había que registrar todas las maletas.

g. Answers will vary.

Practice & Apply

Answers: Empecemos a conversar

4 ESTUDIANTE A

a. ¿Conseguiste un vuelo sin escala?

b. ¿Conseguiste un asiento cerca de la ventanilla?

c. ¿Compraste un boleto sólo de ida?

d. ¿Cambiaste la reservación?

e. ¿Conseguiste un vuelo por la mañana?

f. ¿Hiciste reservaciones en el hotel en Montevideo?

g. ¿Compraste un boleto barato?

h. Questions will vary.

ESTUDIANTE B

a. No, todos hacen escala en Panamá.

b. . . .prefiero estar cerca del pasillo.

c. . . .de ida y vuelta.

d. . . .había que pagar $100 más.

e. . . .conseguí uno a las 3:00.

f. . . .allí nunca hay mucha gente.

g. Por suerte no fue demasiado caro.

h. Answers will vary.

4 comprar un boleto de ida y vuelta a Santiago

A — *¿Compraste un boleto de ida y vuelta a Santiago?*
B — *No, sólo de ida.*

Estudiante A

a. conseguir un vuelo sin escala

b. conseguir un asiento cerca de la ventanilla

c. comprar un boleto sólo de ida

d. cambiar la reservación

e. conseguir un vuelo por la mañana

f. hacer reservaciones en el hotel en Montevideo

g. comprar un boleto barato

h.

Estudiante B

No, sólo de ida.

No, prefiero estar cerca del pasillo.

Por suerte no fue demasiado caro.

No, allí nunca hay mucha gente.

No, conseguí uno a las 3:00.

No, había que pagar $100 más.

No, todos hacen escala en Panamá.

No, de ida y vuelta.

Options

Strategies for Reaching All Students

Spanish-Speaking Students
Ex. 4: Pair Spanish-speaking students if possible.
Ex. 9: Add: *¿Has pasado por la aduana? ¿Qué tuviste que mostrarles a los aduaneros?*

 Un paso más Ex. 12-D

Students Needing Extra Help
Ex. 4: Review preterite verb forms. Pair students who haven't flown before with those who have.
Empecemos a escribir: Answer these questions as a class, to include those who have never traveled.
Ex. 5: Point out that more than one tense will be used.
Ex. 6: Remind students that *te* in the question becomes *me* in the answer. Point out that more than one tense is used.

Cooperative Learning
In pairs, have students choose one of the situations presented in Ex. 4. Have them create a ten-line dialogue acting out that situation. Scenes can be amusing or serious: encourage creativity and wide use of vocabulary. After students have practiced their scene, have each pair present their dialogue to the class. The class should try to guess which situation is being presented.

Pasajeros después de aterrizar en Santo Domingo

Empecemos a escribir

Escribe tus respuestas en español.

5 ¿Tienes pasaporte? ¿Cuánto tiempo hace que lo tienes? ¿Para qué lo necesitaste? Si no tienes uno, ¿a quién conoces que tiene pasaporte? ¿A qué país viajaba cuando lo consiguió?

6 ¿Viajaste en avión alguna vez? ¿Adónde fuiste? ¿Por qué prefiere la gente los vuelos sin escala? ¿Te gusta (o te gustaría) viajar en avión o te da miedo?

7 Cuando viajas, ¿llevas mucho o poco equipaje? Cuando haces la maleta, ¿es difícil decidir qué llevar? ¿Cuál es mejor, facturar el equipaje o llevarlo en la mano? ¿Por qué?

8 En tú opinión, ¿cuáles son las ventajas y desventajas de ser piloto o auxiliar de vuelo? ¿Y las ventajas de ser agente de viajes o empleado(a) de una línea aérea?

9 ¿Sabes cuándo y por qué hay que pasar por la aduana? ¿Crees que los aduaneros deben registrar todas las maletas o no? ¿Por qué?

También se dice

la aeromoza, el aeromozo
la azafata

In addition to saying *facturar,* we also say *chequear.*

Vocabulario para conversar 401

Cultural Notes ☼

(p. 400, left realia)
Portugal lies in the southwestern corner of Europe on the Iberian Plateau facing the Atlantic Ocean. Its Mediterranean climate offers mild winters and hot, dry summers. This ad invites the Spanish tourist to "hurry" or "come flying" to Portugal.

(p. 400, right realia)
Venezuela attracts visitors with such sites as its Amazon jungle, the world's highest waterfall (Cataratas Ángel), and the beaches of las Islas Margarita. Venezuela's population is 67 percent mestizo, 21 percent white, 10 percent black, and 2 percent Indian, including the Warao of the eastern Orinoco Delta and the Yanomami of the Amazonas territory.

(p. 401, photo)
International visitors to the Dominican Republic, which shares the island of Hispaniola with Haiti, land at Las Américas airport in Santo Domingo, the country's capital city. Bartholomew Columbus, brother of Christopher, founded Santo Domingo in 1496, making it the oldest city established by Europeans in the Americas. Many areas in the city have been restored to their colonial style.

Present

Chapter Theme
Tourism

Communicative Objectives
- To discuss tourist accommodations
- To discuss tourist activities

 Transparencies 59–60

 Vocabulary Art BLMs

 Pronunciation Tape 12-2

Grammar Preview
Affirmative and negative *tú* commands are presented here lexically. They are explained on pp. 411–414.

Teaching Suggestions
Preparing students to speak: Use one or two options from each of the categories of Comprehensible Input, Physical Response, or Limited Verbal Response. For a complete explanation of these categories and some sample activities, see pp. T16–T17.

¡El pasaporte, por favor!

Vocabulario para conversar

¿Dónde puedo cambiar cheques de viajero?

la oficina telefónica

la oficina de turismo

la artesanía

la guía

el mercado

el / la turista

la guía

DÓLARES-PESOS

la casa de cambio

402   Capítulo 12

Options

Strategies for Reaching All Students

Spanish-Speaking Students
Ask: *¿Puedes añadir palabras a esta lista? Escríbelas en tu vocabulario personal.*
Exs. 10–11: Pair bilingual with non-bilingual students, if possible.

 Un paso más Ex. 12-F

Students Needing Extra Help
Point out that *turista* is masculine and feminine. Explain that *habitación* loses its accent in the plural. Explain the concept of the long-distance telephone office.
También necesitas . . . : Define "indigenous." Show students that the verb forms of *regatear* and *planear* will look similar. Remind them of *bucear.*

¿Y qué quiere decir . . . ?: Explain the difference between *un viaje* and *una excursión.* Write out the *recomendar* paradigm for students who need to see it.
Ex. 10: Accept any logical answer.

la habitación, pl. las habitaciones

la habitación individual

la habitación doble

el guía

También necesitas . . .

el pueblo	*town*
la pensión, *pl.* las pensiones	*inexpensive lodging*
la naturaleza	*nature*
cambiar	here: *to cash*
disfrutar de	*to enjoy*
incluir: incluye	*to include: it includes*
planear	*to plan*
regatear	*to bargain*
ir: ve; no vayas	*go!; don't go!*
tener cuidado (con): ten cuidado	*to be careful (of / with): be careful!*
indígena	*indigenous, native*
pintoresco, -a	*picturesque*

¿Y qué quiere decir . . . ?
el palacio
el viaje
hacer una excursión
recomendar *(e → ie)*

Vocabulario para conversar   403

Practice

Class Starter Review
On the day following the presentation of vocabulary, you might begin the class with this activity: Describe a situation in which a tourist may find himself or herself in a Spanish-speaking country. Have students write down a solution to the problem. For example: *Tomás necesita información sobre el Museo Nacional. ¿Adónde debe ir? (a la oficina de turismo)*

Answers: Empecemos a conversar

10 ESTUDIANTE A
a. ¿Me recomiendas ver los palacios?
b. . . . visitar una selva tropical?
c. . . . hacer una excursión a las cataratas?
d. . . . hacer un viaje a los pueblos?
e. . . . ir a los lagos y los ríos?
f. . . . hacer una excursión a las montañas?
g. Questions will vary.

ESTUDIANTE B
Answers will vary, but may include:
a. Sí, si te gustan los edificios viejos.
b. . . . gusta la naturaleza.
c. . . . gusta la naturaleza.
d. . . . gustan los lugares pintorescos.
e. . . . gusta pasear en bote.
f. . . . gusta esquiar.
g. Answers will vary.

Enrichment
Ex. 10: To extend this dialogue, *Estudiante A* can ask *Estudiante B* to elaborate by asking, *¿Por qué dices eso?*

Learning Spanish Through Action
STAGING VOCABULARY: *Señalen*
MATERIALS: signs for *el hotel, la casa de cambio, la oficina de turismo, la oficina telefónica, el mercado, la agencia de viajes* placed in different areas of the classroom
DIRECTIONS: Have students imagine they are vacationing in Venezuela. Direct them to point to the place they would go to do the activities you mention.

Practice & Apply

Re-enter / Recycle
Exs. 11 and 14: places in a community from Chap. 8

Answers: Empecemos a conversar

11 ESTUDIANTE A
a. ¿Dónde puedo encontrar un(a) guía?
b. ...comprar artesanías?
c. ...conseguir un boleto de avión?
d. ...buscar un mapa?
e. ...llamar a los Estados Unidos?
f. ...comprar tarjetas postales?
g. ...encontrar una habitación barata?
h. Questions will vary.

ESTUDIANTE B
a. Ve a una oficina de turismo.
b. ...un mercado.
c. ...una agencia de viajes.
d. ...una oficina de turismo / una agencia de viajes / un quiosco.
e. ...la oficina telefónica.
f. ...un quiosco.
g. ...una pensión.
h. Answers will vary.

12 ESTUDIANTE A
a. ¿Prefiere pagar con tarjeta de crédito o con cheques de viajero?
b. ...un hotel o una pensión?
c. ...hacer una excursión al mercado o al Palacio Nacional?
d. ...ir con guía o solo(a)?

Empecemos a conversar

10 ir a los mercados
A —¿Me recomiendas _ir a los mercados_?
B —Sí, si te gusta _regatear_.

Estudiante A
a. ver los palacios
b. visitar una selva tropical
c. hacer una excursión a las cataratas
d. hacer un viaje a los pueblos
e. ir a los lagos y los ríos
f. hacer una excursión a las montañas
g. 🔦

Estudiante B
esquiar   los lugares pintorescos
pasear en bote   los edificios viejos
regatear   la naturaleza
la artesanía indígena 🔦

11 cambiar cheques de viajero
A —¿Dónde puedo _cambiar cheques de viajero_?
B —_Ve a una casa de cambio_.

Estudiante A
a. encontrar un(a) guía
b. comprar artesanías
c. conseguir un boleto de avión
d. buscar un mapa
e. llamar a los Estados Unidos
f. comprar tarjetas postales
g. encontrar una habitación barata
h. 🔦

Estudiante B
la oficina telefónica   una pensión
una casa de cambio   un quiosco
una agencia de viajes   🔦
un mercado
una oficina de turismo

12 una habitación doble / individual
A —¿Prefiere _una habitación doble o una individual_?
B —_Una individual. Viajo solo_.

Estudiante A
a. pagar con tarjeta de crédito / con cheques de viajero
b. un hotel / una pensión
c. hacer una excursión al mercado / al Palacio Nacional
d. ir con guía / solo(a)
e. quedarse en un lugar pintoresco / moderno
f. una habitación al fondo / con ventanas a la calle
g. 🔦

Estudiante B

Options

Strategies for Reaching All Students

Spanish-Speaking Students
Exs. 12–13: Pair bilingual with non-bilingual students, if possible.
Ex. 16: _Haz un folleto o pequeño cartel que anuncie algunos de los lugares de interés turístico en nuestra comunidad._

Students Needing Extra Help
Ex. 12: Brainstorm possible second sentences in the _Estudiante B_ response. _Empecemos a escribir y a leer:_ Answer these questions as a class, to include those who have not traveled before.
Ex. 13: Discuss different types of excursions.
Ex. 14: As a class, review the concept of bargaining.

Ex. 15: Answer questions one at a time as a class to help students stay focused. Write the list of things to be careful of on the chalkboard.
Ex. 16: Generate a list of positive and negative features of your community, then have students use the list to create statements they could make to tourists.

Empecemos a escribir y a leer

Escribe tus respuestas en español.

13 ¿Qué tipo de excursión te gustaría hacer? ¿Disfrutas más de la naturaleza o de las ciudades? ¿Por qué?

14 ¿En qué lugares crees que se puede regatear? ¿Regateaste alguna vez? ¿Dónde? ¿Hay lugares en tu pueblo o ciudad donde se puede regatear?

15 ¿Alguna vez hiciste un viaje a un pueblo, ciudad o país que no conocías? ¿Adónde fuiste? ¿Cómo planeaste el viaje? ¿Fuiste a una agencia de viajes? ¿Con quién(es) viajaste? ¿Qué tuviste que hacer como turista? ¿Con qué debe tener cuidado un(a) turista? Haz una lista para un(a) compañero(a).

> Ten cuidado con el dinero.
> Ten cuidado con . . .
> No vayas al parque por la noche.
> No vayas a . . .

16 Imagina que eres guía en tu comunidad. ¿Qué le recomiendas a un(a) turista?

17 Con un(a) compañero(a), lee los tres anuncios de excursiones. Escoge cuál te gustaría hacer y di por qué.

Ciudad de México · Oaxaca · Mérida

8 días por _sólo_

$440 por persona / hab. doble

Incluye:
- Boleto de ida y vuelta
- 7 noches en hoteles de turista superior
- Transporte diario en autobús con guía en español
- Visita a todas las ruinas, pirámides y lugares pintorescos de la región
- Transporte:
  aeropuerto → hotel → aeropuerto

Santo Domingo

8 días por _sólo_

$520 por persona / hab. individual

Incluye:
- 7 noches en el Hotel Boca Chica (frente al océano)
- Programa completo de deportes acuáticos
- Alimentación completa
- Una camiseta por persona con el logo del hotel
- Transporte:
  aeropuerto → hotel → aeropuerto

Ciudad de Panamá

3 días por _sólo_

$127 por persona / hab. triple

Incluye:
- 2 noches en un hotel turista superior
- Transporte:
  aeropuerto → hotel → aeropuerto
- Transporte todos los días de ida y vuelta a los almacenes en la zona libre*
- Visita al Canal con guía en español

*Zona libre = tax-free

---

e. . . . quedarse en un lugar pintoresco o moderno?
f. . . . una habitación al fondo o con ventanas a la calle?
g. Questions will vary.

ESTUDIANTE B
a.–g. Answers will vary.

Answers: Empecemos a escribir y a leer

13–16 Answers will vary, but look for correct use of the present, preterite, and the impersonal _se_ where appropriate.

17 Answers will vary, but may include the following:
Escogimos el viaje a México porque nos interesan los pirámides / necesitamos un(a) guia / incluye un boleto de ida y vuelta.
Escogimos el viaje a Santo Domingo porque queremos nadar, y además es muy barato porque tiene alimentación completa.
Escogimos el viaje a Panamá porque nos gusta ir de compras y queremos mucho ver el Canal.

 Practice Wkbk. 12-3, 12-4

 Audio Activity 12.2

 Writing Activity 12-C

 Pruebas 12-3, 12-4

 Comm. Act. BLM 12-1

Enrichment
Ex. 14: Additional questions: _¿Te gusta regatear? ¿Por qué sí o no? ¿Conoces a alguien que sepa regatear bien? ¿Cómo es esa persona?_
Ex. 17: To expand this exercise, have students who chose the same trip form groups and plan it.

Practice

Teaching Suggestions
Ex. 1: To prepare for this exercise you may want to ask students to pick up brochures from different Latin American countries at a local travel agency.

Answers:
¡Comuniquemos!
1–3 Answers will vary, but look for a wide variety of chapter vocabulary and correct use of the future tense where appropriate.

Multicultural Perspectives
In rural areas of Colombia, the most practical form of travel is the *chiva* (goat), so called because this converted school bus provides transportation to places only a mountain goat would go. A typical multi-colored, double-decker *chiva* has the destinations it serves written on the bus, along with the name of the company running the service. When people need to travel from one small town to another, they wait at the side of the road and flag down a passing *chiva*. The *chiva* not only carries people from place to place, but doubles as a freight carrier, bringing livestock and agricultural products along with their owners to a given destination. Discuss with students modes of transportation which are unique to a particular region or country.

¡Comuniquemos!

Aquí tienes otra oportunidad para usar el vocabulario de este capítulo.

1 Con un(a) compañero(a), planea un viaje o una excursión a algún país o lugar específico. Hablen de:

- adónde irán
- en qué irán
- qué necesitarán hacer primero
- cuánto tiempo se quedarán
- qué llevarán
- qué harán allá

2 Con un(a) compañero(a), hagan los papeles de un(a) agente de viajes y un(a) cliente.

A — *Quisiera un . . . para ir a . . .*
B — *. . .*
A — *¿Dónde puedo . . . ?*
B — *En . . .*
A — *¿Sabe Ud. si hay que . . . ?*
B — *. . .*

3 Con un(a) compañero(a), hagan los papeles de un(a) auxiliar de vuelo y un(a) pasajero(a). Escojan por lo menos tres de las situaciones que siguen.

A — *Señor (Señorita), por favor, ¿(me) podría . . . ?*
B — *Claro que sí, señor(ita) . . .*
    o: *Lo siento, señor(ita), pero . . .*

1. Tienes sed. El/La auxiliar te ofrece varias bebidas.
2. Quieres leer un periódico y sólo hay revistas.
3. No puedes abrocharte el cinturón de seguridad. Crees que está roto.
4. Quieres cambiar de asiento.
5. Tu maleta es demasiado grande y no puedes ponerla debajo del asiento.
6. Pediste pollo para la cena, pero no hay más.

406   Capítulo 12

¿Por qué tiritar?

La fortaleza de El Morro

¡Pase las vacaciones de invierno en **Puerto Rico!**

Córdoba

La mezquita (hoy la catedral)

donde Ud. encontrará el cruce de las culturas musulmana, judía y cristiana

Options

Strategies for Reaching All Students

Spanish-Speaking Students
Ex. 3: Pair Spanish-speaking students if possible, to prepare this activity and present it to the class. It can be used as a listening comprehension exercise for others, especially if it is recorded.

Students Needing Extra Help
Ex 2: Present a complete model. Provide specific criteria for completing the dialogue.
Ex. 3: Remind students to change the suggestions from the *tú* form to the *yo* form. For the dialogues they develop, point out the necessity for both people to use the *Ud.* form.
¿Qué sabes ahora?: Have students write out this list so they can record their progress.

Cooperative Learning
Have students list three types of excursions they would enjoy on vacation, then circulate through the class to find three others with similar responses. As a group, each must generate one reason why theirs is the ideal vacation. Students will create a poster using words, photos, drawings, etc. Within the group, one pair will be responsible for creating the poster and one pair will generate the reasons why it is ideal.

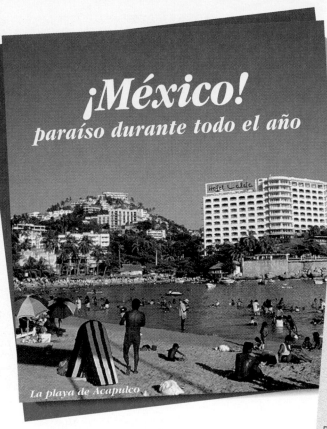

¡México!
paraíso durante todo el año

La playa de Acapulco

⚡⚡⚡

¿QUE TIEMPO HARÁ MAÑANA?

¿Y LOS PROXIMOS DÍAS?

¿TIENE PREVISTO VIAJAR?

No salga sin conocer el tiempo que va a hacer en la zona a la que se dirige.

LLAME AL TELEFONO

903 330 343

SERVICIO 24 HORAS

1️⃣ **COMUNIDAD AUTONOMA DE MADRID**

2️⃣ **CATALUÑA**

3️⃣ **ANDALUCIA Y CANARIAS**

4️⃣ **GALICIA, ASTURIAS, CANTABRIA Y PAIS VASCO**

5️⃣ **LEVANTE, MURCIA Y BALEARES**

6️⃣ **CASTILLA-LEON, RIOJA, NAVARRA Y ARAGON**

7️⃣ **CASTILLA-LA MANCHA Y EXTREMADURA**

Elaborado por: *J. L. Ron*

La Previsión de las próximas 24 horas.

Apdo. 54.082 Madrid. *El coste de la llamada a los servicios 903 incluye el precio de la información o entretenimiento que usted recibe. Benefíciese de las tarifas nocturnas y de días festivos*. Precio llamada e información 60 ptas. minuto. noches y festivos 42 ptas. Sin IVA.

¿Qué sabes ahora?

Can you:

■ discuss travel arrangements?

—Quisiera un ___ de ___ y ___ para ir a Bogotá.

■ ask for recommendations at a tourist office?

—¿Dónde puedo encontrar un(a) ___ barato(a)?

■ suggest what to do and what not to do in your hometown?

—Ve a ___. No ___ a ___.

Vocabulario para conversar 407

Using Realia

Have students compare the two images presented in the top photo on p. 406. Then ask: *¿Qué quiere decir "tiritar?"* (to shiver)

Answers: ¿Qué sabes ahora?

• boleto / ida / vuelta
• Answers will vary, but may include *habitación* or *pensión*.
• Locations will vary; verb should be *vayas*.

 Audio Activity 12.3

Cultural Notes ☀

(p. 406, top photo)
San Juan, Puerto Rico, is one of the oldest cities in the Americas. It was originally settled in 1508, and by 1533 the Spanish settlers and military had begun to build fortifications to protect the island. El Morro castle and the fort of San Cristóbal lie at either end of the viejo San Juan historic section. They are part of the San Juan National Historic Site run by the U.S. National Park Service.

(p. 406, bottom photo)
The Mosque's vast interior space is divided by rows of columns supporting stone piers that carry a second tier of arches, creating a light, airy effect. Construction began in 786 and was finished in 987. Since 1236, it has been used as a cathedral. It remains a breathtaking example of the *mudéjar* style of architecture.

(p. 407, photo)
Acapulco is a popular beach resort with Mexican families and international tourists. Some of the city's most famous beaches are Condesa, Playa Larga, and Revolcadero. The city also has a renowned night life, good restaurants, and many luxury hotels as well as economical *pensiones*.

Present & Apply

Cultural Objective
• To compare accommodations in Spain with those in the U.S.

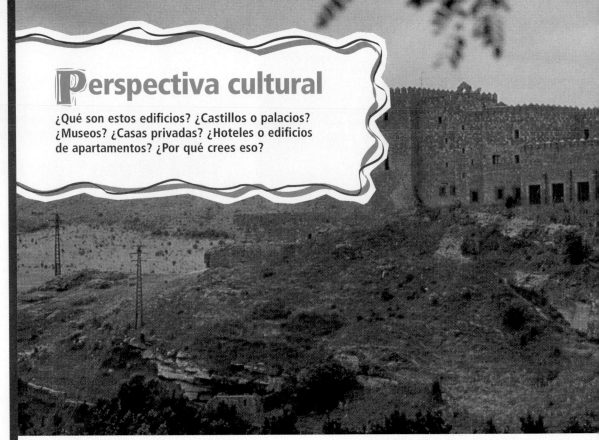

Perspectiva cultural

¿Qué son estos edificios? ¿Castillos o palacios? ¿Museos? ¿Casas privadas? ¿Hoteles o edificios de apartamentos? ¿Por qué crees eso?

El parador de Sigüenza

¿Te gustaría pasar una noche en el Hospital Real fundado por Isabel de Castilla y Fernando de Aragón en 1499? ¿Quisieras quedarte en un castillo construido hace mil años? ¿Qué tal un convento franciscano del siglo dieciséis? ¿O quizás prefieres un edificio que fue primero un templo romano, luego una basílica visigoda y después un convento de la Orden de Santiago? Es posible quedarte en todos estos lugares si vas a España.

En España estos hoteles especiales se llaman *paradores*. En 1926 el gobierno español decidió establecer una cadena de paradores para atraer a los turistas a los lugares donde no había hoteles.

Los primeros paradores estaban a una distancia de un día de viaje uno de otro. Claro que ahora, con las carreteras modernas, el mismo viaje toma mucho menos tiempo. En total, hay 85 paradores en toda España.

Además de paradores, también hay varios tipos de hoteles y albergues (pensiones) para jóvenes en España. Desde la Expo 92 en Sevilla y los Juegos Olímpicos en Barcelona en el mismo año, también es posible pasar la noche en muchas casas privadas. Por lo general, le ofrecen al viajero la habitación y una comida al día. Es una manera muy buena de conocer a la gente y la vida de España.

408 Capítulo 12

Options

Strategies for Reaching All Students

Spanish-Speaking Students
Ask: *Además de hoteles y moteles, ¿qué otros tipos de lugares en los Estados Unidos serían buenos para atraer a los turistas de otros países? Piensa en nuestra área y en diferentes partes del país. Un ejemplo puede ser un rancho de ganado en Texas.*

 Un paso más Ex. 12-G

Students Needing Extra Help
Have students take notes they can use to review in the *¿Lo sabes bien?* culture section. Discuss the types of places in which tourists can stay in the U.S., then compare them to what students see in the photos. Ex. 2: Model a response to the *¿por qué?* question.

Enrichment
Additional questions: *¿Te gustaría tener turistas en tu casa? ¿Por qué sí o no?*

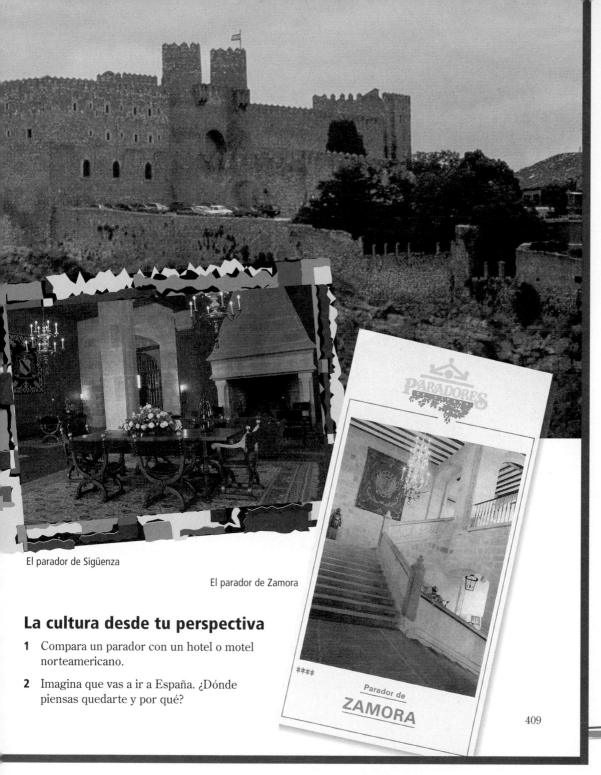

El parador de Sigüenza

El parador de Zamora

La cultura desde tu perspectiva

1 Compara un parador con un hotel o motel norteamericano.

2 Imagina que vas a ir a España. ¿Dónde piensas quedarte y por qué?

Parador de
ZAMORA

409

Cultural Notes ☀

(pp. 408–409, photos)
Parador de Sigüenza, near Guadalajara, was originally a Visigoth castle occupied for a time by the Moors. Famous guests of the castle have included King Ferdinand and Queen Isabela, Cardinal Mendoza, and Juana la Loca.

(p. 409, right photo)
Paradores were historically the lodging of distinguished or respectable travelers. Parador de Zamora, in the medieval city of Zamora, is a Renaissance palace built on the ruins of a Romanesque building.

Teaching Suggestions

A: Point out that if a pronoun is added to a command form of two or more syllables, a written accent is needed, as in *búscalas* (paragraph 1). Provide writing and pronunciation practice.

Answers

A The command forms are *busca, consigue, usa, aprende, habla.* They are the same as the *Ud. / él / ella* forms of the present tense. The *tú* command forms of *viajar, vender,* and *escribir* would be *viaja, vende,* and *escribe.*

B If the command form of *ir* were regular, it would be *va.* It is *ve.* (It is irregular in its ending.)

C The verb forms are *no olvides* and *no seas.* They come from *olvidar* and *ser.* You would tell a friend, *"No factures tu equipaje."*

Gramática en contexto

América Latina: Destino de jóvenes

¿Tienes poco dinero y quieres viajar?
¡Ve a América Latina en cualquier época del año!

Busca una de nuestras pensiones para jóvenes. Están en todas las ciudades grandes y operan todo el año. Búscalas en las oficinas de turismo.

Consigue un carnet estudiantil. Así podrás conseguir descuento en muchos lugares.

Usa el transporte público. Es fácil de usar y siempre barato.

¡Y no olvides! Aprende algunas palabras del idioma—¡y no seas tímido! Habla con la gente. ¡Es amable, alegre . . . vital!

A These tips for student travelers address the reader as *tú.* What are the command forms meaning "look for," "get," "use," "learn," and "talk"? What forms of the present tense are the same? What do you think the *tú* command forms of *viajar, vender,* and *escribir* might be?

B Find the command form of *ir.* What would you expect it to be if it were regular?

C The reader is also urged *not* to do two things. What verbs do you think they come from? How do you think you might tell a friend, "Don't check your baggage"?

410   Capítulo 12

Options

Strategies for Reaching All Students

Students Needing Extra Help
Begin the grammar section of the Organizer. If available, use the grammar section of the Book 1, Chap. 13 Organizer.
Repaso: Mandatos afirmativos con tú: Give additional examples of *tú* commands, isolated and in sentences. Give additional examples of *pon, haz,* and *di* in sentences.

Ex. 1: Remind students that all *Estudiante A* statements will be in the *yo* form, and all the *Estudiante B* responses will be in the *tú* command form. Review the *¡No olvides!* and give further examples before doing the exercise.

Repaso: Mandatos afirmativos con *tú*

You already know how to give affirmative commands to someone you address as *tú*.

> **Pasa** por la aduana.
> **Aprende** a regatear.
> **Escribe** tarjetas postales.

- You also know the irregular command forms *pon (poner)*, *haz (hacer)*, and *di (decir)*. Here are some other verbs that have irregular command forms.

> **salir**
> **Sal** por las escaleras en caso de emergencia.
>
> **ir**
> **Ve** al aeropuerto por lo menos dos horas antes del vuelo.
>
> **ser**
> **Sé** amable con los otros pasajeros.
>
> **tener**
> **¡Ten** cuidado!

¡NO OLVIDES!

Remember that pronouns can be attached to commands. When a pronoun is added to a command form of two or more syllables, a written accent mark is needed.
—¿*Dónde facturo el equipaje?*
—*Factúralo en el mostrador de la línea aérea.*

1 Imagina que estás haciendo un viaje con tu compañero(a).

necesitar una
tarjeta de
embarque

A —*Necesito una tarjeta de embarque.*
B —*Pues, habla con el empleado de la línea aérea.*

a. querer planear un viaje

b. necesitar conseguir cheques de viajero

c. querer saber qué tiempo hace

d. no querer hacer escala

e. preferir otro asiento

f. tener que enviar mi dirección a casa

hablar con el empleado de la línea aérea

escribir una tarjeta postal

preguntarle al auxiliar de vuelo

leer el pronóstico de tiempo

cambiar la reservación

visitar una agencia de viajes

comprarlos en una casa de cambio

Gramática en contexto   411

Present & Practice

Answers

1 ESTUDIANTE A

a. Quiero planear un viaje.
b. Necesito conseguir cheques de viajero.
c. Quiero saber qué tiempo hace.
d. No quiero hacer escala.
e. Prefiero otro asiento.
f. Tengo que enviar mi dirección a casa.

ESTUDIANTE B

a. Pues, visita una agencia de viajes.
b. ...cómpralos en una casa de cambio.
c. ...lee el pronóstico de tiempo.
d. ...cambia la reservación.
e. ...pregúntale al auxiliar de vuelo.
f. ...escribe una tarjeta postal.

Present & Practice

Re-enter / Recycle

Ex. 3: environment and recyclables from Chap. 11

Answers

2 ESTUDIANTE A

a. ¿Dónde pongo la maleta?

b. ¿Qué hago si el avión aterriza de emergencia?

c. ¿Dónde encuentro las maletas?

d. ¿Qué hago en la aduana?

e. ¿Cómo regateo bien?

f. ¿Dónde puedo poner mi pasaporte?

g. ¿Cuándo debo hacer reservaciones?

h. Questions will vary.

ESTUDIANTE B

a. Ponla debajo del asiento.

b. Sal rápido del avión.

c. Ve a la terminal de equipaje.

d. Di lo que tienes en tu maleta.

e. Sé amable con los vendedores.

f. Ten cuidado y guárdalo en un bolsillo.

g. Hazlas en seguida.

h. Answers will vary.

 Practice Wkbk. 12-5, 12-6

 Writing Activity 12-D

---

2 Vas a viajar a otro país por primera vez y le pides consejos *(advice)* a un(a) amigo(a). Por ejemplo:

dónde / cambiar   A — *¿Dónde cambio cheques de viajero?*

cheques de viajero B — *Ve a la casa de cambio.*

a. dónde / poner la maleta

b. qué / hacer si el avión aterriza de emergencia

c. dónde / encontrar las maletas

d. qué / hacer en la aduana

e. cómo / regatear bien

f. dónde / poder poner mi pasaporte

g. cuándo / deber hacer reservaciones

h.

---

ir a la casa de cambio

ir a la terminal de equipaje

hacerlas en seguida

tener cuidado y guardarlo en un bolsillo

ser amable con los vendedores

ponerla debajo del asiento

salir rápido del avión

decir lo que tienes en tu maleta

Los mandatos negativos con *tú*

To form negative *tú* commands with regular verbs, we drop the *o* of the present-tense *yo* form and add the following endings:

hablar
hablo → habl- + **es**   **No hables** ahora.

comer
como → com- + **as**   **No comas** eso.

abrir
abro → abr- + **as**   **No abras** esa puerta.

Notice that *-ar* verbs take the ending *-es* and that *-er* and *-ir* verbs take the ending *-as*.

• In stem-changing verbs the stem change remains.

No devuelvas el boleto todavía.
No recomiendes esa pensión a nadie.
No sigas a esa guía.

412   Capítulo 12

Options

Strategies for Reaching All Students

Students Needing Extra Help

Los mandatos negativos con tú: Give further examples of regular and stem-changing negative commands. Emphasize that forming the negative command requires changes besides just adding *no*.

Ex. 3: Brainstorm possibilities for two additional rules. Have students refer to Book 2, Chap. 11 for ideas.

Ex. 4: Review stem-changing verbs and the rule for forming negative *tú* commands.

Enrichment

Ex. 2: As an in-class written assignment, have students change this exercise by making up entirely new commands or attaching pronouns to commands based on the verb in the original question. For example: *¿Dónde cambio cheques de viajero?* / *Cámbialos en la casa de cambio.*

Ex. 4: Have students work in pairs to generate three additional rules for being a good roommate. You might also have them work in pairs to create rules for riding on a tour bus, going on a field trip *(excursión)*, etc.

412

3 ¿Qué se debe hacer para proteger el medio ambiente? Con un(a) compañero(a), haz estas reglas y por lo menos dos reglas más.

echar las pilas
viejas en la basura   *No eches las pilas viejas en la basura.*

   a. depender sólo de la energía eléctrica
   b. contaminar el agua
   c. echar las botellas de vidrio ni de plástico en la basura
   d. escribir en las paredes de los edificios
   e. cortar las flores
   f. usar lo que no puedes reciclar
   g.

4 Tú y tu compañero(a) tienen una habitación doble en una pensión. Uds. se pelean desde la mañana hasta la noche. Túrnense para ser la persona mandona *(bossy).*

encender
el televisor

A — *No enciendas el televisor.*
B — *¿Por qué?*
A — *Porque no quiero verlo.*

   a. cerrar la ventana
   b. encender la luz
   c. perder las llaves
   d. mostrar mis fotos a nadie

   e. pedir comida ahora
   f. devolver el secador
     de pelo todavía
   g.

Texas. De Todo Un Poco. Y Más.

La iglesia de la misión
San José (1720) en
San Antonio, Texas

Gramática en contexto   413

Class Starter Review
On the day following the presentation of negative *tú* commands, you might begin the class with this activity:
In small groups, have students prepare a list of five rules for the incoming class. The list should include both positive and negative commands. As a class, decide on the five most useful rules.

3 a. No dependas sólo de la energía eléctrica.
b. No contamines el agua.
c. No eches las botellas de vidrio ni de plástico en la basura.
d. No escribas en las paredes de los edificios.
e. No cortes las flores.
f. No uses lo que no puedes reciclar.
g. Answers will vary.

4 Second part will vary.
a. No cierres la ventana. / Porque tengo calor.
b. No enciendas la luz. / . . . quiero dormir.
c. No pierdas las llaves. / . . . no estaré aquí cuando regreses.
d. No muestres mis fotos a nadie. / . . . son malas.
e. No pidas comida ahora. / . . . comeremos muy pronto.
f. No devuelvas el secador de pelo todavía. / . . . necesito usarlo.
g. Answers will vary.

Practice Wkbk. 12-7

Writing Activity 12-E

Cultural Notes

(pp. 412–413, photo)
Catholic missions throughout the Americas functioned as churches, residences, trade schools, and granaries, and were instrumental in Spanish colonization efforts. Of the five missions built near San Antonio, Texas, the most famous is misión San José, known for its beautiful stonework that includes a stone *acequia* (aqueduct) used to bring irrigation water from the San Antonio River to the mission's fields.

(p. 413, realia)
Texas and Mexico have shared much of their histories and key elements of their cultures since 1536, when Cabeza de Vaca led an expedition from Galveston on the Gulf Coast through Texas and down to Mexico City. Spain lost Texas when Mexico declared its independence in 1821. Texas declared itself an independent republic in 1836, and became a state on February 19, 1846. Twenty-five percent of its population is Hispanic, and the majority of those are Mexican American. Commerce and tourism remain important links between Texas and Mexico.

Present & Practice

Re-enter / Recycle

Ex. 5: places in a community from Chap. 8

Answers

5 ESTUDIANTE A

a. No salgas solo(a).

b. No hagas reservaciones en un hotel.

c. No pongas el pasaporte en la maleta.

d. No llegues tarde al aeropuerto.

e. No vayas al centro solo(a) por la noche.

f. No seas maleducado(a).

g. No traigas muchos regalos.

h. No cruces la calle cuando el semáforo está en rojo.

i. Statements will vary.

ESTUDIANTE B

Answers will vary, but could include the following:

a. Sal (con otros miembros de tu grupo).

b. Haz (reservaciones en una pensión).

c. Pon (el pasaporte en el bolsillo de tu chaqueta).

d. Llega (tan temprano como posible).

e. Ve (con un[a] amigo[a]).

f. Sé educado(a).

g. Trae (sólo lo que necesitas).

h. Cruza (sólo cuando está en verde).

i. Advice will vary.

Los mandatos negativos: continuación

Verbs ending in *-car, -gar,* and *-zar* have the following spelling changes in negative *tú* commands in order to maintain the original sound.

-car *(c → qu)*
tocar
toco → to**qu**- + es   **No toques** el piano.

-gar *(g → gu)*
llegar
llego → lle**gu**- + es   **No llegues** tarde.

-zar *(z → c)*
cruzar
cruzo → cru**c**- + es   **No cruces** aquí.

- Verbs whose present-tense *yo* form ends in *-go (caerse, decir, hacer, poner, salir, tener, traer)* form their negative *tú* commands according to the regular rule.

  No pongas la maleta sobre el asiento.
  No hagas ruido en el avión.
  No le **digas** eso a la auxiliar de vuelo.
  No salgas de tu asiento.

- Some verbs, such as *ir* and *ser,* have irregular negative *tú* command forms.

  No vayas al bosque por la noche.
  No seas tímido. Pide lo que necesitas.

5 Imagina que alguien viaja solo(a) por primera vez. Tú y tu compañero(a) le dan consejos. ¿Qué le dicen?

poner la artesanía   A —*No pongas la artesanía en el equipaje.*
en el equipaje   B —*De acuerdo. Ponla en un bolso.*

a. salir solo(a)
b. hacer reservaciones en un hotel
c. poner el pasaporte en la maleta
d. llegar tarde al aeropuerto
e. ir al centro solo(a) por la noche

f. ser maleducado(a)
g. traer muchos regalos
h. cruzar la calle cuando el semáforo está en rojo
i. 🔅

Options

Strategies for Reaching All Students

Students Needing Extra Help

Los mandatos negativos: continuación: On the chalkboard, copy this list of *-car, -gar,* and *-zar* verbs that students know:

buscar	apagar	aterrizar
explicar	colgar	empezar
indicar	despegar	cruzar
picar	entregar	
practicar	jugar	
sacar	llegar	
secar	pagar	
tocar		

Then form their affirmative and negative commands. Repeat with the *-go* verbs, *ir,* and *ser.*

Ex. 5: Brainstorm additional advice to complete the *Estudiante B* response. Point out that the command for *Estudiante A* is negative, but that for *Estudiante B* it is affirmative.

Ex. 6: Have students generate a list of possible activities.

Ahora lo sabes: Have students write out this list so they can record their progress.

Enrichment

As a homework assignment, have students think of a well-known fairy tale, legend, or story and give the main character advice on things not to do or say, places not to go, etc.

414

6 Un estudiante nuevo llega a tu escuela. Con un(a) compañero(a), dile lo que debe hacer y lo que no. Recomiéndale por lo menos ocho cosas. Por ejemplo:

Ve a todos los partidos de fútbol.
Visita . . .
No vayas . . .

ATREVIDA.

Intrépida, decidida, audaz...
así es la nueva gama de maletas y bolsos **Tauro Berry**. Atrevida, especial como tú.
Porque las diferentes formas y tamaños de la línea
Tauro Berry se adaptan a ti.
Van con todo lo que tú más quieres.
Con tus ilusiones. Con tu manera de ser.

TAURO

PON DE MODA TU EQUIPAJE

Ahora lo sabes

Can you:

■ advise a friend or relative what he or she should do?
—___ el boleto, y ___ una reservación en la agencia de viajes.

■ tell a friend or relative what not to do?
—No ___ la maleta grande y no ___ al aeropuerto tarde.

Gramática en contexto 415

Cultural Notes

(p. 415, realia)
This ad brings to mind the flair and daring of the Spanish *taurino* culture, suggesting that the owner of Tauro luggage can be as daring as a bullfighter.

415

Apply

Pronunciation Tape 12-3

Answers: Actividades

1 Answers will vary, but should include the following verb forms:
Ve . . .
Sigue . . .
No tomes . . .
Dobla . . .
No dobles . . .
Busca . . .
No vayas . . .
Compra . . .
Toma . . .
No tomes . . .
Baja . . .

2–3 Answers will vary, but look for correct use of commands where appropriate.

¿Recuerdas?

Play

Video Activity A

Using the Video
The first scene of Chapter 12 is primarily visual, showing Jamie and Carlos in Mexico City visiting el Palacio Nacional, el Palacio de Bellas Artes, and el Museo de Antropología.

Para decir más

Aquí tienes vocabulario adicional que te puede servir para hacer las actividades de esta sección.

rebajar
to lower, to bring down

416   Capítulo 12

Actividades

Esta sección te ofrece la oportunidad de aumentar tus conocimientos de español al integrar lo que aprendiste en este capítulo con lo que aprendiste en capítulos anteriores.

1 Imagina que llega a la escuela un estudiante de un país hispanohablante. En grupo, preparen una lista de direcciones para ir de la escuela a varios lugares importantes o populares. Incluyan un mapa y varios mandatos. Pueden decirle:

- ir a . . .
- seguir por . . .
- no tomar la calle/la carretera . . .
- doblar en la calle . . .
- no doblar en la calle . . .
- buscar . . .
- no ir a . . .

Si hay transporte público, pueden decirle:

- comprar el boleto en . . .
- tomar el autobús/el metro en . . .
- no tomar el número . . .
- bajar en la calle . . .

Options

Strategies for Reaching All Students

Spanish-Speaking Students
Ex. 2: Have students write out this exercise.

 Un paso más Ex. 12-H

Students Needing Extra Help
If there are time constraints, have students do Ex. 2 only.
Ex. 1: Do the map first as a class so that students have a visual to help them. Present a complete model. Point out all the components in giving directions: street names, buildings, directions, etc. Use the vocabulary section of the Book 2, Chap. 10 Organizer.

Ex. 2: Brainstorm possibilities for what to do in an emergency. Review commands.
Ex. 3: Divide this exercise into three distinct parts. Have students do the introductory conversation one day, the pricing and bargaining the next day, and the actual buying and putting it all together on the final day. Present a complete model. You may want to role play this with another teacher, either live or on video.

2 ¿Qué se debe hacer si ocurre una emergencia durante un viaje? En grupo, hablen de eso. Luego, hagan recomendaciones a la clase usando mandatos. ¿Qué debe hacer alguien si . . . ?

- se enferma
- tiene un accidente
- pierde los anteojos o los lentes de contacto
- pierde el pasaporte o el boleto de avión
- alguien le roba

3 Con un(a) compañero(a), hagan los papeles de un(a) turista y un(a) vendedor(a) de artesanías (flores de papel, sombreros, telas, joyas de plata, etc.).

Para comenzar, debes ser muy educado(a) y saludar al (a la) vendedor(a). También debes conversar un poco antes de preguntar el precio. Usa frases como éstas:

- Buenos días/buenas tardes, señor(a).
- ¿Cómo está Ud.?
- ¿Qué tal el día?
- ¿Cómo se llama esto?
- ¡Qué bonito(a) este(a) . . . !
- ¿Dónde lo (la) hacen? ¿Quién lo (la) hace?

Ahora, puedes preguntar el precio. Usa frases como éstas:

- ¿Cuánto cuesta este(a) . . . ?
- ¿Cuánto pide por . . . ?

Para regatear, puedes usar estas frases entre otras:

- ¿Por cuánto me da este(a) . . . ?
- Es un poco caro(a) para mí. ¿Podría . . . ?
- Le doy $___.
- ¿No lo (la) puede rebajar un poco?

Para hacer la compra, puedes usar estas frases entre otras:

- Bueno, lo (la) llevo por $___.
- Está bien. Aquí tiene *(ofreciéndole el dinero)*.
- Muchas gracias.

417

When Jamie and Carlos arrive at el Museo Diego Rivera and see the mural *El sueño de una tarde de domingo en la Alameda,* they imagine Jamie as La Catrina. Later, Jamie and Carlos visit Carolina Beltrán, a lawyer who is reviewing La Catrina's will for them. In Licenciada Beltrán's opinion, the will is valid as long as Jamie lives in Mexico. She advises Jamie to begin legal proceedings in the court of Querétaro to claim La Catrina's property.

 La Catrina: Capítulo 12

Play

 Video Activity B

 **Para entender mejor**

Play

 **Video Activity C**

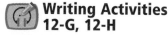 **Writing Activities 12-G, 12-H**

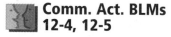 **Comm. Act. BLMs 12-4, 12-5**

Cooperative Learning
As a class, discuss situations in which there may be unwritten rules: traveling, being a tourist in another culture, dating, friendship, talking to an authority figure, etc. Tell pairs of students to select a topic and develop a set of ten rules. One partner will write five affirmative commands, and the other five negative commands. Each command should employ a different verb. Partners should exchange lists to assure appropriateness to the situation. Have students present their lists and discuss them with the class.

Apply

Process Reading
For a description of process reading, see p. 52.

Answers
Antes de leer
Answers will vary, but students may mention:
Check doors and windows to make sure they're locked.
Ask neighbors to pick up the mail.
Put house lights on a timer.
Tell only a few people that you will be away.

Mira la lectura
Answers will vary.

¡Vamos a leer!

Antes de leer

STRATEGY ➤ Using prior knowledge

This is a public service ad about protecting your house before you go on vacation. Make a list in English of six things you think you should do.

Mira la lectura

STRATEGY ➤ Skimming

Now skim the reading selection to get a general idea of what it's about.

ACOSTUMBRE A SU CASA A QUEDARSE SOLA

Este verano, usted va a disfrutar de unas merecidas vacaciones, pero su vivienda se quedará sola, sin su protección. No se preocupe, unas sencillas medidas de seguridad, ayudarán a que su hogar no quede tan vulnerable como usted imagina. Además, las Fuerzas y Cuerpos de Seguridad del Estado, van a dedicar todo su esfuerzo para que a su regreso, encuentre todo tal y como usted lo dejó.

1 Recuerde que la puerta de su casa debe reunir unas condiciones mínimas de seguridad.

2 Haga un inventario de sus efectos personales, indicando marca, tipo y número de fabricación, y procure marcar sus objetos de valor.

3 Compruebe que todas las posibles entradas de la casa quedan perfectamente cerradas, incluyendo las ventanas que dan a patios.

4 No conviene dejar señales visibles de que su vivienda está desocupada: encargue a algún vecino la recogida de la correspondencia de su buzón.

5 No comente su ausencia con personas desconocidas ni deje notas indicando cuando piensa volver.

6 Existen diferentes entidades de crédito que durante sus vacaciones pueden hacerse cargo de sus objetos de valor: no los deje nunca en casa, ni tampoco dinero.

Para más información
llame al:
900 150 000

Ministerio del Interior
Secretaría de Estado para la Seguridad

OPERACION VERANO 91

418 Capítulo 12

Options

Strategies for Reaching All Students

Students Needing Extra Help
Ex. 1: Review vocabulary from Book 2, Chap. 8, and from Book 1, Chap. 10.

Infórmate

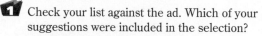

STRATEGY ► Coping with unknown words

1️⃣ Check your list against the ad. Which of your suggestions were included in the selection?

Remember, you already know several ways to figure out unknown words:

- recognizing a cognate
- recognizing a stem that appears in another Spanish word you know
- using the meaning of the phrases before and after the unknown word

2️⃣ What do you think these words mean? Explain to a partner how you figured them out.

merecidas   valor
vivienda   encargue
regreso   recogida
marca   ausencia
fabricación   hacerse cargo de

3️⃣ Now read the selection again and try out your meanings. If you prefer, try out these choices and identify the correct meanings.

1. merecidas
   a. merciful
   b. deserved
   c. safe
2. vivienda
   a. living
   b. life
   c. house
3. regreso
   a. return
   b. regret
   c. leaving
4. marca
   a. mark
   b. brand
   c. stain
5. número de fabricación
   a. serial number
   b. how many you own
   c. manufacturer's phone number

6. valor
   a. bravery
   b. value
   c. validity
7. encargue
   a. drive
   b. put in charge of
   c. send
8. recogida
   a. collecting
   b. recognizing
   c. knowing
9. ausencia
   a. absence
   b. audience
   c. plan
10. hacerse cargo de
    a. to park
    b. to send
    c. to take charge of

Aplicación

Can you understand the meaning of these sentences? Confirm your understanding with a partner.

1. El viaje que le regalaron sus padres era muy merecido.
2. Para su viaje compró una cámara de marca japonesa.
3. En el avión dieron la película *El regreso de Godzilla*.
4. Va a hacer muchas compras; el valor del dólar es alto.

¡Vamos a leer!   419

Cultural Notes

(p. 418, realia)
Summer vacations and holidays, when homes and apartments may be unoccupied for extended periods, are when burglaries are most frequent. For that reason, the Ministerio del interior sponsored this program in 1991 to help homeowners increase their home security. Telephone 900 numbers, similar to 800 numbers in the U.S., are reserved for public service and toll-free calls.

419

Apply

Process Writing
For information regarding developing a writing portfolio, see p. 54.

For information regarding developing a writing portfolio, see p. 54.

¡Vamos a escribir!

¿Prefieres viajar solo(a) o con un grupo? Vamos a comparar un viaje independiente a uno de excursión.

1 Primero, piensa en las ventajas y desventajas de las dos maneras de viajar. Piensa en estas cosas, entre otras:

- el costo
- los compañeros
- la necesidad de planear el transporte y los hoteles
- la oportunidad de conocer un lugar nuevo
- la oportunidad de practicar otro idioma

Escribe un párrafo breve empezando con la frase *Prefiero viajar solo(a) / con un grupo porque …*

Disfruta.

Písalo bien. Estés donde estés.
Porque Europ Assistance está siempre cerca.
Para que nunca te sientas demasiado lejos.

No te preocupes por nada.
Tienes un equipo humano a tu disposición
las 24 horas del día. Cuando tú lo necesites.
Incluso aunque no seas usuario.

Asegúrate de que tu próximo viaje sea
de placer. Hazte socio de Europ Assistance.
Y disfruta.

europ assistance
(91) 597 21 25

En su Banco, Agencia de Viajes o Agente de Seguros y en Cajeros Automáticos de la red Telebanco 4B.

Un policía en Barcelona ayudando a una turista

420 Capítulo 12

Options

420

2 Ahora piensa en la gente que viaja: jóvenes, familias, ancianos *(senior citizens)*. Escoge un tipo de viajero y recomienda la mejor manera de viajar para esta persona. Empieza con la frase *Para (un anciano) es mejor viajar solo/con un grupo porque...*

3 Para distribuir tu trabajo, puedes:

* hacer un debate sobre el tema *Para un(a) jóven es mejor viajar solo(a)*
* enviarlo a la revista o al periódico escolar
* exhibirlo en la escuela o en la sala de clases
* incluirlo en tu portafolio

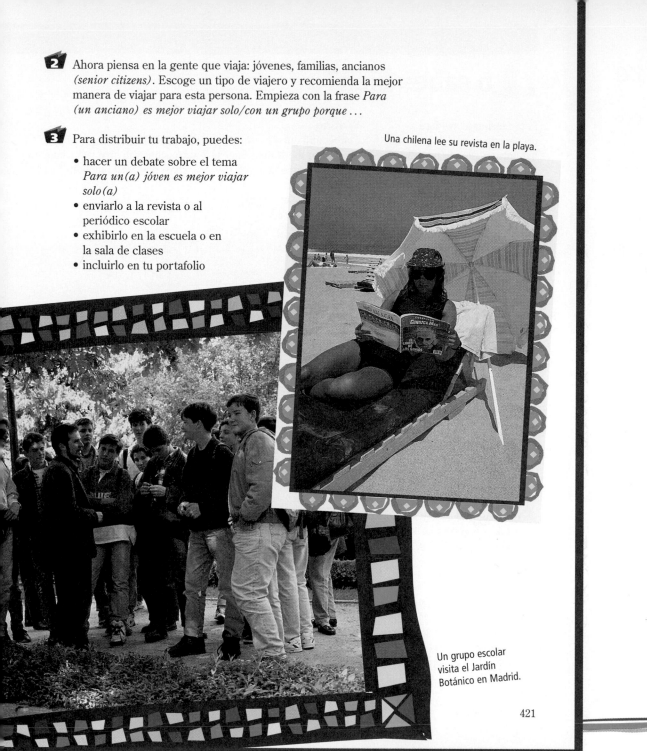

Una chilena lee su revista en la playa.

Un grupo escolar visita el Jardín Botánico en Madrid.

421

(p. 420, bottom photo)
During the 1990s, the Spanish tourism industry has grown to well over 50 million visitors annually. The greatest number of visitors come from Europe (86 percent), followed by Africa (4 percent), and the Americas (3 percent). The majority of tourists say they visit Spain for fun, to visit historic sites, or to increase their understanding of Spanish culture.

(p. 421, top photo)
Just north of the historic Chilean port city of Valparaíso is the famous beach resort of Viña del Mar, whose beaches are filled during the summer months of December, January, and February with vacationers from all over Latin America and Europe. Viña del Mar is noted for its sunshine, good seafood, and beautiful scenery. The city is surrounded by wooded areas, and many scenic gardens explain its nickname, *Ciudad Jardín*.

(pp. 420–421, photo)
Botanical gardens were originally associated with medical schools to train students and to raise medicinal plants. Today they display ornamental plants, drawing visitors to view regional and more exotic plants of special interest. While ethnobotanists continue to study the traditional uses of plants for medicinal purposes, most such gardens today stress cultivation.

Assess & Summarize

Test Preparation

You may want to assign parts of this section as written homework or as an in-class writing activity prior to administering the *Examen de habilidades.*

Teaching Suggestions

The customs form used in the writing section is found on p. 78 of the Vocabulary Art BLMs and on Overhead Transparency 88. Photocopy the BLM for your students.

Answers

Listening: —*Perdón, ¿por dónde queda la terminal de equipaje?*
—*Por este pasillo.*
—*¿Y la aduana?*
—*Está en la salida de la terminal de equipaje, al lado de la casa de cambio.*
—*Muchas gracias.*
The passenger is arriving (he or she is asking for the baggage claim area). It is an international flight (the passenger is asking where the customs area is).

Reading

1. d
2. e
3. b
4. c
5. a

¿Lo sabes bien?

Esta sección te ayudará a prepararte para el examen de habilidades, donde tendrás que hacer tareas semejantes.

Listening

Can you understand when people talk about places at an airport? Is this passenger leaving or arriving? Is it an international flight or not? How do you know?

Reading

This is a notice given to hotel guests. Match the Spanish words with their English meanings.

> **En caso de robo, el primer paso es denunciarlo en la estación de policía más cercana; en caso de emergencias solamente, llamar al 911. Si pierde o le roban el pasaporte, hay que acudir al consulado de su país para su reemplazo temporal.**

1. denunciar   a. *temporary*
2. cercana   b. *go to*
3. acudir   c. *replacement*
4. reemplazo   d. *report*
5. temporal   e. *near*

Writing

Can you fill out a customs form for Spanish-speaking travelers arriving in the United States? Your teacher will give you a copy to fill out. Imagine that you have purchased *at least* one item that has to be declared.

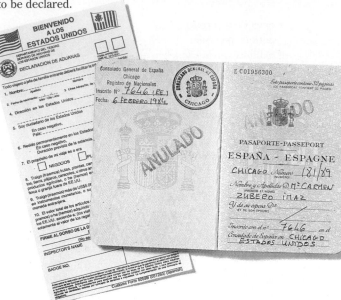

Culture

Can you name three kinds of places to stay in Spain and describe at least one of them?

Speaking

Create a dialogue in which you buy an airline ticket at a travel agency.

A —*¿Cuánto cuesta un boleto de ida y vuelta a Cancún?*
B —*Esta semana la línea aérea Aeroméxico tiene una excursión de seis días a Cancún por sólo $569.*
A —*¿Incluye el hotel?*
B —*Sí, incluye un boleto de ida y vuelta, el hotel y el almuerzo.*
A —*¡Fantástico!*

Options

Strategies for Reaching All Students

Students Needing Extra Help
¿Lo sabes bien?: Have students write out this section so that they can check off what they have mastered. Remind them that this is only a sample of what the real test will be like.
Listening: Remind students that they are listening for only two pieces of information. Brainstorm with students for what words they should be listening.
Reading: Review cognates and recognizing verb stems. Remind students that they prac-

ticed something similar in *Infórmate* in the *¡Vamos a leer!* section.
Writing: Most students will not be familiar with the concept of declaring purchases or the terminology related to it. Explain the idea of declaring and of monetary limits. For items 8, 9, and 10, draw a distinction between the three categories. Have students highlight the main words or phrases. They need not fully understand the fine print on the back of the form; you may, however, want to paraphrase it for them.

Culture: Have students review the notes they took during their first reading of the *Perspectiva cultural.*
Speaking: Remind students not to copy the model directly. Bring in some travel ads that state ticket prices, accommodations, etc. Use the vocabulary section of the Organizer. Limit the number of lines of dialogue. Remind students to use the present tense.

Resumen del capítulo 12

Usa el vocabulario de este capítulo para:

- give advice
- discuss travel arrangements
- make recommendations about what to do and see in your community

to discuss travel arrangements
el viaje
el viajero, la viajera
la agencia de viajes
el /la agente (de viajes)
planear
viajar
la reservación, *pl.* las reservaciones
el boleto (de ida y vuelta)
sólo de ida
el cheque de viajero
el equipaje
la terminal de equipaje
facturar
hacer la maleta
deshacer la maleta
recomendar *(e → ie)*

to describe a plane trip
el aeropuerto
el avión, *pl.* los aviones
la línea aérea
el pasillo
el /la piloto
la puerta
la tarjeta de embarque
la ventanilla
el vuelo
aterrizar
despegar

la escala
sin escala
con destino a
procedente de
el /la auxiliar de vuelo
el empleado, la empleada (de la línea aérea)
abrocharse
desabrocharse
pasar por
registrar
la aduana
el aduanero, la aduanera
el cinturón (de seguridad)
el pasajero, la pasajera

to discuss tourist accommodations
la habitación, *pl.* las habitaciones
una (habitación) doble
una (habitación) individual
la pensión, *pl.* las pensiones

to discuss tourist activities
el /la guía
la guía

la oficina telefónica
el /la turista
la oficina de turismo
hacer una excursión
la casa de cambio
cambiar
la artesanía
el mercado
la naturaleza
el palacio
el pueblo
regatear
indígena
pintoresco, -a

other useful words and expressions
el retraso
conseguir *(e → i)*
disfrutar de
incluir: incluye
tener cuidado (con): ten cuidado
ir: ve; no vayas
a mano

Resumen   423

Writing: Tell students to fill out the forms completely in order to avoid delays in customs.

Culture
1. *paradores:* government-run inns often located in old and historic palaces, castles, or convents
2. hotels
3. youth hostels
4. private homes (which usually provide a room and one meal a day)

Speaking: Dialogues will vary.

¿? **Prueba cumulativa**

¿? **Examen de habilidades**

c **Test Generator**

CAPÍTULO 13

THEME: MEALS

COMMUNICATION

Topics

Food preparation

Nutrition

Fruit

Objectives

To discuss food preparation customs in Spanish-speaking cultures

To name foods

To describe dishes and their ingredients

To discuss cooking

To discuss nutrition

To name snacks and beverages

To make suggestions

CULTURE

Meals and food preparation in Latin America

GRAMMAR

Repaso: Mandatos negativos

El subjuntivo

Ancillaries available for use with Chapter 13

| Multisensory/Technology | Print | Assessment |

Multisensory/Technology

 Overhead Transparencies, 62–66

 Audio Tapes and CDs

 Vocabulary Art Blackline Masters for Hands-On Learning, pp. 68–72

 Classroom Crossword

 Video

 CD-ROM

Print

 Practice Workbook, pp. 125–135

 Writing, Audio & Video Activities, pp. 77–82, 129–131, 175–177

 Communicative Activity Blackline Masters

   Pair and Small Group Activities, pp. 85–90

   Situation Cards, p. 91

 Un paso más: Actividades para ampliar tu español, pp. 74–79

Assessment

 Assessment Program

   Pruebas, pp. 188–198

   Examen de habilidades, pp. 199–202

 Test Generator

Video still from Chap. 13

Regional Cuisine

Many basic foods eaten in Spain and Latin America today have been a part of diets there since pre-Columbian times. Indigenous Latin American staples include potatoes, squash, peppers, and chocolate, but corn is perhaps the most common. The Mexican corn *tortilla* is used rather than bread during meals, and also in the preparation of typical dishes such as *enchiladas* and *tacos*. The *tortilla* is popular in Central America as well, but it is smaller and thicker than its Mexican counterpart. Another popular corn dish in Mexico and Central America is *tamales*. Also known as *nacatamales* in Nicaragua, these can be sweet or spicy, wrapped in corn husks or banana leaves, and will vary in shape and size depending on the region in which they are made. Although *tortillas* and *tamales* are not native to South America, numerous corn dishes are found throughout the continent. In Ecuador, *mote* is a typical part of family meals. It is simply a platter of cooked, large, white corn kernels that is placed in the center of the table: spoonfuls are taken directly rather than placed on individual plates.

Another food staple which dates back to pre-Columbian times is beans. By far, the most common entree in Central America and parts of the Caribbean is black beans and rice. This combination has acquired two colorful names. In Nicaragua, it is known as *gallo pinto* (speckled rooster), and in Costa Rica and Cuba it is referred to as *moros y cristianos* (Moors and Christians, in reference to the Arab invasion of Spain). It is often served with a dry, white cheese on top and accompanied by fried or boiled plantains.

Seafood is also a basic ingredient for those who live along the coasts of Spain and Latin America. Some of the most prized shellfish come from Chile's coastal waters, and are used in many delicious combinations, including the traditional *curanto* (a steaming hot seasoned serving of various shellfish) in southern Chile.

In Spain, the region best known for seafood is Galicia along the northwest coast. One of the most popular dishes there is boiled octopus sliced into medallions and covered with hot olive oil and garlic. The most universally recognized Spanish entree—*paella*—also contains seafood. Originally from Valencia on Spain's east coast, it consists of saffron-seasoned rice, abundant amounts of shellfish in its shell, pork and chicken, and other regional delicacies.

Introduce

Re-entry of Concepts
The following list represents words, expressions, and grammar topics re-entered from Book 1 and Book 2 (Chaps. 4 and 6):

Book 1
numbers 0–31, food, drink, expressing preferences, numbers 32–100

Chapter 4
sports, leisure-time activities

Chapter 6
holidays

Planning

Cross-Curricular Connections

Mathematics Connection *(pp. 446–447)*
Have each student choose a favorite recipe and write it out in Spanish. All directions must be in the command form, with use of the subjunctive encouraged. All the ingredient amounts must be metric. You may want to orchestrate a potluck day so that students can demonstrate these recipes and bring the foods to class.

Health Connection *(pp. 448–449)*
In pairs, have students role play dieticians. They will prepare menus for clients with varying needs: people who must lower their cholesterol or gain weight, vegetarians, people who need low sugar or high protein, etc. Have each pair create two menus and share them with the class.

Spanish in Your Community
Have students determine which restaurants in their community serve foods and dishes from Spain. Have students visit this(these) restaurant(s) for a meal or to talk with the chef. Students may wish to invite a chef or a parent who specializes in Spanish food to visit the class, discuss Spanish food, and perhaps prepare a dish. Students might also want to visit the local grocery store to find out which Spanish foods are available.

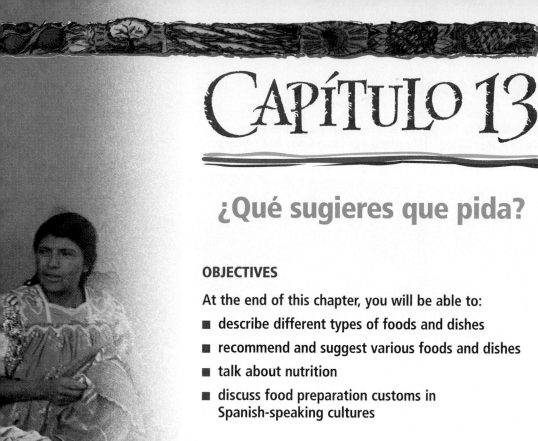

CAPÍTULO 13

¿Qué sugieres que pida?

OBJECTIVES

At the end of this chapter, you will be able to:

■ describe different types of foods and dishes

■ recommend and suggest various foods and dishes

■ talk about nutrition

■ discuss food preparation customs in Spanish-speaking cultures

Mercado de Quetzaltenango, Guatemala

425

Cultural Notes

(p. 424, photo)
Quetzaltenango, also called Xela, is an industrial city and a major trading center for villages in Guatemala's western highlands. Avenida 15 is home to a large market where produce as well as woven and ceramic *artesanía* from the surrounding villages are sold. These two women selling *rábanos* (radishes), *zanahorias,* and *maravillas* (mari-golds) in the market are wearing *huipiles* typical of their home village. Each village has a distinctive *huipil* with a characteristic woven or embroidered design. Often these ornate designs form a cross when the blouse is laid open and flat. The cross shape is emblematic of eternal life and also represents the four cardinal points, the four winds, and the four phases of the moon.

425

Critical Thinking: Classifying Information

Have students make a two-column list with the headings *Bueno(a) para la salud* and *Malo(a) para la salud.* Have them categorize the foods shown in the photos. Using this information, have them make a second list with the headings *Lo que como frecuentemente, Lo que como a veces,* and *Lo que no como nunca.*

Answers: ¡Piénsalo bien!
Answers to inductive questions will vary.

¡Piénsalo bien!

Mira las fotos. Las personas que vemos están hablando de la alimentación. ¿Hay comida en estas fotos que reconoces?

"A toda la familia le gustan las barbacoas y los picnics."

A ti, ¿qué te gusta comer en una barbacoa?

Una familia española disfrutando de un picnic

426   Capítulo 13

Options

Strategies for Reaching All Students

Spanish-Speaking Students
Ask: *¿Cuáles de estas comidas te gustan? ¿Cuáles te gustaría probar? ¿Has probado paella? ¿Te gustó? ¿Cómo se prepara?*

 Un paso más Ex. 13-A

Jóvenes en un restaurante en Cali, Colombia

"Para nosotros, la comida rápida es muy sabrosa. Pero comemos comida más nutritiva en el desayuno y la cena."

¿Cuántas veces a la semana comes comida rápida? ¿Tratas también de comer comida nutritiva frecuentemente?

"¿Hay algo más delicioso que la paella? Para mí, ¡no!"

¿Pruebas comida nueva cuando tienes la oportunidad, o siempre pides lo que sueles comer? ¿Has probado la paella? Si te gustan los mariscos y el arroz, te gustaría mucho la paella.

Comiendo paella en un restaurante al lado del mar, Barcelona

427

Cultural Notes ☀

(p. 427, top photo)
Colombia has many fast-food chains offering the familiar burger and fries combination. For regional variety, though, Colombian street vendors offer many eat-while-you-walk foods, such as *pan de queso* (a ring of cheese bread), *chuzos* (skewers of beef), *tostones* (plantain chips), *buñuelos* (fritters made with corn flour and grated cheese), and a medley of tropical fruit drinks such as *guanábana* (soursop: a large, acid, succulent fruit with short, fleshy spines) and *mora* (mulberry).

(p. 427, bottom photo)
Seafood is abundant in Barcelona, a major Mediterranean seaport. Popular regional dishes include *bullabesa* (fish stew similar to the French *bouillabaisse), zarzuela de mariscos* (an "operetta" of shellfish), *bacalao* (cod), *lenguado* (sole) and *lubina* (sea bass). Catalan cooking combines elements of Spanish and French cuisine, and features spicy sauces including *alli i oli*, garlic-flavored olive oil used for poultry.

Present

Chapter Theme
Cooking

Communicative Objectives
- To name foods
- To describe dishes and their ingredients
- To discuss cooking
- To discuss nutrition
- To name snacks and beverages

 Transparencies 62–63

 Vocabulary Art BLMs

 Pronunciation Tape 13-1

Teaching Suggestions
Preparing students to speak: Use one or two options from each of the categories of Comprehensible Input, Physical Response, or Limited Verbal Response. For a complete explanation of these categories and some sample activities, see pp. T16–T17.

Vocabulario para conversar

¿Quieres probar los camarones?

Vas a necesitar estas palabras y expresiones para hablar sobre la alimentación. Después de leerlas varias veces, practícalas con un(a) compañero(a).

la piña

el durazno

el limón, *pl.* los limones

guisado, -a

el champiñón, *pl.* los champiñones

el espárrago

el camarón, *pl.* los camarones

al horno

a la parrilla

hacer una barbacoa

asado, -a

428   Capítulo 13

Options

Strategies for Reaching All Students

Spanish-Speaking Students
Ask: *¿Puedes añadir algunas palabras a esta lista? Escríbelas en tu vocabulario personal.*

 Un paso más Ex. 13-B

Students Needing Extra Help
Begin the vocabulary section of the Organizer. Separate the foods into categories: fruits, vegetables, condiments, etc. Point out that *champiñón* and *camarón* lose their accents in the plural. Point out that *enlatada* contains the Spanish word *lata,* which they already know. Point out the differences between the cooking terms for students unfamiliar with them.

También necesitas . . . : Remind students that they have seen *dañar* before with a similar meaning. Give examples for *hacer daño a* and *mantenerse sano.* Point out the difference between *el dulce* as a noun and *dulce* as an adjective. Point out that *salado* contains the Spanish word *sal.*

428

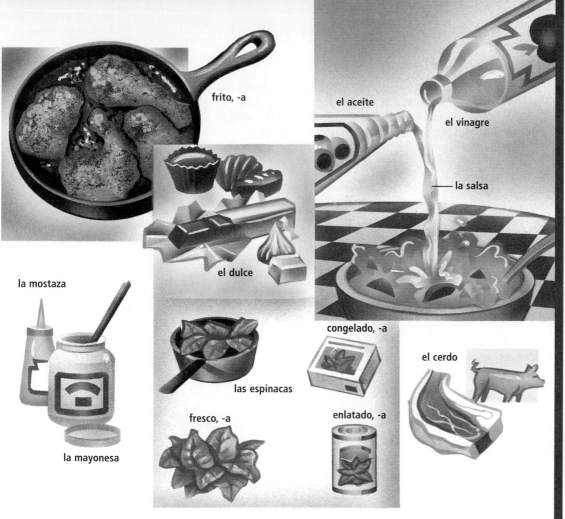

frito, -a

el aceite

el vinagre

la salsa

el dulce

la mostaza

congelado, -a

el cerdo

las espinacas

la mayonesa

fresco, -a

enlatado, -a

También necesitas . . .

la alimentación	nourishment, food	dulce	sweet
hacer daño a	to make ill; not to agree with (food)	grasoso, -a	greasy
		soso, -a	tasteless
mantenerse* sano, -a	to stay healthy		
amargo, -a	bitter		
agrio, -a	sour		
salado, -a	salty		

> **¿Y qué quiere decir . . . ?**
> la caloría   la proteína
> el carbohidrato   la vitamina

*Mantenerse follows the pattern of tener.

Vocabulario para conversar   429

Practice

Reteach / Review: Vocabulary

Before beginning these exercises, you may want to review Chaps. 4 and 12 of Book 1, in which food vocabulary is introduced.

Ex. 2: To extend this exercise, when *Estudiante B* replies that the food is too bitter, salty, etc., *Estudiante A* can offer to add or do something to the food to make it taste better.

Teaching Suggestions

Ex. 1: Point out that *al horno* and *a la parrilla* are expressions whose forms never change. However, *asado, guisado,* and *frito* are adjectives that agree in gender and number with the nouns they follow.

Answers: Empecemos a conversar

1 ESTUDIANTE A

(The adjective chosen may vary.)

a. ¿Quieres probar los camarones fritos?

b. ...el cerdo frito?

c. ...la carne (de res) frita?

d. ...el pollo frito?

e. ...el pescado frito?

f. Questions will vary.

ESTUDIANTE B

a.–f. Answers will vary, but may begin with *Me encanta(n)* and show correct adjective agreement.

Empecemos a conversar

Túrnate con un(a) compañero(a) para ser *Estudiante A* y *Estudiante B*. Reemplacen las palabras subrayadas en el modelo con las palabras representadas o escritas en los recuadros. Si ven 💡 pueden dar su propia respuesta.

1

A — ¿Quieres probar *las papas fritas*?
B — Sí. *Me encantan las papas fritas.*
   o: No. Prefiero *las papas asadas.*

Estudiante A   Estudiante B

a.   b.

c.   d.

e.   f.

430   Capítulo 13

Options

Strategies for Reaching All Students

Spanish-Speaking Students

Exs. 1–2: Pair bilingual with non-bilingual students, if possible.

Students Needing Extra Help

¡No olvides!: If available, have students review the vocabulary sections of Book 1, Chaps. 4 and 12.

Ex. 1: Review cooking terms. Point out that *Estudiante A* has to combine the pictured food with a cooking term.

Ex. 2: Brainstorm other possibilities for the *prefiero* blank. Do the exercise twice, first using the *Estudiante B* response to practice the adjectives, then using the *prefiero* response.

Enrichment

Ex. 1: As homework, have students list three entrées that would appear on a menu in a family restaurant and write brief but detailed descriptions of each one. Tell students that the description should make the food as appealing as possible to the customer. For example, *Carne asada con arroz mexicano sabroso, y verduras frescas y una ensalada de espinacas, lechuga y tomates, servida con nuestra salsa fantástica.*

2

A — ¿Prefieres _café_ o _té_?
B — _Té, por favor. El café es demasiado amargo._
  o: _Ninguno, gracias. Prefiero ____._

Estudiante A

Estudiante B

amargo, -a	grasoso, -a
agrio, -a	dulce
soso, -a	salado, -a

a.

b.

c.

d.

e.

f.

Letrero de
una frutería en
San Francisco

431

2 ESTUDIANTE A
a. ¿Prefieres papas al horno o papas fritas?
b. . . . limones o naranjas?
c. . . . duraznos o manzanas?
d. . . . pollo frito o pollo a la parrilla?
e. . . . jamón o pescado?
f. Questions will vary.
ESTUDIANTE B
a.–f. Answers will vary, but should show correct adjective agreement.

Using Photos
Ask: _Si una yucateca es alguien de Yucatán, ¿de dónde es una mazatleca?_

Cultural Notes

(p. 431, photo)
The nostalgic name of this fruit store in San Francisco's Mission District suggests that the owner may be from Mazatlán, Mexico. The Mission District includes a sizable Hispanic population and is famous for its many murals reflecting the rich cultural influence of Latin America.

431

Practice & Apply

Teaching Suggestions

Ex. 4: Tell students to pretend they are planning a meal for this exercise.

Answers: Empecemos a conversar

3 ESTUDIANTE A

a. ¿Quieres camarones?
b. ... piña?
c. ... pastel?
d. ... dulce?
e. ... vinagre?
f. ... espinacas?
g. Questions will vary.

ESTUDIANTE B

a.–g. Answers will vary.

4 ESTUDIANTE A

a. ¿Qué servimos, espinacas frescas o enlatadas?
b. ... piña fresca o enlatada?
c. ... espárragos frescos o enlatados?
d. ... pescado fresco o enlatado?
e. ... duraznos frescos o enlatados?
f. ... champiñones frescos o enlatados?
g. Questions will vary.

ESTUDIANTE B

a.–g. Answers will vary.

3

A — ¿Quieres *refresco*?
B — *No, gracias. Los refrescos me hacen daño.*
    o: *Sí, un poco, por favor.*

Estudiante A

a.   b.   c.
d.   e.   f.   g.

Estudiante B

___ me hace(n) daño.

No me gusta(n) ___.

Nunca como ___.

Tiene(n) muchas calorías.

4

A — *¿Qué servimos, jamón fresco o enlatado?*
B — *Enlatado. Es más práctico.*
    o: *¿Por qué no servimos ___?*

Estudiante A

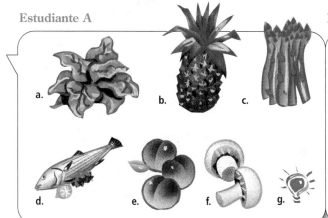

a.   b.   c.
d.   e.   f.   g.

Estudiante B

Tiene(n) más vitaminas.

Es más práctico.

Se consigue(n) durante todo el año.

Es (Son) mejor(es).

Es (Son) muy bueno(a)(s) para la salud.

También podemos servir ___ congelado(a).

432   Capítulo 13

Options

Strategies for Reaching All Students

Spanish-Speaking Students

Exs. 3–4: Pair bilingual with non-bilingual students, if possible.
Ex. 8: *Haz una lista de un menú ideal para un(a) joven. Incluye algo de cada grupo nutritivo. ¿Sigues tú una dieta nutritiva? ¿De qué debes comer más? ¿De qué debes comer menos?*

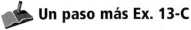 **Un paso más Ex. 13-C**

Students Needing Extra Help

Ex. 3: Give examples of how to fill in the blanks in the *Estudiante B* responses.
Ex. 4: Point out that if *Estudiante B* chooses the *¿por qué?* response, he or she must fill in the blank with an appropriate choice.
Ex. 8: Explain carbohydrates, calories, etc. for students who are unfamiliar with these terms.

Enrichment

Ex. 4: Point out that if students suggest that another food be served, they should give reasons for the suggestion.
Ex. 6: Additional question: *¿Quién prepara la comida cuando hacen barbacoas en tu casa?*

Empecemos a escribir

Escribe tus respuestas en español.

5 ¿Qué frutas y verduras comen en tu casa? Generalmente, ¿son frescas, congeladas o enlatadas? ¿Qué otras cosas enlatadas o congeladas comen? ¿Crees que es mejor comer comidas frescas? ¿Por qué?

6 ¿Cuándo hacen barbacoas en tu casa? Generalmente, ¿qué comidas sirven en una barbacoa? ¿Cuál es tu comida favorita en una barbacoa? ¿Cómo prefieres las carnes—asadas, fritas, al horno o a la parrilla?

7 ¿Le pones aceite y vinagre o alguna otra salsa a la ensalada? ¿A qué le pones mayonesa? ¿Y mostaza?

8 ¿Sabes qué tipos de alimentación tienen muchas calorías? ¿Y pocas? ¿En qué comidas hay muchos carbohidratos? ¿Y proteínas? ¿Qué alimentación debe tener una persona para mantenerse sana?

También se dice

el caramelo
el confite

el ananá

el hongo
la seta

el aderezo
el aliño

el melocotón

el chancho
el cochino
el gorrino
el guarro
el marrano
el puerco

al carbón
a la plancha

rostizado, -a

In addition to *hacer una barbacoa*, we also say *hacer un asado*.

Vocabulario para conversar   433

433

Present

Chapter Theme
Recipes

Communicative Objectives
- To name foods
- To describe dishes and their ingredients
- To discuss cooking
- To discuss nutrition
- To name snacks and beverages
- To make suggestions

 Transparencies 64–65

 Vocabulary Art BLMs

 Pronunciation Tape 13-2

Grammar Preview
The subjunctive is presented here lexically. The explanation is on pp. 443–444.

Teaching Suggestions
Preparing students to speak: Use one or two options from each of the categories of Comprehensible Input, Physical Response, or Limited Verbal Response. For a complete explanation of these categories and some sample activities, see pp. T16–T17.

Vocabulario para conversar

¿De qué está hecha una empanada?

Aquí tienes el resto del vocabulario que necesitas en este capítulo para hablar sobre la alimentación.

hervir *(e → ie)*

revolver *(o → ue)*

el gazpacho

la receta

el chorizo

el pepino

el ajo

el pimiento verde

la masa

el relleno

la empanada

la fresa

la tarta

Options

Strategies for Reaching All Students

Spanish-Speaking Students
Ask: *¿Qué otros ingredientes sabes que se necesitan para completar estas recetas? Escríbelos en tu vocabulario personal.*

 Un paso más Ex. 13-D

Students Needing Extra Help
Point out that *el melón* loses its accent in the plural. Stress that this is canteloupe and not watermelon. Write out the full paradigms for *hervir* and *revolver,* including command forms, for those students who need to see them. If available, use the vocabulary sections of the Organizers from Book 1, Chaps. 4 and 12. Emphasize that a *tortilla española* is an omelet, not a Mexican *tortilla.*

También necesitas . . . : Explain the concept of *las tapas.* Write out the complete *sugerir* paradigm, emphasizing its similarity to *hervir.* Refer to Exs. 10 and 12, where *que pidas* and *que haga* are used in context. Give additional examples.

la calabaza

picar

el huevo duro

la paella

el perro caliente

la tortilla española

la cereza

el melón, *pl.* los melones

la sandía

la ensalada de frutas

También necesitas . . .

el bocadillo	*Spanish sandwich made with French-type roll*
las tapas	*appetizer-size dishes served in restaurants in Spain*
mezclar	*to mix*
sugerir *(e → ie)*	*to suggest*
cocido, -a	*cooked*
(estar) hecho, -a (de)	*(to be) made (of)*
que pidas *(from:* pedir*)*	*that you ask for / order*
que haga *(from:* hacer*)*	*that I do*

¿Y qué quiere decir . . . ?
el cocinero, la cocinera
el ingrediente
cortar

Vocabulario para conversar   435

Practice

Reteach / Review: Vocabulary

Ex. 10: To extend this exercise, *Estudiante B* can ask why *Estudiante A* suggests that particular food with the latter giving his or her reason.

Re-enter / Recycle

Ex. 11: holidays from Chap. 6

Answers: Empecemos a conversar

9 ESTUDIANTE A

a. ¿De qué está hecho el gazpacho?

b. ...hecha la paella?

c. ...hecha una tortilla española?

d. ...hecha una ensalada de frutas?

e. ...hecha una empanada?

f. ...hecho un bocadillo?

g. Questions will vary.

ESTUDIANTE B

a.–g. Answers will vary.

10 ESTUDIANTE A

a. Te sugiero que pidas un bocadillo de ___.

b. ...una empanada de ___.

c. ...unas tapas.

d. ...una tortilla española.

e. ...una sopa de ___.

f. ...un perro caliente.

g. Statements will vary.

ESTUDIANTE B

a.–g. Answers will vary.

Empecemos a conversar

9

A — ¿De qué está *hecho un pastel*?

B — Está *hecho de harina, huevos, leche, mantequilla y azúcar*.

Estudiante A   **Estudiante B**

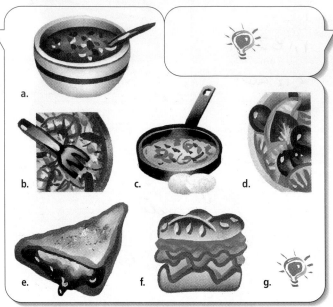

a.

b.   c.   d.

e.   f.   g.

10   un pastel   A — *Te sugiero que pidas un pastel de chocolate*.
      de ___   B — *Sí, buena idea, y además, quiero un café*.
                   o: *No, prefiero una ensalada de frutas*.

Estudiante A   **Estudiante B**

a. un bocadillo de ___   e. una sopa de ___

b. una empanada de ___   f. un perro caliente

c. unas tapas

d. una tortilla española   g.

436   Capítulo 13

Options

Strategies for Reaching All Students

Spanish-Speaking Students

Exs. 9–10: Pair Spanish-speaking students, if possible.

Exs. 11–12: Pair bilingual with non-bilingual students, if possible.

Students Needing Extra Help

Exs. 10 and 12: Explain the subjunctive expressions for meaning only. Avoid discussion of grammar.

Ex. 10: Explain the context of this exercise, (a waiter making suggestions for dinner). Break the expression *Te sugiero que pidas* into parts for students. Brainstorm possibilities for the blanks and for the *Estudiante B* responses.

Ex. 12: Help students match the *Estudiante A* and *Estudiante B* responses before beginning the exercise. Review commands.

11   A —*¿Hacemos <u>pavo</u> para <u>el Día de Gracias</u>?*
       B —*<u>Sí, y tarta de calabaza también</u>.*
          o: *¿Por qué no hacemos ___?*

el Día de Gracias

Estudiante A   **Estudiante B**

a. tu cumpleaños   **b. el picnic**   **c. el Día de la Independencia**

d. la fiesta de sorpresa   **e. la fiesta de graduación**   **f. la barbacoa**   **g.**

12   **el café**   A —*¿Qué quieres que haga para <u>el café</u>?*
                  B —*Primero, <u>hierve el agua</u>.*

Estudiante A   **Estudiante B**

a. la barbacoa   **f. las empanadas**

b. el pastel

c. los camarones fritos   **g.**

d. el gazpacho

e. la paella

picar la cebolla	**mezclar la harina y el azúcar**
cortar los chorizos	
conseguir los perros calientes	**preparar el aceite**
	hervir el agua
revolver el relleno	

11 ESTUDIANTE A
a. ¿Hacemos pastel para tu cumpleaños?
b. . . . bocadillos para el picnic?
c. . . . perros calientes para el Día de la Independencia?
d. . . . empanadas para la fiesta de sorpresa?
e. . . . camarones para la fiesta de graduación?
f. . . . cerdo para la barbacoa?
g. Questions will vary.
ESTUDIANTE B
a.–g. Answers will vary, but should be logical.

12 ESTUDIANTE A
a. ¿Qué quieres que haga para la barbacoa?
b. . . . el pastel?
c. . . . los camarones fritos?
d. . . . el gazpacho?
e. . . . la paella?
f. . . . las empanadas?
g. Questions will vary.
ESTUDIANTE B
Answers will vary, but should include the following *tú* command forms:
a. Primero, consigue los perros calientes.
b. . . . mezcla la harina y el azúcar.
c. . . . prepara el aceite.
d. . . . pica la cebolla.
e. . . . corta los chorizos.
f. . . . revuelve el relleno.
g. Answers will vary.

Practice & Apply

 Practice Wkbk. 13-3, 13-4

 Audio Activity 13.2

 Pruebas 13-3, 13-4

 Comm. Act. BLM 13-1

Empecemos a escribir y a leer

Escribe tus respuestas en español.

13 ¿Has probado alguna vez la comida española? ¿Qué probaste? ¿Dónde? Imagina que estás en un restaurante español. ¿Qué piensas pedir?

14 ¿Qué comida española te gustaría hacer tú mismo(a)? ¿Te gusta la comida con ajo? ¿Y con cebolla?

15 ¿Cómo se prepara el pavo en los Estados Unidos? ¿De qué es el relleno? ¿Cómo ayudarás a preparar el pavo la próxima vez? ¿En qué otras cosas ayudarás? ¿Crees que ser cocinero(a) es una buena profesión? ¿Por qué?

16 Aquí tienes unas recetas para hacer diferentes cosas. Adivina *(guess)* para qué son y completa los nombres de las recetas.

a. ____ de papas

4 papas cocidas	mayonesa
2 huevos duros	sal y pimienta
1 cebolla	

Corta las papas y los huevos. Pica la cebolla. Mezcla todos los ingredientes.

b. ____ vinagreta

2 cucharadas de vinagre
$\frac{1}{2}$ taza de aceite de oliva
sal y pimienta

Con un tenedor, mezcla los ingredientes.

c. ____ de manzanas

5–6 manzanas	$\frac{1}{2}$ taza de azúcar
2 tazas de harina	sal
4 onzas de mantequilla	agua

Antes de comenzar, enciende el horno a 450 grados. Para preparar la masa, mezcla primero la harina y la mantequilla con un tenedor. Después, ponle un poco de sal y agua. Extiende la masa y ponla en un molde. Corta las manzanas y ponlas sobre la masa. Por último, espolvorea el azúcar sobre las manzanas. Ponlo en el horno por 10 minutos. Después, reduce la temperatura a 350 grados y cocina por 30 minutos más.

438 Capítulo 13

Options

Strategies for Reaching All Students

Spanish-Speaking Students
Ex. 15: Additional questions: *¿Se hacen comidas especiales en tu casa? ¿Cuándo se sirven esas comidas?*
Ex. 2: Instead of this exercise, tell students: *Escribe un párrafo sobre el (la) mejor cocinero(a) que conoces. Di por qué crees que es tan bueno(a) y describe una o dos de sus especialidades.*

 Un paso más Ex. 13-E

Students Needing Extra Help
Encourage students to finish all questions.
Ex. 13: Remind students that Spanish, Mexican, and Carribean foods are different from each other. Help them see how regional dishes are based on the ingredients which were originally readily available.
Ex. 14: Use the vocabulary section of the Organizer and the corresponding artwork. Point out that Exs. 15–16 can be completed by students unfamiliar with foreign foods.

Ex. 15: Assign this a few days in advance so that students can ask about it at home or contact the home economics teacher. Model responses to *¿En qué otras cosas ayudarás?* Give details of what a *cocinero(a)* does on a daily basis.
¡Comuniquemos! Ex. 1: Emphasize the health-related phrases suggested here. Model an entire dialogue to encourage students to create responses.
Ex. 2: Present a complete model. Use the vocabulary section of the Organizer. If avail-

¡Comuniquemos!

Aquí tienes otra oportunidad para usar el vocabulario de este capítulo.

1 Compara tu almuerzo con el de un(a) compañero(a).

A —*Para el almuerzo como... ¿Qué comes tú?*

B —*Yo como...*

A —*Me parece que comes mucho(a)/poco(a)... No debes comer tanto(a)/Debes comer más...*

Puedes usar las siguientes frases:

muchas/pocas proteínas   dulce
suficiente carbohidratos   fresco
algunas vitaminas   es mejor

2 Túrnate con un(a) compañero(a) para hablar del mejor cocinero o cocinera que tú conoces.

A —*(Mi abuelita) es la mejor cocinera que conozco.*

B —*¿Por qué?*

A —*Porque hace/Siempre cocina/Sabe preparar...*

3 Consigue una receta de alguna comida que te gusta mucho. Prepara una lista de los ingredientes. Explícale a tu compañero(a) cómo hacerla.

A —*Aquí tienes una receta para hacer un(a)...*

B —*¿De qué está hecho(a)?*

A —*...*

B —*¿Cómo se hace?*

A —*...*

¿Qué sabes ahora?

Can you:

- discuss food preferences and explain why?
  —No me gusta el (la) ___ frito(a) porque es muy ___.
- describe dishes and ingredients?
  —La tortilla española está ___ de ___, ___ y ___.
- suggest to a friend or relative which dishes to order?
  —Te sugiero que ___ un(a) ___.

También se dice

el huevo cocido

el ayote
el zapallo

el chile dulce
el chiltoma
el ají

la salchicha

el melón de agua

Vocabulario para conversar   439

Present & Apply

Cultural Objective

• To discuss the traditional importance of meals and food preparation in Latin America

Multicultural Perspectives

Kitchens, especially during holidays or special events, are the center of most households. In many Latin American countries, the preparation of special dishes involves the entire family. In Puerto Rico, everyone is needed to make *pasteles* for Christmas. These are made from mashed green bananas and seasonings that are then wrapped in banana leaves and steamed. A similar dish is popular in Mexico, where *tamales* are made from meat rolled in cornmeal and wrapped in corn husks that are then steamed. *Nacatamales* are a special holiday treat in some Central American countries. They contain not just corn, but meat, potato, and rice as well. Ask students to share a special event that involves the entire family in food or other preparations.

Perspectiva cultural

¿En qué se parece lo que ves en estas fotos a lo que hacen tú y tu familia? ¿En qué se diferencia?

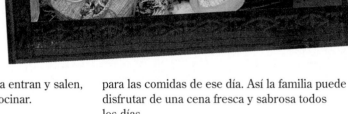

Mercado al lado de la catedral, Granada

Muchas familias latinoamericanas viven en casas o apartamentos pequeños. Los padres trabajan, y padres e hijos comen un almuerzo ligero y cenan platos que se compran ya hechos.

Pero otras familias todavía viven de una manera tradicional. En estas casas, la cocina es un cuarto muy importante. Tiene que ser grande porque se usa todos los días y es un lugar de reunión. La preparación de los platos dura mucho tiempo. Por eso, mientras la madre o la abuela cocina, los miembros de la familia entran y salen, se sientan a charlar y ayudan a cocinar.

En la familia tradicional, la abuela vive con su hijo o hija y sus nietos. Tiene un papel muy importante. Puede encargarse de la casa o cuidar a los niños. Pero sobre todo, se encarga de la comida. Hace las compras por la mañana. Después pasa muchas horas lavando, cortando y preparando los ingredientes de sopas y guisados deliciosos para la cena familiar.

Las familias que viven de una manera tradicional siempre compran por la mañana los ingredientes para las comidas de ese día. Así la familia puede disfrutar de una cena fresca y sabrosa todos los días.

La cultura desde tu perspectiva

1 Compara la cocina tradicional latinoamericana con la norteamericana. ¿Quiénes pasan mucho tiempo en la cocina? ¿Qué hacen?

2 Muchas familias que compran comida fresca todos los días tienen refrigerador y no tienen que hacer las compras tan a menudo. ¿Qué valor cultural tienen estas familias?

440 Capítulo 13

Options

Spanish-Speaking Students
Ask: *Piensa en la cocina de tu mamá o la de tu abuela. ¿Qué crees que recordarás de esa cocina en el futuro? ¿Los olores, los sabores, el calor . . . ? Explica por qué.*

 Un paso más Ex. 13-F

Students Needing Extra Help
Have students take notes to use in the *¿Lo sabes bien?* section.

Enrichment
Additional questions: *¿Cuáles son las ventajas y desventajas de hacer compras todos los días? ¿Cómo es diferente el papel de la abuela en una familia norteamericana de su papel en una familia hispana?*

Preparando camarones en Punta Santiago, Puerto Rico

Una familia cenando en Bogotá

Cultural Notes

(p. 440, photo)
The city of Granada in southeastern Spain was founded by the Moors in about A.D. 750, and was the center of Moorish wealth and culture in the thirteenth century. In 1492, when the armies of Fernando and Isabel took possession of the city, it was the last Moorish stronghold in Europe. The tombs of the king and queen are in the Royal Chapel of Granada's cathedral.

(p. 441, top photo)
Shrimp is a key ingredient in certain Puerto Rican dishes. One such dish is *caldo santo,* eaten during holy week. Ingredients include coconut milk, *recaíto* (a mixture of spices and vegetables), *alcaparrado* (a combination of olives, capers, and pimento), *yuca* (cassava), *yautía* (taro root), *batata* (sweet potato), *ñame* (yam), plantains, shrimp, *bacalao* (salt codfish), blue crab, and red snapper.

441

Preview

Answers

A *Encienda* is from an *-er* verb. The present-tense *tú* form is *enciendes*. The negative *tú* command form is *no enciendas*. It means "we recommend that you light."

B The form of *usar* is *use*. The related form, *use*, is used in negative commands: *No la use nunca . . . .* It is different because it ends in *e* rather than *a*. The verb form *lave* is also different because it ends in *e* rather than *a*.

Multicultural Perspectives

In Argentina, beef is an important part of the economy and of the cuisine. *Gauchos* began the tradition of the *asado criollo,* an outdoor feast featuring meats as the main course. All types of meats—sausages, ribs, steaks, and delicacies such as liver—are cooked *a la parrilla.* Sometimes an entire animal is split open and put on an iron spit to cook slowly as it turns. Different sauces are prepared to accompany the meats. Have students investigate the Pampas region of Argentina and the culture of the *gauchos.*

Gramática en contexto

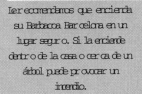

¡Lo felicitamos!
Compró Ud. la mejor barbacoa que se fabrica hoy, la Barbacoa Barcelona.

Le recomendamos que encienda su Barbacoa Barcelona en un lugar seguro. Si la enciende dentro de la casa o cerca de un árbol puede provocar un incendio.

Le sugerimos que use su Barbacoa Barcelona sólo para asar. Nunca la use para hornear o guisar.

Le sugerimos que lave su barbacoa con agua, detergente y un cepillo de metal. ¡Y ahora, que la disfrute! Estamos seguros que estará Ud. satisfecho con su Barbacoa Barcelona.

A A recommendation is made in the first caption. Look at the verb form *encienda.* Is it an *-ar, -er,* or *-ir* verb? What is the present-tense *tú* form? What is the negative *tú* command form? What do you think *Le recomendamos que encienda* means?

B A suggestion is made in the second caption. What form of *usar* is used? What is the related form that you know? How is this different from what you might expect? Find another suggestion in the third caption. How does the verb form that comes after *que* differ from what you might expect?

442   Capítulo 13

Options

Strategies for Reaching All Students

Students Needing Extra Help
Begin the grammar section of the Organizer. Review commands before beginning this section. Emphasize the vowel changes in the command form. Refer to the grammar section of the Chap. 12 Organizer.
Ex. 1: Review negative commands. Brainstorm possible reasons why the child shouldn't do these things. Emphasize the vowel change as a bridge to the subjunctive.

El subjuntivo: Make sure students take careful notes, or have a handout available with this information. Read the explanation and models aloud twice. The second time, when you come to the sentence "We use it to say . . . ," have students tell you the Spanish word for "want," "tell," "suggest," and "recommend." Then give the students the following formula: subject + *querer,* etc. + *que* + other subject + subjunctive.

Emphasize that each sentence will have two subjects and two different verbs, connected by *que.* The subjunctive verb will appear after *que.* Refer to the models to point out the different parts of the formula.

Repaso: Mandatos negativos

You already know how to give negative commands to someone you address as *tú*.

1 Imagina que cuidas a un(a) niño(a) que siempre quiere hacer lo que no debe. Tú le dices que no y él (ella) siempre pregunta por qué. Turnándote con un compañero(a), hagan los dos papeles. Por ejemplo:

beber otro refresco

A —*No bebas otro refresco.*
B —*¿Por qué no?*
A —*Porque te puede hacer daño.*

a. patinar en el pasillo
b. comer más dulces
c. cortar las flores
d. mezclar la sal con el azúcar
e. abrir ese guardarropa
f. saltar a la cuerda en la casa
g. echar los espárragos en la basura

El subjuntivo

Up to now you have been using verbs in the *indicative mood,* which is used to talk about facts or actual events. For example:

Tomás no **come** camarones.
Javier y yo **mezclamos** los ingredientes.
Tú **escribes** toda la receta.

Spanish has another way of using verbs called the *subjunctive mood.* We use it to say what one person does or doesn't want, tell, suggest, or recommend someone else to do. A sentence that includes the subjunctive form has two parts connected by the word *que.* For example:

Sus padres **no quieren que** Tomás **coma** camarones.
La profesora **sugiere que** Javier y yo **mezclemos** los ingredientes.
El cocinero **recomienda que escribas** toda la receta.

Vitaminas de refresco.

Ahora que aprieta el calor, lo mejor es refrescarse con vitaminas. Mucho hielo, agua y zumo de limón. El refresco más natural, más barato y con más vitaminas. Este verano sácale todo su jugo al limón.

Alimentos de España DISFRUTALOS.

Gramática en contexto   443

Present & Practice

Answers

1 ESTUDIANTE A
a. No patines en el pasillo.
b. No comas . . .
c. No cortes . . .
d. No mezcles . . .
e. No abras . . .
f. No saltes . . .
g. No eches . . .

ESTUDIANTE B
Estudiante B responds *¿Por qué no?* throughout, and the subsequent replies of *Estudiante A* will vary, but should be logical.

 Practice Wkbk. 13-5

 Prueba 13-5

 Writing Activity 13-D

Cultural Notes

(p. 443, realia)
This ad suggests that *limonada* is the ideal drink for cooling down during warm weather. Although *refresco* most commonly refers to a soft drink, it literally means "refresher" and can be used to describe any drink that fulfills that meaning.

Present & Practice

On the day folllowing the presentation of the subjunctive mood, you might begin the class with this activity:

Have each student imagine being a waiter or waitress in a Spanish restaurant. They should prepare to share with the class what they would recommend to someone trying Spanish food for the first time.

• We form the present subjunctive of most verbs the same way we form negative *tú* commands. We drop the *-o* of the present-tense indicative *yo* form and add the subjunctive endings.

infinitive *-ar*

que (yo)	hable	que (nosotros) que (nosotras)	hable**mos**
que (tú)	hable**s**	que (vosotros) que (vosotras)	hablé**is**
que Ud. que (él) que (ella)	hable	que Uds. que (ellos) que (ellas)	hable**n**

infinitive *-er/-ir*

que (yo)	com**a** /viv**a**	que (nosotros) que (nosotras)	com**amos** /viv**amos**
que (tú)	com**as** /viv**as**	que (vosotros) que (vosotras)	com**áis** /viv**áis**
que Ud. que (él) que (ella)	com**a** /viv**a**	que Uds. que (ellos) que (ellas)	com**an** /viv**an**

• We form the *yo, tú,* and *Ud./él/ella* forms of the subjunctive of stem-changing verbs the same way as regular verbs. We drop the *-o* of the present-tense *yo* form and add the subjunctive endings.

El camarero quiere que **pruebes**
 la tarta de limón.
El cocinero no quiere que
 hierva el agua.
Te recomiendo que **pidas** una
 tarta de cerezas.

444   Capítulo 13

Options

Strategies for Reaching All Students

Students Needing Extra Help
Rewrite the three subjunctive charts on the chalkboard. Write out separate charts for *comer* and *vivir*. Have students copy the charts. Make sure they include the *que*. Remind them that stem-changing *-ar* and *-er* verbs have the stem change in all except the *nosotros* and *vosotros* forms. There are "boot" verbs in the subjunctive also. Write out some complete paradigms of *-ar, -er,* and *-ir* "boot" verbs *(probar, encender, servir)*.

Before presenting the *-car, -gar,* and *-zar* verbs, remind students that those verbs had a spelling change in the *yo* form of the preterite. In the subjunctive, the change will appear in all forms. Write out the complete paradigms of these verbs on the chalkboard. Have lists available of the verbs students already know that fall into these categories. Practice all irregular verb forms daily.

Ex. 2: Review subjunctive endings. Point out that none of the verbs used here are stem-changing or spelling-change verbs.

444

- Verbs whose infinitives end in *-car, -gar,* and *-zar* have a spelling change in all the forms of the present subjunctive in order to retain the original sound.

-car *(c → qu)*
buscar
Buscamos ajo y cebolla para el gazpacho.
Mamá quiere que **busquemos** ajo y cebolla para el gazpacho.

-gar *(g → gu)*
apagar
Juan apaga la barbacoa con un poco de agua.
Recomendamos que Juan **apague** la barbacoa con un poco de agua.

-zar *(z → c)*
cruzar
Cruzamos la calle para ir a la pescadería.
Sugiero que **crucemos** la calle para ir a la pescadería.

2 ¿Qué les recomienda el médico a sus pacientes que quieren mantenerse sanos?

Gloria /
desayunar cereal, melón y leche

El médico recomienda que Gloria desayune cereal, melón y leche.

a. Tomás / no comer tanta comida salada
b. Sra. González / tomar más vitaminas
c. los estudiantes / escribir una lista de lo que comen
d. (nosotros) / beber ocho vasos de agua al día
e. (tú) / cambiar tu alimentación
f. (yo) / preparar platos de verduras y frutas frescas
g. nadie / comer comida grasosa
h. Graciela y Ricardo / cocinar la carne a la parrilla
i. María Elena y yo / tomar una clase de ejercicio

Una frutería en la Ciudad de México

445

Answers
2 a. El médico recomienda que Tomás no coma tanta comida salada.
b. . . . la Sra. González tome más vitaminas.
c. . . . los estudiantes escriban una lista de lo que comen.
d. . . . bebamos ocho vasos de agua al día.
e. . . . cambies tu alimentación.
f. . . . prepare platos de verduras y frutas frescas.
g. . . . nadie coma comida grasosa.
h. . . . Graciela y Ricardo cocinen la carne a la parrilla.
i. . . . María Elena y yo tomemos una clase de ejercicio.

 Practice Wkbk. 13-6, 13-7

Cultural Notes

Enrichment
As homework, have students list the recommendations the following people would make in the given situation: a teacher advising students on how to prepare for a test, a parent instructing a babysitter on his or her toddler's evening routine, a guidance counselor telling a student how to prepare for a job interview. If they prefer, students can think of people in other situations giving recommendations.

(p. 445, photo)
Most open-air *mercados* in Mexico feature a *frutería*. This one is in the colonial suburb of San Ángel, which lies in the southern section of Mexico City along Avenida Insurgentes, not far from the Universidad Autónoma de México.

Practice

Re-enter / Recycle

Ex. 4: sports and leisure-time activities from Chap. 4

Answers

3 *Estudiante A asks throughout,* *¿Qué quieres que haga?*

ESTUDIANTE B

a. Quiero que piques . . .
b. . . .mezcles . . .
c. . . .abras . . .
d. . . .saques . . .
e. . . .busques . . .
f. . . .apagues . . .
g. . . .cortes . . .
h. Statements will vary.

4 ESTUDIANTE A

a. Mi mamá me dice que monte en bicicleta o a caballo.
b. Mi entrenador(a) me dice que corra . . .
c. Mis amigos me dicen que nade . . .
d. Mi papá me dice que camine . . .
e. Mi abuela me dice que patine . . .
f. Statements will vary.

ESTUDIANTE B

a.–f. Answers will vary.

5 Order may vary, but should include:
Mis padres no quieren que yo escuche cintas cuando cenamos.
. . . use ropa tan sucia.
. . . suba montañas.
. . . me maquille demasiado.
. . . toque mi trompeta a medianoche.

---

3 Túrnate con un(a) compañero(a). Imagina que estás preparando una cena y un(a) amigo(a) está ayudándote. Dile lo que tiene que hacer. Por ejemplo:

lavar los camarones
A — *¿Qué quieres que haga?*
B — *Quiero que laves los camarones.*

a. picar la cebolla
b. mezclar los huevos y la leche
c. abrir la lata de champiñones
d. sacar el pollo congelado
e. buscar chorizos en la carnicería
f. apagar el horno
g. cortar la sandía
h. 💡

4 ¡No sé qué tipo de ejercicio hacer! Todo el mundo me dice algo diferente. Túrnate con un(a) compañero(a). Por ejemplo:

mis hermanas / levantar pesas
A — *Mis hermanas me dicen que levante pesas. ¿Qué me sugieres tú?*
B — *Te sugiero que juegues básquetbol.*

a. mi mamá / montar en bicicleta o a caballo
b. mi entrenador(a) / correr dos kilómetros tres veces a la semana
c. mis amigos / nadar por la mañana
d. mi papá / caminar en el parque
e. mi abuela / patinar por una hora
f. 💡

5 Hay muchas cosas que nuestros padres no quieren que hagamos. Di lo que no te permiten a ti tus padres. Usa los dibujos u otras ideas. Por ejemplo:

Mis padres no quieren que lleve arete.

446   Capítulo 13

Options

Strategies for Reaching All Students

Students Needing Extra Help

Ex. 3: Point out that some of the verbs used here have spelling changes. Remind students that the verb forms will change in the answer. Show them how *quieres* becomes *quiero,* followed by the *que,* and *haga* is replaced by a verb from the list.
Ex. 4: Review the *decir* paradigm. Brainstorm possible suggestions for *Estudiante B.*
Ex. 5: Brainstorm expressions students will need. Make sure students realize that *tocar* is a spelling-change verb.

Ex. 6: Have students match the art with the expressions. Have them tell the correct *tú* form of the subjunctive for the *Estudiante B* verbs. Remind students where to place the object pronouns.
Ex. 7: Present a model. Remind students that they did something similar in Ex. 2, p. 445. Point out that *pedir* and *encontrar* are stem-changing verbs.
Ahora lo sabes: Have students write out this list so that they can record their progress.

Enrichment

Ex. 5: You might extend this exercise by asking students about parentally approved activities. For example: *Mis padres quieren que lleve ropa más o menos como la suya.*

446

6 Imagina que es tu primer día de trabajo en un restaurante. Pregúntale al (a la) cocinero(a) qué hacer.

A —¿*Qué hago con la leche?*
B —*Te sugiero que no la hiervas.*

a.

b.

c.

d.

e.

f.

g.

no hervirla

recomendarla

servirla en seguida

revolverlos con el tomate y la cebolla

encenderlo a 345 grados

probarlo antes de servirlo

devolverlo a la cocina

7 Imagina que quieres organizar una barbacoa con tus compañeros de clase. Diles, a por lo menos siete de ellos, lo que recomiendas que hagan. Usa estos verbos u otros:

cambiar	encontrar	llevar	preparar
cocinar	gastar	pedir	querer
comprar	invitar	pedir prestado(a)	sugerir

Ahora lo sabes

Can you:

- say that you want someone to do something?
  —Quiero que ___ tres cebollas, por favor.
- say that you are telling someone to do something?
  —Le digo a Carlos que ___ unas empanadas para la cena.
- make suggestions and recommendations?
  —Señor, le recomiendo que ___ un café con esa tarta de piña.
  —Le sugiero que no ___ tantos carbohidratos.

Gramática en contexto   447

Apply

Pronunciation Tape
13-3

¿Recuerdas?

Play

 Video Activity A

Using the Video

In Episode 13, as Carlos and Jamie choose from a delicious menu in the Hotel Majestic's restaurant, they talk about the approaching court case against Silvestre Aguilar.

Later, in court, the lawyers of Jamie and Silvestre present their cases about who should be the rightful owner of La Catrina's property. The judge rules that all of it belongs to Jamie.

After the court case, at a big party to celebrate the decision, Demetrio finally introduces Jamie and Carlos to Santana, whose mission is now complete.

Jamie tells Carlos that she feels uncomfortable in her new situation and needs to talk to her family.

Para decir más

Aquí tienes vocabulario adicional que te puede servir para hacer las actividades de esta sección.

el crecimiento
growth

el calcio
calcium

la piel
skin

las grasas
fats

el colesterol
cholesterol

el corazón
heart

la porción, *pl.* **las porciones**
serving

448   Capítulo 13

Actividades

Esta sección te ofrece la oportunidad de aumentar tus conocimientos de español al integrar lo que aprendiste en este capítulo con lo que aprendiste en capítulos anteriores.

1 En grupo, preparen algunas sugerencias para unos visitantes hispanohablantes que quieren probar comida típica de los Estados Unidos. Recomiéndenles restaurantes, a qué hora comer y qué deben pedir. Usen estas frases u otras:

- Yo sugiero que . . .
- Yo recomiendo que . . .

beber	empezar
buscar	pedir
cenar	planear
comer	probar
desayunar	visitar

Options

Strategies for Reaching All Students

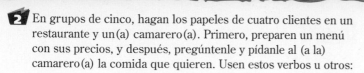

2 En grupos de cinco, hagan los papeles de cuatro clientes en un restaurante y un(a) camarero(a). Primero, preparen un menú con sus precios, y después, pregúntenle y pídanle al (a la) camarero(a) la comida que quieren. Usen estos verbos u otros:

beber	cortar	gastar	recomendar
cambiar	costar	llevar	servir
cocinar	devolver	pedir	sugerir
comer	encontrar	preparar	

3 Dividan la clase en seis grupos. Preparen un informe sobre la alimentación. Usen como base la Pirámide Nutritiva del Departamento de Agricultura de los Estados Unidos. Cada grupo deberá escoger uno de los seis grupos de comida.

Informen sobre:

- qué sustancias nutritivas tienen (proteínas, vitaminas, carbohidratos)
- qué cantidad se debe comer
- qué significa una porción

Usen frases como las siguientes:

- Se recomienda . . .
- Se sugiere . . .
- El Departamento de Agricultura sugiere / recomienda que . . .
- Los médicos dicen que . . .

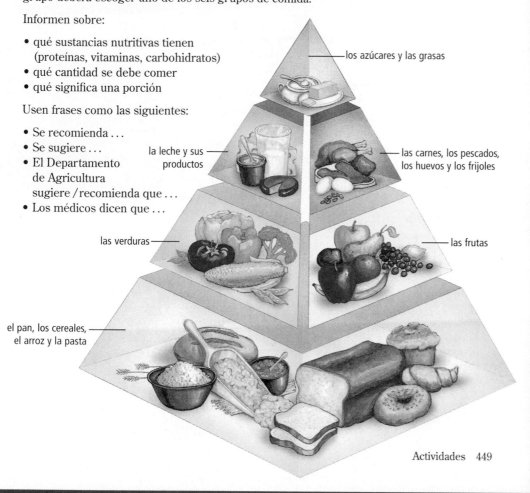

los azúcares y las grasas

la leche y sus productos

las carnes, los pescados, los huevos y los frijoles

las verduras

las frutas

el pan, los cereales, el arroz y la pasta

Actividades 449

La Catrina: Capítulo 13

Play

Video Activity B

Para entender mejor

Play

Video Activity C

Teaching Suggestions
Ex. 2: You may want to elicit some ideas before the groups separate. Students who choose to be waiters (waitresses) may want to use a folded napkin on their arm and a small notebook to take orders.
Ex. 3: Remind students to use additional health-related vocabulary presented for this section to complete the phrase: *Los médicos me dicen que . . . .*

Answers: Actividades
1–3 Answers will vary, but should include correct use of subjunctive.

Writing Activities 13-G, 13-H

Comm. Act. BLMs 13-3, 13-4, 13-5

Cooperative Learning
In groups of four, tell students to imagine they are members of a charity that has decided to purchase $100 worth of food for a family of one adult and three children. Within the group, one pair should make the shopping list, including amounts spent, using foods from the food pyramid on p. 449. When each group is finished they should present the list to the class, letting the class vote on whether or not the food was worth the money.

Apply

Process Reading
For a description of process reading, see p. 52.

Answers
Antes de leer
Answers will vary, but students may say the olive tree originated in Asia Minor. Olive trees grow in the Mediterranean, and the Spaniards introduced the olive tree to Peru, Mexico, Chile, and California.

¡Vamos a leer!

Antes de leer

STRATEGY ➤ Using prior knowledge

Do you know where the olive tree originated? Where do olive trees grow nowadays? How did they get there?

Mira la lectura

STRATEGY ➤ Skimming

Skim the article "El aceite de oliva" to get the gist of it.

El aceite de oliva

El aceite de oliva se extrae de la aceituna, que es el fruto de un árbol llamado olivo. La palabra española se deriva del árabe "azzait."

Su historia El olivo se considera originario de Asia Menor, y desde allí su cultivo se extendió a todos los países del Mediterráneo y a sus islas. En el sur de Europa — Grecia, Italia y España — se cultivaba ya el olivo antes de la era cristiana. Se cree que los fenicios introdujeron el olivo en España. Los romanos y más tarde los árabes intensificaron su cultivo en Andalucía, y desde entonces el olivo es el árbol más representativo de la región andaluza. Los españoles llevaron el olivo a Perú, México, Chile y, más tarde, a California.

El aceite de oliva en la dieta mediterránea
Las propiedades beneficiosas del aceite de oliva residen en su alto contenido en ácido oléico (el ácido mejor absorbido por el organismo humano) y vitamina E.

Este aceite siempre ha constituido uno de los elementos claves de la dieta mediterránea, reconocida en la actualidad como una de las más saludables. La cocina española, tanto tradicional como moderna, utiliza el aceite de oliva en la mayoría de sus platos: ensaladas, salsas, vinagretas, paellas, etc.

Options

Strategies for Reaching All Students

Students Needing Extra Help
Point out that *oliva* and *aceituna* both mean "olive."

Infórmate

By now you have learned many strategies for helping you to understand a reading selection. Read this article carefully. Use what you know about articles and essays, the subject of olive oil, and reading strategies to help you. Which of the following strategies do you think will help you the most?

• Using prior knowledge
• Recognizing word families
• Using cognates

To check your comprehension, read these statements. Some are true, and some are false. Change the false ones to true ones.

1. Los árabes introdujeron el olivo en España.
2. El olivo se cultiva en California.
3. El olivo se cultiva en los países del Mediterráneo.
4. La palabra "olivo" es el nombre del árbol, no de la fruta.
5. El aceite de oliva no es ni bueno ni malo para la salud.

Aplicación

 The olive was brought to the Americas by Europeans. Name three foods that were taken to Europe from the Americas.

 What do some people use in place of olive oil? Where do those foods come from?

Cultural Notes ☀

(p. 450, photo)
Spain is one of the world's leading commercial producers of olives. Fresh olives are too bitter to eat, so they must be treated. In Spain, they are harvested before ripening, and then are soaked in lye to neutralize the oleuropein, the substance causing the bitter taste. The washed olives are then soaked in brine and packaged. The olive may be pitted and stuffed with a hand-rolled pimento. Olive trees may live as long as 1,500 years.

Apply

Teaching Suggestions
Ex. 1: Be sure to exhibit all student work on a bulletin board so that those doing the second exercise can base their work on it.

Process Writing
For information regarding developing a writing portfolio, see p. 54.

¡Vamos a escribir!

¿Comes mucha comida rápida? ¿Debes comer más comida nutritiva y saludable? Vamos a escribir algunas sugerencias.

1 Primero, piensa en las siguientes cosas:

- ¿Qué tipo de comida rápida es saludable?
- ¿Qué comida saludable puede sustituir a la comida rápida?
- ¿Qué meriendas saludables conoces?

Escribe una lista de sugerencias. Luego, ponlas en grupos lógicos. Pídele comentarios a un(a) compañero(a), y sigue los otros pasos del proceso de escribir.

2 Ahora, basándote en las sugerencias de todos los estudiantes, prepara un cartel sobre meriendas saludables. Usa mandatos afirmativos y negativos. Por ejemplo:

No comas dulces.

¡Come uvas!

La uva es la merienda de la naturaleza. Tamaño perfecto para poner en la boca.

Fácil de servir — si quieres sólo una o si quieres muchas.

¡Y el jugo de uvas es delicioso!

452   Capítulo 13

Options

Strategies for Reaching All Students

Students Needing Extra Help
Ex. 1: Divide the class into groups of three. Explain the term "logical groups." Review commands.
Ex. 2: Give students the option of using magazine cutouts. Explain that they should choose one snack and elaborate on its healthful aspects.

3 Para distribuir su trabajo, pueden:

- enviar las sugerencias al periódico o a la revista escolar
- exhibirlas en la sala de clases o en la escuela
- usarlas para preparar un folleto
- enviar los carteles a una escuela primaria donde hay alumnos hispanohablantes
- enviarlos a una clínica que tenga clientes hispanohablantes
- incluir las sugerencias y los carteles en su portafolio

453

Cultural Notes

(p. 453, realia)
Zumo is the most commonly used word for "juice" in Spain, but in some parts of Mexico and Central America, *zumo* refers to the zest: the thin, fragrant, oily outer skin of an orange or lemon. The oil from the zest is combined with alcohol to make flavorings or extracts. The zest itself is bitter, and the vapor it emits when the fruit is peeled or abrased is an eye irritant.

Assess & Summarize

Test Preparation

You may want to assign parts of this section as written homework or as an in-class writing activity prior to administering the *Examen de habilidades.*

Answers

Listening: —*¿Qué pasó?* —(crying) *Un desastre. Los perros calientes se quemaron. ¡Y el perro comió las hamburguesas!* —*No llores. Sugiero que sirvas los perros calientes quemados y que prepares más hamburguesas.* —*No. No vale la pena. Tampoco tenemos mostaza. ¿Por qué no vamos a un restaurante?* The food is being barbecued or grilled.

Reading: The recipe is for an appetizer (guacamole).

Writing: Reasons will vary, but should include subjunctive phrases where appropriate.

Culture: In traditional Latin American homes, the kitchen is central to the home and serves as a gathering place for the family.

Speaking: Dialogues will vary.

¿Lo sabes bien?

Esta sección te ayudará a prepararte para el examen de habilidades, donde tendrás que hacer tareas semejantes.

Listening

Can you understand when people talk about food? Listen as your teacher reads a sample similar to what you will hear on the test. How is this food being cooked?

Reading

Luisa is reading a recipe. Is it for a soup, a main dish, or an appetizer?

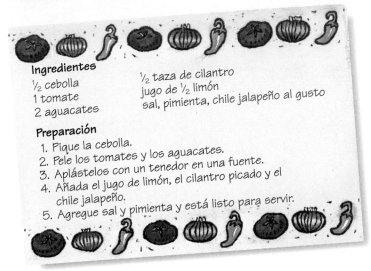

Ingredientes
½ cebolla
1 tomate
2 aguacates
½ taza de cilantro
jugo de ½ limón
sal, pimienta, chile jalapeño al gusto

Preparación
1. Pique la cebolla.
2. Pele los tomates y los aguacates.
3. Aplástelos con un tenedor en una fuente.
4. Añada el jugo de limón, el cilantro picado y el chile jalapeño.
5. Agregue sal y pimienta y está listo para servir.

Writing

The Spanish Club has asked you to help them write a letter suggesting that Spanish and Latin American food be served in the cafeteria. Here is one reason:

Sugerimos que preparen comida que nos ayudará a aprender sobre las culturas de otros países.

Write two more reasons.

454 Capítulo 13

Culture

Can you describe the role of the kitchen in a traditional Latin American home?

Speaking

Create a dialogue with your partner in which you are deciding what to order in a Spanish restaurant.

A —*¿Qué vas a probar primero?*

B —*Pues, me encantan las tapas, pero si como muchas, no podré comer otra cosa.*

A —*Entonces sugiero que pidas sólo unos camarones y unos espárragos frescos.*

B —*Bueno. ¿Y cómo es la paella en este restaurante?*

A —*Sabrosa. Va bien con una ensalada de lechuga y tomate.*

B — . . .

Options

Strategies for Reaching All Students

Students Needing Extra Help
Have students write this out so that they can check off what they have mastered.
¿Lo sabes bien?: Remind students that this is just a sample of what the real test will be like.
Listening: Read more than once. Brainstorm for which words students should be listening. Point out the cooking terms *(al horno, a la parrilla,* etc.) if students do not realize these on their own.

Reading: Brainstorm what ingredients would be found in a main dish or soup recipe. Guide students through the preparation section. Encourage them to use context clues.
Writing: Have students use the Organizer and write two sample suggestions before the test as practice. Brainstorm reasons for serving Spanish and Latin American foods.

Culture: Have students review the notes they took during their first reading of the *Perspectiva cultural.* Give them guidelines for the type and amount of information needed.
Speaking: Use the vocabulary section of the Organizer. Limit the number of lines of dialogue. Present a complete model. Remind students to think about which tenses they need to use.

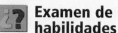

Resumen del capítulo 13

Usa el vocabulario de este capítulo para:

- describe different types of foods and dishes
- recommend and suggest various foods and dishes
- talk about nutrition

to name foods
el camarón, *pl.* los camarones
el cerdo
el perro caliente
el huevo duro
la calabaza
el champiñón, *pl.* los
   champiñones
la cereza
el durazno
la fresa
el limón, *pl.* los limones
el melón, *pl.* los melones
la piña
la sandía
el espárrago
las espinacas

to describe dishes and their ingredients
la paella
el ajo
el chorizo
el gazpacho
el aceite
el vinagre
la salsa
la mayonesa
la mostaza
el pepino
el pimiento verde
la empanada

la masa
el relleno
la ensalada de frutas
la tortilla española
la tarta
agrio, -a
amargo, -a
dulce
grasoso, -a
salado, -a
soso, -a

to discuss cooking
el cocinero, la cocinera
el ingrediente
la receta
estar hecho, -a de
cortar
hervir *(e → ie)*
mezclar
picar
revolver *(o → ue)*
congelado, -a
enlatado, -a
fresco, -a
al horno
a la parrilla
asado, -a
cocido, -a
frito, -a
guisado, -a
hacer una barbacoa

to discuss nutrition
la alimentación
la caloría
el carbohidrato
la proteína
la vitamina
hacer daño a
mantenerse sano, -a

to name snacks and beverages
el bocadillo
el dulce
las tapas

to make suggestions
que haga *(from:* hacer)
que pidas *(from:* pedir)
sugerir *(e → ie)*

Resumen 455

CAPÍTULO 14

THEME: THE OUTDOORS

COMMUNICATION

Topics

Camping

Hiking

Outdoor sports

Wild animals

Objectives

To discuss health problems
tourists may encounter

To discuss camping

To describe nature

To discuss outdoor activities

To discuss plants and animals

CULTURE

Health problems tourists may
encounter

GRAMMAR

*El subjuntivo de ciertos verbos
irregulares*

*El subjuntivo de los verbos
ir y ser*

*El subjuntivo con expresiones
impersonales*

Ancillaries available for use with Chapter 14

Multisensory/Technology

Overhead Transparencies,
67–71

Audio Tapes and CDs

Vocabulary Art Blackline
Masters for Hands-On
Learning, pp. 73–77

Classroom Crossword

Video

CD-ROM

Print

Practice Workbook, pp. 136–146

Writing, Audio & Video Activities,
pp. 83–88, 132–134, 177–180

Communicative Activity
Blackline Masters
   Pair and Small Group
   Activities, pp. 92–97
   Situation Cards, p. 98

Un paso más: Actividades para
ampliar tu español, pp. 79–84

Assessment

Assessment Program
   Pruebas, pp. 203–213
   Examen de
   habilidades, pp. 214–217

Test Generator

Video still from Chap. 14

Parques y reservas nacionales

Latin America has many undeveloped regions providing travelers the opportunity to experience many unusual animal and plant species. National parks and biological reserves have been established to preserve a region's ecology and, in some instances, promote eco-tourism, a concept started in the mid-1980s. Three such parks are worth special mention.

The lush and pristine Monte Verde Cloud Forest Reserve, in subtropical mountains along Costa Rica's continental divide, consists of some 48,000 acres that are home to a proliferation of plant and mammal species, including almost 500 emerald green and pink *quetzal* birds, held sacred among the pre-Columbian peoples of Mesoamerica. Another of its more unusual animal species is the delicate golden toad, which despite bold efforts to maintain ecological balance in the reserve, is on the verge of extinction. Entrance fees to Monte Verde, as well as to other national parks, have fostered the creation of more scientific institutes and educational programs dedicated to protecting the environment.

In stark physical contrast to Monte Verde is Chile's Torres del Paine National Park and Biosphere Reserve, offering one of the most dramatic landscapes in our hemisphere, with glaciers and ice fields, steep-rising jagged peaks, gentle plateaus, lakes, rivers, and waterfalls. Animal species include the South American condor, ducks, geese, flamingos, swans, small herds of guanaco (cousin of the llama), and Patagonian pumas. Despite its harsh, windy climate, tourism to the region has increased dramatically in recent years. Many come merely to relish the park's distinctive arctic beauty, while others engage in such activities as hiking, mountain climbing, and kayaking. The 450,000-acre park is considered one of Latin America's most well-managed and successful parks.

Perhaps the most well known of all the national parks and biological reserves in the world are the Galápagos Islands, approximately 600 miles from Ecuador's Pacific coast. Consisting of some 70 volcanic islands, they were discovered in 1835 by Charles Darwin who arrived at his theory of evolution based on environmental adaptation by observing that many of the islands contained their own unique animal species. Among the species inhabiting the Galápagos today are sea lions, giant tortoises, the flightless cormorant, and the albatross. To preserve this important natural habitat, the surrounding waters have been declared a marine reserve. Visitors are allowed to visit only a handful of the islands and must be accompanied by guides who educate them about the area's ecology and help enforce the islands' strict rules.

Introduce

Re-entry of Concepts
The following list represents words, expressions, and grammar topics re-entered from Book 1 and Book 2 (Chaps. 2–11):

Book 1
leisure-time activities, personality traits, nature, environmental dangers, animals, transportation

Chapter 2
personal hygiene items

Chapter 3
clothing

Chapter 4
leisure-time activities

Chapter 5
behavior

Chapter 11
environment

Planning

Cross-Curricular Connections

Geography Connection *(pp. 460–461)*
In groups of four, have students plan a camping trip to a site in a Spanish-speaking country. Within each group, they should choose a specific location and locate it on a map. Then they should describe the topographical and / or climatic features that influenced their choice, and which outdoor activities are available in the summer months.

Science Connection *(pp. 476–477)*
Have students choose one of the animals, plants, or natural features from this chapter and write a brief article for a science magazine. Without revealing their chosen subject, students should write three paragraphs: one describing its physical characteristics and special attributes, one telling its importance to the Earth or to our civilization, and one making recommendations as to how we can help conserve or protect it. Tell students to use as much chapter vocabulary and as many subjunctive phrases as possible. The following day, have students read their paragraphs aloud to the class, who must then guess the identity of the subject.

CAPÍTULO 14

¡Me encanta la naturaleza!

OBJECTIVES

At the end of this chapter, you will be able to:

- discuss popular outdoor activities
- describe the natural environment
- express attitudes and opinions about the environment
- explain why it may be unwise to drink the water in unfamiliar places

Campamento en un valle cerca de El Cotopaxi, Ecuador, el volcán activo más alto (5.896 m.) del mundo

457

Spanish in Your Community
Have students go to a national park or park district office and interview the park director concerning the information available to the local Hispanic community. Have them present this to the class. If none is available, have students collect information in English to use as a model to create a Spanish brochure to present to the national park or park district office.

Cultural Notes

(p. 456, photo)
INEFAN *(Instituto Ecuatoriano Forestal y de Áreas Naturales y Vida Silvestre)* administers Cotopaxi National Park, which lies along the Pan American Highway, south of Quito. The park is a destination for people interested in hiking up to the snowline of Mt. Cotopaxi (19,346 ft.) or for those wishing to view some of the wildflowers, lichens, birds, and majestic scenery of the mountain's lower slopes and protected gorges. Among the other parks administered by INEFAN are the Galápagos Islands.

Cultural Objective

• To discuss health problems tourists may encounter

Critical Thinking: Summarizing Information

Have students describe the three photos. Write responses on the chalkboard, and then have students summarize what the photos have in common.

Answers: ¡Piénsalo bien!
Answers will vary.

¡Piénsalo bien!

Mira las fotos. Los estudiantes que vemos están hablando de la naturaleza. ¿Te gustaría viajar a estos lugares? ¿Por qué sí o por qué no?

"Cuando hace buen tiempo, nos gusta mucho dar caminatas por el bosque."

¿Disfrutas mucho de la naturaleza? ¿Dan caminatas tú y tus amigos? ¿Dónde? ¿Hay bosques donde vives? Si hay bosques, ¿cómo son?

En el parque nacional de Ordesa, en los Pirineos, España

458   Capítulo 14

Options

Strategies for Reaching All Students

Spanish-Speaking Students
¿En cuáles de estas actividades te gustaría participar? ¿En cuáles ya has participado?

 Un paso más Ex. 14-A

Cultural Notes

(p. 458, photo)
The Parque Nacional de Ordesa y Monte Perdido was founded in 1918 to protect the natural environment of the central Pyrenees. The park includes many varieties of pine, fir, larch, beech, and poplars. Several species of protected wildlife live there, including boar, chamois (a small type of antelope), and the *Capra Pyrenaica* mountain goat.

Campamento en la Cordillera Vilcanota, Perú

"Me gustaría ir de camping a las montañas: poca gente, aire puro, agua limpia de la nieve . . ."

¿Fuiste de camping alguna vez? ¿Adónde fuiste? ¿Cuándo lo hiciste? ¿Con quiénes? ¿Por cuánto tiempo?

"Sólo una foto más . . . ¡No te muevas, iguana!"

¿Tienes una cámara? ¿De qué sacas fotos? ¿De la gente? ¿De tu familia y tus amigos? ¿De los edificios? ¿De los animales y la naturaleza?

En las islas Galápagos de Ecuador

(p. 459, top photo)
This campground is set up in the Cordillera Vilcanota near Cuzco, Peru. While other Latin American countries have single *cordilleras* (mountain ranges) running through them, Peru's Andes are characterized by a number of separate but converging ranges. The Peruvian Andes are much wider than ranges to the north or south and have several sharp, snow-covered peaks that are favored by experienced mountain climbers.

(p. 459, bottom photo)
The six Galápagos Islands, called *Las Islas Encantadas* by Spanish explorers, lie 600 miles off the coast of Ecuador. It is believed that the Incas may have journeyed to the islands in large ocean-going rafts. Charles Darwin's observations of life on the islands led to his theory of evolution described in *The Origin of Species.* Each island carries an English name as well as a Spanish one. Located at the southeastern extreme of the group is Hood Island *(Isla Española).* The Galápagos are an Ecuadorian national park and wildlife sanctuary.

Present

Chapter Theme
Camping

Communicative Objectives
• To discuss camping
• To describe nature
• To discuss plants and animals

 Transparencies 67–68

 Vocabulary Art BLMs

 Pronunciation Tape 14-1

Grammar Preview
Several subjunctive phrases are presented here lexically. The explanation of the subjunctive of certain irregular verbs is on p. 475.

Teaching Suggestions
Preparing students to speak: Use one or two options from each of the categories of Comprehensible Input, Physical Response, or Limited Verbal Response. For a complete explanation of these categories and some sample activities, see pp. T16–T17.

Reteach / Review: Vocabulary
También necesitas . . . : Remind students of the other meaning of the word *roto* (broken).

Vocabulario para conversar

¿Das caminatas a menudo?

Vas a necesitar estas palabras y expresiones para hablar sobre la naturaleza. Después de leerlas varias veces, practícalas con un(a) compañero(a).

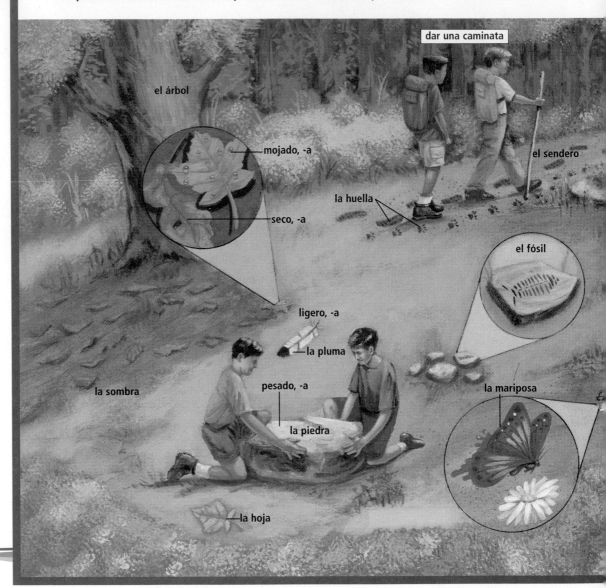

dar una caminata

el árbol

mojado, -a

seco, -a

el sendero

la huella

el fósil

ligero, -a

la pluma

la sombra

pesado, -a

la piedra

la mariposa

la hoja

Options

Strategies for Reaching All Students

Spanish-Speaking Students
Ask: *¿Sabes otras palabras que se relacionen a este tema? Escríbelas en tu vocabulario personal.*

 Un paso más Ex. 14-B

Students Needing Extra Help
Begin the vocabulary section of the Organizer. Point out the word families of *el abrelatas, seco, caminata,* and *pesado. También necesitas . . . :* Give examples of how *que lo hagamos, pongamos,* and *recojamos* are used in sentences.

Enrichment
Have students make two lists: one headed *Lo que es necesario llevar,* the other headed *Lo que está en la naturaleza.* Tell students to place the new vocabulary under the appropriate heading.

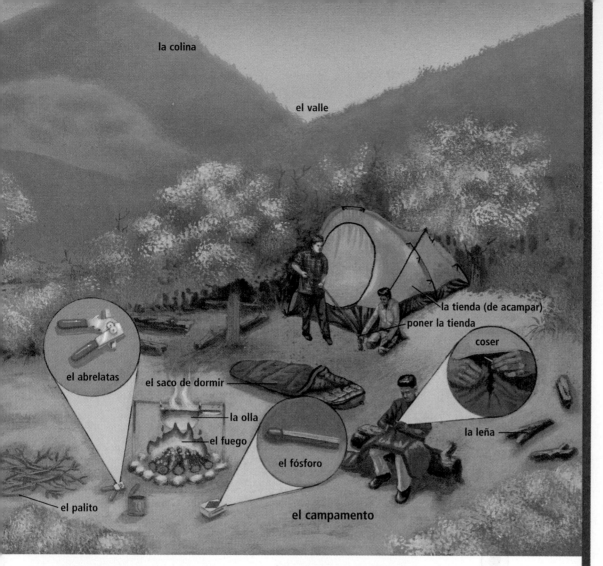

la colina

el valle

la tienda (de acampar)

poner la tienda

coser

el abrelatas

el saco de dormir

la olla

el fuego

la leña

el fósforo

el palito

el campamento

Class Starter Review
On the day following the initial presentation of vocabulary, you might begin the class with this activity:
Have students name items they would carry in their backpack to go on a camping trip.

También necesitas . . .

recoger ($g \to j$) to pick up, to gather
roto, -a here: torn
al aire libre outdoors

¿Y qué quiere decir . . . ?	
contaminado, -a	que lo (la) hagamos
ir de camping	que lo (la) pongamos
secar ($c \to qu$)	que lo (la) recojamos

Vocabulario para conversar   461

Learning Spanish Through Action
STAGING VOCABULARY: *Levanten, Señalen*
MATERIALS: reproductions of vocabulary transparency or Vocabulary Art BLMs
DIRECTIONS: Tell students to listen to the story of a recent camping trip. Have students raise or point to items as you mention them. For example: *Llegamos al campa-*

mento temprano. Pusimos la tienda (de acampar) y luego sacamos el abrelatas y la olla de la mochila pesada. Hicimos un fuego con palitos secos debajo de un árbol en la sombra y cocinamos la comida. ¡Qué bonito es comer al aire libre, lejos de la ciudad contaminada!

Practice

Reteach / Review: Commands

Ex. 1: As a variation of this exercise, have students redo it with *Estudiante B* using a negative command first, and then an affirmative command to tell *Estudiante A* what to do. For example: *¿Qué hago? El plato está roto. / Pues, no lo uses. Usa otra cosa.*

Answers: Empecemos a conversar

1 ESTUDIANTE A

a. ¿Qué hago? La leña está mojada.

b. ...El agua está contaminada.

c. ...La olla está sucia.

d. ...La tienda (de acampar) está rota.

e. ...El abrelatas está roto.

f. ...La mochila está demasiado pesada.

g. Statements will vary.

ESTUDIANTE B

Answers will vary, but may include the following:

a. Pues, tendrás que secarla.

b. ...hervirla.

c. ...lavarla.

d. ...coserla.

e. ...buscar otro.

f. ...sacarle algo.

g. Answers will vary.

Empecemos a conversar

Túrnate con un(a) compañero(a) para ser *Estudiante A* y *Estudiante B*. Reemplacen las palabras subrayadas en el modelo con palabras representadas o escritas en los recuadros. Si ven 💡 pueden dar su propia respuesta.

1   A —*¿Qué hago? El plato está roto.*
       B —*Pues, tendrás que usar otra cosa.*

roto

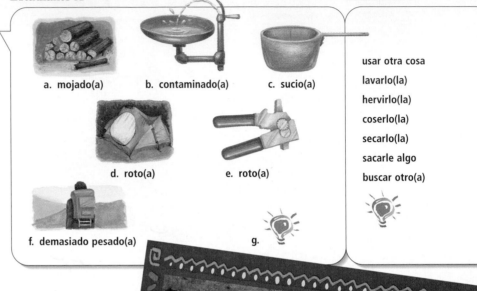

Estudiante A

a. mojado(a)   b. contaminado(a)   c. sucio(a)

d. roto(a)   e. roto(a)

f. demasiado pesado(a)   g.

Estudiante B

usar otra cosa

lavarlo(la)

hervirlo(la)

coserlo(la)

secarlo(la)

sacarle algo

buscar otro(a)

La etiqueta en esta mariposa sirve para que los científicos estudien su migración. Millones de mariposas monarcas pasan el invierno en México.

462   Capítulo 14

Options

Strategies for Reaching All Students

Spanish-Speaking Students
Exs. 1–2: Pair bilingual with non-bilingual students, if possible.
Ex. 3: Pair Spanish-speaking students, if possible.

Students Needing Extra Help
Ex. 2: Review location words. Discuss the details of the picture. Remind students of the change in the object pronoun at the beginning of the *Estudiante B* response.

Enrichment
Ex. 2: To extend this exercise, have *Estudiante A* respond affirmatively to *Estudiante B*'s question. Either student can continue by suggesting another place to look for the item in question.

2

A — *No encontré los champiñones.*
B — *¿Los buscaste en la sombra, debajo de los árboles?*

Estudiante A

a.

b.

c.

Estudiante B

d.

e.

f.

Vocabulario para conversar   463

2 ESTUDIANTE A
a. No encontré las huellas.
b. . . . los fósiles.
c. . . . las flores.
d. . . . las piedras.
e. . . . las mariposas.
f. . . . la leña.

ESTUDIANTE B
Answers will vary, but may include the following:
a. ¿Las buscaste en el sendero?
b. ¿Los . . . en la colina?
c. ¿Las . . . en el valle?
d. ¿Las . . . en el río?
e. ¿Las . . . sobre las flores?
f. ¿La . . . en el bosque?

Cultural Notes

(p. 462, photo)
The butterfly reserve at El Rosario, Michoacán, lies in the mountains between Morelia, Michoacán, and Toluca, Mexico. From November through February every year, millions of monarch butterflies migrate to this area from the north, covering the branches of the area's tall pine trees.

463

Practice & Apply

Re-enter / Recycle

Ex. 7: leisure-time activities and sports from Chap. 4

3 ESTUDIANTE A

a. ¿Qué se debe hacer con los fósforos?

b. ...el fuego?

c. ...la basura?

d. ...la tienda (de acampar)?

e. ...los palitos?

f. ...la leña?

g. ...la sopa?

h. Questions will vary.

ESTUDIANTE B

Answers will vary, but may include the following:

a. Es necesario que los busques.

b. ...lo apagues.

c. ...la recojas.

d. ...la pongas.

e. ...los enciendas.

f. ...la consigas.

g. ...la hagas.

h. Answers will vary.

3

A —¿Qué se debe hacer con *el agua*?

B —Es necesario que *la hiervas*.

Estudiante A

Estudiante B

a. b. c.

d. e.

f. g. h.

Estudiante B

apagues

busques

consigas

enciendas

hagas

hiervas

pongas

recojas

seques

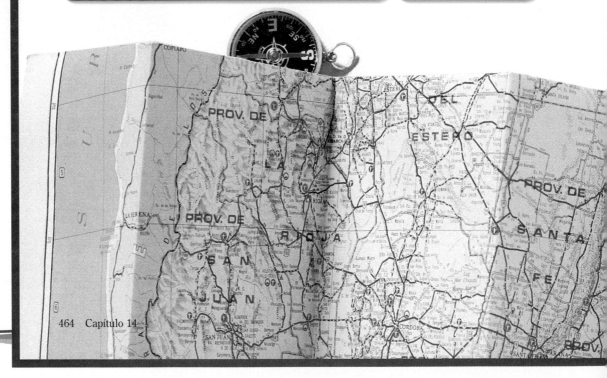

464   Capítulo 14

Options

Strategies for Reaching All Students

Spanish-Speaking Students

Ex. 7: *¿Qué se puede hacer cerca de donde vives? ¿En qué estación del año te gusta más estar al aire libre?*

 Un paso más Ex. 14-C

Students Needing Extra Help

Ex. 3: Put this exercise in context. Have students decide on the object pronouns and match them to the verbs before beginning this activity.

Ex. 4: Decide on which area the students should base the activity before beginning this exercise. Have information available if a specific place is chosen. Brainstorm camping activities and important related information.

Ex. 5: Brainstorm things to be careful of. Explain the expressions that begin with *¿con qué . . . .*

Ex. 6: Brainstorm possible answers.

Ex. 8: Give students a specific number of things to be included on the lists. Use the vocabulary section of the Chap. 11 Organizer.

Empecemos a escribir

Escribe tus respuestas en español.

4 ¿Fuiste a un campamento alguna vez o te gustaría ir a alguno? ¿Adónde? ¿Qué actividades hay en un campamento que te gustan mucho? ¿Crees que es importante saber cocinar si vas de camping? ¿Qué más es importante saber?

5 Si das una caminata en el campo, ¿con qué hay que tener cuidado? ¿Con qué hay que tener cuidado en el bosque? ¿Qué te gusta hacer cuando das una caminata?

6 ¿Qué se necesita para hacer un fuego? ¿Cómo se enciende? ¿Cómo se apaga? ¿Cómo se puede proteger el bosque de un incendio?

7 ¿Qué te gusta hacer al aire libre?

8 ¿Crees que es importante llevar cosas ligeras cuando vas de camping? Haz una lista de lo que hay que llevar y una de lo que no se debe llevar. Haz una lista de lo que te gustaría recomendarle a alguien para que no contamine ni haga ningún daño a la naturaleza.

También se dice

la fogata

la cerilla
el cerillo

el abridor de latas

la loma

el caminito

la pisada

la roca

Este joven argentino va de camping a los Andes.

Vocabulario para conversar   465

Cultural Notes

Enrichment

Additional questions: *Hay personas que nunca van de camping porque no les gusta nada la idea de pasar sus vacaciones en un campamento. ¿Por qué crees que piensan así? ¿Crees que tienen razón?*

Cooperative Learning

Using the question in Ex. 7, have students interview three classmates. They should then form a pair with someone they did not interview and share the responses they received. Have pairs prepare a graph illustrating their combined results and present it to the class.

(p. 465, photo)
Aconcagua, in Argentina, rises 22,834 feet. Although the Andes reach their highest elevations around Aconcagua, the relatively short distance across the mountains between Santiago de Chile and Mendoza, Argentina, makes this crossing well traveled. These mountains are rocky and dry with low, scrubby vegetation. On the Argentine side, orange, pink, red, crimson, and black rock formations color the landscape.

Present

Communicative Objectives
- To describe nature
- To discuss outdoor activities
- To discuss plants and animals

 Transparencies 69–70

 Vocabulary Art BLMs

 Pronunciation Tape 14-2

Teaching Suggestions

Preparing students to speak: Use one or two options from each of the categories of Comprehensible Input, Physical Response, or Limited Verbal Response. For a complete explanation of these categories and some sample activities, see pp. T16–T17.

Vocabulario para conversar

¿Qué ves en el desierto?

Aquí tienes el resto del vocabulario que necesitas en este capítulo para hablar sobre la naturaleza.

la ardilla
el amanecer
el búho
el venado
la venada
la rana
la serpiente
el lobo, la loba
el parque nacional

el desierto
la espina
el atardecer
el cacto

Options

Strategies for Reaching All Students

Spanish-Speaking Students
¿Puedes añadir otras palabras relacionadas al tema? Escríbelas en tu vocabulario personal.

 Un paso más Ex. 14-D

Students Needing Extra Help
Point out the feminine form of *el lobo*. Remind students of the word family for *atardecer (tarde)*. Divide the vocabulary into three sections: animals, activities, and equipment.
También necesitas . . . : Remind students that *salvaje* and *silvestre* both mean "wild."

Learning Spanish Through Action
STAGING VOCABULARY: *Señalen*
MATERIALS: Photos or posters of vacation spots
DIRECTIONS: Place the various photos or posters around the room and describe them, having students indicate which one is being described.

el elefante

el gorila

el coyote

la ballena

la balsa

navegar en balsa

la canoa

navegar en canoa

la tabla (de surf)

hacer surf

la vela

hacer surf de vela

la moto acuática

hacer moto acuática

hacer esquí acuático

el trampolín, pl. los trampolines

dar saltos

escalar montañas

También necesitas . . .

el animal salvaje	*wild animal*
la planta silvestre	*wild plant*
venenoso, -a	*poisonous*

¿Y qué quiere decir . . . ?
el oxígeno
doméstico, -a
peligroso, -a
los animales en peligro de extinción

Vocabulario para conversar 467

Practice

Re-enter / Recycle
Ex. 9: leisure-time activities and sports from Chap. 4
Ex. 11: environment from Chap. 11

Reteach / Review: Vocabulary

Ex. 10: Have students choose three settings for which they have already learned vocabulary, and list the objects, animals, or people they would see if they went there. For example: *En la fiesta habrá pastel y una piñata. En el parque habrá árboles, flores y ardillas.*

Answers: Empecemos a conversar

9 ESTUDIANTE A

a. ¿Qué te gustaría hacer este verano, hacer moto acuática o bucear?

b. ...hacer surf o navegar en balsa?

c. ...escalar montañas o hacer esquí acuático?

d. ...navegar en canoa o hacer surf de vela?

e. ...montar en bicicleta o patinar?

f. ...jugar béisbol o dar saltos?

g. Questions will vary.

ESTUDIANTE B

a.–g. Answers will vary.

10 ESTUDIANTE A

a. Si voy a un océano, ¿qué puedo hacer?

b. ...una selva tropical, ¿qué puedo ver?

Empecemos a conversar

9

A —¿Qué te gustaría hacer este verano, <u>dar caminatas o montar a caballo</u>?

B —<u>Montar a caballo. Es más divertido</u>.

o: *Ni una cosa ni la otra. Prefiero ___.*

¡NO OLVIDES!

Do you remember these words associated with sports?

bucear
correr
esquiar
los esquíes
el campeón, la campeona
el entrenador, la entrenadora
la piscina

Estudiante A   Estudiante B

a.

b.

c.

d.

e.

f.

g.

468   Capítulo 14

Options

Strategies for Reaching All Students

Spanish-Speaking Students
Exs. 9 and 11: Pair bilingual with non-bilingual students, if possible.
Ex. 10: Pair Spanish-speaking students, if possible.

Students Needing Extra Help
Ex. 9: Brainstorm possible adjectives that describe the preferred activity. Point out that if students choose the second response, they need to fill in the blank following *Prefiero* with another activity.
Ex. 10: Brainstorm what students might do or see in these particular places.

Ex. 11: Avoid discussing the subjunctive. Match *Estudiante A* and *B* responses as a class. Encourage students to incorporate their own ideas into the answers. Accept all logical answers.

10

ver

A — *Si voy a un río, ¿qué puedo ver?*
B — *Ranas, peces, serpientes y plantas silvestres.*

Estudiante A

a. hacer   b. ver   c. ver

d. hacer   e. hacer   f. ver   g.

Estudiante B

11 los bosques   A — *¿Por qué es necesario que protejamos los bosques?*
B — *Porque allí viven los animales salvajes.*

Estudiante A

a. los desiertos
b. los océanos
c. los parques nacionales
d. los elefantes
e. las selvas tropicales
f. el medio ambiente
g. los búhos
h.

Estudiante B

allí viven los animales salvajes
están en peligro de extinción
los seres humanos los están matando
sus plantas y árboles nos dan oxígeno
necesitamos aire y agua limpios
allí viven los lobos y los coyotes
allí viven las ballenas y los peces
allí protegen la naturaleza

c. ...un parque nacional, ¿qué puedo ver?
d. ...un lago, ¿qué puedo hacer?
e. ...un bosque, ¿qué puedo hacer?
f. ...un desierto, ¿qué puedo ver?
g. Questions will vary.
ESTUDIANTE B
a.–g. Answers will vary.

11 ESTUDIANTE A
a. ¿Por qué es necesario que protejamos los desiertos?
b. ...los océanos?
c. ...los parques nacionales?
d. ...los elefantes?
e. ...las selvas tropicales?
f. ...el medio ambiente?
g. ...los búhos?
h. Questions will vary.
ESTUDIANTE B
Answers will vary, but may include:
a. Porque allí viven los lobos y los coyotes.
b. ...allí viven las ballenas y los peces.
c. ...allí protegen la naturaleza.
d. ...los seres humanos los están matando.
e. ...sus plantas y árboles nos dan oxígeno.
f. ...necesitamos aire y agua limpios.
g. ...están en peligro de extinción.
h. Answers will vary.

 Comm. Act. BLM 14-1

Enrichment
Ex. 9: To extend this exercise, have *Estudiante A* ask *Estudiante B* to elaborate on the answer. For example, *¿Por qué crees que es más divertido?* or *¿Por qué prefieres ése?*

Cooperative Learning
Make signs for each of the sports listed on pp. 466–467 and post them around the room. Tell students they have received a scholarship to a summer camp that specializes in one of these sports. Give students time to decide which they would choose,

and ask them to move to that location in the room. When all groups are formed, have each student tell the members of his or her group one reason why he / she chose that sport. Groups should combine the reasons and present a list to the class.

Practice & Apply

Re-enter / Recycle
Ex. 16: clothing from Chap. 3

Answers: Empecemos a escribir y a leer

12–15 Answers will vary.

16 a. Para protegerte del zumaque te recomiendo que nunca camines sin zapatos.
b. ... que uses ...
c. ... que lleves ...
d. ... que te abroches ...
e. ... que lleves ...
f. Answers will vary.

Practice Wkbk.
14-3, 14-4

Audio Activity 14.2

Writing Activities
14-B, 14-C

Pruebas 14-3, 14-4

Empecemos a escribir y a leer

Escribe tus respuestas en español.

12 ¿Cómo es el desierto? ¿Qué animales hay? ¿Qué no hay en un desierto?

13 ¿Cómo es el campo donde vives? ¿Qué animales hay? ¿Qué se puede hacer? ¿Se pueden hacer deportes acuáticos? ¿Cuáles? ¿Cuáles haces tú? ¿Cuál prefieres? ¿Cuál te parece el deporte acuático más peligroso? ¿Y el más divertido? ¿Por qué?

14 ¿Te gusta ver los amaneceres o los atardeceres? Describe uno de los dos. ¿Por qué no es prudente quedarse en el bosque después del atardecer?

15 ¿Qué animales salvajes te dan miedo? ¿Por qué? ¿Por qué se debe tener cuidado con algunos animales? ¿Con cuáles? ¿Y con qué plantas? ¿Por qué?

16 Lee el texto sobre el zumaque venenoso. Luego, dale recomendaciones de la lista a un(a) compañero(a). Agrega *(add)* otra recomendación tuya.

El zumaque venenoso abunda en los Estados Unidos. Causa una alergia muy dolorosa y en algunos casos muy peligrosa, sobre todo para los niños pequeños. Para protegerte del zumaque te recomiendo que:

a. nunca caminar sin zapatos
b. usar guantes si quieres recoger flores o plantas silvestres
c. llevar camisas de manga larga y pantalones largos
d. abrocharse todos los botones de la camisa
e. llevar siempre la camisa dentro de los pantalones y los pantalones dentro de las botas
f. 💡

Mono araña en la selva panameña

Una foca con su recién nacido en las islas Galápagos

DEVOLVAMOS A QUITO SU ALEGRÍA

SEMBREMOS ARBOLITOS

INSCRIBÁMONOS EN EL DEPARTAMENTO DE PARQUES Y JARDINES
Venezuela y Chile esquina
Teléfonos: 580055/580067
ext. 123 132

De sus viveros el Municipio nos entregará miles de árboles tradicionales para sembrarlos y cuidarlos en todos los barrios de Quito.

Hagamos de Quito un gran jardín

Options

Strategies for Reaching All Students

Spanish-Speaking Students
Ex. 15: *¿Crees que debemos proteger estos animales? ¿Por qué?*
Ex. 2: *Escoge una actividad. Escribe un párrafo que dice cómo se puede evitar hacerle daño a la naturaleza y a la vez, disfrutar de la actividad.*

 Un paso más Exs. 14-E, 14-F

Students Needing Extra Help
Ex. 12: Use the vocabulary section of the Organizer. Have information available about desert activities.
Ex. 14: Brainstorm adjectives to describe the sunrise and sunset.
Ex. 15: If available, use the vocabulary section of the Book 1, Chap. 13 Organizer. Use the vocabulary section of the Chap. 9 Organizer.
Ex. 16: Do *a.* as a class. Point out that *b.–e.* are affirmative suggestions.

¡Comuniquemos! Ex. 1: Present a complete model. Have students set up columns for each category and brainstorm possible answers. Use the vocabulary section of the Organizer.
Ex. 2: Present a complete model. Brainstorm positive and negative aspects of each activity.
¿Qué sabes ahora?: Have students write out this exercise to record their progress.

¡Comuniquemos!

Aquí tienes otra oportunidad para usar el vocabulario de este capítulo.

1 En grupo, hablen de adónde quisieran ir durante las vacaciones y por qué.

A —*¿Te gustaría ir a un desierto?*
B —*A un desierto, no. Allí no hay . . . Hay que llevar . . . Prefiero . . .*
C —*A mí me gustaría ir a un desierto porque . . .*

2 Habla con un(a) compañero(a) sobre algunas actividades o deportes que le pueden hacer daño a la naturaleza. Por ejemplo:

coleccionar plantas silvestres   hacer moto acuática
esquiar   ir de camping
hacer esquí acuático   ir de pesca

A —*¿Qué piensas de hacer moto acuática?*
B —*Creo que es un . . .*
A —*Estoy de acuerdo, pero . . .*

3 Habla con un(a) compañero(a) sobre el campamento ideal. Hablen sobre:

• dónde está el campamento
• cómo es el campo por allí
• qué animales se pueden ver allí
• si es necesario hacer una reservación
• qué hay que llevar
• si hay agua, electricidad, servicios, duchas, etc.
• qué se puede hacer y qué no se puede hacer

¿Qué sabes ahora?

Can you:

■ talk about water sports?

—Me encanta ___. Es un deporte ___, pero muy divertido.

■ discuss our natural environment?

—En el estado donde vivo hay ___, ___ y ___.

■ talk about protecting animals and the environment?

—Es necesario que protejamos los ___ porque ___.

También se dice

el tecolote
la lechuza

la culebra

surfear

hacer saltos de trampolín
hacer clavados

la piragua

hacer alpinismo

Vocabulario para conversar   471

Cultural Notes ☀

Enrichment
Ex. 12: *¿Qué cosas debes llevar si vas a visitar el desierto por algunas horas?*
Ex. 16: *¿En qué lugar te gusta más la naturaleza: los desiertos, los océanos, los bosques, los ríos o las selvas tropicales? ¿Por qué?*

(p. 470, top photo)
The spider monkey, small with a notably long tail, is a genus found only in the Americas. It is characterized by long, slender limbs, a rudimentary thumb, and a prehensile tail. Chocó Indians, who inhabit the province of Darién, in eastern Panama, have traditionally hunted spider monkeys using blow guns and bows and arrows.

(p. 470, bottom photo)
Although many of the species of animals found on the Galápagos are unique, others, such as the California sea lion, may be found elsewhere. This animal is known for its intelligence and memory and is popular in zoos and marine shows since it is easily trained. The California sea lion's coat is brown, but appears black when wet. Galápagos park regulations protect the sea lion.

Present & Apply

Cultural Objective
• To discuss health problems tourists may encounter

Multicultural Perspectives
Major cities in Latin America use water filtration systems much like those in the U.S. In rural areas, however, the quality of water can be dramatically lower. Many people do not have potable water: they have to obtain their drinking water from rivers contaminated by animals and farm runoff.

Untreated water carries many diseases and is one of the leading causes of infant mortality in Latin America. Intestinal bacteria can affect infants through prolonged diarrhea, which causes dehydration and sometimes death. Rural areas also experience outbreaks of other water-born diseases such as cholera, typhoid, and hepatitis. Have students research the efforts of Latin American governments and world health organizations to provide clean water throughout the region. Ask students to share their findings with the class.

Perspectiva cultural

¿Hay comida y bebidas que puedes identificar en las fotos? Imagina que vas a ir a estos lugares. ¿Qué comida comerás? ¿Qué bebidas beberás? ¿Cuáles no? ¿Por qué?

Imagina que estás visitando la ciudad de Guadalajara en México con unos compañeros. Hace mucho calor y tienen sed. En un quiosco ven a un vendedor de aguas frescas. Tiene botellas grandes de vidrio que contienen pedazos de hielo y de naranjas, piñas o sandía flotando en el líquido refrescante. Algunos de tus compañeros quieren comprar un vaso de agua fresca. Otros no. ¿Qué harás tú?

¿Es verdad que los turistas no deben beber el agua en ciertos países? Toda agua contiene microbios. Diversos países usan diversos sistemas para purificarla. Y, por lo general, la gente está acostumbrada al agua de su país. En otras palabras, el agua no le hace daño porque suele beberla. Por eso, los viajeros deben tomar precauciones para no tener problemas.

¿Qué precauciones debes tomar? Primero, bebe sólo agua hervida o agua mineral que se venda en botella. Cepíllate los dientes con esa misma agua. No bebas bebidas hechas con agua regular. No comas verduras o frutas lavadas con agua regular. Pela la fruta. Si quieres, antes de viajar, puedes pedirle a tu médico que te recete un antibiótico para protegerte.

Además del agua, hay otras causas de problemas del estómago. En la mayoría de los casos, se deben a la deshidratación o al cansancio (fatigue), no al agua.

La cultura desde tu perspectiva

1 ¿Por qué los microbios les hacen daño a algunas personas y a otras no?

2 ¿Qué le puedes decir a un(a) turista que está en los Estados Unidos por primera vez que te pregunta si debe beber el agua?

Vendedor de aguas frescas en el mercado de San Miguel de Allende, México

472 Capítulo 14

Options

Strategies for Reaching All Students

Spanish-Speaking Students
Ex. 2: After this exercise, have students answer in writing: *Como dice el artículo, hay otras causas de problemas del estómago, además del agua, para los turistas. ¿Qué consejos les darías a los turistas para no sentirse mal cuando viajen? Haz una lista.*

 Un paso más Ex. 14-G

Students Needing Extra Help
Have students take notes to be used later in the culture section of *¿Lo sabes bien?*
Ex. 1: You might want to change *los microbios les hacen* to *el agua les hace.*

Enrichment
As an additional assignment, have students research advice given in guidebooks regarding food, drink, and general health questions for people traveling to foreign countries. Have them prepare a brief report to share with the class, naming the guidebook and the recommendations given.

Answers will vary, but should include the following ideas:

1 All water contains microbes, but we are all accustomed to the water in our own region. When we travel to a foreign country, the different microbes in the water may cause illnesses.

2 Take these precautions: Drink and brush your teeth with only bottled or boiled water. Don't drink anything made with tap water. Don't eat fruits or vegetables washed in tap water, and peel all fruit before eating.

Vendedor de aguas frescas pelando un mango en el parque de Chapultepec

Perspectiva cultural   473

Cultural Notes ☼

(pp. 472–473, photos)
Glass jars filled with *aguas frescas* are a familiar sight in any Mexican market or *zócalo.* Three common *aguas* are *horchata, agua de jamaica,* and *agua de tamarindo. Horchata* is made with rice, blanched almonds, cinnamon, sugar, and water. *Agua de jamaica* is made from calyxes of the hibiscus blossom, sugar, and water. Tamarind pods are shelled and then boiled with sugar and water to prepare *agua de tamarindo.*

Preview

Reteach / Review: Subjunctive

B: As a review, ask students to compare the subjunctive forms *cruces* and *apagues* with the corresponding *yo* forms of the present tense, and ask how the stem changes in the subjunctive.

Answers

A The two examples are *es importante limpiar* and *es necesario quitar.* The word *que* follows *es necesario.* It changes (from *haces* to *hagas).* The infinitive of *hagas* is *hacer.* The negative *tú* command form is *no hagas.*

B The verbs are *uses,* from *usar; cruces,* from *cruzar;* and *apagues,* from *apagar.* You would use the subjunctive form *lleves.*

𝔊ramática en contexto

Para hacer un fuego

Primero, es importante limpiar bien el área. Es necesario quitar las piedras, los palos y las hojas del lugar.

El fuego debe quedar limitado al área que escogiste. Para eso es necesario que hagas un círculo con piedras en el centro del área.

Pon palitos y papeles dentro del círculo. Es importante que uses palitos secos. Si están mojados, será difícil encenderlos.

Luego, pon la leña sobre los palitos y los papeles. Es importante que cruces los palitos y la leña para permitir la entrada del aire

Al final, enciende los palitos de abajo con un fósforo. Pronto se encenderá la leña. Recuerda: Es muy importante que apagues el fuego antes de acostarte o de salir del área.

A You have seen *es importante* and *es necesario* followed by infinitives. Find two examples in the first caption. In the second caption, the writer is saying that it is necessary for someone to do something. What word follows *es necesario?* What happens to the verb form after *que?* What is the infinitive of *hagas?* What is the negative *tú* command form?

B Each of the other captions contains a suggestion using *es importante.* Look at the verbs that follow *que* and identify the infinitive of each. What form of *llevar* would you use to complete this sentence: *Es importante que tú (llevar) fósforos secos?*

474 Capítulo 14

Options

Strategies for Reaching All Students

Students Needing Extra Help
Have students begin the grammar section of the Organizer. Tell them to take careful notes.
A: Write the expressions on the chalkboard as students find them.
B: Write the three *Es importante . . .* sentences on the chalkboard. Underline *uses, cruces,* and *apagues.* Have students identify

the infinitive of each verb form. Point out that all are *-ar* verbs if they do not see this on their own. Write the new sentence on the chalkboard, leaving room for students to supply the correct form of *llevar.*
El subjuntivo de ciertos verbos irregulares: Write out the complete paradigm of the listed verbs.

Ex. 1: Match the responses as a class. Write the model on the chalkboard, underlining the parts that change. Review the placement of object pronouns. Brainstorm possible *Estudiante B* responses.

El subjuntivo de ciertos verbos irregulares

As in negative commands, irregular verbs that add a *g* to the stem in the present-tense *yo* form (including *caerse, decir, hacer, poner, salir, tener,* and *traer*) also have a *g* in the present subjunctive.

hacer → hag-o → **haga**
tener → teng-o → **tenga**

Mi papá quiere que yo **haga** esquí acuático.
Mi mamá quiere que **tengamos** mucho cuidado.

¡NO OLVIDES!
We form the present subjunctive of most verbs in the same way we form negative *tú* commands. Add the subjunctive endings to the stem of the present-tense *yo* form.

1 La directora del campamento les da recomendaciones a un grupo de excursionistas.

los mosquitos

A — *¿Qué debemos hacer con tantos mosquitos?*
B — *Les recomiendo que traigan repelente.*

a. con las tiendas de acampar
b. con los fuegos
c. con los fósforos
d. en las caminatas
e. con los animales salvajes
f. con las latas
g. con lo que hay que llevar

ponerlos en un lugar seco
hacer una mochila con sólo cosas necesarias
no salir muy lejos del campamento
traer un abrelatas
no hacerlos cerca de las tiendas
no ponerlas donde hay piedras
tener mucho cuidado con ellos

Ahora tú, dales otras tres recomendaciones a los excursionistas.

h. con las flores y las plantas silvestres
i. con la comida
j. con la leña y los palitos

Gramática en contexto   475

Present & Practice

 Practice Wkbk. 14-5, 14-6

 Writing Activity 14-D

Present & Practice

Re-enter / Recycle

Ex. 2: behaviors from Chap. 5

Answers

2 ESTUDIANTE A

a. ¿Me recomiendas que vaya a un desierto?

b. ¿Le . . . que vaya a un parque nacional?

c. ¿Nos . . . que vayamos a un lago?

d. ¿Les . . . que vayan a un campamento?

e. ¿Me . . . que vaya a una selva?

f. ¿Nos . . . que vayamos a una ciudad?

g. Questions will vary.

ESTUDIANTE B

Answers may include:

a. Sí. Y te recomiendo también que seas prudente con el agua.

b. . . . le . . . sea obediente a las reglas.

c. . . . les . . . no sean tímidos(as) de nadar.

d. . . . les . . . sean limpios(as) con la comida.

e. . . . te . . . seas paciente para ver los animales.

f. . . . les . . . sean sociables con la gente.

g. Answers will vary.

El subjuntivo de los verbos *ir* y *ser*

Ir and *ser* have irregular subjunctive forms. They are just like the negative *tú* command forms.

(yo)	**vaya / sea**	(nosotros) (nosotras)	**vayamos / seamos**
(tú)	**vayas / seas**	(vosotros) (vosotras)	**vayáis / seáis**
Ud. (él) (ella)	**vaya / sea**	Uds. (ellos) (ellas)	**vayan / sean**

2 Pregúntale a un(a) compañero(a) qué recomienda.

me

A — ¿*Me recomiendas que vaya a una playa?*
B — *Sí. Y te recomiendo también que seas prudente con la tabla de surf.*

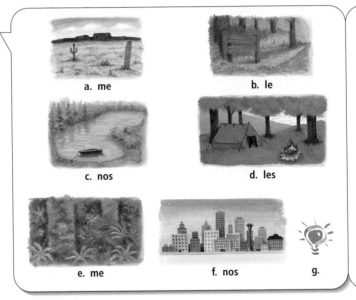

a. me   b. le

c. nos   d. les

e. me   f. nos   g.

paciente

(no) desobediente

ordenado, -a

(no) desordenado, -a

limpio, -a

sociable

(no) tímido, -a

(no) perezoso, -a

476   Capítulo 14

Options

Strategies for Reaching All Students

Students Needing Extra Help
Review the negative *tú* command forms of *ir* and *ser*. Refer students to the grammar section of the Chap. 12 Organizer. Point out that there is a written accent mark on *vayáis*.
Ex. 2: Do this exercise as a class, separating it into two parts. First, do the exercise eliminating the *ser* + adjective phrase. Repeat the exercise, including the *ser* + adjective phrase, choosing one adjective to repeat throughout.

El subjuntivo con expresiones impersonales: Refer to the captions in the art in the *Gramática en contexto* section. Give additional examples of using infinitives as opposed to the subjunctive. Have students keep a running list of subjunctive expressions. Review regular subjunctive using the Chap. 12 Organizer. Write the *yo* forms of those verbs on the chalkboard.

Enrichment
El subjuntivo de los verbos ir *y* ser: As homework, have students think of a place (restaurant, school, theater, hospital, etc.) to which they would never recommend that anyone go, and give three reasons why.
El subjuntivo con expresiones impersonales: Ask pairs of students to create sayings about life in general using the expressions presented. Encourage students to be humorous and creative. Let them share their sayings with the class.

El subjuntivo con expresiones impersonales

You know how to make suggestions and recommendations using certain impersonal expressions with the infinitive. For example:

Es mejor dar una caminata por la mañana.

When we want to specify *who* should do something, we use the subjunctive.

Es mejor que Samuel y sus amigos vayan de camping a un parque nacional.

Some of the expressions that we use this way are *es mejor, es necesario*, and *es importante*.

¿Es necesario que yo vaya con ellos?
Es importante que regresen antes del atardecer.

Navegando en canoa en
el Río Napa, Ecuador

Dando una caminata en
las montañas de California

477

Class Starter Review
On the day following the presentation of the subjunctive with impersonal expressions, you might begin the class with this activity: In pairs, have students take turns telling each other precautions that must be taken when going camping. For example: *Es importante que traigas agua pura.*

Multicultural Perspectives
Tortuguero National Park in Costa Rica is the most important breeding area in the world for the green sea turtle. From July to October, up to 3,000 female turtles come to Tortuguero to nest. A female may come ashore two or three times to nest, each time laying over 100 eggs. Because this is one of the most scientifically studied areas, tourists can sometimes participate in the tagging of female turtles to see if they return to the same nesting place. This type of ecotourism is a new way to experience exotic places. Ask students if they know of other areas which promote ecotourism.

 Practice Wkbk.
14-7, 14-8

 Writing Activities
14-E, 14-F

 Pruebas 14-5, 14-6

Cultural Notes

Cooperative Learning
In pairs, have students use the adjectives in Ex. 2 on p. 476 to create six recommendations for a classmate who is running for class president. Each student is responsible for three recommendations and the rationale behind them. As a pair, students should prioritize their recommendations and present them to the class.

(p. 477, right photo)
The Oriente region of Ecuador drops from the eastern side of the Andes to the headwaters of the Amazon River. The Napo River is the major tributary of the Amazon. Those traveling alone, who don't mind rustic accomodations, can begin a trip at Puerto Napo in a motorized canoe, stopping for the night in guest houses, army posts, and settlers' homes.

Practice & Apply

Teaching Suggestions

Ex. 3: To further practice the subjunctive, you may want to repeat this exercise using *todos, alguien,* and *algunos* as subjects.

Answers

3 ESTUDIANTE A

a. ¿Qué debemos hacer para ver los animales salvajes?
b. ...dar una caminata larga?
c. ...cocinar al aire libre?
d. ...poner la tienda de acampar?
e. ...escalar una montaña?
f. ...proteger el bosque?
g. ...proteger la comida de las hormigas?
h. Questions will vary.

ESTUDIANTE B

a. Es necesario que seamos pacientes y que estemos callados.
b. ...que llevemos agua pura para beber.
c. ...que recojamos palitos y leña para el fuego.
d. ...que quitemos las piedras.
e. ...que llevemos una cuerda.
f. ...que apaguemos bien el fuego.
g. ...que la guardemos en el coche.
h. Answers will vary.

3 Túrnate con un(a) compañero(a) para decir qué es mejor, qué es necesario o qué es importante hacer en un campamento.

proteger el parque nacional

A — ¿Qué debemos hacer para proteger el parque nacional?
B — Es necesario que recojamos toda la basura.

a. ver los animales salvajes
b. dar una caminata larga
c. cocinar al aire libre
d. poner la tienda de acampar
e. escalar una montaña
f. proteger el bosque
g. proteger la comida de las hormigas

recoger toda la basura
quitar las piedras
guardarla en el coche
llevar agua pura para beber
ser paciente y estar callado(a)
recoger palitos y leña para el fuego
llevar una cuerda
apagar bien el fuego

4 Dile a un(a) compañero(a) lo que quisieras hacer este verano. Tu compañero(a) te dará algunas ideas.

escalar una montaña

A — Este verano quisiera escalar una montaña.
B — Es importante que consigas unas botas buenas.

a. hacer ...
b. ir a ...
c. ir de camping ...
d. navegar en ...
e. practicar ...
f. recoger ...
g. ver ...
h. viajar ...

es necesario que ...
es importante que ...
es mejor que ...

478   Capítulo 14

Options

Strategies for Reaching All Students

Students Needing Extra Help
Ex. 3: If possible, divide the class into groups with at least one experienced camper in each. Review verbs from Chap. 13. Remind students to use only the *nosotros* form.

Ex. 4: Brainstorm possible completions for the *Estudiante A* statement and the *Estudiante B* response.
Ahora lo sabes: Have students write out this list so they can record their progress.

Subiendo un árbol en la selva de San Blas, Panamá

Todos los días, miles de animales salvajes mueren o son capturados ilegalmente en el mundo sin que parezca importarle a nadie.

Y si nadie hace algo para evitarlo, dentro de poco muchas especies animales y vegetales van a desaparecer para siempre. Algunas de ellas, imprescindibles para fines médicos, industriales o para el equilibrio ecológico de nuestro entorno.

Para que esto no suceda, existen normas que protegen a las especies en peligro de extinción. Como el Convenio de Washington, al que se adscribió España en 1986, por el cual se regula el Comercio Internacional de Especies Amenazadas (CITES).

No obstante, continúan entrando ilegalmente en España animales procedentes de Africa y América, en tránsito hacia otros países europeos o para ser comercializados en nuestro país.

En ADENA trabajamos día a día para combatir casos como éste. Para proteger nuestro patrimonio natural y hacer respetar los acuerdos internacionales que algunos parecen haber olvidado.

Por eso, si quieres que en el mundo siga habiendo otros animales, hazte socio de ADENA. Con tu ayuda lo conseguiremos.

DENTRO DE POCO NO HABRA MAS ANIMALES QUE ESTOS

Ahora lo sabes

Can you:

- tell someone what it is necessary, important, or advisable to do?
  —Es mejor que (nosotros) ___ la tienda antes de comer.
- recommend that someone not go somewhere?
  —Te recomiendo que no ___ al desierto en el verano.
- say that it is important for someone not to be a certain way?
  —Es importante que los niños no ___ maleducados.

Gramática en contexto   479

4 Answers for *Estudiante A* will vary, but should include the construction *quisiera* + inf. Answers for *Estudiante B* will also vary, but look for *es necesario / importante / mejor que* + subjunctive.

Answers: Ahora lo sabes
- pongamos
- vayas
- sean

 Practice Wkbk. 14-9, 14-10

 Audio Activities 14.4, 14.5

 Pruebas 14-7, 14-8

 Comm. Act. BLM 14-2

Cultural Notes

(p. 479, photo)
The archipelago of 365 San Blas Islands lies just off the Caribbean coast of Panama. Rain forests, such as the one in San Blas, have a characteristic structure generally consisting of several layers: the ground surface, the undergrowth, and the upper canopy, or treetops. Many animals live out their entire lifespan in only one of these layers. This forest reserve is significant because wild areas in other parts of Panama are being encroached upon by developers.

(p. 479, realia)
Spain's unique geographic location makes it an important European port of entry. Unfortunately, illegal smuggling of wildlife has been known to follow this same route. By combatting this activity in its own territory, the Spanish government helps to stem the mistreatment of wildlife internationally. These two stone lions are at the entrance of the Spanish Parliament.

Apply

Using the Video

In Episode 14, Jamie calls her parents in Los Angeles and tells them about the inheritance. They advise her not to give up her opportunity to go to college by staying in Mexico to see to the property. Later, Jamie explains to Carlos her decision to return to Los Angeles and donate the Hacienda La Jacaranda to Operación Aztlán. In a declaration before a judge, she adds that the Hotel will still belong to her family.

The final scene takes place at the train station, where Jamie and Felipe are saying good-bye to everyone they have met. Felipe and María agree to stay in touch and see each other again. Carlos promises Jamie he will visit Los Angeles and wait for her to return to Querétaro.

Actividades

Esta sección te ofrece la oportunidad de aumentar tus conocimientos de español al integrar lo que aprendiste en este capítulo con lo que aprendiste en capítulos anteriores.

1 Escoge por lo menos cuatro lugares que te gustaría visitar. Un(a) compañero(a) te hará sugerencias. Pueden usar el dibujo y las frases siguientes. Por ejemplo:

A — *¿Qué recomiendas que haga si voy al océano?*
B — *Te sugiero que traigas mucho bronceador. Te recomiendo que hagas surf de vela y que seas muy prudente.*

- aprender a . . .
- ir a . . .
- divertirse
- ser prudente
- no ser desordenado(a) / demasiado atrevido(a)
- escalar la montaña
- ponerse / quitarse

- hacer una excursión en coche / autobús / tren
- navegar en . . .
- traer . . .
- salir / llegar antes del amanecer / atardecer
-

Options

Strategies for Reaching All Students

Spanish-Speaking Students
Ex. 1: Give students this alternative assignment: *Escribe un párrafo acerca de lo que se puede hacer en dos de los lugares. Incluye también unas advertencias o alguna precaución que debe tomar el turista.*

 Un paso más Ex. 14-H

Students Needing Extra Help
If time is a factor, do only one activity.
Ex. 1: Brainstorm possibilities to complete the verb phrase used in the *Estudiante B* response. Review the rule for forming the subjunctive of reflexive verbs. Remind students that *ponerse* is also irregular.
Ex. 2: Have maps available as models. Divide the class into five groups, assigning one of the bulleted items to each group to

brainstorm, make the signs, and place them appropriately. Create a larger version of the original map and display it. Have each group add information to it. Present complete models of the travel agent / tourist conversation.
Ex. 3: Brainstorm suggestions for success. Have students sign their names, or take a picture of the class and put it on the list.

2 En grupo, hagan un mapa físico del área donde viven ustedes (incluyendo la ciudad y el campo) o de algún lugar imaginario. Pónganle letreros *(signs)* al mapa para indicar:

- los lugares de interés
- las estaciones y el clima
- la geografía
- las actividades divertidas, turísticas y deportivas
- el transporte

Luego, hagan los papeles de agentes de viaje y turistas. Pueden usar frases como las siguientes:

Les sugerimos que ...
Para ir a ... es necesario que ...
Es importante que ...

3 En grupo, piensen en el año escolar que termina. ¿Qué hicieron para tener éxito en la clase de español? Preparen algunas sugerencias para los estudiantes nuevos. ¿Qué les recomiendan que hagan y que no hagan? Usen frases como éstas:

- Es necesario /importante (que) ...
- Les sugerimos /les recomendamos que ...
- El (la) profesor(a) quiere que ...

Pueden escribir sus sugerencias en un cartel y ponerlo en la pared de la sala de clases para los estudiantes del año próximo.

Actividades   481

 La Catrina: Capítulo 14

Play

 Video Activity B

 Para entender mejor

Play

 Video Activity C

Teaching Suggestions
Ex. 2: Students' choice of which area to map should be determined by how much time the class can devote to this activity.

Answers: Actividades
1–3 Answers will vary, but should include correct use of subjunctive where appropriate.

 Writing Activities 14-G, 14-H

 Comm. Act. BLMs 14-3, 14-4, 14-5

Apply

Process Reading

For a description of process reading, see p. 52.

Answers
Antes de leer

Answers will vary, but students may mention that they would expect to find pictures of the endangered plants or animals, and a description of what the area will be like.

Mira la lectura

Answers will vary, but students may say that Ecuador has more than twice the species of animals and plants than all of North America. Just one river of the Equatorial Amazon contains 473 species of fish; compared to only 70 in the European continent. Ecuador also is home to over 20 percent of the world's population of birds.

¡Vamos a leer!

Antes de leer

STRATEGY ➤ Using prior knowledge

Ecotourism is travel to areas that need protection because they have endangered species of plants and/or animals. What would you expect to find in an ad for ecotours?

Mira la lectura

STRATEGY ➤ Scanning

Scan the ad to find three attractions in Ecuador for travelers who are interested in protecting the environment.

Entre las miles de especies que viven en las islas Galápagos, hay piqueros (pájaros de patas azules), muchos tipos de iguanas terrestres y marinas y tortugas gigantes que tienen cientos de años.

Infórmate

STRATEGY ➤ Coping with unknown words

1 Read the ad carefully and make a list of words you don't know. Underline the ones that you think are important to know. Work with a partner to figure them out. Then use a dictionary to verify the meanings.

2 Now read the ad again. Then read the following sentences based on it. Some are true and some are false. Change the false sentences to true ones.

a. Hay más especies de peces en Ecuador que en Europa.

b. No hay montañas en Ecuador.
c. Hay sólo dos tipos de bosques en Ecuador.
d. Samoa Turismo tiene un catamarán y un yate a motor.
e. Los Estados Unidos tiene un número mayor de especies animales y vegetales que Ecuador.

Aplicación

What would be an attractive destination in the United States for an ecotourist? Write three sentences in Spanish telling why.

482   Capítulo 14

Options

Strategies for Reaching All Students

Spanish-Speaking Students
Investiga algún lugar en otro país que se presta al ecoturismo. Di dónde es, qué tipo de lugar es (una selva tropical, un río, un cañón, etc.) y qué se puede ver allí.

Students Needing Extra Help
Mira la lectura: Emphasize scanning and the fact that students are looking for three pieces of information.
Infórmate: Emphasize the strategy for coping with unknown words. Limit the number of words on the list. Do the activity as a class, one paragraph at a time, until students learn the technique. On the chalkboard, write a list of words students don't understand.
Aplicación: Brainstorm possible locations.

Cultural Notes

(p. 482, left photo)
Blue-footed boobies are a type of gannet, or fish-eating off-shore sea bird. During courtship, male boobies fly toward their future mates, exposing the brilliant blue soles of their feet as they land. Since there are few natural predators on the islands, boobies show little fear when observed close-up by humans.

ECUADOR:
¡Bienvenido a la experiencia!

La primera consideración de Samoa Turismo al ofrecerle visitar Ecuador es naturaleza, mezclada con comodidad, seguridad y mucha simpatía.

Visitar nuestro país de apenas 283.561 kilómetros cuadrados, realmente es una hermosa experiencia; es uno de los países de mayor biodiversidad de la Tierra, tomando en cuenta su pequeña superficie, y con una riqueza florística excepcional que corresponde al 50% de la flora de Brasil y al 10% de la flora mundial.

Posee más del doble de especies animales y vegetales que toda Norteamérica y podemos citar que en un solo río de la Amazonía ecuatoriana habitan 473 especies de peces mientras que todo el continente europeo tiene 70.

En Sudamérica existen 3.500 especies de aves y en todo el mundo 8.600, en Ecuador viven 1.800 especies que representarían más del 20% de la avifauna mundial.

Posee tres de los puntos excepcionales para la conservación de las especies: las estribaciones orientales de los Andes, el bosque lluvioso noroccidental y los bosques secos, semihúmedos y húmedos tropicales.

Samoa Turismo también le brinda la oportunidad de visitar las Islas Galápagos, una de las maravillas naturales del mundo, Patrimonio de la Humanidad y la selva Amazónica, considerada el pulmón de la tierra.

Al ofrecerle nuestros servicios, Samoa Turismo garantiza una operación segura, en nuestros propios yates: **"American Enterprise"**, lujoso catamarán para 16 pasajeros y 8 tripulantes; y **"Samoa I"**, yate a motor, clase turista superior para 12 pasajeros y 6 tripulantes, además de su **"Amazon Jungle Resort Village"** en la selva Amazónica ecuatoriana y sus demás servicios en el resto del país, Andes y Costa que harán de su visita algo realmente inolvidable.

SAMOA TURISMO
Bienvenido a la experiencia ...

(map labels)
ISLAS GALÁPAGOS
ECUADOR
0°   0°
OCÉANO PACÍFICO
AMÉRICA DEL SUR
OCÉANO ATLÁNTICO

(p. 482, center photo)
Although the name "iguana" is generally applied to any herbivacious lizard with a dorsal crest, the Galápagos iguanas are a unique genus of lizard. The Galápagos marine iguana, which grows to as much as five feet, uses its tail to swim and dive. It grazes on underwater seaweed, and the Galápagos land iguana feeds on berries and cactus.

(p. 482, right photo)
The Galápagos tortoise is an ancient animal that existed in Texas and other parts of the southwestern U.S. some 25,000 years ago. The majority of them live today near the Alcedo volcano on the island of Isabela. Behaving in a manner typical of many Galápagos animals, the tortoise demonstrates little fear of humans. The giant tortoises weigh as much as 600 pounds and have a natural life span of 100 years or more.

Galápagos is Spanish for "tortoise" and the animal has come to symbolize the uniqueness of the islands' reptiles, birds, and plants. About 10,000 of these animals remain in the wild.

Apply

Teaching Suggestions

Ex. 1: Display all student work so that students doing the second task can choose a poet about whom to write.

Process Writing

For information regarding developing a writing portfolio, see p. 54.

¡Vamos a escribir!

Vamos a escribir unos poemas haiku. Los poemas haiku tienen tres líneas. La primera tiene 5 sílabas, la segunda tiene 7 y la tercera tiene 5. Por lo general, tratan de la naturaleza y de los sentimientos que inspira.

1 Para empezar, piensa en los lugares al aire libre que te gustan más, por ejemplo, un parque, un bosque o una playa. ¿Qué sientes cuando estás en uno de esos lugares? Trata de expresar tus sentimientos de una manera muy concreta y sencilla. Aquí hay unos ejemplos.

En el desierto,
la serpiente descansa.
Comió ardilla.

Al aire libre,
las hojas, el sendero,
tú y yo, tristes.

Montañas altas,
dar una caminata,
estoy cansado.

Cuenta las sílabas. No olvides que necesitas 5, 7 y 5 sílabas. Pídele sus comentarios a un(a) compañero(a) y revisa tu haiku si quieres.

484   Capítulo 14

Options

Strategies for Reaching All Students

Students Needing Extra Help
Explain haiku format. Have English-language haiku available. Use the vocabulary section of the Organizer.
Ex. 2: Give examples of the type of short biography found on book jackets. Pair students who like the same poem.

2 Un libro de poesía generalmente tiene datos sobre los poetas y las poetisas. Escoge un haiku que te gusta mucho y entrevista al (a la) compañero(a) que lo escribió. Luego, haz una nota biográfica sobre él o ella. Incluye estos datos:

- cómo se llama
- cuándo y dónde nació
- qué actividades le gustan más
- cuánto tiempo hace que escribe poesía
- qué piensa ser en el futuro

3 Para distribuir su trabajo, pueden:

- hacer un libro que se llama *La naturaleza en haiku*
- enviar su trabajo al periódico o revista escolar
- enviarlo a un periódico o revista local
- exhibirlo en la sala de clases o en otro lugar de la escuela
- incluirlo en su portafolio

You may want to assign parts of this section as written homework or as an in-class writing activity prior to administering the *Examen de habilidades.*

Answers

Listening: —*¡Qué aventura! Estábamos dando una caminata cuando Julio decidió escalar una montaña. Pero, ¿qué le pasó? De repente, ¡se cayó en un cacto! No se lastimó mucho, pero todavía tiene unas espinas que le duelen mucho. Ahora siempre les dice a sus amigos, "Es mejor que lleven zapatos especiales para escalar montañas."*
While mountain climbing, Julio fell on a cactus and hurt himself on the thorns.

Reading: You might see this sign in a national park.

Writing: Statements will vary; look for the subjunctive following each of the phrases.

Culture: A foreigner traveling in the U.S. might have an upset stomach because he or she is unaccustomed to the water, or because of dehydration or fatigue.

Speaking: Dialogues will vary.

¿Lo sabes bien?

Esta sección te ayudará a prepararte para el examen de habilidades, donde tendrás que hacer tareas semejantes.

Listening

Can you understand when people talk about outdoor activities? Listen as your teacher reads a sample similar to what you will hear on the test. What happened to Julio?

Reading

How well can you understand signs that deal with wildlife? Where might you see this sign?

En este lugar hay lobos, venados, coyotes y serpientes de muchas especies. Algunos de estos animales están en peligro de extinción. Por lo tanto les pedimos que sigan por el sendero, que tengan cuidado con los animales que encuentren y que tomen precauciones contra las plantas venenosas.
Se prohibe encender fuegos.

Writing

This is an excerpt from a brochure that gives advice on camping. Finish statements 2 to 4.

1. Es importante que lleven fósforos secos.
2. Se recomienda que ...
3. Es mejor que ...
4. Es necesario que ...

Culture

Can you explain why a foreigner traveling in the United States might have stomach upsets?

Speaking

You and your partner have gone camping. Create a dialogue in which you solve a problem. Here is an example:

A —*¡Vaya! ¡Los fósforos están mojados!*

B —*Yo sé encender palitos con un lente de mis anteojos.*

A —*¡No me digas! ¿De verdad?*

B —*Créeme. Pero necesito que me ayudes.*

A —*Bueno. ¿Qué hago?*

B —*Primero, busca palitos y hojas secas. Luego, ...*

Options

Strategies for Reaching All Students

Students Needing Extra Help

¿Lo sabes bien?: Remind students that this is just a sample of what the test will be like.
Listening: Read the sample more than once. Remind students they only need to listen for one piece of information. Brainstorm words students should be listening for.
Reading: Remind students to use context clues.
Writing: Have students use the Organizer to write sample suggestions as practice.

Culture: Have students review the notes they took during their first reading of the *Perspectiva cultural.* Encourage them to give an explanation rather than a short answer.
Speaking: Use the vocabulary section of the Organizer. Limit the number of lines of dialogue. Encourage students to use the subjunctive. Brainstorm problems that might arise on a camping trip and their possible solutions.
Have students write out this exercise so that they can check off what they have mastered.

Resumen del capítulo 14

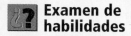

Usa el vocabulario de este capítulo para:

- discuss popular outdoor activities
- describe the natural environment
- express attitudes and opinions about the environment

to discuss camping
ir de camping
al aire libre
el campamento
la tienda (de acampar)
poner la tienda
el saco de dormir
el fósforo
el fuego
la leña
el palito
el abrelatas
la olla
ligero, -a
pesado, -a
mojado, -a
seco, -a
contaminado, -a
roto, -a

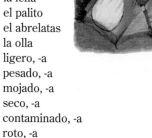

to describe nature
el amanecer
el atardecer
el desierto
el parque nacional
la colina
el valle
el fósil
la huella
la piedra
el sendero
la sombra

to discuss outdoor activities
dar una caminata
dar saltos
el trampolín, *pl.* los
    trampolines
escalar montañas
hacer esquí acuático
hacer moto acuática
la moto acuática
hacer surf
hacer surf de vela
la tabla (de surf)
la vela
navegar en balsa
la balsa
navegar en canoa
la canoa

to discuss plants and animals
el animal salvaje
la ardilla
la ballena
el búho
el coyote
el elefante
el gorila
el lobo, la loba
la mariposa
la pluma
la rana
la serpiente
el venado, la venada
los animales en peligro de
    extinción
doméstico, -a
peligroso, -a
venenoso, -a
el árbol
la hoja
el cacto
la espina
la planta silvestre

other useful words and expressions
el oxígeno
coser
recoger
secar

Verbos

Regular Verbs

estudiar	PRESENT INDICATIVE	estudio, estudias, estudia; estudiamos, estudiáis, estudian
	PRESENT SUBJUNCTIVE	estudie, estudies, estudie; estudiemos, estudiéis, estudien
	PRETERITE	estudié, estudiaste, estudió; estudiamos, estudiasteis, estudiaron
	IMPERFECT	estudiaba, estudiabas, estudiaba; estudiábamos, estudiabais, estudiaban
	FUTURE	estudiaré, estudiarás, estudiará; estudiaremos, estudiaréis, estudiarán
	TÚ COMMANDS	estudia, no estudies
	PRESENT PARTICIPLE	estudiando

comer	PRESENT INDICATIVE	como, comes, come; comemos, coméis, comen
	PRESENT SUBJUNCTIVE	coma, comas, coma; comamos, comáis, coman
	PRETERITE	comí, comiste, comió; comimos, comisteis, comieron
	IMPERFECT	comía, comías, comía; comíamos, comíais, comían
	FUTURE	comeré, comerás, comerá; comeremos, comeréis, comerán
	TÚ COMMANDS	come, no comas
	PRESENT PARTICIPLE	comiendo

vivir	PRESENT INDICATIVE	vivo, vives, vive; vivimos, vivís, viven
	PRESENT SUBJUNCTIVE	viva, vivas, viva; vivamos, viváis, vivan
	PRETERITE	viví, viviste, vivió; vivimos, vivisteis, vivieron
	IMPERFECT	vivía, vivías, vivía; vivíamos, vivíais, vivían
	FUTURE	viviré, vivirás, vivirá; viviremos, viviréis, vivirán
	TÚ COMMANDS	vive, no vivas
	PRESENT PARTICIPLE	viviendo

Reflexive Verbs

lavarse	PRESENT INDICATIVE	me lavo, te lavas, se lava; nos lavamos, os laváis, se lavan
	PRESENT SUBJUNCTIVE	me lave, te laves, se lave; nos lavemos, os lavéis, se laven
	PRETERITE	me lavé, te lavaste, se lavó; nos lavamos, os lavasteis, se lavaron
	IMPERFECT	me lavaba, te lavabas, se lavaba; nos lavábamos, os lavabais, se lavaban
	FUTURE	me lavaré, te lavarás, se lavará; nos lavaremos, os lavaréis, se lavarán
	TÚ COMMANDS	lávate, no te laves
	PRESENT PARTICIPLE	lavándose

Stem-Changing Verbs *(You will learn the forms that are in italics next year.)*

cerrar (e → ie)

PRESENT INDICATIVE	cierro, cierras, cierra; cerramos, cerráis, cierran
PRESENT SUBJUNCTIVE	cierre, cierres, cierre; *cerremos, cerréis, cierren*
PRETERITE	cerré, cerraste, cerró; cerramos, cerrasteis, cerraron
IMPERFECT	cerraba, cerrabas, cerraba; cerrábamos, cerrabais, cerraban
FUTURE	cerraré, cerrarás, cerrará; cerraremos, cerraréis, cerrarán
TÚ COMMANDS	cierra, no cierres
PRESENT PARTICIPLE	cerrando

Other verbs that follow the pattern of **cerrar: despertarse, pensar,** *and* **recomendar.**

dormir (o → ue)

PRESENT INDICATIVE	duermo, duermes, duerme; dormimos, dormís, duermen
PRESENT SUBJUNCTIVE	duerma, duermas, duerma; *durmamos, durmáis, duerman*
PRETERITE	dormí, dormiste, durmió; dormimos, dormisteis, durmieron
IMPERFECT	dormía, dormías, dormía; dormíamos, dormíais, dormían
FUTURE	dormiré, dormirás, dormirá; dormiremos, dormiréis, dormirán
TÚ COMMANDS	duerme, no duermas
PRESENT PARTICIPLE	durmiendo

empezar (e → ie)

PRESENT INDICATIVE	See *cerrar.*
PRESENT SUBJUNCTIVE	empiece, empieces, empiece; *empecemos, empecéis, empiecen*
PRETERITE	empecé, empezaste, empezó; empezamos, empezasteis, empezaron
IMPERFECT	See *cerrar.*
FUTURE	See *cerrar.*
TÚ COMMANDS	See *cerrar.*
PRESENT PARTICIPLE	See *cerrar.*

jugar (u → ue)

PRESENT INDICATIVE	juego, juegas, juega; jugamos, jugáis, juegan
PRESENT SUBJUNCTIVE	juegue, juegues, juegue; *juguemos, juguéis, jueguen*
PRETERITE	jugué, jugaste, jugó; jugamos, jugasteis, jugaron
IMPERFECT	jugaba, jugabas, jugaba; jugábamos, jugabais, jugaban
FUTURE	jugaré, jugarás, jugará; jugaremos, jugaréis, jugarán
TÚ COMMANDS	juega, no juegues
PRESENT PARTICIPLE	jugando

llover (o → ue)

PRESENT INDICATIVE	llueve
PRESENT SUBJUNCTIVE	llueva
PRETERITE	llovió
IMPERFECT	llovía
FUTURE	lloverá
PRESENT PARTICIPLE	lloviendo

nevar (e → ie)

PRESENT INDICATIVE	nieva
PRESENT SUBJUNCTIVE	nieve
PRETERITE	nevó
IMPERFECT	nevaba
FUTURE	nevará
PRESENT PARTICIPLE	nevando

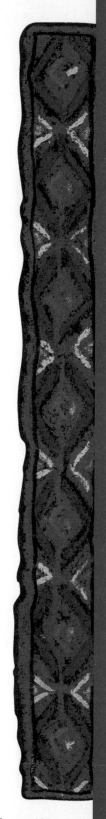

pedir (e → i)	PRESENT INDICATIVE	pido, pides, pide; pedimos, pedís, piden
	PRESENT SUBJUNCTIVE	pida, pidas, pida; *pidamos, pidáis, pidan*
	PRETERITE	pedí, pediste, pidió; pedimos, pedisteis, pidieron
	IMPERFECT	pedía, pedías, pedía; pedíamos, pedíais, pedían
	FUTURE	pediré, pedirás, pedirá; pediremos, pediréis, pedirán
	TÚ COMMANDS	pide, no pidas
	PRESENT PARTICIPLE	pidiendo

Other verbs that follow the pattern of pedir: **conseguir, despedirse, seguir, servir,** *and* **vestirse.**

perder (e → ie)	PRESENT INDICATIVE	pierdo, pierdes, pierde; perdemos, perdéis, pierden
	PRESENT SUBJUNCTIVE	pierda, pierdas, pierda; *perdamos, perdáis, pierdan*
	PRETERITE	perdí, perdiste, perdió; perdimos, perdisteis, perdieron
	IMPERFECT	perdía, perdías, perdía; perdíamos, perdíais, perdían
	FUTURE	perderé, perderás, perderá; perderemos, perderéis, perderán
	TÚ COMMANDS	pierde, no pierdas
	PRESENT PARTICIPLE	perdiendo

| **poder** (o → ue) | See Irregular Verbs. |

preferir (e → ie)	PRESENT INDICATIVE	prefiero, prefieres, prefiere; preferimos, preferís, prefieren
	PRESENT SUBJUNCTIVE	prefiera, prefieras, prefiera; *prefiramos, prefiráis, prefieran*
	PRETERITE	preferí, preferiste, prefirió; preferimos, preferisteis, prefirieron
	IMPERFECT	prefería, preferías, prefería; preferíamos, preferíais, preferían
	FUTURE	preferiré, preferirás, preferirá; preferiremos, preferiréis, preferirán
	TÚ COMMANDS	prefiere, no prefieras
	PRESENT PARTICIPLE	prefiriendo

Other verbs that follow the pattern of **preferir: divertirse, encender, hervir, mentir, sentirse,** *and* **sugerir.**

probar (o → ue)	PRESENT INDICATIVE	pruebo, pruebas, prueba; probamos, probáis, prueban
	PRESENT SUBJUNCTIVE	pruebe, pruebes, pruebe; *probemos, probéis, prueben*
	PRETERITE	probé, probaste, probó; probamos, probasteis, probaron
	IMPERFECT	probaba, probabas, probaba; probábamos, probabais, probaban
	FUTURE	probaré, probarás, probará; probaremos, probaréis, probarán
	TÚ COMMANDS	prueba, no pruebes
	PRESENT PARTICIPLE	probando

Other verbs that follow the pattern of **probar: acostarse, colgar, encontrar, mostrar, probarse,** *and* **recordar.**

| **querer** (e → ie) | See Irregular Verbs. |

soler (o → ue)	PRESENT INDICATIVE	suelo, sueles, suele; solemos, soléis, suelen
	PRESENT SUBJUNCTIVE	suela, suelas, suela; *solamos, soláis, suelan*
	PRETERITE	solí, soliste, solió; solimos, solisteis, solieron
	IMPERFECT	solía, solías, solía; solíamos, solíais, solían
	FUTURE	soleré, solerás, solerá; soleremos, soleréis, solerán
	TÚ COMMANDS	suele, no suelas
	PRESENT PARTICIPLE	soliendo

Other verbs that follow the pattern of **soler: devolver** *and* **revolver.**

Verbs with Spelling Changes

actuar (u → ú)

PRESENT INDICATIVE	actúo, actúas, actúa; actuamos, actuáis, actúan
PRESENT SUBJUNCTIVE	actúe, actúes, actúe; actuemos, actuéis, actúen
PRETERITE	actué, actuaste, actuó; actuamos, actuasteis, actuaron
IMPERFECT	actuaba, actuabas, actuaba; actuábamos, actuabais, actuaban
FUTURE	actuaré, actuarás, actuará; actuaremos, actuaréis, actuarán
TÚ COMMANDS	actúa, no actúes
PRESENT PARTICIPLE	actuando

Other verbs that follow the pattern of **actuar: graduarse**.

apagar (g → gu)

PRESENT INDICATIVE	apago, apagas, apaga; apagamos, apagáis, apagan
PRESENT SUBJUNCTIVE	apague, apagues, apague; apaguemos, apaguéis, apaguen
PRETERITE	apagué, apagaste, apagó; apagamos, apagasteis, apagaron
IMPERFECT	apagaba, apagabas, apagaba; apagábamos, apagabais, apagaban
FUTURE	apagaré, apagarás, apagará; apagaremos, apagaréis, apagarán
TÚ COMMANDS	apaga, no apagues
PRESENT PARTICIPLE	apagando

Other verbs that follow the pattern of **apagar: despegar, entregar, investigar, llegar, navegar,** *and* **pagar**.

buscar (c → qu)

PRESENT INDICATIVE	busco, buscas, busca; buscamos, buscáis, buscan
PRESENT SUBJUNCTIVE	busque, busques, busque; busquemos, busquéis, busquen
PRETERITE	busqué, buscaste, buscó; buscamos, buscasteis, buscaron
IMPERFECT	buscaba, buscabas, buscaba; buscábamos, buscabais, buscaban
FUTURE	buscaré, buscarás, buscará; buscaremos, buscaréis, buscarán
TÚ COMMANDS	busca, no busques
PRESENT PARTICIPLE	buscando

Other verbs that follow the pattern of **buscar: explicar, indicar, picar, practicar, sacar, secar(se),** *and* **tocar**.

conocer (c → zc)

PRESENT INDICATIVE	conozco, conoces, conoce; conocemos, conocéis, conocen
PRESENT SUBJUNCTIVE	conozca, conozcas, conozca; conozcamos, conozcáis, conozcan
PRETERITE	conocí, conociste, conoció; conocimos, conocisteis, conocieron
IMPERFECT	conocía, conocías, conocía; conocíamos, conocíais, conocían
FUTURE	conoceré, conocerás, conocerá; conoceremos, conoceréis, conocerán
TÚ COMMANDS	conoce, no conozcas
PRESENT PARTICIPLE	conociendo

Other verbs that follow the pattern of **conocer: desobedecer, obedecer,** *and* **parecer**.

creer (e → y)

PRESENT INDICATIVE	creo, crees, cree; creemos, creéis, creen
PRESENT SUBJUNCTIVE	crea, creas, crea; creamos, creáis, crean
PRETERITE	creí, creíste, creyó; creímos, creísteis, creyeron
IMPERFECT	creía, creías, creía; creíamos, creíais, creían
FUTURE	creeré, creerás, creerá; creeremos, creeréis, creerán
TÚ COMMANDS	cree, no creas
PRESENT PARTICIPLE	creyendo

Other verbs that follow the pattern of **creer: leer**.

Verbos   491

cruzar (z → c)	PRESENT INDICATIVE	cruzo, cruzas, cruza; cruzamos, cruzáis, cruzan
	PRESENT SUBJUNCTIVE	cruce, cruces, cruce; crucemos, crucéis, crucen
	PRETERITE	crucé, cruzaste, cruza; cruzamos, cruzasteis, cruzaron
	IMPERFECT	cruzaba, cruzabas, cruzaba; cruzábamos, cruzabais, cruzaban
	FUTURE	cruzaré, cruzarás, cruzará; cruzaremos, cruzaréis, cruzarán
	TÚ COMMANDS	cruza, no cruces
	PRESENT PARTICIPLE	cruzando

Other verbs that follow the pattern of **cruzar: lanzar.**

dirigir (g → j)	PRESENT INDICATIVE	dirijo, diriges, dirige; dirigimos, dirigís, dirigen
	PRESENT SUBJUNCTIVE	See *escoger.*
	PRETERITE	See *escoger.*
	IMPERFECT	See *escoger.*
	FUTURE	See *escoger.*
	TÚ COMMANDS	See *escoger.*
	PRESENT PARTICIPLE	See *escoger.*

empezar (z → c)   See Stem-Changing Verbs.

escoger (g → j)	PRESENT INDICATIVE	escojo, escoges, escoge; escogemos, escogéis, escogen
	PRESENT SUBJUNCTIVE	escoja, escojas, escoja; escojamos, escojáis, escojan
	PRETERITE	escogí, escogiste, escogió; escogimos, escogisteis, escogieron
	IMPERFECT	escogía, escogías, escogía; escogíamos, escogíais, escogían
	FUTURE	escogeré, escogerás, escogerá; escogeremos, escogeréis, escogerán
	TÚ COMMANDS	escoge, no escojas
	PRESENT PARTICIPLE	escogiendo

Other verbs that follow the pattern of **escoger: proteger(se)** *and* **recoger.**

incluir (i → y)	PRESENT INDICATIVE	incluyo, incluyes, incluye; incluímos, incluís, incluyen
	PRESENT SUBJUNCTIVE	incluya, incluyas, incluya; incluyamos, incluyáis, incluyan
	PRETERITE	incluí, incluiste, incluyó; incluimos, incluisteis, incluyeron
	IMPERFECT	incluía, incluías, incluía; incluíamos, incluíais, incluían
	FUTURE	incluiré, incluirás, incluirá; incluiremos, incluiréis, incluirán
	TÚ COMMANDS	incluye, no incluyas
	PRESENT PARTICIPLE	incluyendo

Other verbs that follow the pattern of **incluir: destruir.**

jugar (g → gu)   See Stem-Changing Verbs.

Irregular Verbs *(You will learn the forms that are in italics next year.)*

| caerse | PRETERITE | me caí, te caíste, se cayó; nos caímos, os caísteis, se cayeron |

For all other forms, see **traer** *and Reflexive Verbs.*

dar	PRESENT INDICATIVE	doy, das, da; damos, dais, dan
	PRESENT SUBJUNCTIVE	*dé, des, dé; demos, deis, den*
	PRETERITE	di, diste, dio; dimos, disteis, dieron
	IMPERFECT	daba, dabas, daba; dábamos, dabais, daban
	FUTURE	daré, darás, dará; daremos, daréis, darán
	TÚ COMMANDS	da, *no des*
	PRESENT PARTICIPLE	dando

decir	PRESENT INDICATIVE	digo, dices, dice; decimos, decís, dicen
	PRESENT SUBJUNCTIVE	diga, digas, diga; digamos, digáis, digan
	PRETERITE	dije, dijiste, dijo; dijimos, dijisteis, dijeron
	IMPERFECT	decía, decías, decía; decíamos, decíais, decían
	FUTURE	diré, dirás, dirá; diremos, diréis, dirán
	TÚ COMMANDS	di, no digas
	PRESENT PARTICIPLE	diciendo
estar	PRESENT INDICATIVE	estoy, estás, está; estamos, estáis, están
	PRESENT SUBJUNCTIVE	*esté, estés, esté; estemos, estéis, estén*
	PRETERITE	estuve, estuviste, estuvo; estuvimos, estuvisteis, estuvieron
	IMPERFECT	estaba, estabas, estaba; estábamos, estabais, estaban
	FUTURE	estaré, estarás, estará; estaremos, estaréis, estarán
	TÚ COMMANDS	está, *no estés*
	PRESENT PARTICIPLE	estando
haber	PRESENT INDICATIVE	hay
	PRESENT SUBJUNCTIVE	*haya*
	PRETERITE	hubo
	IMPERFECT	había
	FUTURE	habrá
hacer	PRESENT INDICATIVE	hago, haces, hace; hacemos, hacéis, hacen
	PRESENT SUBJUNCTIVE	haga, hagas, haga; hagamos, hagáis, hagan
	PRETERITE	hice, hiciste, hizo; hicimos, hicisteis, hicieron
	IMPERFECT	hacía, hacías, hacía; hacíamos, hacíais, hacían
	FUTURE	haré, harás, hará; haremos, haréis, harán
	TÚ COMMANDS	haz, no hagas
	PRESENT PARTICIPLE	haciendo
ir	PRESENT INDICATIVE	voy, vas, va; vamos, vais, van
	PRESENT SUBJUNCTIVE	vaya, vayas, vaya; vayamos, vayáis, vayan
	PRETERITE	fui, fuiste, fue; fuimos, fuisteis, fueron
	IMPERFECT	iba, ibas, iba; íbamos, ibais, iban
	FUTURE	iré, irás, irá; iremos, iréis, irán
	TÚ COMMANDS	ve, no vayas
	PRESENT PARTICIPLE	*yendo*
mantenerse	See *tener* and Reflexive Verbs.	
nacer	PRETERITE	nací, naciste, nació; nacimos, nacisteis, nacieron
poder	PRESENT INDICATIVE	puedo, puedes, puede; podemos, podéis, pueden
	PRESENT SUBJUNCTIVE	pueda, puedas, pueda; *podamos, podáis, puedan*
	PRETERITE	pude, pudiste, pudo; pudimos, pudisteis, pudieron
	IMPERFECT	podía, podías, podía; podíamos, podíais, podían
	FUTURE	podré, podrás, podrá; podremos, podréis, podrán
	TÚ COMMANDS	puede, no puedas
	PRESENT PARTICIPLE	*pudiendo*
poner	PRESENT INDICATIVE	pongo, pones, pone; ponemos, ponéis, ponen
	PRESENT SUBJUNCTIVE	ponga, pongas, ponga; pongamos, pongáis, pongan
	PRETERITE	puse, pusiste, puso; pusimos, pusisteis, pusieron
	IMPERFECT	ponía, ponías, ponía; poníamos, poníais, ponían
	FUTURE	pondré, pondrás, pondrá; pondremos, pondréis, pondrán
	TÚ COMMANDS	pon, no pongas
	PRESENT PARTICIPLE	poniendo

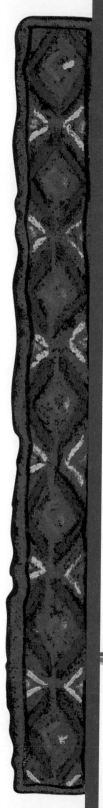

Verbos   493

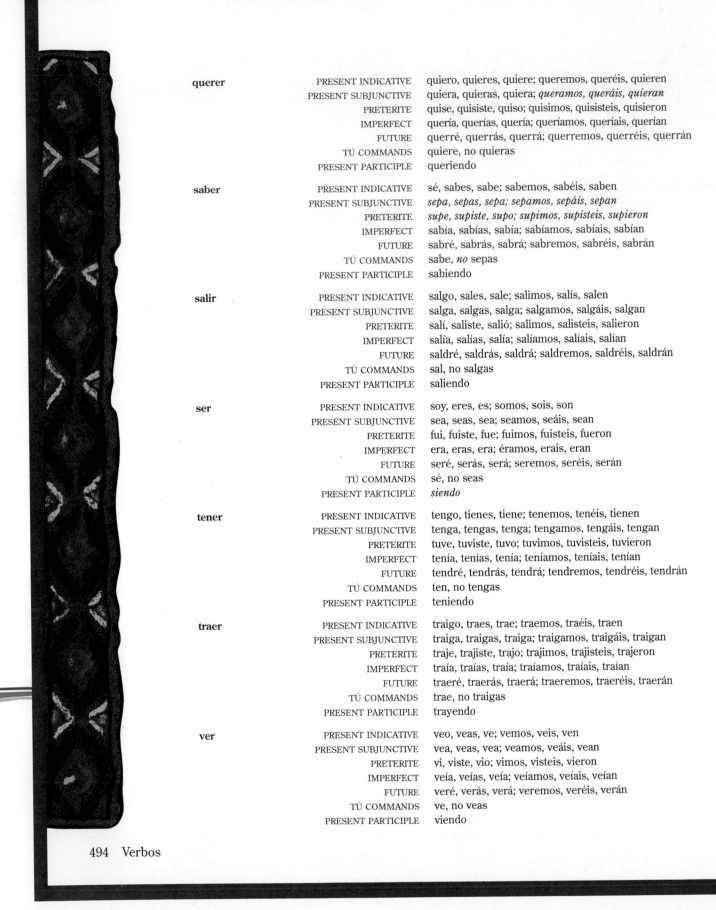

querer	PRESENT INDICATIVE	quiero, quieres, quiere; queremos, queréis, quieren
	PRESENT SUBJUNCTIVE	quiera, quieras, quiera; *queramos, queráis, quieran*
	PRETERITE	quise, quisiste, quiso; quisimos, quisisteis, quisieron
	IMPERFECT	quería, querías, quería; queríamos, queríais, querían
	FUTURE	querré, querrás, querrá; querremos, querréis, querrán
	TÚ COMMANDS	quiere, no quieras
	PRESENT PARTICIPLE	queriendo
saber	PRESENT INDICATIVE	sé, sabes, sabe; sabemos, sabéis, saben
	PRESENT SUBJUNCTIVE	*sepa, sepas, sepa; sepamos, sepáis, sepan*
	PRETERITE	*supe, supiste, supo; supimos, supisteis, supieron*
	IMPERFECT	sabía, sabías, sabía; sabíamos, sabíais, sabían
	FUTURE	sabré, sabrás, sabrá; sabremos, sabréis, sabrán
	TÚ COMMANDS	sabe, *no* sepas
	PRESENT PARTICIPLE	sabiendo
salir	PRESENT INDICATIVE	salgo, sales, sale; salimos, salís, salen
	PRESENT SUBJUNCTIVE	salga, salgas, salga; salgamos, salgáis, salgan
	PRETERITE	salí, saliste, salió; salimos, salisteis, salieron
	IMPERFECT	salía, salías, salía; salíamos, salíais, salían
	FUTURE	saldré, saldrás, saldrá; saldremos, saldréis, saldrán
	TÚ COMMANDS	sal, no salgas
	PRESENT PARTICIPLE	saliendo
ser	PRESENT INDICATIVE	soy, eres, es; somos, sois, son
	PRESENT SUBJUNCTIVE	sea, seas, sea; seamos, seáis, sean
	PRETERITE	fui, fuiste, fue; fuimos, fuisteis, fueron
	IMPERFECT	era, eras, era; éramos, erais, eran
	FUTURE	seré, serás, será; seremos, seréis, serán
	TÚ COMMANDS	sé, no seas
	PRESENT PARTICIPLE	*siendo*
tener	PRESENT INDICATIVE	tengo, tienes, tiene; tenemos, tenéis, tienen
	PRESENT SUBJUNCTIVE	tenga, tengas, tenga; tengamos, tengáis, tengan
	PRETERITE	tuve, tuviste, tuvo; tuvimos, tuvisteis, tuvieron
	IMPERFECT	tenía, tenías, tenía; teníamos, teníais, tenían
	FUTURE	tendré, tendrás, tendrá; tendremos, tendréis, tendrán
	TÚ COMMANDS	ten, no tengas
	PRESENT PARTICIPLE	teniendo
traer	PRESENT INDICATIVE	traigo, traes, trae; traemos, traéis, traen
	PRESENT SUBJUNCTIVE	traiga, traigas, traiga; traigamos, traigáis, traigan
	PRETERITE	traje, trajiste, trajo; trajimos, trajisteis, trajeron
	IMPERFECT	traía, traías, traía; traíamos, traíais, traían
	FUTURE	traeré, traerás, traerá; traeremos, traeréis, traerán
	TÚ COMMANDS	trae, no traigas
	PRESENT PARTICIPLE	trayendo
ver	PRESENT INDICATIVE	veo, veas, ve; vemos, veis, ven
	PRESENT SUBJUNCTIVE	vea, veas, vea; veamos, veáis, vean
	PRETERITE	vi, viste, vio; vimos, visteis, vieron
	IMPERFECT	veía, veías, veía; veíamos, veíais, veían
	FUTURE	veré, verás, verá; veremos, veréis, verán
	TÚ COMMANDS	ve, no veas
	PRESENT PARTICIPLE	viendo

VOCABULARIO ESPAÑOL-INGLÉS

This *Vocabulario* contains all active vocabulary from PASO A PASO 1 and 2.

A dash (—) represents the main entry word. For example, **al** — after **el horno** means **al horno.**

The number following each entry indicates the chapter in which the word or expression is presented. A Roman numeral (I) indicates that the word was presented in PASO A PASO 1.

The following abbreviations are used: *adj.* (adjective), *dir. obj.* (direct object), *f.* (feminine), *fam.* (familiar), *ind. obj.* (indirect object), *inf.* (infinitive), *m.* (masculine), *pl.* (plural), *prep.* (preposition), *pron.* (pronoun), *sing.* (singular).

a, al *(a + el)* at; to (I)
la **abeja** bee (9)
el **abogado, la abogada** lawyer (11)
abrazarse to hug, to embrace (6)
el **abrelatas** can opener (14)
el **abrigo** coat (I)
abril April (I)
abrir to open (I)
abrocharse to fasten (12)
el **abuelo, la abuela** grandfather, grandmother (I)
los **abuelos** grandparents (I)
aburrido, -a boring (I)
aburrir to bore (I)
  —se to be bored (4)
acampar: la tienda de — tent (14)
el **accidente** accident (9)
acción: la película de — action film (10)
Acción *see* **Día**
el **aceite** oil (13)
acondicionado *see* **aire**
acostarse *(o → ue)* to go to bed (2)
la **actividad** activity (2)
el **actor, la actriz** actor, actress (I)
la **actuación** acting (10)
actuar to act (10)
acuático, -a *see* **esquí, moto**
acuerdo: estar de — to agree (I)
además in addition, besides (9)
adiós good-by (I)
¿adónde? (to) where? (I)
la **aduana** customs (12)
el **aduanero, la aduanera** customs agent (12)
aérea: la línea — airline (12)
el **aeropuerto** airport (12)
afeitar:
  —se to shave (8)
  la crema de — shaving cream (8)
  la máquina de — razor (8)
la **agencia de viajes** travel agency (12)
el/la **agente (de viajes)** (travel) agent (12)
agosto August (I)

agrio, -a sour (13)
el **agua** *f.* water (I)
el **aguacate** avocado (I)
ahora now (I)
ahorrar to save (7)
el **aire** air (I)
  al —libre outdoors (14)
  el — acondicionado air conditioning (7)
el **ajedrez** chess (4)
el **ajo** garlic (13)
alegre happy, festive (4)
el **alemán** German *(language)* (1)
la **alergia** allergy (9)
alérgico, -a (a) allergic (to) (9)
el **álgebra** *f.* algebra (1)
algo something (I)
  — más something else (I)
el **algodón** cotton (3)
alguien someone, somebody (I, 3)
alguno (algún), -a some (I, 1)
  —a vez ever (I)
la **alimentación** nourishment, food (13)
allí there (I)
  — está there it is (I)
el **almacén** department store (I)
el **almuerzo** lunch (I)
  en el — for lunch (I)
alto, -a tall (I)
el **alto: la señal de —** stop sign (8)
el **aluminio** aluminum (I)
amable kind, nice (I)
el **amanecer** dawn, sunrise (14)
amargo, -a bitter (13)
amarillo, -a yellow (I)
el **ambiente** atmosphere (I)
  el medio —environment (I, 11)
la **ambulancia** ambulance (9)
la **amenaza** threat (I)
el **amigo, la amiga** friend (I)
el **análisis** medical test (9)
anaranjado, -a orange *(color)* (I)
el **anillo** ring (7)
el **animal** animal (I, 5)
  el—de peluche stuffed animal (5)

el **aniversario (de boda)** (wedding) anniversary (6)
anoche last night (I)
los **anteojos (de sol)** (sun)glasses (I, 7)
antes de + *verb* before + *verb* + -ing (2)
antialérgico, -a non-allergenic (9)
el **antibiótico** antibiotic (9)
antiguo, -a old, traditional (I)
antipático, -a unfriendly, unpleasant (I)
el **anuario** yearbook (2)
el **anuncio** ad, commercial (I)
el **año** year (I)
  a los ... —s at the age of ... (6)
  el — Nuevo New Year's Day (6)
  ¿cuántos — tienes? how old are you? (I)
  cumplir —s to have a birthday (6)
  la fiesta de fin de — New Year's Eve party (I)
  el fin de — New Year's Eve (6)
  tener ... —s to be ... years old (I)
apagar to turn off (I, 7); to blow out *(candles)* (6)
el **aparato** appliance, device (7)
el **apartamento** apartment (I)
aprender to learn (I)
apretado, -a tight *(clothing)* (3)
aquel, aquella; aquellos, -as that (over there); those (over there) (3)
aquél, aquélla; aquéllos, -as *pron.* that one (over there); those (over there) (3)
aquí here (I)
  — está here it is (I)
  por — around here (I)
la **araña** spider (9)
el **árbol** tree (I, 14)
la **ardilla** squirrel (14)
el **arete** earring (I, 7)
el **argumento** plot (10)
el **armario** locker (1)
arreglar to clean up (I)
arrestar to arrest (10)

el **arroz** rice (I)
el **arte** art (I, 4)
las—s **marciales** martial arts (2)
la **artesanía** handcrafts (12)
artístico, -a artistic (I)
asado, -a roasted (13)
el **ascensor** elevator (8)
asco: ¡qué —! yuck! that's disgusting! (I)
así, así so-so, fair (I)
el **asiento** seat (1)
la **aspiradora** vacuum cleaner (I)
pasar la — to vacuum (I)
el/la **astronauta** astronaut (11)
el **atardecer** sunset (14)
aterrizar to land (12)
atractivo, -a attractive (I)
atrevido, -a bold, daring (I)
el **auditorio** auditorium (1)
el **autobús** bus (I)
la parada del — bus stop (I)
automático, -a automatic (11)
el/la **auxiliar de vuelo** flight attendant (12)
la **avenida** avenue (I)
aventura: la película de —s adventure film (I)
el **avión** airplane (12)
¡ay! ouch! (I)
ayer yesterday (I)
la **ayuda** help, assistance (10)
ayudar to help (I)
el **azúcar** sugar (I)
azul, *pl.* **azules** blue (I)

bailar to dance (I, 6)
el **bailarín, la bailarina** dancer (11)
el **baile** dance (I, 6)
baja: el sube y — seesaw (5)
bajo, -a short *(height)* (I)
la **ballena** whale (I, 14)
el **balón** *(inflated)* ball (4)
la **balsa** raft (14)
navegar en — to go river rafting (14)
bañarse to take a bath (2)
el **banco** bank (I)
la **banda** band (2)
la **bandera** flag (1)
el **baño** bathroom (I)
el traje de — bathing suit (I)
barato, -a cheap, inexpensive (I)
la **barbacoa** barbecue (13)
hacer una — to have a barbecue (13)
basado, -a (en) based (on) (10)

básquetbol: jugar — to play basketball (I)
bastante rather, quite (I, 4)
la **basura** garbage (I)
el **bate** (baseball) bat (4)
beber to drink (I)
la **bebida** beverage (I)
el **béisbol** baseball (I)
besarse to kiss (6)
la **biblioteca** library (I)
la **bicicleta** bicycle (I, 4)
montar en — to ride a bike (4)
bien well (I)
la **biología** biology (1)
el **bisabuelo, la bisabuela** great-grandfather, great-grandmother (6)
el **bistec** steak (I)
blanco, -a white (I)
el **bloque** block *(toy)* (5)
la **blusa** blouse (I)
la **boca** mouth (I)
el **bocadillo** Spanish-style sandwich (13)
la **boda** wedding (6)
el **boleto (de ida y vuelta)** (round-trip) ticket (12)
el **bolígrafo** pen (I)
los **bolos** bowling (4)
el **bolsillo** pocket (3)
el **bolso** gym bag, book bag (1); purse (3)
el **bombero, la bombera** firefighter (8)
la estación de —s fire station (8)
el **bombillo** light bulb (7)
bonito, -a pretty (I)
el **bosque** woods (11)
la **bota** boot (I)
el **bote** rowboat (I)
pasear en — to row (I)
la **botella** bottle (I, 11)
el **botín** half boots (3)
el **botón** button (3)
el **brazo** arm (I)
el **bronceador** suntan lotion (I)
bucear to skin-dive (I)
bueno (buen), -a good (I)
bueno OK, fine, all right (I)
la **bufanda** muffler, scarf (I)
el **bufet de ensaladas** salad bar (1)
el **búho** owl (14)
el **burrito** burrito (I)
buscar to look for (I)
el **buzón** mailbox (8)

el **caballero: la ropa para —s** men's wear (8)
el **caballo** horse (10)
montar a — to ride a horse (10)
la **cabeza** head (I)
tener dolor de — to have a headache (I)
el **cacto** cactus (14)
la **cadena** chain (7)
caerse to fall down (9)
el **café** coffee (I)
la **cafetería** cafeteria (1)
la **caja** cashier's station (8)
el **cajero, la cajera** cashier (3)
el **cajón de arena** sandbox (5)
la **calabaza** pumpkin (13)
la **calamina** calamine lotion (9)
el **calcetín** sock (I)
la **calculadora** calculator (I)
la **calefacción** heating (7)
el **calentador** heater (7)
caliente: el perro — hot dog (13)
callado, -a quiet (I)
la **calle** street (I)
calor:
hace — it's hot (out) (I)
tener — to be hot *(person)* (I)
la **caloría** calorie (13)
la **cama** bed (I)
la **cámara** camera (I)
el **camarero, la camarera** waiter, waitress (I)
el **camarón** shrimp (13)
cambiar to change (10); to cash (12)
el **cambio** change (11)
la casa de — currency exchange (12)
caminar to walk (5)
caminata: dar una — to go hiking (14)
el **camión** truck (5)
la **camisa** shirt (I)
la **camiseta** T-shirt (I)
el **campamento** campground (14)
el **campeón, la campeona** champion (4)
el **campeonato** championship (4)
camping: ir de — to go camping (14)
el **campo** countryside (I)
el **canal** (TV) channel (I)
la **canción** song (2)
la **canoa** canoe (14)
navegar en — to go canoeing (14)
canoso: pelo — gray hair (I)
cansado, -a tired (I)

el/la **cantante** singer (11)
cantar to sing (I, 2)
el **capítulo** chapter (1)
la **cara** face (2)
el **carbohidrato** carbohydrate (13)
cariñoso, -a affectionate, loving (I)
la **carne (de res)** beef (I)
el **carnet de identidad** ID card (7)
la **carnicería** butcher shop (8)
caro, -a expensive (I)
la **carpeta** pocket folder (I)
　　la — de argollas three-ring
　　　binder (I)
la **carretera** highway (8)
el **carrusel** merry-go-round (5)
la **carta** letter (I)
　　a la — a la carte (I)
el **cartel** poster (I)
la **cartera** wallet (3)
el **cartón** cardboard (I, 11)
la **casa** house (I)
　　la — de cambio currency
　　　exchange (12)
　　en — at home (I)
　　la especialidad de la — house
　　　specialty (I)
casado, -a (con) married (to) (6)
casarse (con) to marry, to get
　　married to (6)
el **casco** helmet (4)
el **casete** cassette (4)
casi almost (I)
caso: en — de in case of (7)
castaño: pelo — brown (chestnut)
　　hair (I)
el **catálogo** catalog (3)
las **cataratas** waterfall (I)
la **catedral** cathedral (I)
catorce fourteen (I)
la **cebolla** onion (I)
la **celebración** celebration (6)
celebrar to celebrate (6)
la **cena** dinner (I)
central central (7)
el **centro** center (I); downtown (8)
　　el — comercial mall (I)
cepillarse (los dientes) to brush
　　(one's teeth) (2)
el **cepillo** brush (8)
　　el — de dientes toothbrush (8)
cerca (de) near (I)
el **cerdo** pork (13)
el **cereal** cereal (I)
la **cereza** cherry (13)
cero zero (I)
cerrar *(e → ie)* to close (I)
el **césped** lawn (I)

el **cesto de la ropa sucia** laundry
　　hamper (3)
el **chaleco** vest (3)
el **champiñón** mushroom (13)
el **champú** shampoo (I)
el **chandal** sweatsuit (3)
la **chaqueta** jacket (I)
el **chaquetón** car coat (3)
charlar to chat (6)
el **cheque** check (3)
　　el — de viajero traveler's check
　　　(12)
el **chile** chili pepper (I)
　　el — con carne beef with beans
　　　(I)
　　el — relleno stuffed pepper (I)
el **chocolate** hot chocolate (I)
el **chorizo** sausage (13)
el **churro** churro (I)
cien one hundred (I)
la **ciencia ficción** science fiction (I)
las **ciencias** science (I)
　　— de la salud health (science)
　　　(I)
　　— sociales social studies (I)
el **científico, la científica** scientist
　　(10)
ciento uno, -a; ciento dos; etc.
　　101, 102, etc. (I)
cinco five (I)
cincuenta fifty (I)
el **cine** movies, movie theater (I)
el **cinturón** belt (3)
　　el — de seguridad seatbelt (12)
la **ciudad** city (I)
el **clarinete** clarinet (2)
claro: ¡— que sí/no! of course
　　(not) (I)
claro, -a light *(color)* (3)
la **clase (de)** class; kind, type (I)
　　después de las —s after school
　　　(I)
　　la sala de —s classroom (I)
clásico, -a classical (4)
la **clínica** clinic (I)
el **club** club (2)
el **coche** car (I)
cocido, -a cooked (13)
la **cocina** kitchen (I)
cocinar to cook (I)
el **cocinero, la cocinera** cook (13)
el **codo** elbow (9)
la **colección** collection (5)
coleccionar to collect (5)
colgar *(o → ue)* to hang (3)
la **colina** hill (14)
el **collar** necklace (I, 7)

el **color** color (I)
　　¿de qué —? what color? (I)
　　en —es in color (I)
el **columpio** swing (5)
la **comedia** comedy, sitcom (I)
el **comedor** dining room (I)
el **comentario (sobre)** review (of)
　　(10)
comer to eat (I)
los **comestibles** groceries (I)
cómico, -a comical (I)
la **comida** meal, food (I)
como like, as (I)
　　tan + *adj.* + — as + *adj.* + as (1)
　　tanto(s), -a(s) + noun + — as
　　　much (many) + *noun* + as (3)
¿cómo? how? (I)
　　¿— eres? what are you like? (I)
　　¿— estás/está Ud.? how are
　　　you? (I)
　　¡— no! certainly! (I)
　　¿— se dice . . . ? how do you
　　　say . . . ? (I)
　　¿— se llama(n)? what is
　　　his/her/their name? (I)
　　¿— te llamas? what's your
　　　name? (I)
la **cómoda** dresser (I)
cómodo, -a comfortable (I)
el **compañero, la compañera**
　　classmate (I)
la **composición** composition (1)
comprar to buy (I)
compras:
　　hacer las — to shop (8)
　　ir de — to go shopping (I)
　　el programa de — home
　　　shopping show (10)
la **computadora** computer (1)
la **comunidad** community (I)
con with (I)
el **concierto** concert (I)
　　concursos: el programa de —
　　　game show (10)
　　congelado, -a frozen (13)
　　conmigo with me (I)
conocer *(c → zc)* to know, to be
　　aquainted with (I, 1)
conseguir *(e → i)* to get, to obtain
　　(12)
el **consejero, la consejera** counselor
　　(1)
el **consejo estudiantil** student
　　council (2)
consentido, -a spoiled *(child)* (5)
conservar to conserve, to save (I, 7)
contaminado, -a contaminated,
　　polluted (I, 14)

contaminar to pollute (11)
contestar to answer (1)
contigo with you (I)
el contrabajo bass (2)
el control remoto remote control (7)
la corbata necktie (I, 3)
el coro chorus, choir (2)
el correo post office (I)
correr to run, to jog (4)
cortar to cut (I, 13)
—se to cut oneself (9)
corto, -a short (length) (I)
la cosa thing (I)
coser to sew (14)
costar (o → ue) to cost (I)
el coyote coyote (14)
crédito: la tarjeta de — credit card (3)
creer to think, to believe (I)
creo que sí (no) I (don't) think so (I)
la cremallera zipper (3)
el crimen crime (10)
el/la criminal criminal (10)
el cruce intersection (8)
el crucigrama crossword puzzle (4)
cruzar to cross (8)
el cuaderno spiral notebook (I)
la cuadra block (I)
cuadrado, -a square (I)
el cuadro picture (I)
cuadros: a — plaid, checked (3)
¿cuál(es)? what? which? which one(s)? (I)
cuando, ¿cuándo? when (I)
de vez en — sometimes (7)
¿cuánto? how much? (I)
¿— (tiempo) hace que . . . ? how long has it been since . . . ? (I)
¿cuántos, -as? how many? (I)
¿— años tiene . . . ? how old is . . . ? (I)
cuarenta forty (I)
cuarto, -a quarter; fourth (I)
y — (time) quarter after, quarter past (I)
el cuarto room (I)
cuatro four (I)
cuatrocientos four hundred (I)
la cucaracha cockroach (9)
la cuchara spoon (I)
el cuchillo knife (I)
el cuello neck (I)
el suéter de — alto turtleneck (3)
la cuenta bill (restaurant) (I)

la cuerda rope (5)
saltar a la — to jump rope (5)
el cuero leather (I)
de — (made of) leather (I)
el cuerpo body (I)
cuidado: tener — (con) to be careful (with / of) (12)
cuidar niños to baby-sit (2)
el cumpleaños birthday (I, 6)
¡feliz —! happy birthday! (I)
la fiesta de — birthday party (I)
la tarjeta de — birthday card (I)
cumplir años to have a birthday (6)
el cuñado, la cuñada brother-in-law, sister-in-law (6)

damas: la ropa para — ladies' wear (8)
las damas checkers (4)
dañar to damage (10)
daño: hacer — a to make ill, not to agree with (food) (13)
dar to give (I)
— + movie or TV program to show (I)
— una caminata to go hiking (14)
— miedo a to scare (I)
— saltos to dive (14)
—se la mano to shake hands (6)
(me) da igual it's all the same (to me) (3)
de, del (de + el) from; of; — 's, — s' (I)
— + material made of (I)
— nada you're welcome (I)
— postre for dessert (I)
¿— veras? really? (I)
debajo de under(neath) (I)
deber ought to, should (I)
decir to say, to tell (I)
¿cómo se dice . . . ? how do you say . . . ? (I)
—se "¡Hola!" to say hello (6)
¡no me digas! really?, you don't say! (I)
¿qué quiere — . . . ? what does . . . mean? (I)
se dice . . . it is said (I)
la decoración decoration (I)
dedicarse (a) to be involved in; to devote oneself (to) (11)
el dedo finger (I)
el — del pie toe (I)
delante de in front of (I)
demasiado too (I)
dental: la seda — dental floss (8)

el/la dentista dentist (I)
depender (de) to depend (on) (I, 2)
los deportes sports (I)
deportista athletic (I)
el/la deportista athlete (11)
deportivo, -a adj. sports (I)
depositar to deposit (I)
derecha: a la — (de) to the right (of) (I)
derecho, -a right (I)
el derrumbe landslide (10)
desabrocharse to unfasten (12)
el desastre disaster (4)
desayunar to have breakfast (2)
el desayuno breakfast (I)
descansar to rest (I)
el descuento: la tienda de —s discount store (I)
desde (que + verb) since, from (6)
desear: ¿qué desea Ud? may I help you? (I)
el desfile parade (4)
el desierto desert (14)
desobedecer (c → zc) to disobey (5)
desobediente disobedient (5)
el desodorante deodorant (8)
desordenado, -a messy (I)
despedirse (e → i) (de) to say goodby (to) (6)
despegar (plane) to take off (12)
el despertador alarm clock (2)
despertarse (e → ie) to wake up (2)
después de + inf. after + verb + -ing (I, 2)
destino: con — a going to (12)
destruir to destroy (10)
la desventaja disadvantage (11)
el/la detective detective (10)
el programa de —s detective show (I)
el detector de humo smoke detector (7)
detrás (de) behind (I)
devolver (o → ue) to return (something) (I)
el día day (I)
buenos —s good morning (I)
el — de fiesta holiday (6)
el plato del — daily special (I)
¿qué — es hoy? what day is it? (I)
todos los —s every day (I)
el Día de (Acción de) Gracias Thanksgiving (6)
el Día de los Enamorados Valentine's Day (6)
el Día de la Independencia Independence Day (6)

el **Día de la Madre** Mother's Day (6)
el **Día del Padre** Father's Day (6)
el **Día de la Raza** Columbus Day (6)
la **diapositiva** slide (1)
dibujar to draw (I)
el **dibujo** drawing (I)
  los **—s animados** cartoons (I)
el **diccionario** dictionary (I)
diciembre December (I)
diecinueve nineteen (I)
dieciocho eighteen (I)
dieciséis sixteen (I)
diecisiete seventeen (I)
los **dientes** teeth (2)
  el cepillo de — toothbrush (8)
  diez ten (I)
difícil difficult, hard (I)
digas *see* **decir**
el **dinero** money (I)
el **dinosaurio** dinosaur (5)
la **dirección** address (8); direction (10)
el **director, la directora** *(school)* principal (1); *(film)* director (10)
dirigir *(g → j)* to direct (10)
el **disco** disk (4)
  el — compacto compact disk (4)
  el — (de hockey) (hockey) puck (4)
disfraces: la fiesta de — costume party (I, 4)
disfrutar de to enjoy (12)
la **distancia** distance (8)
la **diversión** fun, entertainment (4)
  el parque de —es amusement park (I)
divertido, -a amusing, funny (I)
divertirse *(e → ie)* to have fun (4)
divorciado, -a (de) divorced (from) (6)
doblar to turn (8)
doble double (12)
doce twelve (I)
el **documental** documentary (I)
el **dólar** dollar (I)
doler *(o → ue)* to hurt, to ache (I)
dolor: tener — de . . . to have a . . . ache (I)
doméstico, -a domestic (14)
domingo Sunday (I)
  el — on Sunday (I)
donde, ¿dónde? where (I)
dormir *(o → ue)* to sleep (I)
  el saco de — sleeping bag (14)
el **dormitorio** bedroom (I)
dos two (I)
doscientos two hundred (I)
ducharse to take a shower (2)

dulce sweet (13)
el **dulce** candy (13)
durar to last (I)
el **durazno** peach (13)
duro: el huevo — hard-boiled egg (13)

echar to throw out, to dump (11)
económico, -a economical (11)
la **edad: ¿a qué —?** at what age? (6)
el **edificio** building (1)
la **educación** education (11)
educado, -a polite, well-mannered (5)
educativo, -a educational (I)
efectivo: (el dinero) en — cash (3)
los **efectos especiales** special effects (10)
eficiente efficient (11)
el **ejercicio** exercise (I, 1)
  hacer — to exercise (I)
el **el** the *m. sing.* (I)
él he; him *after prep.* (I)
la **electricidad** electricity (7)
eléctrico, -a electric (7)
el **elefante** elephant (I, 14)
elegante elegant (I, 3)
ella she; her *after prep.* (I)
ellos, ellas they; them *after prep.* (I)
el **embarque: la tarjeta de —** boarding pass (12)
la **emergencia** emergency (7)
  en caso de — in case of emergency (7)
  la sala de — emergency room (9)
emocionante exciting, funny (I)
la **empanada** turnover (13)
empatar to tie *(in scoring)* (4)
empezar *(e → ie)* to begin, to start (I)
el **empleado, la empleada** employee (12)
en in, at, on (I)
  — + *vehicle* by (I)
Enamorados *see* **Día**
enamorarse (de) to fall in love (with) (10)
encantado, -a delighted (I)
encantar to love (I)
encender *(e → ie)* to light (6); to turn on (7)
la **enchilada** enchilada (I)
encima (de) on (top of) (I)
encontrar *(o → ue)* to find (3)
  —se *(o → ue)* to meet (6)
la **energía** energy (I, 7)

enero January (I)
la **enfermedad** illness (9)
la **enfermería** nurse's office (I)
el **enfermero, la enfermera** nurse (9)
enfermo, -a ill, sick (I)
enfrente (de) facing, opposite, in front of (I)
enlatado, -a canned (13)
la **ensalada** salad (I)
  el bufet de —s salad bar (1)
  la — de frutas fruit salad (13)
enseñar to teach (I)
la **entrada** entrance (8)
entre between, among (I)
entregar to deliver (I); to hand in (1)
el **entrenador, la entrenadora** coach (4)
la **entrevista** interview (10)
  el programa de —s talk show (I)
enviar to send, to mail (I)
el **equipaje** baggage (12)
  la terminal de — baggage claim (12)
el **equipo** team (2)
  el — de sonido stereo (I)
la **erupción** eruption (10)
la **escala** stopover (12)
  sin — nonstop (12)
escalar montañas to go mountain climbing (14)
la **escalera** stairs (8)
  la — mecánica escalator (8)
la **escena** scene (10)
el **escenario** stage (1)
escoger *(g → j)* to choose (I, 3)
escolar *adj.* school (1)
esconder to hide *(something)* (10)
  —se to hide (10)
escribir to write (I, 1)
  ¿cómo se escribe . . . ? how do you spell . . . ? (I)
  —se to write each other (6)
el **escritor, la escritora** writer (11)
el **escritorio** desk (I)
escuchar to listen (to) (I)
la **escuela** school (I)
ese, -a; -os, -as that; those (I, 3)
ése, -a; -os, -as *pron.* that one; those (3)
el **esmalte de uñas** nail polish (8)
eso: por — that's why (I)
el **espacio** space (11)
la **espalda** back (I)
el **español** Spanish *(language)* (I)
el **espárrago** asparagus (13)
especial special (6)

Vocabulario español-inglés 499

499

la **especialidad de la casa** house specialty (I)
el **espejo** mirror (I)
la **espina** thorn, spine (14)
las **espinacas** spinach (13)
el **esposo, la esposa** husband, wife (6)
el **esquí** ski (4)
    el **— acuático** water skiing (14)
    hacer — acuático to water ski (14)
esquiar to ski (I)
la **esquina** corner (I)
la **estación** season; station (I)
el **estadio** stadium (I)
el **estante** shelf (7)
estar to be (I)
    ¿cómo estás/está Ud.? how are you? (I)
    la sala de — family room (I)
este, -a; -os, -as this; these (I, 3)
éste, -a; -os, -as *pron.* this one; these (3)
el **estómago** stomach (I)
    tener dolor de — to have a stomachache (I)
estornudar to sneeze (9)
el/la **estudiante** student (I)
estudiantil *adj.* student (2)
estudiar to study (I)
la **estufa** stove (I)
exagerado, -a exaggerated (10)
el **examen** exam, test (1)
excelente excellent (10)
la **excursión** excursion, short trip (12)
    hacer una — to take an excursion (12)
éxito: tener — to be successful (10)
explicar to explain (1)
explorar to explore (I, 11)
la **exposición (de arte)** (art) exhibit (4)
la **extinción: en peligro de —** endangered (I, 14)
extracurricular extracurricular (2)
el/la **extraterrestre** alien (10)

la **fábrica** factory (I)
fácil easy (I)
fácilmente easily (2)
facturar to check *(baggage)* (12)
la **falda** skirt (I)
faltar to be lacking, to be missing (I)
la **familia** family (I)
familiar *adj.* family (6)
fantástico, -a fantastic (I)

la **farmacia** drugstore (I)
fascinante fascinating (I)
fascinar to fascinate (I)
febrero February (I)
la **fecha** date (I)
¡felicidades! congratulations! (6)
felicitar to congratulate (6)
¡feliz cumpleaños! happy birthday! (I)
feo, -a ugly (I)
la **fiebre** fever (I)
    tener — to have a fever (I)
la **fiesta** party (I, 3)
    el día de — holiday (6)
    la — de cumpleaños birthday party (I, 6)
    la— de disfraces costume party (I, 4)
    la — de fin de año New Year's Eve party (I, 6)
    la — de sorpresa surprise party (I, 6)
fila: hacer — to line up, to stand in line (1)
el **fin:**
    el— de año New Year's Eve (6)
    el — de semana on the weekend (I)
    la fiesta de — de año New Year's Eve party (I)
físico, -a: la educación —a physical education (I)
el **flan** flan (I)
la **flauta** flute (2)
flojo, -a loose *(clothing)* (3)
la **flor** flower (I, 6)
floreado, -a flowered (3)
la **floristería** flower shop (8)
fondo: al — in the back (8)
formar parte de to be a part of (I)
el **fósforo** match (14)
el **fósil** fossil (14)
la **foto** photo (I)
    sacar —s to take pictures (I)
la **fotografía** photography (10)
el **fracaso** failure (10)
el **francés** French *(language)* (1)
el **fregadero** sink (7)
los **frenillos** braces (9)
la **fresa** strawberry (13)
fresco, -a fresh (13)
fresco: hace — it's cool outside (I)
el **frijol** bean (I)
    los —es refritos refried beans (I)

frío:
    hace — it's cold outside (I)
    tener — to be cold *(person)* (I)
frito, -a fried (13)
la **fruta** fruit (I)
la **frutería** fruit store (8)
el **fuego** fire (14)
    los —s artificiales fireworks (6)
fuerte strong (9)
fui, fuiste *see* **ir, ser**
funcionar to work, to function (7)
el **fútbol** soccer (I)
    el — americano football (I)
el **futuro** future (11)

el **galán** *(film)* hero (10)
ganar to earn money (2); to win (4)
    —se la vida to earn a living (11)
la **ganga** bargain (I)
el **garaje** garage (I)
la **garganta** throat (I)
    las pastillas para la — throat lozenges (I)
    tener dolor de — to have a sore throat (I)
gastar to spend (8); to waste (11)
el **gato** cat (I)
el **gazpacho** gazpacho (I, 13)
el **gemelo, la gemela** twin (I)
generalmente usually, generally (I)
generoso, -a generous (I)
¡genial! great! wonderful! (I)
la **gente** people (I)
la **geografía** geography (1)
la **geometría** geometry (1)
gigante: la pantalla — big screen TV (11)
el **gimnasio** gymnasium (I)
el **gol** goal (4)
el **golf** golf (4)
el **gorila** gorilla (I, 14)
la **gorra** cap (3)
el **gorro** ski cap (I)
las **gotas (para los ojos)** (eye)drops (9)
la **grabadora** tape recorder (I)
gracias thank you (I)
las **Gracias** *see* **Día**
gracioso, -a funny (I)
la **graduación** graduation (6)
graduarse to graduate (6)
grande big, large (I, 3)
la **grapadora** stapler (1)
grasoso, -a greasy (13)
la **gripe** flu (I)
    tener — to have the flu (I)
gris gray (I)

el **guacamole** avocado dip (I)
el **guante** glove (I)
guapo, -a handsome, good-looking (I)
guardar to put away, to keep (3)
el **guardarropa** closet (I)
la **guardería infantil** day-care center (5)
la **guerra** war (11)
el/la **guía** guide (12)
la — guidebook (12)
la — **telefónica** phone book (I)
el **guión** script (10)
guisado, -a stewed (13)
el **guisante** pea (I)
la **guitarra** guitar (I)
gustar to like (I)
me (te) gustaría I'd (you'd) like … (I)

haber:
hay there is / are (I)
hubo there was / were (10)
la **habitación** hotel room (12)
hablar to talk, to speak (I)
—**se** to talk to each other (6)
se habla is spoken (8)
hacer to do, to make (I)
hace + *(time)* … ago (I)
hace + *(time)* + **que** it's been *(time)* since (I)
— **ejercicio** to exercise (I)
se hace(n) con … it's (they're) made with … (I)
hambre: tener — to be hungry (I)
la **hamburguesa** hamburger (I)
la **harina** flour (I)
hasta until (I)
— **luego** see you later (I)
hay there is /are (I)
— **que** + *inf.* it's necessary to (I, 2)
hecho, -a (de) made (of) (I, 13)
el **hecho** fact (I, 10)
la **heladería** ice cream shop (8)
helado: el té — iced tea (I)
el **helado** ice cream (I)
el **hermano, la hermana** brother, sister (I)
los **hermanos** brothers; brother(s) and sister(s) (I)
la **heroína** heroine (10)
hervir *(e → ie)* to boil (13)
hice, hiciste *see* **hacer**
el **hielo** ice (4)
el **hijo, la hija** son, daughter (I)
los **hijos** sons; children (I)
la **historia** history (1)

histórico, -a historic(al) (8)
el **hockey** hockey (4)
la **hoja** leaf (14)
la — **de papel** sheet of paper (I)
¡hola! hi!, hello! (I)
el **hombre** man (I)
el — **de negocios** businessman (11)
la **hora** period ; time (I)
¿a qué —? at what time? (I)
¿qué — es? what time is it? (I)
el **horario** schedule (I)
la **hormiga** ant (9)
el **horno** oven (7)
al — baked (13)
horrible horrible (I)
el **horror** horror (4)
el **hospital** hospital (I)
el **hotel** hotel (I)
hoy today (I)
— **no** not today (I)
hubo *see* **haber**
la **huella** footprint (14)
el **hueso** bone (9)
el **huevo** egg (I)
el — **duro** hard-boiled egg (13)
humano, -a human (11)
humo: el detector de — smoke detector (7)
humor: de buen / mal — in a good / bad mood (2)
el **huracán** hurricane (10)

ida *see* **boleto**
sólo de — one way (12)
la **identidad: el carnet de** — ID card (7)
la **identificación** identification (7)
el **idioma** language (1)
la **iglesia** church (I)
igual: (me) da — it's all the same (to me) (I)
igualmente likewise (I)
impaciente impatient (I)
el **impermeable** raincoat (I)
el **incendio** fire (7)
el **extinguidor de** —**s** fire extinguisher (7)
incluir to include (12)
incómodo, -a uncomfortable (I)
indicar to indicate, to show, to point out (8)
indígena indigenous, native (12)
individual: la habitación — single room (12)
infantil *see* **guardería**
la **infección** infection (9)
la **información** information (10)

el **informe** report (1)
el **inglés** English *(language)* (I)
el **ingrediente** ingredient (I, 13)
el **insecticida** insecticide (9)
el **instrumento** instrument (2)
inteligente intelligent (I)
el **interés** interest (I)
interesante interesting (I)
interesar to interest (I)
internacional international (10)
la **inundación** flood (10)
investigar to investigate (10)
el **invierno** winter (I)
la **invitación** invitation (I, 6)
el **invitado, la invitada** guest (I)
invitar to invite (I, 6)
la **inyección** injection, shot (9)
poner una — to give an injection (9)
ir to go (I)
— **a** + *inf.* to be going to + *verb* (I)
izquierda: a la — **(de)** to the left (of) (I)
izquierdo, -a left (I)

el **jabón** soap (I)
el **jaguar** jaguar (I)
el **jamón** ham (I)
el **jarabe (para la tos)** cough syrup (9)
los **jeans** jeans (I)
joven *adj.* young (I)
el/la **joven** young man, young woman (I)
los **jóvenes** young people (I)
las **joyas** jewelry (I)
las **judías verdes** green beans (I)
jueves Thursday (I)
el — on Thursday (I)
el/la **juez** judge (11)
el **jugador, la jugadora** player (4)
jugar *(u → ue)* to play (I)
el **juguete** toy (5)
de — *adj.* toy (5)
el **jugo** juice (I)
julio July (I)
junio June (I)

el **kilómetro** kilometer (8)
el **kindergarten** kindergarten (5)

la the *f.sing.*; her, it *dir. obj. pron.* (I)
los **labios** lips (8)
el lápiz de— lipstick (8)
el **laboratorio** laboratory (1)

lado: al — de next to, beside (I)

el **ladrón, la ladrona** thief (10)

el **lago** lake (I)

la **lámpara** lamp (I)

la **lana** wool (3)

lanzar to shoot (6)

el **lápiz** pencil (I)

    el **— de labios** lipstick (8)

largo, -a long (I)

las the *f.pl.;* them *dir. obj. pron.* (I)

lástima: ¡qué —! that's too bad! what a shame! (I)

lastimar to hurt (I)

la **lata** can (I, 11)

el **lavadero** laundry room (I)

la **lavadora** (clothes) washer (7)

el **lavaplatos** dishwasher (7)

lavar to wash (I)

    —se (la cara, etc.) to wash (one's face, etc.) (2)

le *ind. obj. pron.* (to) him, her, it, you (I)

la **lección** lesson (1)

la **leche** milk (I)

la **lechuga** lettuce (I)

leer to read (I)

lejos (de) far (from) (I)

la **leña** firewood (14)

los **lentes de contacto** contact lenses (7)

les *ind. obj. pron.* (to) them (I)

levantar to lift (4)

    —se to get up (2)

leve light, minor (9)

libre: al aire — outdoors (14)

la **librería** bookstore (I)

el **libro** book (I)

la **liga** league (4)

ligero, -a light *(weight)* (14)

el **limón** lemon, lime (13)

la **limonada** lemonade (I)

limpiar to clean (I)

limpio, -a clean (I)

la **línea aérea** airline (12)

la **linterna** flashlight (7)

la **liquidación** sale (3)

    estar en — to be on sale (3)

liso, -a plain (3)

literario, -a literary (2)

la **literatura** literature (1)

llamar to call (I)

    —se to be named (I)

la **llave** key (7)

el **llavero** keychain (7)

llegar to arrive (I)

llevar to wear; to take, to carry along (I)

llorar to cry (5)

llover *(o → ue)* to rain (I)

llueve it rains, it's raining (I)

la **lluvia** rain (I)

lo *dir. obj. pron.* him, it (I)

    — que what (3)

    — siento I'm sorry (I)

el **lobo, la loba** wolf (I, 14)

local local (10)

el **locutor, la locutora** announcer (10)

la **lona** canvas (3)

los the *m.pl.; dir. obj. pron.* them (I)

    — + day of week on (I)

luego then, if (I)

el **lugar** place (I)

el **lujo** luxury (7)

la **Luna** moon (11)

lunes Monday (I)

    el **—** on Monday (I)

la **luz** light (I)

la **madera** wood (I)

    de — (made of) wood (I)

la **madre** mother (I)

el **maíz** corn (I)

mal badly (I)

    menos — que . . . it's a good thing that . . . (I)

    me siento — I feel ill (I)

maleducado, -a rude, impolite (5)

la **maleta** suitcase (I, 12)

    (des)hacer la — to (un)pack (12)

malo, -a bad (I)

manera: de ninguna — not at all (I)

la **manga** sleeve (3)

la **mano** hand (I)

    a — by hand (12)

    darse la — to shake hands (6)

    hecho, -a a — handmade (I)

el **mantel** tablecloth (I)

mantenerse sano, -a to stay healthy (13)

la **mantequilla** butter (I)

la **manzana** apple (I)

mañana tomorrow (I)

la **mañana** morning (I)

    de/por la — in the morning (I)

el **mapa** map (1)

el **maquillaje** make-up (8)

maquillarse to put on makeup (8)

el **mar** sea (I)

el **marcador** marker (I)

la **mariposa** butterfly (14)

los **mariscos** seafood (9)

marrón brown (I)

martes Tuesday (I)

    el **—** on Tuesday (I)

marzo March (I)

más more, *adj.* + -er (I)

    el/la/los/las — + *adj.* the most + *adj.*, the *adj.* + -est (I, 1)

la **masa** dough (13)

matar to kill (10)

las **matemáticas** mathematics (I)

la **materia** school subject (1)

mayo May (I)

la **mayonesa** mayonnaise (13)

mayor older (I)

    el **—** the oldest, biggest (I)

me *obj. pron.* me (I)

mecánico, -a: la escalera —a escalator (8)

el **mecánico, la mecánica** mechanic (11)

media:

    una hora y — an hour and a half (I)

    — hora *f.* half an hour (I)

    y — half-past (I)

mediano, -a medium *(in sizes)* (3)

la **medianoche** midnight (I)

la **medicina** medicine (9)

el **médico, la médica** doctor (I)

medio: *(número)* **y —** and a half *(in sizes)* (3)

el **medio ambiente** environment (I, 11)

el **mediodía** noon (I)

mejor better (I)

    el/la — the best (I)

el **melón** cantaloupe (13)

menor younger (I)

menos:

    el/la/los/las — + *adj.* the least + *adj.* (I, 1)

    — mal que . . . it's a good thing that . . . (I)

    por lo — at least (2)

mentir *(e → ie)* to lie (5)

el **menú** menu (I)

menudo: a — often (I)

el **mercado** market (12)

la **merienda** afternoon snack (I)

    de — for a snack (I)

el **mes** month (I)

la **mesa** table (I)

    la — de noche night table (7)

metal: de — (made of) metal (I)

meter un gol to score a goal (4)

el **metro** subway (I); meter *(measurement)* (8)

mezclar to mix (13)

mi, mis my (I)
mí me *after prep.* (I)
el **microondas** microwave (oven) (7)
el **miembro** member (2)
  ser — de to be a member of (2)
mientras while (8)
miércoles Wednesday (I)
  el — on Wednesday (I)
mil one thousand (I)
la **milla** mile (8)
el **minuto** minute (I)
mío, -a my, (of) mine (7)
el **mío, la mía** mine (7)
mismo, -a same (2)
  lo — the same thing (I)
  (yo) — myself (7)
el **mocasín** loafer (3)
la **mochila** backpack (I)
la **moda** fashion (3)
  estar de — to be fashionable (3)
moderno, -a modern (I)
mojado, -a wet (14)
molestar to bother, to annoy (5)
la **moneda** coin (7)
el **monstruo** monster (10)
la **montaña** mountain (I)
montar:
  — a caballo to ride horseback (10)
  — en bicicleta to ride a bike (I, 4)
el **monumento** monument (I)
morado, -a purple (I)
la **mosca** fly (9)
el **mosquito** mosquito (9)
la **mostaza** mustard (13)
el **mostrador** counter (8)
mostrar *(o → ue)* to show (7)
la **moto acuática** jet skiing (14)
  hacer — to jet ski (14)
el **muchacho, la muchacha** boy, girl (I)
mucho, -a a lot of, much (I)
  —as veces many times (I)
  —gusto pleased / nice to meet you (I)
los **muebles** furniture (I)
las **muelas: tener dolor de —** to have a toothache (I)
muerto, -a dead (6)
la **mujer** woman (I)
  la — de negocios business-woman (11)
las **muletas** crutches (9)
la **muñeca** doll (5); wrist (9)
el **muñeco** action figure (5)
el **músculo** muscle (9)
el **museo** museum (I)

la **música** music (I)
musical *adj.* musical (I, 2)
  el video — music video (4)
el **músico, la música** musician (11)
muy very (I)

nacer to be born (6)
nacional national (14)
nada nothing, not at all (I)
  de — you're welcome (I)
nadar to swim (I)
nadie no one (I)
la **naranja** orange (I)
la **nariz** nose (I)
la **naturaleza** nature (12)
navegar *see* **balsa, canoa**
la **Navidad** Christmas (6)
necesario, -a necessary (2)
la **necesidad** necessity (7)
necesitar to need (I)
los **negocios** business (11)
  el hombre / la mujer de — businessman, businesswoman (11)
negro, -a black (I)
  en blanco y — in black and white (I)
nevar: nieva it snows, it's snowing (I)
ni . . . ni neither . . . nor, not . . . or (I)
el **nieto, la nieta** grandson, grand-daughter (6)
la **nieve** snow (I)
el **nilón** nylon (3)
ninguno (ningún), -a no, not any (I, 8)
  —a parte nowhere, not anywhere (I)
el **niño, la niña** boy, girl (5)
  cuidar niños to baby-sit (2)
  los niños children (5)
no no, not (I)
  ¿no? don't you?, aren't I?, etc. (I)
la **noche** evening (I)
  buenas —s good evening, good night (I)
  de la — at night (I)
  por la — in the evening (I)
la **Nochebuena** Christmas Eve (6)
el **nombre** name (I)
nos *obj. pron.* us (I)
nosotros, -as we (I); us *after prep.* (I)
la **nota** grade (1)
las **noticias** news (I)
novecientos nine hundred (I)

la **novela** novel (11)
noventa ninety (I)
noviembre November (I)
el **novio, la novia** boyfriend, girlfriend (I)
nuestro, -a our (I); (of) ours (7)
el **nuestro, la nuestra** ours (7)
nueve nine (I)
nuevo, -a new (I)
  de — again (6)
el **número** number (I); (shoe) size (3)
nunca never (I)

o or (I)
obedecer *(c → zc)* to obey (5)
obediente obedient (5)
la **obra de teatro** play (4)
el **obrero, la obrera** laborer (11)
el **océano** ocean (I, 11)
ochenta eighty (I)
ocho eight (I)
ochocientos eight hundred (I)
octavo, -a eighth (I)
octubre October (I)
ocupado, -a busy (I)
ocurrir to occur, to happen (10)
el **oeste: la película del —** western (I)
la **oficina** office (1)
el **oído** ear (I)
  tener dolor de — to have an earache (I)
el **ojo** eye (I)
la **olla** pot (14)
once eleven (I)
la **operación** operation (9)
ordenado, -a neat, tidy (I)
el **oro** gold (7)
  de — (made of) gold (7)
la **orquesta** orchestra (2)
oscuro, -a dark *(color)* (3)
el **oso** bear (I, 5)
el **otoño** fall, autumn (I)
otro, -a another, other (I)
el **oxígeno** oxygen (14)

paciente *adj.* patient (I)
el **padre** father (I)
  los —s parents (I)
la **paella** paella (13)
pagar to pay (I)
la **página** page (1)
el **país** country (I)
el **pájaro** bird (I, 5)
el **palacio** palace (12)
el **palito** twig; *pl.* kindling (14)

Vocabulario español-inglés 503

el **palo (de golf, de hockey)** golf club, hockey stick (4)

el **pan** bread (I)

    el **— tostado** toast (I)

la **panadería** bakery (8)

la **pantalla** screen (11)

los **pantalones** pants (I)

las **pantimedias** pantyhose (I)

el **pañuelo** scarf (3)

la **papa** potato (I)

    la **— frita** French fry (I)

el **papel** paper (I); part, role (10)

    hacer el — (de) to play the part (of) (10)

    la **hoja de —** sheet of paper (I)

    para for, in order to (I)

la **parada del autobús** bus stop (I)

el **paraguas** umbrella (I)

    parecer to appear, to seem (7)

la **pared** wall (1)

el **pariente, la parienta** relative (I, 6)

el **parque** park (I)

    el **— de diversiones** amusement park (I)

la **parrilla: a la —** grilled (13)

    partes: por todas — all over, everywhere (3)

    participar (en) to participate (in) (2)

el **partido** match, game (I, 4)

    pasado, -a last, past (I)

el **pasajero, la pasajera** passenger (12)

el **pasaporte** passport (I)

    pasar to pass; to happen (I)

    — la aspiradora to vacuum (I)

    —lo bien / mal to have a good / bad time (I, 4)

    ¿qué pasa? what's the matter? (I)

el **pasatiempo** pastime, hobby (I)

    pasear:

    ir a — to take a walk (I)

    — en bote to row (I)

el **pasillo** aisle (12)

la **pasta dentífrica** toothpaste (I)

el **pastel** cake (I, 6)

la **pastilla** pill (I, 9)

el **patín** skate (4)

    patinar to skate (I)

    — sobre hielo to ice skate (4)

el **patio de recreo** playground (5)

el **pavo** turkey (6)

la **paz** peace (11)

    pedir *(e → i)* to ask for, to order (I)

    — prestado, -a (a) to borrow (from) (4)

    peinarse to comb one's hair (2)

el **peine** comb (7)

    pelearse to fight (5)

la **película** film, movie (I)

el **peligro** danger (I, 14)

    en — de extinción endangered (I, 14)

    peligroso, -a dangerous (14)

    pelirrojo, -a red-haired (I)

el **pelo** hair (I, 2)

    el **secador de —** hair dryer (7)

la **pelota** ball (4)

    peluche:

    el **animal de —** stuffed animal (5)

    el **oso de —** teddy bear (5)

    pensar *(e → ie)* to think (I)

    — + *inf.* to plan (I)

la **pensión** inexpensive lodging (12)

    peor worse (I)

    el/la **—** the worst (I)

el **pepino** cucumber (13)

    pequeño, -a small (I, 3)

    de — as a child (5)

    perder *(e → ie)* to lose (4)

    perdón excuse me (I)

    perdonar to excuse, to pardon (8)

    perdone (Ud.) excuse me, pardon me (8)

    perezoso, -a lazy (I)

el **perfume** perfume (8)

el **periódico** newspaper (I, 2)

    permitir to permit, to allow (1)

    se permite it's allowed (1)

    pero but (I)

el **perro** dog (I)

    el **— caliente** hot dog (13)

la **persona** person (I)

el **personaje** character (10)

    personal personal (I)

    pesado, -a heavy (14)

las **pesas** weights (4)

    pesca: ir de — to go fishing (I)

la **pescadería** fish store (8)

el **pescado** fish *(cooked)* (I)

el **pez,** *pl.* **los peces** fish *(live)* (5)

el **piano** piano (2)

la **picadura (de insecto)** insect bite, sting (9)

    picante spicy, peppery, hot *(flavor)* (I)

    no — mild *(flavor)* (I)

    picar to sting (9); to chop (13)

el **picnic** picnic (4)

    hacer un — to have a picnic (4)

el **pie** foot (I)

    a — walking, on foot (I)

    el **dedo del —** toe (I)

la **piedra** rock, stone (14)

la **piel** fur (I)

la **pierna** leg (I)

la **pila** battery (7)

el/la **piloto** pilot (12)

la **pimienta** pepper *(seasoning)* (I)

el **pimiento verde** green pepper (13)

la **piña** pineapple (13)

el **pintor, la pintora** painter (11)

    pintoresco, -a picturesque (12)

la **pirámide** pyramid (I)

la **piscina** pool (I)

el **piso** story, floor (I)

la **pistola (de agua)** (water) pistol (5)

la **pizarra** chalkboard (I)

    planear to plan (12)

el **planeta** planet (11)

la **planta** plant (I, 14)

el **plástico** plastic (I, 3)

    de — (made of) plastic (I)

la **plata** silver (7)

    de — (made of) silver (7)

el **plátano** banana (I)

el **platillo** saucer (I)

el **plato** dish, plate (I)

    el **— del día** daily special (I)

la **playa** beach (I)

la **plaza** town square (I)

la **pluma** feather (14)

    poco: un — (de) a little (I)

    poder *(o → ue)* can, to be able (I)

    ¿podría(s)? could you? (8)

el **polen** pollen (9)

el/la **policía** police officer (10)

    la — the police (I)

la **política** politics (11)

el **político, la política** politician (11)

el **pollo** chicken (I)

el **polvo** dust (9)

    poner to put, to place (I)

    —la mesa to set the table (I)

    —se to put on *(clothing, make-up, etc.)* (8)

    —una tienda to pitch a tent (14)

    por for (I, 9); *(+ place)* by, through, at (8)

    — aquí around here (I)

    — eso that's why, therefore (I)

    — la mañana / la tarde / la noche in the morning / afternoon / evening (I)

    — lo menos at least (2)

    ¿— qué? why? (I)

    — supuesto of course (I, 11)

    — todas partes all over, everywhere (3)

    porque because (I)

    portarse (bien / mal) to behave (well / badly) (5)

la **posesión** possession (7)
el **postre** dessert (I)
    de — for dessert (I)
practicar to practice (I)
práctico, -a practical (I)
preferir *(e → ie)* to prefer (I)
la **pregunta** question (1)
    hacer una — to ask a question (1)
preguntar to ask (1)
preparar to prepare (I)
presentar to introduce (I)
    te presento a . . . I'd like you to meet . . . (I)
prestado, -a: pedir — (a) to borrow (from) (4)
prestar to lend (4)
primaria: la escuela — elementary school (5)
la **primavera** spring (I)
primero (primer), -a first (I)
el **primo, la prima** cousin (I)
principal *adj.* main, principal (10)
probar *(o → ue)* to try, to taste (I)
    —se to try on (3)
el **problema** problem (1)
procedente de arriving from (12)
la **profesión** profession (11)
el **profesor, la profesora** teacher (I)
el **programa** program (I)
prohibir to prohibit (1)
    se prohibe it's prohibited (1)
el **pronóstico del tiempo** weather forecast (I)
propio, -a own (7)
proteger(se) *(g → j)* to protect (oneself) (I, 9)
la **proteína** protein (13)
próximo, -a next (1)
el **proyector** projector (1)
prudente cautious (I)
la **prueba** quiz (1)
público, -a public (8)
pude, pudiste *see* **poder**
el **pueblo** town (12)
la **puerta** door (I); gate (12)
pues well *(to indicate pause)* (I)
la **pulsera** bracelet (I, 7)
    el reloj — wristwatch (I, 7)
las **puntadas** stitches (9)
    hacer — to stitch *(surgically)* (9)
punto: en — sharp, on the dot (I)
puntualmente on time (I)
el **pupitre** student desk (I)
puro, -a pure, clean (I)
puse, pusiste *see* **poner**

que that, who (I)
    lo — what (3)
¿qué? what? (I)
    ¿de — es...? what's it made of? (3)
    ¡— + *adj.*! how + *adj.*! (I)
    ¿— tal? how's it going? (I)
    ¿— tal es . . . ? how is . . .? (10)
quedar to fit; to be located (I)
    —se (en la cama) to stay (in bed) (I)
el **quehacer (de la casa)** (household) chore (I)
quemar(se) to burn (oneself) (9)
querer *(e → ie)* to want (I)
    ¿qué quiere decir ...? what does ... mean? (I)
    quisiera(s) I'd / you'd like (I, 11)
la **quesadilla** quesadilla (I)
el **queso** cheese (I)
¿quién(es)? who? whom? (I)
la **química** chemistry (1)
quince fifteen (I)
quinientos five hundred (I)
quinto, -a fifth (I)
el **quiosco (de periódicos)** newsstand (8)
quisiera *see* **querer**
quitar la mesa to clear the table (I)
quitarse to take off *(clothing, make-up, etc.)* (8)

el **radio** radio (set) (7)
la **radiografía** X-ray (9)
    sacar una — to take an X-ray (9)
la **rana** frog (14)
la **raqueta (de tenis)** (tennis) racket (4)
rayas: a — striped (3)
la **Raza** *see* **Día**
razón: (no) tener — to be right (wrong) (I)
la **reacción** reaction (9)
real real (I)
realista realistic (I)
la **receta** prescription (9); recipe (13)
recetar to prescribe (9)
recibir to receive (I)
el **reciclaje: el centro de —** recycling center (I)
reciclar to recycle (I, 11)
recoger *(g → j)* to gather, to pick up (I, 14)
recomendar *(e → ie)* to recommend (12)

recordar *(o → ue)* to remember (5)
recreo: el patio de — playground (5)
el **recuerdo** souvenir (I)
redondo, -a round (I)
reducir *(c → zc)* to reduce (I, 11)
el **refresco** soft drink (I)
el **refrigerador** refrigerator (I)
regalar to give a gift (I, 6)
el **regalo** gift (I)
    la tienda de —s gift shop (I)
regatear to bargain (12)
registrar to inspect, to search (12)
la **regla** ruler (I)
regresar to come back, to return (I)
regular so-so, fair (I)
el **relleno** filling (13)
el **reloj** clock (1)
    el — (pulsera) wristwatch (I, 7)
reparar to repair, to fix (7)
repartir to deliver (2)
repasar review (1)
el **repelente** insect repellent (9)
la **reservación** reservation (12)
el **resfriado** cold (I)
la **respuesta** answer (1)
el **restaurante** restaurant (I)
el **retraso** delay (12)
la **reunión** gathering, get-together (I, 6)
la **revista** magazine (I, 2)
revolver *(o → ue)* to stir (13)
el **río** river (11)
robar to rob (10)
el **robot** robot (5)
rock: la música — rock music (4)
la **rodilla** knee (9)
rojo, -a red (I)
romántico, -a romantic (I)
el **rompecabezas** jigsaw puzzle (4)
romperse to break *(a bone)* (9)
la **ropa** clothes (I)
    la — para caballeros men's wear (8)
    la — para damas ladies' wear (8)
    la — para niños children's wear (8)
rosado, -a pink (I)
roto, -a broken (9); torn (14)
rubio, -a blonde (I)
la **rueda: la silla de —s** wheelchair (9)
las **ruinas** ruins (I)

Vocabulario español-inglés   505

sábado Saturday (I)

    el — on Saturday (I)

saber to know (how) (I, 4)

sabroso, -a delicious, tasty (I)

el **sacapuntas** pencil sharpener (1)

sacar to take; to take out (I)

    — dinero to withdraw money (I)

    — fotos to take pictures (I)

    — una buena / mala nota to get a good / bad grade (1)

    — un libro to check out a book (I)

el **saco de dormir** sleeping bag (14)

sacudir to dust (I)

la **sal** salt (I)

la **sala** living room (I)

    la — de clases classroom (I)

    la — de emergencia emergency room (9)

    la — de estar family room (I)

salado, -a salty (13)

la **salida** exit (8)

salir to go out, to leave (I)

la **salsa** sauce, dressing (I, 13)

saltar a la cuerda to jump rope (5)

saltos: dar — to dive (14)

la **salud** health (I)

saludar to greet (6)

salvaje wild *(animals)* (14)

la **sandía** watermelon (13)

el **sandwich** sandwich (I)

la **sangre** blood (9)

sano, -a healthy (13)

el **saxofón** saxophone (2)

el **secador de pelo** hair dryer (7)

la **secadora** (clothes) dryer (7)

secar to dry (14)

    —se (el pelo) to dry (one's hair) (2)

la **sección** section (8)

seco, -a dry (14)

el **secretario, la secretaria** secretary (11)

sed: tener — to be thirsty (I)

la **seda dental** dental floss (8)

seguida: en — right away (I)

seguir *(e → i)* to follow; to continue (8)

según according to (2)

segundo, -a second (I)

la **seguridad:**

    el cinturón de — seatbelt (12)

    el sistema de — security system (11)

seis six (I)

seiscientos six hundred (I)

el **sello** stamp (I)

la **selva** forest (I)

    la — tropical rain forest (I)

el **semáforo** traffic light (8)

la **semana** week (I)

    el fin de — on the weekend (I)

el **semestre** semester (I)

sencillo, -a simple (3)

el **sendero** path (14)

sensacionalista sensationalistic (10)

sentir:

    lo siento I'm sorry (I)

    —se *(e → ie)* to feel (9)

la **señal de alto** stop sign (8)

señor Mr.; sir (I)

señora Mrs.; ma'am (I)

señorita Miss; miss (I)

separado, -a (de) separated (from) (6)

separar to separate; to sort (I, 11)

septiembre September (I)

séptimo, -a seventh (I)

ser to be (I)

el **ser humano** human being (11)

serio, -a serious (I)

la **serpiente** snake (I, 14)

el **servicio: la estación de —** gas station (I)

los **servicios** restroom (8)

la **servilleta** napkin (I)

servir *(e → i)* to serve (I)

sesenta sixty (I)

setecientos seven hundred (I)

setenta seventy (I)

sexto, -a sixth (I)

si if, whether (I)

sí yes; do + *verb (emphatic)* (I)

siempre always (I)

siete seven (I)

la **silla** chair (I)

    la — de ruedas wheelchair (9)

el **sillón** armchair (I)

silvestre wild *(plants)* (14)

simpático, -a nice, friendly (I)

sin without (2)

sintético, -a synthetic (3)

el **síntoma** symptom (9)

el **sistema de seguridad** security system (11)

sobre about; on (I)

    patinar — hielo to ice skate (4)

el **sobrino, la sobrina** nephew, niece (6)

sociable outgoing (I)

el **sofá** sofa (I)

el **sol** sun (I)

    los anteojos de — sunglasses (I)

    hace — it's sunny (I)

    tomar el — to sunbathe (I)

solar solar (11)

soler *(o → ue) + inf.* to be in the habit of (I, 2)

solo, -a alone (I)

sólo only (I)

soltero, -a single, unmarried (6)

la **sombra** shade (14)

sonido: el equipo de — stereo (I)

la **sopa** soup (I)

soportar to tolerate, to stand (4)

la **sorpresa: la fiesta de —** surprise party (I, 6)

soso, -a tasteless (13)

el **sótano** basement (I)

su, sus his, her; your *formal;* their (I)

el **sube y baja** seesaw (5)

subir to climb (I)

sucio, -a dirty (I)

la **sudadera** sweatshirt (I)

el **suelo** floor (3)

sueño: tener — to be sleepy (I)

suerte: por — luckily (1)

el **suéter** sweater (I)

    el — de cuello alto turtleneck (3)

suficiente sufficient, enough (7)

sugerir *(e → ie)* to suggest (13)

el **sujetapapeles** paper clip (1)

el **supermercado** supermarket (I)

supuesto: por — of course (I, 11)

surf:

    hacer — to surf (14)

    hacer — de vela to windsurf (14)

    la tabla de — surfboard (14)

suyo, -a (of) his, her (of hers), your (of yours), their (of theirs) (7)

el **suyo, la suya** yours, his, hers, theirs (7)

la **tabla (de surf)** surfboard (14)

tacaño, -a stingy (I)

el **taco** taco (I)

el **tacón** heel (I, 3)

tal:

    ¿qué —? how's it going? (I)

    ¿qué — es . . . ? how is? (10)

la **talla** clothing size (3)

el **tamaño** size (3)

también also, too (I)

el **tambor** drum (2)

tampoco neither, not either (I)

tan + *adj.* + **como** as + *adj.* + as (1)

tanto, -a + noun + **como** as much / many + *noun* + as (3)

las **tapas** Spanish-style appetizers (13)

tarde late (I)

la **tarde** afternoon (I)

buenas —s good afternoon, good evening (I)

de/por la — in the afternoon (I)

la **tarea** homework (I)

la **tarjeta** card (I)

la — de crédito credit card (3)

la — de embarque boarding pass (12)

la — postal post card (I)

la **tarta** pie (13)

el **taxi** taxi (I)

la **taza** cup (I)

el **tazón** bowl (I)

te *fam. obj. pron.* you (I)

el **té** tea (I)

el — helado iced tea (I)

el **teatro** theater (I)

la obra de — play (4)

el **técnico, la técnica (de computadoras)** (computer) technician (11)

la **tecnología** technology (11)

la **tela** fabric, cloth (3)

telefónico, -a: la oficina —a telephone office (12)

el **teléfono** telephone (I)

el número de — phone number (I)

por — on the telephone (I)

el — con video video telephone (11)

el — público public (pay) phone (8)

la **telenovela** soap opera (I)

la **tele(visión)** television (I)

el **televisor** TV set (7)

el **templo** temple (I)

temprano early (I)

el **tenedor** fork (I)

tener to have (I)

¿qué tienes? what's wrong? (I)

— que + *inf.* to have to (I)

el **tenis** tennis (I)

los **tenis** sneakers (I)

tercer, -a third (I)

la **terminal de equipaje** baggage claim (12)

terminar to end (I)

el **terremoto** earthquake (10)

terrible terrible (I)

terror: la película de — horror film (I)

ti you *fam. after prep.* (I)

el **tiempo** time; weather (I)

hace buen/mal — the weather is nice/bad (I)

el pronóstico del — weather forecast (I)

¿qué — hace? what's the weather like? (I)

tener — de + *inf.* to have time + *inf.* (4)

la **tienda** store (I)

poner una — to pitch a tent (14)

la — (de acampar) tent (14)

la **Tierra** Earth (I, 11)

el **tigre** tiger (I)

tímido, -a shy (5)

el **tío, la tía** uncle, aunt (I)

los tíos uncles; aunts and uncles (I)

típico, -a typical (I, 10)

el **tobillo** ankle (9)

el **tobogán** slide (5)

el **tocacintas** tape player (7)

tocar to play (I)

todavía still (I)

— no not yet (I)

todos, -as all; everyone (I)

— los días every day (I)

tomar to take (I)

— el sol to sunbathe (I)

el **tomate** tomato (I)

tonto, -a silly, dumb (I)

la **tormenta** storm (10)

la **tortilla** tortilla (I)

la — española potato and onion omelet (13)

la **tortuga** turtle (5)

la **tos** cough (9)

el jarabe (para la —) cough syrup (9)

toser to cough (9)

tostado: el pan — toast (I)

el **tostador** toaster (7)

trabajador, -a hardworking (I)

trabajar to work (I)

traer to bring (I)

el **tráfico** traffic (11)

el **traje** suit (I, 3)

el — de baño bathing suit (I)

el **trampolín** diving board (14)

el **transporte** transportation (8)

tratarse de to be about (10)

travieso, -a mischievous, naughty (5)

trece thirteen (I)

treinta thirty (I)

el **tren** train (I)

el — de juguete train *(toy)* (5)

tres three (I)

trescientos three hundred (I)

el **triciclo** tricycle (5)

montar en — to ride a tricycle (5)

triste sad (I)

la **trompeta** trumpet (2)

tu, tus your *fam.* (I)

tú you *fam.* (I)

turismo: la oficina de — tourist office (12)

el/la **turista** tourist (12)

el **tutor, la tutora** tutor (2)

tuve, tuviste *see* tener

tuyo, -a your, (of) yours (7)

el **tuyo, la tuya** yours (7)

último, -a last (4)

la **uña** fingernail (8)

el esmalte de —s nail polish (8)

único, -a only (I)

la **universidad** university (11)

uno (un), una a, an, one (I)

es la una it's one o'clock (I)

— one, a person (2)

unos, -as a few, some (I)

usar to use (I, 1); to wear (3)

usted (Ud.) you *formal sing.* (I)

ustedes (Uds.) you *formal pl.* (I)

la **uva** grape (I)

la **vaca** cow (I)

las **vacaciones** vacation (I)

ir de — to go on vacation (I)

valer: (no) vale la pena it's (not) worthwhile (I)

el **valle** valley (14)

el **vaquero, la vaquera** cowboy, cowgirl (10)

el **vaso** glass (I)

¡vaya! my goodness! gee! wow! (I)

el **vecino, la vecina** neighbor (5)

veinte twenty (I)

veintiuno (veintiún) twenty-one (I)

la **vela** candle (6); sail (14)

el **venado, la venada** deer (14)

la **venda** bandage (8)

el **vendedor, la vendedora** salesperson (3)

vender to sell (I)

— se to be sold (8)

venenoso, -a poisonous (14)

la **ventaja** advantage (11)

la **ventana** window (I)

la **ventanilla** *(plane)* window (12)

el **ventilador** electric fan (7)
ver to see, to watch (I)
  a — let's see (I)
  —se to see each other (6)
el **verano** summer (I)
veras: ¿de — ? really? (I)
la **verdad** truth (5)
  ¿—? isn't that so?, right? (I)
verde green (I)
la **verdulería** greengrocer (8)
las **verduras** vegetables (I)
el **vestido** dress (I)
vestirse *(e → i)* to get dressed (2)
el **veterinario, la veterinaria**
  veterinarian (11)
la **vez,** *pl.* **las veces** time (I)
  a la — at the same time (I)
  alguna — ever (I)
  a veces at times, sometimes (I)
  de — en cuando sometimes (7)
  dos veces twice (I)
  muchas veces many times (I)
  una — one time, once (I)
viajar to travel (12)
el **viaje** trip, voyage (12)
  la agencia de —s travel agency
   (12)
  el / la agente de —s travel
   agent (12)

el **viajero, la viajera** traveler (12)
  el cheque de — traveler's check
   (12)
la **víctima** victim (10)
la **vida** life (I)
  ganarse la — to earn a living
   (11)
  el programa de hechos de la
   — real fact-based program (I)
el **video** video (4)
la **videocasetera** VCR (I)
el **videojuego** video game (I)
el **vidrio** glass (I, 11)
  de — (made of) glass (I)
viejo, -a old (I)
el **viento** wind (I)
  hace — it's windy (I)
viernes Friday (I)
  el — on Friday (I)
el **vinagre** vinegar (13)
la **violencia** violence (10)
violento, -a (10)
el **violín** violin (2)
el **virus** virus (9)
visitar to visit (I)
la **vitamina** vitamin (13)
vivir to live (I)
el **vóleibol** volleyball (I)

voluntario(a): trabajar como —
  to volunteer (2)
vomitar to vomit (9)
vosotros(as) you *pl.* (I)
el **vuelo** flight (12)
  el/la auxiliar de — flight
   attendant (12)
vuelta *see* **boleto**

y and (I)
ya already (I)
  — no no longer, not anymore (I)
el **yeso** cast (9)
yo I (I)

la **zanahoria** carrot (I)
la **zapatería** shoe store (I)
el **zapato** shoe (I)
  los —s de tacón alto high-
   heeled shoes (I, 3)
el **zoológico** zoo (I)

ENGLISH-SPANISH VOCABULARY

This *Vocabulary* contains all active vocabulary from PASO A PASO 1 and 2.

A dash (—) represents the main entry word. For example, **to — for** following **to ask** means **to ask for.**

The number following each entry indicates the chapter in PASO A PASO 2 in which the word or expression is first introduced. Two numbers indicate that it is introduced in one chapter and elaborated upon in a later chapter. A Roman numeral (I) indicates that the word was presented in PASO A PASO 1.

The following abbreviations are used: *adj.* (adjective), *dir. obj.* (direct object). *f.* (feminine), *fam.* (familiar), *ind. obj.* (indirect object), *inf.* (infinitive), *m.* (masculine), *pl.* (plural), *prep.* (preposition), *pron.* (pronoun), *sing.* (singular).

a, an un, una (I)
able: to be — poder *(o → ue)* (I)
about sobre (I)
   to be — tratarse de (10)
accident el accidente (9)
according to según (2)
ache el dolor (I)
acquainted: to be — with
   conocer (I, 1)
to **act** actuar (10)
acting la actuación (10)
action:
   — figure el muñeco (5)
   — film la película de acción (10)
activity la actividad (2)
actor, actress el actor, la actriz (I)
ad el anuncio (I)
addition: in — además (9)
address la dirección, *pl.* las direcciones (8)
advantage la ventaja (11)
adventure film la película de aventuras (I)
affectionate cariñoso, -a (I)
after después (de) (I)
   — + *verb* **+ -ing** después de + *inf.* (2)
   — school después de las clases (I)
afternoon la tarde (I)
   — snack la merienda (I)
   good — buenas tardes (I)
   in the — por la tarde (I)
again de nuevo (6)
age:
   at the age of... a los... años (6)
   at what — ? ¿a qué edad? (6)
ago hace + *(time)* ... (I)
to **agree** estar de acuerdo (I)
   not to — with *(food)* hacer daño a (13)
air el aire (I)
   — conditioning el aire acondicionado (7)
airline la línea aérea (12)

airplane el avión, *pl.* los aviones (12)
airport el aeropuerto (12)
aisle el pasillo (12)
alarm clock el despertador (2)
algebra el álgebra *f.* (1)
alien el / la extraterrestre (10)
all todo, -a (I)
   — over por todas partes (3)
   — right bueno (I)
   — the same (to me) (me) da igual (3)
allergic (to) alérgico, -a (a) (9)
allergy la alergia (9)
to **allow** permitir (1)
   it's —ed se permite (1)
almost casi (I)
alone solo, -a (I)
already ya (I)
also también (I)
aluminum el aluminio (I)
always siempre (I)
ambulance la ambulancia (9)
among entre (I)
amusement park el parque de diversiones (I)
amusing divertido, -a (I)
and y (I)
animal el animal, *pl.* los animales (I, 5)
   stuffed — el animal de peluche (5)
   wild — el animal salvaje (14)
ankle el tobillo (9)
anniversary el aniversario (6)
announcer el locutor, la locutora (10)
to **annoy** molestar (5)
another otro, -a (I)
answer la respuesta (1)
to **answer** contestar (1)
ant la hormiga (9)
antibiotic el antibiótico (9)
any: not — ningúno (ningún), -a (I, 8)

anywhere: not — ninguna parte (I)
apartment el apartamento (I)
appetizers *(Spanish-style)* las tapas (13)
apple la manzana (I)
appliance el aparato (7)
April abril (I)
arm el brazo (I)
armchair el sillón, *pl.* los sillones (I)
around here por aquí (I)
to **arrest** arrestar (10)
to **arrive** llegar (I)
arriving from procedente de (12)
art el arte (I, 4)
   — exhibit la exposición, *pl.* las exposiciones de arte (4)
artistic artístico, -a (I)
as:
   — + *adj.* **—** tan + *adj.* + como (1)
   — much (many) + *noun* **+ —** tanto, -a (tantos, -as) + *noun* + como (3)
to **ask** preguntar (1)
   to — a question hacer una pregunta (1)
   to — for pedir (I)
asparagus el espárrago (13)
assistance la ayuda (10)
astronaut el / la astronauta (11)
at en; a (I); por (8)
athlete el / la deportista (11)
athletic deportista (I)
atmosphere el ambiente (I)
attractive atractivo, -a (I)
auditorium el auditorio (1)
August agosto (I)
aunt la tía (I)
   —s and uncles los tíos (I)
automatic automático, -a (11)
autumn el otoño (I)
avenue la avenida (I)
avocado el aguacate (I)
   — dip el guacamole (I)

to **baby-sit** cuidar niños (2)
back la espalda (I)
   in the — al fondo (8)
backpack la mochila (I)
bad mal, -a (I)
   to have a — time pasarlo mal (I, 4)
baggage el equipaje (12)
   — claim la terminal de equipaje (12)
baked *adj.* al horno (13)
bakery la panadería (8)
ball la pelota (4); *(inflated)* el balón, *pl.* los balones (4)
banana el plátano (I)
band la banda (2)
bandage la venda (8)
bank el banco (I)
barbecue la barbacoa (13)
   to have a — hacer una barbacoa (13)
bargain la ganga (I)
to **bargain** regatear (12)
baseball el béisbol (I)
based (on) basado, -a (en) (10)
basement el sótano (I)
basketball el básquetbol (I)
bass el contrabajo (2)
bat *(baseball)* el bate (de béisbol) (4)
bath: to take a — bañarse (2)
bathing suit el traje de baño (I)
bathroom el baño (I)
battery la pila (7)
to **be** estar; ser (I)
   to — about tratarse de (10)
beach la playa (I)
beans los frijoles (I)
   green — las judías verdes (I)
   refried — los frijoles refritos (I)
bear el oso (I)
because porque (I)
bed la cama (I)
   to go to — acostarse *(o → ue)* (2)
bedroom el dormitorio (I)
bee la abeja (9)
beef la carne (de res) (I)
before + *verb* + *-ing* antes de + *inf.* (2)
to **begin** empezar *(e → ie)* (I)
to **behave (well / badly)** portarse (bien / mal) (5)
behind detrás (de) (I)
to **believe** creer (I)
belt el cinturón, *pl.* los cinturones (3)
beside al lado de (I)
besides además (9)

best el / la mejor (I)
better mejor (I)
between entre (I)
beverage la bebida (I)
bicycle la bicicleta (I, 4)
   to ride a — montar en bicicleta (I, 4)
big grande (I)
   — screen TV la pantalla gigante (11)
bike *see* **bicycle**
bill *(restaurant)* la cuenta (I)
binder (3-ring) la carpeta de argollas (I)
biology la biología (1)
bird el pájaro (I, 5)
birthday el cumpleaños (I)
   — card la tarjeta de cumpleaños (I)
   — party la fiesta de cumpleaños (I, 6)
   happy —! ¡feliz cumpleaños! (I)
   to have a — cumplir años (6)
bite *(insect)* la picadura (9)
to **bite** *(insect)* picar (9)
bitter amargo, -a (13)
black negro, -a (I)
   in — and white en blanco y negro (I)
block la cuadra (I); *(toy)* el bloque (5)
   how many —s (from . . .)? ¿a cuántas cuadras (de . . .)? (I)
blond rubio, -a (I)
blood la sangre (9)
blouse la blusa (I)
to **blow out** *(candles)* apagar (6)
blue azul (I)
boarding pass la tarjeta de embarque (12)
body el cuerpo (I)
to **boil** hervir *(e → ie)* (13)
bold atrevido, -a (I)
bone el hueso (9)
   to break a — romperse (9)
book el libro (I)
   — bag el bolso (1)
bookstore la librería (I)
boot la bota (I)
   half — el botín, *pl.* los botines (3)
to **bore** aburrir (I)
bored: to be — aburrirse (4)
boring aburrido, -a (I)
born: to be — nacer (6)
to **borrow (from)** pedir prestado, -a (a) (4)
to **bother** molestar (5)

bottle la botella (I, 11)
bowl el tazón, *pl.* los tazones (I)
bowling los bolos (4)
boy el muchacho (I); el niño (5)
boyfriend el novio (I)
bracelet la pulsera (I, 7)
braces los frenillos (9)
bread el pan (I)
to **break** *(a bone)* romperse (9)
breakfast el desayuno (I)
   for — en el desayuno (I)
   to have — desayunar (2)
to **bring** traer (I)
broken roto, -a (9)
brother el hermano (I)
   —s and sisters los hermanos (I)
   —-in-law el cuñado (6)
brown marrón, *pl.* marrones; *(hair)* castaño (I)
to **brush** *(one's teeth, hair, etc.)* cepillarse (los dientes, el pelo, etc.) (2)
building el edificio (1)
to **burn** quemar (9)
   to — oneself quemarse (9)
burrito el burrito (I)
bus el autobús, *pl.* los autobuses (I)
   — stop la parada del autobús (I)
business los negocios (11)
   —man, —woman el hombre / la mujer de negocios (11)
busy ocupado, -a (I)
but pero (I)
butcher shop la carnicería (8)
butter la mantequilla (I)
butterfly la mariposa (14)
button el botón, *pl.* los botones (3)
to **buy** comprar (I)
by por; + *vehicle* en (I)

cactus el cacto (14)
cafeteria la cafetería (1)
cake el pastel (6)
calamine lotion la calamina (9)
calculator la calculadora (I)
to **call** llamar (I)
calorie la caloría (13)
camera la cámara (I)
campground el campamento (14)
camping: to go — ir de camping (14)
can poder *(o → ue)* (I); la lata (I, 11)
   — opener el abrelatas (14)
candle la vela (6)

candy el dulce (13)
canned enlatado, -a (13)
canoe la canoa (14)
    to go —ing navegar en canoa (14)
cantaloupe el melón, *pl.* los melones (13)
canvas la lona (3)
cap la gorra (3)
    ski — el gorro (I)
car el coche (I)
    — coat el chaquetón, *pl.* los chaquetones (3)
carbohydrate el carbohidrato (13)
card la tarjeta (I)
    ID — el carnet de identidad (7)
cardboard el cartón (I, 11)
careful: to be — (of / with) tener cuidado (con) (12)
carousel el carrusel (5)
carrot la zanahoria (I)
carte: a la — a la carta (I)
cartoons los dibujos animados (I)
case: in — of en caso de (7)
cash (el dinero) en efectivo (3)
to cash cambiar (12)
cashier el cajero, la cajera (3)
    —'s station la caja (8)
cassette el casete (4)
cast el yeso (9)
cat el gato (I)
catalog el catálogo (3)
cathedral la catedral (I)
cautious prudente (I)
CD el disco compacto (4)
to celebrate celebrar (6)
celebration la celebración, *pl.* las celebraciones (6)
center el centro (I)
    recycling — el centro de reciclaje (I)
    shopping — el centro comercial (I)
central central (7)
cereal el cereal (I)
chain la cadena (7)
    key— el llavero (7)
chair la silla (I)
chalkboard la pizarra (I)
champion el campeón, *pl.* los campeones; la campeona (4)
championship el campeonato (4)
change el cambio (11)
to change cambiar (10)
channel el canal (I)
chapter el capítulo (1)
character el personaje (10)
to chat charlar (6)

cheap barato, -a (I)
check el cheque (3)
to check *(baggage)* facturar (12)
    to — out a book sacar un libro (I)
checked *(design)* a cuadros (3)
checkers las damas (4)
cheese el queso (I)
chemistry la química (1)
cherry la cereza (13)
chess el ajedrez (4)
chestnut(-colored) castaño, -a (I)
chicken el pollo (I)
    — soup la sopa de pollo (I)
child el niño, la niña (5)
    as a — de pequeño, -a (5)
    only — el hijo único, la hija única (I)
children los niños (5)
    —'s wear la ropa para niños (8)
chili pepper el chile (I)
chocolate: hot — el chocolate (I)
choir el coro (2)
to choose escoger *(g → j)* (I, 3)
to chop picar (13)
chore el quehacer (I)
    household — el quehacer de la casa (I)
chorus el coro (2)
Christmas la Navidad (6)
    — Eve la Nochebuena (6)
church la iglesia (I)
churro el churro (I)
city la ciudad (I)
clarinet el clarinete (2)
class la clase (de) (I)
classical clásico, -a (4)
classmate el compañero, la compañera (I)
classroom la sala de clases (I)
clean limpio, -a; puro, -a (I)
to clean limpiar (I)
    to — up arreglar (I)
to clear the table quitar la mesa (I)
to climb subir (I)
clinic la clínica (I)
clock el reloj (1)
    alarm — el despertador (2)
to close cerrar *(e → ie)* (I)
closet el guardarropa (I)
cloth la tela (3)
clothes la ropa (I)
club el club, *pl.* los clubes (2)
coach el entrenador, la entrenadora (4)
coat el abrigo (I)
    car — el chaquetón, *pl.* los chaquetones (3)

cockroach la cucaracha (9)
coffee el café (I)
coin la moneda (7)
cold frío, -a (I)
    to be (very) — tener (mucho) frío (I)
    to have a — tener (un) resfriado (I)
    it's — out hace frío (I)
to collect coleccionar (5)
collection la colección, *pl.* las colecciones (5)
color el color (I)
    in — en colores (I)
    what —? ¿de qué color? (I)
Columbus Day el Día de la Raza (6)
comb el peine (2)
to comb one's hair peinarse (2)
comedy la comedia (I)
comfortable cómodo, -a (I)
comical cómico -a (I)
commercial el anuncio (de televisión) (I)
community la comunidad (I)
compact disc el disco compacto (4)
composition la composición (1)
computer la computadora (1)
    — technician el técnico, la técnica de computadoras (11)
concert el concierto (I)
congratulations! ¡felicidades! (6)
to congratulate felicitar (6)
to conserve conservar (I, 7)
contact lenses los lentes de contacto (7)
to contaminate contaminar (11)
contaminated contaminado, -a (I, 11)
cook el cocinero, la cocinera (13)
to cook cocinar (I)
cooked cocido, -a (13)
cool: it's — out hace fresco (I)
corn el maíz (I)
    — tortilla la tortilla de maíz (I)
corner la esquina (I)
to cost costar *(o → ue)* (I)
costume party la fiesta de disfraces (I, 4)
cotton el algodón (3)
cough la tos (9)
    — syrup el jarabe (para la tos) (9)
to cough toser (9)
could you…? ¿podría (Ud.) / podrías (tú) + *inf.?* (8)

English-Spanish Vocabulary   511

counselor el consejero, la consejera (1)
counter el mostrador (8)
country el país (I)
countryside el campo (I)
course: of — claro que sí (I); por supuesto (I, 11)
cousin el primo, la prima (I)
cow la vaca (I)
cowboy, cowgirl el vaquero, la vaquera (10)
coyote el coyote (14)
credit card la tarjeta de crédito (3)
crime el crimen (10)
criminal el / la criminal (10)
to cross cruzar (8)
crossword puzzle el crucigrama (4)
crutches las muletas (9)
to cry llorar (5)
cucumber el pepino (13)
cup la taza (I)
currency exchange la casa de cambio (12)
customs la aduana (12)
— agent el aduanero, la aduanera (12)
to cut cortar (I)
to — oneself cortarse (9)

daily special el plato del día (I)
to damage dañar (10)
dance el baile (I, 6)
to dance bailar (I, 6)
dancer el bailarín, la bailarina (11)
danger el peligro (I, 14)
dangerous peligroso, -a (14)
daring atrevido, -a (I)
dark (color) oscuro, -a (3)
date la fecha (I)
what's today's —? ¿cuál es la fecha de hoy? (I)
daughter la hija (I)
dawn el amanecer (14)
day el día (I)
every — todos los días (I)
day-care center la guardería infantil (5)
dead muerto, -a (6)
December diciembre (I)
decoration la decoración, pl. las decoraciones (I)
deer el venado, la venada (14)
delay el retraso (12)
delicious sabroso, -a (I)
delighted encantado, -a (I)
to deliver repartir (2)

dental floss la seda dental (8)
dentist el / la dentista (I)
deodorant el desodorante (8)
department store el almacén, pl. los almacenes (I)
to depend (on) depender (de) (I, 2)
to deposit depositar (I)
desk el escritorio; (student) el pupitre (I)
desert el desierto (14)
dessert el postre
for — de postre (I)
to destroy destruir (10)
detective el / la detective (10)
— show el programa de detectives (I)
device el aparato (7)
to devote oneself (to) dedicarse (a) (11)
dictionary el diccionario (I)
difficult difícil (I)
dining room el comedor (I)
dinner la cena (I)
for — en la cena (I)
dinosaur el dinosaurio (5)
to direct dirigir (g → j) (10)
direction la dirección, pl. las direcciones (10)
director (film) el director, la directora (10)
dirty sucio, -a (I)
disadvantage la desventaja (11)
to disagree no estar de acuerdo (I)
disaster el desastre (4)
discount store la tienda de descuentos (I)
disgusting: that's — ! ¡qué asco! (I)
dish el plato (I)
dishwasher el lavaplatos (7)
disk el disco (4)
disobedient desobediente (5)
to disobey desobedecer (c → zc) (5)
distance la distancia (8)
to dive dar saltos (14)
diversion la diversión, pl. las diversiones (4)
diving board el trampolín, pl. los trampolines (14)
divorced (from) divorciado, -a (de) (6)
to do hacer (I)
documentary el documental (I)
dog el perro (I)
doll la muñeca (5)
dollar el dólar (I)
domestic doméstico, -a (14)
door la puerta (I)

dot: on the — en punto (I)
double doble (12)
dough la masa (13)
downtown el centro (8)
to draw dibujar (I)
drawing el dibujo (I)
dress el vestido (I)
party — el vestido de fiesta (I)
dressed: to get — vestirse (e → i) (2)
dresser la cómoda (I)
to drink beber (I)
drops las gotas (9)
drugstore la farmacia (I)
drum el tambor (2)
dry seco, -a (14)
to dry secar (14)
to — one's hair secarse el pelo (2)
dryer:
clothes — la secadora (7)
hair — el secador de pelo (7)
dumb tonto, -a (I)
to dump echar (11)
dust el polvo (9)
to dust sacudir (I)

ear el oído (I)
—ache el dolor de oído (I)
early temprano (I)
to earn ganar (2)
to — a living ganarse la vida (11)
earring el arete (I, 7)
Earth la Tierra (I, 11)
earthquake el terrremoto (10)
easily fácilmente (2)
easy fácil (I)
to eat comer (I)
economical económico, -a (11)
education la educación (11)
educational educativo, -a (I)
efficient eficiente (11)
egg el huevo (I)
hard-boiled — el huevo duro (13)
eight ocho (I)
— hundred ochocientos (I)
eighteen dieciocho (I)
eighth octavo, -a (I)
eighty ochenta (I)
either: not — no ... tampoco (I)
elbow el codo (9)
electric eléctrico, -a (7)
— fan el ventilador (7)
electricity la electricidad (7)
elegant elegante (I, 3)

elementary school la escuela primaria (5)
elephant el elefante (I, 14)
elevator el ascensor (8)
eleven once (I)
else: anything — algo más (I)
to **embrace** abrazarse (6)
emergency la emergencia (7)
— **room** la sala de emergencia (9)
in case of — en caso de emergencia (7)
employee el empleado, la empleada (12)
enchilada la enchilada (I)
to **end** terminar (I)
endangered en peligro de extinción (I, 14)
energy la energía (I, 7)
English (*language*) el inglés (I)
to **enjoy** disfrutar de (12)
enough suficiente (7)
entertainment la diversión, *pl.* las diversiones (4)
entrance la entrada (8)
environment el medio ambiente (I, 11)
eruption la erupción, *pl.* las erupciones (10)
escalator la escalera mecánica (8)
evening la noche (I)
good — buenas noches / tardes (I)
in the — por la noche / tarde (I)
ever alguna vez (I)
every day todos los días (I)
everyone todos, -as (I)
everywhere por todas partes (3)
exaggerated exagerado, -a (10)
exam el examen, *pl.* los exámenes (1)
excellent excelente (10)
exciting emocionante (I)
excursion la excursión, *pl.* las excursiones (12)
to take an — hacer una excursión (12)
to **excuse** perdonar (8)
— **me** perdón (I); perdone (Ud.) (8)
exercise el ejercicio (I, 1)
to **exercise** hacer ejercicio (I)
exhibit (*art*) la exposición, *pl.* las exposiciones (de arte) (4)
exit la salida (8)
expensive caro, -a (I)
to **explain** explicar (1)

to **explore** explorar (I)
extracurricular extracurricular (2)
eye el ojo (I)
— **drops** las gotas para los ojos (9)

fabric la tela (3)
face la cara (2)
facing enfrente (de) (I)
fact el hecho (I, 10)
—**-based program** el programa de hechos de la vida real (I)
factory la fábrica (I)
failure el fracaso (10)
fair regular; así, así (I)
fall el otoño (I)
to **fall (down)** caerse (9)
to — in love (with) enamorarse (de) (10)
family la familia (I); *adj.* familiar (6)
— **room** la sala de estar (I)
fan (*electric*) el ventilador (7)
fantastic fantástico, -a (I)
far (from) lejos (de) (I)
to **fascinate** fascinar (I)
fascinating fascinante (I)
fashion la moda (3)
fashionable: to be — estar de moda (3)
to **fasten** abrocharse (12)
father el padre (I)
—**'s Day** el Día del Padre (6)
feather la pluma (14)
February febrero (I)
to **feel** sentirse (*e → ie*) (9)
how do you —? ¿cómo te sientes? (I)
festive alegre (4)
fever la fiebre (I)
to have a — tener fiebre (I)
few: a — unos, unas (I)
fifteen quince (I)
fifth quinto, -a (I)
fifty cincuenta (I)
to **fight** pelearse (5)
filling el relleno (13)
film la película (I)
to **find** encontrar (*o → ue*) (3)
finger el dedo (I)
fingernail la uña (8)
— **polish** el esmalte de uñas (8)
fire el incendio (7); el fuego (14)
— **extinguisher** el extinguidor de incendios (7)
— **station** la estación de bomberos (8)

firefighter el bombero, la bombera (8)
firewood la leña (14)
fireworks los fuegos artificiales (6)
to shoot — lanzar fuegos artificiales (6)
first primero (primer), -a (I)
fish (*cooked*) el pescado (I); (*live*) el pez, *pl.* los peces (5)
— **store** la pescadería (8)
to go —ing ir de pesca (I)
to **fit** quedar (I)
five cinco (I)
— **hundred** quinientos (I)
to **fix** reparar (7)
flag la bandera (1)
flan el flan (I)
flashlight la linterna (7)
flight el vuelo (12)
— **attendant** el / la auxiliar de vuelo (12)
flood la inundación, *pl.* las inundaciones (10)
floor (*story*) el piso (I); el suelo (3)
floss: dental — la seda dental (8)
flour la harina (I)
— **tortilla** la tortilla de harina (I)
flower la flor (I, 6)
— **shop** la floristería (8)
flowered floreado, -a (3)
flu la gripe (I)
to have the — tener gripe (I)
flute la flauta (2)
fly la mosca (9)
folder la carpeta (I)
to **follow** seguir (*e → i*) (8)
food la comida (I); la alimentación (3)
foot el pie (I)
on — a pie (I)
football el fútbol americano (I)
footprint la huella (14)
for para; por (I)
— + *time expression* por (9)
forest la selva (I)
rain — la selva tropical (I)
fork el tenedor (I)
forty cuarenta (I)
fossil el fósil (14)
four cuatro (I)
— **hundred** cuatrocientos (I)
fourteen catorce (I)
French (*language*) el francés (1)
— **fries** las papas fritas (I)
fresh fresco, -a (13)
Friday viernes (I)
on — el viernes (I)

English-Spanish Vocabulary   513

513

fried frito, -a (13)
friend el amigo, la amiga (I)
friendly simpático, -a (I)
frog la rana (14)
from de (I); desde (6)
front: in — of enfrente de; delante de (I)
frozen congelado, -a (13)
fruit la fruta (I)
   — salad la ensalada de frutas (13)
   — shop la frutería (8)
fun: to have — divertirse *(e → ie)* (4)
to **function** funcionar (7)
funny gracioso, -a; emocionante; divertido, -a (I)
fur la piel (I)
furniture los muebles (I)
future el futuro (11)

game el partido (I, 4)
   — show el programa de concursos (10)
garage el garaje (I)
garbage la basura (I)
garlic el ajo (13)
gas station la estación de servicio (I)
gate la puerta (12)
to **gather** recoger (14)
gathering la reunión, *pl.* las reuniones (I, 6)
gazpacho el gazpacho (13)
gee! ¡vaya! (I)
generally generalmente (I)
generous generoso, -a (I)
geography la geografía (1)
geometry la geometría (1)
German *(language)* el alemán (1)
to **get** conseguir *(e → i)* (12)
   to — up levantarse (2)
get-together la reunión, *pl.* las reuniones (I, 6)
gift el regalo (I)
   — shop la tienda de regalos (I)
   to give a — regalar (I, 6)
girl la muchacha (I); la niña (5)
girlfriend la novia (I)
to **give** dar (I)
   to — a gift regalar (I, 6)
   to — an injection poner una inyección (9)
glass el vaso (I); *(material)* el vidrio (I, 11)
   (made of) — de vidrio (I)
glasses los anteojos (I, 7)

glove el guante (I)
   baseball — el guante de béisbol (4)
to **go** ir (I)
   to be —ing to + *verb* ir a + *inf.* (I)
   to — fishing ir de pesca (I)
   — on! ¡vaya! (I)
   to — on a trip hacer una excursión (12)
   to — on vacation ir de vacaciones (I)
   to — shopping ir de compras (I)
   to — to bed acostarse *(o → ue)* (2)
   to — to school ir a la escuela (I)
   to — through pasar por (12)
goal el gol (4)
going to con destino a (12)
gold el oro (7)
   (made of) — de oro (7)
good bueno (buen), -a (I)
   — afternoon buenas tardes (I)
   — evening buenas noches (I)
   — morning buenos días (I)
   — night buenas noches (I)
   it's a — thing that . . . menos mal que . . . (I)
golf el golf (4)
   — club el palo (de golf) (4)
good buen(o), -a (I)
   to have a — time pasarlo bien (I, 4)
good-by adiós (I)
   to say — (to) despedirse *(e → i)* (de) (6)
good-looking guapo, -a (I)
goodness: my —! ¡vaya! (I)
gorilla el gorila (I, 14)
grade la nota (1)
   to get a good / bad — sacar una buena / mala nota (1)
to **graduate** graduarse (6)
graduation la graduación, *pl.* las graduaciones (6)
granddaughter la nieta (6)
grandfather el abuelo (I)
grandmother la abuela (I)
grandparents los abuelos (I)
grandson el nieto (6)
grape la uva (I)
gray gris, *pl.* grises (I)
   — hair pelo canoso (I)
greasy grasoso, -a (13)
great! ¡genial! (I)
great-grandfather / grandmother el bisabuelo, la bisabuela (6)

green verde (I)
   — beans las judías verdes (I)
   — pepper el pimiento verde (13)
greengrocer la verdulería (8)
to **greet** saludar (6)
grilled a la parrilla (13)
groceries los comestibles (I)
guest el invitado, la invitada (I)
guide el / la guía (12)
guidebook la guía (12)
guitar la guitarra (I)
gym el gimnasio (I)
   — bag el bolso (1)

habit: to be in the — of soler *(o → ue)* + *inf.* (I, 2)
hair el pelo (I)
   to comb one's — peinarse (2)
   — dryer el secador de pelo (7)
half:
   and a — *(in sizes)* y medio (3)
   — an hour media hora (I)
   — boots el botín, *pl.* los botines (3)
   —-past y media (I)
ham el jamón (I)
hamburger la hamburguesa (I)
hamper: laundry — el cesto de la ropa sucia (3)
hand la mano (I)
   by — a mano (12)
   —made hecho, -a a mano (I)
   to shake —s darse la mano (6)
to **hand in** entregar (1)
handcrafts la artesanía (12)
handsome guapo, -a (I)
to **hang** colgar *(o → ue)* (3)
to **happen** pasar (I); ocurrir (10)
   what —ed to you? ¿qué te pasó? (9)
happy alegre (4)
hard difícil (I)
hard-boiled egg el huevo duro (13)
hard-working trabajador, -a (I)
to **have** tener (I)
   to — fun divertirse *(e → ie)* (4)
   to — a good / bad time pasarlo bien / mal (I, 4)
   to — time + *inf.* tener tiempo de + *inf.* (4)
   to — to tener que + *inf.* (I)
he él (I)
head la cabeza (I)
   —ache el dolor de cabeza (I)

health la salud (I); *(class)* las ciencias de la salud (I)
healthy sano, -a (13)
   to stay — mantenerse sano, -a (13)
heater el calentador (7)
heating la calefacción (7)
heavy pesado, -a (14)
hello! ¡hola! (I)
helmet el casco (4)
help la ayuda (10)
to **help** ayudar (I)
   may I — you? ¿qué desea (Ud.)? (I)
her *adj.* su, sus (I); suyo, -a (7); *dir. obj. pron.* la; *ind. obj. pron.* le (I)
here aquí (I)
   around — por aquí (I)
   — it is aquí está (I)
hero *(film)* el galán, *pl.* los galanes (10)
heroine la heroína (10)
hers el suyo, la suya, los suyos, las suyas (7)
hi! ¡hola! (I)
to **hide** esconder(se) (10)
high-heeled shoes los zapatos de tacón alto (I, 3)
highway la carretera (8)
hiking: to go — dar una caminata (14)
hill la colina (14)
him *dir. obj. pron.* lo; *ind. obj. pron.* le (I)
his *adj.* su, sus (I); suyo, -a (7); *pron.* el suyo, la suya, los suyos, las suyas (7)
historic(al) histórico, -a (8)
history la historia (1)
hobby el pasatiempo (I)
hockey el hockey (4)
   — puck el disco (de hockey) (4)
   — stick el palo (de hockey) (4)
holiday el día de fiesta (6)
home la casa (I)
   — shopping show el programa de compras (10)
homework la tarea (I)
horrible horrible (I)
horror el horror (4)
   — movie la película de terror (I)
horse el caballo (I, 10)
   to ride —back montar a caballo (10)
hospital el hospital (I)
hot *(flavor)* picante (I)
   to be — *(person)* tener calor (I)
   it's — out hace calor (I)

hot dog el perro caliente (13)
hotel el hotel (I)
   — room la habitación, *pl.* las habitaciones (12)
house la casa (I)
   — special la especialidad de la casa (I)
household chore el quehacer de la casa (I)
¡how! qué + *adj.* (I)
how? ¿cómo? (I)
   — are you? ¿cómo estás /está (Ud.)? (I)
   — long has it been since . . . ¿cuánto (tiempo) hace que . . . ? (I)
   — many? ¿cuántos, -as? (I)
   — much? ¿cuánto? (I)
   — old is . . . ? cuántos años tiene . . . ? (I)
   —'s it going? ¿qué tal? (I)
   — is...? ¿qué tal es...? (10)
to **hug** abrazarse (6)
human being el ser humano (11)
hundred cien; ciento (I)
hungry: to be — tener hambre (I)
hurricane el huracán, *pl.* los huracanes (I)
to **hurt** doler *(o → ue);* lastimarse + *part of body* (I)
husband el esposo (6)

I yo (I)
ice el hielo (4)
   to — skate patinar sobre hielo (4)
ice cream el helado (I)
   — shop la heladería (8)
iced tea el té helado (I)
identification la identificación (7)
   — card la carnet de identidad (7)
if si (I)
ill enfermo, -a (I)
   to feel — sentirse *(e → ie)* mal (I)
   to make — hacer daño a (13)
illness la enfermedad (9)
impatient impaciente (I)
impolite maleducado, -a (5)
in en (I)
   — order to para + *inf.* (I)
to **include** incluir (12)
Independence Day el Día de la Independencia (6)
to **indicate** indicar (8)
indigenous indígena (12)
inexpensive barato, -a (I)
   — lodging la pensión, *pl.* las pensiones (12)

infection la infección, *pl.* las infecciones (9)
information la información (10)
ingredient el ingrediente (I, 13)
injection la inyección, *pl.* las inyecciones (9)
   to give an — poner una inyección (9)
insect el insecto (9)
   — bite la picadura (de insecto) (9)
   — repellent el repelente (9)
insecticide el insecticida (9)
to **inspect** registrar (12)
instrument el instrumento (2)
intelligent inteligente (I)
interest: place of — el lugar de interés (I)
to **interest** interesar (I)
interesting interesante (I)
international internacional (10)
intersection el cruce (8)
interview la entrevista (10)
to **introduce** presentar (I)
to **investigate** investigar (10)
invitation la invitación, *pl.* las invitaciones (I, 6)
to **invite** invitar (I, 6)
   involved: to be — in dedicarse (a) (11)
it *dir. obj.* lo (I)

jacket la chaqueta (I)
jaguar el jaguar (I)
January enero (I)
jeans los jeans (I)
to **jet ski** hacer moto acuática (14)
jet skiing la moto acuática (14)
jewelry las joyas (I)
jigsaw puzzle el rompecabezas (4)
to **jog** correr (4)
judge el / la juez, *pl.* los / las jueces (11)
juice el jugo (I)
   orange — el jugo de naranja (I)
July julio (I)
to **jump (rope)** saltar (a la cuerda) (5)
   — rope la cuerda (5)
June junio (I)

to **keep** guardar (3)
key la llave (7)
   —chain el llavero (7)
to **kill** matar (10)
kilometer el kilómetro (8)
kind *adj.* amable; la clase (I)

kindergarten el kindergarten (5)
kindling los palitos (14)
to **kiss** besarse (6)
kitchen la cocina (I)
knee la rodilla (9)
knife el cuchillo (I)
to **know** conocer (*c → zc*) (I, 1); saber (I, 4)
    to **— how** saber (I, 4)

lab(oratory) el laboratorio (1)
laborer el obrero, la obrera (11)
lacking: to be — faltar a (I)
ladies' wear la ropa para damas (8)
lake el lago (I)
lamp la lámpara (I)
to **land** aterrizar (12)
landslide el derrumbe (10)
language el idioma (1)
large grande (I, 3)
last pasado, -a (I); último, -a (4)
    — night anoche (I)
to **last** durar (I)
late tarde (I)
    see you —r hasta luego (I)
laundry hamper el cesto de la ropa sucia (3)
laundry room el lavadero (I)
lawn el césped (I)
    to mow the — cortar el césped (I)
lawyer el abogado, la abogada (11)
lazy perezoso, -a (I)
leaf hoja (14)
league la liga (4)
to **learn** aprender (I)
least el / la / los / las menos + *adj.* (I)
    at — por lo menos (2)
leather el cuero (I)
    (made of) — de cuero (I)
to **leave** salir (I)
left izquierdo, -a (I)
    to the — (of) a la izquierda (de) (I)
leg la pierna (I)
lemon el limón, *pl.* los limones (13)
lemonade la limonada (I)
to **lend** prestar (4)
lenses: contact — los lentes de contacto (7)
less menos (I)
    more or — más o menos (I)
lesson la lección, *pl.* las lecciones (1)
letter la carta (I)

lettuce la lechuga (I)
library la biblioteca (I)
to **lie** mentir (*e → ie*) (5)
life la vida (I)
to **lift** levantar (4)
light *(color)* claro, -a (3); *(minor)* leve (9); *(weight)* ligero, -a (14)
light la luz, *pl.* las luces (I)
    — bulb el bombillo (7)
    traffic — el semáforo (8)
to **light** encender (*e → ie*) (6)
to **like** gustar a (I)
    I'd (you'd) — quisiera(s); me (te) gustaría (I)
likewise igualmente (I)
lime el limón, *pl.* los limones (13)
line: to — up hacer fila (1)
lips los labios (8)
lipstick el lápiz (*pl.* los lápices) de labios (8)
to **listen (to)** escuchar (I)
literary literario, -a (2)
lit(erature) la literatura (1)
little pequeño, -a (I)
    a — un poco (de) (I)
to **live** vivir (I)
living: to earn a — ganarse la vida (11)
living room la sala (I)
loafer el mocasín, *pl.* los mocasines (3)
local local (10)
located: to be — quedar (I)
locker el armario (1)
lodging: inexpensive — la pensión, *pl.* las pensiones (12)
long largo, -a (I)
to **look (at)** mirar (I)
    to — for buscar (I)
loose *(clothing)* flojo, -a (3)
to **lose** perder (*e → ie*) (4)
lot: a — of mucho, -a (I)
love: to fall in — (with) enamorarse (de) (10)
to **love** encantar (I)
loving cariñoso, -a (I)
luckily por suerte (1)
lunch el almuerzo (I)
    for — en el almuerzo (I)
luxury el lujo (7)

ma'am señora (I)
made hecho, -a (I, 13)
    it's — of… es de… (3)
    — of de + *material* (I)
    what's (it) — of ? de qué es…? (3)

magazine la revista (I)
to **mail** enviar (I)
mailbox el buzón, *pl.* los buzones (8)
main principal (10)
to **make** hacer (I)
make-up el maquillaje (8)
    to put on — maquillarse (8)
mall el centro comercial (I)
man el hombre (I)
many muchos, -as (I)
    as — as tantos, -as + *noun* + como (3)
map el mapa (1)
March marzo (I)
market el mercado (12)
marker el marcador (I)
married (to) casado, -a (con) (6)
    to get — (to) casarse (con) (6)
martial arts las artes marciales (2)
match *(game)* el partido (I); el fósforo (14)
mathematics las matemáticas (I)
matter: what's the —? ¿qué pasa? (I)
May mayo (I)
mayonnaise la mayonesa (13)
me *obj. pron.* me; *after prep.* mí (I)
meal la comida (I)
mechanic el mecánico, la mecánica (11)
medical test el análisis, *pl.* los análisis (9)
medicine la medicina (9)
medium *(in sizes)* mediano, -a (3)
to **meet** encontrarse (*o → ue*) (6)
    I'd like you to — te presento a… (I)
    pleased to — you mucho gusto; encantado, -a (I)
member el miembro (2)
    to be a — of ser miembro de (2)
men's wear la ropa para caballeros (8)
menu el menú (I)
merry-go-round el carrusel (5)
messy desordenado, -a (I)
metal el metal (I)
    (made of) — de metal (I)
meter *(measurement)* el metro (8)
microwave oven el microondas (7)
midnight la medianoche (I)
mild *(flavor)* no picante (I)
mile la milla (8)
milk la leche (I)

mine el mío, la mía, los míos, las mías (7)
minor leve (9)
minute el minuto (I)
mirror el espejo (I)
mischievous travieso, -a (5)
miss (la) señorita (I)
miss: to be —ing faltar a (I)
to **mix** mezclar (13)
modern moderno, -a (I)
Monday lunes (I)
   on — el lunes (I)
money el dinero (I)
monster el monstruo (10)
month el mes (I)
monument el monumento (I)
mood: in a good / bad — de buen / mal humor (2)
moon la Luna (11)
more más (I)
   — or less más o menos (I)
morning la mañana (I)
   good — buenos días (I)
   in the — por la mañana (I)
mosquito el mosquito (9)
most: the — el / la / los / las más + *adj.* (I)
mother la madre (I)
   —'s Day el Día de la Madre (6)
mountain la montaña (I)
   to go — climbing escalar montañas (14)
mouth la boca (I)
movie la película (I)
   —s el cine (I)
   — theater el cine (I)
   to show a — dar una película (I)
to **mow the lawn** cortar el césped (I)
Mr. (el) señor (I)
Mrs. (la) señora (I)
much mucho, -a (I)
   as — as tanto, -a + *noun* + como (3)
   how —? ¿cuánto? (I)
muffler la bufanda (I)
muscle el músculo (9)
museum el museo (I)
mushroom el champiñón, *pl.* los champiñones (13)
music la música (I)
   — program el programa musical (I)
   — video el video musical (4)
musical musical (I)
musician el músico, la música (11)

mustard la mostaza (13)
my mi, mis (I); mío, -a (7)
myself (yo) mismo, -a (7)

nail *see* **fingernail**
name el nombre (I)
   my — is me llamo (I)
   what's your —? ¿cómo te llamas? (I)
named: to be — llamarse (I)
napkin la servilleta (I)
national nacional (14)
native *adj.* indígena (12)
nature la naturaleza (12)
naughty travieso, -a (5)
near cerca (de) (I)
neat ordenado, -a (I)
necessary: it's — to hay que + *inf.* (I, 2); es necesario (2)
necessity la necesidad (7)
neck el cuello (I)
necklace el collar (I, 7)
necktie la corbata (I, 3)
to **need** necesitar (I)
neighbor el vecino, la vecina (5)
neither . . . nor ni . . . ni (I)
nephew el sobrino (6)
never nunca (I)
new nuevo, -a (I)
   — Year's Day el Año Nuevo (6)
   — Year's Eve el fin de año (6)
news las noticias (I)
newspaper el periódico (I, 2)
newsstand el quiosco (de periódicos) (8)
next próximo, -a (1)
   — to al lado (de) (I)
nice amable; simpático, -a (I)
niece la sobrina (6)
night la noche (I)
   at — de la noche (I)
   good — buenas noches (I)
   last — anoche (I)
   — table la mesa de noche (7)
nine nueve (I)
   — hundred novecientos (I)
nineteen diecinueve (I)
ninety noventa (I)
no no (I)
   — longer ya no (I)
nobody, no one nadie (I)
nonallergenic antialérgico, -a (9)
nonstop sin escala (12)
noon el mediodía (I)
nor: neither . . . — ni . . . ni (I)
nose la nariz (I)

not no (I)
   — anymore ya no (I)
   — at all de ninguna manera (I)
   — yet todavía no (I)
notebook el cuaderno (I)
nothing nada (I)
nourishment la alimentación (13)
novel la novela (11)
November noviembre (I)
now ahora (I)
nowhere ninguna parte (I)
number el número (I)
   phone — el número de teléfono (I)
nurse el enfermero, la enfermera (9)
   —'s office la enfermería (I)
nylon el nilón (3)

obedient obediente (5)
to **obey** obedecer *(c → zc)* (5)
to **obtain** conseguir *(e → i)* (12)
to **occur** ocurrir (10)
ocean el océano (I, 11)
October octubre (I)
of de (I)
   — course claro que sí (I); por supuesto (I, 11)
office la oficina (1)
   telephone — la oficina telefónica (12)
   tourist — la oficina de turismo (12)
often a menudo (I)
oil el aceite (13)
ok bueno (I)
old viejo -a; antiguo, -a (I)
   how — is . . . ? ¿cuántos años tiene . . . ? (I)
older mayor (I)
omelet *(Spain)* la tortilla española (13)
on en; sobre (I)
   — the dot en punto (I)
   — time puntualmente (I)
   — top (of) encima (de) (I)
once una vez (I)
one uno (un), una (I); *(a person)* uno (2)
   it's — o'clock es la una (I)
   —-way sólo de ida (12)
onion la cebolla (I)
only sólo (I)
   — child el hijo único, la hija única (I)
to **open** abrir (I)
operation la operación, *pl.* las operaciones (9)

opposite enfrente (de) (I)
or o (I)
   not . . . — ni . . . ni (I)
orange anaranjado, -a; la naranja (I)
   — juice el jugo de naranja (I)
orchestra la orquesta (2)
order: in — to para + *inf.* (I)
to order pedir *(e → i)* (I)
other otro, -a (I)
ouch! ¡ay! (I)
ought to deber (I)
our nuestro, -a (I)
ours el nuestro, la nuestra, los
   nuestros, las nuestras (7)
outdoors al aire libre (14)
outgoing sociable (I)
oven el horno (7)
over: all — por todas partes (3)
owl el búho (14)
own propio, -a (7)
oxygen el oxígeno (14)

to pack hacer la maleta (12)
paella la paella (13)
page la página (1)
painter el pintor, la pintora (11)
palace el palacio (12)
pants los pantalones (I)
pantyhose las pantimedias (I)
paper el papel (I)
   — clip el sujetapapeles, *pl.* los
     sujetapapeles (1)
   sheet of — la hoja de papel (I)
parade el desfile (4)
to pardon perdonar (8)
   — me perdone (Ud.) (8)
parents los padres (I)
park el parque (I)
   amusement — el parque de
     diversiones (I)
part: to be a — of formar parte de
   (I)
part *(film, play)* el papel (10)
   to play the — (of) hacer el
     papel (de) (10)
to participate (in) participar (en) (2)
party la fiesta (I)
   birthday — la fiesta de cumple-
     años (I, 6)
   costume — la fiesta de disfraces
     (I, 4)
   New Year's Eve — la fiesta de
     fin de año (I, 6)
   surprise — la fiesta de sorpresa
     (I, 6)
to pass pasar (I)
passenger el pasajero, la pasajera
   (12)

passport el pasaporte (I)
past:
   half-— y media (I)
   quarter — y cuarto (I)
pastime el pasatiempo (I)
pastry el pastel (I)
path el sendero (14)
patient *adj.* paciente (I)
to pay pagar (I)
pea el guisante (I)
peace la paz (11)
peach el durazno (13)
pen el bolígrafo (I)
pencil el lápiz, *pl.* los lápices (I)
   — sharpener el sacapuntas, *pl.*
     los sacapuntas (1)
people la gente (I)
pepper la pimienta (I)
   green — el pimiento verde (13)
   stuffed — el chile relleno (I)
peppery picante (I)
perfume el perfume (8)
period la hora (I)
to permit permitir (1)
   it's —ted se permite (8)
person la persona (I)
   a — uno (2)
personal personal (I)
phone el teléfono (I)
   on the — por teléfono (I)
   pay — el teléfono público (8)
   — book la guía telefónica (I)
   — number el número de teléfono
     (I)
photo la foto (I)
photography la fotografía (10)
physical education la educación
   física (I)
physician el médico, la médica (I)
piano el piano (2)
to pick up recoger (I, 14)
picnic el picnic (4)
   to have a — hacer un picnic (4)
picture el cuadro (I)
picturesque pintoresco, -a (12)
pie la tarta (13)
pill la pastilla (9)
pilot el/la piloto (12)
pineapple la piña (13)
pink rosado, -a (I)
pistol la pistola (5)
to pitch a tent poner una tienda (14)
place el lugar (I)
   — of interest el lugar de interés
     (I)
to place poner (I)
plaid a cuadros (3)
plain liso, -a (3)
to plan pensar + *inf.* (I); planear (12)

plane el avión, *pl.* los aviones (12)
planet el planeta (11)
plant la planta (I, 14)
plastic el plástico (I, 3)
   (made of) — de plástico (I)
plate el plato (I)
play la obra de teatro (4)
to play jugar *(u → ue)* (I)
   to — the part (of) hacer el
     papel (de) (10)
player el jugador, la jugadora (4)
playground el patio de recreo (5)
pleased to meet you mucho gusto;
   encantado, -a (I)
plot el argumento (10)
pocket el bolsillo (3)
   — folder la carpeta (I)
to point out indicar (8)
poisonous venenoso, -a (14)
police la policía (I)
   — officer el / la policía (10)
   — station la estación de policía
     (I)
polish: nail — el esmalte de uñas
   (8)
polite (bien) educado, -a (5)
politician el político, la política (11)
politics la política (11)
pollen el polen (9)
to pollute contaminar (11)
polluted contaminado, -a (I, 14)
pool la piscina (I)
pork el cerdo (13)
possession la posesión, *pl.* las
   posesiones (7)
post card la tarjeta postal (I)
poster el cartel (I)
post office el correo (I)
pot la olla (14)
potato la papa (I)
   baked — la papa al horno (I)
   French-fried — la papa frita (I)
practical práctico, -a (I)
to practice practicar (I)
to prefer preferir *(e → ie); gustar más
   (I)
to prescribe recetar (9)
prescription la receta (9)
to prepare preparar (I)
pretty bonito, -a (I)
principal *(school)* el director, la directora (1); *adj.* principal (10)
problem el problema (1)
profession la profesión, *pl.* las
   profesiones (11)
program el programa (I)

to **prohibit** prohibir (1)
    it's —ed se prohíbe (1)
projector el proyector (1)
to **protect (oneself)** proteger(se)
    (g →j) (I, 9)
protein la proteína (13)
public público, -a (8)
puck el disco (de hockey) (4)
pumpkin la calabaza (13)
pure puro, -a (I)
purple morado, -a (I)
purse el bolso (3)
to **put** poner (I)
    to — away guardar (3)
    to — on *(clothes)* ponerse (8);
    (make-up) maquillarse (8)
pyramid la pirámide (I)

quarter cuarto, -a (I)
    — past y cuarto (I)
quesadilla la quesadilla (I)
question la pregunta (1)
    to ask a — hacer una pregunta
    (1)
quiet callado, -a (I)
quite bastante (4)
quiz la prueba (1)

racket: tennis — la raqueta de
    tenis (4)
radio *(set)* el radio (7)
raft la balsa (14)
    to go —ing navegar en balsa
    (14)
rain la lluvia (I)
to **rain** llover *(o → ue)* (I)
    it's —ing llueve (I)
raincoat el impermeable (I)
rain forest la selva tropical (I)
rather bastante (I)
razor la máquina de afeitar (8)
reaction la reacción, *pl.* las
    reacciones (9)
to **read** leer (I)
real real (I)
realistic realista (I)
really? ¿de veras?; ¡no me digas! (I)
to **receive** recibir (I)
recipe la receta (13)
to **recommend** recomendar *(e → ie)*
    (12)
to **recycle** reciclar (I, 11)
recycling center el centro de
    reciclaje (I)
red rojo, -a (I)
    —-haired pelirrojo, -a (I)
to **reduce** reducir *(c → zc)* (I, 11)

refrigerator el refrigerador (I)
relative el pariente, la parienta (I, 6)
to **remember** recordar *(o → ue)* (5)
remote control el control remoto
    (7)
to **repair** reparar (7)
repellent el repelente (9)
report el informe (1)
reservation la reservación, *pl.* las
    reservaciones (12)
to **rest** descansar (I)
restaurant el restaurante (I)
restroom los servicios (8)
to **return** regresar; devolver *(o → ue)*
    (I)
review (of) el comentario (sobre)
    (10)
to **review** repasar (1)
rice el arroz (I)
to **ride:**
    to — a bike montar en bicicleta
    (4)
    to — horseback montar a caballo
    (10)
right derecho, -a (I)
    to be — tener razón (I)
    —? ¿verdad? (I)
    — away en seguida (I)
    to the — (of) a la derecha (de)
    (I)
ring el anillo (7)
river el río (11)
roasted asado, -a (13)
to **rob** robar (10)
robot el robot, *pl.* los robots (5)
rock la piedra (14); *(music)* la
    música rock (4)
role el papel (10)
    to play the — (of) hacer el
    papel (de) (10)
romantic movie la película
    romántica (I)
room el cuarto (I); *(hotel)* la
    habitación, las habitaciones
    (12)
rope la cuerda (5)
    to jump — saltar a la cuerda (5)
round redondo, -a (I)
    —-trip ticket el boleto de ida y
    vuelta (12)
to **row** pasear en bote (I)
rowboat el bote (I)
rude maleducado, -a (5)
ruins las ruinas (I)
ruler la regla (I)
to **run** correr (4)

sad triste (I)
sail la vela (14)
salad la ensalada (I)
    fruit — la ensalada de frutas
    (13)
    — bar el bufet de ensaladas (1)
    — dressing la salsa (13)
sale la liquidación, *pl.* las liquida-
    ciones (3)
    to be for — se vende (8)
    to be on — estar en liquidación
    (3)
salesperson el vendedor, la vende-
    dora (3)
salt la sal (I)
salty salado, -a (13)
same mismo, -a (2)
    it's all the — (to me) (me) da
    igual (3)
    the — thing lo mismo (I)
sandbox el cajón, *pl.* los cajones de
    arena (5)
sandwich el sandwich (I); *(Spanish-
    style)* el bocadillo (13)
Saturday sábado (I)
    on — el sábado (I)
sauce la salsa (I)
saucer el platillo (I)
sausage el chorizo (13)
to **save** conservar (I, 7); ahorrar (7)
sax(ophone) el saxofón, *pl.* los
    saxofones (2)
to **say** decir (I)
    how do you — . . . ? ¿cómo se
    dice . . . ? (I)
    it is said . . . se dice . . . (I)
    to — good-by (to) despedirse
    (e → i) (de) (6)
    to — hello decirse "¡Hola!" (6)
    you don't — ! ¡no me digas! (I)
to **scare** dar miedo a (I)
scarf la bufanda (I); el pañuelo (3)
scene la escena (10)
schedule el horario (I)
school la escuela (I); *adj.* escolar
    (1)
    after — después de las clases (I)
    elementary — la escuela
    primaria (5)
science las ciencias (I)
    — fiction la ciencia ficción (I)
scientist el científico, la científica
    (10)
to **score (a goal)** meter (un gol) (4)
screen la pantalla (11)
    big — TV la pantalla gigante (11)

English-Spanish Vocabulary   519

script el guión, *pl.* los guiones (10)
sea el mar (I)
seafood los mariscos (9)
to search *(baggage)* registrar (12)
season la estación, *pl.* las estaciones (I)
seat el asiento (1)
seatbelt el cinturón, *pl.* los cinturones de seguridad (12)
second segundo, -a (I)
secretary el secretario, la secretaria (11)
section la sección, *pl.* las secciones (8)
security system el sistema de seguridad (11)
to see ver (I)
 let's — a ver (I)
 to — each other verse (6)
seesaw el sube y baja (5)
to sell vender (I)
semester el semestre (I)
to send enviar (I)
sensationalistic sensacionalista (10)
to separate separar (I, 11)
separated (from) separado, -a (de) (6)
September septiembre (I)
serious serio, -a (I)
to serve servir *(e → i)* (I)
to set poner (I)
 — the table poner la mesa (I)
seven siete (I)
 — hundred setecientos (I)
seventeen diecisiete (I)
seventh séptimo, -a (I)
seventy setenta (I)
to sew coser (14)
shade la sombra (14)
to shake hands darse la mano (6)
shampoo el champú (I)
sharp en punto (I)
sharpener: pencil — el sacapuntas (1)
to shave afeitarse (8)
shaving cream la crema de afeitar (8)
she ella (I)
shelf el estante (7)
shirt la camisa (I)
 T-— la camiseta (I)
shoe el zapato (I)
 high-heeled —s los zapatos de tacón alto (I)
 — store la zapatería (I)
to shoot fireworks lanzar fuegos artificiales (6)

to shop hacer las compras (8)
shopping:
 to go — ir de compras (I)
 — center el centro comercial (I)
 short *(height)* bajo, -a (I); *(length)* corto, -a (I)
shorts los pantalones cortos (I)
shot la inyección, *pl.* las inyecciones (9)
 to give a — poner una inyección (9)
should deber + *inf.* (I)
show el programa (I)
 game — el programa de concursos (10)
 home shopping — el programa de compras (10)
to show *movie or TV program* dar (I); mostrar *(o → ue)* (7); indicar (8)
shower: to take a — ducharse (2)
shrimp el camarón, *pl.* los camarones (13)
shy tímido, -a (5)
sick enfermo, -a (I)
 to feel — sentirse *(e → ie)* mal (I)
silly tonto, -a (I)
silver la plata (7)
 (made of) — de plata (7)
simple sencillo, -a (3)
since desde (que + *verb*) (6)
 it's been *(time)* — hace + *(time)* + que (I)
to sing cantar (I, 2)
singer el / la cantante (11)
single *(unmarried)* soltero, -a (6); *(room)* individual (12)
sink el fregadero (7)
sir señor (I)
sister la hermana (I)
sister-in-law la cuñada (6)
sitcom la comedia (I)
six seis (I)
 — hundred seiscientos (I)
sixteen dieciséis (I)
sixth sexto, -a (I)
sixty sesenta (I)
size el tamaño (3); *(clothing)* la talla (3); *(shoe)* el número (de zapatos) (3)
skate el patín, *pl.* los patines (4)
to skate patinar (I)
 to ice — patinar sobre hielo (4)
ski el esquí, *pl.* los esquíes (4)
 — cap el gorro (I)
to ski esquiar (I)

to skin-dive bucear (I)
skirt la falda (I)
to sleep dormir *(o → ue)* (I)
sleeping bag el saco de dormir (14)
sleepy: to be — tener sueño (I)
sleeve la manga (3)
slide *(photograph)* la diapositiva (1); *(playground)* el tobogán, *pl.* los toboganes (5)
small pequeño, -a (I)
smoke detector el detector de humo (7)
snack *(afternoon)* la merienda (I)
 for a — de merienda (I)
snake la serpiente (I, 14)
sneakers los tenis (I)
to sneeze estornudar (9)
snow la nieve (I)
to snow nevar *(e → ie)* (I)
 it's —ing nieva (I)
soap el jabón (I)
 — opera la telenovela (I)
soccer el fútbol (I)
social studies las ciencias sociales (I)
sock el calcetín, *pl.* los calcetines (I)
sofa el sofá (I)
soft drink el refresco (I)
solar solar (11)
sold: to be — venderse (8)
some unos, unas (I); alguno (algún), -a (1)
someone, somebody alguien (I, 3)
something algo (I)
 — else algo más (I)
sometimes a veces (I); de vez en cuando (7)
son el hijo (I)
 —s; —s and daughters los hijos (I)
song la canción, *pl.* las canciones (2)
sorry: I'm — lo siento (I)
to sort separar (I)
so-so así, así; regular (I)
soup la sopa (I)
sour agrio, -a (13)
souvenir el recuerdo (I)
space el espacio (11)
 — heater el calentador (7)
Spanish español, -a; *(language)* el español (I)

special especial (6)
   daily — el plato del día (I)
   — effects los efectos especiales (10)
spell: how do you — . . . ? ¿cómo se escribe . . . ? (I)
to **spend** gastar (8)
spicy picante (I)
spider la araña (9)
spinach las espinacas (13)
spine *(on plant)* la espina (14)
spoiled *(child)* consentido, -a (5)
spoken: is — se habla (8)
spoon la cuchara (I)
sports los deportes (I)
   — program el programa deportivo (I)
spring la primavera (I)
square cuadrado, -a (I)
squirrel la ardilla (14)
stadium el estadio (I)
stage el escenario (1)
stairs la escalera (8)
stamp el sello (I)
to **stand** soportar (4)
   to — in line hacer fila (1)
stapler la grapadora (1)
to **start** empezar *(e → ie)* (I)
station la estación, *pl.* las estaciones (I)
to **stay** quedarse (I)
   to — in bed quedarse en la cama (I)
   to — healthy mantenerse sano, -a (13)
steak el bistec (I)
stereo el equipo de sonido (I)
steward, stewardess el / la auxiliar de vuelo (12)
stewed guisado, -a (13)
still todavía (I)
sting *(insect)* la picadura (9)
to **sting** *(insect)* picar (9)
stingy tacaño, -a (I)
to **stir** revolver *(o → ue)* (13)
to **stitch** *(surgically)* hacer puntadas (9)
stitches las puntadas (9)
stomach el estómago (I)
   —ache el dolor de estómago (I)
stone la piedra (14)
stopover la escala (12)
stop sign la señal de alto (8)
store la tienda (I)
   clothing — la tienda de ropa (I)
   department — el almacén, *pl.* los almacenes (I)
   discount — la tienda de descuentos (I)

storm la tormenta (10)
story *(of a building)* el piso (I)
stove la estufa (I)
strawberry la fresa (13)
street la calle (I)
striped a rayas (3)
strong fuerte (9)
student el / la estudiante (I)
   — council el consejo estudiantil (2)
to **study** estudiar (I)
stuffed animal el animal de peluche (5)
subject *(in school)* la materia (1)
subway el metro (I)
   — station la estación del metro (I)
successful: to be — tener éxito (10)
sufficient suficiente (7)
sugar el azúcar (I)
to **suggest** sugerir *(e → ie)* (13)
suit el traje (I, 3)
   bathing — el traje de baño (I)
suitcase la maleta (I, 12)
summer el verano (I)
sun el sol (I)
to **sunbathe** tomar el sol (I)
Sunday domingo (I)
   on — el domingo (I)
sunglasses los anteojos de sol (I, 7)
sunny: it's — hace sol (I)
sunrise el amanecer (14)
sunset el atardecer (14)
suntan lotion el bronceador (I)
supermarket el supermercado (I)
to **surf** hacer surf (14)
surfboard la tabla (de surf) (14)
surprise party la fiesta de sorpresa (I, 6)
sweater el suéter (I)
   turtleneck — el suéter de cuello alto (3)
sweatshirt la sudadera (I)
sweatsuit el chandal (3)
sweet dulce (13)
to **swim** nadar (I)
swimming pool la piscina (I)
swing el columpio (5)
symptom el síntoma (9)
synthetic sintético, -a (3)
system el sistema (11)

table la mesa (I)
   to clear the — quitar la mesa (I)
   night — la mesa de noche (7)
   to set the — poner la mesa (I)
tablecloth el mantel (I)

taco el taco (I)
to **take** llevar; sacar; tomar (I)
   to — a bath bañarse (2)
   to — off *(clothes, make-up, etc.)* quitarse (2); *(aircraft)* despegar (12)
   to — out sacar (I)
   to — pictures sacar fotos (I)
   to — a shower ducharse (2)
   to — a walk ir a pasear (I)
to **talk** hablar (I)
   to — to each other hablarse (6)
talk show el programa de entrevistas (I)
tall alto, -a (I)
tape player el tocacintas, *pl.* los tocacintas (7)
tape recorder la grabadora (I)
to **taste** probar *(o → ue)* (I)
tasteless soso, -a (13)
tasty sabroso, -a (I)
taxi el taxi (I)
tea el té (I)
   iced — el té helado (I)
to **teach** enseñar (I)
teacher el profesor, la profesora (I)
team el equipo (2)
technican el técnico, la técnica (11)
technology la tecnología (11)
teddy bear el oso de peluche (5)
teeth las muelas (I); los dientes (2)
telephone el teléfono (I); *see also* **phone**
   — office la oficina telefónica (12)
   video — el teléfono con video (11)
television la tele(visión) (I)
   — set el televisor (7)
   to watch — ver la tele(visión) (I)
to **tell** decir (5)
temple el templo (I)
ten diez (I)
tennis el tenis (I)
   — racket la raqueta de tenis (4)
tent la tienda (de acampar) (14)
   to pitch a — poner una tienda (14)
terrible terrible (I)
test el examen, *pl.* los exámenes (1)
   medical — el análisis, *pl.* los análisis (9)
Thanksgiving el Día de (Acción de) Gracias (6)
thank you gracias (I)

that que (I); ese, esa; (I, 3); aquel, aquella (3)
  isn't — so? ¿verdad?(I)
  — one ése, ésa, (I, 3); aquél, aquélla (3)
  —'s too bad! ¡qué lástima! (I)
  —'s why por eso (I)
the el, la, los, las (I)
theater *(movie)* el cine; el teatro (I)
their su, sus (I); suyo, -a (7)
theirs el suyo, la suya, los suyos, las suyas (7)
them *dir. obj. pron.* los, las; *after prep.* ellos, ellas; *ind. obj. pron.* les (I)
then luego (I)
there allí (I)
  — is / are hay (I)
  — it is allí está (I)
  — used to be había (5)
  — was / were había (5); hubo (10)
  — will be habrá (11)
therefore por eso (I)
these estos, -as (I, 3); *pron.* éstos, -as (3)
they ellos, ellas (I)
thief el ladrón, *pl.* los ladrones; la ladrona (10)
thing la cosa (I)
to **think** creer; pensar *(e → ie)* (I); parecer (que) (7)
  I (don't) — so creo que sí (no) (I)
  to — about pensar en (I)
third tercer, -a (I)
thirsty: to be — tener sed (I)
thirteen trece (I)
thirty treinta (I)
this este, esta (I, 3)
  — one éste, ésta (3)
thorn la espina (14)
those esos, -as (I, 3); aquellos, -as (3); *pron.* ésos, -as; aquéllos, -as (3)
thousand mil (I)
threat la amenaza (I)
three tres (I)
  — hundred trescientos (I)
  —-ring binder la carpeta de argollas (I)
throat la garganta (I)
  sore — el dolor de garganta (I)
  — lozenges las pastillas para la garganta (I)
through por (8)
to **throw out** echar (11)
Thursday jueves (I)
  on — el jueves (I)

ticket el boleto (12)
tidy ordenado, -a (I)
tie la corbata (I, 3)
to **tie** *(in scoring)* empatar (4)
tiger el tigre (I)
tight *(clothing)* apretado, -a (3)
time la hora; el tiempo; la vez (I)
  at the same — a la vez (I)
  at —s a veces (I)
  at what — ¿a qué hora ? (I)
  to have a good / bad — pasarlo bien / mal (I, 4)
  many —s muchas veces (I)
  on — puntualmente (I)
  what — is it? ¿qué hora es? (I)
tired cansado, -a (I)
to a (I)
  in order — para + *inf.* (I)
toast el pan tostado (I)
toaster el tostador (7)
today hoy (I)
  not — hoy no (I)
toe el dedo del pie (I)
to **tolerate** soportar (4)
tomato el tomate (I)
  — soup la sopa de tomate (I)
tomorrow mañana (I)
too también (I); demasiado (I)
toothache el dolor de muelas (I)
toothbrush el cepillo de dientes (8)
toothpaste la pasta dentífrica (I)
top: on — of encima de (I)
torn roto, -a (14)
tortilla la tortilla (I)
tourist el / la turista (12)
  — office la oficina de turismo (12)
town el pueblo (12)
  — square la plaza (I)
toy el juguete (5); *adj.* de juguete (5)
traffic el tráfico (11)
  — light el semáforo (8)
train el tren (I)
  — station la estación del tren (I)
transportation el transporte (8)
to **travel** viajar (12)
travel agency la agencia de viajes (12)
  — agent el/la agente de viajes (12)
traveler el viajero, la viajera (12)
  —'s check el cheque de viajero (12)
tree el árbol (I, 14)
tricycle el triciclo (5)
  to ride a — montar en triciclo (5)

trip el viaje (12)
  short — la excursión, *pl.* las excursiones (12)
truck el camión, *pl.* los camiones (5)
trumpet la trompeta (2)
truth la verdad (5)
to **try** probar *(o → ue)* (I)
  to — on probarse *(o→ ue)* (3)
T-shirt la camiseta (I)
Tuesday martes (I)
  on — el martes (I)
turkey el pavo (6)
to **turn** doblar (8)
  to — off apagar (I, 7)
  to — on encender *(e → ie)* (7)
turnover la empanada (13)
turtle la tortuga (5)
  —neck (sweater) el suéter de cuello alto (3)
tutor el tutor, la tutora (2)
twelve doce (I)
twenty veinte (I)
twice dos veces (I)
twig el palito (14)
twin el gemelo, la gemela (I)
two dos (I)
  — hundred doscientos (I)
type la clase (I)
typical típico, -a (I, 10)

ugly feo, -a (I)
umbrella el paraguas (I)
uncle el tío (I)
uncomfortable incómodo, -a (I)
under(neath) debajo de (I)
to **unfasten** desabrocharse (12)
unfriendly antipático, -a (I)
university la universidad (11)
unmarried soltero, -a (6)
to **unpack** deshacer la maleta (12)
unpleasant antipático, -a (I)
until hasta (I)
to **upset** *(one's stomach)* hacer daño a (13)
us *obj. pron.* nos; *after prep.* nosotros, -as (I)
to **use** usar (I)
usually generalmente (I)

vacation las vacaciones (I)
  to go on — ir de vacaciones (I)
to **vacuum** pasar la aspiradora (I)
vacuum cleaner la aspiradora (I)
Valentine's Day el Día de los Enamorados (6)
valley el valle (14)

VCR la videocasetera (I)
vegetable la verdura (I)
  — soup la sopa de verduras (I)
very muy (I)
vest el chaleco (3)
veterinarian el veterinario, la veterinaria (11)
victim la víctima (10)
video el video (4)
  — game el videojuego (I)
vinegar el vinagre (13)
violence la violencia (10)
violent violento, -a (10)
violin el violín, *pl.* los violines (2)
virus el virus (9)
to **visit** visitar (I)
vitamin la vitamina (13)
volleyball el vóleibol (I)
to **volunteer** trabajar como voluntario (2)
to **vomit** vomitar (9)
voyage el viaje (12)

waiter, waitress el camarero, la camarera (I)
to **wake up** despertarse *(e → ie)* (2)
to **walk** caminar (5)
walking a pie (I)
wall la pared (1)
wallet la cartera (3)
to **want** querer *(e → ie)* (I)
war la guerra (11)
to **wash** lavar (I)
  — one's face, hair, etc. lavarse la cara, el pelo, etc. (2)
washer:
  clothes — la lavadora (7)
  dish— el lavaplatos (7)
to **waste** gastar (11)
watch el reloj (pulsera) (I, 7)
to **watch** ver (I)
water el agua *f.* (I)
  — pistol la pistola de agua (5)
  to — ski hacer esquí acuático (14)
  — skiing el esquí acuático (14)
waterfall las cataratas (I)
watermelon la sandía (13)
we nosotros, -as (I)
to **wear** llevar (I); usar (3)
weather el tiempo (I)
  the — is nice (bad) hace buen (mal) tiempo (I)
  — forecast el pronóstico del tiempo (I)
  what's the — like? ¿qué tiempo hace? (I)

wedding la boda (6)
  — anniversary el aniversario (de boda) (6)
Wednesday miércoles (I)
  on — el miércoles (I)
week la semana (I)
weekend el fin de semana (I)
weights las pesas (4)
  to lift — levantar pesas (4)
welcome: you're — de nada (I)
well bien (I); *(to indicate pause)* pues (I)
well-mannered (bien) educado, -a (5)
western la película del oeste (I)
wet mojado, -a (14)
whale la ballena (I, 14)
what ¿qué? (I); lo que (3)
wheelchair la silla de ruedas (9)
when ¿cuándo?; cuando (I)
where? ¿dónde?; donde (I)
  from —? ¿de dónde? (I)
  (to) —? ¿adónde? (I)
whether si (I)
while mientras (8)
white blanco, -a (I)
  in black and — en blanco y negro (I)
who? whom? ¿quién(es)? (I)
why ¿por qué? (I)
  that's — por eso (I)
wife la esposa (6)
wild *(animal)* salvaje (14); *(plant)* silvestre (14)
to **win** ganar (4)
wind el viento (I)
window la ventana (I); *(plane)* la ventanilla (12)
to **windsurf** hacer surf de vela (14)
winter el invierno (I)
with con (I)
  — me conmigo (I)
  — you contigo (I)
to **withdraw** *(money)* sacar (I)
without sin (2)
wolf el lobo, la loba (I, 14)
woman la mujer (I)
  young — la joven (I)
wonderful fantástico; ¡genial! (I)
wood la madera (I)
  (made of) — de madera (I)
woods el bosque (11)
wool la lana (3)
to **work** trabajar (I); *(machines)* funcionar (7)
worse peor (I)
worst el / la (los / las) peor(es) (I)

worthwhile: it's (not) — (no) vale la pena (I)
wow! ¡vaya! (I)
wrist la muñeca (9)
  —watch el reloj pulsera (I, 7)
to **write** escribir (I, 1)
  to — to each other escribirse (6)
writer el escritor, la escritora (11)
wrong:
  to be — no tener razón (I)
  what's —? ¿qué tienes? (I)

X-ray la radiografía (9)
  to take an — sacar una radiografía (9)

year el año (I)
  to be . . . —s old tener . . . años (I)
  New —'s Day el Año Nuevo (6)
  New —'s Eve el fin de año (6)
  New —'s Eve party la fiesta de fin de año (I)
yearbook el anuario (2)
yellow amarillo, -a (I)
yes sí (I)
yesterday ayer (I)
you *fam.* tú ; *formal* usted (Ud.); *pl.* ustedes (Uds.); *dir. obj. pron.* lo, la, los, las; *fam. dir. obj. pron.* te; *ind. obj. pron.* le, les; *fam. after prep.* ti (I)
young *adj.* joven (I)
  —er menor, *pl.* menores (I)
  — lady la joven (I)
  — man el joven (I)
  — people los jóvenes (I)
your tu, tus *fam.;* su, sus *formal & pl.* (I); tuyo, -a; suyo, -a (7)
yours *fam.* el tuyo, la tuya, los tuyos, las tuyas; *formal & pl.* el suyo, la suya, los suyos, las suyas (7)
yuck! ¡qué asco! (I)

zero cero (I)
zipper la cremallera (3)
zoo el zoológico (I)

English-Spanish Vocabulary 523

Índice

In almost all cases, structures are first presented in the Vocabulario para conversar, where they are practiced lexically in conversational contexts. They are explained later, usually in the Gramática en contexto section of that chapter. Light-face numbers refer to pages where structures are initially presented or, after explanation, where student reminders occur. Bold-face numbers refer to pages where structures are explained or otherwise highlighted.

ACKNOWLEDGMENTS

Illustrations   Iskra Johnson: p. **IV**; Jim Starr: p. **V**; Lane Dupont: p. **V**; Rick Clubb: p. **VII**; Andy Lendway: p. **IX**; Rod Vass: p. **IX**; Rick Clubb: p. **X** (top 2); Peg Magovern: p. **X** (bottom 1); Jim Starr: p. **XI**; Richard Stergulz: p. **XI**; Mapping Specialists Limited: pp. **XII-XV**; Iskra Johnson: pp. **8-9**; Elizabeth Wolf: pp. **10-11**; Scott Snow: p. **17**; Susan Aiello: pp. **75, 86, 210-211, 438, 484**; Kevin Bapp: pp. **42-43**; Andrea Barrett: pp. **162-166, 169-171, 176, 189, 216-217**; Robert Burger: pp. **337, 345-346**; John Ceballos: pp. **418-419**; Rick Clubb pp. **194-201, 203, 208, 210, 212, 221, 276, 364-367, 369, 380, 384, 391**; Guy Crittenden: pp. **480-481**; Lane Dupont: pp. **62-63, 65-69, 71, 76-77, 80, 89, 245**; John Edens: p. **174**; George Eisner: pp. **344, 354, 356, 406**; Susan Greenstein: pp. **448, 454**; Doug Henry: p. **310**; Robin Hotchkiss: pp. **348-349**; Andy Lendway: pp. **215, 296-302, 304-306, 312, 315-316, 318, 325, 446**; Jude Maceren: pp. **451-452**; Peg Magovern: pp. **282, 311, 410, 417**; James Mellett: pp. **128-141, 145, 147, 157, 281, 390, 442**; Steve Musgrave: pp. **351, 355, 387, 444, 484**; Andy Myer: pp. **52-53, 152-153, 320-321**; Ortelius Design: p. **286**; Julie Pace: pp. **94-105, 112, 114-115, 122-123**; Leif Peng: pp. **396-398, 401-403, 423, 474**; Donna Perrone: pp. **222-223**; Bob Shein: p. **485**; Ken Smith: pp. **64, 68**; Scott Snow: pp. **322-323, 449**; Jim Starr: pp. **30-37, 44-46, 48-49, 51, 56-57, 116, 357, 370-373, 388, 391, 428-437, 439, 446-447, 455**; Richard Stergulz: pp. **460-469, 470, 476, 484, 487**; Joe Scrofani: pp. **260-269, 271, 272-273, 278-279, 281, 283, 291**; Rod Vass: pp. **226-235, 237, 242-244, 255, 330-333, 335-336, 338-339, 350**; Gary Yealdhall: pp. **50, 182-183, 240**; John Zielinsky: p. **108**

Photography   **Front Cover:** Haroldo Castro/FPG International; **Back Cover:** F. Catala-Roca, Barcelona; **II:** F. Catala-Roca, Barcelona; **V:** (c)Frerck/Odyssey/Chicago; **VI:** (t)©Robert Fried; (c)©Owen Franken; (b)Chip & Rosa Maria de la Cueva Peterson; **VII:** (t)Stuart Cohen/Comstock; (b)Martha Cooper/Viesti Associates; **VIII:** (t)©Jack Parsons; (c)Ric Ergenbright Photography; (b)Stuart Cohen/Comstock; **IX:** ©Joe Viesti; **XI:** ©Mary Altier; **XVI:** ©Owen Franken; **2:** (l)David R. Frazier Photolibrary; (c)©Tony Arruza; (r)©Glenn Randall; **3:** ©Tony Arruza; **5:** (l)©Cynthia Lum/Sports Light; (r)Focus On Sports; **6:** Arthur Tilley/FPG International; **7:** Frerck/Odyssey/Chicago; **16:** (t)Yoram Kahana/Shooting Star; (b)Joel Holzman/Shooting Star; **18:** © José Luis Martín Mena, courtesy Semana; **19:** ©Hoviv, courtesy ¡Hola!; **20:** (t)Chris Sharp/DDB Stock Photo; (c)©D. Donne Bryant; (b)Frerck/Odyssey/Chicago; **22-23:** ©1994 Gary Braasch; **23:** (tl)©Glenn Randall; (tr)Stuart Cohen/Comstock; (b)©1994 Gary Braasch; **24-25:** ©Jack Parsons; **26-27:** ©Ken Laffal; **28:** Robert Fried/DDB Stock Photo; **29:** Frerck/Odyssey/Chicago; (tr)Scala/Art Resource, NYC, ©ARS, New York; **38:** Chip & Rosa Maria de la Cueva Peterson; (inset) Frerck/Odyssey/Chicago; **40:** Victor Englebert; **41:** (t)Nancy D'Antonio; (b)Chip & Rosa Maria de la Cueva Peterson; **47:** ©Robert Fried; **51:** Chip & Rosa Maria de la Cueva Peterson; **55:** Chip & Rosa Maria de la Cueva Peterson; **58-59:** ©Bob Daemmrich Photography; **60:** (l)Chip & Rosa Maria de la Cueva Peterson; (r)©Joe Viesti; **61:** (t)The Museum of Modern Art, New York. Mrs. Simon Guggenheim Fund. Photograph ©1995 The Museum of Modern Art.; (b)©Owen Franken; **72:** Chip & Rosa Maria de la Cueva Peterson; **73:** (t)©Robert Fried; (b)Nancy D'Antonio; **74:** Courtesy NASA; **79:** ©Owen Franken; **80:** Frerck/Odyssey/Chicago; **83:** (t)Robert Fried/DDB Stock Photo; (b) Victor Englebert; **84:** Bob Daemmrich/Stock Boston; **86:** ©Richard Lord; **87:** (tl)David R. Frazier Photolibrary; (tr)Courtesy NASA; (bl)©Beryl Goldberg Photographer; (br)©Richard Lord; **90-91:** E. Narichoque/Comstock; **92:** ©Robert Fried; **93:** (t)David R. Frazier Photolibrary; (b)©Owen Franken; **100-101:** ©Robert Fried; **103:** David R. Frazier Photolibrary; **106-107:** David R. Frazier Photolibrary; **110:** Suzanne L. Murphy/DDB Stock Photo; **113:** (t)David R. Frazier Photolibrary; (b)©Beryl Goldberg Photographer; **116:** ©Owen Franken; **117:** (t)©Owen Franken; (b)©Robert Fried; **118:** ©Owen Franken; **120:** (t)David R. Frazier Photolibrary; (bl)Nancy D'Antonio; (br)Chip & Rosa Maria de la Cueva Peterson; **121:** ©Chip & Rosa Maria de la Cueva Peterson; (b)M. Antman/The Image Works; **124-125:** ©Robert Fried; **126:** (t)Cameramann International, Ltd.; (b)Chip & Rosa Maria de la Cueva Peterson; **127:** ©Owen Franken; **130:** Tony Freeman/PhotoEdit; **131:** ©Jacques Halber; **133:** ©Bob Daemmrich Photography; **137:** (l)Chip & Rosa Maria de la Cueva Peterson; (r)Peter Menzel; **139:** Susan Watts/Retna, Ltd.; **142-143:** Bob Schalkwijk/Art Resource, NY; **144:** Courtesy Foreign Imported Productions & Publishing, Inc.; **148:** Art Gingert/Comstock; **151:** Frerck/Odyssey/Chicago; **154:** (t)©Krasner/Trebitz-E.R.S.; (b)©Mary Altier; **155:** ©Robert Fried; **158-159:** ©Joe Viesti; **160:** (t)Stuart Cohen/Comstock; (b)©Tony Arruza; **161:** The Metropolitan Museum of Art, The Jules Bache Collection, 1949 (49.7.41); **168:** ©Tony Arruza; **172:** UPI/Bettmann; **173:** ©Beryl Goldberg Photographer; **175:** David J. Sams/Stock Boston; **179:** ©Robert Fried; **180:** ©Tony Arruza; **181:** Frerck/Odyssey/Chicago; **184:** Courtesy of the Pittsburgh Pirates Baseball Club/Photo by Dave Arrigo; **185:** (t)UPI/Bettmann; **186:** Cameramann International, Ltd.; **187:** (t) D. Boroughs/The Image Works; (b)Chip & Rosa Maria de la Cueva Peterson; **190-191:** ©Peter Menzel, Material World; **192:** (t)©1994 Fernando Botero/VAGA, NY, courtesy the Marlborough Gallery; (b)Scala/Art Resource; **193:** Pablo Picasso, Family of Saltimbanques, Chester Dale Collection, ©1995, National Gallery of Art, Washington; **202:** (l)©Robert Fried; (r)Mary Altier; **204:** Chip & Rosa Maria de la Cueva Peterson; **206-207:** ©Martha Cooper/Viesti Associates; **207:** (t)©Joe Viesti; (b)Ann Trulove/Unicorn Stock Photos; **209:** Diego Goldberg, Material World/Peter Menzel; **213:** Allan Landau for ScottForesman, courtesy Mexican Fine Arts Center, Chicago; **217:** ©Richard Lord; **218:** Peter Millen/The Image Bank; **218-219:** ©Joe Viesti; **219:** (inset)Steve Vidler/Leo de Wys, Inc.; **222-223:** ©Beryl Goldberg Photographer; **224:** ©Joe Viesti; **225:** B. Barbey/Magnum Photos; **233:** M. Antman/The Image Works; **236:** ©Joe Viesti; **238:** (t)Lee Boltin Picture Library; (b)Frerck/Odyssey/Chicago; **239:** Ric Ergenbright Photography; **247:** Daniel Aubry/Odyssey/Chicago; **248:** (r)H. Gans/The Image Works; **249:** ©Jack Parsons; **252:** (artifacts) Lee Boltin Picture Library; **253:** ©Joe Viesti; **256-257:** ©B.W. Hoffmann/envision; **258:** ©Owen Franken/Stock Boston; **259:** (t)Stuart Cohen/Comstock; (b)©Owen Franken; **264:** (t)Ric Ergenbright Photography; (b)Collection of the Art Museum of the Americas, OAS, Washington, D.C.; **264-265:** ©Tom Gibson/envision; **270:** ©Beryl Goldberg Photographer; **274-275:** ©Miriam Lefkowitz/envision; **284:** ©Robert Fried; **285:** (l)Beryl Goldberg Photographer; (r)Stuart Cohen/Comstock; **288:** (t)The Metropolitan Museum of Art, H.O. Havemeyer Collection, Bequest of Mrs. H.O. Havemeyer, 1929.; (b)©Joe Viesti; **289:** Courtesy Michael Realty Company, Toledo, OH; **292-293:** Tom McCarthy/PhotoEdit; **294:** (l)Alyx Kellington/DDB Stock Photo; (r)Chip & Rosa Maria de la Cueva Peterson; **295:** Chip & Rosa Maria de la Cueva Peterson; **304-305:** Nancy D'Antonio; **308:** Chip & Rosa Maria de la Cueva Peterson; **309:** (t)David R. Frazier Photolibrary; (b)M. Rangell/The Image Works; **313:** Frerck/Odyssey/Chicago; **314-315:** ©Joe Viesti; **317:** ©Owen Franken/Stock Boston; **319:** (t)©Owen Franken; (b)©Tony Arruza; **326-327:** R. Crandall/The Image Works; **328:** ©Jeffrey J. Foxx; **329:** (t)Stuart Cohen/Comstock; (b)Larry Mangino/The Image Works; **334:** Photofest; **335:** The Kobal Collection; **341:** (t)©Owen Franken; (b)Jack Demuth for ScottForesman; **342-343:** Courtesy Coral Picture Corporation/Radio Caracas Television, Venezuela; **347:** (t)Frerck/Odyssey/Chicago; (b)©Beryl Goldberg Photographer; **352-353:** ©William Dyckes; **360-361:** Erica Lanser/Black Star; **362:** (t)©Robert Fried; (b)Larry Mangino/The Image Works; **363:** David R. Frazier Photolibrary; **369:** ©Peter Menzel; **375:** (t)Michael Fogden/Bruce Coleman; (b)©Walt Anderson; **376:** (t)David Simson/Stock Boston; (b)©Peter Menzel; **377:** ©Beryl Goldberg Photographer; (inset)Robert Frerck/Tony Stone Images, Inc.; **378-379:** Courtesy NASA; **382:** ©William Dyckes; **386:** Courtesy Universidad Nacional Antónoma de México, Instituto de Ingeniería, Sunrayce '95, Proyecto Tonatiuh; **387:** Daniel Aubry/Odyssey/Chicago; **392-393:** Frerck/Odyssey/Chicago; **392-395:** Byron Crader/Ric Ergenbright Photography; **394:** (t)©Beryl Goldberg Photographer; (b)P&G Bowater/The Image Bank; **395:** ©Beryl Goldberg Photographer; **401:** Martha Cooper/Viesti Associates; **406:** (t)David R. Frazier Photolibrary; (b)©Beryl Goldberg Photographer; **407:** David R. Frazier Photolibrary; **408:** (inset) Courtesy Parador de Zafra; **408-409:** Courtesy Parador de Sigüenza; **409:** (bl)Courtesy Parador de Sigüenza; (br)Courtesy Parador de Zamora; **412-413:** ©Robert Fried; **416-417:** cultural objects courtesy Rosi Marshall; wall hanging courtesy Michelle Ryan; Byron Crader/Ric Ergenbright Photography; **420:** ©Owen Franken; **420-421:** ©Beryl Goldberg Photographer; **421:** (t)David R. Frazier Photolibrary; **422-423:** Byron Crader/Ric Ergenbright Photography; **424-425:** Miriam Lefkowitz/envision; **426:** David R. Frazier Photolibrary; **427:** (t)Victor